D0968512

SETTLING DISPUTES
in SOVIET SOCIETY

STUDIES OF THE RUSSIAN INSTITUTE
COLUMBIA UNIVERSITY

Photo Marshall MacDuffie

A MOSCOW PEOPLE'S COURT

SETTLING DISPUTES
in SOVIET SOCIETY

The Formative Years of Legal Institutions

by *JOHN N. HAZARD*

COLUMBIA UNIVERSITY PRESS *New York* 1960

The transliteration system used in this series is based on the Library of Congress system with some modifications.

THE RUSSIAN INSTITUTE OF COLUMBIA UNIVERSITY

THE RUSSIAN INSTITUTE was established by Columbia University in 1946 to serve two major objectives: the training of a limited number of well-qualified Americans for scholarly and professional careers in the field of Russian studies, and the development of research in the social sciences and the humanities as they relate to Russia and the Soviet Union. The research program of the Russian Institute is conducted through the efforts of its faculty members, of scholars invited to participate as Senior Fellows in its program, and of candidates for the Certificate of the Institute and for the degree of Doctor of Philosophy. Some of the results of the research program are presented in the Studies of the Russian Institute of Columbia University. The faculty of the Institute, without necessarily agreeing with the conclusions reached in the Studies, believe that their publication advances the difficult task of promoting systematic research on Russia and the Soviet Union and public understanding of the problems involved.

The faculty of the Russian Institute are grateful to the Rockefeller Foundation for the financial assistance which it has given to the program of research and publication.

STUDIES OF THE RUSSIAN INSTITUTE

SOVIET NATIONAL INCOME AND PRODUCT IN 1937 *Abram Bergson*

THROUGH THE GLASS OF SOVIET LITERATURE: VIEWS OF RUSSIAN SOCIETY
Edited by *Ernest J. Simmons*

THE PROLETARIAN EPISODE IN RUSSIAN LITERATURE, 1928–1932
Edward J. Brown

MANAGEMENT OF THE INDUSTRIAL FIRM IN THE USSR: A STUDY IN SOVIET
ECONOMIC PLANNING *David Granick*

SOVIET POLICIES IN CHINA, 1917–1924 *Allen S. Whiting*

UKRAINIAN NATIONALISM, 1939–1945 *John A. Armstrong*

POLISH POSTWAR ECONOMY *Thad Paul Alton*

LITERARY POLITICS IN THE SOVIET UKRAINE, 1917–1934
George S. N. Luckyj

THE EMERGENCE OF RUSSIAN PANSLAVISM, 1856–1870
Michael Boro Petrovich

BOLSHEVISM IN TURKESTAN, 1917–1927 *Alexander G. Park*

THE LAST YEARS OF THE GEORGIAN MONARCHY, 1658–1832
David Marshall Lang

LENIN ON TRADE UNIONS AND REVOLUTION, 1893–1917
Thomas Taylor Hammond

THE JAPANESE THRUST INTO SIBERIA, 1918 *James William Morley*

SOVIET MARXISM: A CRITICAL ANALYSIS *Herbert Marcuse*

THE AGRARIAN FOES OF BOLSHEVISM: PROMISE AND DEFAULT OF THE RUS-
SIAN SOCIALIST REVOLUTIONARIES, FEBRUARY TO OCTOBER, 1917
Oliver H. Radkey

SOVIET POLICY AND THE CHINESE COMMUNISTS, 1931–1946
Charles B. McLane

PATTERN FOR SOVIET YOUTH: A STUDY OF THE CONGRESSES OF THE KOMSO-
MOL, 1918–1954 *Ralph Talcott Fisher, Jr.*

THE EMERGENCE OF MODERN LITHUANIA *Alfred Erich Senn*

THE SOVIET DESIGN FOR A WORLD STATE *Elliot R. Goodman*

SETTLING DISPUTES IN SOVIET SOCIETY: THE FORMATIVE YEARS OF LEGAL
INSTITUTIONS *John N. Hazard*

Preface

A PROFESSIONAL MAN begins early to consider the part played by his profession in society. The lawyer delves into anthropological materials to study the emergence in primitive communities of institutions with which he is daily concerned in his practice. He examines legal systems in modern states to compare the methods which each has developed to meet problems well known to him in his own jurisdiction.

An increasing number of persons are asking whether the experience of the Russian Revolution can illuminate the role of legal institutions in modern society. Every one knows that the Russian revolutionaries entered upon their task determined to start anew with social organization. They were vociferous in their denial of advantages to be found in courts as they had known them in the past. They promised to show the world how a system for settling disputes could be made simple, and some of them wrote with the expectation that even their simple "court" would eventually become unnecessary as society moved toward the goal of communism. Formalities, legal procedure, representation by lawyers, and technical language: all of these elements of courts as they had been known in the Empire were to be abolished.

It is the purpose of this volume to test with Soviet data the thesis that modern man can settle his disputes with simplicity, without elaborately organized tribunals, without legal representation, without complicated laws, and without a labyrinth of rules of procedure and evidence. No society offers the perfect testing ground because extraneous factors enter to influence its development. Soviet society is no exception. Its evolution has not occurred on the basis of pure reason in a completely new environment. Civil war, world war, world public opinion, and the heritage of the past in the thinking of Soviet citizens have all influenced the result. Yet in no modern society since the French Revolution has there been such a generally accepted will among those who make policy to simplify judicial procedure. It is for this reason that the Soviet experience offers an unusual opportunity to make a test.

This study is concerned with disputes between citizens. All mature societies have found it desirable to substitute for the blood feud and less violent forms of redress several types of procedure. The degree of public importance attached to action exciting conflict has been the determinant of the type of procedure provided by the state to give satisfaction to the aggrieved party. It is as often a criminal court as a civil court, arbitration tribunal, or administrative agency. Soviet society has been no exception. Consequently, considerable space in the study has of necessity been devoted to the evolution of criminal jurisdiction and procedure alongside civil jurisdiction and procedure.

The study is not concerned directly with crimes against the state, nor with the operations of security agencies designed to preserve the power of those who rule. This segment of Soviet activity has already been examined and described in detail by scholars of several lands and by individuals who have experienced the severity of Soviet security measures. There is no need to repeat what is well known in this already long study. Still, the tribunals and procedures developed by Soviet jurists to resolve disputes between citizens have often been influenced by the character and procedure of institutions devised to assure the security of the Soviet state. For this reason the evolution of certain security institutions and procedures has been introduced when pertinent to an understanding of otherwise inexplicable development in the less political arena.

Although it is appreciated that no outsider can discover the whole story of the evolution of any Soviet institution, even when it bears only indirectly on state security, there is a considerable written record of events in the fields treated in this study, and this record is particularly full for the formative years. It is this record that has served as the foundation for this study, verified to the extent possible during three and a half years' residence in the U.S.S.R. in the mid-1930's as a fellow of the Institute of Current World Affairs of New

York delegated to study Soviet law. While the results cannot be all that might be wished, they may serve at least to indicate the outlines of a thesis for others to challenge and thus advance the exploration of the subject.

To the author's colleagues in the Russian Institute of Columbia University, to the financial assistance provided by the Institute, to the reviewers of previous books who have suggested a study of institutions and procedure, to all who have given advice, the author is greatly indebted.

J. N. H.

Columbia University
New York, New York
January, 1960

CONTENTS

1. *MAKING A BEGINNING* — 1
   The Theory of Change — 3
   A New Judiciary — 5
   Liquidating Prerevolutionary Problems — 9
   Practice in the Local Courts — 13
   Practice in the District Courts — 14
   The Applicable Law — 16
   Cases before the Courts — 19
   The District Courts Lose Importance — 24
   Procedural Guidance to Courts — 25
   Hostility to Formality — 28

2. *STRIVING FOR SIMPLICTY* — 34
   Lawyers Begin to Practice — 35
   Lawyers in the District Courts — 37
   Judges Want Lawyers in Court — 40
   Steps toward a Salaried Bar — 43
   The People's Court Act of 1918 — 47
   Specialization in the Courts — 51
   The Transition to the New System — 57
   A Summary of Achievements — 61

3. *STEPS TOWARD CENTRALIZATION* — 64
   Revolutionary Consciousness and Legal Situations — 68
   Centralizing Control over Local Departments of Justice — 72
   The Civil War Encourages Centralization — 78
   Parallel Developments in the Ukraine — 83
   Ukrainian Centralization of Authority — 87

4. *SEEKING THE BEST OF BOTH WORLDS* — 94
   Directing Uniformity — 96
   Assuring Information from Below — 99
   The Third Congress Reviews the Experience — 103

Shortcomings of the Bar   106
New Controls for the Judges   109
Introducing the Reform by Ministerial Instruction   112
The People's Court Act of 1920   116
Reducing Authority of Local Judges   120
Centralization at Key Points   123

5. *RECONSTRUCTION*   128
Supreme Control over Courts   131
Private Enterprise Gains a Reprieve   136
Revived Civil-Law Relationships   142
Restraint of Bourgeois Elements   145
The Fourth Congress of Persons Engaged in the Administration
    of Justice   148
The Debate Over a Unified Court System   152
Establishing a State Prosecutor   156
Reestablishing the Bar   159
Implementing the Plans   162
A Glimpse at Court Activity   166
Parallelism of Institutions   172

6. *CRYSTALLIZATION OF THE COURT STRUCTURE*   176
Strengthening the General Courts   179
Presenting the Draft Judiciary Act   183
The New General Courts   186
The New Judges   190
The Specialized Courts   195
The Supreme Court of the Republic   199
Reform in the Smaller Republics   204
The Federal Supreme Court   209
A Federal Judiciary Act   212
Building for the Years   214

7. *THE WATCHMAN*   217
Planning State Prosecution   218
Public Debate of the Plan   224
The Politburo Intervenes   227
The Statutes Enacting the Reform   230
The Right to Intervene   235
Examples from Practice   240
The Impact of Federation   243

8. *PROFESSIONALIZING THE BAR*   247
Legislation of 1922   250
Ukrainian Improvements   254

Contents

Implementation of the New Policy	258
Organizing the Moscow Bar	262
Limitations on Numbers of Lawyers	264
The Right to Counsel	267
Procedural Revision in 1923	272
"Underground Practice"	276
A Canon of Ethics	281
Decisions on Legal Ethics	283
Legal Ethics and Soviet Social Theory	291
The Influence of Federation	297
9. PROCEDURE TO THE FORE	301
A New Code of Criminal Procedure Takes Form	305
A Procedural Bill of Rights	309
The Police Inquiry	313
The Preliminary Investigation	315
Transmission to Court	319
The Trial	321
Judicial Review	327
The Audit Procedure	333
The Rules of Evidence	335
The Revolutionary Tribunals	337
Krylenko's Evaluation of 1922	340
10. A SECOND STEP IN PROCEDURAL REFORM	342
Early Reaction to Procedural Reform	343
Dreams of Simplification	353
The Revision of 1923	355
Ukrainian Proposals for Revision	364
Judicial Experience with Procedure	369
The Fifth Congress of Persons Engaged in the Administration of Justice	376
Kurskii's Proposed Amendments	380
Amendments of 1924	383
Federal Principles of Criminal Procedure	388
11. CIVIL PROCEDURE CAPS THE CLIMAX	396
Protection Against Bourgeois Cleverness	397
The General Principles in the New Code	405
Presentation of a Claim and the Trial	411
Rules of Evidence	414
Execution of Judgment	420
Levy upon Property and Garnishment	423
Procedure on Appeal	426
Special Proceedings	426

The Fifth Congress of Persons Engaged in the Administration
of Justice   427
Renewed Emphasis on Unification of Courts   431

12. *REFINING PROCEDURE IN PRACTICE*   436
State Arbitration Commissions   439
Refinement of Procedural Detail   441
Opportunities for Private Arbitration   443
Federal Concern with Civil Procedure   449
Problems Arising in Commodity Exchanges   451
Practical Problems in the General Courts   456
Judgments in Search of General Policy   463

13. *FROM SIMPLICITY TO COMPLEXITY AND FORMALITY*   477

BIBLIOGRAPHY   492

TABLE OF STATUTES AND ORDERS   509

TABLE OF CASES   517

INDEX   519

SETTLING DISPUTES
in SOVIET SOCIETY

Chapter 1

MAKING A BEGINNING

A SORDID DISPUTE over the ownership of a samovar and the matter of appropriate terms of detention for a gang of thieves who had robbed an old woman at gunpoint were the first two matters to come before the new court created in Moscow after the Russian Revolution.[1] It had not been easy to organize the first sitting. Although the government had ordered the creation of the new "people's courts" to replace the court system inherited from the tsars, nothing had been done. The judge of the new Moscow court later reminisced that every one had hoped that somehow it might have been possible to postpone the task of creating a new judiciary until some of the many more pressing problems that had fallen on the shoulders of the Moscow city government might have been solved. The hope was blasted when the justices of the peace who had continued to sit after the Revolution refused to serve longer.

It was mid-December, 1917, when the first court opened its doors.[2] It had been almost impossible to find a courtroom. The central government had ordered the messengers in the old justice of the peace courts to take possession of the property and courtrooms, but the Moscow court messenger overplayed his part and sealed up the court offices one night with the aid of some of the Red Guards. His action angered the justices of the peace to such an extent that they refused to evacuate the premises, and they seem to have had enough power to hold the courtroom. The city soviet tried to woo them by offering them the opportunity of standing for election to the new court, as the law permitted, but they would not be bribed. The courtroom remained closed to the officials of the new regime.

---

[1] A. R. Kadich, "O narodnom sudie (iz lichnykh vpechatlienii)," *Proletarskaia revoliutsiia i pravo*, No. 2 (August 15, 1918), p. 24.

[2] Actually December 16, 1917. See D. I. Kurskii, "Otchët otdiela sudoustroistva Narodnago Komissariata Iustitsii," *ibid.*, No. 1 (August 1, 1918), p. 39.

A little dirty room in an old wooden house, foul with stale air, reeking with the smell of burning charcoal, heated up just before the evening session began, dimly lighted with a single kerosene lamp: this was the setting for the first case of the first "people's court" in Moscow. For want of personnel, it had been decided to open only two chambers of the new court to hear disputes between working people. The chambers to hear disputes carried over from pre-revolutionary times and involving the bourgeoisie were not yet to be organized.

A significant part of the public was not receptive at all to the idea of courts in the new Russia. The judge of the first court reported that a characteristic refrain from those who appeared to press their claims against fellow citizens was: "And that fellow said to me, 'You can't do anything to me because there are no courts any more!'" Borrowed money was not repaid, and creditors reported that they were taunted with the refrain, "There are no courts!" Complaints against rowdies and public nuisances were prefaced in court by statements that the offenders had refused to conform to the needs of society "because there are no courts." The judge of the first court explained that his first task was to instill in the minds of the people among whom he sat the fact that his fledgling court in its miserable setting, crowded in the main with the very poor and the small artisans of Moscow, was a completely real institution.

No one respected the dignity of the new court. Parties to suits sat on the benches wearing their hats, replying to questions without rising from their places, while a hum of conversation among those waiting to be heard drowned out the hearing. Even the minor state officials lacked respect for the court. The policemen on duty made no effort to stop conversations between spectators and those brought in under arrest. Prison wardens demanded in the form of an ultimatum that their prisoners' cases be heard immediately, or the prisoners would be taken back to prison again.

Revolt against authority was in the air. Had not the Revolution freed the common man from the necessity to obey! Almost immediately after the "October days" there had been promulgated the "Declaration of Rights of the Peoples of Russia."[3] It was a

<hr />

[3] Decree of November 2, 1917, [1917–1918] I *Sobranie Uzakonenii i Rasporiazhenii Rabochago i Krest'ianskago Pravitel'stva RSFSR*, No. 2, item 18.

document expressed primarily in terms of emancipation from authority: peasants were to be emancipated from landlords, soldiers were to be emancipated from the authority of generals, workmen were to be emancipated from the duty to obey capitalist factory owners. The spirit of the new-found freedom was summed up in the declaration's phrase, "All that is alive and vital is being freed from the hated chains."

THE THEORY OF CHANGE

Courts of the old regime had been reviled since the time of the Communist Manifesto. Taking hold of the phrase "Your jurisprudence is but the will of your class made into a law for all," Lenin had sought to impress upon his readers that the tsarist courts had been class courts designed to preserve a hostile capitalist class in power and not to administer anything which could be called abstract justice. It was not easy for his admirers, especially for those who lacked sophistication, to make the transition required after the Revolution to respect for the authority of a new court. Some even doubted that courts would be needed any more. There was much material in the pamphlets with which the revolutionaries had wooed the masses before 1917 to encourage thinking along such lines.

Courts had been described by Lenin as being among the instrumentalities of the state apparatus, one of the instruments of power.[4] They were to be required during a period following the Revolution to hold in subjection the defeated classes, but eventually they were to become unnecessary. The growth of a classless society would, according to the pamphlets written by those who had instigated revolution, make unnecessary an apparatus designed to suppress some classes for the benefit of a ruling class. In consequence, the instrumentalities of the state, which included among their number

---

All dates through January 31, 1918, are given in accordance with the Julian calendar in force in Russia at the time. By decree published January 26, 1918, *ibid.*, No. 19, item 289, the Gregorian calendar was adopted for all dates beginning with February 14, 1918, which would have been February 1, 1918, under the Julian calendar.

[4] "A court is an organ of state power. Liberals sometimes forget that. It is a sin for a Marxist to forget it." V. I. Lenin, "K voprosu ob iavke na sud Bol'shevistskikh liderov" [July 8, 1917], in Lenin, *Sochineniia* (4th ed.; Moscow, 1949–1950), XXV, 155. Quoted with other remarks by Lenin about courts in N. V. Krylenko, *Lenin o sude i ugolovnoi politike, k desiatiletiiu so dnia smerti, 1924–1934* (Moscow, 1934), p. 44.

the system of the courts, would eventually have no function to perform and would cease to exist.[5]

Lenin included in his analysis the opinion that the process of withering would require much time and that no one could tell when it would be completed, but some of his colleagues expected the period to be short. No one could know in 1917 when the courts would no longer be required to keep order in the community in favor of its new master, the working class. While the leaders of the Revolution seem to have appreciated that the transition to a society without courts would take time, the public generally had little conception of the magnitude of the task of creating a new social order, and it was with this public that the new judges had to deal.

The first decree on the new court system appeared only after a month of consideration. It had been Communist gospel ever since Lenin had adopted the Paris Commune of 1871 as his model that it was of primary importance in making a successful revolution to break up the apparatus of the old state.[6] In terms of action this meant ousting the bureaucrats themselves, including the judges of the old courts, and Lenin made this specific in discussing the draft decree.[7]

One of the leading figures in the process of preparation of the first decree has reported that there was fear that law was too complex to place in the hands of the inexperienced, and that for this reason the old judges should be retained, at least for a while.[8] He reports that there was agreement that the judges in the new Soviet courts must be close to the people and coming from the very heart of the people. Further, there was agreement that until society was no longer divided into classes, the new court must be a class court defending the interests of the toiling elements of the population.

The difficulty was met when it became necessary to apply the class principle in the selection of the new judges. At this point the nonlawyers among the policy makers were frightened by the thought that there would not be enough legally trained persons to

---

[5] For Lenin's thesis on the withering away of the state, see Lenin, *The State and Revolution* (Moscow, 1935), pp. 81–99.

[6] See *ibid.*, pp. 40–44.

[7] See Lenin, *Sochineniia* (3d ed.; Moscow, 1928–1937), XXII, 424.

[8] P. I. Stuchka, "Proletarskaia revoliutsiia i sud," *Prol. rev. i pravo*, No. 1 (August 1, 1918), p. 5.

become judges, although not a few of the former lawyers had indicated their sympathy for the ideas of communism. Yet the lawyers in the group of policy makers would not permit themselves to be frightened out of destruction of the old court apparatus. They felt assured that with the abolition of the old civil law—a process which was progressing under their eyes as decrees nationalized large-scale productive property and began to reduce private enterprise to modest proportions—the civil relationships of the future would be as easily understood by the layman as by the lawyer. Laws were to be drafted in simple terms, and the complexity of the past was not expected to be permitted to confuse those without legal training.

A NEW JUDICIARY

The first decree on the new courts[9] abolished the three levels of general courts inherited from the tsars as well as the commercial courts which had been functioning in Petrograd, Moscow, Odessa, and Warsaw. Under the laws of the Empire,[10] as reformed in 1864, the general courts had been designed to provide a forum for the trial of all but relatively minor offenses and for the settling of civil disputes except those of small value, the value varying with the type of claim involved.

Apart from the general courts there had been two systems of courts of inferior jurisdiction, the "volost" courts and the "justice of the peace" courts. The volost courts had been created by the Emancipation Act of 1861 to provide a state-sponsored tribunal for the peasantry to replace the "village" courts previously functioning among the serfs. Jurisdiction in the volost courts, as they continued to exist up to the time of the Revolution, had been limited to petty civil claims and criminal prosecutions among the peasants. Control was maintained over them by an agent of the Ministry of the Interior.

[9] November 24, 1917, [1917–1918] I *Sob. Uzak. RSFSR*, No. 4, item 50. The date of adoption is given as November 22, 1917, in a history of Soviet decrees published by the Institute of Marxism-Leninism under the Central Committee of the Communist Party of the Soviet Union and the Institute of History of the USSR Academy of Sciences, *Dekrety Sovetskoi vlasti* (Moscow), I (1957), 85.

[10] For a summary of the judicial structure of the Russian Empire, see Samuel Kucherov, *Courts, Lawyers and Trials under the Last Three Tsars* (New York, 1953), pp. 43–50.

The justice of the peace courts had survived to 1917 in many urban and rural communities of the country, after periods of Imperial displeasure causing their abolition at times in some parts of the Empire. They had jurisdiction over civil claims up to five hundred rubles in value, in contrast to the jurisdiction of the volost courts of one hundred rubles, and in some cases they could go higher, as with real-property actions. Their criminal jurisdiction at the time of the Revolution was likewise limited, largely to crimes for which the penalties might be fines up to three hundred rubles in value or imprisonment for periods not exceeding eighteen months.

The precise line of demarcation of jurisdiction between the general courts and the inferior courts was not clearly designated, so that borderline cases had to be decided by the courts themselves. In view of this fact, which would make necessary a discussion of the case law as well as the details of the statutes, no more will be said here of the details of jurisdiction. For the student of Soviet courts it is important, however, to know that the Soviet authorities inherited a structural pattern which included two court systems, and this fact left its imprint on the decrees of 1917 and 1918.

While the first Soviet decree on the new courts abolished the general court system and declared that subsequently a decree would issue concerning the courts which would replace it, it adopted a different approach to the courts concerned with the cases touching most closely the people in whose name the Revolution had been fought. It suspended the activity of the justice of the peace courts, substituting for the existing justices local courts to be composed of a single professional judge, "professional" in the sense that he was to be employed full time as a judge but not "professional" in the sense that he would necessarily be a lawyer, and two lay judges. The lay judges were to be chosen in turn for each session of the court from a panel prepared for the purpose.

Jurisdiction in the new court was set at a maximum of three thousand rubles[11] for civil cases and over crimes for which a penalty

[11] The value of the ruble at the time is suggested by salary scales. Professional judges received 750 rubles per month in 1918 and court messengers 350 rubles per month. See Cherliunchakevich, "Otchët o dieiatel'nosti miestnykh narodnykh sudov goroda Moskvy za pervuiu tret' 1918 goda," *Prol. rev. i pravo*, No. 2 (August 15, 1918), p. 36.

of up to two years' imprisonment was provided by law. Appeals were to be forbidden unless the judgment exceeded one hundred rubles or there had been a sentence in excess of seven days' detention. In such event there might be a request for a review of the record by a meeting of all judges in the county called together as a "congress" from time to time for the purpose. In no event was there to be a complete retrial of the case as had been permitted in the appellate procedure of the Empire.

The delay in establishing the new courts to replace the justices of the peace of the old regime has already been indicated as it developed in Moscow, which although not yet the capital of the new Russia was considered to be the model for the country. The local court was established even more slowly in other cities. Vitebsk reported that the new court opened its doors only in mid-January of 1918, while Gorodok seems to have been unable to commence its judicial activities until April, 1918.[12]

Evidence of the reason for the delay is to be found in a report from the province of Samara on the problems it had met in creating the new courts.[13] Not until the end of December, 1917, had the provincial soviet formed a "Provincial Commissariat of Justice." It was early January, 1918, before the Provincial Commissariat was able to take the steps required by the first decree on the courts when it acquired the property and files of the former district court of the province and of the justice of the peace courts of the principal cities. Similar steps in the villages of the province had to await the sending of an instruction to the various county soviets to establish "County Commissariats of Justice" to absorb the old courts and create the new. Relations with the Commissariat of Justice in the capital are not mentioned at all in the report, although the acting Commissar, P. I. Stuchka, had created a section in the Commissariat for the establishment of courts on December 12, 1917,[14] and the direction of this section was shown to have been assumed by the incoming Commissar, the Socialist Revolutionary

[12] For notice of opening days in various provinces, see "Khronika," *ibid.*, No. 5–6 (October 1–15, 1918), pp. 78–79.

[13] N. N. Lotov, "Deiatel'nost' Samarskogo Gubernskogo Komissariata Iustitsii," *ibid.*, No. 2–4 (12–14) (February-April, 1919), pp. 86–100.

[14] [1917–1918] I *Sob. Uzak. RSFSR*, No. 9, item 127.

I. N. Shteinberg, when he published the work plan for the Commissariat on December 19, 1917.[15]

The uneven introduction of the new court system was made the subject of an apologetic explanation by Stuchka months later when he followed Shteinberg to become the second Commissar of Justice.[16] He confirmed the implication of the Samara report, namely, that the central authorities had been unable to take part directly in the process of replacing the courts of the old regime with the new Soviet courts. The central authorities had had to content themselves with the issuance of general directives. Stuchka admitted that the change to the new system had been slow in some places, while in others the activities of the old courts had been terminated by local authorities even before the publication of the first decree on the courts. Some communities had established what they had called their "revolutionary people's courts." Others had placed the administration of law and order in the hands of local "investigation committees," while others had established "revolutionary tribunals." These latter bodies were formally sanctioned only in the first decree on the courts in an article authorizing their creation to deal with cases of alleged counterrevolution,[17] but the Commissar's account suggests that they had been established even before the publication of the decree and that they had become the local court for all matters, although presumably their activities were largely in the criminal field. It can hardly be imagined that in the temper of the first few months after the Revolution there would have been many civil claims brought to court for adjudication.

The opening of the new local courts had occurred almost everywhere by the first of the new year of 1918. By July of 1918 the new courts were functioning in two thirds of all of Russia, not excluding the villages. Presumably the statistics concerned only that part of the country which was subject to control by the new regime.

The authors of the first decree on the courts indicated in their decree their expectation that the formal court system established by the state might be replaced at an early opportunity by a system

[15] *Ibid.*, No. 12, item 171. Shteinberg had been named Commissar on December 14, 1917. *Ibid.*, No. 9, item 128.
[16] Stuchka, "Otchët Narodnago Komissara Iustitsii," *Prol. rev. i pravo*, No. 1 (August 1, 1918), p. 33.
[17] Art. 8.

for settling disputes without state intervention. Under the Empire, arbitration had not been organized by a state agency, but it had been arranged by various commercial organizations like those to be found elsewhere in Europe. Now the new decree provided that if the parties so desired, they might refer disputes in civil cases to an arbitration court on which a special decree was to issue subsequently.[18] Not only were aggrieved citizens to be permitted to take their property and contract disputes to such a tribunal, but they were permitted to go before the tribunal with cases involving violation of the criminal laws if the offense fell in that category of case established by the Imperial Criminal Code as subject to prosecution only if the injured party requested prosecution—in short, the criminal cases in which the state had no interest transcending the desires of the injured party for revenge.

The settlement outside of court of disputes of a minor character involving no great danger to the welfare of the community became later a goal of importance to the Soviet policy makers. The first decree marks the first step in implementing a policy which will be found to appear in various forms with the evolution of the Soviet system for settling disputes in society.

LIQUIDATING PREREVOLUTIONARY PROBLEMS

By February, 1918, the new regime indicated its preparedness to attack the problem of cases held over from the courts of the old regime and the problem of new disputes of a character involving more property and more serious offenses than those included within the jurisdiction of the court created by the November decree. In its second decree on the courts[19] the government established what

[18] Art. 6. The decree was issued February 3, 1918. [1917–1918] I *Sob. Uzak. RSFSR*, No. 28, item 366. Its provisions are set forth in Chapter XII.
[19] [1917–1918] I *Sob. Uzak. RSFSR*, No. 26, item 420. This decree bears no date in the official collection where it was published on March 7, 1918, as item 420. It appears between items 346 and 348, seemingly being item 347 and misnumbered, for a second item 420 appears subsequently in its proper place. Nevertheless the decree was cited soon after publication by the Commissar of Justice as item 420 and noted as having been published on January 12, 1918, in the newspaper of the Workers'-Peasants' Government. See Stuchka, *Narodnyi sud v voprosakh i otvietakh* (Moscow, 1918), p. 73. A historian currently gives the date of approval by the Council of People's Commissars as January 30, 1918. See M. V. Kozhevnikov, *Istoriia Sovetskogo suda 1917–1956*

it called a "District People's Court" to try cases exceeding the
jurisdiction of the local people's court. In contrast to the local courts,
the district courts were to be comprised of more judges than the
people's courts, and there was greater emphasis upon professionalism.
Thus, all questions before trial were to be decided by a bench of
three professional judges, and the trial itself, if it concerned a civil
claim, was to be heard by three professional judges, supplemented
by four lay judges; and if criminal by a bench of twelve lay judges
and two alternate lay judges, chaired by one of the members of the
staff of professional judges assigned to the court. All professional
judges were to be named and subject to recall by the district soviet,
while the lay judges were to be chosen from a panel prepared by
the provincial soviets or by the city soviets in the large cities on
the basis of lists of candidates submitted by the borough soviets in
the cities or the village soviets in the countryside. Nothing was said
of requirements that the professional judges have legal training,
although in its last article the decree permitted judges of the courts
of the old regime to be selected for the new courts. In fact, most of
the professional judges were legally trained, to the annoyance of
a man who was to become Commissar of Justice after Stuchka and
was eventually to undo the work of the draftsmen of the second
decree.[20]

Appeals from decisions of the new district courts were forbidden
in the form permitted under Imperial law, but there was to be
permitted under the name of "cassation" a review of the record
without the calling of witnesses and the verification of documents.
In substance, this meant that the record was to be subject to review
for errors by a panel of judges elected for the purpose from among

---

gody (Moscow, 1957), p. 30. Another current historian sets the date of first
publication in *Izvestiia TsIK i Petrogradskogo Soveta* as February 20, 1918.
See V. A. Ivanov, "Organizatsiia suda i prokuratury," in *Sorok let sovetskogo
prava 1917–1957* (Leningrad, 1957), I, 569. The theory that the numbering
of the decree as item 420 was an editorial error is supported by a republication
thirty-eight years later in a collection of documents as item 420 (347). See
S. A. Golunskii, ed., *Istoriia zakonodatel'stva SSSR i RSFSR po ugolovnomu
protsessu i organizatsii suda i prokuratury 1917–1954: Sbornik dokumentov*
(Moscow, 1955), p. 40. Lenin's amendments to the draft are set forth in
Dekrety Sovetskoi vlasti, pp. 463–66. This work dates the decree February 15,
1918. It says of the citation, "Item marked incorrectly as 420."

[20] See Kurskii, "Otchët," pp. 45–46.

their own number by all district people's court judges in each province. Remand for new trial was to be permitted not only if errors thought to be substantial had been committed, but also if the reviewing court found the decision to be clearly unjust in substance.

To assure uniformity in the practice of the provincial "cassational" courts, a "supreme court control" was ordered established in the capital. Its members were to be chosen for one-year terms by the members of the provincial "cassational" courts from among their own members and were to serve for one-year terms, subject to recall either by the district courts or by the soviets. Uniformity was to be established by court orders based upon divergencies found in this review of the work of the "cassational" courts. Should the control body find that any law had proved in practice to be contrary to what it believed to be the popular concept of justice, the legislative organ was to be informed of the necessity of publishing a new law. Decisions of the control body, could be revoked by the legislative organ, thus establishing in practice the principle later to become more clearly enunciated, namely, that under the Soviet system of government there should be no separation of powers between the various branches of government, all of them being responsible to the agency entrusted with the legislative function.

Although the second decree on the courts was published in February, it was not until April that the authorities began to establish the new district people's courts.[21] They never established the provincial "cassational" courts and the supreme court control.[22] The delay was explained by the then Commissar of Justice as caused by the fact that the district courts' judges were mostly judges of the former courts, and this fact called forth noticeable opposition in the provinces. The Commissar claimed that his Commissariat had opposed the establishment of the court of superior jurisdiction from the beginning, but this opposition had not caused the Commissariat to delay in putting the second decree into effect. He declared that his Commissariat was working on a draft of a new law to be intro-

---

[21] See Stuchka, "Otchët," p. 33.

[22] See A. I. Denisov, ed., *Istoriia sovetskogo gosudarstva i prava* (Moscow, 1949), p. 53.

duced in the very near future to create a single court of general jurisdiction under which the local people's courts defined in the first decree might absorb the jurisdiction of the district people's courts created by the second decree.

Some of the local people's courts, notably those in Petrograd, tried to expand the jurisdiction of the local courts beyond the statutory limits of the first decree and to absorb the work of the district people's court, thus creating the single court of which the Commissariat was dreaming. On June 4, 1918, the Petrograd interdistrict meeting of local judges and representatives of the local soviets framed a resolution asking that all criminal and civil cases be transferred from the district courts to the local courts, and that the district courts be abolished.[23] In reply to the resolution the Commissariat explained that the second decree on the courts could not but be observed as an act of supreme Soviet authority; further, the district courts were already functioning in Petrograd, Omsk, Tomsk, Tobolsk, Barnaul, Novo-Nikoliaevsk, Vladimir, Kostroma, Riazan, Viatka "and elsewhere." Finally, it was said that to have burdened the local people's courts with cases inherited from the past would have deprived them of the possibility of administering justice in the innumerable current cases because they would have been forced to deal with highly complicated civil and criminal cases for which they were not fitted.

Some of the indecision as to the role of the district courts may have been the result of the fact that the decree establishing them had issued from the government at a time when it was a coalition of Bolsheviks and members of the left wing of the Socialist Revolutionary party. The latter group had placed one of its members, I. N. Shteinberg, to whom reference has already been made, in the post of Commissar of Justice. He had assumed his duties on December 10, 1917, to remain until March 4, 1918. It will be seen that the first decree creating the simplified system of local courts preceded his regime in the Commissariat, and that the third decree followed it.

Shteinberg was a lawyer who was not prepared to agree with his Bolshevik colleagues that the Revolution must swing very far to the left and discard accepted standards of law and order. In his

[23] Text published in *Prol. rev. i pravo*, No. 1 (August 1, 1918), p. 72.

memoirs[24] he recounts two instances when he stood out against
Bolshevik terror and opposed Lenin's position. It is possible that
his stabilizing influence was felt in the preparation of the second
decree with its emphasis upon a court staffed generally with persons trained in the law and authorized to function under the principles of the prerevolutionary codes of procedure. The Bolsheviks
later claimed that the influence of the Socialist Revolutionaries
accounted for the legality of the early decree, but an American
student of the matter in the early 1930's concluded that such an
explanation was not entirely correct. He noted the fact that the
Instruction on the Rules for the Courts, which was signed in July,
1918, by Stuchka, who had replaced Shteinberg when the Bolsheviks
assumed the justice portfolio, contained elements of the second
decree.[25]

PRACTICE IN THE LOCAL COURTS

The Moscow court is said to have been the local people's court
which conformed most closely to the requirements of the first
decree.[26] Some indication of the popularity of this court as an
instrument for the settlement of disputes is to be found in its increasing activity in the civil sphere. In January, 1918, 376 civil cases
were heard in the various local Moscow courts. In spite of the
fact that calendar reform reduced February to a half month, 650
cases of a civil nature were heard in that month. In March the
civil cases increased to 2,203, and in April they totaled 3,339, or 31
percent of the work of the courts reporting their statistics.[27] The
Commissariat of Justice concluded that the local courts had not
only become a part of the life of the community, but, with each
month, they were embracing new fields of legal relationships among
the broad masses of the population—in short, they seem to have
been becoming popular.

Attention was called especially to the growth in the number of

[24] See I. N. Steinberg, *In the Workshop of the Revolution* (New York,
1953), pp. 69–72, 77–81. The author's name when used in the text herein is
transliterated in accordance with the system used throughout rather than in
the simplified form used by the author after he came to New York.

[25] See Judah Zelitch, *Soviet Administration of Criminal Law* (Philadelphia,
1931), p. 23.

[26] See Kurskii, "Otchët," p. 39.   [27] *Ibid.*, p. 40.

civil cases heard and to the fact that they were increasing at a rate much faster than the criminal cases. In fact, the burden of civil cases was said to have been the principal reason for having to increase the staffs of the people's courts to four persons (a clerk, a senior and junior assistant, and a messenger), which was said to exceed the staffs of the former justice of the peace courts.

When the figures for May and June, 1918, were added to those published earlier, it was found that the number of civil cases had increased six times over those filed in January, while the criminal cases had only doubled in number over the same period.[28] An analysis of the types of cases of a civil nature indicated that the total of 3,393 civil cases for June, 1918, was divided as follows: 1,935 were suits on various types of contract and tort claims, 847 were suits for divorce, while 611 were protective proceedings, usually for maintenance (*okhranitelnye*). Very few cases were being appealed to the "congress" of people's judges. Of over 13,000 civil cases heard in the first six months of 1918, only 232 were appealed, of which 53 percent had been disposed of by June 30. Of the cases concluded, the trial court's decision was affirmed in 54 percent; changes in the trial court's opinion were made in 42 percent, and 4 percent were cases which were withdrawn before a decision.[29]

By the autumn of 1918 the number of local people's courts had increased so that there were throughout the entire Russian Republic 3,267 local people's courts, with 337 "congresses" of local court judges sitting as "cassational" tribunals to review their work. In the Moscow province there were 142 local courts, and in the Petrograd province 138.[30]

PRACTICE IN THE DISTRICT COURTS

The Petrograd District People's Court has left a report[31] of its activities, which suggests the type of work being done by these superior courts established by the second decree on the courts. It

[28] "O dvizhenii del v Sovete mestnykh narodnykh sudei i mestnykh narodnykh sudakh goroda Moskvy s 1-go ianvaria po 1-oe iiulia 1918 g.," *Prol. rev. i pravo*, No. 5–6 (October 1–15, 1918), p. 32.

[29] *Ibid.*, pp. 34–35.

[30] "Svedeniia o deiatel'nosti mestnykh narodnykh sudov i sovetov narodnykh sudei v guberniiakh respubliki," *ibid.*, No. 8–9–10 (November 15–December 15, 1918), pp. 73–74.

[31] "Khronika," *ibid.*, pp. 140–41.

inherited some 10,000 cases which had been pending in the District, Circuit, Commercial, and Supreme Court (Governing Senate) of the former regime. To examine this huge volume of cases the court established three chambers: criminal, civil, and a special chamber to hear cases involving claims for damages resulting from death or loss of working capacity. Work was begun in mid-April when the selection of cases inherited from the past had been completed. The judges had been chosen from persons trained in the law: two former judges of the former district courts, and the others former clerks of court, provincial justices of the peace, court investigators, and a few lawyers. The report declares that these latter were not those who had formerly had well-known law practices.

Court sessions had been initiated with the participation of lay judges on May 21 and were held thereafter once a month for two weeks at a time. They heard the civil cases and claims for damages resulting from death or loss of working capacity. The first session of the criminal department was not until September 9, 1918. While most of the civil cases filed with the court were inherited from the past, the figure being 5,200 for the period of the report (apparently to October 1, 1918), there were 681 new civil cases. Of the 5,881 cases, 1,090 had been disposed of in the preliminary sitting, while 299 had gone to trial. The department handling the personal injury cases had 3,879 cases inherited from the past, and 2,050 cases filed since the Revolution. Of these, 364 cases were disposed of at the preliminary sitting, and 835 had gone to trial by the time of the report. The criminal department inherited 1,567 cases from the past, and received 535 cases prosecuted since the Revolution.

The work of several other district courts was analyzed at the end of June, 1918.[32] The Tver District Court had begun sessions on May 13, 1918, with a docket of 619 cases. After preliminary examination the court transferred 330 of these to the local people's court; 5 cases were transferred to the revolutionary tribunals as involving serious charges of counterrevolution; 23 cases involving juvenile delinquents were transferred to the newly created Commissions on Juveniles, and 119 cases were dismissed. The Orlov District Court held two sittings in the month of May, 1918, at which it heard ten cases with lay judges, in eight of which the accused was convicted,

[32] See Kurskii, "Otchët," pp. 46–47.

and then it went on circuit to the city of Karachev in which it heard ten more cases in four days, as the result of which two more accused persons were convicted. The Novgorod District Court held its first sitting for two days in the first week of June, 1918, to hear eight cases, in which five of the accused were convicted. The Vitebsk District Court began trying criminal cases at the beginning of June with a bench of lay judges drawn exclusively from local factories, and the civil cases were tried on June 20 and 21, 1918. In the Riazan District Court legal specialists were found to have had considerable influence, for attention was first given to establishing a system of preliminary investigation, and two sets of court rules were drafted, one entitled "Temporary Rules for the Investigating Commissions," and the other entitled "Concerning Candidates for Court Positions (Senior and Junior)."

THE APPLICABLE LAW

No drafts of codes were ready for the new courts when they were brought into existence. Only the outlines of a family code were published in December, 1917, to be followed in October, 1918, with a full code.[33] The second code, concerning labor law, was published in December, 1918. Consequently the new Soviet courts had little to guide them in the form of legislation from the hands of the new policy makers. To meet the need for guidance, the first decree on the courts had instructed the new people's courts to use as a guide the laws of the ousted government to the extent that they had not been revoked by the Revolution and were not contrary to the revolutionary conscience and revolutionary consciousness of the judges. The second decree instructed the district people's courts to be guided by the civil and criminal laws existing up to that time to the extent that they had not been revoked by decrees of the Central Executive Committee and Council of People's Commissars and did not conflict with socialist justice. While the formula had been changed slightly in the second decree, it was essentially the same with its authorization to use the laws of the past, tempered by each

[33] For an account of substantive law in the USSR see John N. Hazard, *Law and Social Change in the U.S.S.R.* (London, 1953).

court's concept of the type of justice consonant with Soviet Russia's
new variety of socialism.

Placing the right to develop law in the hands of the court exercising its own concept of socialist justice gave rise, apparently, to
some questions when the judges retired to formulate a decision
concerning the fate of one of the workmen for whom the new
regime had expressed its primary concern. It has been reported that
the concept of the Soviet court as a "proletarian class court" was
not equivalent to deciding all cases in favor of the proletarian or
the poor peasant and against his opponent.[34] Yet the urge to favor
the workman regardless of the merits was said to have been very
strong, so much so that in chambers when the judges retired to
decide the case, there was hardly a session in the first Moscow
people's court in which it was not necessary to discuss this theme
exhaustively. The professional judge of this court has reported that
in the first six months of his practice, however, there was not a
case in which this primitive view of the class character of the court
had triumphed. He declared that even when the lay judges had
been tempted to be impassioned and partial, they had restrained
themselves. This view is not shared by some of those who later fled
Soviet jurisdiction to take refuge in the West.

The Moscow judges of this early time showed themselves ready to
decide the applicable law and to defend their decisions against the
inroads of the politicians, for on March 30, 1918, after the sentence
of one of the local courts had been set aside by one of the borough
soviets of Moscow, the general assembly of judges adopted a resolution to the effect that the court when it is acting within its special
competence must be guaranteed full and exclusive authority.[35] The
resolution was introduced by one E. B. Pashukanis who was to be
elected on May 11, 1918, as one of the three permanent members
of the seven-man presidium created at that time to assume organizational and administrative direction over the Moscow local people's
courts. In this act the man who was later to rise to the highest point
in the hierarchy of Soviet lawyers by becoming Director of the
Institute of Soviet Construction and Law, Vice-President of the

---

[34] See Kadich, "O narodnom sudie," p. 26.
[35] See Cherliunchakevich, "Otchët," p. 34.

Communist Academy, member of the constitutional drafting committee which prepared the constitution of 1936, and author of major theoretical treatises, made his first public play in favor of the independence of the judiciary and against the interference of the local soviets representing the political and administrative officials of the community. In the light of his dismissal, denunciation and probable death in 1937 under criticism as an "enemy of the people," this first recorded act of resistance to direct political intervention in court activity has interest to outsiders trying to understand this complicated man.[36]

Some of those who participated in discussion of the first decree as it was being drafted are reported to have been opposed to reference to the old laws, while a few were opposed to the application of written law in general.[37] The Commissar of Justice seems to have been realistic about the lasting influence of legal tradition. He declared that it was true that the old laws were being burned, but that it was not enough to burn the ancient codes in order to erase their influence from the memories and upon the attitudes of man. The formula adopted in the first two decrees was, apparently, recognition that the old laws would naturally continue to have influence, but at the same time it was a warning to all that they might not be applied if they were in conflict with the discernible policy of the new order.

Although reproached by the right wing for this derogation from the old laws, the Commissar quoted Marx in support of the thesis that the social structure does not rest upon law, but the laws reflect the social structure.[38] It followed, in the Commissar's opinion, that the law must change to meet the needs of the new society, and the formula of the first two decrees was designed to achieve this end. It was the hope of the Commissar that the judges, who had been made as free and independent of the old written law as was

---

[36] Pashukanis was rehabilitated posthumously in 1956 following Stalin's death, but Stalin's charges against him were not published. See "Za podlinno nauchnuiu razrabotku korennykh voprosov nauki istorii sovetskogo gosudarstva i prava," *Sovetskoe gosudarstvo i pravo* No. 6 (1956), p. 10. For a record of the denunciation and the texts of the principal works of Pashukanis and his denouncers, see V. I. Lenin *et al.*, *Soviet Legal Philosophy* (20th Century Legal Philosophy Series; Cambridge, Mass., 1951).

[37] See Stuchka, "Proletarskaia revoliutsiia," p. 3.

[38] *Ibid.*, p. 4.

possible, would create in their decisions the most valuable material with which to establish new codes of law. The second decree had ordered that any departure from prerevolutionary law be accompanied by a reasoned opinion to provide material for new norms. The Commissar admitted that in reading the decisions of the people's judges he was finding some strange and absurd decisions, but he thought that the majority were cases based on life, not in the sense of enthusiasm for ancient custom as the manifestation of what was called "moldy folk wisdom," but in the sense of a true understanding of the developing new social structure in all of its details. To a common-law lawyer of the Anglo-American school, the Commissar seems to be saying that a common-law system which grows with the times has real advantages in pointing the way to social reformers who are not entirely sure of the direction in which they want to lead. With their centuries of tradition of code law, the revolutionary leaders of the new Russia were consciously choosing at this time the common-law method of development as best suited to the needs of the early revolutionary period.

CASES BEFORE THE COURTS

Decisions of some of the new courts in the early months will give evidence of the influence of the former codes upon the courts, and the extent to which even the district courts were prepared to depart from the old rules. Two criminal cases inherited from prerevolutionary times by the Tver district court have been recorded. One Daletskii was prosecuted under a statute of June 6, 1917, for having urged publicly on July 9, 1917, the murder of the head of the provisional government, Alexander Kerenskii. The court decided that as Kerenskii had since fled the country and had been declared an outlaw, any further legal action in the case would be contrary to the socialist concept of justice of the toiling people of the Russian Social Democratic Soviet Republic and the scruples of the people's court. Daletskii was ordered released and the case closed.[39] In the other case[40] one Danilov, a youth of eighteen years of age, was prosecuted under the articles of the Imperial Criminal Code

[39] *Case of Daletskii,* in Kurskii, "Otchët," pp. 46–47.
[40] *Case of Danilov, ibid.,* p. 46.

for an attempt to kill a nineteen-year-old girl. He was found guilty and sentenced to two years in prison with loss during that time of his good name, of the confidence of society, and of his family and property rights. The court felt itself torn between the sense of justice of the lay judges which required an obvious allowance for youth under the circumstances of the case and the law of the government which had been overthrown, which the judges set forth in scrupulous detail in the decision. The court also referred frequently to the amnesty of March 17, 1917.

Two cases also inherited from the past were brought before the Nizhegorod District Court with similar examination of conscience on the part of the judges. One Abramov, forty-two years of age, was accused of having broken into a sawmill on the night of March 27, 1917, with the aid of another and with having stolen a drive belt valued at three hundred rubles. He was convicted on his own admission of guilt and sentenced to internment in the correctional establishment for two years with loss of all rights and privileges pertaining to his person and to his status, and to pay court costs if able.[41] The other case involved the theft of a horse with its harness and sleds by one Serafimovich, twenty-four years of age, on January 4, 1917, from a peasant in Nizhny-Novgorod. He was convicted, but the court declared that it was taking into consideration the mitigating facts that he was in a desperate situation at the time of the theft and had subsequently frankly admitted his guilt. The sentence was set at hard labor in prison for one year and five months, of which one year and four months would be considered as having been served, that being the time he had already been under guard awaiting trial.[42]

The greatest difficulty in utilizing the Imperial codes as guides was found to lie in persuading the lay judges that the rule of the Imperial Code was still appropriate. The lay judges are said to have refused entirely to apply the penalties prescribed by the old code.[43] They wanted to fit the punishment to the particular circumstances of each individual case, taking into consideration the circumstances

[41] *Case of Abramov,* in Kurskii, "Zamietki o narodnom sudie," *Prol. rev. i pravo,* No. 2 (August 15, 1918), pp. 17–18.

[42] *Case of Serafimovich, ibid.,* p. 18.

[43] See Speranskii, "Narodnye zasedateli (Lichnye vpechatleniia)," *ibid.,* No. 5–6 (October 1–15, 1918), pp. 28–29.

of the environment, and having in mind the rehabilitation of the criminal rather than his punishment. The lay judges had particular difficulty with the idea of the conditional sentence, generally refusing to use it, seeing in it a sort of compromise. They used to say: "If he is guilty, he should be convicted. If he is not guilty, he should be acquitted. If he committed the crime because of poverty, that fact should be found, and he should be freed."

The distillers of illegal liquor were insufferable to the lay judges, and they were not content with the penalties prescribed for violating the Imperial excise tax law. They thought that the mild statutes issued before the Revolution were completely unsatisfactory when the illegal distillers were speculators, or wealthy peasants, or those who stole grain to make alcohol.

Officials who committed crimes and accepted bribes, especially when they were elected Soviet officials, were judged severely by the lay judges. In the opinions the lay judges stated that such crimes as bribery, extortion, and fraud discredited the idea of Soviet authority, and that offenders in these categories were actually undoing the socialist revolution, which was cause for no mercy.

Property crimes, especially theft and robbery from the gardens of landlords, were looked upon more leniently by the lay judges, who thought that the thieves should not be punished under the articles of the Imperial Code since they showed, although in very crude form, the undercurrents of revolutionary sentiments. Even attempts to murder were looked upon with leniency, each one being examined in the light of the conditions of life at the moment of the attempt.

The local people's courts are also reported as having decided complex cases. Under the law they were concerned with matters of postrevolutionary origin. Some had to do with situations in which the court was called upon to give effect to the policies of the new government. Thus, when one L'vov brought suit against the manager of a store belonging to the heirs of one Kondratov, the suit was dismissed because it was found at the trial that the building had been requisitioned by the county soviet for its own use. The court declared that any suit would have to be brought against the soviet as the responsible party.[44] Likewise a suit brought by a former workman, one Mogil'shchikov, against the owner of a factory, was dis-

[44] *L'vov* v. *Kondratov,* in Kurskii, "Zamietki o narodnom sudie," *ibid.,* p. 21.

missed because it was found that the factory was one in which a workers' committee had been established on whom the employment of workers had come to depend. The court stated that the owner was no longer concerned with the internal affairs of the factory. The court added that the workers' committee in the factory had offered to continue the plaintiff at work, but that for some reason he had refused to accept the employment.[45]

In a divorce action involving the Bykovs, the wife had complained that she could not reconcile herself to return to her husband, and that the village communal society had ordered her father to pay fifteen hundred rubles in the event of divorce to compensate the husband for damages suffered during the marriage. At the trial the husband declared that he would consent to the divorce if the fifteen hundred rubles were paid. The court granted the divorce, but refused to give effect to the village community's order.[46]

Two civil actions were brought against the Vishivsk village communal society for damages caused to fields of crops by animals belonging to the society. In one a peasant Bazhenov sued for damages caused to his clover patch. The suit was dismissed because in the court's opinion the plaintiff had failed to prove that the damage had been caused by the society's animals rather than by a single animal belonging to some other individuals. Further, although the field had been fenced, the fence was in such bad repair that the plaintiff could be accused of negligence in protecting his own property.[47] Citation was made to the laws of the Empire. In the other action[48] against the same village communal society, the opposite result was reached when one Kormakov sued for one hundred forty rubles damage to his field of oats. Judgment was given for the plaintiff because the court was convinced by the testimony of witnesses that the herd belonging to the village communal society had spent the night close to the field and because of that fact they could have entered the field. Further, hoof prints had been found leading in the direction of the village herd.

A horse trade came before another court for examination on suit

[45] *Mogil'shchikov* v. *Factory Committee, ibid.*
[46] *Bykova* v. *Bykov, ibid.*
[47] *Bazhenkov* v. *Vshivskii Village Community, ibid.,* p. 19.
[48] *Kormakov* v. *Vshivskii Village Community, ibid.*

brought by one Omonina to set it aside because of fraud.[49] The facts indicated that Omonina had traded her horse to one Kaliaganov for the latter's horse plus a cash payment of ninety rubles. After the trade Omonina discovered that her newly acquired horse was weak and emaciated, and she decided that she would rather have her own horse back. At the trial Kaliaganov admitted the trade and the weak and emaciated condition of the horse, but he claimed that this condition had developed as the result of Omonina's failure to feed the horse properly. After hearing the witnesses, the court concluded that Kaliaganov had taken advantage of Omonina; that he had sought to conceal the condition of his horse by throwing into the deal the ninety ruble cash payment; that he had influenced the testimony of some witnesses at the trial; and that it could be presumed that Omonina would have cared for the horse properly as her own property. On the basis of the appropriate article of the Imperial Code, the deal was ordered set aside. Each party was to return to the other the horse in its possession, and Omonina was to repay the ninety rubles received as added inducement to proceed with the trade. Further, Kaliaganov, as the party at fault, was ordered to pay the plaintiff's expenses of twenty rubles incurred in bringing the case to court, and to pay also the expenses of the court of ten rubles.

In commenting upon the handling of these cases, Kurskii, who was later to become Commissar of Justice, concluded that the local people's courts were already providing a wealth of material from which it was possible to measure the ability of the local courts as well as to determine the character of revolutionary genius in developing law.[50] He felt that it was premature to draw any general conclusions of far-reaching character, but he thought it possible to say that if the district people's courts could not free themselves of the snares of the old criminal laws with all of their special points, such as variations in penalty depending upon whether the property was valued at more than three hundred rubles, then it would be the fault first of all of the old lawyers among them. He hoped that it would be possible to utilize the third decree on the court, which had just been promulgated at the time he wrote, to leave with the

[49] *Omonina v. Kaliaganov, ibid.,* p. 20.   [50] See *ibid.,* p. 22.

district courts only a few really serious cases and thus clear the way for the eventual creation of a single people's court for all types of jurisdiction.

THE DISTRICT COURTS
LOSE IMPORTANCE

The third decree on the courts, of which Kurskii had spoken, had been issued on July 20, 1918.[51] It marked a step toward the single people's court, for it reduced the jurisdiction of the district courts and increased the jurisdiction of the local courts. While the local courts had been limited by the first decree to civil suits involving claims up to three thousand rubles and over crimes for which a penalty of two years' imprisonment was provided by law, the new decree increased the civil jurisdiction. The local courts now could hear claims up to ten thousand rubles and try crimes for which law or socialist consciousness authorized penalties up to five years' imprisonment. The jurisdiction of the district courts was defined as including criminal cases involving attempts to commit murder, rape, robbery, banditry, to engage in counterfeiting of paper money, bribery, and black marketing (speculation). The crimes of bribery and black marketing had previously been within the exclusive jurisdiction of the revolutionary tribunals established by the first decree on the courts to protect the state against counterrevolution. Appeals from decisions were to be permitted in the same criminal cases as under the first decree, namely, when the sentence was in excess of seven days' imprisonment, but the value of the civil judgment from which an appeal might be taken was raised from the minimum of three hundred rubles set by the first decree to five hundred rubles.

A change was made in the character of the bench authorized to hear civil cases in the district courts. The bench was materially reduced in size from the requirement of the second decree that it be composed of three professional judges supplemented by four lay judges, for the new district court bench was to be composed of but one professional judge from the civil department of the court and four lay judges.

The authority granted in the second decree to establish a "supreme

[51] [1917–1918] I *Sob. Uzak. RSFSR*, No. 52, item 589.

court control" to assure uniformity in the practice of the provincial "cassational" courts, and the authority to create provincial "cassational" courts was revoked in favor of the establishment of a temporary "Cassational Court" to be established in Moscow to hear civil and criminal appeals from the district courts. It was to be composed of a president and his deputy, named by the People's Commissariat of Justice and confirmed by the Central Executive Committee of the Republic, and of eight members selected by the Central Executive Committee from a list of nominees to be prepared by August 1, 1918, by the district people's courts and the various "councils" of local people's judges. All judges were subject to recall by the Central Executive Committee of the Republic.

The running of the various statutes of limitations which had been suspended earlier from the first day of the Revolution was to recommence on August 1, 1918, so that the defense of laches might be introduced thereafter in appropriate cases. With this provision, the third decree struck a procedural note which was in contrast to the attitude of the earlier months, when formal procedural matters were in general disrepute. The first decree on the courts had established no rules of procedure for the local people's courts. Accounts of the operations of the first courts contain no reference to procedure.

PROCEDURAL GUIDANCE TO COURTS

The need for some procedural guidance seems to have been felt early by the new judges, for there is a report of a special meeting of judges called to study the subject in Moscow from which there issued on April 15, 1918, a "Temporary Instruction on the Organization and Work of the Local People's Courts." [52] This instruction is said to have contained a detailed statement on the method of conducting a criminal case, the principal elements of which had been projected as early as January 28, 1918. On May 18, 1918, general instructions on the procedure to be followed in conducting a civil case had been adopted by a general meeting of judges.

The district courts had not been left in procedural confusion, for the second decree on the court had provided that civil and criminal

[52] See Cherliunchakevich, "Otchët," p. 34.

cases should be conducted in accordance with the provisions of the
codes of 1864 to the extent that these had not been revoked by
decrees of the Central Executive Committee and Council of People's
Commissars and did not conflict with the concept of justice of the
toiling classes.[53] The district courts were not to follow slavishly the
procedural rules. They were to reject arguments based on formal
rules of procedure,[54] and to admit or obtain any evidence they
thought pertinent.[55] Since the district courts, unlike the local courts,
seem always to have included legally trained persons upon the
bench, there was presumably no problem of knowing how to conduct a case. It is not surprising, therefore, that the early periodicals
contain no complaints or discussion on procedure.

A first instruction on court procedure for the local people's courts
was issued by the Commissariat of Justice over Stuchka's signature
on July 23, 1918.[56] It devoted most of its attention to criminal cases,
but its provisions also treat of problems in civil cases when they
require special mention. While its opening sections merely repeat
the material on structure of the court as they had been set forth in
the first decree on the court, and on jurisdiction as modified by the
third decree, new material is introduced on the conduct of a case.
The court's work is defined from the period of preliminary investigation, this task having been placed upon the single professional judge
of the local people's court in simple criminal cases and upon the
investigation commission established by the second decree on the
courts for the work of the district courts, when the case was "more
complicated." There was no definition of the factor to be used in
determining complexity. While the investigating committee might
begin an investigation on its own initiative, the case might not be
brought to trial without the consent of the court. This provision
suggests that the draftsmen of the rules had little confidence in
what amounted to a "police" agency, especially when it had been
created to serve the legally minded district courts, and wished to
maintain control over its activities by the judiciary of the local courts
for whom it was now to perform services.

The principle of court initiative in the commencement of cases
was adopted in the first rules, it being provided that the local judge

---

[53] Art. 8.   [54] Art. 12.   [55] Art. 14.
[56] [1917–1918] I *Sob. Uzak. RSFSR,* No. 53, item 597.

might call a citizen for questioning if he thought that there had been a violation of law, or if a member of the local soviet or a state official requested that court proceedings be instituted. If the judge concluded from the questioning that the individual concerned should be held under guard, he might give such an order on his own initiative, but he was required to obtain ratification of his act by the full bench at its next sitting. When a case was to be brought to trial, the full dossier had to be presented to the court, including the substance of all of the interrogation, examination of evidence and facts thought to be material to the case, together with the accusation, which was comparable to an indictment.

The local people's professional judge was instructed to acquaint himself with this file before the trial to determine whether the accusation was properly formulated and supported by sufficient evidence to merit a trial, and then to set a day for trial if the facts warranted it. He was also to order taken such measures as seemed necessary to assure the presence of the defendant. The decision as to the measures to be taken to assure the presence of the defendant at his trial had to be submitted to the "college" of the local people's court, defined as the group of all professional judges in the court plus two lay judges. Should the court conclude on the preliminary review of the file that the case was outside the jurisdiction of the local people's courts, as that jurisdiction had been defined by decrees one and three, it was to forward the case to the appropriate court for action. If the defendant had been placed under guard, the hearing of his case was to be given priority over all other cases before the court.

Interested parties were to be summoned by a registered letter or orally, stating the reason for the summons and the consequences for failure to appear. The rules were quite detailed as to what the court was to do when the trial opened: determine who was there, determine whether the case could be heard under the circumstances, it being provided that failure of an interested party to appear might be considered inconsequential by the court. In the absence of a defendant a copy of the sentence or of the civil judgment was to be sent to him. If a party wished to call witnesses, the court was authorized to determine whether their testimony was to be pertinent. Experts might be called when necessary, except that if the case required the analysis of material evidence this had to be performed by experts before trial.

Witnesses, experts, and the parties were not to be sworn, but to be informed that false testimony subjected them to prosecution. In this provision the draftsmen probably reflected the Communist party's denial of the existence of God, for a state led by atheists had no reason to ask its witnesses in court to swear before their Maker to tell the truth. The reason formally given for eliminating the oath was not so basic, however. It was explained that in view of the separation of church and state, there could no longer be an oath in court.

Trials were to be in public unless the court thought special circumstances required that the doors be closed. Witnesses who had not testified were not to be permitted to be present while other witnesses were testifying, so as to avoid the possibility of a change in testimony in the light of what had been overheard.

The trial was to open with the calling of the court to order by the professional judge. The floor was then to be given to the plaintiff in a civil case, or to the complainant in a criminal case, for a brief statement of his understanding of the facts. Thereafter the court was to formulate the accusation or the civil complaint in legal terms, and ask the accused whether he pleaded guilty, or recognized his civil liability. The defendant was then to be given his hearing. In the event of admission of guilt or liability, the court was authorized to proceed immediately to the decision without the hearing of witnesses. If the defendant denied responsibility, the witnesses were to be called one by one to testify, their testimony being written into the form of a statement to be signed by them. If they were illiterate, this fact was to be stated in the record. When all testimony had been given and the final arguments had been made by any representatives of the parties present, the parties were themselves to be given an opportunity to say their final word, the defendant always being permitted to speak last.

HOSTILITY TO FORMALITY

The hostility of the draftsmen to formal rules was expressed in an article reading:

In hearing both criminal and civil cases, the local people's court is not cramped by any formal considerations, and it is permitted to admit any evidence it wishes under the circumstances of the case, and to demand it of persons who have it. Also the local people's court may reject any reference to the lapse of prescriptive time or of any other period of limitation, and in spite of any formal objections it may decide clearly just demands.

In this rule the draftsmen had adopted the substance of principles established in the second decree on the courts for the purpose of guiding the district people's courts. The provision of this principle in the new rules for the local courts emphasizes the desire of the rulers of the new Russia to reaffirm faith in informality and simplicity in legal procedures at a time when a set of procedural rules, even though rudimentary in form, was being adopted for the local courts.

Examination of the new rules indicates that emphasis is upon proceedings before trial. The draftsmen appear to have been influenced strongly by the continental procedure, common to the Russian Empire as well as to Western European countries, of preparing an exhaustive examination of the case before trial. Trials on the Continent look to the common-law lawyer like a verification of the work of the preliminary examiner rather than a proceeding *de novo* in which no one knows in advance what evidence will be produced, as was, and still is, the case in most common-law jurisdictions in which the court has only the indictment of the grand jury in the criminal case or the complaint of the plaintiff in the civil case before it when the trial begins. Soviet lawyers wanted, apparently, to continue the Continental practice, at least in simplified form.

A system of court costs was established for the first time in the July 23, 1918, set of rules for the local people's courts. It was the same as that established previously for the district people's courts. In civil cases a fee was to be charged on all claims over 100 rubles at the rate of 2 percent of the amount from 100 rubles to 3,000 rubles, and at the rate of 3 percent if the amount fell between 3,000 rubles and 100,000 rubles. If the amount was over 100,000 rubles, a fee of 4 percent was to be charged, except that the court was permitted to waive the court fee if it concluded that the party had inadequate means. Since the local people's courts had no jurisdiction at this time over suits involving more than 10,000 rubles, it is to be wondered if the draftsmen merely copied the rates for the district courts without making the necessary adjustment.

Costs of the winning party were also to be awarded the winner, except that instead of proved costs the court might charge not more than 10 percent of the amount adjudged or denied to the losing party, of which amount as much as the court found suitable would be ordered paid to the winning party, and the balance was to be paid to the treasury. This provision was also copied from the decree concerning the district courts.

As an additional guide to judges in the local people's courts, the Russian Communist party published a handbook by Stuchka during the summer of 1918.[57] Professing to be only "an unofficial guide with alphabetical index and appendix containing the decrees of the Workers'-Peasants' Government which are most important for the People's Court," the handbook appears to have been intended as an indication of the minimum of legal knowledge required of a professional judge in the new Soviet court. Because of its structure, it provides some evidence of the laws which the courts were required to apply. In the section on crime they included only the decrees on bribery; on confiscation of share capital of former private banks; on prohibition of payment of coupon interest and dividends; on the state monopoly over the printing of notices or advertisements in the newspapers, in books, and in posters; on the state monopoly over employment offices; on the prohibition of transactions concerning real property; on speculation and on the jurisdiction of courts (Decree No. 3).

Decrees relating to jurisdictional matters were printed in the new people's court handbook in the following order: jurisdiction of courts (Decrees No. 1 and No. 2); jurisdiction of the arbitration tribunal; jurisdiction of the commission on minors; the moratorium on the payment of debts; and jurisdiction of the revolutionary tribunals.

Civil-law matters were represented by the decrees on marriage, divorce; abolition of inheritance; judicial recognition of death in the event of long absence; prohibition of gifts in excess of 10,000 rubles; and the eight-hour day.

[57] Stuchka, *Narodnyi sud v voprosakh i otvietakh* (Moscow, 1918).

Stuchka explained in the introduction that the handbook had been commenced in December, 1917, as soon as the people's courts had begun to function, but publication had been delayed by several inescapable matters, and then the evacuation of Petrograd in the face of the German advance after the failure of the first Brest-Litovsk conference had further delayed publication. He stated that he had planned an official commentary, but that had proved to be impossible, and so he was sending his manuscript to the press. He dated his introduction "April 30, 1918," but the book was obviously delayed until summer, for it includes decrees of July, 1918.

Stuchka reminded his readers that the Revolution had been fought without any clear idea of the final form of the new code; that the matter of the form of the new courts had been in even greater discussion, and that the new people's court was only at that time beginning to work itself into shape. Not only were the names of the old courts dying, but their very functions were changing to be replaced by new functions. The court was losing its former formal character, and soon there would be no formality to which it would be required to adhere. In consequence the court rules would have a new character, not being compulsory under all circumstances, but compulsory only to the extent that the court was convinced of their value. He thought it obvious that some articles of the decrees on the courts had been so thoroughly accepted as to be incontestable, but he felt that there was still room for imaginative development by the new judges in all of the purely technical parts of a trial, such as the means of summoning parties, the gathering of evidence, the means of investigation, etc.

Guidance to the judges who could read the handbook was presented in fatherly fashion. Thus, in response to the question "How should a witness be examined?" Stuchka wrote:

First of all establish the identity of the witness and his relationship to the parties; then propose to him that he explain what he knows about the case, or ask the parties to put the necessary questions pertaining to the case. The court at all times guides the examination, putting even questions of its own, and it terminates the examination only when it finds that the examination has been exhaustive or the matter has been clarified sufficiently.[58]

[58] *Ibid.,* p. 21.

In discussing the evaluation of evidence, Stuchka instructed his readers, "the court is not limited by anything in evaluating the testimony of witnesses in accordance with its own conviction. It can accept the truthfulness of one witness against six contrary witnesses. It may without any explanation of the reasons for its evaluation decide freely whether a given witness has proved a given fact." [59]

The relation of the new court to law in general was stated: "We are not anarchists, rejecting all law, since we stand for the planned development of society—i.e., for the widest possible application of the law of the working class. But we are now in the transitional stage, and law has not succeeded in reorganization in fact, or let us say, it has rushed forward without yet actually assuming general compulsory force." [60]

The difficult matter of developing a revolutionary legal consciousness was explained in two paragraphs:

All law is a certain regulation, a public definition of the mutual relationships of people in a given society. When these mutual relationships change, the whole superstructure, in the form of legal norms (rules) must, therefore, also change. But these mutual relationships of people do not all change at once nor is the change similar in all places. A lively imaginative development must occur in new social relationships, but of course, not by some direct route, but rather through trial and error, and in consequence there appears a new legal consciousness, that is, an internal conviction, first of a few individuals, and later of a group, and then of a whole class, and finally of all mankind.

This revolutionary legal consciousness must become a standard of the people's judges especially entrusted with the confidence of the people and of their lay judges, as they decide what given old law or custom must be considered abrogated or changed. It is obvious that this process will give rise to some even undesirable lack of stability, that it will necessitate a noticeable vacillation in law, but the task of the highest organs of the workers'–peasants' government concerned with following this matter is to discern everything correctly and to establish it so that it becomes fixed and to introduce it into new laws which will reflect in desirable manner the change from the past. [61]

When one reviews the events of the first nine months of the new regime, it is evident that the officials were very slow to put into practice the new Soviet court system decreed within one month after victory at the Winter Palace. When the new system became

---

[59] *Ibid.*, p. 22.   [60] *Ibid.*, pp. 29–30.   [61] *Ibid.*, pp. 31–32.

effective, it proved to be most primitive, lacking completely in formality and guided by no procedural rules. Within four months after the Revolution a supplementary system of courts was established with jurisdiction over cases remaining from prerevolutionary times, as well as over new cases of considerable seriousness as measured by the types of penalties authorized or the amount of the civil claim.

While the supplemental system of courts was staffed with professional men on the bench and authorized to use procedural codes of the Empire as a guide, even this district court was expected to depart from formalities when they could lead to what was believed to be an unjust result. The life of the supplementary courts was expected to be short, for the Commissariat of Justice expressed hostility to the idea of a permanent court system like that of the Empire with two types of courts, one for the small cases and one for the more important cases, whether civil or criminal.

By July, 1918, a step towards the concept of a single court of original jurisdiction was introduced by the third decree on the courts,[62] after some of the local courts had been taking the law into their own hands and expanding their jurisdiction at the expense of the district courts. Perhaps to prepare these local courts for eventual assumption of complete jurisdiction there was adopted in the same month as the expansion of their competence a set of procedural rules designed, presumably, to formalize the rudimentary procedures found to have been desirable in the handling of a legal action. The draftsmen reasserted their fear of formalities however, for they took pains to direct the court never to let formalities stand in the way of a just decision.

Legal formality appears from the records to have been a major casualty of the Russian Revolution during the first nine-month period, although the impending introduction of a single court of general jurisdiction seems to have required the elaboration of at least a rudimentary set of rules to be followed in the conduct of cases.

[62] Decree of July 20, 1918, [1917–1918] I *Sob. Uzak. RSFSR*, No. 52, item 589.

Chapter 2

STRIVING FOR SIMPLICITY

ELIMINATION of the professional prosecutor and of the professional defender was an aim of those who created the new Soviet court system. The concept of simplicity espoused for the settlement of disputes between citizens appears to have originated in a desire to use as a model the tribunal of primitive societies, in which a wise man heard his aggrieved fellow clansmen and dispensed what he thought necessary to avoid a recurrence of the blood feud. The Soviet draftsmen were prepared to make their wise man a professional in the sense that he would devote full time to his position, although they kept him from losing touch with reality by seating at his side two laymen who would be replaced at short intervals to provide a clue as to the thinking of the community.

The Soviet draftsmen manifested their confidence in the ability of this three-judge court to work without the assistance of others in applying the rules of common sense to the disputes brought before it. There were to be no full-time state prosecutors or members of a bar to advise the court on what to do under the circumstances. The new Soviet trial was not to be a contest between experts who manipulated the rules of law and of procedure before a referee who would subsequently decide the issues largely on the basis of the skilfullness of their performance.

The earliest decree, in November of 1917,[1] took a few steps in the direction of the early Soviet ideal. The professional bar of old Russia was abolished, together with the prerevolutionary system of prosecutors and court investigators. The new professional judges were instructed to become their own investigators, at least until matters might be organized otherwise, while any blameless citizen of either sex having civil rights was to be permitted to appear as

[1] November 24, 1917, [1917–1918] I *Sobranie Uzakonenii i Rasporiazhenii Rabochago i Krest'ianskago Pravitel'stva RSFSR,* No. 4, item 5, sec. 2.

accuser or defender before the court from the moment the investigation began. Special commissars were to be appointed to take possession of the files of the old courts, prosecutors' offices, and investigating agencies so as to make available material from the past required for the handling of cases which might be carried over from early regimes. All clerks of the old agencies were ordered to remain at their posts under the supervision of the new commissars. The preservation of these agencies with their personnel seems to have been more to assure the availability of information from the past, if that were required, and perhaps to avoid antagonizing the clerical staffs who would otherwise have lost their jobs as the result of the Revolution, than preparation of cadres to man a complicated new set of judicial agencies. As has already been seen, even these measures failed to aid the first Moscow local people's court as it began its operations in December, 1917. Not even a courtroom could be obtained from the inheritance of the past.

LAWYERS BEGIN TO PRACTICE

Lawyers of the old regime must have begun to appear under the permissive provisions of the first decree, for a Soviet chronicler of events of the early period explains that in most cases when a representative of a party appeared, he was a lawyer who had made an agreement with the party to do so.[2] The first decree had not forbidden the payment of lawyers' fees and, since the matter remained open, some lawyers apparently were willing to risk displeasure in practicing their profession.

Statistics published at the time suggest that lawyers appeared rarely. When they did appear, it was usually in an appeal to the congress of people's judges from the decision of the local people's court. The Moscow congress of local people's judges reported[3] that in the period from January 1, 1918, to July 15 of the same year there had been representatives of the accused in 28.2 percent of the 415 cases appealed to it. The presence of a defender may have been of some slight advantage to a person convicted of crime at the time,

---

[2] See E. S. Rivlin, *Sovetskaia advokatura* (Moscow, 1926), p. 18.
[3] See A. Molochkov, "Advokaty—pravozastupniki—sud'i—assistenty," *Proletarskaia revoliutstla i pravo*, No. 7 (November 1, 1918), p. 24.

for in 5.1 percent of the cases in which defenders appeared the defendant was acquitted, as compared with acquittal on appeal of only 3 percent of the defendants who appeared without a defender. Some advantage is evident also in the reduction of sentences, for 35.1 percent of the defendants who had been represented by a defender had their sentences reduced as compared with 32.6 percent of those not represented. The greatest advantage was gained from utilizing the skill of the attorney to convince the congress of judges that a new trial was necessary. This happened in 32.5 percent of the cases of defendants who were represented by attorneys, as compared with only 23.5 percent of the cases in which no attorneys appeared. In commenting on this fact, a contemporary author states that the lawyers were effective in finding purely formal elements in the procedure which necessitated a new trial, but not in lessening penalties or in clearing their clients entirely.[4]

Lawyers appeared before the congress of Moscow local people's court judges even less often in civil cases than in criminal cases, for the statistics show that in the period up to June 19 (about one month shorter than the period for criminal appeals), both parties had been represented in only 3 percent of the 201 cases heard; the appellant had been represented by an attorney in another 16 percent of the cases; no respondents had been represented by attorneys when the appellant was not represented; while in 81 percent of the cases no attorneys had appeared for either side.[5] The statistics indicate that the presence of an attorney was of advantage in securing a modification of the judgment, but not in having the judgment set aside in its entirety. No judgments were set aside in their entirety in cases in which attorneys appeared either for one or both parties, while 12.7 percent of the judgments against which the parties argued without counsel were set aside. A considerable advantage seems to have been obtained in reducing a judgment if one retained an attorney, for such reductions occurred in 50 percent of the cases when both parties had attorneys, 48.4 percent when the appellant alone had an attorney, and in only 36.7 percent when there were no attorneys at all.

Statistics in the new courts are compared with those of the pre-revolutionary court of similar type with limited jurisdiction, namely,

[4] *Ibid.*, p. 25.   [5] *Ibid.*, p. 26.

the Moscow Congress of Justices of the Peace, to show that lawyers appeared in a higher percentage of criminal cases under the new regime than under the old.[6] In the prerevolutionary period from March 6 to July 15, 1916, lawyers appeared to defend clients on criminal appeal in only 11.2 percent of the 794 cases coming before the congress of Justices of the Peace. Their success was largely in obtaining an acquittal, although more of the unrepresented defendants were amnestied or pardoned than were the represented ones.

No statistics are available to indicate the number of cases in the postrevolutionary local people's courts in which attorneys appeared, or in which members of the family sought to aid in the defense of a citizen. The cases appealed from the local courts constituted only a small part of the cases heard (2.5 percent of the criminal cases and 2.8 percent of the civil cases). It is explained that since only a small number of the parties were represented on appeals, which were assumed to be the serious cases, it could be considered evident that in the great mass of cases, both civil and criminal, coming before the local people's courts, there was no "servant of the law" present.[7]

LAWYERS IN THE DISTRICT COURTS

The opening of the district courts in February, 1918, to dispose of criminal and civil cases inherited from the old regime and to try cases of considerable seriousness called for a different approach to professional assistance in the trial. As has been indicated in the first chapter, the judges of the new district court were largely men trained in law before the Revolution. In this aspect there was a marked contrast to the local people's courts in which the judges, even the full-time ones, were chosen more for their loyalty to the principles of the Revolution than for their learning in the law.

With this combination of circumstances, namely, the inheritance from the past of cases involving complicated points of law, and a judiciary which had been accustomed to the assistance of attorneys in considering the application of the law to the circumstances of the case, the arrangements made by the second decree on the courts fall into a more familiar pattern. Lawyers were to be permitted to

[6] *Ibid.*, pp. 27–28.   [7] *Ibid.*, p. 31.

appear on a professional basis. Further, the courts were to be permitted to call to their aid professional accusers, although these were not yet organized as state prosecutors. They were to be selected from members of the local bar in much the same fashion as the county police in England retain a local solicitor to prosecute their case before the local magistrate's court if it seems serious enough to require more than presentation by the Chief Constable.

To formalize the arrangement, the second decree on the courts provided for the establishment of a college by each local soviet in which would be enrolled persons selected by the soviet and subject to dismissal by the soviet. Members of the college were to be available to the courts for the selection of a person to assist with the prosecution of a criminal case or to accept the court's assignment to defend a person brought before it. The parties themselves might retain attorneys from the college. They could not select persons from outside the college if a fee was to be paid. The statute did not abolish the principle of the first decree on the court that any person meeting the requirements of that decree might also appear on behalf of a party or as an accuser, for it specifically provided that one accuser and one defender might appear at the trial in addition to the official accuser and defender chosen from the panel maintained by the college.

Personal representatives, whether paid or not, might be excluded from the preliminary investigation of a criminal case by the new investigating commission established by the decree if the commission thought that exclusion was necessary in the interest of discovering the truth. With the creation of the investigating commission, composed of three persons chosen by the local soviet and authorized to call upon the services of the local police and the Red Guard for help, the policy makers made available to the district courts what they had not provided for the local people's courts, namely, a full-time agency to prepare criminal cases before trial. In this additional way the simple structure of the court system provided by the first decree was abandoned although it must be noted that the change related only to the work of the district courts.

Although a professional bar was developed for the purpose of the district courts, it evoked little enthusiasm from the rank and file of the people who sat as lay judges on the courts. A contemporary account[8] by the president of the district court in Vitebsk of the work of the lay judges on his court declares that during the first two months of the work of the court (June 10 to August 10, 1918) there had been about one hundred criminal cases and twenty-five civil cases brought before the court. The criminal cases usually involved violation of the excise tax, largely in connection with the illegal distilling of liquor. The next most numerous type of cases in the order of their frequency involved attempted murders, property crimes, crimes by officials in their official capacity, bribery, fraud, and extortion. The lay judges had been called exclusively from the factory workers and poorest peasantry living around the city, and the preponderant majority of them belonged to the Communist party. Before this court there appeared as public accusers and defenders, presumably at the request of the court, members of the local soviet's executive committee who were members of the Communist party, but had no legal training. Some public accusers had been military jurists, former assistants to military prosecutors or former military judges. Former members of the bar are said to have refused persistently to appear as prosecutors, but they did appear occasionally as defenders.

Gratitude was expressed by the judge in his written account to those party members who had served as defenders for their services in searching for the truth and for their fearless exposition of the facts of the case. Defenders who appeared in arrangement with the accused were reported to have aided not at all in the cases, whether they were professionals who worked for a fee or private persons. The lay judges are said to have felt that these persons who were hired to defend against whatever might come were blindly claiming the innocence of their clients, without regard to the facts of the case or to common sense. When the judges retired to chambers to discuss the case and reach a decision, the lay judges criticized these lawyers severely and called them "hired consciences." They often asked the professional judge why such windbags were permitted to defend accused persons.

[8] See Speranskii, "Narodnye zasedateli (Lichnye vpechatleniia)," *ibid.*, No. 5–6 (October 1–15, 1918), p. 27.

JUDGES WANT LAWYERS IN COURT

Absence of professional legal assistance in the local people's courts disturbed the thoughtful judges in these inferior courts after the introduction of a professional college for the district courts. The judge of the first Moscow local people's court ended his reminiscences[9] of his first few months' work with the observation that in the "big" cases the absence of lawyers had been a "sore point" in the work of the court. He explained that with all the efforts he had made to give the accused the opportunity to defend himself with all defenses permitted, such as through the testimony of relatives who were always invited to say their piece about the accused, as well as in response to direct prompting and leading questions by the court, the accused was not in general on an equal footing with the other parties when there was no experienced lawyer present to serve as a counterweight to the accusation which was supported by the municipal police. The judge felt that since the people's court had become strengthened with the passage of time, it was necessary to rectify the defect and establish as the first step a criminal bar attached to the local people's court. He closed his remarks by saying that it was impossible to ask of the court, as was being asked at the time, that it be at the same time both an accuser and a defender; that the judge be in a word "a twentieth-century Solomon."

The sentiments of the judge of the first Moscow court were shared by the judges of the other Moscow courts, for in early June, 1918, a resolution was adopted by the general meeting of the Moscow professional local court judges in favor of establishing a college of legal defenders. The college was to be started by the opening of a register of persons wishing to enter the college. Special precautions were to be taken to see that the population was not exploited by undercover solicitors of business, as was said to be common, especially in divorce cases.[10]

The resolution suggests that professional lawyers were functioning even in the local courts by appearing within the limitations

[9] See A. R. Kadich, "O narodnom sude (iz lichnykh vpechatlienii)," *ibid.*, No. 2 (August 15, 1918), pp. 29–30.
[10] See Cherliunchakevich, "Otchët o dieiatel'nosti miestnykh narodnykh sudov goroda Moskvy za pervuiu tret' 1918 goda," *ibid.*, p. 35.

established by the first decree, as friends of the parties, but that they were behaving in an unprincipled way because there was no organization of the bar to perform the usual duties of self-policing. The judges believed so thoroughly by this time in the necessity of an organized bar for the local courts that they were prepared to set one up before statutory authority was given. It was not long, however, before their action was ratified and made the rule for all.

The rules which established the first formalities of a procedural character for the conduct of the affairs of the local courts also included provisions about a bar.[11] Under these rules practice before the local courts was to be limited to members of a college of defenders, whether the lawyers were paid or not. No provisions were made for the establishment of such colleges, and it is probable that several communities had established their own colleges as the Moscow judges had done before the publication of the new rules. The draftsmen of the instruction were not entirely certain, apparently, that professional lawyers would be a help, for the rules permitted the local court to refuse to permit the appearance of lawyers in uncomplicated civil cases and in divorce cases. Again the evidence indicates that the chief trouble with business-getters was in the divorce field.

To make it clear that the new rules did not exclude the nonprofessional representative of the party before the court, the rules declared that there might be such persons as defenders in a criminal case or attorneys in a civil case, but these might be only close relatives, such as parents, children, sisters, and spouses as well as officials of state or social agencies and of nationalized enterprises. The omission of brothers as possible unpaid family defenders is not explained.

The narrowing of the group of persons given the right to appear as an attorney to those belonging to a bar was found by a contemporary commentator[12] to be the beginning of a desirable tendency. He felt that by making all professional participants in the trial belong to a college of defenders there was provided the sole assurance possible that there would not be concealed under the

[11] See Instruction on the Organization and Activity of Local People's Courts, [1917–1918] I *Sob. Uzak. RSFSR*, No. 53, item 597, sec. 23.

[12] See Molochkov, "Advokaty," p. 33.

flag of free legal aid unconscionable exploitation of the population and attempts to delay the organization of legal procedure along new lines. He felt that it would have been insufficient to require that those who appeared for a fee belong to a bar and to permit any blameless citizen with civil rights to appear without a fee, although this would have had the advantage of destroying the lawyers' monopoly. It would not, however, have guaranteed the destruction of the old Tsarist institution of the bar and its personnel, which were considered a potential brake upon the speedy and fundamental reform of the courts. It was feared that many undesirable persons might take cases without a fee and argue in a formal way so as to force the judges to make a compromise with their socialist legal consciences. Further, the court, by hearing the old lawyers, might cultivate socially antagonistic forces cloaked with special technical experience and representing private interests. The new rules, by limiting the right to appear—except for relatives and representatives of Soviet agencies—to members of a bar over which strict control might be maintained, seem to have been thought to assure the absence from court of skilled opponents of the regime, unless perhaps such a one were a parent or child of the accused.

It is tempting to imagine that in this possibility might lie the explanation for the exclusion of brothers from the group of relatives permitted to appear. The policy makers might have expected that of all the relatives of an accused person, a brother might alone be a scheming hostile lawyer, since a father would presumably be too old and emotionally interested in the case and a child too young to argue effectively as a clever opponent of the regime. Only a brother might seek to use the case more as a means of influencing the development of Soviet law in a harmful direction than as a means of defending the accused. A political explanation of this nature, while plausible and tempting, is probably inaccurate, for this was a time of hasty draftsmanship. It may be that brothers were omitted from the list of defenders because of an oversight.

July, 1918, was a month of great significance in developing the formal structure of the new Soviet state. The month of July marked the adoption of the first constitution of the R.S.F.S.R. The constitution had been in committee since April, 1918, and many drafts had been debated. On June 3, 1918, a draft approved by the drafting commission had been published in the daily press, but it was announced as incomplete. The omitted sections were promised for a subsequent issue, and one of them was declared to concern the court.[13] Yet two days later,[14] when the draft was republished as the "second draft," it contained no provisions on the court, and none were in the constitution as finally adopted on July 10, 1918.[15] The courts were mentioned only in connection with the granting to the Central Executive Committee of authority to organize the courts and legal procedure.[16] One Soviet author has said that reference to the courts was omitted because the draftsmen wanted to emphasize that they were rejecting Montesquieu's theory of separation of powers. Perhaps his explanation is correct, or it may be that the constitutional draftsmen were not yet ready to fix the court system in constitutional form. The Montesquieu theory could have been avoided by including a statement that the judiciary was subservient to the legislature. It is possible that the policy makers of July, 1918, wished to retain flexibility to permit them to eliminate the district people's courts as soon as they might be able to do so, and it would have been pointless to write them into the constitution. As the course of events later proved, it was not necessary to wait long before making the change to a single court system represented by an augmentation of what had been the local people's courts.

STEPS TOWARD A SALARIED BAR

The newly organized bar was discontented with its position from the outset.[17] Those lawyers who now controlled it seem not to have been prepared to return by degrees to the status of the bar before the Revolution. The attitude of the postrevolutionary lawyers must have been motivated by two interests: a desire to be organized in such a way that the bar's service relation to the court rather than to one party before the court might be emphasized, and by a desire to be paid by the state rather than by the citizen whom the lawyer represented.

[13] See concluding paragraph of draft in "Konstitutsiia sovietskoi vlasti," *Prol. rev. i pravo*, No. 3–4 (September 1–15, 1918), p. 52.

[14] See *ibid.*, p. 69.

[15] See *ibid.*, p. 91 and also [1917–1918] I *Sob. Uzak. RSFSR*, No. 51, item 582.

[16] Art 49 (n).   [17] See Molochkov, "Advokaty," p. 33.

The new ferment was manifested in public at the same time as the new rules were being adopted for the conduct of business by the local people's courts. In early July, 1918, delegates to a Second All-Russian Congress of Provincial Commissars of Justice gathered in Moscow. A resolution was introduced concerning the method of payment of legal defenders in which there was expressed the desire that members of the bar should be paid monthly wages by the state.[18] Opponents of the resolution argued on the floor of the Congress that it was financially impossible for the state treasury to pay legal defenders, and secondly it would be bad for morale, as the salaried lawyers might reduce the intensity of their labors if they received a wage. Proponents argued that funds could be obtained to meet the wage bill by creating a special tax on law suits, while the tendency to laziness could be defeated if the Soviets who appointed the defenders used vigorously their right to dismiss them from the college. Following the debate the vote indicated the extent to which the new type of thinking had spread. Only five voices were raised against the resolution, while all the rest voted for a fixed monthly wage for legal defenders.

The vote for a fixed wage had no immediate effect, for the rules as they were adopted on July 23 contained no provisions for a salaried bar; but within four months the new attitude was to influence the next primary step in the development of the Soviet court. In arguing for the change to a salaried bar, one author declared the intent of the lawyers in the new Russia to leave behind them the concept of the private little shop, the concept of the private hireling, to enter what was called "the noble arena of social service."

To meet the fears of those who recalled the age-long tradition of the lawyer in seeking to maintain his independence of the state, it was argued that the old efforts had been truly progressive when the state was a representative of the bourgeoisie and its courts decided cases in the interests of the bourgeoisie.[19] In such circumstances the lawyer by remaining independent so that he might defend his client without fear or favor was thought to have preserved his freedom to protect the interests of the mass of members who made up society against the interests of the few who ruled the state. With the Russian

[18] *Ibid.*, pp. 33–34.   [19] *Ibid.*, pp. 34–35.

Revolution, the situation was said to have changed. The state now was declared to be the defender of the masses. It had changed roles with society. From a former instrument of oppression of the toiling masses, it was said to have gone into their own hands, and in doing so to have been transformed from a factor of social stagnation into a factor of social progress. Society, which in opposing the state in bourgeois society had been a progressive factor, was thought to have become a conservative social force with the transfer of state authority to the hands of the revolutionary classes of the proletariat and poorest peasantry. It was reported that the Commissariat of Justice was working on a draft of a new statute which would create "a college of defenders, accusers, and representatives of parties in civil suits," which would provide that members were to be elected by the soviets on the same basis as other officials of the Soviet Republic, in consequence of which the members would receive a salary of the same amount as that established for the local people's judges.

From the argument in favor of a salaried bar as the servant of the new state, it is clear that the proponent, if he be given the benefit of the assumption that he was writing sincerely and without tongue in cheek, could not conceive of abuse of authority on the part of the new state. Independence could be relinquished by the bar because all officials of the state, whether judges, accusers, or defenders, had only one interest, namely, determination of the truth, and all could be trusted to search for it. In doing so, they would search as a team, each one having a specialized role to play, but each sharing consciously in the team effort. How foreign was this view to that of the partisans of the adversary procedure of the common law, and of modern variations of western European codes! Such partisans believe the truth to be more elusive and to be discoverable, if at all, by a healthy contest between parties with conflicting interests before a judge who attempts to determine the truth from what is assumed to be a complete collection of the facts by those who naturally wish to introduce every shred of evidence that can help their case.

An approach reminiscent of the civil-service panel system in use in other lands for purposes of selecting state employees was to be followed in selecting the accuser and defender in each case under the proposed rules for the new bar. The court was to receive from the college before each sitting a list of persons available for assignment, from which the court was to select an accuser and a defender. A defender was to be required whenever requested by an accused if the authorized penalty might be deprivation of freedom. In lesser criminal cases the court was to decide whether it thought a defender desirable. Thus, the accused could only move to have a defender selected, and the court would be the agency to name one.

In civil cases the parties wishing to be represented would apply to the governing board of the college, but the latter might refuse to provide an attorney. In such an event the aggrieved party was to have the right to appeal the denial to the court before whom the suit was to be brought. If attorneys appeared in a criminal or a civil case, the court would exact from the party concerned a fee to be paid into court.

The new scheme was thought to provide a means of reforming the institution of the bar, but it was declared that it by no means exhausted the question of replacement of the old institution by the new. It was considered impossible to remake the lawyers merely because they were to be named by the court or the college to the case and were to be paid a wage as a state servant. All of these elements were considered purely formal, although they were thought to be important symbols. It was said that the symbolic change had to be followed by a substantive change in thinking on the part of the lawyers; they must appreciate that they now worked as members of a team in court rather than as the representative of an individual. Lawyers were advised to learn to subordinate private interests to the public policy established by the state and to do so by means of whatever measures seemed to be expedient. The lawyer had to come to think of himself as an "assistant to the judge." This role of assistant was thought to express most succinctly the new role, and to do so effectively enough to suggest that it be used to express the relationship which should exist not only in a court, but in other purely administrative bodies which also were charged with the settlement of various types of disputes.

The draft of a new statute on defenders, accusers, and representatives of the parties in civil suits was evidently withheld from public view until the great reform of the court system to be introduced on

November 30, 1918, in the form of a People's Court Act.[20] In this act the Commissariat of Justice was able to effect the plan of its dreams, if we may surmise those dreams from the statements of Commissar Kurskii in the months leading up to the act. Now at last it seems to have been thought possible to strike a blow for simplicity, to throw out all reference to the laws of the past and to abolish the district courts with their heritage of legalisms and their bench of legally trained professionals. It had taken a year to clean up the leavings of the past, for the new decree came nearly thirteen months after the Revolution, but the new broom was to sweep clean.

THE PEOPLE'S COURT ACT OF 1918

Appearing over the signature of Kurskii as Commissar of Justice as well as over the signatures of the president and secretary of the issuing authority, the Central Executive Committee, the People's Court Act of 1918[21] introduced nothing that could have been a surprise to anyone who had followed the writing of Kurskii and his colleagues both before and after he had become Commissar in succession to Stuchka. The local people's court was expanded to become the sole court in the new Russia, with jurisdiction over all criminal and civil cases, except those of a political nature. The political cases were reserved for the revolutionary tribunals which made no pretense of being courts of law. No mention was made of the abolition of the district people's courts, although this was to be the logical consequence of the creation of general jurisdiction in the new courts. An Instruction[22] was soon published over Kurskii's name ordering the district courts to complete liquidation by January 15, 1919, and in exceptional cases with the permission of the chief of the legal department of the provincial executive committee by February 1, 1919. All civil cases in process of review were to be transferred to the reviewing authorities created by the new decree.

[20] People's Court Act of the RSFSR, November 30, 1918, [1917–1918] I *Sob. Uzak. RSFSR*, No. 85, item 889.

[21] *Ibid.*

[22] Instruction on Putting into Effect the Statute on a Unified People's Court (undated), *Prol. rev. i pravo*, No. 8–9–10 (November 15—December 15, 1918), p. 127.

Judges of the abandoned district courts might be utilized as judges in the new court or on the review tribunal, although authorities were cautioned that the reviewing authorities in the new system must be composed of persons about whose loyalty to the new regime there could be no question. Most of these were to be Communists who had knowledge of the technical operations of the local people's courts which had advanced to become the sole court of the land.

Reference to laws of prerevolutionary governments was forbidden by the new decree, the judges being admonished to apply decrees of the new government, and in the absence of appropriate decrees or gaps in the decrees to be guided by their socialist concept of justice.[23] Through this measure the draftsmen made unnecessary knowledge of the old law, which had been important until the conclusion of the cases inherited from the past. By this rule the new decree made unnecessary the employment on the bench of persons schooled in the old law, as had been necessary in the district courts during the preceding months, and the door was opened to the unrestricted development of the imagination of the judges bent upon creating principles for a new legal system. Each case thereafter would be decided on the basis of common sense, revolutionary expediency and a residual concept of law to produce whatever result the judges thought suitable under the circumstances. As will be seen from later decrees, the result was a wide variation of views requiring ultimate codification in the interest of establishing uniformity.

The section concerning the new "college of defenders, accusers, and representatives of the parties in civil suits" followed the lines predicted a month earlier by the author already quoted. They made of the bar a salaried civil service available to the court and selected by it from a panel submitted by the administration of the college. Salaries were fixed at the same level as those of the professional judges of the courts in which the attorneys were to appear as prosecutors or defenders. There was, however, carried over from the July rules permission for a litigant to introduce as his or her attorney a close relative, and the degree of kinship was set forth in almost identical terms as it had been defined in the July rules. The one addition was the word "brother," suggesting that the earlier

[23] People's Court Act, sec. 22.

omission of this relative had been a drafting error in July, although it may have been calculated for the reasons suggested above.

Attorneys were not to be permitted as a matter of right in all cases. If the case involved a criminal charge of attempt on life, the causing of serious injury or harm, rape, robbery, counterfeiting of currency and documents, bribery, and speculation in goods on rations or monopolized, the defendant had an absolute right to the designation of an attorney.[24] In other cases the court was free to deny the defendant's request for an attorney, except that an attorney was always to be permitted in the less serious criminal cases if the court called for an accuser from the college. In all cases an attorney might be denied admittance to the preliminary investigation if it was felt by the court on the suggestion of the investigating commission that his presence might hinder the disclosure of the true facts.[25]

The investigating commissions adopted for the local courts in the July rules were continued under the new Act.[26] These commissions seem to have met a need of the district courts for which they had been created originally by the second decree of February, 1918. The value of professional investigating agencies to the local people's courts had been recognized already by the draftsmen of the July rules. Now the investigating commissions became fixed among the agencies of the new regime. They existed to investigate serious cases going beyond the capabilities of the municipal police. Every investigating district was to have an investigating commission to be composed of a president and two members, all to be chosen and subject to recall by the city soviet in large cities, and by the county soviet in the countryside. The draftsmen of the decree had in mind for the investigating commissions a task needing skill in its performance, for they required the nominees not only to have political rights under the provisions of the new constitution of July, 1918, but also to have had either special schooling or practical experience in the duties which they were to perform. The commission was authorized to request assistance in its work from the local police or from any state or social agency, or from any private person or state official.

In the requirement that the nominees for the investigating com-

---

[24] *Ibid.*, sec. 43.   [25] *Ibid.*, sec. 34.   [26] *Ibid.*, secs. 28–33.

missions have political rights under the constitution, the draftsmen sought to make certain that the commission members would support the political aims of the new regime. The new constitution had contained two articles concerning the franchise, one listing the categories of persons who might vote or be elected to office,[27] and the other listing the categories of persons who might not vote or be elected to office.[28] Political rights were to be limited to persons who earned their living by productive work useful to society, persons engaged in domestic operations which enabled the former to follow their calling, soldiers in the army and navy, and citizens in the categories mentioned who were incapacitated for work.

Those who were denied the right to vote and hold office as potential, if not actual, enemies of the new regime were listed as those who employed others for the sake of profit, those who lived on a return on investments, private businessmen, agents and middlemen, monks and priests, agents and employees of the former police and its services as well as members of the former ruling dynasty, the mentally deranged and those under wardship, and finally, persons convicted of infamous or mercenary crimes for as long a period as the court might fix in the sentence.

A similar limitation applied to those eligible for the post of judge under the new statute,[29] but it was not new as it applied to judges. It had been established by the July rules of 1918.[30] The test of presumed loyalty to the regime had to be met by proving one's status, and then one had to prove qualifications as a person with the necessary skills. These were not limited as narrowly as with the investigators. A prospective judge was considered qualified, once he had met the political test of electoral rights, if he had theoretical or practical preparation for the post, or if he had the experience of having worked in a proletarian organization, these being listed as the Communist party, trade unions, workers' cooperatives, factory committees, and agencies of the Soviet state apparatus.[31] By this definition of the qualifications required to be a judge the draftsmen

---

[27] See Constitution RSFSR, Art. 64, in [1917–1918] I *Sob. Uzak. RSFSR*, No. 51, item 582.

[28] *Ibid.*, Art. 65.   [29] People's Court Act, sec. 12.

[30] Instruction on the Organization and Activity of Local People's Courts, sec. 4.

[31] People's Court Act, sec. 12.

emphasized that political experience in the new regime was thought by them to be as important as knowledge of the law. In making this equation the draftsmen seem to have reaffirmed the faith expressed by Stuchka months earlier when he explained that the first decree on the court had taken the position that legal education was not necessary to be a judge in the new Russia because the problems of the future were to be sufficiently simple to be understood by a layman as well as by a lawyer. Once again in the People's Court Act of November, 1918, the policy makers of the new regime seem to have been preparing for the development of a simple system for settling disputes within society.

To assure selection of the types of people desired as judges on the court, they were to be named from a list of nominees prepared in the cities by the executive committees of the borough soviets and confirmed by a general meeting of the borough soviet itself.[32] In the country districts the nominations were to be made by the executive committees of the soviets in the villages, and the selection from the list of nominees was to be made by the executive committee of the county soviet under whom the various village soviets functioned. Through this two-step process in the country districts, there was established control over the selection process, perhaps because the peasants of the villages were not trusted to choose people in whom the worker-dominated leadership of the new state had complete confidence.

SPECIALIZATION IN THE COURTS

The new Soviet court was to take various forms, depending upon the type of problem to be solved. The concept of benches constituted in different ways to meet different needs had been suggested as early as the first decree on the courts of the preceding year, in which it had been provided that the professional judge sitting alone would conduct the preliminary investigation of a criminal case[33] to be tried subsequently by himself and two lay judges to make a bench of three judges.[34]

[32] *Ibid.*, sec. 13.
[33] Decree No. 1 on the Court, sec. 3, [1917–1918] I *Sob. Uzak. RSFSR*, No. 4, item 50.
[34] *Ibid.*, sec. 2.

With the introduction of a system of district courts to hear the cases inherited from the past and the more serious of the new civil and criminal cases, the concept of differently constituted benches for civil and criminal cases was introduced. The criminal bench was to have a single professional judge as president and twelve lay judges with two alternates, while the civil bench was to have three professional judges and four lay judges.[35] With the third decree which reduced the number of cases to be tried by the district court as a result of increasing the jurisdiction of the local courts, the bench of judges for civil cases in the district courts was changed to require the presence of only one professional judge with the four lay judges.[36] No change was made in the standard bench of three judges in the local courts even though their jurisdiction had been increased considerably, and the July rules reaffirmed that the standard bench of one professional and two lay judges was to be the bench of the local courts for both civil and criminal cases.[37]

The new People's Court Act of November 30, 1918, introduced an approach to the bench of the new single court which combined some of the features of the district courts, which were being abolished by the Act, and of the local people's courts, which were being developed as the nucleus of the new single court. The criminal bench for serious cases of attempts on life, the causing of serious injury or harm, rape, robbery, counterfeiting of currency and documents, bribery and speculation in goods on rations or monopolized was to be composed of one professional judge and six lay judges,[38] while the bench for lesser criminal cases and all civil cases was to be what had become traditional for the local courts, namely, a single professional judge and two lay judges, unless the professional judge thought that one of the less serious criminal cases required six lay judges.[39]

Some have thought that the differentiation between serious criminal cases and those of less serious character as well as civil cases was in order to provide a form of "jury" for the prosecutions which could result in heavy penalties. Serious criminal cases under the laws

[35] Decree No. 2 on the Court, sec. 3, *ibid.*, No. 26, item 420 (347).
[36] Decree No. 3 on the Court, sec. 7, *ibid.*, No. 52, item 589.
[37] Instruction on the Organization and Activity of Local People's Courts, sec. 20.
[38] People's Court Act, sec. 7. [39] Sec. 8.

of the Empire had been tried with a jury, and the second decree, in establishing the district courts with much of the same jurisdiction, had continued the jury in the form of lay judges sitting with a professional judge. Now the People's Court Act continued the jury, but reduced its size by half for the serious criminal cases to be tried by the new single court.

A professional judge sitting alone was authorized by the new act not only to make the decisions necessary before trial as to the form of detention thought necessary to assure the defendant's presence at the trial and the progress of the investigation by the police, but also to hear suits for divorce and suits which were not contested.[40] The single judge was also directed to make reviews of the detention of all persons within the court's district to determine whether they were being held in accordance with orders properly issued.

The lay judges were placed in complete equality with the professional judge when they sat with him. They could share in the decision of all questions of fact and law, and when the bench included six lay judges, the president might be either the professional judge or one of the others, as the bench itself should decide. When the bench included only two lay judges, the president was always to be the professional judge.[41] Decisions in both criminal and civil cases were to be by majority vote, the dissenting judges being authorized, as had been the case in the July rules, to present a minority opinion which had to be included in the record so as to be available for review.

The positive role to be played by the judge in managing the case, even the civil case, rather than sitting back as a referee while the lawyers argued the case for the prosecution and defense or for the civil plaintiff and defendant was indicated. Even in a civil case the court was authorized to call to court persons with special knowledge when that was required.[42] Here was reaffirmation of faith in the wise man of the primitive tribunal who settled disputes by doing all that he thought necessary when a complaint was brought before him. He was not required to limit his investigation by any rules of procedure placing a burden of proof upon the parties if he thought that the peace of the community and justice demanded his intervention on behalf of a side unable to further its own interests.

[40] Sec. 6.   [41] Sec. 10.   [42] Sec. 11.

The same theme reappears in the provisions of the act relating to the procedure to be used at the trial. In the main it is similar to that established by the July rules. The court might initiate the action if it believed prosecution necessary.[43] The court might accept such evidence as it wished without any restraint in the form of exclusionary rules of evidence. This point was reinforced by a clearer wording than had been chosen in the July rules, for the November act permitted in express words the exclusion of a witness after determining the nature of the facts he was expected to establish.[44] In the July rules a similar right of exclusion had been implied but not stated.[45] The November act introduced a new article permitting the court before hearing a witness to establish the relationships existing between the party concerned and the witness in the case.[46] From these articles it is evident that the draftsmen of the November act saw the court as an active participant in the conduct of the trial rather than a passive referee awaiting disclosure of detail through the examination and cross examination of the witnesses. An explanation at the time confirmed that the new act was limiting the adversary procedure of the past by giving the judges broad powers of intervention. In making their choice, the draftsmen adopted a position which was to continue down to the present day, and which has since been expressed by the phrase that the judge is the "boss" (*khoziain*) of the trial. As in western Continental courts, the Soviet judge even today takes the initiative in examining and cross-examining witnesses, and the prosecutor and defender, when they appear at all, fill in details which seem to them to have been overlooked by the judge's intervention.

The formal adoption by the July rules of the Investigating Commission as the agency of preliminary examination in the serious criminal case found reflection in the new act's procedural provisions, for the presiding judge was instructed to follow his opening speech in which he would inform the defendant of his right to challenge the professional judge or the lay judges[47] and request that they step off the bench because of possible involvement in the case by a presentation of the report of the Investigating Committee setting

---

[43] Sec. 53.   [44] Sec. 60.

[45] Instruction on the Organization and Activity of Local People's Courts, sec. 22.

[46] People's Court Act, sec. 61.   [47] Sec. 58.

forth its conclusions.[48] In other cases the court was to formulate its own accusation, just as it had been instructed to do in all cases under the July rules.

No hearing was required if the court concluded that the defendant's admission of guilt or of civil liability was sufficient.[49] This had been inaugurated as the rule in July, and it was repeated in November.

A procedure for review was established in almost the same form as had existed previously. Once again it was stated that the review was to take the form only of examination of the record. There was to be no hearing of witnesses at the second level, not even if the person seeking review had not been present at the trial below.[50] All restriction on review was removed.[51] In the July rules it had been provided that sentences of less than seven days' imprisonment and civil judgments in an amount less than five hundred rubles could not be the subject of review. The right was extended by the November act in so many words not only to the parties, but to any agency taking part in the proceedings, and even to the executive committee of the local soviet.[52] By this insertion the new act indicated that political authorities might seek to set aside a decision, although they were expected to act through legal procedures rather than by simple order of their own body. Perhaps the draftsmen had in mind the resolution of the Moscow judges some months earlier protesting against the direct intervention of a local soviet to set aside a decision of the court through assumption of judicial authority.

The reviewing unit remained the congress of judges, now to be called the council of people's judges, as it had been called in the July rules as an alternative to the word "congress." It was to be organized at a higher level than previously, when the reviewing district had been the county or the city. Now it was to be the province or the great cities of Moscow or Petrograd.[53] Its judges were to be named by a general meeting of the judges of the reviewing district, but this selection had to be ratified by the executive committee of the provincial soviet, thus preserving political control over the choice. The council was to be composed of a president,

[48] Sec. 65.   [49] Sec. 67.   [50] Sec. 59.   [51] Sec. 75.   [52] Sec. 75 (note).
[53] Sec. 81 (note).

his deputy, two to five full-time judges, and the judges of the district, who would sit in rotation. Not all members of the council would sit on every review, for the bench was to number five, of which two would be permanent members of the staff, and three the rotating members. This provision marked a change in the July provisions, when the bench was defined as "not less than three judges." Any appeals from individual rulings of the trial court were to be heard by only three judges.

The powers of the reviewing authority were reduced from what they had been in the July rules, according to which sentences or judgments could be reduced, a party could be released, or a new trial ordered.[54] Under the November act the reviewing bench could not reduce a sentence or release a party completely. It could only order a new trial. The trial under the new act was to be before a different court in the same district[55] and the reviewing authority was to send back a full statement of the reasons for ordering a new trial.[56] These reasons were to explain why the retrial was ordered under the provisions set forth in the November act. In the statement or reasons for ordering a new trial there was again a change from the July rules, which had said that a decision might be set aside "because of formal violations, found to be substantial." Under the new act the reasons were to be "in the event that there are found substantial violations or incorrect application of decrees, especially violation of the forms of court procedure, and also in the event that the investigation has been incomplete." By choosing to mention the forms of court procedure specifically, the draftsmen seem to have emphasized more than they had been prepared to do in July the importance to the judicial process of formality. As in the July rules the reviewing authority was permitted to set aside a sentence and call for a new trial if "it was clearly an injustice." No definition of an injustice was offered, but presumably, the provision gave the reviewing bench an opportunity to find that the expression of revolutionary conscience set forth by the trial court was not its own idea of what a good revolutionary should think. In setting aside a decision from below, the reviewing authority was not to be limited to the issues raised in the complaint of the appellant.[57]

Some suggestion of the amount to be sought in civil suits and

[54] Secs. 89 and 92.   [55] Sec. 92.   [56] Sec. 91.   [57] Sec. 90.

the extent to which the draftsmen had changed their ideas of reasonable court fees is to be found in the section of the November act concerned with these matters.[58] Whereas the July rules had adopted without editing the provisions of the second decree relating to the fees in the district courts, to establish a fee scale applying to suits over which the local courts did not have jurisdiction at the time, the November act was obviously drafted with care. Even though the new court had unlimited jurisdiction in contrast to the limit of 10,000 rubles for the court which it was absorbing, the November act set a scale of fees mentioning a top bracket which began at 10,000 rubles instead of the 100,000 rubles of the former rules. Further, it removed the exemption from fees formerly attaching by the July rules to suits claiming up to five hundred rubles, and the fee was to be 1 percent of the claim. The second bracket was set at from 500 to 3,000 rubles for which the fee was set at 3 percent. The third bracket ran from 3,000 to 10,000 rubles with a fee of 5 percent instead of the old fee of 3 percent for this bracket, while suits claiming over 10,000 rubles were to pay a fee of 10 percent. The November act introduced a stamp tax on each document received in a civil or criminal action. For one conversant with the American revolutionaries' aversion to stamp taxes nearly a century and a half earlier, the stamp tax provisions of the new Act have interest. The same set of fees and stamp taxes were to apply to requests for review.

Costs of the parties were treated in the same manner as in July, for the court was to award the winner all his court costs and the expenses of the attorney. Further, he was to be given a judgment for any other expenses or damages suffered as a result of the litigation. The same was to apply in a criminal case when the defendant was acquitted.[59]

THE TRANSITION TO THE NEW SYSTEM

Commissar Kurskii was proud of his new courts. In his speech[60] explaining the act to the Central Executive Committee he singled

---

[58] Sec. 94.   [59] Sec. 97.

[60] See D. I. Kurskii, "O edinom narodnom sude," *Prol. rev. i pravo*, No. 1 (11) (January, 1919), pp. 16–19.

out for attention points which he believed to be of primary interest in the new legislation. The new courts, as the heirs of the local people's courts, would be near to the people as the local courts had been, and they would act quickly instead of slowly and mechanically as the district courts were found to have functioned. The new court would have a bench of one professional judge and six lay judges for serious criminal cases, indicating capacity to hear cases of any measure of difficulty, but no single court would be limited in its activity to the specific precinct to which it was assigned. Unlike the former local people's court, it would be a court of the whole district along with the other courts assigned to the other precincts in the same district. In consequence it could be assigned the difficult cases from any other precinct if it had shown itself especially competent in dealing with such cases. Specialization seems to have been anticipated by Kurskii among the various courts of a district.

Authority to discard reference to the old laws of the Empire was the third factor noted by Kurskii as important in the new court, and liberation from any formality in the taking of evidence was a fourth factor. The freedom of the court was even to extend to the changing of measures of punishment set in the new regime's own postrevolutionary decrees, so long as a full explanation of the reason for the change was given. This provision was expected to provide material for reconsideration of policy when the decree was brought up for review at a later time. Further, the prohibition of review of small cases had been removed, and the new reviewing authority was organized on the level of the province rather than the county. This was explained as a change which had been made possible because so few cases were being sent forward for review that the county congresses of people's judges had little to do. Kurskii praised this change as making possible a greater unification of control and a wider unification of practice in court procedures. Finally, Kurskii hailed the change in the structure of the college of defenders.

Perhaps to assure himself and his colleagues that he had fostered the right plan, Kurskii permitted his Commissariat's journal to publish three pages of telegrams[61] from twelve provincial congresses of judges and a telegram from the judges of the new Belorussian

---

[61] *Ibid.*, pp. 124–26.

Republic,[62] praising him as the true inspirer and author of the November People's Court Act. A clue as to how these telegrams originated is to be found in the account of the first meeting of the Yaroslavl Provincial Council of People's Judges after the promulgation of the November act. Sixty-two judges met on December 28 and 29, 1918, to represent all counties of the province. Before the session began, the judges who were members of the Communist party are said to have caucused and to have resolved to have the congress send a congratulatory telegram to Lenin, Kurskii, and Sverdlov, the latter of whom as President of the Central Executive Committee had also signed the decree. The meeting was opened by the acting chief of the judicial section of the provincial commissariat of justice. Reports were given by the presiding justice of the local people's court of each county, and a presiding judge was elected for the new provincial council of people's judges. Work of the new court in accordance with the November 30, 1918 decree began on December 29, 1918. Again a considerable delay after the promulgation of a decree before it could be put into effect was manifested.

A report[63] of the Vitebsk Provincial Commissariat of Justice indicates how the work of the district people's court had begun to taper off toward the end of 1918 and the work of the local people's courts had begun to increase. The Vitebsk district court continued to function right up to January 15, 1919. During the period beginning September 1, 1918, to the end of the court's life, it heard sixty-seven criminal cases and nine civil cases. Its criminal cases concerned primarily violation of the old Imperial excise tax law in the form of illegal manufacture and sale of wines and spirits. The number of cases of a civil nature had dropped to nine from the twenty-four which had been heard in the preceding two and a half months. This drop was reported to have been due to the fact that the third

[62] Belorussia had declared its independence as a Soviet type of republic on January 1, 1919. In its declaration it stated that it was solidly allied with the Russian federation and in section 10 that all decrees of the RSFSR were placed in force on the territory of Belorussia. See A. I. Denisov, ed., *Istoriia sovetskogo gosudarstva i prava* (Moscow, 1949), p. 170. For the text of the declaration, see *Istoriia sovetskoi konstitutsii v dekretakh i postanovleniiakh sovetskogo pravitel'stva, 1917–1936* (Moscow, 1936), p. 99.

[63] See Speranskii, "Otchët o deiatel'nosti Vitebskogo gubernskogo Komissariata iustitsii za period vremeni s sentiabria 1918 goda po ianvar' 1919," *Prol. rev. i pravo*, No. 1 (11) (January, 1919), p. 104.

decree on the court had increased the jurisdiction of the local people's courts at the expense of the district courts. Of the nine cases, three had involved claims of less than 10,000 rubles, one had involved a claim of more than 10,000 rubles, while five plaintiffs had not expressed their demands in terms of a specific sum of money. Total recovery in the cases had been 22,185 rubles 98 kopeks. In addition to the cases brought to trial, the court had disposed of two hundred motions from September 1, 1918, to the end of its life. The Commissariat was of the opinion that such limited business unquestionably did not justify the existence of such a large agency as the district court had come to be, but it thought that the court had played its part. The experienced jurists upon it had served as technical assistants while the local people's judges were learning the substance of judicial work and the technique of court activity. As a result of this activity there had developed new cadres of the people's courts, most of whom were prepared to assume the new duties thrust upon them by the November People's Court Act.

The increasing activity of the local people's courts prior to the inauguration of a single people's court under the November 30, 1918, decree is evidenced by the Vitebsk provincial report.[64] By September, 1918, there functioned in the city of Vitebsk and in the county within which it lay four courts in boroughs of the city itself and nine courts in the county outside the city limits. In November, 1918, an additional court was opened within the city limits. From September 1, 1918, to January 1, 1919, 8,056 cases were filed in the various courts of the city and county. Of this number, 656 were directed to the still-existing district courts because of lack of jurisdiction in the local courts; 700 were dismissed for other reasons, and 3,958 were tried. This left on the calendar for subsequent disposition 2,749 cases. Of the cases which had been tried, most were criminal prosecutions, the statistics indicating that 3,214 were criminal cases, 647 were civil suits, and 97 were divorce actions.

The ratio of civil suits was higher in some of the other counties of the province. Thus, in the county of Gorodok, which included the city of that name, the criminal cases numbered 1048, the civil cases 674, and the divorce cases 13 for a total of 1,735 cases disposed of by the five local courts of the county. A similar picture, although

[64] *Ibid.*, p. 113.

with a smaller total number of cases, is drawn by the statistics for the county of Sebezh, for in that county the eight local courts heard 808 criminal cases, 478 civil cases, and 25 divorce cases for a total of 1,311. The four courts in Polotsk county reported statistics only for November, 1918. They tried only 154 cases, of which 84 were criminal prosecutions, 69 were civil suits, and one was a divorce action. The ten courts of Nevelsk county in the same month of November, 1918, heard 400 cases, of which 266 were criminal, 125 were civil, and 9 were divorce actions.

The same Vitebsk provincial report indicates that the investigating commissions, which had been given a place by the July rules in the investigation of serious criminal prosecutions begun in the local courts, were not yet engaged in a large percentage of the criminal cases examined. Presumably, the court with the help of the local police found itself able to bring together enough information to make a decision possible. The statistics published at the time concern a three-month period as compared with the four-month period of the court statistics, but they indicate in some measure the nature of the Investigating Commission's activity. Thus, in Gorodok county, the Investigating Commission completed investigations of 147 cases in three months, while the courts of the county were trying 1048 criminal cases in a period only one month longer. The report comments that the work of the investigating commissions was sometimes slow, but critics were reminded by the author that the commissions often had to travel outside the county to collect evidence.

A SUMMARY OF ACHIEVEMENTS

The accomplishment in the legal field by the end of 1918 seems to have been what the Communist party had hoped for. The Eighth Communist Party Congress meeting in March, 1919, adopted a new program[65] for the party to replace the outdated program which had remained unchanged since 1903. The prerevolutionary program[66] had set only two goals with respect to courts of law:

[65] See *VKP (B) v rezoliutsiiakh i resheniiakh s"ezdov, konferentsii i plenumov TsK* (5th ed.; Moscow, 1936), Part I, p. 290.

[66] *Ibid.*, Part I, p. 20. For English translation with Lenin's 1917 proposals for revision, see V. I. Lenin, *Selected Works* VI (Moscow, 1935), 118.

(1) the right of all persons to sue any official in the usual manner before a court with a jury, and (2) the election of judges by the people. Lenin had suggested a change in the program in June, 1917, in the period between revolutions, but it had contained nothing radical in the sections relating to courts. He urged the retention unchanged of the right to sue officials, but enlargement of the second principle to read: "Election by the people of judges and other officials, both civil and military, with the right to recall any of them at any time by decision of a majority of their electors." The "October" came before the program was rewritten, so that the contemporary opinions of the Bolshevik leaders as to what the courts should be in the new Russia were not reflected in the party program at the time they seized power. Not until 1919 was official expression given to policy in the adoption of a new program.

The section on the judiciary in the 1919 Communist party program summarized the steps which had been taken prior to its publication and set the goal for the future. As the expression of Communist intentions, the section deserves to be set forth in full. In translation published by the Communist International [67] it reads:

Proletarian democracy, taking power into its own hands and finally abolishing the organs of domination of the bourgeoisie—the former courts of justice—has replaced the formula of bourgeois democracy: "judges elected by the people" by the class watchword: "judges elected from the working masses and only by the working masses," and has applied the latter in the organization of law courts, having extended equal rights to both sexes, both in the election of judges and in the exercise of the function of judges.

In order to induce the broad masses of the proletariat and the poorest peasantry to take part in the administration of justice, a bench of jury-judges sitting in rotation under the guidance of a permanent judge is introduced and various labor organizations and trade unions must impanel their delegates.

The Soviet Government has replaced the former endless series of courts of justice with their various divisions, by a very simplified, uniform system of People's Courts, accessible to the population, and freed of all useless formalities of procedure.

The Soviet Government, abolishing all the laws of the overthrown governments, commissioned the judges elected by the Soviets to carry out the will of the proletariat in compliance with its decrees, and in cases

[67] See William E. Rappard *et al.*, *Source Book on European Governments* (New York, 1937), Part V, pp. 19–20.

of absence or incompleteness of decrees, to be guided by socialist conscience.

Constructed on such a basis, the courts of justice have already led to a fundamental alteration of the character of punishment, introducing conditional sentence on a wide scale, applying public censure as a form of punishment, replacing imprisonment by obligatory labor with the retention of freedom, and prisons by institutions of training, and applying the principle of comradely tribunals.

The All-Russian Communist party, in order to assist the further development of the courts of justice on these lines, will strive to induce all workmen without exception to perform judicial duties and finally replace the system of punishment by measures of an educational character.

The new Soviet judiciary seems to have developed by early 1919 into the ideal form envisioned by the Russian revolutionaries in their writings on the subject. At this moment of success, however, the civil war which had been rumbling around the edges of what had been the Empire began to creep toward the heart of the new state. Forces of the opposition began to have threatening successes, and even Lenin wondered whether his new regime could survive. Concurrently with the various defeats of the civil war the new regime moved to terminate the extensive freedom previously granted to local authorities to handle their own affairs. A trend toward direction from above became manifest.

Chapter 3

STEPS TOWARD CENTRALIZATION

JUBILATION was the theme of the Commissar of Justice when he turned his attention in early 1919 to the development of a new system of law. He pointed with pride to the provisions of the People's Court Act of 1918 giving to each individual court the authority to provide criminal penalties of different character from those set in the law as long as the reasons were stated, and releasing each court from any responsibility to observe formal restrictions on the types of evidence to be admitted.

The uniqueness of the Soviet court seemed so apparent to the Commissar that he was moved to write:

Neither Roman law nor subsequent bourgeois law gave such authority to a judge. Perhaps we can find some analogy in more ancient primitive law. But one has only to consider the whole complexity of contemporary social relationships and to contrast these with the primitive usage which was developed into a norm by the elders, by custom, and by other sources of primitive law to grasp the immeasurable difference between the sources of primitive law and of the new law created by the proletarian revolution.[1]

In spite of the Commissar's exultation over what he took to be the nearly primitive independence and authority of each local court, it was becoming evident that in practice guidance was being provided to these local courts by the central authorities. This guidance took several forms, the most noticeable being the lengthening list of decrees concerned with defining certain acts as crimes. The Commissar listed on four pages of his 1919 article the separate statutes which had been adopted during the first seventeen months of the life of the new regime. He grouped them impressively as one might arrange the chapters of a criminal code, but they were still

---

[1] D. I. Kurskii, "Novoe ugolovnoe pravo," *Proletarskaia revoliutsiia i pravo*, No. 2–4 (12–14) (February–April, 1919), p. 24.

less numerous than would have been the articles of a criminal code, and he declared that there were "very few norms forbidding under fear of punishment the commission of some act or other."

Most of the decrees specifically defining crime had to do with the protection of the state against dangerous acts: instigation to treason, counterrevolutionary activity, refusal to answer a call to military service, bribery of state officials, refusal to till the land in accordance with orders from local authorities, violation of the rules relating to the use and distribution of metals, trade in monopolized goods, or refusal to report surplus grain. Only one group of items on the Commissar's list had to do with the intervention of the state in personal relationships, and this group had very tenuous standing in law as it existed in 1919.

The group of actions relating to personal relationships were classed by the Commissar under the rubric "Crimes against the Individual." He then listed attempts on life, the causing of serious bodily injury or mutilation, rape, and robbery. Citation is made by the Commissar to the People's Court Act of 1918 as authority for inclusion of the items among the prohibited activities. The notable step taken by the Commissar in enlarging on his own initiative the areas in which guidance was to be given by the authorities at the center to local judges becomes apparent when one studies the People's Court Act of 1918 to which he refers. It creates no such crimes against the person. It refers to them only in describing the form of the bench to be required when charges of crimes of this nature were to be tried. The only possibility of considering crimes against the person as already within the body of Soviet law is to assume that they had to be found punishable under the authority given the new Soviet courts, in the absence of decree, to punish acts which seemed to them to violate their social consciousness of law.

In considering the Commissar's position as revealed by his inclusion of crimes against the individual in the list of crimes specifically established by legislation of the new regime when they had not yet been so established, the conclusion is suggested that the Commissar was no longer prepared on this point to follow established policy in leaving to individual initiative at the local level the determination of what should become the law of the new Russia. The Commissar seems to have decided to go farther than his government and to guide the local judges along a path which the Commissar thought desirable.

The Commissar's inclusion of crimes against the individual and against personal property in his list of specifically defined crime is the more surprising because of an article written in the same issue of the Commissariat's journal. Its author thought it remarkable that no statutes of the new regime had defined acts against the individual and against personal property as criminal.[2] In reviewing the decrees of the new regime defining crime, the author noted that "two types of criminal activity representing a significant part of all crime remained without any regulation whatever." He thought this omission the more remarkable because property relationships had been changed markedly by the Soviet regime since the Revolution. He declared that the absence of decrees in this field was not the result of accident but the consequence of a definite policy adopted at the outset of the regime's existence, namely, the desire to give to local initiative in the legal field the opportunity to develop itself in establishing its own rules. He concluded that this desire had lost its reason for existence by early 1919 because the authorities in the central government had begun to guide local government in all other fields of public life. The gap in the field of defined crimes, made by the absence of a decree on crimes against the person and against personal property, seemed to him to have become noticeable.

The ripeness of the times for codification of law by the central authorities appears to have been a matter of differing opinion in early 1919. One author is seen to have thought that centralization had progressed far enough in other fields to make it possible to add to the list of defined crime, while the government gave no outward signs of departing from its policy of giving local initiative full rein. The Commissar of Justice seems to have taken a middle ground. He said nothing about desiring to see codification speeded, but he found it desirable to turn policy in this direction for some crimes, and he was ready to read into the People's Court Act of 1918 some provisions which were not there in order to support his position. In doing so, he risked putting himself among the believers in natural law, among whom it can be presumed that he would not wish to have been in

---

[2] Iak. Berman, "K voprosu ob ugolovnom kodekse sotsialisticheskogo gosudarstva," *ibid.*, p. 49.

view of the Marxist denial of the validity of the natural-law theory. He took this risk because it could have been said of him that he was declaring that certain acts were assuredly violation of the social consciousness of law, and by so doing he was equating social consciousness of law with the law of nature. The acts he selected as criminal violation of the social consciousness of law would have been accepted by believers in natural law as in violation of the law of nature.

Guidance by the central authorities as to the rules to be used in handling disputes over civil-law relationships was more limited in early 1919 than is seen to have been the case in the criminal field. There had been two separate statutes in 1917,[3] followed by a code of October, 1918, on marriage, divorce, and guardianship;[4] a law of April 27, 1918, on inheritance;[5] and a code of labor laws in December, 1918.[6] The courts were free in 1919 to improvise on other matters in the civil field, for the People's Court Act of 1918 had forbidden further citation of the Imperial law to which the judges of the first year had been referring.

In reviewing the situation as it stood at the beginning of 1919, it is evident that while inroads upon the freedom of each judge to make his own law had begun to appear on the statutory side, the policy of headquarters still called for the preservation of this freedom except in some cases critical for the continued existence of the regime. While the government as a whole was not yet prepared to codify, its Commissar of Justice found it difficult to hold his hand. He was prepared to dictate the types of activity which must surely be penalized as violating the "social consciousness of law." He seems also to have been ready to provide guidance to local courts in another form, for in the first issue of his Commissariat's journal for 1919 he made suggestions as to the direction in which local courts were to be encouraged to exercise their judicial discretion. The Commissar made these suggestions in an article sum-

[3] Decree on Civil Marriage, Children and Vital Statistics Registries, December 18, 1917, and Decree on Divorce, December 19, 1917, [1917–1918] I *Sobranie Uzakonenii i Razporiazhenii Rabochago i Krest'ianskago Pravitel'stva RSFSR*, No. 10, item 152, and No. 11, item 160.

[4] Code of Laws on Acts of Civil Status, Marriage, Family and Guardianship RSFSR, October (undated) 1918, *ibid.*, No. 76–77, item 818.

[5] Abolition of Tsarist Inheritance Law, April 27, 1918, *ibid.*, No. 34, item 456.

[6] Code of Labor Laws RSFSR, December (undated) 1918, *ibid.*, No. 87–88, item 905.

marizing what he believed to be the good features of the work of the people's courts.[7] Since the new unified court provided by the People's Court Act of 1918 had only just begun to function at the first of the year 1919, the Commissar had to choose his examples from the work of the district courts, against which he had fought for months and whose existence he had finally succeeded in terminating by legislation.

REVOLUTIONARY CONSCIOUSNESS AND LEGAL SITUATIONS

Seven cases concerned with personal rights were chosen by the Commissar of Justice as examples to be followed by the courts of 1919. In the first one[8] Smirnov had been accused of corrupting a thirteen-year-old girl in the autumn of 1916 by paying her to have sexual relations with him. He was the landlord of the apartment in which she and her family had a room. There were no witnesses, but the Moscow District People's Court on July 1, 1918, thought that the corruption had been established sufficiently by the medical evidence, the testimony of the girl's school teacher, and the testimony of the accused. The court found that as a result of the corruption, society had lost a useful worker, healthy in mind and body. Although the Imperial law was said to have had no provisions making such action criminal, the revolutionary consciousness of the public was found not to permit Smirnov to go unpunished since his action had in it the elements of a crime both against society and against the person of the girl, a fact which required the creation of a new norm of law. In consequence, Smirnov was convicted and sentenced to public censure and the payment of court costs.

The murder on June 4, 1918, of a Red Army soldier by another soldier, named Poliakovich, was the subject of a prosecution in the Petrograd District People's Court on September 11, 1918.[9] At the trial it was established by the testimony of the accused and of a witness that the killing had occurred in a place outside the Army barracks when both were intoxicated. The accused's defense was that he had been incited to murder by the proposal of his drinking

---

[7] Kurskii, "Iz praktiki narodnogo suda," *Prol. rev. i pravo*, No. 1 (11) (January, 1919), p. 29.

[8] *Case of Smirnov, ibid.,* p. 29. [9] *Case of Poliakovich, ibid.,* p. 30.

companion that they steal funds from the regimental treasury, but this allegation was found not to have been proved. Having heard the public accuser and the defender appointed in the case, the court concluded that bearing in mind the admission of guilt by the accused and his plea in his final words before the court for leniency, the following were the factors which governed the decision: (1) even if the motive for the killing had been proved, it would not have been reason to acquit the accused, for there must have been no prior acquaintance between the parties to allow such a defense, and there must have been some group or gregarious psychological influence; (2) the killing occurred without prior planning and as the result of intoxication; (3) such relationships, especially with a fellow soldier, are inexcusable for Red Army soldiers, since they must value the good name of the Red Army; (4) the punishment might be lenient because the murdered man had also been intoxicated, as was proved by medical testimony. The accused was sentenced to five years' deprivation of freedom, but the court ordered taken into account the fact that he had been held under guard since June 5, 1918. After serving the sentence, the defendant was to be restored to all civil and political rights. The court added that had there not been found reasons for leniency, the penalty would have been double in length.

A charge of attempted robbery on May 23, 1918, had also been brought before the same court on September 11, 1918, by a houseowner, Makarov.[10] The court concluded that the guilt of the accused, Piniagin, had not been proved, but there was reason to take measures against him. He had been shown at the trial to belong to the category of idealistic anarchists, but his plans for the activities which took place in an apartment at 42 Raz'ezhaia Street were found to have included nothing that would indicate an intent to enrich himself personally at the expense of another. There was also no evidence to prove that the revolver and bomb which were found upon his person had threatened the life of any one. In consequence Piniagin was acquitted of the charge, but the court concluded that in the light of the explanation given by the accused that he had sought to requisition a room for himself in the apartment, the accused should be found guilty of unauthorized requisition, and he

[10] *Case of Piniagin, ibid.*, p. 32.

was sentenced to six months' deprivation of freedom, his three and a half months under guard being taken into consideration in a reduction of the time yet to be served.

Embezzlement of 21,953 rubles was charged against one Batov in the Petrograd District People's Court on September 10, 1918.[11] The accused admitted his guilt, and three witnesses were called to prove it. A public accuser and a defender named by the court participated, after which the court found

(1) that Batov had committed the embezzlement, although not by deliberate design and also not as the result of exceptional external circumstances over which he had no control but because of his weak will in not being able to resist desires common among persons of his age and position (carousal and cards), (2) that the preceding twenty-five year irreproachable service of Batov and the absence of other reprehensible circumstances in his life permit in the given case a show of leniency, and (3) that in view of the character of the crime conditional sentence is inadmissible since it might set an undesirable precedent for the masses of persons holding positions of responsibility, similar to that of Batov's terms and conditions of work.

Batov was sentenced to imprisonment for one year, with consideration of the time already served under guard since July 26, 1918. After completion of the term he was to be restored to full civil and political rights.

The civil cases held up by the Commissar as examples of good court work in the eyes of the new leaders were three from the Voronezh District People's Court. The first involved a suit brought by Nesterenko against the Southeast Railway Company for 10,000 rubles in damages.[12] The case had been commenced in 1906 in the pre-revolutionary district court, but had come to trial only on July 26, 1918. The years of delay in reaching the stage of trial were singled out by the Commissar for comment as indicating the inexcusable red tape of the old court procedure. The facts proved at the trial were these: a fifteen-year-old student, Nesterenko, was waiting for the train on April 23, 1906, at the station of Kopamishch. He had to wait a long time and decided to go into a little glade close at hand to pick flowers. When he heard the train's whistle, he ran back to the station, and jumped on the step of one of the cars, but the train

<hr>

[11] *Case of Batov, ibid.*, pp. 32–33.
[12] *Nesterenko v. Obshchesto Iugo-vostochnykh zh. d., ibid.*, pp. 33–34.

had already begun to move. The conductor who was standing on the platform struck him in the chest, and he fell backward so that the wheel of the railway car smashed his right foot. It had to be amputated. At the trial the railway moved for further adjournment to permit the examination of experts to determine whether the plaintiff was able to work. The judges at the trial took note of the fact that there was already a medical opinion that because of the shock suffered at the time the plaintiff had lost his capacity to work for all time, and that he had developed an hysteria which reduced his mental capacities by one third. The judges could imagine no employment for which the plaintiff was now suited. In the light of these considerations the judges refused to hear new experts, and they stated in their decision that they as people of the world knew better than experts what was necessary to hold a job both before the Revolution and since, and in reliance on their consciousness they could achieve justice without the help of new experts. Taking into consideration the contributory negligence of the plaintiff, the judges gave judgment for the plaintiff in the amount of 41 rubles a month from the date of the accident to February 27, 1918, and 166 rubles 66 kopeks a month from that date until his death or until a system of social insurance should be introduced into the country.

Maintenance of a child was the subject of the second suit held up as a good example by the Commissar.[13] Zemlianikova sought 100 rubles a month from Kodorov with whom she had lived for three years and to whom she had borne a child. He had subsequently discarded her and married another woman. Judgment was given for the plaintiff but her request for expenses incurred in bringing suit was denied because one of the lay judges convinced the others that since Kodorov was a workman and lived solely on his wages, and since he now had to support two families, it would be like putting a noose around his neck to require him to pay costs.

A suit for maintenance was the third exemplary case.[14] It had been brought by Livenshtein, a woman of education, against her husband to whom she had been married in a religious ceremony when he was still a student. Soon after the ceremony they had

[13] *Zemlianikova v. Livenshtein, ibid.,* p. 35.
[14] *Livenshtein v. Livenshtein, ibid.*

separated, and the court concluded from the letters introduced in evidence that the marriage had been fictitious solely to permit the plaintiff to escape from the difficult situation in which some one had placed her. It is reported that as soon as the members of the court had retired for consultation, one of the women lay judges had said: "Naturally, we must dismiss the suit; they have no children, and a woman must work the same as a man to earn her livelihood. These are not times when a wife can represent herself as living in a hothouse and ask for maintenance from her husband." The other judges agreed with this view. The judges would not, however, give judgment for costs to the husband on the ground that he was himself responsible, for he had entered into the marriage without sufficient consideration.

Kurskii brought his account of the above cases to a close with this statement: "These decisions are shot through with the spirit of unhindered imagination. They are as far from the opinion of a legally trained judge as they are from the heartless form of the old written law, and at the same time they are just in high degree." [15]

CENTRALIZING CONTROL OVER
LOCAL DEPARTMENTS OF JUSTICE

The trend toward centralization emerging in 1919 finds reflection in the measures taken on January 30 to bring the local "Commissariats of Justice" more closely under the supervision of the central government's Commissariat, if not to make of them branch offices of the Moscow authorities. In an instruction[16] published over Kurskii's signature the former provincial "commissariats" of justice were to be replaced by provincial "departments" of justice organized within the framework of the provincial soviets. By the instruction each provincial soviet was directed to choose from its own number a chief of the new "department" to be installed by the central government's Commissariat of Justice.

The new department of justice in each province was to be divided

[15] *Ibid.*
[16] Charter for Departments of Justice in the Provincial Executive Committees, Instruction of the People's Commissariat of Justice, January 30, 1919, *ibid.*, pp. 147–50. Also published in [1919] I *Sob. Uzak. RSFSR*, No. 2, item 29.

into sections with operating functions including advising the provincial soviet's executive committee on legal matters coming before
it, editing instructions to be issued by the executive committee,
informing the executive committee of illegal acts of local officials,
instructing state offices in proper accounting procedures, informing
the Commissariat of Justice and the financial section of the provincial soviet of income and expenditures of state offices under the
Commissariat's jurisdiction, organizing and supervising the people's
courts, the revolutionary tribunals, the investigating commissions,
the colleges of accusers, defenders and representatives in civil suits,
and the court executioners, calling of congresses of people's court
judges in the county seats, instigating the preparation of lists of
persons to sit in courts as lay judges, nominating candidates to be
appointed by the Soviets as members of the investigating commissions, generally supervising the work of the police in preliminary
investigation, organizing legal aid to the population in the form
of consultation points, collecting statistics on the work of the courts
and investigating committees for transmission to the Commissariat
of Justice, preparing lists of convicted persons for transmission to
the Commissariat of Justice, and organizing and supervising the
prisons and detention points. Expenses of the provincial departments of justice were to be borne by the Commissariat of Justice
at the center.

Complete subordination of the departments to the central government's authorities in Moscow was avoided by the introduction of a
"college" with which the chief of the department was required to
work. The members of this college were to be named by the executive committee of the provincial soviet, and they were to have the
right to protest to the executive committee of the provincial soviet
any action of the head of the department with which they could
not agree although the action was to be put into effect in spite of
this protest until such time as it might be set aside by the executive
committee. Their authority was further strengthened by a provision
that the staff of sections of the department could be named by the
chiefs of each section, but they had to be approved by the college of
the department. In spite of this emphasis upon the authority of the
college, the impression is left that the central authorities had the
upper hand, since they installed the head of the department, his

decisions were to go into effect when made in spite of the college's
lack of agreement, and the expenses of the department were to be
met by the headquarters rather than the executive committee of the
provincial soviet. Moscow and Petrograd were declared to be
equivalent to provinces for the purpose of establishing departments
of justice within them. No mention was made of the future for
the former county commissariats of justice.

A subsequent instruction of March 10, 1919,[17] outlined in detail
the structure and authority of the departments to be established
in cities of Moscow and Petrograd. The close link to be maintained
with the central government's authorities was reiterated in a provision that the departments were to be transmission agencies for
the organizational and administrative measures sponsored by the
Commissariat of Justice, and that the departments were to be held
accountable for their actions to the Commissariat of Justice as well
as to the city soviet of which they were structurally an administrative arm. Cognizance was taken of the fact that the people's judges
in the two largest cities had already established strong administrative agencies in the form of the presidiums of the council of people's
judges, for the instruction provided that in performing their supervisory duties over the activities of the people's courts, they should
act "through and in contact with" the presidium of the council of
people's judges.

While the internal structure of the departments was to take the
form established by the instruction of January 30, 1919, on the
subject, there was manifest in the specialized instruction issued by
the Commissariat to implement the decree for Moscow and Petrograd a tendency to utilize existing agencies at the borough level
within each of the great cities. It was provided in the instruction
that where a borough juridical department existed, the city's department of justice should delegate some of its functions to it, while
other of its functions should be performed at the borough level
by members of the college of the city department assigned for the
specific purpose or by "instructors" designated for the task. If no
borough juridical department existed in a given borough, the city's

[17] Instruction on Application of the Charter for Departments of Justice in the
Cities of Moscow and Petrograd, *Prol. rev. i pravo*, No. 2–4 (12–14) (February–
April, 1919), pp. 109–11. Also published in [1919] I *Sob. Uzak. RSFSR*,
No. 10–11, item 119.

department was authorized to utilize the services of the legal adviser to the borough soviet.

The functions to be delegated to the borough juridical departments were listed as: legal advice to the borough soviet, editing of instructions to be issued by the borough soviet, preliminary review of complaints filed with the borough soviet against the actions of local officials on the payroll of the soviet, investigation of allegations of violation by state enterprises of the rules governing their operation with transfer to the investigating commission or to a people's court of the file if criminal activity were discovered, review of the work of the local consultation point providing legal advice to the population, auditing payments of sums collected by the court executioners, preparation of lists of persons to stand as candidates for selection as people's judges, as members of the investigating commissions, as members of the college of defenders, accusers and representatives in civil suits, and preparation of lists of persons to serve as lay judges in the people's courts. Further, the city departments were authorized to place upon the borough departments the duty to call periodic meetings of the people's judges of the boroughs, of the investigating commissions, and of the colleges of defenders, accusers, and representatives in civil suits, so that these groups might be kept in touch with the functions of the legal departments. Such meetings were said not to be permitted to replace the regular meetings of the judges, the investigators, and the lawyers to discuss matters arising in the performance of their functions. Finally, the borough departments were instructed to arrange for periodic oral reports to the borough soviet by people's judges and by members of the other court agencies on the character of their work and on the incidence of crime in the borough.

Certain functions were specifically excluded by the instruction from the list of matters to be delegated to the borough departments, namely, direct control over the people's judges and the other court agencies, which was to be provided only by the presidium of the people's judges to which all complaints were to be referred. Likewise complaints against the activities of the colleges of defenders, accusers, and representatives in civil suits were to be referred to the council of the college, with notice also to the department of justice for the whole city.

In contrast to the situation established for the provincial departments, to which the city departments of Moscow and Leningrad were made equivalent, the expenses of the borough legal departments were to be paid by local funds and not by the People's Commissariat of Justice. By this particular provision the central authorities removed from their budget an item of expense which they probably thought unnecessary for the purpose of maintaining the control of the center. It may have seemed enough to establish the control of the purse over the provincial or big-city departments on the assumption that the chiefs of the provincial or big-city departments could continue control over the borough departments even without control of the purse, since the latter were responsible only to the department in the provincial or big-city soviet. There was no sharing of responsibility with the local soviet such as had been provided in the decree of January 30, 1919, for the provincial and big-city departments.

The method in which the newly created department of justice in each province was to perform its functions at the county level was left unexplained by the decree of January 30, 1919. Prior to that time the former "commissariats of justice" in the provinces had acted through "commissariats of justice" in the various counties, but the latter seem to have been considered as local bodies responsible locally rather than as arms of the central authorities concerned with the preservation of order. To be sure they received "proposals" from higher authorities, but they were appointed and financed locally, and it can be presumed that without the power of the purse or the power to employ and dismiss, the central authorities had to rely on persuasion and the psychological stimulus evoked by a sense of the much-vaunted brotherhood of the proletarians to obtain a suitable response to the "proposals." Not until publication of a special instruction dealing with the organization in the counties did the situation become clarified.

The special instruction dealing with the organization in the counties[18] bears no date, but its publication in the journal of the Commissariat of Justice at the same time as the dated instruction relating to the organization of law enforcing agencies in Moscow and in

[18] Instruction on Application of the Charter for Provincial Departments of Justice, *Prol. rev. i pravo*, No. 2–4 (12–14) (February–April, 1919), pp. 107–9.

Petrograd suggests that it appeared at about the same time in March, 1919. Under this instruction the meeting of judges in each county was authorized to elect a "bureau" or executive committee at a session to which members of the investigating commissions and of the colleges of defenders, accusers, and representatives in civil suits were to be admitted with a consultative vote. This "bureau" was given the same functions as the legal departments of the borough soviets in Moscow and Petrograd, and the impression is given that they replaced the "commissariats of justice" in each county. They could concern themselves not only with affairs of the courts, but with the affairs of the investigating commissions and colleges of defenders, accusers, and representatives in civil suits as well. In cases where the interests of these two agencies were concerned, their representatives had full votes.

A link was to be maintained under the terms of the instruction between the new "bureau" and the county soviet by a provision in the instruction requiring the president of the county meeting of judges or some other judge to make a report to the executive committee of the county soviet on the work of the court agencies in the county, on the character of crime in the county and on the punitive measures applied by the courts. Further, the president of the executive committee of the county soviet was to be invited to attend the county meeting of judges.

The instruction suggests that the authorities were prepared to leave with the local citizenry much more authority over the preservation of order in the various counties than they were prepared to leave to the local authorities in the cities of Moscow and Petrograd. Perhaps the central authorities in the Commissariat of Justice in Moscow felt that it was still desirable to develop initiative at the local level through such a mechanism, although the explanation seems more plausible that Moscow and Petrograd were convenient for control through the center, while the outlying counties were too far away to permit the frequent communication which is necessary for any highly centralized system of government.

THE CIVIL WAR ENCOURAGES
CENTRALIZATION

A consideration of the military developments of the time will indicate the problem faced by the central Soviet authorities in the spring of 1919 in maintaining communication with outlying parts of the country. The forces of the opposition under Admiral Kolchak in Siberia were having great success. The city of Perm had been captured, and Ufa fell in March, 1919. General Denikin began an offensive through the Ukraine toward Moscow in mid-May, 1919, and his armies captured the key cities of Kharkov, Ekaterinoslav, and Tsaritsyn during June. The Soviet counterattack failed, and Denikin marched on to reach a line of Voronezh-Orel-Chernigov-Odessa by mid-October before the tide began to turn. In the north General Yudenich attacked Petrograd from Estonia and occupied Gatchina not far from the city.

Dissension within the Communist party may also have contributed to the anxiety of the central authorities and to the pressure being exerted by some high party officials for further centralization of the state apparatus. Competing factions within the party were struggling for recognition, and new members were being admitted in such numbers that it was difficult to teach them the discipline advocated by Lenin as essential to strong party ties and to assure performance of party orders transmitted from the center to the provinces. Local leaders were prone to make their own decisions, abetted by the recurring severance of communications as the Red Army suffered defeats. In the absence of a strong, disciplined, centralized Communist party reaching down into the remote areas of the country, Lenin and his colleagues in Moscow may have been moved to proceed faster with centralization of the state apparatus than would have been needed had they been able to rely upon more subtle instruments of guidance over local soviets formed by individuals frequently intoxicated with the new experience of wielding power.

The defeats of the civil war were reflected in the measures taken by the Soviet policy makers to keep order. Attention seems to have been focused on protection of the state, and the record of development of a system of law and legal agencies to settle disputes between citizens almost disappears from Soviet literature. The journal of the People's Commissariat of Justice was discontinued with the issue appearing in April, 1919, not to reappear until December, 1921. The Russian Republic's official collection of laws for the period shows the emphasis to have been upon expansion of the powers of the agencies concerned with counterrevolution and acts endangering the state. On February 17, 1919,[19] the Cheka, which had become well known as the sword of the new regime, was continued in its authority to act promptly through its three-man tribunals in exacting retribution from those found guilty of armed insurrection and of such other crimes as might be listed in a declaration of martial law in a given area.

Military revolutionary tribunals were established by decree of February 4, 1919,[20] on a pattern rather similar to that of the revolutionary tribunals which had been authorized by the first decree on the courts of November 24, 1917, to provide jurisdiction over political offenses committed by civilians. The new tribunals were to try all cases of political offenses and crimes of a military character within the army. On April 12, 1919,[21] a revision of the statute on the civilian revolutionary tribunals which handled political offenses was published. On April 3, 1919,[22] the local police together with their investigative arm which served the criminal courts were ordered financed from the state budget and staffed by persons approved by the Commissariat of Internal Affairs. Rules for the formation of a river police under the Commissariat of Internal Affairs were published on April 23, 1919.[23]

The highly nervous condition of the central authorities at the time is illustrated by a decree of a state of siege in Petrograd on

[19] Decree on the All-Russian Extraordinary Commission, [1919] I *Sob. Uzak. RSFSR*, No. 12, item 130.

[20] Statute on Revolutionary Military Tribunals, *ibid.*, No. 13, item 131.

[21] Statute on Revolutionary Tribunals, *ibid.*, item 132.

[22] Decree on the Soviet Workers'-Peasants' Militia, *ibid.*, item 133.

[23] Charter on the River Soviet Workers'-Peasants' Militia, *ibid.*, No. 18, item 213. This police had been authorized by decree of July 25, 1918, [1917–1918] *ibid.*, No. 55, item 608, but it seems to have functioned without a charter until April, 1919.

May 2, 1919,[24] with a statement in its preamble that a radio report had been picked up that night from Paris in which it had been announced that the Finnish government had sent an ultimatum to the Russian government threatening war unless the Soviet government stopped its attack on Karelia. The decree's preamble declared that no ultimatum had been received, and no Soviet attack was in progress against Karelia, but that to be ready for a Finnish attack the state of siege was being declared. The military commander was authorized to requisition such property as he needed, to impress citizens into work for the army, and to clean the army's rear of counterrevolutionary elements.

The impact of the advance of the opposition forces upon the agencies concerned with the preservation of order is illustrated by a decree of May 21, 1919,[25] concerning the liquidation of the affairs of evacuated local soviets, requiring them to complete their liquidation in not more than seven days if they were a soviet of a province, after which they were to seal up their archives without making an inventory and deliver them to the local soviet or provincial soviet where they happened to be at the time, to deposit such moneys as might remain in the local soviet's treasury at the state bank, to send a report of their activities to the All-Russian Central Executive Committee, to send a report of their finances to the Moscow State Bank, and to deliver any arms and ammunition to the local army commander. Within six weeks the situation had deteriorated to such an extent that a decree of July 9[26] ordered the members of the executive committee of all evacuated soviets and the personnel of all agencies of the soviet to report for duty at the front if physically able to serve in the army.

Strict measures were introduced to centralize administration and to limit the freedom of citizens where the safety of the state might be endangered by exercise of such freedom. On April 24, 1919, a decree[27] forbade the issuance of passports for departure abroad by

[24] Decree Declaring Petrograd, and the Petrograd, Olonets and Cherepovets Provinces in a State of Siege, and on Measures for the Defense of Petrograd, [1919] *ibid.*, No. 19, item 219.

[25] Instruction on the Liquidation of All Evacuated Soviets, *ibid.*, No. 20, item 246.

[26] Decree on the Procedures for Evacuating Local Executive Committees and Offices of Soviets, *ibid.*, No. 35, item 352.

[27] Decree on the Procedure for Issuing Passports for Abroad, *ibid.*, No. 18, item 211.

any but the Commissariat of Foreign Affairs, and the clearance of the Commissariat of Internal Affairs and of the Commissariat for Military Affairs was required. On April 15, 1919, compulsory work camps were ordered established by the provincial offices of the Cheka, to be centrally administered after establishment by the Commissariat of Internal Affairs.[28] These camps were to receive persons committed to them by the Cheka, the revolutionary tribunals, the people's courts and other Soviet agencies. Workmen were forbidden to leave their jobs without the consent of management by a decree of April 12, 1919,[29] and on June 25, 1919,[30] labor books to contain the employment record of all workers over the age of sixteen in Moscow and Petrograd were ordered introduced to serve as a means of personal identification, as well as the basis for the distribution of ration books and social insurance and proof that each citizen was participating in the productive process.

By the autumn of 1919 the tide had begun to turn. Admiral Kolchak had been defeated in Siberia, although he was not executed until April of the following year. The Soviet government controlled the territory as far east as Irkutsk. General Denikin had been stopped in October. On November 8, 1919, Lloyd George stated that the Bolsheviks could not be conquered by arms. The Soviet authorities seem to have sensed ultimate victory. On November 5, 1919, they issued a decree[31] saying that while the Soviet government had been forced to take the severest forms of repression in order to preserve the first republic of toilers in the face of siege by hostile armies and when its rear was infiltrated with counterrevolutionaries, it had now achieved improvement and had strengthened its forces. An amnesty was decreed in honor of the second anniversary of the Revolution. All persons whose crimes against the working class did not require further deprivation of freedom were to be released, if they had been sentenced to a term of less than five years, and had not committed an act in a group or as part of a conspiracy having

[28] Decree on Camps for Forced Labor, *ibid.*, No. 12, item 124. Enlarged by decree of May 17, 1919, *ibid.*, No. 20, item 235.

[29] Decree on Forbidding Voluntary Transfer of Soviet Office Workers from One Agency to Another, *ibid.*, No. 18, item 204.

[30] Decree on Introducing Labor Books in the Cities of Moscow and Leningrad, *ibid.*, No. 28, item 315.

[31] Amnesty on the Second Anniversary of the October Revolution, *ibid.*, No. 55, item 525.

as its aim armed attack on the Soviet government, or had not shown clearly mercenary motives in a non-political act. If a sentence had been for longer than five years, it was to be reduced to five years, or the criminal might be released. The amnesty applied to persons whether sentenced by a court or by a revolutionary tribunal or by an administrative body such as the Cheka, an executive committee, or an administrative department.

By the amnesty the central government gave further evidence of a developing trend toward centralization of the process of making decisions as to social danger. While the courts, the revolutionary tribunals, the Cheka and other administrative bodies having the power to imprison had been deciding for themselves without much detailed guidance from the center what activities violated social consciousness, the central authorities now indicated their willingness to intervene to establish categories of persons for whom they recommended release from prison. By so doing the central authorities provided a common yardstick of danger, saying, in effect, that as a general rule persons who had been sentenced for offenses lacking in critical danger to the very life of the new regime were to be presumed to be no longer sufficiently dangerous to require imprisonment. The central authorities did not yet go as far as they were to go in later years in opening prison doors without regard to a review of the record of each case. The first amnesty of 1919 left to the local courts, the revolutionary tribunals, the Cheka, and the other administrative agencies the final decision as to the future imprisonment of each person previously sentenced by them. The amnesty decree established what seems to have been a national policy of reducing sentences and a presumption of no continuing danger from specified categories of criminals, but it permitted the local authorities to apply the policy and to decide whether the presumption was rebutted by the evidence accumulated in each individual file.

A further step in the direction of codification of law, with its implication of reduced authority for local judges in exercising their social consciousness was taken on December 12, 1919.[32] The Commissariat of Justice published "a basic aid" in criminal law in which a definition was given for law in general, criminal law in gen-

[32] Decree on the Basic Principles for the Criminal Law of the RSFSR, *ibid.*, No. 66, item 590.

eral, and Soviet criminal law in particular, after which articles established the types of punishment to be given in court sentences; the matters to be considered in determining the appropriate punishment; exemption of minors, the insane and those who acted in self-defense; the seriousness to be attributed to attempts, preparation for crime, and complicity; the function of the suspended sentence; and the territorial jurisdiction of the criminal laws of the R.S.F.S.R.

The December "basic aid" did not define any specific crime. Each judge was left to his own resources to apply the specialized decrees which had been published or to apply his social consciousness, but there was now provided for his guidance a definition to make his task somewhat easier. Soviet criminal law was defined as "having as its function during the transitional period of the dictatorship of the proletariat between capitalism and communism the protection by means of repression of the system of social relations which accord to the interests of the toiling masses."

Stuchka has explained that the definition of law in general which appeared in the 1919 decree was adopted by the governing body of the Commissariat of Justice rather hastily and more as a matter of flair than after exhaustive study of the subject.[33] He admitted later that he had been pleasantly surprised that the definition had in general stood up under criticism, even though there was no fundamental study of the meaning of its various popularly used words, such as "society, class, class interest, etc." What he said of the general definition of law was probably applicable to the specific definition of Soviet criminal law as well, for there was in 1919 very little agreement on the meaning of such words as "dictatorship of the proletariat," the "transitional period," and "communism" itself.

PARALLEL DEVELOPMENTS
IN THE UKRAINE

While the Russian Republic had been experimenting in the fashion indicated during the years 1917 and 1918, the Ukraine had been in the throes of a military struggle for control. The first Soviet-spon-

---

[33] See Introduction to P. I. Stuchka, *Revoliutsionnaia rol' prava i gosudarstvo* (2nd ed.; Moscow, 1923), p. 5 (reprinted from first edition of 1921).

sored decrees began to issue from the new Soviet capital of the Ukraine only in January, 1919. Military affairs seem to have concerned the government more than arrangements to settle civilian disputes. The first decree on courts,[34] published on January 14, 1919, concerned only military personnel and civilians in the theater of military operations when accused of committing military crimes. These were defined in the decree as "espionage, causing of harm to military units, etc." For the trial of such charges there was established a system of military tribunals at four levels; a disciplinary court at the company level, a regimental court, a court for an army, and a cassational-appellate court under the Military-Revolutionary Council of the Ukrainian Soviet Army.

Although the first courts concerned protection of the state rather than disputes between individuals, some of the elements of the first decree bear examination since they throw light upon the thinking in the Ukraine on the judicial process. The decree established no code of military law, nor were the military tribunals provided with a code of procedure. As in the Russian Republic's first efforts to establish a mechanism for the trial of cases, it is indicated that the Ukrainians relied largely on the intuition of their new judges to do what was necessary to preserve the new regime. The decree stated simply, "The only source of court activity is revolutionary conscience." Procedure was treated with the enunciation of a few fundamentals. Judges were directed to conduct their courts in accordance with the principles of (a) expediency, (b) impartiality, (c) directness, (d) equality of prosecution and defense, (e) public trial, and (f) trial on the basis of oral examination of the parties and witnesses rather than on documents alone. Sentences were to be supported by a majority vote of the judges. The parties were to be permitted to have counsel, and in serious cases the court was required to employ the services of both an accuser and a defender. A written record of the trial was to be kept.

The principles established in the decree on military courts were developed further in mid-February when the civilian courts were established. This step was not taken, however, until the new Ukrainian government had appointed on January 29, 1919, a People's

---

[34] [1919] I *Sobranie Uzakonenii i Rasporiazhenii Raboche-Krest'ianskogo Pravitel'stva Ukrainy,* No. 1, item 9.

Commissar of Justice to sit as a member of the Council of People's Commissars.[35] No official designated for such duties had been included in the list of department chiefs installed in the first decrees of the new government.[36] Presumably the leaders of the new state felt that the establishment of civilian courts was in second place on their list of priorities at a time of vigorous military action.

Even before the publication of the decree on the new civilian courts, the government gave its attention to the organization of local administration of legal matters. On February 8, 1919, a general statute on local government[37] included provisions for the creation of departments of justice in each provincial, city, and county soviet. The decree gave no indication of the relationship to be maintained between the local departments of justice and the ministry in Kharkov. One can imagine that at this time of confusion on the battlefield it was as tenuous as that established in 1918 in the Russian Republic.

Evidence of centralization of authority appears for the first time in the decree of February 9, 1919, establishing a local police force.[38] This evidence is to be found in the provision that the local police departments were to be organized not by the local soviets which they were to serve but by the People's Commissariat of Internal Affairs in the Republic's capital of Kharkov.

The first general statute on the civil courts was published as a "temporary" measure on February 19, 1919.[39] The influence upon the draftsmen of the experience of the Russian Republic in the preceding fifteen months is noticeable, for the Ukrainian government introduced its court system in the model already in existence in the Russian Republic at the time the Ukrainians drafted their statute rather than in the model of the Russian Republic's first decree on the courts. The same wording was used in the decree as the Russians had used to abolish the old system, but the new system created to replace it indicated that the Ukrainians were prepared to jump the experiment of the Russians during their first year with a system of local and district courts. There was no "district court" at all in the Ukrainian statute, and nothing was said about limits of jurisdic-

[35] *Ibid.*, No. 4, item 52b.
[36] Decree of January 14, 1919, *ibid.*, No. 2, item 16.
[37] *Ibid.*, No. 7, item 86, sec. 22.   [38] *Ibid.*, item 96.
[39] *Ibid.*, No. 11, item 141.

tion. The Ukrainians adopted the concept of the single court for all civil and criminal cases, except those having to do with counter-revolution, treason, espionage, crimes by officials and sabotage, speculation, and such other serious crimes as might be designated. For these serious crimes involving the safety of the new regime, there was established a system of "revolutionary tribunals" similar to the system existing in the Russian Republic.

By utilizing the experience of the Russian Republic and introducing its court pattern in the form of the Russian Republic rather than in some completely different pattern, the Communists of the Ukraine who controlled the new government seem to have established the principle later to find reflection even in Poland, Rumania, Bulgaria, Hungary, Czechoslovakia, and Albania. It is the principle against which Marshal Tito revolted when he took Yugoslavia out of the Soviet orbit in 1948. In general terms the principle might be stated as follows: Each new state to adopt the Soviet system of government will do so on the pattern of the U.S.S.R., although minor modifications will be permitted to meet special situations existing in the new state. No extensive experimentation with other forms will be permitted. Not until the Gomulka revolt in Poland in 1956 was there a relaxation of the requirement of conformity, and even that had limits.

Having followed the Russian pattern as it stood in 1919 rather than in 1917, the new Soviet Ukraine said nothing of applying pre-revolutionary law, subject to such changes as seemed necessary to bring it to accord with revolutionary consciousness. The judges were instructed by the Ukrainian decree to apply such decrees of the new government as had been enacted, and in the absence of decree to seek guidance "in the first instance in the interests of the socialist revolution, and then in the socialist concept of law." While the formula is not identical with that in force in the Russian Republic in 1919, it bears close similarity. As in the Russian Republic the judges were authorized to feel no limitations in establishing a procedure for trial which would disclose the truth. The bench of judges was to vary in size as it did in the Russian Republic at the time, namely, from a professional judge with six lay judges for the trial of serious offenses, to one judge with two lay judges for the trial of other crimes and civil suits. Appeals were to lie to a council of people's judges to be composed of three professional judges, which might set aside a sentence or decision if there had been a substantial violation of law going to the heart of the sentence or decision, or in the event that the sentence or decision seemed clearly to be unjust. The case was then retried by a people's court, with a different bench of judges from that of the first trial. In contrast to the authority granted to the council of people's judges in the Russian Republic, the Ukrainian government authorized the council not only to remand for new trial but also to hear the case itself as a trial court when augmented with the number of lay judges required under the circumstances.

While the Ukrainian statute authorized the presence of accusers and defenders at the trial, and declared that accusers and defenders should be provided by a college of accusers and legal defenders in turn, the statute departed from the pattern set by the Russian Republic's decree of November 30, 1918, for it contained no details as to the character of this college, nor did the Ukrainian decree establish court fees.

UKRAINIAN CENTRALIZATION OF AUTHORITY

Centralization of authority was indicated early as the principle on which the Ukrainian system of legal administration was to be built. Whereas the Russian Republic's authorities had preferred to leave the evolution of law to the imagination of each individual court, the Ukrainian authorities placed in the juridical departments of the provincial, city, and county soviets, which had been established on the Russian Republic's pattern,[40] the authority to see to the uniform interpretation of the laws "in the spirit of Soviet legislation and the social consciousness of law." [41] Further, the juridical departments of the local soviets were given the authority to appear as a party in all criminal and civil matters before the local courts and to protest any civil judgment or criminal sentence as unjust to the council of peo-

[40] Decree on the Legal Departments of the Provincial, County and City Executive Committees, February 25, 1919, *ibid.*, No. 15, item 164.

[41] Circular on the Overseeing by the Legal Departments of the Provincial Executive Committees of the Conformity to Law of Sentences and Judgments of the Judicial Establishments under their Jurisdiction, March 8, 1919, *ibid.*, No. 23, item 252.

ple's judges concerned. If the procedural process of review had been completed before the discovery of a departure from Soviet legislation or the principle of socialist legal consciousness, the matter was to be reported to the People's Commissariat of Justice at Kharkov.

The People's Commissariat of Justice had already been provided with a statute[42] establishing within it a department of "Control and Investigation" with the task of performing general and current audit of the activities of court and investigatory authorities of the Republic as well as of the juridical departments of the local soviets. On April 15, 1919, the Commissar of Justice proposed to all local soviets that they establish within the juridical departments of their executive committees a control and investigation section in which the work of following the activities of local courts would be concentrated.[43]

Having assumed responsibility for coordination of the work of the various local people's courts, the People's Commissariat of Justice moved quickly to establish its regulatory authority in several fields relating to the administration of law. An order was issued on March 20, 1919, directing the juridical departments of the provincial and county executive committees to estabilsh a section for legal advice to the executive committee and to other soviet offices, and to the population generally.[44] A lengthy instruction informed the local executive committees of the procedure to be followed in giving free legal advice to the population.[45] On March 21, 1919,[46] the Commissariat was given the right by a decree of the Council of Ministers of the Ukraine to set aside or amend orders of the provincial executive committees concerning the number of revolutionary tribunals and the places in which they were to sit in the province, as well as orders concerning the number of persons to be placed on the roster of

[42] Decree on the Charter of the People's Commissariat of Justice, March 1, 1919, *ibid.,* No. 18, item 195.

[43] Order on Establishing Control-investigation and Administrative (General) Sections within the Legal Departments of the Executive Committees (addition to Art. 164), *ibid.,* No. 36, item 432.

[44] Order on Establishing a Section for Legal Advice within the Legal Departments of the Provincial and County Executive Committees, *ibid.,* No. 30, item 327.

[45] Instruction on Establishing Consultation Points to Provide Free Legal Aid to the Population, March 20, 1919, *ibid.,* item 328.

[46] Decree on Amending Secs. 3 and 6 of the "Temporary Charter of People's Courts and Revolutionary Tribunals," *ibid.,* No. 32, item 347.

members of the college of accusers and legal defenders, special court investigators, and revolutionary tribunals. This right was extended on April 16, 1919, to permit the Commissariat as well as provincial executive committees to set aside or amend orders of local soviets establishing the number and territorial jurisdiction of people's courts, as well as the number of lay judges, investigators, court executioners, and members of the college of accusers and legal defenders to be elected.[47]

The audit jurisdiction of the Commissariat seems to have required elaboration by mid-April, for on April 15, 1919, the Council of People's Commissars of the Ukraine established a new ninth department of the People's Commissariat of Justice to be known as "the Supreme Court Control."[48] Its function was to centralize the permanent and current audit of the activity of all local courts in the Ukrainian Socialist Soviet Republic, and especially to see to the uniformity of decision in civil and criminal cases by the courts. The "Control and Investigation Department" of the Commissariat, which had formerly performed this function, was limited in jurisdiction to audit of the work of the investigating authorities and the juridical departments of the local executive committees, and of such of the court activities as might be assigned to it by the Commissariat.

A tenth department was ordered established in the Commissariat of Justice on the following day, April 16, 1919, to be entitled "The Supreme Court of Cassation."[49] Its function was to hear appeals from sentences of the revolutionary tribunals. Its authority was to set aside sentences if there had been a substantial violation of a law or of an instruction of the People's Commissariat of Justice or if there had been a clear miscarriage of justice. The case might be remanded for new trial or decided by the Supreme Court itself, but in this situation the court had to invite accusers and defenders to appear in accordance with the usual rules. On retrial, a revolutionary tribunal was required to accept the interpretation of the law given by the Supreme Court.

[47] Decree on the Procedure for Reviewing Sentences of Revolutionary Tribunals, *ibid.*, No. 36, item 437.

[48] Decree on Establishing a Ninth Department of the People's Commissariat of Justice—the Supreme Court Control, *ibid.*, No. 37, item 443.

[49] Decree on Establishing a Tenth Department of the People's Commissariat of Justice—the Supreme Court of Cassation, *ibid.*, item 444.

Not until June 29, 1919, was an instruction[50] published by the Commissariat of Justice of the Ukraine establishing a procedure for the Supreme Court of Cassation of the Commissariat. Under its provisions the court was to be composed of a president and judges named by the Commissariat. When it received an appeal, it was to verify compliance with all procedural rules of appeal and then refer the file to the "court control department," which was to return it within forty-eight hours so that a date might be set for trial. In the event that the case involved the interpretation of a law or the application of the criteria of the "spirit of socialist consciousness of law," the court control department was to arrange a hearing on this subject and to invite to the discussion of the question representatives of the "legal advice department" as well as a representative of the department engaged in establishing rules and controlling the structure of the courts. Each of these two departments was to have an advisory voice at the meeting. Not later than one day before the session of the Supreme Court of Cassation, the court control department was to give to the Supreme Court of Cassation its ruling on the applicable law. The Supreme Court of Cassation's function was to determine the facts only. As an aid in this process the Supreme Court of Cassation was to establish a college of accusers and a college of legal defenders on whom it might call for assistance in the review of the case. New evidence might be introduced on the argument of the case, if the court thought it pertinent, and the accused was permitted to say his final words. A simple majority of the judges decided the matter.

Guidance in matters of substantive law was much less extensive in the Ukrainian Republic of this period than in the Russian Republic. The Council of People's Commissars of the Ukrainian Republic was authorized on March 18, 1919,[51] to legislate as well as to administer, probably because it alone could meet under conditions of occupation of much of the Republic. Much of the legislation came from the Council, therefore, rather than from the Central Executive Committee of the Soviets, which had been authorized by the

---

[50] Instruction on the Mutual Relations between the Cassational Department of the Supreme Court of Cassation and the Court Control Department of the People's Commissariat of Justice, *ibid.*, Part II, item 150.

[51] Order Granting Temporarily to the Council of People's Commissars Rights in the Sphere of Legislating and General Administration, *ibid.*, Part I, item 207.

Ukrainian constitution of March 14, 1919,[52] to function as the supreme authority in the intervals between the infrequent meetings of the Ukrainian Congress of Soviets.

What legislation there was in the Ukraine paralleled that of the Russian Republic. There was a decree on marriage,[53] and a decree on divorce,[54] decrees limiting the sale of immovables[55] and nationalizing all philanthropic enterprises,[56] a decree abolishing the tsarist inheritance system,[57] a decree on the settlement of industrial disputes,[58] and a considerable number of decrees instructing the administrative authorities and the courts as to the measures to be taken with respect to cases held over from the past. It seems to have been the desire of the authorities to reduce the litigation by eliminating all prerevolutionary cases from the dockets unless one of the parties requested that they be continued.[59] If such cases were pressed, the juridical departments of the executive committees of the provincial soviets were to assemble the materials from the files of the old court. Thereafter the file was to be forwarded to the agency concerned, these being indicated for civil cases as follows: (a) if the case had been in process of appeal on the law to the highest court of the Empire, it was to be referred to the council of people's judges at the domicile of the defendant; (b) if the case had been in process of trial in the court of original jurisdiction or in process of retrial in the intermediate court of appeal, it was to be retried by the new people's court; (c) if the case had passed through the intermediate court, and the statute of limitations on cassation had not expired at the time of abolition of the old courts, it was to

[52] Constitution of the Ukrainian Socialist Soviet Republic, March 14, 1919, Art. 10, *ibid.*, No. 19, item 204.

[53] Decree on Civil Marriage and the Introduction of Books for Acts of Civil Status, February 20, 1919, *ibid.*, No. 12, item 144.

[54] Decree on Divorce, February 20, 1919, *ibid.*, item 145.

[55] Decree Forbidding Sales of Immovables, March 4, 1919, *ibid.*, No. 21, item 227.

[56] Decree on Nationalization of All Philanthropic Enterprises, March 4, 1919, *ibid.*, item 228.

[57] Decree on Abolition of Inheritance, March 11, 1919, *ibid.*, No. 24, item 268.

[58] Instruction on the Procedure for Examining Disputes between Employers and Workers, March 14, 1919, *ibid.*, No. 27, item 295.

[59] Decree on the Procedure and Conditions for Terminating Civil Suits in Process in Judicial Establishments Abolished by the Decree on the Court, February 25, 1919, *ibid.*, No. 12, item 145a.

be directed to the council of people's judges at the domicile of the defendant. The councils of people's judges were instructed to consider the basis of appeal, and to apply former law to these pre-revolutionary cases only to the extent that it did not conflict with the socialist conception of law. If the appeal was on the basis of procedural law of the Empire, it was to be allowed only if the point in issue remained a matter of procedural law under the first decree on the courts of the Ukrainian Republic.

As in the Russian Republic, the constitution of the Ukrainian Republic[60] contained no articles relating to the court system. The judiciary as a branch of government was left without constitutional status. It could be formed and reformed as the Congress of Soviets or its Central Executive Committee desired. Once again was demonstrated the Soviet rejection of the concept of separation of powers so dear to the American political philosopher, and by this rejection the Soviet draftsmen left the way open for experimentation.

Experimentation within the pattern of the Russian Republic was suspended for a while with the overrunning of the Ukraine in June, 1919. The collection of decrees terminates with the instruction establishing the structure and procedure of the Supreme Court of Cassation to review appeals from the sentences of the revolutionary tribunals. The collection was not to reappear until 1920, but in its six months of publication it had provided testimony to the early thinking of Ukrainian Communists of the time on the matter of settling disputes in the new Ukrainian Soviet society. It is evident that the Ukrainian politicians were concerned more with survival of their state than with development of an elaborate system for settling disputes, but enough appears to make it certain that they were moving in the same direction as the Russian Republic.

For both the Russian and Ukrainian Republics in what had been the former Russian Empire the trend was clearly in the direction of centralization of authority in 1919, although the Ukrainian Republic seems to have been moving faster in that direction than the Russian Republic, perhaps because of the pressures exerted by the civil war. In the Russian Republic there appears to have been a continuing desire to proceed with experimentation at the local level in the hope of developing more fully a body of law and procedure suitable to

[60] Constitution of the Ukrainian SSR, *ibid.*, No. 19, item 204.

the needs of the new Soviet society. At the same time the Commissar of Justice of the Russian Republic was moving in the direction of codification and establishment of fundamental principles of policy at the capital rather than in the local courtroom. The Ukrainians seem to have been prepared or to have found it necessary for their survival to declare more openly their reliance upon the capital for guidance, although they were not yet setting down in print details of the new law they would like to see applied. They preferred to rely on a mechanism of coordination to establish uniformity rather than upon extensive codification.

Chapter 4

SEEKING THE BEST
OF BOTH WORLDS

THE INCREASING NEED for centralization in the interest of uniformity
had begun by 1920 to press for formal recognition over continuing
independence of the trial judge. The policy makers of the new Soviet
republics seem to have hoped to preserve the best of both worlds:
uniformity on the one hand and flexibility on the other. The latter
concept was linked closely with the desire of the leadership to avoid
complexity in the judicial process, not only so that the judges might
be free to fit their decisions to the requirements of each case without
being bound by complex rules, but also because complexity was still
associated in the minds of the people with the discredited formalities
of Imperial Russian procedures.

The times were trying in early 1920 for those who favored continuing experimentation by local authorities in the search for a
perfect law and procedure. Although the tide was turning in the
civil war, the Bolsheviks had not yet been victorious on all fronts.
The Ukraine was still in tumult. It even had no civil administration.
Its affairs were in the hands of an "All-Ukrainian Revolutionary
Committee" concerned primarily with the conduct of military operations. Not until February 20 was there published a decree bringing
the work of this committee to an end and organizing a new Council
of People's Commissars with a People's Commissar of Justice among
its members.[1] The government was declared as functioning again on
the following day in a decree over the signatures of the President of
the Ukrainian Central Executive Committee and of the various
newly-named Commissars.[2] A Congress of Soviets was called for

[1] [1920] I *Sobranie Uzakonenii i Rasporiazhenii Raboche-Krest'ianskogo
Pravitel'stva Ukrainy*, No. 1, item 1.
[2] *Ibid.*, item 4.

April 15, 1920, presumably to reestablish official liaison with local communities.[3]

The Ukrainian Commissar of Justice began to act immediately upon matters relating to the judicial process. Within a week three instructions were issued. One ordered that all persons accused of crime be made the subject of an indictment to be prepared within two days if the case was before a revolutionary tribunal and three days if before a court.[4] Representatives of the college of accusers had to be present if the accused was to be brought before a revolutionary tribunal or a people's court with six lay judges. In the less politically important cases the people's judge alone was to prepare the indictment. The legal departments of the county or city executive committees were ordered to see that all imprisonments were regularized in this fashion.

Speeding up of the preliminary investigation was the subject of the second instruction with the establishment of a time schedule and the requirement that the investigator inform the accused of the allegations within forty-eight hours after the decision to begin prosecution.[5] Sanctions were provided by a declaration that failure to adhere to the rules constituted a crime by an official and was to be punished by court or disciplinary action. The third instruction[6] required trial in a people's court to begin within a week, and in a revolutionary tribunal within two weeks of the decision to prosecute. The courts and the revolutionary tribunals were told to inform the provincial legal departments of the date of the trial and the substance of the charge within twenty-four hours of the setting of the case for trial.

From the Commissar's instructions it is clear that he had decided to keep informed of all that went on within the Republic when it concerned court activity. He was not yet directing the activity of local agencies but he was placing himself in a position to continue, if he wished, the centralization of authority which had been emerging as a prominent part of the pattern of government in the Ukraine before it had been completely overrun by the White armies.

[3] The congress was later postponed until May 15, 1920. See *ibid.*, No. 7, item 118.
[4] *Ibid.*, No. 1, item 18.   [5] *Ibid.*, item 19.   [6] *Ibid.*, item 20.

DIRECTING UNIFORMITY

Within the Russian Republic the Commissariat of Justice was also evidencing its concern with the progress of affairs in the people's courts. In its first circular of 1920, issued on January 20,[7] it complained of lack of uniformity in the application of law, of red tape, of misuse of the power to penalize, of leniency, and of illegal assumption of jurisdiction over some types of disputes. The growing tendency of the central authorities to intervene in the affairs of local courts was clearly manifest.

Lack of uniformity was criticized in the varying rates of acquittal in the respective provinces. The Commissar called attention to the "excessive variation" in the number of acquittals and convictions. The legal departments were ordered to investigate the reasons to learn whether it was due to the particular individuals who sat on the courts. The variations were reported as extending from 20 percent acquittals in the city of Petrograd to 59 percent acquittals in Tula Province, 56 percent acquittals in Vitebsk, 54 percent in Riazan, 54 percent in Voronezh, 51 percent in Astrakhan, 50 percent in Vologda, 48 percent in Penza and Tambovsk, 47 percent in Pskov, and 46 percent in Nizhegorod. The Commissar noted that the rate of acquittals was highest in provinces in which there were no Communist party members as judges (Novgorod, Ufa, and Orenberg), and in provinces in which Communist judges were in the minority (Gomel, Viatka, and Tambovsk). The judges in these provinces were asked to use Communists as investigators, and also to put them into positions as judges.

Delays in some provinces were criticized, it being stated that in various places the number of cases awaiting investigation and trial had increased progressively to the point where they exceeded the cases which had been completed. The courts in these provinces were ordered to clear up first the cases of those who had been long in prison awaiting trial as well as uncontested cases, for example, those concerning divorce. Those responsible for the delays were

[7] RSFSR Narodnyi Komissariat Iustitsii, ianvaria 20 dnia 1920g, tsirkuliar No. 1. This circular has not been found in any of the various collections of documents or Commissariat circulars but only in the original. In its text it erroneously cites the 1918 decree requiring precise observance of the law as being in the volume of laws for 1919. See paragraph 4 of the circular.

ordered discovered and prosecuted under the law of November 8, 1918, requiring precise observance of the laws.[8]

Even though the People's Court Act still permitted the judges to vary penalties and also to reduce them below those set in specific decrees, the Commissar took issue with what had been going on. He thought the penalties for illegal manufacture of liquor and for drunkenness in public places impermissibly light. He ordered the judges to adhere strictly to the law of December 19, 1919,[9] as published on January 1, 1920, setting the penalty of imprisonment at not less than five years and confiscation of all property for the distilling, transportation, storage, and sale of spirits and its substitutes, and at not less than one year for public drunkenness and the public drinking of hard liquors. He criticized also the light penalties which had been given in many provinces for speculation, crimes by officials, and failure to observe the rules of labor discipline. While he restated in connection with these three crimes the rule of the statute on the people's courts to the effect that the judges might reduce penalties below those set in the pertinent statutes, he reminded his readers that this could be done only when the sentence contained a full explanation of the reasons for the leniency.

Some penalties were being misapplied, in the opinion of the Commissar. There were too many fines being levied, and there was insufficient use of the new penalty under which a person was to be required to work at an assigned job for a fixed period of time but without being placed under guard. As to the fines, the Commissar noted that in many provinces fines constituted over 50 percent of the penalties, and in some provinces they were 60 percent of the penalties. He cautioned that fines were never to be linked with the provision that in the event that the convicted person had no property with which to pay the fine, he was to serve a specified term in prison. They were to be used only when their enforcement would materially affect the convicted person as a form of total or partial confiscation of his property.

As to the new penalty of required work, the Commissar declared

---

[8] [1918] I *Sobranie Uzakonenii i Rasporiazhenii Rabochego i Krest'ianskogo Pravitel'stva RSFSR*, No. 90, item 908.

[9] Decree on Forbidding in the Territory of the RSFSR Distilling and Sale of Spirits, Strong Drinks, and Alcoholic Substances Not Suited for Drinking, [1920] *ibid.*, No. 1–2, item 2.

that in some provinces the penalty had fallen into disuse. He indicated that while the courts in Saratov Province had sentenced criminals to such a penalty in 28 percent of the cases during the first quarter of 1919, the use of the penalty had fallen to 3 percent during the second quarter. Similarly in Vologda Province the use of the penalty had fallen from 18 percent to 9 percent in the same period, while in Vitebsk Province the decrease had been from 9 percent to 4 percent. In many provinces the rate of application of the new penalty was said to be only 3 percent. Courts were ordered to use the new penalty in place of fines, or together with fines, and to apply it in all cases where the individual did not require isolation from the community for the latter's safety. The departments of justice in the provinces and counties were ordered to see that the penalty was used in the circumstances for which it was designed.

The one matter of civil strife with which the Commissar was concerned in his January 20, 1920, instruction was the dispute over division of land use. Under 1918 legislation all land had become the property of the state,[10] but its use was to be distributed by the local soviets to the toiling peasantry. The Commissar reminded the courts that any dispute involving the division of the use of the land among members of a family, as well as a dispute over the division of buildings upon the land or tools with which to work the land was to be decided by the village or county land department of the respective soviet. It was not to be decided by a court. On the other hand, the court had jurisdiction over all disputes concerning the division among members of a family of money, clothing, furniture, and other movable property not related to the tilling of the land as well as over disputes which might arise from the use of the land but which were of a type calling for prosecution for crime, such as the appropriation without authority of meadows or of stores of produce, and the causing of damage to fields by failure to control cattle. By this provision the Commissar indicated the predominant type of dispute in the countryside and the administration's determination to provide a court procedure for the settlement of those disputes which did not concern the allocation of the use of the land. Allocation of use seems to have been in a special category

[10] Decree on Nationalization of the Land, State Farms, February 19, 1918, [1918] *ibid.*, No. 25, item 346.

for which the policy makers were not prepared to resort to a court. They preferred the administrative officer of the land department, perhaps because he represented the Russian tradition of settling land disputes through the community, but perhaps also because they may have had greater confidence in his application of revolutionary favoritism of poor peasants over rich peasants.

ASSURING INFORMATION FROM BELOW

The sense of independence felt by the local courts may be indicated by a final complaint in the Commissar's instruction of January 20, 1920. He states that even though statistical information on the work of the courts had been requested of the provincial departments of justice beginning with July 1, 1919, there was as yet no information from nine provinces (Nizhegorod, Simbirsk, Penza, Tula, Smolensk, Tver, Novgorod, Viatka and Riazan). While some of the provinces failing to report were far from the capital, others, such as Tula and Tver, were within a hundred miles. The Commissar complained that without information the Commissariat could not provide any review of the activities of the courts and of the quality of the judges, nor could it answer questions on jurisdiction, for which there was said to be great need.

The Ukrainian Republic soon manifested the same concern with lack of information. On March 30, 1920,[11] the Council of People's Commissars ordered all departments of provincial and county executive committees to send two copies of their orders and instructions to the legal departments of their executive committees, and all Commissariats to send to the Commissariat of Justice two copies of their orders and instructions.

The interrelationship of central authorities and local soviets was made the subject at about the same time in the Russian Republic of a decree establishing a charter for village soviets.[12] The village soviets were ordered to execute all orders received from higher soviet authority, and to give assistance to all representatives of

[11] Decree on the Requirement that All Orders Issued by People's Commissariats, Authorized Agencies and Departments of Executive Committees be Transmitted to the People's Commissariat of Justice and to the Legal Departments of the Respective Executive Committees, [1920] I *Sob. Uzak. Uk.*, No. 6, item 89.

[12] Charter for Village Soviets, February 15, 1920, [1920] I *Sob. Uzak. RSFSR*, No. 11, item 68.

higher authority in carrying out their tasks. Further, the village soviets were to publish and explain all decrees and orders of higher soviet authority, and to hold responsible all citizens who violated the laws. Clearly, the central authorities in both the Russian and Ukrainian Republics were moving in the direction of strict responsibility to the central government. Local government was developing as an arm of the central authorities rather than as the loosely related and almost autonomous unit which had been envisioned by a large part of the peasantry at the time of the Revolution. There was to be no support for the autonomous local soviet as it had been espoused by the left Socialist Revolutionaries in the third congress of soviets in January, 1918, and also as desired by a broad movement even within the Communist party opposing increasingly centralized control from Moscow.

A statute on village soviets, worded identically to that of the Russian Republic, was adopted in the Ukraine on July 3, 1920,[13] after the promulgation on the preceding day of a series of decrees defining the functions of the various higher levels of government.[14] By these decrees the very close relationship between the two constitutionally independent republics was indicated. This close relationship was to reappear frequently in the following months as the Russian Republic led the way in another reorganization of the institutions concerned with the settlement of disputes. There was always, however, a lag of weeks, and sometimes of months in the adoption in the Ukraine of measures found desirable in the Russian Republic's experience. Thus, it was not until April 16, 1920,[15] that the Ukrainian Republic adopted the criminal penalty which had been favored by the Russian Commissar of Justice's circular of January 20, 1920, namely, required work without guard at a place designated by the local soviet's department for punishment. The Ukrainian decree provided that 5 percent of the wages of the convicted person were to be withheld by the employer and paid over to the local department for punishment to help meet the expenses of keeping a record of the sentence. Violation of the obliga-

[13] Statute on Village Soviets, [1920] I *Sob. Uzak. Uk.*, No. 11, item 216.
[14] *Ibid.*, items 209–15.
[15] Order on Persons Condemned to Social Compulsory Labor without Deprivation of Freedom, *ibid.*, No. 7, item 117.

tion to work subjected the violator to new penalties to be set by the court at his place of work or at his domicile.

Both the Russian and Ukrainian Republics were introducing in the spring of 1920 specific obligations upon segments of the population to perform social duties. These obligations were stated to have their legal foundation in the general labor obligation established in the labor code of the Russian Republic[16] and in a corresponding statute of the Ukrainian Revolutionary Committee.[17] On March 2, 1920, the Ukrainian government's committee on general labor duty in the field of public health had established an obligation upon all to assist in public health matters.[18] On March 7, 1920 the Commissariat of Justice ordered all Ukrainians who had formerly been judges or lawyers in the old regime but who were now working in Soviet agencies to register within a week upon pain of prosecution for desertion.[19] On May 11, 1920,[20] the Russian Republic's Council of Commissars ordered the registration of all persons with legal education regardless of age or sex, even though they might be serving in the Army. Any registered person was subject to assignment to work in agencies of the Commissariat of Justice or in agencies of other commissariats requiring legal assistance. The Ukrainian Republic adopted an identically worded decree on June 5, 1920.[21]

Utilization of persons registered as having had legal education was assured by the creation in the Russian Republic on May 18,

[16] "For all citizens of the Russian Socialist Federated Soviet Republics, with the exceptions stated in Articles 2 and 3, a duty to perform labor is established," Art. 1, Code of Laws on Labor, RSFSR, December (undated) 1918, [1917–1918] I *Sob. Uzak. RSFSR*, No. 87–88, item 905.

[17] A decree of April 16, 1920, on the procedure for putting this obligation to work into effect through the committees of labor appears in *ibid.*, No. 7, item 114. The original establishment of the obligation has not been found in the journals available for examination.

[18] Decree of March 2, 1920, was referred to in order of April 17, 1920, on drawing the attention of the population of the Ukrainian SSR to their obligation to perform labor during "Cleanup Week" because of a typhus epidemic. [1920] I *Sob. Uzak. Uk.*, No. 7, item 119. The journal said to contain the March 2, 1920, order has not been available for examination.

[19] Decree on Registration of Specialists for Court Units, *ibid.*, No. 2, item 32.

[20] Decree on Registration of Persons with Higher Legal Education, [1920] I *Sob. Uzak. RSFSR*, No. 47, item 211.

[21] Decree on Using Practicing Jurists, [1920] I *Sob. Uzak. Uk.*, No. 12, item 235.

1920, of legal-consultation sections within all commissariats and other central agencies of the government.[22] Among the tasks of the newly created sections was the giving of advice on contracts made by the agency with private persons, both in their making and when they were the subject of dispute, as well as the giving of advice on claims against the enterprise for injury or damages suffered by private persons. The sections were also to represent the commissariat in actions brought by or against it in the courts of the Republic. The chief of the section was to be named by the Commissariat of Justice, as were the various consultants in the number required by the commissariat which was to use their services. The employees of such sections were to remain responsible to the Commissariat of Justice, and were required to refer to the consultation department of the Commissariat of Justice any matters of policy arising in practice or any disagreement as to the state of the law as it might arise in the work of the consultation department. The cost of the legal consultants in the new departments was to be borne by the Commissariat of Justice until such time as the budgets of the various commissariats served by the new departments could reflect the new expense, presumably by tapping new sources of income.

Local soviets in the Ukraine appear to have given the central authorities difficulties in maintaining the authority of the courts, for on June 4, 1920, the Commissariat of Justice of the Ukrainian Republic issued a circular declaring that some local administrative agencies had been interfering with the work of the revolutionary tribunals and of the courts by setting aside or refusing to execute their sentences and judgments.[23] The Commissariat ordered its court-investigation department to write to all local soviets' legal departments instructing them to observe with care those articles of the Statute on the People's Court in which it was provided that any change or setting aside of sentences or judgments of people's courts could be effected only in the manner provided in the statute. Administrative agencies or individuals interfering with the work of the people's courts were ordered to be prosecuted.

[22] Statute for Legal Consultation Sections in People's Commissariats and in All Central Offices RSFSR, [1920] I *Sob. Uzak. RSFSR*, No. 51, item 221.

[23] Circular on Noninterference by Local Organs of Authority in the Affairs of People's Courts and Revolutionary Tribunals, [1920] I. *Sob. Uzak. Uk.*, No. 12, item 225.

Perhaps to meet the demand of local governmental authorities for more effective use of the channels open for setting aside or changing sentences deemed harmful to governmental interests, the Ukrainian Commissar of Justice issued on June 6, 1920, a circular[24] noting that the preponderant majority of appeals from the people's courts were filed by the defendant, while there were many violations of procedure and substantive law against which appeals should have been taken on behalf of the accuser. The provincial departments of justice were ordered to instruct all colleges of accusers subject to their jurisdiction that appeals were not only their right but their duty under such circumstances. They were ordered to use this right of appeal whenever they found a violation of any decree or order of the state or any incorrect action violating the principles of the soviet system of government and of the socialist concept of law.

To assure uniformity through centralized control all appeals were ordered by a circular of the same day[25] to be in two copies, one of which was to be forwarded immediately by the provincial council of people's judges which received it to the court control department of the Commissariat of Justice. When an opinion had been rendered, the provincial council of people's judges was ordered to forward to the same department a copy of its opinion containing the reasons for the decision and also containing a statement of the date on which the copy of the appeal had been forwarded, perhaps so that the file clerk could put the two documents together, or perhaps as a reminder that the first document should have been filed previously.

THE THIRD CONGRESS REVIEWS
THE EXPERIENCE

A general review of the work of the courts and the agencies which assisted them began on June 25, 1920, in what was called the Third Congress of persons engaged in the administration of justice. While the Commissar of Justice provided reporters on the various subjects to be discussed, there seems to have been a group of dissenters from the official position prepared to make their views known. One

[24] Circular No. 13 on Cassational Complaints Against Court Orders by Social Accusers, *ibid.*, item 238.

[25] Circular No. 16 on the Procedure for Forwarding Cassational Complaints, *ibid.*, item 239.

Kozlovskii attacked the system of lay judges by declaring: "It is time once and for all to finish with this institution, which was born of liberalism and which is at the present time unnecessary under the dictatorship of the proletariat." [26]

Liberalism has a special meaning for Soviet authors, and to appreciate the possible logic of Kozlovskii's argument the Westerner must take note of that meaning. A Soviet dictionary defines liberalism as "a political trend which was progressive when it was born in defending the freedom of the bourgeoisie during the epoch of the bourgeois revolution, but which became reactionary when it had established its political rule." [27] In concrete terms liberalism means to Soviet authors a philosophy of protection of the individual against the absolutist state. Since the Soviet regime had declared that it had smashed the absolutist state and had replaced it with a state of the people, any suggestion that the people needed to be protected against the arbitrary action of a professional judge by being represented directly in the courts through laymen on the bench could logically have been called an insult to the good faith of the policy makers of the new government. Seen in this light Kozlovskii's argument could have been expected to invite support from the leadership of the congress. He was, however, to be disappointed in what must have been his expectation, for the representative of the Commissariat of Justice, Cherliunchakevich, who had been the first presiding judge in the Moscow Council of People's Judges, replied that lay judges were necessary

so that the court would always be the most living, the most authentic echo of that concept of law which had currency among the population; so that in the decision and sentence of a court there would be made apparent that concept of the people, and so that the court and so-called "public opinion" would not present two points of view having nothing in common, as had been the case in the former court.

To make his view effective, the speaker introduced a resolution that "in the panel of lay judges available for service in turn there must be included every last toiler having the right to vote and to be elected to the soviets." The congress adopted the resolution, and

---

[26] See Ia. L. Berman, *Ocherki po istorii sudoustroistva RSFSR c predisloviem N. V. Krylenko* (Moscow, 1924), p. 37.

[27] S. P. Obnorskii, ed., *Slovar' russkogo iazyka* (Moscow, 1949), p. 328.

thus indicated the readiness of the majority to follow the leadership of Kurskii in broadening the base of the lay-judge system rather than in eliminating it.

The Congress suggested some other changes in the system of law agencies as they had been established by the People's Court Act of 1918. It proposed that there be established a more centralized procedure to be followed in the appointment and recall of the judges in the people's courts and in the provincial councils of judges; that there be established "special sessions" of the people's court and a new "standing" court,[28] that the structure of the investigating commissions be changed, and that the college of accusers, defenders, and representatives in civil suits be revised. The nature of these changes and the reasons for them are given in some detail by Commissar Kurskii in an article written soon after the congress.[29]

Commissar Kurskii emphasized that the congress of persons engaged in the administration of justice had decided to continue the basic principle of the single people's court, namely, that it should be composed of two elements, the professional judge and the lay judges sitting together with equal rights as a college. The congress did not thereby, however, indicate that it supported the "collegiate" principle of organization for law agencies regardless of the function to be performed. Thus, the congress opposed the "collegiate" form as it had existed in the investigation of criminal charges. The commission structure of the investigating organ was declared undesirable and no longer in accord with the requirements of practice.

The investigating agency had taken the form of a board or group of persons when it had been established in 1918 to assist the overworked judges on the most complicated of the cases brought before them. Kurskii explained that the idea of a commission of three persons who were required to reach, in consultation with each other, all conclusions on the facts had grown out of the necessity of the 1918 period when the state had as yet been unable to train enough persons of proletarian origin in the techniques of investigation. In consequence, many of the investigators had been employees of the former courts of the Imperial regime. They could be useful in performing technical functions, and in teaching proletarians the

[28] See Berman, *Ocherki,* p. 38.
[29] See D. I. Kurskii, "Novoe polozhenie o narodnom sude," dated 1920. Published in D. I. Kurskii, *Izbrannye stat'i i rechi* (Moscow, 1948), p. 64.

art of investigation, but they had to be watched lest they commit political errors or even attempt sabotage of the new regime. By placing a person of proletarian origin with them, the state provided a trusted agent who could serve as a political supervisor and also learn the techniques of the trade. Kurskii reported that by degrees the members of the commission had found it possible, and even necessary, to divide the cases before the commission among themselves for preliminary preparation. They later came together to ratify the decision taken by the individual who had been assigned to a particular case. This process of division of labor had been speeded by the necessity of sending a single investigator to remote places to collect evidence. As a result of these developments, Kurskii found it possible easily to revise the law so as to make the transition from group investigation to individual investigation because the transition had already occurred in fact. The Commissar thought that the political danger which had been feared two years earlier had been erased with the passage of time, for during the intervening period sufficient proletarians had been trained to carry on the investigative function.

SHORTCOMINGS OF THE BAR

The organization of the bar seems to have been the major subject of discussion at the June congress. In his summary of the events of the congress, Kurskii devoted most of his space to the matter, reviewing the history of the problem as it appeared to require emphasis and then stating the current issues.[30] In what seems, by comparison with the events of the past—events which have been reviewed in the preceding chapters of this study in some detail— to have been a telescoping and simplification in which some important detail was lost, Kurskii stated that the structure of the bar had gone through three stages of experimentation.

The first stage in Kurskii's explanation was said to have rested upon the theory that all citizens were to be recognized by the proletariat as having equal rights. Rights were to be denied to individuals rather than to classes, and such individual denials were to occur only when a citizen had tried to harm the interest of

[30] *Ibid.*, pp. 65–67.

socialist development. In reflection of this philosophy the system of legal representation in court had been organized to permit all citizens to appear as accusers or defenders before the courts regardless of their social origins.

The first stage quickly proved to be undesirable in conditions of civil war, and, according to Commissar Kurskii, the role of defender actually fell into the hands of lawyers of the Imperial bar. The role of the defender was said to have been used as a means of agitating against the economic and social bases of the Soviet system of government, and in particular to discredit the people's courts. Further, the lawyers were said to have used their position and talents in civil cases to make under-the-table agreements. In the light of this experience, the second decree on the courts of January, 1918, had reestablished a professional bar from which persons were to be selected for representational purposes and to whom a fee was to be paid. Although this measure of control through the organization of a bar could have avoided the designated evils of the first stage, it was not permitted to do so, because the same decree continued some of the system of the first stage in that it permitted one accuser and one defender to step forward from the onlookers in the court room. Kurskii calls this provision a "relic of the illusions which had not yet been outlived."

Kurskii explains this "relic" as an effort to leave open the door to relatives and friends to appear as defenders. By opening the door, however, the draftsmen, in Kurskii's review, made possible the employment as "friends" of persons who could not gain admission to the new bar. Kurskii finds that the system of the second decree bore within itself the seeds of its own destruction in that it permitted the payment of fees, which he described as having been used as a means of making excess profits. He indicated further that the new bar had been unable to attract proletarian elements with the consequence that it was ill equipped for its task because it was of limited numbers and only somewhat qualified. The great bulk of the members of the former Imperial bar had remained outside and were said to have fought against the new system, presumably through the loophole left for "friends" who might come forward to the defense in the courtroom.

The third stage indicated by Kurskii was said to have been

ushered in by the People's Court Act of November 30, 1918. Kurskii found here an effort to make a transition to the concept of a broadly based system of legal aid and advice for the working class. The new law looked upon lawyers as state officials who were to aid the court in providing a complete elucidation of all of the circumstances concerning the accused or the parties to a civil suit. Lawyers were made by the new law equal to the people's judges and they were paid by the state at the same salary scale as the judges. Defense attorneys were required by the law in all cases when there was a special accuser or when the case was of the serious type requiring trial before a bench containing six lay judges.

The experience of eighteen months with the system established in November, 1918, had indicated, according to Kurskii, that trials with six lay judges were so few as to require the presence of a defender in only a small percentage of the cases before a court, and further, the number of cases in which a special accuser was present was even smaller, so that there were almost no cases in which a defender was required on this count. Finally, in Kurskii's words, the number of lawyers appearing in court had been necessarily small because there were so few members of the bar available for the service. In consequence of their small numbers, the lawyers had been forced of necessity to confine their activities to consultation.

Kurskii found an opportunity at this point to restate some of the principles which he had always thought popular, namely, that the simplification of court procedures under the Soviet system had made it possible for the untrained individual to conduct his case without benefit of legal representation, and second, that the number of civil cases requiring legal representation had been greatly reduced in urban areas because the number of contracts had been reduced. Presumably, he was referring to the effect of the nationalization decrees upon private enterprise. Kurskii admitted that in the village communities there were still a number of civil disputes, but these, he said, were being handled largely by friends and relatives who acted as the legal representatives. Kurskii seems to have been pleased to report that in the summaries of the work of the various provinces it was frequently stated by delegates to the congress that the institution of the bar was unnecessary in the people's courts.

The draftsmen of the new judiciary act, which was reported to have been in preparation after, if not during, the congress, were said by Kurskii not to have taken the completely negative view of many of the delegates to the congress. The draftsmen, and presumably this meant Kurskii himself, were stated as being of the opinion that lawyers were necessary in the Soviet system, but that the colleges of defenders must become centers for consultation available to those appearing before the people's courts, the provincial councils of judges, and the departments of justice of the county and province soviets. The draftsmen favored the organization of legal defense as a compulsory labor duty. Such a duty would correspond to the practice in other fields where skilled persons were drafted to perform the functions for which they had been trained. Kurskii thought it logical that persons trained in the law and with competency be drawn into the business of consultation even though they might not be available or qualified for one reason or another to assume the full position of a member of the college of defenders. He found that the basis for such an approach to legal consultation as a labor duty had been laid by the decree requiring all lawyers to register, from which there had been made available lists of all legally trained persons. The task remaining was to create an apparatus to put the labor duty for lawyers into effect. Until the apparatus had been established, the lawyers should, in his words, "be made available in necessary cases at the offices of the departments of justice of the county and provincial soviets."

NEW CONTROLS FOR THE JUDGES

Kurskii found two other matters which required comment in the proceedings of the congress, namely, the recall of people's judges and the right of a judge to reduce a sentence below the minimum limit set in the law.[31] Kurskii thought that the existing system of recall by local soviets had proved to be unsatisfactory, in that the order of recall had not included within it the reasons for the order.

[31] *Ibid.,* p. 68.

In consequence it had lacked educational value both for the recalled judge and for those responsible for the election of judges. Further, since the recall had not been required to state reasons, it was not infrequently based upon plain arbitrariness. To avoid such action in the future, the congress favored the introduction of a requirement that all appointments of people's judges by local soviets be approved by the executive committee of the provincial soviet, and recalls would be permitted only by the executive committee of the provincial soviet. Under the new rules the recalls were to contain the reasons for the recall, and the opinion of the provincial department of justice had to be attached.

As for the lowering of penalties below standards set in the law, Kurskii pointed out that the proposed new statute would abolish the judge's right to free a person without penalty, but that the right to reduce a penalty would be preserved subject to restrictions. The compromise position favored by the new draft was to permit a judge who thought that the application of a law would work an undesirable result to request a pardon from the Central Executive Committee of the Russian Republic if he believed there should be no penalty at all, and in the event that he favored some penalty but not as severe a one as provided by law, he was to give the reasons in full in his opinion, presumably so that the council of people's judges sitting at the provincial level might set aside his opinion if it did not agree.

The desire to preserve the independence of the judge in the face of the tendency toward centralization appears again in the closing remarks of Commissar Kurskii. He declared that the new provisions were intended as a corrective in favor of greater conformity to policy in the sentences of the people's judges, but that the new provisions also had as their purpose the preservation of the right in the court to set aside or reduce a sentence if the application of the law would require a conflict with the internal conviction of the judges. Kurskii stated that the new measures did not restrict the judges in selecting the measures they thought suitable. From this distance it is hard to tell whether Kurskii honestly believed that the local judge should be left with authority to do as he wished, or whether he was merely trying to preserve the appearance of avoiding the centralization toward which his measures were leading because he knew that many of his hearers still looked upon strong central government as anathema. It is hard to imagine that a judge in a remote locality would have forwarded to the capital in Moscow his recommendation that a pardon be granted, or that he would often risk reversal by the council of people's judges at the provincial level by sending up an opinion for examination even if its reasoning seemed particularly cogent. One would have had to have been a rugged individual to do this often, and even at this early period in Soviet history the nonconforming citizen risked being branded a saboteur, particularly if he had in his background a history of association with any of the legal institutions of the Empire.

One point which had been discussed at some length at the congress is not included in Kurskii's review of the affair. Perhaps he was not happy with a development which was forced upon him by circumstances. In January his circular had bemoaned the fact that the people's courts were falling behind in their work, often to the point of having more cases undecided on their dockets than they had already decided since their creation. The Third Congress proposed a plan to speed up consideration of cases. It suggested the creation of a "standing" bench of the people's courts in each provincial capital and in the county seats.[32] This bench was to be composed of lay judges chosen in the usual way and of one professional judge, sitting in turn in accordance with a system of rotation to be prepared by the council of people's judges in the provincial capital and by the legal department of the county soviet in the county seats. This "standing" court was to hear immediately all cases of persons who had been arrested if those responsible for their arrest thought that no special investigation was required to establish facts.

In addition to the "standing" court, there was proposed a "special session" of the people's court.[33] It appears that both the Cheka and the revolutionary tribunals had been exercising the right given them by law to transfer to the jurisdiction of the people's courts some of the cases which seemed appropriate for trial in the usual manner. These were said to have been cases of large-scale speculation with commodities under monopoly or ration, serious crimes by officials, willful violation of labor duty, cases involving illegal traffic in

[32] See Berman, *Ocherki*, p. 39.   [33] *Ibid.*, p. 38.

li·[uor, and exemption from military service because of religious conviction. It was feared by members of the congress that with respect to the latter two types of action very lenient attitudes could be expected from lay judges who were now to be chosen on a universal basis rather than on a selective basis. It was said that the public was "soft" on drunkenness and religious prejudice.

The same Cherliunchakevich who had spoken for the Commissariat in favor of broadening the base in the selection of lay judges argued against leaving with the people's court some of the cases of the type mentioned. He said: "Since the hearing of claims for exemption from military service because of so-called religious convictions requires from the judges certain political firmness and political development in order to apply the decrees correctly, it is therefore necessary to create a 'special session' to hear this category of case." These courts were to be under the presidency of a member of the presidium of the council of people's judges if sitting in the provincial capital, and of a member of the legal department of the county soviet if sitting in a county seat, while the lay judges upon them were to be chosen from a list of specially qualified citizens.

Three years later a historian[34] of the early period was prepared to admit that the concept of a "special session" to hear very serious cases, at first limited to criminal, but later also having civil, jurisdiction, violated the principle of a "single people's court" as that principle had been established by the People's Court Act of November 30, 1918. Considering the vigorous struggle conducted by Kurskii throughout 1918 to establish the principle of a single court by abolishing the district courts formed under the second decree on the courts, it is not surprising that he did not emphasize this aspect of the work of the Third Congress.

INTRODUCING THE REFORM BY
MINISTERIAL INSTRUCTION

The stage had been laid by the Third Congress of persons engaged in the administration of justice for the revision of the structure of agencies established by the People's Court Act of 1918. The decisions taken at the Congress seem to have established a

[34] *Ibid.,* pp. 38 and 40.

policy for the Ukrainian Republic as well as for the Russian Republic, for both began to adopt nearly identical measures thereafter. At some points the Ukraine found it necessary to catch up with its more experienced colleague. Thus, the Ukrainian Commissar of Justice published on August 4, 1920,[35] as a Ukrainian circular the Russian Republic's circular of December 12, 1919. This had established a definition of criminal law and the major principles to be observed in applying the criminal law. No effort was made to disguise the fact that the Ukraine was accepting the Russian circular without change, for the Russian circular was referred to as the source of the Ukrainian circular. The Ukraine seems to have been abandoning by this time all semblance of independent thought in defining the major lines of its development.

Distribution of responsibility for the creation of the new "standing" session of the people's courts and of the "special session" of the same courts was made the subject of a circular issued over Kurskii's signature on August 27, 1920.[36] The circular seems also to have been used to put together in one convenient document a statement of the functions of the departments of justice of the provinces, the council of people's judges of the province, the "bureau of justice" of the counties, the people's courts, the court investigators and the court marshals known as court executioners. In seven pages of printed text the tasks of each agency are listed. Most of the articles concern matters with which the agencies had been concerned for some months, but some were obviously adopted to put into effect the decisions of the Third Congress. Thus, the provincial department of justice is listed as having the function of initiating what Americans would call impeachment proceedings against judges of any of the courts as well as against investigators. The provincial executive committee was to decide the question, but until its decision the department of justice might suspend the accused from duty in the event of clear abuses. The same procedure was to be followed in the event that a department of justice in a province objected to the appointment of an individual or group of individuals by the county executive committees.

[35] Circular on Guiding Fundamentals for Criminal Law, [1920] I *Sob. Uzak. Uk.*, No. 22, item 438.

[36] RSFSR Narodnyi Komissariat Iustitsii, avgusta 27 dnia 1920 g., Tsirkuliar No. 20. Charter for local organs of justice.

The council of people's judges in each province and the county bureaus of justice were authorized to establish the "special sessions" of the people's courts of which the congress had spoken. The instruction introduces a new element, for it provides that such "special sessions" were to have jurisdiction not only over those cases referred by the Cheka and the provincial revolutionary tribunals but also over the most important cases falling within the general jurisdiction of the people's courts. The same authority was given for the establishment of the "standing" session of the people's courts.

The investigator is spoken of in the singular in the instruction, rather than as a commission, which indicates the transition from the collegiate system to which Kurskii had made reference. Among the investigator's functions was that of guiding the local police in the investigation of the case, and of issuing warrants for arrest, search, and seizure of documents. Other indications of increased authority for the investigator are to be found in provision of the right to participate in the selection of members of the county bureau of justice. The right to be present at all provincial meetings of persons engaged in court affairs and to vote on matters coming before the county councils of judges having to do with investigation was continued from the previous law. There was created a gradation in the investigating apparatus for the first time, in that there was established within the Commissariat of Justice a "court investigator for the most important cases," who was to undertake an investigation if ordered to do so by the Central Executive Committee of the Republic as the principal interim policy agency between meetings of the Congress of Soviets, by the Council of People's Commissars or by the collegium of the Commissariat of Justice as the policy board of the Commissariat. A similar investigator for the most important cases was established in each provincial department of justice to act on the initiative of the provincial executive committee, the department of justice of the provincial executive committee, and the council of people's judges of the province. Such special investigators were to be nominated by the provincial executive committee's department of justice, but approved by the Commissariat of Justice.

With both the "special session" of the people's courts for serious cases and the investigators for serious cases, there appears at this

time a return to the concept of stratification on the basis of "seriousness." Since the revolutionary tribunals and the Cheka continued to
function to ferret out and punish those political enemies who were
really or presumably seeking to overthrow the regime, the inspiration of new institutions for the "serious" cases seems to have come
from the conclusion that the people's courts and the investigators
as constituted by the 1918 legislation were inadequate to the task
posed by the complicated nonpolitical case, especially when the
subject matter of the case touched upon a matter with which the
public generally had sympathy because of its own appreciation of
human frailty such as drunkenness. In mid-1920, the policy makers
seem to have been prepared to retreat to a two-level court system,
although they were not yet ready to admit it in the terminology
of the time. They still talked of the "single people's court," pretending, apparently, that simplicity of structure was still a characteristic
of the Soviet court system.

The court executioners, or marshals, were treated briefly in the
circular of August 27, 1920. Reference was made to a special instruction of the Commissariat of Justice to be issued on the subject,
but it was indicated that they were responsible to the provincial
council of people's judges, and that they functioned not only in
executing judgments and sentences of the people's courts, but also
in attaching items of value for the protection of a plaintiff who
might win his suit, protecting property which was in dispute, and
in selling inventoried property to meet penalties levied by agencies
of the state.

The actual establishment of the "standing" session and of the
"special session" of the people's courts waited for another instruction
of the Commissariat of Justice, dated September 16, 1920.[37] The
ground had been sufficiently laid so that the instruction introduced
no new elements. The point was made even clearer than in the
earlier instruction that the "special session" was to have general
jurisdiction beyond that relating to the specific crimes listed, for it
was provided that the People's Commissariat of Justice, the departments of justice in the provinces, the bureaus of justice in the
counties, and the council of people's judges in the provinces might

---

[37] Order on Special Sessions of the People's Court and of Standing Sessions,
[1920] I *Sob. Uzak. RSFSR*, No. 100, item 541.

on their own initiative or at the request of other agencies transfer any case to the "special session's" jurisdiction if it was found that the case had great public importance. The instruction made it clear that the "special session" was to be guided procedurally by the People's Court Act of 1918, without any exception. In this provision there is an implication that this "special session" was a sufficient departure from the single-court system to require re-affirmation that it was to be subject exactly to the same rules as the courts engaged with lesser matters. Again Kurskii seems to have felt it necessary to face possible critics.

THE PEOPLE'S COURT ACT
OF 1920

With the preliminary steps out of the way, the People's Court Act of 1920[38] must have come as an anticlimax. The wonder is that, with so many of the proposals of the Third Congress of persons engaged in the administration of justice already in effect as a result of the instructions of the Commissariat of Justice, it took so long to promulgate a comprehensive law. Perhaps the difficulty lay in completing arrangements for the new plan of legal representation. It alone of the major changes proposed in June had not been put into effect at the time of promulgation of the new act.

The college of accusers, defenders, and representatives of parties in civil suits was split by the new act along functional lines. The function of accusing was placed in a new institution to be organized in each province by the provincial department of justice. This agency would decide on the number of accusers required and would nominate appropriate persons to be commissioned for the task by the various provincial soviets' executive committees. When a people's court or interested parties or government agencies thought an accuser necessary in a case, the request would be filed with the provincial department of justice which would make the necessary assignment of personnel. The provincial department of justice might also assign an accuser to a case on its own initiative. A government agency which had instigated a prosecution or a trade union might also introduce its representative into court to prosecute a case.

[38] October 21, 1920, *ibid.*, No. 83, item 407.

A professional prosecuting staff of state's attorneys was brought into being by the new institution, although it was not yet thought of in such terms. More steps were taken in this direction by a circular issued by the Commissariat of Justice on November 23, 1920,[39] by which the new accusers were placed on an equal footing with the people's courts, and were directed to appear in all cases in which the complexity and conflicting character of the evidence suggested that the court would benefit by the application of adversary procedure. A Soviet historian[40] of the period said three years later that he saw in the new institution the seed of the prosecutor's office of the future, with one exception—the accusers were not limited to this work alone but were permitted to perform other work as well.[41] This part-time feature was criticized by the historian as having permitted the weakening of their tie to the courts with the result that many accusers became only occasional participants in trials.

The abrupt separation of the accusing function from the defending function was explained later as having been made necessary because the agency with combined functions had not provided "that firm permanent basis for an institution inalienably linked with the whole court organization." [42] Again the explanation is given that "the old liberalism with respect to this institution had already become dangerous." Another author[43] writing in 1926 explained that the linking of the accusers to the defenders, which had been the case during the period between the 1918 and the 1920 acts, had permitted illegal deals. It is stated that there were cases in which an accused reached agreement with the defender and the accuser to prosecute lightly and to defend vigorously. Finally it came to pass that in Leningrad, all but one member of the college had been brought into court for disciplinary action. It was said that the system of state defense as it had been established in 1918 had become so discredited that it had lost completely the confidence of the court.

---

[39] Instruction on the Organization of Prosecution and Defense in Court, *ibid.*, No. 100, item 543.
[40] See Berman, *Ocherki*, p. 43.
[41] This authorization was contained in sec. 4.
[42] See Berman, *Ocherki*, p. 43.
[43] See E. S. Rivlin, *Sovetskaia advokatura* (Moscow, 1926), p. 21.

The policy makers seem to have reached the conclusion that the judges could not probe the case sufficiently with their own questions. They needed help from some one who would present the strong points against the accused, and that some one had to be a person employed, at least part time, especially for the purpose. Further, he needed to be completely separate from the lawyers who would defend the accused so that there would be less possibility of an under-the-table agreement to prosecute with less than full vigor. The new institution of accusers was the result.

The function of defending was treated differently. The existing system of a paid staff of lawyers to perform the function as an aid to the court had collapsed. There was to be no attempt to create a new institution under better circumstances. By the new act there was to be another experiment. The executive committees of borough, city, and county soviets were ordered to prepare lists of persons with legal training in accordance with an instruction to be issued by the Commissariat of Justice. The courts were then to call upon persons included on the list when a lawyer was required, either in the opinion of the party or of the court itself.

The persons listed by the various executive committees were not to be persons without other activity.[44] They were to be persons with legal education employed by government agencies or elsewhere, presumably on work having no bearing on their function as a defender. The employing agency was required by law to release its employee when a call for legal aid service was received and to pay his regular salary while he performed his service. Service was to be demanded for not more than six days in any six-month period. If the legally trained persons on the panel were already all occupied on assignment or had already served their term, the court was to be permitted to fill the position by calling upon one of the consultants regularly employed by the provincial executive committee's department of justice to advise state agencies. If a person engaged in agriculture or as an artisan or in housework was called, he was to be paid from public funds during periods of service a *per diem* fee equivalent to the established minimum wage for the community.

Persons not on the approved panel of defenders or called from

[44] Instruction on the Organization of Prosecution and Defense in Court, sec. 7.

the departments of justice might appear in court in both criminal and civil actions if they were close relatives (specified as parents, children, spouses, brothers, and sisters) or if they were consultants or representatives of soviet agencies and assigned for the purpose.[45] The statute referred particularly to representatives of labor unions or of factory committees to which an accused person might belong. If a party requested admission of a defender, the court was to decide whether to admit him to the case, taking into consideration the character of the case and the person concerned. The court was advised to admit attorneys if a party was not fully capable of understanding legal actions or was a foreigner. Any appeal from denial by a court of permission to appear had to be held for inclusion in the general appeal against the decision.

The act was silent on the presence of a representative during the period of investigation before trial. It was stated later by the 1926 historian to whom reference has been made that this silence meant exclusion of the lawyer during the investigatory stage, and it was explained that the newly introduced system of individual investigation rather than board investigation had resulted in closed hearings into which a lawyer could not be permitted to come,[46] without losing the supposed advantage of secrecy at this stage in the attempt to solve the crime.

The preparation of the panels was guided later by the instruction of November 23, 1920, issued by the Commissariat of Justice.[47] While the lists were to be approved and issued by the several provincial soviets' executive committees, they were to be prepared locally by people's courts, revolutionary tribunals, provincial councils of judges, trade unions, and Communist party organizations at the request of the bureaus of justice of the county and provincial executive committees. Since the legal-assistance function was to be a labor duty, any person chosen by a court to appear and refusing to do so was subject to prosecution.

The system established by the 1920 act was later characterized as lacking completely an organization.[48] It was not a bar but a

---

[45] *Ibid.*, sec. 8.
[46] See Rivlin, *Sovetskaia advokatura*, p. 22.
[47] Instruction on the Organization of Prosecution and Defense in Court, sec. 7.
[48] See Berman, *Ocherki*, p. 44.

telephone book of approved names. When considered together
with some of the other events of the times, the new provision seems
to have represented one more attempt by Commissar Kurskii and
his colleagues to retain as much as possible of the simplicity of
court institutions for which the Soviet system had been noted in
1917. This simplicity had been slipping away with the passage of
the years in the search for uniformity and efficiency, and the officials
of the Commissariat appear to have been unhappy about it.

REDUCING AUTHORITY OF LOCAL JUDGES

Together with the dramatic innovations of the new type of legal
aid and the introduction of a second level of courts of original jurisdiction, the People's Court Act of 1920 included a few provisions
worthy of note in that they laid the base for greater centralization
and less independence for the local judges. Thus, the new statute
required that the number of courts in a province be determined
solely by the provincial soviet's executive committee.[49] With this
provision the county soviet's executive committee lost the authority
which it had shared with the provincial soviet's executive committee under the 1918 act to determine the needs of its county.
The new act also revoked the provision of the 1918 act authorizing
the election of one of the six lay judges as presiding justice when
the people's court met with six lay judges. Under the 1920 act only
the professional judge might preside.[50] Further, sentences were to
contain much fuller statements of fact and reasoning, and were to
include specifically data on the age, profession, Communist party
status, and domicile of the defendant.[51] Presumably this information
was desired to place the provincial council of judges in a position
to act with political wisdom in deciding what to do with the appeal.

The structure of the appellate bench was changed to reduce the
number of required judges from five to three.[52] A suggestion that
the draftsmen were hoping to speed the settlement of cases on
appeal is supported not only by the new provision but by a reduction in the time permitted for appeal from one month to two
weeks.[53]

[49] Instruction on the Organization of Prosecution and Defense in Court,
sec. 3.
[50] Sec. 11.   [51] Sec. 75.   [52] Sec. 83.   [53] Sec. 79.

Finally, all reference to court fees was eliminated from the decree, although the court might fine a party who brought suit without honest reason, and a judgment might award costs of preparing and defending a suit to the party in whose favor the suit was decided.[54]

The change from a board of investigators to a single investigator resulted in one measure designed, apparently, to benefit the accused. He might challenge the investigator for personal prejudice,[55] a privilege which may not have seemed so necessary under the former board system of investigation in which a personally prejudiced investigator would presumably have been outvoted by his two colleagues, particularly since the investigations were then public.

The Ukrainian Republic adopted its People's Court Act[56] but a few days after the Russian Republic. While it was essentially the same as that of the Russian Republic, it was not identical as were some of the other Ukrainian decrees. The Ukraine retained its 1919 formula as to the law to be applied in the absence or incompleteness of decrees. The Ukraine directed the judge to look in the first instance to the interests of the socialist revolution and thereafter to the socialist concept of law.[57] The Russian Republic adhered to its 1918 formulation including only the socialist concept of law as the guide in the absence of statute.[58] The Ukrainian statute was silent as to the force of prerevolutionary law, while the Russian statute forbade reference to the old law.[59] The Ukraine permitted a party to request a new trial in the event of discovery of new evidence,[60] while the Russian statute was silent on the subject. The Ukraine said specifically that there were to be no court fees levied against the parties,[61] while the Russian statute only implied that there would be none by removing the former provisions on court fees.

The 1920 acts indicated clearly that complexity was emerging to harass those who believed in simplicity, but the proponents of simplicity seem to have been able to do little of importance to retard the trend. They had doffed their hats to their early hopes of

[54] Sec. 96.   [55] Sec. 52.
[56] People's Court Act, October 26, 1920, [1920] I *Sob. Uzak. Uk.*, No. 25, item 536.
[57] Sec. 27.   [58] Sec. 22.   [59] Sec. 22 (note).   [60] Sec. 80.   [61] Sec. 82.

simplification by establishing a system of legal aid which lacked formal features. Their most obvious obeisance to the old idea was put in the very opening phrase of the acts of 1920, both in the Russian Republic and in the Ukraine. There was repeated the declaration of the earlier acts being replaced by the new acts, namely, that within the boundaries of each Republic there functioned but a single people's court. Subsequent articles of the acts indicated the falsity of this declaration, for there was established a new higher level of court of original jurisdiction for serious civil and criminal cases. The draftsmen seem to have wanted to close their eyes to this unpleasant concession, although they cannot but have known what they were doing. Only three years later an authorized historian felt it possible to say that the familiar declaration as to the simple structure of the soviet court system was violated even before it was promulgated by the creation of the "special session" of the people's court in response to the demands of the June congress.

Simplicity was apparently to be the keynote of proceedings in the regular people's courts engaged in trying the bulk of the non-complicated and nonpolitical cases in which were reflected the usual disputes of Soviet society. The People's Court Act of 1920[62] carried out the decisions of the Third Congress by declaring that the panels from which lay judges were to be chosen for these courts were to include all toilers having the right to vote and to be elected to office in the soviets. Panels were to be prepared every six months by trade unions and factory committees in urban communities and by village soviets in the countryside. After preparation the lists were to be sent to the city or county soviet's executive committee for approval and promulgation. Judges, including one alternate, were to be named from the panel for each case and to serve for that case alone, and in any event for not more than six days. During the period of service lay judges were to receive their regular wages at their place of work, and in the event of self-employment to receive a per diem from the treasury at the rate declared as the minimum for the community concerned.

The political reason for the newly enunciated all-inclusive character of the panels was restated in an instruction issued by the

[62] Secs. 16–20.

Commissariat of Justice on November 6, 1920,[63] to implement the act. The leadership indicated that it was not interested primarily in the reason given at the time of the Third Congress for the all-inclusive panel, namely, the bringing of public opinion to bear on the decision. The reason appears in the instruction to have been adult education. In so many words it is declared: "Without mass participation of toiling people it will be impossible to instill in the political laggards of the population a proletarian concept of law and familiarity with new Soviet law as decreed by the workers'-peasants' government." The Marxist hope of ultimate withering away of the repressive force of the state as the population became educated on a new economic base seems to have found expression in the broadened institution of the lay judge.

A group of especially qualified lay judges was expected to develop out of repeated court service, according to the terms of the Commissariat's instruction. These were to be called "shock groups," and it was from these superior citizens that the trade unions, factory committees, and village executive committees were to prepare a second set of panels. Citizens on these panels were to be chosen for service as lay judges on the new "special sessions" of the people's courts engaged in hearing cases of complicated and serious character.

CENTRALIZATION AT KEY POINTS

The period of revision of the court structure was chosen as appropriate to revise and restate the pattern of organization of the Russian Republic's People's Commissariat of Justice itself and of the local police system. It was three years since the Commissariat had published its organization chart. Even though the decrees of 1919 and 1920 had referred to departments of the Commissariat not listed in the instructions of 1917,[64] to which reference has already been made, there had been no detailed statement of or-

---

[63] Instruction on the Procedure for Establishing Lists of Lay Judges, [1920] I *Sob. Uzak. RSFSR*, No. 100, item 542.

[64] Instruction on Abolition of Former Division of the Commissariat of Justice into Departments and on Establishing a New Division, December 12, 1917, [1917–1918] *ibid.*, No. 9, item 127, and Instruction on the Plan of Work of the People's Commissariat of Justice, December 19, 1917, *ibid.*, No. 12, item 171.

ganization published in the laws. On November 26, 1920,[65] the gap was filled by an instruction listing eleven departments as replacing the six departments established in 1917.

The growth of concern on the part of the Commissariat for activities on every level within the apparatus occupied with maintenance of order is reflected in the reorganization. New departments of court control, of investigation, and of consultation take their place in the structure, while the old department of publications was split into its component parts of editing and printing. The old department of administration was split into administration on the one hand and preparation of a budget for the Commissariat on the other. The former departments of legislation and codification were combined, while the department of punishment seems to have been kept about the same as in 1917, as was the department concerned with the establishment of the courts.

The local police system, called in Soviet parlance the "militia" to distinguish it in the public mind from the tsarist police against which insurrection had been fostered was also brought under a new charter. While the first decree on the police of October 28, 1917,[66] had called upon each local soviet to establish its own police force, the order of the Commissariat of Internal Affairs of October 13, 1918,[67] had produced one of the earliest indications of the future policy of complete subordination of the local soviets to the center. All provincial police chiefs were to be named and dismissed under the 1918 order by provincial executive committees, subject to the approval of the People's Commissariat of Internal Affairs. Police chiefs in cities and county districts were to be named and dismissed by the respective city or county soviet's executive committee, but subject to the approval of the provincial soviet's executive committee.[68] All police chiefs were required to execute orders of the superior agency from whom approval of their appointment was obtained.[69]

The principle of strict centralization of the police apparatus at

[65] Order on the Departments of the People's Commissariat of Justice, [1920] *ibid.*, No. 90, item 465.

[66] Decree on the Workers' Militia, [1917–1918] *ibid.*, No. 1, item 15.

[67] Instruction on the Organization of the Workers'-Peasants' Militia, *ibid.*, No. 75, item 813.

[68] Secs. 13, 14.   [69] Secs. 32, 34.

all levels under the Commissariat of Internal Affairs was restated in the decree of June 10, 1920.[70] Some suggestion that the local executive committees had not understood their subordination to the center in this sphere is to be found in a provision of the new decree telling the local executive committee that they had no right to set aside an order of the Commissariat's Department for the Militia.[71] If the local soviet objected to an order, its recourse was a complaint over the head of the Department for the Militia to the Commissar himself. If the local soviet objected to refusal of the provincial executive committee's department for the militia to approve appointment or removal of a county police chief, appeal might be taken to the presidium of the provincial soviet's executive committee. Likewise a disgruntled provincial soviet might appeal blocking of its appointment or dismissal of a provincial police chief by the Commissariat's Department for the Militia to the Commissar.[72]

Dictation by central police authorities became a legal possibility with the 1920 decree, for it permitted the appointment of a police chief by the authority normally having only the approving function if no suitable local candidates were proposed.[73] An executive committee of the soviet concerned could only file a reasoned objection to the appointment. The statute was silent on the agency with whom the objection might be filed.

The year 1920 was brought to a close with one further manifestation of the extent to which the central authorities had been reducing the area within which the local judges were permitted to exercise their own sense of socialist justice in settling disputes. There was published a 268-page systematized collection of the most important decrees for the period 1917–20.[74] For the first time the enactments of the first years were arranged according to subject matter. With one volume a local judge could have equipped himself to find easily the basic laws of his Republic as they were in force at the outset of the year 1921.

The collection seems not to have been prepared to meet the needs of the local judge, however, and in this fact lies the notable

[70] Decree on the Workers'-Peasants' Militia, [1920] *ibid.*, No. 79, item 371.
[71] Sec. 15 (note).   [72] Secs. 21, 22.   [73] Sec. 22 (note).
[74] *Sobranie uzakonenii i rasporiazhenii rabochego i krest'ianskogo pravitel'stva, sistematicheskii sbornik vazhneishikh dekretov 1917–1920* (Moscow, 1920). [On the outside cover the date is given as 1921.]

feature. Commissar Kurskii in his introduction declares that the volume was edited to meet a need felt especially during the Second Congress of the Communist International, which had met in Moscow in late July, 1920. It was stated that many of the foreign Communists had asked for material on the legislation of the Soviet Republic. They had found it very difficult to utilize the periodical official journal with its lack of organization by subject matter and its mass of minute detail. As further indication of the intentions of the editors to help their foreign comrades, the collection was published simultaneously in German, French, and English as well as in Russian.

The collection of 1920 strikes the note of world revolution which was much in the air. The invading Polish armies had been defeated and pushed back to the gates of Warsaw itself in mid-August of 1920, at which point the expectation of the Bolsheviks of a new Soviet Poland was temporarily dashed by defeat, but Soviet territory in the southwest had been cleared of foreign troops.

The final battles of the civil war at home were being fought in 1920. The White armies under General Wrangel were defeated in October after the collapse of their July offensive. Wrangel and his troops retreated through the Crimea, which was entered by the Red Army in November. The areas south of the Caucasus fell under Soviet domination during the year. Azerbaidzhan established a Soviet regime on April 27, 1920, while Armenia began to operate under Soviet principles on November 29, 1920. Georgia alone in the Transcaucasian area had not been conquered by the end of 1920, but victory was to be achieved early the next year, on March 19, 1921.

Hopes were high for further spread of the Soviet system by early 1921. Only the far east within the boundaries of what was later to become the U.S.S.R. remained beyond the reach of Soviet law. Soviet decrees were being published not only for the effect they were expected to have within the country itself but also for the propaganda advantage they might give to the Soviet government in spreading its influence throughout Europe and Asia. Under such circumstances it may have seemed necessary further to centralize authority in the interest of uniformity. The record of 1920 makes it clear that while Soviet policy makers still looked longingly back upon the flexibility which they had decreed in 1917 and while they occasionally took steps to try and preserve elements of it, they were moving away from the local judge as the source of a new and imaginative system of law and judicial administration.

Chapter 5

RECONSTRUCTION

THE CIVIL WAR had been won by 1921, but much of the country was in ruins. Starving, ill-clothed, and unemployed citizens roamed the land. Their demand for action on their behalf presented the government with a problem which could not be ignored. It was the major issue before the Eighth Russian Congress of Soviets meeting on the eve of the new year.

A declaration "to all of the toilers of Russia" was the principal resolution of the Eighth Congress. It sought to cheer the people with ringing words:

Comrade workers, the three years of the Revolution have been for you a time of the greatest suffering and want. You have starved during these years as you have never starved before. But starvation did not drive you to your knees before capital. It did not induce you to turn back, to waiver in your faith in the proletarian state as the sole power which can bring the country out of unheard of disaster. . . . Toilers of Russia, in this three years of the greatest deprivation, of bloody losses, you have won for yourselves the right to peaceful work. We shall devote all our resources to providing that work. . . .[1]

Disintegration of the body politic was being felt not only in the soviets but in the Communist party as well. In March of 1921 the Kronstadt garrison revolted with the participation of dissident Communists. That the revolt extended beyond the military was evident to Lenin, for he ordered a purge of the party from top to bottom to eliminate those who opposed his leadership. He was determined to restore discipline to party ranks in preparation for the difficult times which he anticipated when the economic

[1] Declaration to All the Toilers of Russia, Eighth All-Russian Congress of Soviets of Workers, Peasants, Red Armymen, and Cossak Deputies (December 23–29, 1920), [1921] I *Sobranie Uzakonenii i Rasporiazhenii Rabochego i Krest'ianskogo Pravitel'stva RSFSR*, No. 1, item 13, appendix 3.

reforms then being formulated were put into effect to speed reconstruction.

Reconstruction was to be the theme of state action during 1921. The needs of the human body were so great that the leaders of the state showed themselves willing to make sacrifices of economic principles to restore the national economy. But bodily needs were not the sole forces moving the people. The Eighth Congress indicated that there was another growing complaint of which it had to take cognizance, namely, overcentralization of authority. A reversal of policy in this field seems also to have been desired by the public.

All offices of the Republic Government's Commissariats at local governmental levels were ordered abolished.[2] Work on the village and city level in the future was to be conducted solely through the departments of the executive committees of the provincial and county soviets. Exceptions to this rule were to be permitted only when arranged with the consent of the All-Russian Executive Committee or of its Presidium. The decree of the previous year permitting Commissariats to levy disciplinary fines upon members of the executive committees of local soviets was ordered reviewed by the Presidium of the Central Executive Committee.[3] The order of November 25, 1920, establishing rules for the naming of fully empowered representatives of central agencies to operate at the local levels was also to be reviewed.[4]

Elections to local soviets were ordered held to rejuvenate the bodies which had carried on for long periods without elections during the civil war. Soviets were to be created in all cities to meet at least twice a month. Executive committees of village and county soviets were to meet at least once a week, while those for the provinces were to meet at least every two weeks. Enlarged meetings of the executive committees to which deputies from the soviets who did not sit on the executive committees would be invited were ordered called at specified intervals. The agendas for these meetings were to include for discussion matters of national concern and not solely issues of local interest.

[2] Decree on the Soviet Structure, Chap. IV, sec. 4, *ibid.*, item 1.
[3] *Ibid.*, Chap. IV, sec. 6. [4] *Ibid.*, sec. 7.

Demands of the peasants and city workmen for direct participation in government rather than through representatives who had become professional and permanent seem to have been reflected in these acts of the Eighth Congress of Soviets. At the top level itself, the All-Russian Central Executive Committee as the constitutionally constituted policy-making body of the state during the periods between congresses of Soviets appears to have resented the assumption of policy-making functions by the Council of People's Commissars. A resolution of the congress demanded that all decrees establishing general rules for political and economic conduct as well as all decrees changing fundamentally the existing practice in state agencies must be communicated to the Central Executive Committee.[5] A staff of up to three hundred persons was authorized to permit the keeping of a watchful eye on the administration.[6]

While seeking to reestablish the participation of the general public in policy-making organs both at the center and on the local level, the congress indicated that the spirit of local autonomy fostered during late 1917 in local soviets was not to be restored. The resolution provided that orders of local soviets and of their executive committees might be set aside by soviets at higher levels, as well as by the executive committees of these higher soviets and by the All-Russian Central Executive Committee.[7]

Implementation of the resolutions followed soon after. City soviets were ordered restored in counties where they had ceased to function,[8] and new elections for local soviets were ordered held under the auspices of the various provincial executive committees.[9] Directions for the calling of meetings to which representatives of the lower soviets should be invited to meet with members of the executive committee of the next higher soviet appeared.[10] There were also instructions to local soviets to forward their complaints against orders of the Commissariats to the People's Commissariat of

---

[5] *Ibid.*, sec. 1.   [6] *Ibid.*, sec. 5.   [7] *Ibid.*, sec. 1.

[8] Circular on Organizing City Soviets of Workers' and Peasants' Deputies, February 8, 1921, *ibid.*, No. 11, item 71.

[9] Circular on Regular Preelection of Soviets and on the Calling within a Fixed Time of Congresses of Soviets, February 8, 1921, *ibid.*, item 72.

[10] Circular Order on Calling of Regular Widely Representative Meetings of Representatives of Village Soviets, Volost Executive Committees and County Executive Committees, February 8, 1921, *ibid.*, No. 12, item 77.

Internal Affairs, which was to report on the subject to the Council of People's Commissars.[11]

SUPREME CONTROL OVER COURTS

While attention was being directed in early 1921 toward popularization of government and a measure of decentralization of administration, the reverse trend was intensified in the organization of the courts. The People's Court Act of 1920 had included one three-line note as a novel provision in the section which had otherwise repeated the provisions of the 1918 act on the work of the provincial councils of people's judges.[12] In this note it had been provided that the People's Commissariat of Justice would have the right of supreme control over criminal sentences and civil decisions of the people's courts and of the councils of people's judges in each province. The act gave no particulars of the new institution, but it left the formulation of details to a subsequent statute.

Details were published in a decree of March 10, 1921.[13] They went as far as to establish what was called two years later by the official Soviet historian "the prelude to the organization of a supreme cassational court." [14] In short, they introduced into the soviet court structure a supreme court to become the pinnacle of a three-step judicial system.

The Commissariat of Justice had indicated on November 26, 1920,[15] that its own internal structure had been altered to include a new department to be called "department of court control" with the task of "reviewing by way of audit individual sentences and decisions of people's courts, reopening cases because of newly discovered circumstances, routing of complaints and appeals from individual citizens and agencies presented to the People's Com-

[11] Decree on the Procedure for Communicating between Local Executive Committees and the Council of People's Commissars, February 10, 1921, *ibid.*, item 82.
[12] People's Court Act of 1920, [1920] I *Sobranie Uzakonenii i Rasporiazhenii Raboche-Krest'ianskogo Pravitel'stva Ukrainy*, No. 25, item 536, sec. 84 (note).
[13] Decree on Charter for Superior Judicial Control, *ibid.*, No. 15, item 97.
[14] See Ia. L. Berman, *Ocherki po istorii sudoustroistva RSFSR c predisloviem N. V. Krylenko* (Moscow, 1924), p. 45.
[15] Charter of the People's Commissariat of Justice, [1920] I *Sob. Uzak. RSFSR*, No. 90, item 465.

missariat of Justice which concern the illegal action of officials or private persons." With the decree of March 10, 1921, the work of the new department was outlined in even broader terms.

The correct and uniform application by all courts of legislation of the R.S.F.S.R. in accordance with the policy of the government was set by the March decree as the task of the new department of the Commissariat. To assure the achievement of this task, the department was given general supervision over the activities of the courts and authority to issue guiding instructions and orders concerning existing law, as well as the right to declare a sentence or decision as of no effect, even though it had already gone into effect, if it violated the law. Finally it was authorized to reopen any case, no matter how much it had been reviewed, if newly discovered circumstances required reopening.

Grounds for setting aside a sentence or decision of a court were defined as (a) clear violation of or failure to apply laws of the Soviet state, (b) illegal assumption of jurisdiction, as when a court took jurisdiction over a dispute concerning the use of the land or over a matter to be handled otherwise under the general measures established by the state, (c) clear conflict between the sentence or decision with the guiding principles of Soviet legislation or with the general policy of the government.

Review might be instigated by the action of the Commissariat itself, by agencies of the central government or by a provincial executive committee. If a complaint was to be filed by a local official or a private person, the appropriate channel was indicated as being the department of justice in the provincial executive committee, or the Commissariat itself. In the latter case, the Commissariat was required to obtain the opinion of the collegium of the responsible provincial department of justice. The local view on the matter seems to have been desired by the central authorities.

The reopening of a case because of newly discovered circumstances was to be permitted when new evidence relating to the innocence of the accused was found, when it was established after the trial that the sentence or decision had been based upon false testimony or fraudulent documents, or when it was discovered that the court had entertained venal or other improper motives in reaching the decision. In such cases the Commissariat was to request the trial court for an opinion of the allegations, and if the Commissariat concluded ultimately that retrial was necessary, the case was returned to the proper court for action.

The introduction of a form of supreme court was explained later as having been made necessary by the variation which had appeared in the practice of the provincial councils of judges. The decentralization of the appellate process which had been an element of the court system up to that time was found to require a corrective in the form of centralized leadership from the Commissariat of Justice.[16]

The provincial departments of justice in the exercise of their right to give an opinion on complaints filed by local government offices or private persons found guidance in a circular issued by the Commissariat at a later date.[17] The provincial department was to forward to the Commissariat a conclusion not only when the provincial department suggested review by the Commissariat's department of court control but also when it decided that no action was required. In exceptional cases the provincial department might even suspend execution of a sentence if it thought that the complaint was justified. It was not required to wait for a decision of the Commissariat on its suggestions. This latter exceptional authority was said to have caused confusion in the appellate procedure, because it created in effect another appellate court. The situation was said to have introduced into the already "not entirely clear" relationships between the provincial department of justice and the provincial council of judges "still more fogginess." [18]

A sampling of the review practice of the new department of supreme court control indicates three types of activity: interpreting statutes, filling gaps in the law, and choosing on policy grounds between two conflicting policies.

The interpretation of the Family Code's limitation on the time of commencing a paternity suit was questioned in the first decision.[19] The Tambovsk Provincial Council of Judges had refused on August

[16] See Berman, *Ocherki*, p. 45.
[17] Circular No. 47. Text not found in available collections. Substance described in Berman, *Ocherki*, p. 46.
[18] See Berman, *Ocherki*, p. 46.
[19] *Eremina* v. *Medvedev, Ezhenedel'nik sovetskoi iustitsii*, No. 3 (January 15, 1922), p. 10, Case I.

14, 1921, to hear an appeal brought by an alleged father against a finding of paternity by the trial court on the ground that the Family Code required the filing of an appeal before the birth of the child. The department declared on November 23, 1921, that the Family Code's provision required only that a mother seeking maintenance for herself during the advanced stages of pregnancy was required to bring suit to establish paternity within three months before the child's birth. It did not bar an appeal which was not brought within the period indicated. The department went further to declare that the appeal was justified because the trial court had heard a contested paternity case without the presence of the alleged father, and this was in violation of the code.

The filling of a gap in the law occurred in a case involving the rights of a bona fide purchaser.[20] At the time of the department's decision in December, 1921, there had not yet been enacted a civil code, so that there was no statutory rule on the subject. The suit had been brought by one Samokhvalov against one Komarov to obtain goods claimed to be wrongfully in the possession of the latter. In proof of ownership the plaintiff introduced in evidence a bill of sale for the goods, stating that he had not taken possession at the time of purchase but had left the goods with the seller, one Kon'kova. The defendant introduced in evidence a bill of sale from the husband of Kon'kova. The trial court had held for the defendant as a bona fide purchaser, although it had not examined the goods to determine whether they were the same goods as had been sold previously to the plaintiff. The department of supreme court control declared that it had only one question on which it wished to speak, namely, the question of the rights of the defendant as a bona fide purchaser if it were found on retrial that the goods were those originally purchased by the plaintiff.

On the point of law to be applied to a bona fide purchaser, the department laid down the rule that a bona fide purchaser may keep goods purchased in good faith from an apparent owner, provided that the apparent owner has not committed a crime in obtaining them. As reason for such a rule the department declared that the precision necessary to civil-law relationships made it impossible to permit a bona fide purchaser to be deprived of possession of goods

[20] *Samokhvalov* v. *Komarov, ibid.*, Case II.

simply because the original owner had given someone a bill of sale to the goods. The department suggested that its rule was not harsh because a purchaser could protect himself by taking possession of the goods at the time of purchase or by not paying for the goods in advance of their receipt. The department explained further that the claimant had a remedy in a suit for damages against the seller. In closing its opinion the department indicated its attitude toward violation of procedural law. It had found some procedural violations in the case, but it believed them inconsequential and not influencing the correct decision of the case.

Choice between competing policies was necessary in a dispute over housing space coming before the department of supreme court control in late December, 1921.[21] The trial court had evicted a woman from a room in an apartment shared by several families because she had used her neighbor's sewing machine without permission and was constantly stirring up rows and conflict. The court stated that it had become impossible for the other tenants to live with the woman. Her husband then intervened to argue that it was against public policy to separate a man and wife by force. The department of supreme court control stated the public policy underlying the eviction saying that each person must be held responsible for his or her acts regardless of marital status; that a quarrelsome woman cannot be permitted to remain in an apartment solely because her husband conducts himself admirably; and that the law did not require that a husband and wife live together. On the contrary it provided that they need not live together in the same building after marriage. The department sought, apparently, to mitigate the harshness of its rule by saying that the husband had the opportunity to move with his wife to other quarters if he wished to remain with her. The department did not make clear that the rule permitting a husband and wife to live separately had been enacted to liberate women from the obligation of living with their spouses against their will, and that it was merely permissive. It could hardly have been said to support an argument that they could be required to live separately, nor did the department indicate that the housing shortage of the time was such that the finding of other quarters to which to move would have been exceedingly difficult if

---

[21] *Case of Vasil'eva, ibid.,* No. 2 (January 8, 1922), p. 10, Case II.

not impossible, so that the couple was probably in fact being separated.

To the outsider in search of Soviet experience that may throw light upon the possibilities of preserving a simplified court structure in a modern industrial society, the decree of March 10, 1921, with its provisions for a supreme reviewing agency in the Commissariat of Justice suggests that the requirement of uniformity in the governmental process had become elemental. Whether it was because order could not be maintained unless all citizens in all parts of the country were treated alike or whether it was because the Soviet leadership with its view of the state function could not conceive of letting the local community move in directions opposite to those desired by that leadership is hard to determine.

It is obvious from all Soviet political literature that a few men have felt that they have analyzed correctly the elements governing the course of social history and, in consequence, that they can tell what goals are most advantageous to mankind and what general steps need to be taken to achieve those goals. They seem to have been prepared to permit experimentation during the early years for the purpose of determining the detail of their new legal system. Yet, on the other hand, they came progressively to the conclusion within the first three years that this experimentation could not be permitted to proceed to such an extent that basic lines established by the Communist party's leaders as essential to the success of the new regime's plans became obliterated. Experimentation there would be, but after March, 1921, one single agency would have as its duty the maintenance of uniformity at those points which were considered crucial to the success of the new regime.

PRIVATE ENTERPRISE GAINS
A REPRIEVE

Reconstruction was pressed by various means in 1921. First and foremost among those means stood in the minds of Soviet policy makers the development of the economy through state enterprise. The policy of emphasis upon what was called the "socialist sector" was in accord with the principles espoused by the leaders of the

Revolution who had placed their faith in state-owned industry. To further this policy there was enacted a decree establishing a state planning commission on February 22, 1921.[22] Development of a planning mechanism was related closely to the philosophy of the Bolsheviks, for state industry could be expected to produce at its best only if it were coordinated. The new planning commission would provide the coordination.

Real surprise was provided by a second step toward reconstruction. It came soon after the introduction of state planning. It was a reprieve to private enterprise. No one pretended that it did not mark a change in policy, and to indicate that fact it was called the "New Economic Policy." Its purpose was to utilize private initiative in restoring the devastated economy by increasing production and facilitating distribution. For the student of Soviet legal institutions it was a step of vast importance, for it was to influence for years the entire course of Soviet law.

The decrees introducing the new policy into the life of the country began with the peasantry. Under the conditions of civil war the peasants had been required to give of their produce all that was not actually required for their own family consumption. Since the state officials determined what the family could be expected to require, the peasants found themselves on starvation rations. Their reaction was traditional of the East European peasantry in times of strife: to hide the surplus and make certain in the future that production would not create much more than the family required. The peasants could see no advantage to them in working to produce crops from which they received no benefit. They had no sense of social duty.

The opening measure of the New Economic Policy was the decree establishing a "tax in kind."[23] Under its provisions each peasant family was to deliver to the state a predetermined percentage of its production, and the balance of the crop was to be left with the family for its own use. The extent of the reduction in the amount

[22] Charter for the State General Planning Commission, [1921] I *Sob. Uzak. RSFSR*, No. 17, item 106.
[23] Decree on Replacing Produce and Raw Material Assessments with a Tax in Kind, March 21, 1921, *ibid.*, No. 26, item 147. This decree was duplicated in the Ukraine by decree of March 27, 1921, [1921] I *Sob. Uzak. Uk.*, No. 5, item 143.

of produce to be taken from the peasants has been indicated by a table published in late 1921.[24] It coordinated the various decrees establishing the new rate of tax to give the following picture. The collections of wheat were set for 1921 at 240,000,000 poods[25] as compared with a budgeted collection of 423,000,000 poods under the system in existence during the preceding season. Potatoes were to be collected at the rate of 60,000,000 poods, as compared with a collection of 112,000,000 poods during the preceding year. Collections of meat were to drop from 25,460,000 poods to 6,500,000 poods, while flax was to be reduced from 5,100,000 poods to 340,000 poods. The lower rate of collection was admitted to be inadequate for the needs of the country, but the peasants were expected to produce a surplus over their own requirements, and this was to be obtained for public needs by making it profitable to the peasants to dispose of it.[26]

The manner in which the disposition of agricultural surpluses was to be made profitable to the peasants of the Russian Republic and of the Ukraine was indicated almost immediately in both republics. The free market was to be reopened, and a decree in each republic authorized the peasants to buy and sell their surpluses.[27] Artisans and small-scale manufacturers were given the same freedom by both republics within two months. Local state agencies were ordered to permit peasants, artisans, and small-scale producers to sell their produce as long as they did not utilize raw materials provided by the state for other purposes under contract.[28] Within a week identical decrees in both republics extended the right to trade to everyone.[29]

[24] See Foreword by R. Arskii to *Severo-zapadnoe promyshlennoe biuro VSNKh, sbornik dekretov i postanovlenii po novoi ekonomicheskoi politike* (2 vols.; Petrograd, 1921–22) I, xiv.

[25] Decree on the Size of the Tax in Kind on Produce for 1921–1922, March 28, 1921, [1921] I *Sob. Uzak. RSFSR,* No. 26, item 148.

[26] See Arskii, in *Promyshlennoe biuro,* p. xiv.

[27] Decree on Free Exchange, Purchase and Sale of Agricultural Products in Provinces Completing Delivery of their Assessment, March 28, 1921, [1921] I *Sob. Uzak. RSFSR,* No. 26, item 149. The Ukraine's similar measure was dated April 13, 1921, [1921] I *Sob. Uzak. Uk.,* No. 5, item 164.

[28] Decree on Guiding Directives to Organs of Authority with Regard to Small and Artisan Production and Artisan Agricultural Cooperatives, May 17, 1921, [1921] I *Sob. Uzak. RSFSR,* No. 47, item 230. The Ukraine's similar measure was dated June 21, 1921. See [1921] I *Sob. Uzak. Uk.,* No. 11, item 320.

[29] Decree on Trade, May 24, 1921, [1921] I *Sob. Uzak. RSFSR,* No. 40, item 212, and Ukrainian decree of April 19, 1921, [1921] I *Sob. Uzak. Uk.,*

This meant that the middleman might return as a merchant to sell in the markets, bazaars, and even in covered stores. The extent to which the policy makers were willing to go in utilizing private enterprise to restore the economy became apparent in a provision permitting the sale of state-owned produce through agents. Preference in the selection of agents was to be given to cooperative stores as distributors, but even the private retailer could be selected for the purpose in individual situations.

Industrial activity with employed labor was permitted to private enterprisers under certain restrictions by decrees adopted by both republics in the early summer of 1921. The first breach in the wall against private industry was made by a decree authorizing citizens to lease from provincial councils of national economy such of the nationalized industries as were offered on a leasehold basis.[30] Two days later citizens were also authorized to establish their own new enterprises employing from ten to twenty workmen, the maximum to be fixed within those limits for each type of industry by the Supreme Council of National Economy.[31] The whole philosophy of the new policy as a reprieve to private enterprise was set forth on August 9, 1921, in the Russian Republic and on August 30, 1921, in the Ukrainian Republic.[32] In the two identical decrees the respective Councils of People's Commissars assigned specific tasks to the various agencies of government, including the trade unions.

Restoration of a measure of private enterprise in production and commerce had its effect upon the development of legal institutions and of the law. It had become evident during the period of civil war that courts had found themselves concerned increasingly with the criminal case. While reference was made by the Commissar of Justice in his circular of January 20, 1920, as has been indicated

---

No. 7, item 193. Noteworthy in this instance is that the Ukraine enacted its decree before the RSFSR. The latter's decree is in almost identical form as that of the Ukraine.

[30] Decree on the Procedure for Leasing Enterprises under the Jurisdiction of the Supreme Council of National Economy, July 5, 1921, [1921] I *Sob. Uzak. RSFSR*, No. 53, item 313 and Ukrainian decree of August 8, 1921, [1921] I *Sob. Uzak. Uk.*, No. 15, item 425.

[31] Decree on Artisans and Small Industry, July 7, 1921, [1921] I *Sob. Uzak. RSFSR*, No. 53, item 323.

[32] Instruction of the Council of People's Commissars on Putting into Effect the Beginnings of the New Economic Policy, *ibid.*, No. 59, item 403, and [1921] I *Sob. Uzak. Uk.*, No. 16, item 490.

earlier,[33] to disputes among the peasantry over land use and the division of household property, most of the provisions of the circular concerned the criminal case. When the Commissariat of Justice revived its official journal in December, 1921, there was extensive statistical treatment of criminal cases before the courts,[34] but civil cases were looked upon as so unimportant that no statistics were given on them.

Near disappearance of civil suits just prior to the introduction of the New Economic Policy in 1921 was confirmed by an author in 1922. In bemoaning the lack of interest in the problem of the execution of civil judgments, he indicated that the reason was to be found in the steady reduction of civil-law relationships and private commerce over the first four years of the life of the Russian Republic. He laid this steady reduction in civil-law activity to the abolition of private ownership of real property, to the absence from the market of many items of household use, and to the disappearance from legal trade of the big items which are normally the subject of private suit.[35]

Statistics published by the courts of Moscow city and province also confirm the relative insignificance of civil law matters.[36] During the six-month period (April 1 to October 1, 1920), the courts heard only 6,886 cases. A year later during a similar six-month period the same courts heard 10,233 cases as a result of the increase in private enterprise. Even with this increase in cases, the proportion of civil cases remained low on the calendar of the courts, being only 11 percent of the total. Criminal prosecutions accounted during this period in 1921 for 83 percent of the work of the courts, while divorce actions were 6 percent.

The tendency of the state seems even to have been to withdraw from the settlement of some types of civil disputes common to society prior to 1921. Evidence in support of this conclusion is to be found in the revived official journal in the only article concerned

[33] See circular No. 1, January 20, 1920, discussed *supra*, Chapter Four, note 7.
[34] See E. Tarnovskii, "Dvizhenie prestupnosti v predelakh RSFSR po svedeniiam mestnykh sudov za 1919–1920 gg," *Proletarskaia revoliutsiia i pravo*, No. 15 (December 15, 1921), p. 3.
[35] See M. Braginskii, "Ispolnenie sudebnykh reshenii," *Ezhenedel'nik sovetskoi iustitsii*, No. 2 (January 8, 1922), pp. 5–6.
[36] See T. P., "Narodnye sudi g. moskvy i moskovskoi gub. v 1921 g.," *ibid.*, No. 6 (February 5, 1922), pp. 2–4.

with civil law, namely, an article on marriage law.[37] Its author, in reviewing the problem of family relations, concluded: "Now, almost three years after publication of the code, so little remains of the old social conditions which served as the basis for the rules of marriage law that the time has come for its complete abolition, i.e., for recognition of marriage as the personal affair of each individual citizen, in which affair state authority must not interfere."

The interference of the state in the settlement of disputes arising before the introduction of the New Economic Policy seems to have been legitimate in the minds of the vocal members of the community primarily in those disputes which had led to violence, or from which violence might be expected to appear if the state did not provide an orderly means of isolation through the criminal courts.

Evidence in support of this conclusion is to be found in an instruction to the state investigators, published in October, 1920.[38] Eight types of crime were listed as requiring the attention of the investigator: murder and attempts to murder, bodily injury, rape, robbery, arson, counterfeiting of currency and documents, bribery of officials, and speculation. One additional crime is referred to, namely, larceny, but it is indicated that since this was a less terrible crime, it did not require investigation by an investigator but by the people's judge.

The list of crimes on which instruction in matters to be investigated is given contains presumably the full gamut of offenses with which the investigators would have to deal. As such, it presents a reasonably accurate source of information on the type of case being tried by Soviet courts in late 1920. The first five of the categories listed relate either to violent disputes which had occurred or to the source of disputes which could have been expected to follow commission of the crime if the state had not intervened. While the crimes in the latter three categories appear to be related more directly to the enforcement of state policies than to the settling or prevention of disputes in Soviet society, it is possible that if the

[37] See A. Zelenetskii, "O nashem brachnom prave," *Prol. rev. i pravo,* No. 15 (December 15, 1921), p. 17.
[38] Instruction to People's Investigators on the Conduct of Preliminary Investigations, Special Part, in RSFSR, *1917–1922 g. sistematicheskii sbornik dlia sudebnykh deiatelei* (Petrograd, 1922), I, 153. The date of the circular is given as October, 1920, in its original form as distributed by the Commissariat.

state had not intervened to check crimes of this character, social unrest arising out of inequality of treatment by bribed officials or as the result of forged documents or because of the opportunities to purchase scarce commodities upon the black market might have been expected.

Further evidence of the type of action with which the courts of the time were concerned is to be found in the statistical summary published in 1921, to which reference has been made.[39] The author noted that crime had increased in 1920 over the figures for 1919 by 26 percent in the twenty-five provinces for which statistics were available. The clue to the type of crime is to be found in the author's comments on the wide variation between the various provinces. He found that those provinces which lay in northern Russia and along the Volga had the highest rate of increase. These were said to be the provinces of the consumers and of the farming regions which had suffered in the crop failure of 1920. The rate of crime in the producing provinces had fallen, as it had also in Moscow and Petrograd, but the reasons were said to have been different. It was a noted fact that both Moscow and Petrograd had lost about half of their populations, the statistics showing that the exodus since 1917 had been 45 percent for Moscow and 51 percent for Petrograd. City dwellers had found it necessary to return to the countryside to escape starvation, leaving a smaller population in each city and thus reducing the number of crimes. The implication of the report is that crime in the Russia of 1920 was being caused primarily by want, and that most of the 1,187,169 criminal cases in the people's courts during that year had concerned robbery and larceny.

REVIVED CIVIL-LAW RELATIONSHIPS

Attention was turned in ever-increasing degrees to civil-law relationships and to the prevention and settlement of civil disputes with the declaration of the New Economic Policy in 1921. The burden was to be heavy upon the institutions concerned with the administration of justice and the maintenance of order. The first measure indicating the new concern of the authorities with civil-law

[39] Tarnovskii, "Dvizhenie prestupnosti," p. 4.

matters was a circular of the Commissariat of Justice addressed to all departments of justice in the provinces, and bearing the date of August 13, 1921.[40] In its opening paragraph it set the stage for the development of the next six years by saying: "The New Economic Policy of the R.S.F.S.R. urgently requires that the organs of justice adjust their staffs to the demands provoked by the rebirth of the economic life of the country. People and groups participating in this work must be provided with all of the means both to regulate their mutual rights and duties and to obtain fitting protection of all of their legal rights."

A notarial desk was ordered established by the circular in all provincial departments of justice and all county bureaus of justice.[41] The notary was to examine every contract and agreement to make certain that it did not violate Soviet legislation. He was to witness all powers of attorney concerned with the management of property, and to record each such document in a book whose pages were to be tied together and sealed with the official seal. A notarial fee was to be paid into the state treasury. Its rate was set at .5 percent if the amount involved did not exceed 500,000 rubles, 1 percent of the amount if it was between 500,000 and 5,000,000 rubles, and 1.5 percent on agreements involving greater sums. If the value of the contract could not be determined, the fee was to be 10,000 rubles.[42] Due to the fact that inflation was rampant at the time, as evidenced by the fact that the 422 page volume of decrees concerning the New Economic Policy, to which reference has been made, was marked as selling for 120,000 rubles, the fees were not really large.

People's courts were ordered to certify the authenticity of copies, the authenticity of signatures, the identity of individuals, family status, the loss of documents, and also to issue certifications as to

[40] RSFSR, Narodnyi Komissariat Iustitsii, otdel pervy, sudoustroistva i nadzora, avgusta 13 dnia 1921 goda, No. 36. This circular has been found only in the original, not in the collections.
[41] A notarial desk was also ordered established under all provincial and county legal departments in the Ukraine. See Decree on Notarial Functions, September 27, 1921, [1921] I *Sob. Uzak. Uk.*, No. 19, item 554.
[42] An identical table of fees was adopted in the Ukraine, Order of October 18, 1921, on Establishing Fees Payable to the Republic through the People's Commissariat of Justice, *ibid.*, No. 21, item 599. The Ukrainian decree also reintroduced fees for filing civil suits, graduated from 1 to 5 percent of the amount claimed.

the right to perform acts relating to property, such as the receipt of money orders and valuable parcels, wages, distributions in kind, etc. In doing so, the people's courts were ordered to follow the same rules as those established for the notaries, except that they were not to charge fees until a special instruction on the subject should be issued.

A "special session" court for civil cases, similar to that created by the People's Court Act of 1920 for serious criminal cases, was ordered established by the circular "to hear the most complicated and large-scale cases." It was to be organized under the auspices of the provincial council of judges and county bureaus of justice. The president of each court was to be entrusted, either by the presidium of the provincial council of judges or by the bureau of justice of the county executive committee, to a member of the presidium of the provincial council of judges or of the bureau of justice, or to one of the people's judges. In the latter event, the people's judge had to be a member of the Communist party and fully familiar with all of the new legislation relating to economic affairs as well as with the fundamental economic policies and the structure of civil law relationships brought into being with the development of commerce.

People's judges in the new civil court were to be chosen from the special panel prepared for the "special sessions" having criminal jurisdiction. Cases were to be placed upon the docket of the new court either by a people's court, or by a county bureau of justice or by the provincial council of people's judges. The order had to contain the reasons for requesting this special procedure.

The framers of the circular seem to have feared that the new civil court might be idle, for they provided that in the event of inactivity because of an insufficient number of cases, it might hear cases which were on the calendar of the "special session" for criminal cases. Both civil and criminal "special sessions" were to make use of the same court staffs, so that they became, in effect, chambers of the same court. In this fashion the way was paved for the introduction during the court reform of 1922 of a second level of courts having original jurisdiction in both civil and criminal matters.[43]

[43] By circular No. 8 of February 28, 1921, the criminal chamber had been given jurisdiction over all crimes by state officials "to eliminate the possibility of any local influences and to assure greater impartiality at the trial." See *1917–1922 g. sistematicheskii sbornik*, I, 213.

RESTRAINT OF BOURGEOIS ELEMENTS

Fear lest the New Economic Policy be utilized by subversive bourgeois elements to regain economic power and ultimately to unseat the regime established by the Communist party is reflected in the rules for the new civil chamber of the court of "special session." As has been indicated, judges had to be well versed in the policies of the administration, and they had to be members of the Communist party, if they were selected from the ranks of the people's judges. Apparently, members of the presidiums of the councils of people's judges and of the bureaus of justice of the county executive committees were by this time either all Communists, or otherwise trusted, for the instruction of August 13, 1921 found it unnecessary to express the Communist-membership requirement in listing them as having the qualifications to serve as judges in the new civil courts of the special session.

The same fear of bourgeois penetration is to be found in a decree of August 25, 1921,[44] calling upon the departments of justice and the other agencies concerned with the maintenance of order to secure the most experienced and most desirable persons as staff. The chiefs of the provincial departments of justice were not to be replaced by new people unless the circumstances were exceptional, and the Commissariat of Justice had to be informed of any proposed substitution and the compelling reasons for it as well as the person proposed to fill the vacancy. If the local executive committee could not agree with the view of the Commissariat on the proposed substitution, the dispute was to be referred to the Presidium of the All-Russian Central Executive Committee in Moscow.

To provide coordination of the work in each province, each provincial department of justice was ordered to create immediately, if it did not already have such an institution, a "college" or advisory committee within the department. It was to be composed of the chief of the department together with the president of the revolutionary tribunal, the president of the council of people's judges, and the chief of the prison department of the provincial executive com-

---

[44] Decree on Strengthening the Activity of Local Organs of Justice, [1921] I *Sob. Uzak. RSFSR*, No. 63, item 456. The Ukraine's decree of September 14, 1921, is identical: [1921] I *Sob. Uzak. Uk.*, No. 17, item 529.

mittee. All people's judges were to be issued an identity card indicating their right to instigate trials, to verify detentions under
guard, and to supervise the conduct of investigations by the police.
The card was also to declare that no people's judge or investigator
might be arrested without notification at the same time to the
presidium of the local provincial soviet either directly or through
the county or provincial bureau of justice.

The issuance of documents to judges and investigators required
knowledge of the entire personnel of the courts and investigation
offices throughout the country, and such knowledge did not exist.
Five days before the decree of August 25, Kurskii sent out Circular
No. 37[45] to all provincial departments of justice, councils of people's
judges, and revolutionary tribunals castigating them for failing to
report their personnel. In the words of the Commissar, "not a
single department of justice has complied with Circular No. 850
of September 30, 1919, as a result of which the organizational work
of the People's Commissariat of Justice is being slowed." Department
chiefs were ordered to report their staff by September 15, 1921,
on pain of prosecution. The lack of information seems to have
extended even beyond the names of people, for the Commissar
also ordered the preparation within each province by September
15 of a list containing addresses of all courts and investigating
offices, as well as of county bureaus of justice, special sessions of
the people's courts, standing courts, and legal aid bureaus, together
with a statement of staff vacancies.

Fees for the civil plaintiff were restored in the Ukrainian Republic by decree of October 30, 1921,[46] in a statute also establishing
a notariate and a scale of fees for his services similar to that established in the Russian Republic by the instruction already discussed.
The Russian instruction on the notariate had not included a section
on court fees, however, nor did such a section appear elsewhere
in the Russian Republic's collection of laws for 1921. On the record,
at least, it appears that the Ukraine was the first to appreciate that
the reprieve to private enterprise brought with it the possibility of
greatly increased costs of court activity in the civil sphere. Having

---

[45] Circular No. 37, August 20, 1921. See *1917–1922 g. sistematicheskii
sbornik,* I, 293.
[46] [1921] I *Sob. Uzak. Uk.,* No. 21, item 599, sec. A.

abolished fees specifically in the People's Court Act of 1920, the Ukrainian policy makers appear to have decided that there was no reason for the state to subsidize the litigation of private enterprisers under the conditions of the New Economic Policy. The scale of court fees established by the October 30, 1921, decree was 1 percent on claims up to 1,000,000 rubles, 2 percent on claims up to 10,000,000 rubles, 3 percent on claims up to 50,000,000 rubles, 4 percent on claims up to 100,000,000 rubles, and 5 percent on claims exceeding 100,000,000 rubles. Fees were to be charged at the time of filing a claim or counterclaim.

A schedule of fees for legal advice was also established in the same decree by the Ukraine. In civil cases the lawyer was to charge for one consultation 3,000 rubles; for the preparation of a document in the case, 5,000 rubles; for the preparation of a contract, 3,000 rubles if the amount involved was less than 100,000 rubles and 5 percent if the amount involved exceeded 100,000 rubles. Fees for advice in criminal cases were substantially lower, being 1,000 rubles for oral advice, and 3,000 rubles for the preparation of a petition, application for appeal, or other court paper.

The value of money at the end of 1921 is indicated by the price of a collection of decrees and court orders published by the Commissariat of Justice in Petrograd. Its first volume was listed as costing 50,000 rubles. The collection stated in the preface by its editor that during the first four years of practice there had not been published a single collection of material including all questions of court structure, procedure, and the administrative agencies of the Commissariat of Justice. The new collection was published because of the "approaching new events in the field of law in connection with the New Economic Policy, the birth of civil law, of a bar, of a prosecutor's office, and also because of the undeviating continued application of revolutionary legality." The editor foresaw the difficulty which was to develop with his collection, for he warned his readers that some parts of the collection might become out of date before publication because of the quickly changing legislation of the times. The author's expectations proved to be correct, for a Fourth Congress of persons engaged in the administration of justice was called for January 26, 1922, to consider the changes in law made necessary by the events of the preceding nine months.

The attitude of the policy makers on the eve of 1922 was indicated by Kurskii at a speech in honor of the fourth anniversary of the founding of the Moscow People's Court. He declared:

The old rule that a court shall decide by itself what is criminal and not criminal requires change. We have already worked out a criminal code. The same is true of procedural law. . . . Every citizen must know by what court and for what offense he is being tried and what punishment is possible. In civil law the time has also come to establish firmly a whole set of rules. . . . We are leaving behind the short slogans in the field of law and are going on to a complicated system of laws in an exceptionally difficult economic and political atmosphere.[47]

THE FOURTH CONGRESS OF PERSONS ENGAGED IN THE ADMINISTRATION OF JUSTICE

The keynote of the Fourth Congress of persons engaged in the administration of justice was set by Commissar Kurskii in his opening speech.[48] He indicated the task as being discussion of the desirability of unifying the revolutionary tribunals and the people's courts into a single-court system, of introducing uniformity into the application of the law as between the city and the village, of sending the people's courts out of the county seats on circuit to bring them closer to the peasants, of introducing new laws to foster the stability required in the commercial relations encouraged under the New Economic Policy, of creation of an office of the prosecutor, and of complete reorganization of the system of defenders to bring it under state control.

The Fourth Congress was to develop in the field of legal organization the principles which had been enunciated in general terms at the Ninth All-Russian Congress of Soviets which had met in Moscow from December 23 to 29, 1921.[49] Lenin had declared at that time that during the preceding year no Russian or foreign capitalists had attacked the new Soviet regime with arms. The year had been marked by restoration of commercial and diplomatic rela-

---

[47] Reported in "Chetyrekhletie moskovskogo narodnogo suda," *Ezh. sov. iust.*, No. 1 (January 1, 1922), p. 9.

[48] See D. I. Kurskii, *Izbrannye stat'i i rechi* (Moscow, 1948), pp. 69–80.

[49] For principal resolutions of the Ninth Congress, see A. Ia. Vyshinskii, ed., *S"ezdy sovetov RSFSR v postanovleniiakh i rezoliutsiiakh* (Moscow, 1939), pp. 193 *et seq.*

tions with neighboring states. A peace treaty had been signed with Poland on March 18, 1921, and diplomatic relations had been established between Finland and Estonia. A commercial treaty had been signed on March 16, 1921, with England in which the Russian Republic had been recognized *de facto*. Germany had signed a commercial agreement on May 6, 1921, and Italy had taken a similar step on December 26, 1921. Temporary commercial agreements had been signed with Norway and Austria in November and December, 1921. Countries in the east had also signed treaties establishing relations during the year, these being with Iran on February 26, 1921, with Afghanistan on February 28, 1921, with Turkey on March 16, 1921, and with a region of China which the Russians chose to recognize as the Mongolian People's Republic on November 5, 1921.

The numerous commercial treaties of 1921 provided Kurskii with what seems to have been a *force majeure* making him recommend a new policy in the field of law. It can be imagined that for a man of Kurskii's apparent devotion to a simplified court system, applying a simple system of law which would be understandable to the masses, the events of 1921 and their implications for the system to which he had devoted his energies aroused misgivings. He tried to suggest that there was no real change. To do this, he opened his speech by saying that the slogans of 1918, that is, the slogans of revolutionary legality and of a single people's court, were still the guiding principles not only of the people engaged in administering justice but of the broadest masses of workers and peasants. He spoke also of the years since 1918 in which there had been developed a system of administrative bodies to fight with counterrevolution, leaving the people's courts to deal solely with the types of cases which had previously come before the justice of the peace courts and the volost courts of the Empire. He suggested that this arrangement of matters was rather pleasing to him, and that he would not have recommended a change had it not been for the conditions brought about by the New Economic Policy. He declared: "Deep internal economic reasons were necessary to make these already well-rooted methods of deciding questions give place to that great task which stands before us today, the task of installing a regime of law." He hastened to quiet any fears that might have arisen that the Revolution was being betrayed by adding that the regime of law would be completely original in the worker-peasant state.

Responsibility for requiring the development of a new system was placed partly on the capitalist states with which the new Soviet Republics had concluded commercial treaties. Kurskii told his workers that when the question of the agenda for a congress at Genoa was being discussed, Lloyd George had said that Soviet Russia would have to establish a known system of legal norms which would permit other countries to have permanent relations with her. Kurskii added as an aside that "We shall see what these juridical norms shall be and who in the last analysis will dictate them," but he admitted that the commercial treaties raised some practical problems because they put forward demands for specified guarantees of property and persons.

The main responsibility for the necessity of making a change in the law was put by Kurskii upon the New Economic Policy. He indicated that it was necessary to enlist private capital in reconstruction, and that he envisaged stock corporations, in which foreign capital would share with the Soviet state in ownership.

Simplicity was still a dream of Kurskii's. He admitted that the laws of the first four years had sometimes been complicated. He reminded his hearers that the Ninth Congress of Soviets had demanded that the new laws relating to the use of the land be drafted so as to be understandable to the masses. The agencies through which the laws were to be administered were to be partly reorganized and partly created anew. Having set the stage, Kurskii then turned to the concrete problems to be met in this reconstruction of institutions.

Unification of the court system to combine the political courts and the people's courts was said to have been a question raised in several provincial congresses of persons engaged in the administration of justice. Kurskii indicated that it was a question which was open for discussion at the congress, but he did not conceal his desires. He thought that it was as yet impossible to eliminate the Cheka and the revolutionary tribunals because there were still counterrevolutionary threats in the republics and disruption of traffic on the railroads. He thought that if there were a unified court system, there would be problems in bringing the new combined political and people's courts close to the villages and to the workers of the cities. To prove how necessary it was to woo the people with courts operating close to them, he quoted a peasant speaker at the Ninth Congress of Soviets who had asked that the people's courts be lifted out of the county seats and be established in every peasant volost. Kurskii thought this impossible, but he did favor a traveling court which would sit in the village communities when it was necessary rather than sitting always in the county seat. He reported that there were many voices raised to give the people's court jurisdiction over all disputes in the countryside, including those having to do with the use of land. He thought it impossible, apparently, to invent a court which would be sufficiently intimate to meet the desires of the peasantry on the one hand and sufficiently firm to struggle effectively with politically hostile elements on the other.

Variation in the work of the people's courts in the villages and in the cities was another matter worrying Kurskii. He reported that although the people's courts were supposed to be united in a single system, there was in fact very great variation in the manner in which they treated crime. The courts in Kaluga Province were said to have gathered statistics on the treatment of crime in the cities and in the villages, with the result that it had become known that theft was punished seven times more severely in the rural communities than in the cities, while the courts in the villages were more lenient than the city courts when the crime was the distilling of illegal liquor or crimes against public order. To provide for uniformity, a new criminal code was being hurried into existence,[50] Kurskii explained. The judges were not, apparently, to be permitted to depart in the future from the penalties set in the law for crimes believed to be important in protecting the Soviet social structure. For crimes considered relics of the bourgeois past, Kurskii was prepared to continue the freedom which the judges had been enjoying in fixing the sentences to meet the situations as they analyzed them.

Although Kurskii with his influential voice opposed unification of the revolutionary tribunals with the people's courts into a single system, he was challenged by one of his colleagues in the Commissariat. N. V. Krylenko, who was to follow Kurskii in 1928 as

---

[50] The draft of the criminal code was published in *Prol. rev. i pravo*, No. 15 (December 15, 1921), pp. 87–95.

Commissar of Justice, presented a resolution to unite the two systems, but it was voted down. Years later, in 1937, when Krylenko was to lose his position and be denounced as an enemy of the people in the purge of those who had supported E. B. Pashukanis, this proposal may have been considered as evidence that he was intentionally lenient with counterrevolutionary elements in wanting to abolish the separate system of revolutionary tribunals.

THE DEBATE OVER A
UNIFIED COURT SYSTEM

The debate over the unification of the courts was later said to have been long and heated and the basic one of the Fourth Congress,[51] resting as it did on the difficulty of finding a compromise between the desire to organize the court so that it would be close to the people and the desire to maintain a court for political struggle with enemies of the regime. The spokesman for the Commissariat, one Lunin, declared: "The time for aggravated class warfare has not passed. A political court is extraordinarily necessary." He referred to "the petty-bourgeois conditions" and the domestic and foreign capitalist conditions of the times. He found that with the new precise procedural norms which were to be adopted, the people's courts were not prepared to meet the challenge of the enemy.[52]

Support for a unified system in which the revolutionary tribunals would be amalgamated with people's courts was urged by Krylenko on the ground that there already existed unity in the structure and principles of the two courts, and there was unity in the practice of the two courts in the field.[53] He thought that Lunin's comments of a political character were insufficient reason for maintaining two systems. He proposed a compromise in which a single system of courts would be established subject to the review of an appellate court. All courts in the single system would then be organized with

---

[51] See Berman, *Ocherki*, p. 51.
[52] For a summary of Lunin's speech see "IV Vserossiiskii s"ezd deiatelei sovetskoi iustitsii, doklady tov. Lunina i tov. Krylenko o sudoustroistve," *Ezh. sov. iust.*, No. 5 (January 29, 1922), p. 10.
[53] The summary cited in footnote 52 does not make this view clear, but Berman reports that Krylenko took this position. See Berman, *Ocherki*, p. 51.

strict observance of the concept of a class court. The judges would not be subject to removal by local soviets, and there would be a special system for selecting lay judges. This proposal would have reversed the decisions of the 1920 congress of persons engaged in the administration of justice, when it had been decided to continue the close ties between local soviets and the people's courts and to provide for service of every single citizen at one time or another as a lay judge. Krylenko seems to have been willing to increase centralization of authority and the political character of the people's courts so as to obtain the elimination of the very political and highly centralized revolutionary tribunals.

Krylenko urged adoption of a three-step court system with the bottom level occupied by a people's court comprised of two or six lay judges to be chosen by the provincial soviet's executive committee as the character of the case might require, and sitting without a professional judge; a second level to be the existing council of people's judges augmented by lay judges chosen from among the presidents of the lower courts, this council of people's judges to have original jurisdiction over all criminal cases and appellate jurisdiction over appeals in civil cases tried in the first instance by the people's courts; and a third level to be occupied by a Supreme Court of Criminal Cassation. The Supreme Court would provide unity in the practice of the courts by hearing the criminal appeals and by serving as a supervisory agency over all of the people's courts in the local communities.

Such a scheme seems to have had as its object placing all civil cases in the hands of lay judges close to the people who would settle them in accordance with the will of the community, raising all criminal cases to a higher level in which they would be heard by politically more developed, and hence less lenient, professionals who would retain their touch with the masses through a system of lay judges who had gained experience by presiding in cases in the local courts, and providing centralized control in a Supreme Court, which would serve not only as a bench to hear appeals but as an auditing agency charged with periodic examination on its own initiative of the work of lower courts to see whether they were conforming to the basic policies of the regime.

The compromise finally adopted by the Fourth Congress was not

Krylenko's, but it represented a considerable change over the existing situation.[54] It preserved two systems of courts, one for politically oriented cases and the other for everything else, both civil and criminal. While it preserved the two systems, it sought to establish uniformity through a single control point rather than the two supreme control points which were existing at the time in the form of the Supreme Revolutionary Tribunal and the Department of Supreme Judicial Control in the Commissariat of Justice. It sought to narrow the authority of the politically oriented side of the court system. These principles were to be accomplished by the following specific changes.

The principle of a single people's court would be reaffirmed, the court being designated as an organ of the dictatorship of the proletariat, and the masses being drawn into its work. There would be established at the center a supreme authoritative court, which would unite in itself all appellate jurisdiction from all types of courts (both revolutionary tribunals and people's courts). The jurisdiction of the revolutionary tribunals would be defined with precision, and they would no longer be permitted to enlarge their jurisdiction. The people's courts would retain their professional judges and the collegial form of bench, namely, one professional judge and two lay judges or one professional judge and six lay judges as the seriousness of the case required, but serious attention was to be given to the selection of lay judges and to their preparation for service. The special chamber of the Cheka with its authority to intern for periods up to five years in labor camps the "parasitic elements" of society who appeared to be dangerous even though it was impossible to find evidence of crime justifying a criminal prosecution[55] was to be abolished. The "standing courts" of the people's courts would be continued to cope with matters requiring attention without delay, such as desertion from the army or refusal to serve in the army, and red tape in administrative offices. These "standing" courts would also continue to try promptly the noncomplicated cases. There would be preserved the "special sessions" of the people's courts for

[54] See Berman, *Ocherki*, p. 52. The text of the resolution is printed in "Rezoliutsii s"ezda," *Ezh. sov. iust.*, No. 5 (January 29, 1922), p. 13.

[55] The authority of the Cheka tribunals is set forth in the Decree on Revolutionary Tribunals, dated March 18, 1920. [1920] I *Sob. Uzak. RSFSR*, No. 22–23, item 115, sec. 1 (note).

both criminal and civil cases, but they would be attached only to the councils of people's judges in the provincial centers and no longer also to the bureaus of justice of the executive committees of the county soviets, as they had been under the 1920 circular creating them. The side of the "special session" for criminal cases would have jurisdiction over crimes having great social and political importance. The side for civil cases would be given jurisdiction over a new type of case expected to arise under conditions of the New Economic Policy, namely, suits against the state "arising out of concession contracts, leases, and other contracts in which the state was a party, suits brought by former factory owners for the return of their factories by the state." The bench of the "special session" for civil cases was to be composed of especially qualified persons chosen from a special panel maintained for the purpose.

Such statistics as there were at the time suggested that the number of criminal cases in the revolutionary tribunals was relatively small compared to the number of criminal prosecutions in the people's courts. The figures for the year 1920 indicated that 86 percent (1,187,169 cases), of the criminal cases had gone before the people's courts, while the military revolutionary tribunals had heard 2 percent (23,447) of the cases, and the other revolutionary tribunals 12 percent (167,162).[56] If these figures were reported accurately, it is possible to guess at the motives of the two elements which had debated in the Fourth Congress the future of the court system. Krylenko may have felt that the work of the revolutionary tribunals had been reduced to such a low level that they should be absorbed into the basic people's court system in the interest of simplicity of court structure. Yet his political training caused him to fear that in such a single system organized along the existing lines of the people's courts, the masses would have a preponderant influence, and the masses were held by the Soviet leaders to be as yet unprepared for the strict discipline necessary to achieve goals set by the policy makers, involving as they did the negation of many concepts which had been taken for granted as universal by the peasant and urban communities of prerevolutionary times. In consequence, Krylenko was prepared to put the new single court which he espoused into the hands of people who could be presumed

[56] See Tarnovskii, "Dvizhenie prestupnosti," p. 12.

to be politically literate, and his scheme was designed to bring that about.

The majority, influenced by Commissar Kurskii, appears to have felt differently about retaining the intimate ties between the people's court and the masses. Whether the majority acted out of real concern for a belief in the wisdom of the masses in developing rules and procedures for settling disputes at their own level cannot be determined with assurance. The majority may have felt that the masses were not yet prepared to accept political leadership from a favored few who claimed their position because of an alleged superior understanding of the forces motivating the course of history. Certainly they would have had reason for such feelings as there was plenty of evidence at the time indicating that mass support for the policies of the regime was lacking. The only fact that is clear from the discussion is that the majority spoke in terms of retaining intimate links between the court system and the masses of the people. At the same time the majority took a position which indicated that they were aware of political danger to the regime in the determined opponents of the regime. To meet the two problems—namely, retaining close relations with the masses on the one hand, and eliminating individual enemies of the regime on the other—they favored a two-sided court system, even though it complicated the court structure and violated their espoused principle of a single court.

ESTABLISHING A STATE PROSECUTOR

Discussion of the desirability of reinstituting the office of state prosecutor along lines parallel to that of the office in the Empire was said by Kurskii in his opening speech at the Fourth Congress to be general. He spoke of articles in the press and of trial balloons in the provincial congresses of persons engaged in the administration of justice. He reported that these trial balloons raised by the Commissariat of Justice had met with sharp criticism, yet he felt that the matter had to be discussed in detail and in businesslike fashion at the Fourth Congress. He sought to quiet opposition by saying that the new office would, of course, be organized to put into effect revolutionary legality, which presumably would assure that it would not return to the hated activity of the tsarist office. He indicated that its most important function would be the concentration in its own hands of the investigating organization and in overseeing searches.

A form of prosecutor's office had been introduced in 1920 with the separation of the function of prosecuting from the function of defending. Both functions had remained a matter of local organization. The plan presented to the Fourth Congress went well beyond the existing situation. As Kurskii indicated in his opening speech, the proposed office would not limit itself to prosecution in terms of organization of the accusation before the court. It was to absorb the investigating organs. When Krylenko presented the plan to the Congress, the new office was seen to be an important innovation.[57] It was to be the watchdog of legality, the state's own inspector general, in seeing to the orderly functioning of the state's own offices. Krylenko summed it up:

The Prosecutor of the Republic, the provincial people's prosecutor, the deputy people's prosecutor must be places to which every person can go with a statement that his rights have been infringed from his point of view, and consequently this agency must have enough authority to set the matter right and to determine whether there has really been a violation of law, and further, it must have the right to act not only on the initiative of another but on its own initiative, not only to cut short a violation but also to prevent a violation of law.[58]

To create an agency capable of performing such functions, Krylenko proposed that the new agency be established parallel to the court, not having priority over the court or being subject to the court; that it be placed on a permanent basis functioning continuously; that it be organized on a strictly centralized basis, each level being responsible to the next highest level up to the Prosecutor's Department of the Commissariat of Justice which would name all prosecutors from top to bottom of the hierarchy; that in all cases it be independent of local soviets; and that it be given complete power to supervise and direct the investigating apparatus.

The defenders of the powers of local soviets entered the debate vigorously in opposition to the centralized control and absence of any responsibility to local soviets, especially to the departments of

[57] For a summary see "IV Vserossiiskii s"ezd deiatelei sovetskoi iustitsii, doklad tov. Krylenko o prokurature," *Ezh. sov. iust.*, No. 5 (January 29, 1922), pp. 11–12.

[58] See Berman, *Ocherki*, pp. 52–53.

justice of the executive committees on the provincial and county soviet levels. When the vote was taken, the majority favored the proposal of the Commissariat of Justice as amended by Krylenko to favor complete independence of local authorities. The resolution[59] declared as necessary for the prosecutor's office that it be from top to bottom free of local influence; that it be named and recalled solely by order of the Prosecutor of the Republic; that the local prosecutor as watchdog of the law have the right of consultative vote in the meetings of the executive committees of the local soviets; and that the local prosecutors be free from having to perform their duties in accordance with any decisions of the provincial soviet's department of justice.

Since the investigating organization was to be brought under the prosecutor's office, the matter was discussed at the Fourth Congress in terms of unification.[60] All of the existing separate systems of investigating organs, that of the people's courts, that of the revolutionary tribunals, that of the Cheka, that of the department of justice of the provincial soviet's executive committee, and that of the "militia department" of the provincial executive committee, were to be combined into a single system attached administratively to the courts but subject to the supervision of the prosecutor's office.

Organizationally the new unified investigating system would consist of three departments: the county investigator who would investigate cases to be tried by a people's court with six lay judges and such other cases as might be transferred by the prosecutor or the people's court; the investigator for the most important cases having unusual social concern, these being determined by the provincial prosecutor, the council of people's judges in the province or the executive committee of the provincial soviet, and approved by the Commissariat of Justice; and the investigator for such of the cases within the jurisdiction of the revolutionary tribunals as might be referred to it by the Prosecutor of the Republic, the prosecutor of the province, the executive committee of the provincial soviet, and the revolutionary tribunal itself. While the investigators were all subject to the provincial prosecutor as to the legality of their acts,

[59] Text of the resolution not published with other resolutions, but summarized. See "Preniia po dokladu tov. Krylenko o prokurature," *Ezh. sov. iust.*, No. 5 (January 29, 1922), pp. 11–12.
[60] For text of resolution, see *ibid.*, p. 13.

any quarrel between the investigator and the prosecutor was to be settled by the court. The Fourth Congress also decided that the local police must be subject to the prosecutor and the investigator in their investigative work, and that the police's powers to make arrests, to hold under guard, and to conduct a search and seizure must be strictly limited to exceptional cases when necessary to disclose a crime. No police office was to be permitted to hold a person under guard for more than twenty-four hours without obtaining the approval of an investigator or a judge, and a statement of the charge had to be given to the accused within another twenty-four hours.

While the delegates to the Fourth Congress indicated in the vote on the police that they had little confidence in the ability of the police to resist the temptations of power, they acted in reverse fashion in the matter of the investigator. The question was raised as to whether a defense attorney ought to be permitted to be present at the preliminary investigation to advise and protect his client's rights. The delegates voted against the presence of a defense attorney on the ground that "the correct organization of supervision by the prosecutor and the right to appeal to the court against the acts of the investigator are sufficient guarantee against the misuse by the investigator of his power." [61] By this resolution the die was cast in favor of a system which was to last to 1958, and with exception for juvenile offenders thereafter, although it has been subjected to criticism by Soviet authors, some of whom as prosecutors have wanted to introduce the check which a lawyer can provide against mistakes.[62]

REESTABLISHING THE BAR

The system of maintaining a list of available legal defenders rather than organizing a bar was declared a failure in Kurskii's opening speech. He concluded that the state must interfere if it wished to prevent the practice of law from becoming an aspect of

---

[61] See Berman, *Ocherki,* p. 55.

[62] See proposal of Bredikhin, prosecutor for the investigating department of the Kuibyshev provincial prosecutor's office, in "Predlozheniia chitatelei k razrabotke proektov uk i upk SSSR," *Sotsialisticheskaia zakonnost',* No. 1 (January, 1947), p. 22.

private enterprise. He felt that representation of clients had to be organized in institutional form, and the new institution had to be brought under state supervision. The Fourth Congress was asked to discuss the qualifications to be required of members of the bar and the best means by which state control could be maintained.

The expansion of personal and property rights as a result of the introduction of the New Economic Policy and the growing desire to hold all agencies of the state to the observance of law in their activities underlay the discussion of the matter of the bar at the Fourth Congress. It was assumed that these factors required that the institution of defenders in court be regulated as a permanent part of the court organization.[63] There were two functions to be performed, the defense of a client before a court and the providing of legal advice and assistance to the population generally. To meet these needs every one at the congress seemed to desire the creation of a college of defenders which would be tied to the courts in being subject to supervision and disciplinary action, but which would at the same time have partial autonomy and independence, and have the right to elect from its own members an executive board.

Fear lest the new bar revert to the traditions of the prerevolutionary bar gave rise to a search for conditions which would make of it a body of persons aware of their function in the framework of society generally rather than as a body of persons interested primarily in earning a living. The bar was to be conscious of its duty to defend the unfortunate person who found himself in the dock regardless of his ability to pay for a lawyer as well as to protect the person able to pay.

A proposal was brought into the meeting by the first presiding judge of the Moscow Council of People's Judges, Cherliunchakevich, as the spokesman for the Commissariat of Justice.[64] The lawyers were to be organized into an institution which would be autonomous and self-governing but under specified control of the executive committees of the provincial soviets in the admission of members. The new bars in each province were to be self-supporting rather than on state salary, as had been the case from 1919 to 1920, in that they were to be authorized to reach agreement with clients on fees.

[63] See Berman, *Ocherki*, p. 55.
[64] See E. S. Rivlin, *Sovetskaia advokatura* (Moscow, 1926), p. 25.

The question of fees aroused a lively debate. Those opposed to the fee system said that it would give rise as it had in the past to loss of confidence in the bar on the part of the judges, and that it would cause the concept of the practice of law as a means of earning a living to be dominant over the concept of the practice of law as a service to society, and that this would result in inadequate defense of the working masses who constituted the majority of cases before the courts. One opponent is reported as having asked why the accuser was not also to receive a fee from the defendant if the defendant's lawyer was to be paid by him. To this remark Krylenko retorted: "A comrade asks why the accuser is to receive nothing. I should like to see the accused who would pay me for accusing him." [65]

The resolution adopted after the debate conformed largely to the proposal of the Commissariat of Justice. The institution was to be a college of defenders (or advocates) in each province, whose members would be appointed by the executive committee of the provincial soviet on the nomination of the provincial council of people's judges. The members were not to be permitted to have any other employment. The provincial council of people's judges was to organize each college and to establish its rules. There was to be an executive bureau for each college chosen by the members from among their own number, but confirmed on the recommendation of the council of people's judges by the executive committee of the provincial soviet. Payment of fees was to be regulated under rules which would provide that persons having no property would be exempt from any duty to pay, while workmen in state and private enterprises, clerks in state offices and enterprises would pay a fee in accordance with a tariff established by the Commissariat of Justice. Only in instances when the clients came from other groups were the fees subject to no regulation but to negotiation between the lawyer and the client.

A link with the informalities of the past was retained in that persons not members of the college were to be permitted to defend a client under limited circumstances. Such persons were to be permanent employees of state offices and enterprises when the matter concerned his employer as well as members of trade unions

[65] *Ibid.*, p. 26.

or other social organizations to which the defendant or civil litigant belonged provided that authorization for appearance as attorney was given by the trade union. Finally, close relatives might appear, and in exceptional situations persons having the confidence of the court.

The executive bureau was to be given the task of general supervision over the affairs of the college and control over the individual member to make certain that he performed his duty. It was to be determined when no fee was to be paid and when a fee in accord with the rate set in the tariff was to be exacted. The executive bureau was to be responsible for all funds of the college and to organize at the request of the local people's court any consultation center thought necessary for providing legal advice to the population.

IMPLEMENTING THE PLANS

The decisions of the Fourth Congress were slowly put into legislative form in the Russian and Ukrainian Republics during the months that were to follow. First to appear were the two statutes on the state prosecutor's office to be established in the respective People's Commissariats of Justice.[66] Then followed the statutes in each republic on the college of advocates.[67] A statute on the state notary was published in the autumn,[68] and finally there appeared in each republic the judiciary act reorganizing the system of courts.[69]

The new institutions were to be provided extensive guidance in

[66] Statute on Prosecutor's Supervision, May 28, 1922, [1922] I Sob. Uzak. RSFSR, No. 36, item 424. Similar charters were adopted in other republics. See order of June 28, 1922, [1922] I Sob. Uzak. Uk., No. 28, item 440; order of June 26, 1922, [1922] Sobranie Uzakonenii i Rasporiazhenii Raboche-Krest'ianskogo Pravitel'stva BSSR, No. 5, item 83, and order of July 11, 1922, [1922] Sobranie Uzakonenii i Rasporiazhenii Raboche-Krest'ianskogo Pravitel'stva AzSSR, No. 7, item 241. The four orders may be compared conveniently by examining Sovetskaia prokuratura v vazhneishikh dokumentakh (Moscow, 1956), pp. 212–24.

[67] Order Establishing a Charter for the College of Advocates, May 26, 1922, [1922] I Sob. Uzak. RSFSR, No. 36, item 425, and Ukrainian order of October 2, 1922, [1922] I Sob. Uzak. Uk., No. 43, item 630.

[68] Decree Establishing a Charter for the State Notary, October 4, 1922, [1922] I Sob. Uzak. RSFSR, No. 63, item 807, amended June 13, 1923, [1923] ibid., No. 57, item 552. The Ukrainian decree is dated April 20, 1923: [1923] I Sob. Uzak. Uk., No. 13, item 232.

[69] Judiciary Act, RSFSR, October 31, 1922, [1922] I Sob. Uzak. RSFSR, No. 69, item 902. Judiciary Act, Ukrainian SSR, December 16, 1922, [1922] I Sob. Uzak. Uk., No. 54, item 779.

the substantive law to be applied, and the procedure to be followed. A Criminal Code,[70] a Code of Criminal Procedure,[71] a Code of Labor Law,[72] a Land Code,[73] and a Civil Code appeared in that order in the Russian Republic during 1922.[74] Not until early in 1923, however, was the new Code of Civil Procedure[75] promulgated to complete the collection of codes with which the law-enforcing institutions were to work.

The Institute of Soviet Law, which had been opened at the end of 1920[76] to develop the subject of law through study of its problems in theory and practice, published the first number of its journal on May 15, 1922. Kurskii introduced the new journal with a statement of the "first tasks in studying Soviet law." [77] He spoke out against the metaphysical tendency he found in a contemporary German theorist's book on the influence of the Revolution upon law, and said that in contrast to the German's approach Soviet jurists must study the concrete manifestations of the development of the new law, in short, they must not separate theory from practice. He found that Soviet law during the preceding four and a half years had developed constantly in moving through at least three stages: the period of destruction of the old law and the creation of temporary transitional norms, the period of militant Communism, and finally the period of state capitalism. He called for an analysis which would permit the further development of a new contemporary system of Soviet law as a result of generalization, of "the distilling of principles" from the practice, especially at the moment when little by little there was

[70] Criminal Code, RSFSR, decree effective June 1, 1922 (no precise date given to the decree), [1922] I *Sob. Uzak. RSFSR,* No. 15, item 153.
[71] Code of Criminal Procedure, RSFSR, Decree of May 25, 1922, [1922] *ibid.,* No. 20–21, item 230, effective July 1, 1922. Effective date extended to August 1, 1922, by decree of July 8, 1922, *ibid.,* No. 44, item 539. This was done to await establishment of the office of prosecutor.
[72] Code of Laws on Labor, RSFSR, October 30, 1922, *ibid.,* No. 70, item 903, effective November 15, 1922.
[73] Land Code, RSFSR, October 30, 1922, *ibid.,* No. 68, item 901, effective December 1, 1922.
[74] Civil Code, RSFSR, October 31, 1922, *ibid.,* No. 71, item 904, effective January 1, 1923.
[75] Code of Civil Procedure, RSFSR, July 7, 1923, *ibid.,* No. 46–47, item 478, effective September 1, 1923.
[76] See "Otchët o deiatel'nosti instituta sovetskogo prava za 1921 god i 1-iu polovinu 1922 goda," *Sovetskoe pravo* (Moscow), No. 2 (July, 1922), p. 139.
[77] See D. Kurskii, "Blizhaishie zadachi izucheniia sovetskogo prava," *ibid.,* No. 1 (May 15, 1922), p. 3.

being established a certain stability in the legal superstructure in connection with the international and economic policies of the previous year.

Because of the relationship between international and economic policies and the new legal structure, Kurskii urged that analytical legal study put in first place Soviet international law, which he thought to be of great practical importance. He suggested analysis of all Soviet treaties to permit generalization. His second choice for study was federalism as it had developed within the Russian Republic. He urged that the theorists find the new elements which Soviet experience had introduced into this subject. In third and fourth place he put the law of concessions and civil law. Finally he listed criminal law. In this ranking Kurskii manifested the change in attitude which had occurred since 1920, when criminal law had received almost the entire attention of lawmakers and writers. Kurskii could now foresee a wide range of disputes on the international and national level requiring the attention of the men designated to work out a new system for settling such disputes.

Considerable opportunity for imaginative development was anticipated for those who would seek to generalize from practice. D. Magerovskii, in an article following that by Kurskii in the new law review, declared: "Law is that sphere of social relationships to which Marxist thought has turned its attention less than to all other aspects of social relationships. . . . We know extraordinarily little about the law of the transitional period [from capitalism to Communism]." [78] The author seems to have been suggesting that Marxist dogma was not to be a limitation on the imaginative generalization of practice, for he found no such dogma in the field of law. Magerovskii was not without influence, for he was a member of the three-man commission which was to establish a plan for widespread legal education later in the year. [79]

Discussion of the new principles of law was popular at the time. In addition to the journal appearing with the authorization of the Commissariat of Justice and containing official notices as well as

[78] See D. Magirovskii, "Sovetskoe pravo i metody ego izucheniia," *ibid.*, p. 24.
[79] See "Organizatsiia iuridicheskikh shkol v rossii," *Ezh. sov. iust.*, No. 39–40 (October 27–November 4, 1922), p. 36.

theoretical articles,[80] and the law review of the new Institute of Soviet Law,[81] a third journal appeared in June, 1922.[82] Its editors declared in its first issue that it was to contribute to the development of law by basing study upon the best legal inheritance from the past and upon consideration of the new political legal ideas.[83] Judging from its contents, which included theoretical articles, guides to new legislation, and instructions and summaries of court decisions, this journal was designed for practitioners and written by men trained in law before the Revolution but sympathetic to the new regime. It seems to have represented an attempt to bring traditional forms of legal analysis to the problems of Soviet society and to create a blend of old and new to avoid unfettered enthusiasm for the new alone.

It is from this June journal that the new emphasis upon legal education becomes evident. A Law Department was reported to have been established by order of the Council of Ministers on March 4, 1921, in the Faculty of Social Sciences of the Moscow State University.[84] It declared that its 1922 enrollment was 1,100 students (763 men and 337 women) in its three-year course, with 566 of these in the entering class (443 men and 123 women).[85] Its curriculum contained courses on every branch of law, and its professors included many of the important legal experts of the time. They were men who had gained reputations even before the Revolution. Presumably they were now accepted to reintroduce the complex law of the past for the New Economic Policy in a blend with the spirit of the Revolution. Many of them were not members of the Communist party.

Institutes of law were opened outside of Moscow. One such Institute opened its doors on January 17, 1922, in the Faculty of Social Sciences in the remote Turkestan State University in Central Asia.[86] Its program was modest, with four chairs: (1) history and theory of

---

[80] *Ezhenedel'nik sovetskoi iustitsii* (Moscow).
[81] *Sovetskoe pravo* (Moscow).   [82] *Pravo i zhizn'* (Moscow).
[83] "Nashi zadachi," *ibid.*, No. 1 (1922), p. 3.
[84] "Novyi uchebnyi plan pravovogo otdeleniia fakul'teta obshchestvennykh nauk," *ibid.*, p. 113.
[85] "Akademicheskaia khronika, pravovoe otdelenie fakul'teta obshchestvennykh nauk Moskovskogo Gosudarstvennogo Universiteta," *ibid.*, No. 3 (1922), p. 88.
[86] "Pravovoi institut pri F. O. N. turkestanskogo gosudar. univer.," *ibid.*

law, (2) public law, (3) local law including Moslem law, and (4) criminal and civil law. No report is given of the number of its students.

A GLIMPSE AT COURT ACTIVITY

Starvation in the spring of 1922 brought grim cases before the courts in the famine areas of Central Asia. Two orders for detention pending completion of investigation were printed in the law review.[87] In one the accusation was that Sultangarei Mukhametzianov, aged 42 and living in the village of Aniaseva of Kirgizianov volost, had killed a human being for the purpose of eating his flesh. So as to prevent repetition of the offense he was ordered taken into custody on March 4, 1922, pending completion of the investigation. A similar order issued from the same court on the same day against Samigull, aged 42 years, and Khatir, aged 57, of the village of Enikulova, to prevent their hiding from the court during the investigation of the charge that they had killed a human being and eaten his flesh.

Civil cases were also reported in the law review to indicate that the civil work of the courts in 1922 was beginning to have general interest to the practitioner. From the seven cases selected by one author for publication in the practitioner's law review[88] it is evident that the maintenance of children after divorce of the parents ranked as a major matter of dispute among citizens at this time, for five of the cases concern this problem. The brief summaries of the seven cases suggest the type of civil dispute being settled by the courts even before the introduction of the reforms accompanying the emergence of the New Economic Policy during the latter half of the year 1922. The decisions are those of the Moscow Council of People's Judges, which was sitting as an appellate tribunal to hear complaints against decisions of the people's courts throughout the province.

A divorced wife sued her former husband to obtain maintenance

[87] *Case of Mukhametzianov*, and *Case of Samigull and Khatir* (both names are spelled differently at different places in the report), *ibid.*, No. 1 (1922), p. 112.
[88] Ia. A. Khazin, "Sudebnaia khronika, iz praktiki moskov. soveta narodnykh sudei," *ibid.*, pp. 85–87.

for a child born to them after the divorce.[89] The trial court gave judgment for the divorced wife in the amount of half of the former husband's wages at his factory job, plus one third of the payments in kind which he was also receiving in accordance with the practice of the time. No indication was given in the opinion as to how the payments in kind were to be divided, nor why the fraction differed for the money wages and the payments in kind. The defendant appealed on the ground that the two parts of the judgment were in contradiction, presumably because the fractional share to be awarded the wife differed. In its decision of June 1, 1922, the council of people's judges held that the judgment had been correct, and the appeal was denied.

A divorced wife sued in the second case not only for maintenance of a child born of the marriage but also for a return of those articles which she had brought to the marriage as dowry.[90] The trial court refused to order the return of the articles specified on the ground that it had not been proved that they were part of the dowry, but it gave judgment in favor of the plaintiff in the amount of one half of her former husband's wages. He appealed, saying that he had left his mother's home in which he had been living and had re-married, so that he now lived with a second wife, her mother and her brother, and he could not afford to pay one half of his wages to support his child. The council of people's judges in a decision of June 1, 1922, set aside the judgment as to the share of the wages because the trial court had not taken evidence on the family situation or the wealth of the former husband. The council added that if this had been done, it would have affirmed the judgment. Presumably there was a rehearing on this issue.

Support was provided to a trial court when consideration had been given to a former husband's wealth in a third action brought by a divorced wife for maintenance of her three children of the mar-riage, the eldest of which was only six-and-a-half years of age.[91] The defendant had filed a counterclaim for articles which he alleged to be his although remaining in the apartment formerly occupied by the whole family. The trial court gave judgment in the amount of one quarter of the defendant's wages, but it rejected the counter-

[89] *Pilach* v. *Pilach, ibid.,* Part III, Case 1, p. 86.
[90] *Matina* v. *Skvortsov, ibid.,* Part III, Case 2.
[91] *Bogoliubskaia* v. *Bogoliubskii, ibid.,* Part III, Case 3, p. 87.

claim for want of payment of the court fee. It declared itself ready to hear the counterclaim separately upon payment of the fee. The defendant appealed on the ground that the court in giving its judgment had not considered his wealth or his family status, and there was no reason to separate the counterclaim for a separate hearing. The council of people's judges rejected the appeal in its decision of June 1, 1922.

Ownership of specific items of property acquired during the marriage but claimed by one of the parties after divorce provided the basis for a dispute settled in the fourth case.[92] Under the 1918 Family Code[93] which was still in force at the time, marriage of urban residents did not create community property of items acquired during the marriage. A divorced wife brought suit not only for maintenance of a child of the marriage but also for a sewing machine which she claimed to be hers but which her former husband refused to release. In reply the defendant offered to pay 100,000 rubles a month maintenance, but he refused to give up the sewing machine, saying that it had been purchased with his wages; not for his wife with whom he was already in strained relations but for the use of other persons in his household. He declared that his wife was working in a factory and receiving wages of her own, and he never gave to her a share of his own wages. Witnesses were called in support of his claim, and they testified to the truth of all his statements. The former wife testified that the sewing machine had been purchased with money from her own wages, and further that the defendant had some land, and she asked for produce from that land to feed the child. The trial court granted the plaintiff's request in that it ordered the defendant to provide the former wife with 10 poods of rye and 25 poods of potatoes from the 1922 harvest. It also ordered that the sewing machine be delivered to the former wife, on condition that she give it to her daughter on the latter's majority.

The defendant's appeal from the decision of the trial court declared that the court had failed to decide the only question before it, namely, who owned the sewing machine, and that the granting of the machine to the mother to be held for the daughter

---

[92] *Spiridonova* v. *Chesnov*, *ibid.*, Part III, Case 5, p. 87.
[93] Art. 105.

until her majority introduced a new concept, the concept of inheritance during one's lifetime. In spite of these rather cogent arguments from what would seem to be the legal point of view, the council of people's judges affirmed the judgment below.

Property ownership in a peasant household gave rise to the dispute settled in the fifth case. Under the law of the time, peasant households continued to hold marital property in community as they had done under Russian customary law before the Revolution.[94] A peasant couple had been separated and all of its property divided between the parties. Most of the chattels had been divided according to mouths to feed; the fodder had been divided in accordance with the cattle given to each party, while the farm and its implements had been divided equally. The divorced wife, to whom a child had been born within six weeks after the divorce, sued her former husband for maintenance of the child in the amount of one half of his earnings.[95] At the trial the defendant offered either to give his former wife the half of the farm and its implements which he had received, from which she would have to support the child, or to take the child for rearing himself. The plaintiff refused to accept either proposal.

Faced with the alternatives, the trial court decided to give the child to the father because there was no possibility of determining the amount represented by one half of the earnings of the father, nor was it possible to give to the mother the father's share in the farming operation unless she accepted it, and this she refused to do. The mother appealed, and the council of people's judges upheld her, saying that in giving the child to the father the trial court "had not discussed his property status to determine precise and definite facts as to what the father would use to support the child." The case was remanded to a different people's court for retrial, at which time the father repeated his offer in the alternative, and the mother again refused. The court then without raising the questions asked by the council of people's judges in their first decision and without discussing the proposals of the parties as to how they might support the child decided to take from the mother a part of

[94] This situation which had continued to exist in spite of the apparently contrary rule of Art. 105 of the 1918 Family Code was formalized by the Land Code of the RSFSR, 1922, Arts. 66–67.

[95] *Sporova v. Sporov, Pravo i zhizn'*, No. 3 (1922), Part III, Case 4, p. 87.

the land to which she had been given the use on the division and to obligate the father to work this land for the benefit of the child. The plaintiff again appealed, but the council of people's judges decided on the second occasion to affirm the judgment below.

Commercial relationships appeared in the two other cases reported as an indication of the work of the courts in mid-1922. One case involved a suit for shoes which had been ordered and paid for.[96] The trial court found on the basis of written evidence presented to it that the claim was well founded, but it went further. Finding that the defendant was systematically failing to execute the orders placed with him, the trial court fined him one hundred rubles. The council of people's judges affirmed the judgment and the fine.

A horse trade presented the court with an unusually complicated problem in the other contract case.[97] From the complaint it appeared that one Sulimov had asked one Maerov to accompany him to the neighboring village to advise him in buying a horse, since Sulimov had no knowledge of horses. On the way Maerov proposed that Sulimov buy his four-year-old horse, which although quite thin and having a sore on his back was nevertheless in good health and suited to the light work of Sulimov's small farm. The two left the road to look at the horse, and enlisted the help of one Perov to examine the horse. During the examination one of the group remarked that the horse was not well and suggested that they call upon the veterinarian in the neighboring village, but Maerov replied that he had already been to the veterinarian's and had received a report that the matter was trifling. Sulimov then in reliance upon the statement agreed to pay forty million rubles for the horse. When Maerov stated that he needed the money immediately, they agreed to go to Moscow on Monday, February 27, 1922, to get the money. The payment was made, and it was agreed to leave the horse for the time with Maerov. On the following day Maerov's wife in going to feed the horse noticed that it was getting no better. On the contrary, it was unable longer to stand. A few days later the woman hired three people early in the morning to remove the half-dead horse from her stable.

[96] *Drozdov* v. *Kalinin, ibid.*, Part I, p. 85.
[97] *Sulimov* v. *Maerov, ibid.*, Part II, p. 86.

On his return on Saturday, March 4, 1922, Sulimov called the veterinarian who pronounced the horse hopeless, and the horse died subsequently. Sulimov then claimed that he had been swindled and asked for the return of his forty million rubles. At the trial on March 22, 1922, the plaintiff stated in further explanation that the veterinarian to whom Maerov said he had gone for an opinion on the horse had never examined it. All of the plaintiff's allegations were found to have been proved by the plaintiff's witnesses and by examination of the defendant. The trial court found that the plaintiff had not established that he had been swindled, but it ordered Maerov to return one-half of the purchase price to make good the damage. The court declared that it was taking into consideration the relative wealth of the parties and the damage suffered. Both parties appealed the judgment, and the decision was set aside as lacking support in evidence. Presumably a second trial was held.

From the civil cases published on the eve of the 1922 legal reforms it is evident that the people's courts were applying a homely type of wisdom in support of property rights and the sanctity of contract. There was as yet no law of contracts to guide the court in the latter two cases, although there was a Code of Family Law dating from 1918 to provide guidance in the disputes over marital property and the maintenance of children after divorce. In most of the cases cited the trial courts had not adhered to rules familiar in non-Soviet jurisdictions and soon to be adopted in part in their own. They had sought to reach a decision of an original character.

The originality of the court decisions of 1922 may have been the result of lack of legal education rather than unusual imagination. Statistics on the people's court judges of the city of Moscow and Moscow Province in 1921 indicated that of the 149 professional judges only 21 had legal education. Of the rest, 5 had college education, 20 had middle-school education, and 103 had elementary-school education or less. Their qualifications seem to have been in large measure their political reliability. Eighty were members of the Communist party and the rest nonparty people.[98]

In the work of the provincial council of people's judges in the cases reported, there is evident an effort to balance orthodoxy from

---

[98] T. P., "Narodnye sudy g. moskvy i moskovskoi gub. v 1921 g.," *Ezh. sov. iust.*, No. 6 (February 5, 1922), p. 3.

the legal point of view with what was being called "revolutionary expediency." In the seven cases indicated the council varied between upholding the novel solutions proposed by the people's courts and what would have been a more orthodox solution. Kurskii probably felt confident that his courts had not yet reverted to the attitudes of the tsarist courts.

Labor disputes were also crowding the courts in 1922. Statistics on the court's work as a criminal court to hear complaints brought by the labor inspectors who were no longer permitted to close down a manufacturing establishment or levy a fine on their own authority indicate a notable rate of activity. Reports from thirty-three provinces of the Russian Republic for the period January to June, 1922,[99] indicated that there had been 940 such cases in the people's courts, which was said to be but 15 percent of the work of the courts in labor law. The nature of employers is indicated by the fact that 61 percent of the prosecutions were of private employers. Managers of state enterprises accounted for 28.4 percent, while cooperatives were prosecuted in 10.6 percent of the cases. Offenses involved were violation of the limitations on the length of the working day, child labor, and female labor; violation of wage minimums and failure to pay promptly; violation of sanitary and safety regulations; failure to report accidents promptly; violation of regulations on employment through labor exchanges; failure to pay social-insurance premium; attempts to bribe labor inspectors; failure to perform orders of the labor inspector; and illegal dismissal of workers.

PARALLELISM OF INSTITUTIONS

A review of the events of the first four years indicates that simplicity in structure had disappeared from the judiciary. Despite professions that there existed but a single court of general jurisdiction, there had been brought into existence a bifurcated system. On the one side were the revolutionary tribunals dealing with matters deemed to be essential to the life of the regime, namely, discipline in the army, protection of transportation, and attempts to overthrow the regime. While there had been a determined at-

[99] Vl. Zaitsev, "Sudebnye dela po okhrane truda v ianvare-sentiabre 1922 g.," *Sovetskoe pravo*, No. 2 (5) (1923), pp. 97 and 99.

tempt led by Krylenko at the Fourth Congress of persons engaged in the administration of justice to abolish these specialized courts, it had failed. On the other side and in contrast to the revolutionary tribunals there were the people's courts dealing primarily with disputes between citizens and with the maintenance of public order.

Neither side of the bifurcated structure was simple in form. Although there had been a statute in 1921[100] purporting to unite the various types of revolutionary tribunal, there had in fact occurred almost no reduction in the complex of tribunals.[101] There had been only coordination of their activity in a Supreme Revolutionary Tribunal which could hear appeals and also try exceptionally important cases referred to it by the Central Executive Committee. The people's courts were even more complex. Original jurisdiction in both civil and criminal matters lay in most instances in the courts to be found in every ward of the cities and on circuit in the rural communities, but original jurisdiction in both civil and criminal matters lay also in a more experienced and trusted tribunal to be found in the provincial capitals and known as the "special session" of the people's court.

Appellate jurisdiction over the regular people's courts was to be found in the council of people's judges in each provincial capital. Although the council had been instituted as a body composed of the judges in the people's courts called to sit in review of the work in each county, it had become a professional and permanent body, with only a reminder of its close relationship to the local courts in the provision for participation on its bench of a minority of local judges sitting in rotation.

Review over the people's court branch of the bifurcated system had become centered in a form of supreme court organized as a department of the People's Commissariat of Justice. It was recommended in January, 1922, by the Fourth Congress that it be made into a supreme court for the revolutionary tribunals as well. While appeals did not lie to this department from the people's courts as they would to an ordinary supreme court, requests for review could be filed with it by a number of agencies, and it could act upon its own initiative. Practice indicated that it accepted petitions

[100] Decree on Uniting All Revolutionary Tribunals of the Republic, June 23, 1921, [1921] I *Sob. Uzak. RSFSR*, No. 51, item 294.
[101] See Berman, *Ocherki*, p. 34.

from disgruntled parties to suits and became almost traditional in its operations.

As aids to the court there had developed a prosecutor's office, a bar, and an office of the investigator. To provide a means of avoiding disputes before they degenerated into matters requiring court intervention in the interest of the peace of the community there had been created a notary's office. As a first line of defense against disorder in the community there had been established a highly centralized system of local police.

In the light of developments during the first four years, there is little wonder that an appropriate word of characterization was needed, yet Kurskii preferred to evade the issue. Speaking to the Fourth Congress in early 1922 he suggested that he would accept either of two approaches to the bifurcation. It could be looked upon as a unified people's court system or as one comprising the parallel institutions of the courts and the revolutionary tribunals. He was not insistent on the acceptance of either approach, but he was adamant on one point. Both parts must keep close to the masses —linked in the villages to the peasantry and in the cities to working-men's organizations. A close link with the masses was in Kurskii's mind the feature making the Soviet legal system unique.[102]

No Soviet leader could have afforded politically, nor would he have wanted, to suggest that the wheel had turned full circle with the reintroduction of complexity and centralization into the legal institutions of the new Russia. For Bolsheviks an institution derives its character from its function. The appearance by late 1921 of institutions having prerevolutionary names and seeming to be charged with age-old functions in keeping social order was not a full retreat from the principles of the Revolution, although some Communists began to have their doubts. Kurskii tried to calm them by emphasizing the link with the masses.

What had caused the emergence by the end of 1921 of a complex system of legal institutions functioning under centralized control? Kurskii chose to note the pressure from bourgeois elements for recognition of formality as essential to the proper function of Lenin's neo-capitalism. But Kurskii made no apologies for centralism. This

<hr />

[102] See D. I. Kurskii, "Rol' i znachenie sovetskoi iustitsii v sviazi s novoi ekonomicheskoi politikoi," in Kurskii, *Izbrannye stat'i*, p. 77.

was an element which he had helped to establish with his early articles setting a line for judicial decisions and his draftsmanship of centralizing measures. This was a measure not to be confused by his followers with the policy of centralism sponsored by the tsars.

During the years that were to follow the civil war faded into history; private enterprise flowered but only to succumb to the state-enterprise policy of the five-year plans. Finally Stalin devised a system to circumvent the law and its agencies when they stood in the way of what he thought necessary to create a personal dictatorship. Thus, the institutions were chipped away at the corners and sometimes at vital points, but the legal system of mid-twentieth century was built in form, at least, on the foundation laid by Kurskii and his colleagues. For that reason the remaining chapters will examine institution by institution the ideas and decisions of those having the task of devising a legal structure to meet the needs and anticipated dangers of the New Economic Policy as it emerged from 1922 to 1925.

Chapter 6

CRYSTALLIZATION OF THE COURT STRUCTURE

EXPERIMENTATION with flexibility in settling disputes in Soviet society was nearly at an end by 1922. Pressures for predictability had become so great with the reprieve granted to private enterprise that a crystallization of the court structure had become a primary task of the Commissar of Justice. It was he who was charged with preparation of a judiciary act to fix the court structure for the foreseeable future. Having heard the advice of his colleagues assembled in a nation-wide meeting for the purpose of reviewing the alternatives, the Commissar set out to draft the decrees.

Commissar Kurskii's thinking seems always to have been dominated by his desire for simplicity in the court structure. In 1918 while he was still Deputy Commissar he had been angered by the introduction above the level of the people's court of a specially qualified court for complicated civil and criminal cases. On his elevation to the post of Commissar in the summer of 1918, he had set out to undo the work of his predecessors so as to introduce a single court of general jurisdiction.

The People's Court Act of late 1918 had marked the victory of Kurskii's policy of simplicity, but the victory had been short-lived. It had proved necessary by the summer of 1920 to erect a court of greater experience and more political reliability than had been found in the usual people's court. Kurskii might have attempted to improve the quality of the people's court so that all cases could have been tried by learned and politically conscious judges. This he had not done, perhaps because he could not have mustered a sufficient number of learned and politically conscious men and women quickly, but also probably because he was opposed in principle to the idea of taking a step which would have removed the courts from the level of the masses. To avoid making such a far-reaching concession to the need of the times, he had been prepared to make a different concession which must have seemed less of a retreat from principle. He had indicated that he was willing to reintroduce into the Soviet scene a second court of original jurisdiction to specialize in the complex and politically important cases, while the people's court concentrated its attention on the routine dispute.

Kurskii might have argued in customary Marxist fashion that the new superior court of 1920 was different in quality from the one which he had succeeded in eliminating from the scene in late 1918. He might have said that the 1918 court had been composed in large measure of judges held over from the Imperial regime and applying the procedural and substantive law codes of the Empire to the extent that their provisions did not seem to violate the principles of the Revolution. He could have said that his new superior court marked a sharp contrast because it was composed of new men and women having had no relationship to the courts of the Empire but selected because of the skill which they had evidenced in the work of the people's courts. Further, his new judges were applying a procedural and substantive law which was being created by the new regime. In spite of the availability of this argument that the new court had changed in quality from the 1918 "district court" against which he had fought so vigorously, Kurskii writes as if he had been worried by what he found it necessary to do.

To persuade the public and perhaps even himself that no real sacrifice had been made in principle, he had called the new court a "special session" of the people's court, and he placed in the opening article of the People's Court Act of 1920 his statement of faith, namely, that the Soviet court system was unitary. Actually it was not, and even Kurskii's colleagues were prepared to say that article one was violated by the articles which came after it establishing the "special session."

The system of multiple courts of original jurisdiction obviously had come to stay in 1920 in spite of Kurskii's pretense of loyalty to the unitary system. Kurskii appears even to have become willing to see it established as the permanent system in the new judiciary act being drafted in 1922. The only question remaining in Kurskii's mind seems to have been whether the new act should countenance a great many different courts of original jurisdiction, or whether it should permit the existence of only a few. To clarify this question he had permitted his colleague Krylenko to bring into the Fourth Congress of persons engaged in the administration of justice a proposal to eliminate the separate system of revolutionary tribunals which had expanded their activities since their creation by the first decree on the courts in 1917. Krylenko was prepared to amalgamate the revolutionary tribunals with the courts, but at a cost to the courts which appeared too high to Kurskii.

Krylenko's draft came into conflict with the other principle fostered by Kurskii, namely, the principle of popularity of the court system. Kurskii had emphasized on many occasions that the courts must be close to the people, by which he, apparently, meant that they had to be staffed by the rank and file of the public and had to be physically located so that a long trip to the county seat would not be required to find a tribunal to settle a dispute. Krylenko's draft would have sacrificed this principle of popularity, for it called for a court of sufficient political responsibility to assume what had been the work of the revolutionary tribunals. Krylenko would not have let every one sit on the bench of the new court. He called for politically conscious judges, and there were not many such people in the new Russia. Statistics had shown that the benches of the people's courts were staffed with persons less than half of whom were Communist party members, and these figures related only to the professional judges. The laymen who sat with the professionals were even less likely to have had the political training which the party required of its members.

Faced with the necessity of professionalizing and thus depopularizing the courts if they were to assume the work of the revolutionary tribunals, Kurskii turned away from Krylenko's proposal of amalgamation. The Fourth Congress under his leadership resolved against it and accepted continuation of the revolutionary tribunals as specialized courts of original jurisdiction, although the wish was expressed that their activities be coordinated within the judicial system by making them subject to the leveling influence of a supreme court which would also be the pinnacle of the system of people's courts.

STRENGTHENING THE GENERAL COURTS

Although Kurskii was prepared, when forced to do so by the apparent political need, to sacrifice the principle of a unitary court system in order to continue the revolutionary tribunals, he showed himself completely opposed to any plan which would have permitted the Cheka also to maintain its special tribunal for the punishment of citizens believed to be dangerous to the regime. He wrote in enthusiastic support of the policy of extermination of these tribunals as it has been enunciated by the Ninth Congress of Soviets at the very end of 1921.

Kurskii's part in the abolition of the Cheka's tribunals by the Ninth Congress may have been large. In the Congress' resolution, published on the morning of December 30, 1921,[1] tribute had been paid to "the heroic work performed by the Cheka in the most critical moments of the civil war," but after that tribute had come the guillotine. The resolution stated that the strengthening of Soviet authority both within and outside the country had permitted a narrowing of the Cheka's activity so as to place the task of struggling with violation of law upon the courts. The Central Executive Committee's Presidium was directed to revise the statute on the Cheka within the shortest possible time so as to effect the changes.

The Cheka was abolished entirely by the decree of February 6, 1922.[2] Its investigative functions were transferred to a newly created State Political Administration within the Commissariat of Internal Affairs, while its trial jurisdiction was transferred to the revolutionary tribunals and the courts. The world knows that the abolition of the Cheka eventually became a mockery, for the State Political Administration, known by its Russian initials as the G.P.U., subsequently became renowned for severity equal to that of the Cheka, but at the time of the change Kurskii and his colleagues seem to have considered themselves victorious over what they believed to be an overly zealous political police. In less than a

[1] Resolution on the All-Russian Extraordinary Commission, [1922] I *Sobranie Uzakonenii i Rasporiazhenii Rabochego i Krest'ianskogo Pravitel'stva RSFSR*, No. 4, item 42.

[2] Decree on the Abolition of the All-Russian Extraordinary Commission and on the Rules for Conducting Searches, Seizures, and Arrests, *ibid.*, No. 16, item 160.

week Kurskii's journal published his explanation of the tasks placed upon the Commissariat of Justice by the transfer to its agencies of the former court functions of the Cheka.[3]

Kurskii noted that the former chief of the Cheka, Latsis, had defined his agency in 1921 as "not being an investigating commission, nor a court, nor a tribunal, but a battle agency acting on the domestic front in the civil war and using in its struggle methods of investigating commissions, of courts, of tribunals and of armed forces." Kurskii thought that this description proved that the Cheka had exercised the functions of a court even though this was denied in the opening phrase. Kurskii believed that the new policy required that all future violations of law be tried either by a court or a revolutionary tribunal, depending upon the character of the violation.

The transfer to the courts of the cases formerly tried by the Cheka was expected nearly to break the back of the courts, according to an article by Kurskii's colleague Lisitsyn in the same issue of the law review.[4] The author reminded his readers that the decree had required the Cheka to deliver to the courts and to the revolutionary tribunals within two weeks all pending cases involving "speculation, crimes by officials, etc." The newly created G.P.U. was to limit its activities to apprehending those committing counterrevolutionary acts, banditry, espionage, theft from railroads and waterways, smuggling and crossing of the frontier without permission. Procedural limitations were created on the G.P.U. It was to inform the accused within two weeks of the charges against him and to take the case to court within two months or ask for continuance from the Presidium of the Central Executive Committee to permit further investigation.

The Moscow Cheka is reported to have proposed to the Moscow Council of People's Judges to accept immediately all cases in process before Cheka tribunals, regardless of the state of investigation. The Council of People's Judges is said to have faced the dilemma of refusing the cases or of overloading itself to the point at which its regular work would have been disorganized. Lisitsyn suggested that agreement should be reached between the Cheka

[3] D. Kurskii, "Reorganizatsiia organov chresvychainoi repressii i zadachi NKIu," *Ezhenedel'nik sovetskoi iustitsii*, No. 7 (February 12, 1922), p. 2.
[4] A. Lisitsyn, "K uprazdneniiu VChK," *ibid.*, pp. 2–3.

in each province and the departments of justice of each provincial soviet as to which cases should be discontinued, and which should be carried through the stage of investigation by the Cheka and turned over in completed form to the courts and the revolutionary tribunals for trial. It was admitted that the new functions placed upon the courts and revolutionary tribunals would require increasing their number and their "quality."

The demand for improved quality of the courts appears to present a lesson for a study of the means of settling disputes between citizens. The work of the Cheka had been the preservation of state power through terror and the quick destruction of opposition to the regime. The Cheka had not had great influence upon the people's courts except as it had fostered a spirit of intolerance in the community generally. For this reason the Cheka has not been discussed in this study. Yet at this point in the history of the progress of events in 1922 the impact of the abolition of the Cheka upon the work of the courts settling disputes between citizens becomes important. To absorb the political responsibilities formerly performed by the Cheka, the courts were asked to improve their quality. The word "quality" seems to have meant at this time thorough grounding in political concepts and class consciousness as well as somewhat greater educational achievement generally. With each step in the direction of general education and political responsibility the courts moved one step away from the people, for the people lacked both of these qualities. With each step the courts reduced their popular character.

Kurskii was, apparently, cognizant of his problem. Strengthening the courts as politically conscious and learned institutions meant sacrifice of popularity. He took steps which seem to have been directed to countering the trend by giving the courts jurisdiction over a greater number of popular problems. He spoke out against continuing the jurisdiction of administrative boards under the jurisdiction of the People's Commissariat of Internal Affairs to administer fines for small offenses. He wanted this work done by the courts.[5] He demanded that an end be put to the practice of administrative agencies which had been interfering in relationships

[5] D. I. Kurskii, "Ugolovnyi kodeks 1922 goda," in *Izbrannye stat'i i rechi* (Moscow, 1926), p. 86.

having a purely property nature.[6] He felt that the draft for the new civil code eliminated this interference by placing all disputes of a civil-law character in the courts.

The multitudinous disputes over land usage, which had been decided up to that time by a board in the land department of each local soviet, were suggested as suitable for decision by courts instead of the local soviets.[7] Likewise the multitudinous disputes over the right to housing space, which had been handled by the communal economy department of each municipal soviet, were to be transferred to courts.[8] Both types of dispute related closely to the lives of the people, one group concerning the peasants and the other group the urban workmen. By putting jurisdiction of such disputes in the courts, the masses and the judges could not but be brought closer together, to what must have appeared to Kurskii and his colleagues their mutual advantage.

Another step toward popularization of the courts was a suggestion that the trade-union disciplinary tribunals be abolished with transfer of jurisdiction to the courts.[9] The courts had been active up to that time in prosecutions of factory managers and owners for violation of labor law, but disciplining the workers had been the task of the union's disciplinary tribunals. These tribunals had been permitted to reprimand, to deprive of electoral rights, to suspend, to dismiss, and even to commit to a concentration camp. The tribunals are said to have enlarged their jurisdiction in practice so that they had become in fact a special criminal court. Sometimes they had assumed civil jurisdiction as well. Most of their cases involved thefts, but they also tried charges of misuse of authority by supervisors, personal insult to supervisors, and sabotage. They had been brought under supervision of the council of people's judges in each province by decree of April 5, 1921, placing a representative of the council in all provincial meetings of members of the labor disciplinary tribunals. The Commissariat of Justice had also sought to supervise their activities, for it had ordered its local agencies to participate

[6] *Ibid.*, p. 97.
[7] "Doklad t. Lisitsyna o poriadke rassmotreniia zemel'nykh i zhilishchnykh del," *Ezh. sov. iust.*, No. 6 (February 5, 1922), p. 11.
[8] *Ibid.*
[9] D. Rodin, "Rabochie professional'nye ditsiplinarnye tovarishcheskie sudy (k ikh uprazdneniiu)," *Pravo i zhizn'*, No. 1 (June, 1922), p. 40.

in the organization of the disciplinary tribunals by a circular of April 14, 1921.

The trade unions had subsequently taken the initiative in amalgamating the work of the tribunals with the courts, but presumably after Communist party consideration of the problem. By resolution of February 28, 1922, the All-Russian Central Council of Trade Unions had declared it expedient to abolish the tribunals, and a request that this be done had been transmitted to the Council of People's Commissars and the Central Executive Committee. One more avenue through which the courts could be brought close to the problems of the masses had been opened, and one more competitor with the courts as an agency for settling disputes had been eliminated.

PRESENTING THE DRAFT
JUDICIARY ACT

Krylenko was charged with the task of presenting to the fourth session of the Central Executive Committee of the Russian Republic the draft prepared by the Commissariat of Justice to effect the changes recommended in the court structure of the Republic.[10] In the months since the January meeting of persons engaged in the administration of justice, the way had been prepared for statutory enactment of the changes that had been recommended, but the draft was not identical with the plan approved by the January meeting. The most noticeable change from the January plan was the proposed elimination of the general revolutionary tribunals.

There was to be retained the highly specialized military tribunal for offenses affecting the strength of the army and the tribunal before which charges of offenses against transportation were tried, but the debate as to the desirability of incorporating all revolutionary tribunals into the general court system seems to have been resolved in a compromise. The solution fell between Krylenko's demand for complete incorporation of all revolutionary tribunals and Kurskii's demand that the general courts remain unburdened

---

[10] For text of draft, see *Ezh. sov. iust.*, No. 34 (September 16, 1922), pp. 17–20; and *ibid.*, No. 36.

with the political responsibilities which would be thrust upon them if amalgamation were to occur. The proposed draft indicated that there was to be partial amalgamation. This proposal brought closer the unified court system of which the leaders had always spoken, but it was not a complete victory for the unifiers.

The draftsmen showed themselves desirous of continuing their policy of pretending that the court system was a unitary one, even though it was not. As they had done in the 1920 act, they again sought to emphasize the unitary feature by opening the 1922 act with an article declaring that there would function upon the territory of the R.S.F.S.R. a "unitary system of judicial institutions," composed of a people's court with a single professional judge, a people's court with a professional judge and two lay judges, a provincial court, and a Supreme Court of the Republic. The draft proceeded to establish additional courts, however, although nothing was said in the preamble of the draft to call attention to these exceptions to the unitary system or to explain why they were necessary. This omission aroused Krylenko, perhaps because he thought that if attention were called in the preamble to the existence of the exceptional courts, they might eventually be amalgamated in the general court system because of the embarrassing conflict with basic principle which they presented.

To effect his plan, if his actions can be taken as evidence of such a plan, Krylenko introduced on the floor of the fourth session of the Central Executive Committee at its sitting of October 31, 1922, a proposal to incorporate a new Article Two in the draft.[11] In this article he wanted to declare why there existed special courts alongside the system of people's courts. With what appears to have been tongue in cheek, Krylenko said: "In order to escape somehow from the proposition that the unity of our system is being violated in some manner, it is necessary to introduce a second article." The article disclosed the complexity which was to be found in the court system in spite of the simple declaration of unity appearing in Article One. It read:

In order to try cases of special categories, in view of the special complexity of such cases and of the necessity of special knowledge and ex-

[11] RSFSR—IV sessiia Vserossiiskogo Tsentral'nogo Ispolnitel'nogo Komiteta, IX sozyva, 23–31 oktiabria 1922 g. (Stenograficheskii otchët), biulleten' No. 8, 1 noiab. 1922 g. (Moscow, 1922), p. 1.

perience for their review, and in consideration of the special danger of certain categories of criminal actions for the military strength of the Republic or for its economic prosperity, there shall exist temporarily alongside the unitary system of people's courts of the R.S.F.S.R. the following special courts: (a) military tribunals for cases involving crimes endangering the strength and might of the Red Army, (b) military-transport tribunals for cases of especially serious crimes endangering transportation, (c) special labor sessions of the people's courts for cases concerning crimes arising out of violation of the code of labor law, (d) land commissions for land cases, (e) a central and local arbitration commission organized under the Council of Labor and Defense and under the provincial economic councils for cases involving disputes over property rights between state agencies.

Krylenko had, apparently, obtained the prior consent of the legislative commission to his proposed amendment. This commission had been formally appointed on the opening day of the session on October 23, 1922. It included the prior Commissar of Justice, Stuchka, and Kurskii as the Commissar of the time as well as Krylenko, Milyutin, Sosnovskii, Dagodov, Krol', Antonov-Ovsenko, Ozol, Sol'ts, Narimanov, Samur'skii, and Riazanov.[12] In his speech in presentation of the draft judiciary act just prior to the appointment of the commission, Krylenko had not emphasized the presence in the Act of provisions creating a varied court system. On the contrary he had opened his remarks by emphasizing that the draft introduced in place of the existing two systems of courts a single system of courts "outside of which there may not be, at least there ought not to be, any other judicial agencies." [13]

In the final moments of his speech, Krylenko declared his antagonism to the special courts by saying:

The inadequacy of the system, with which we must struggle, is that there is fitted into it such commissariat courts as the military and transport courts, even though in reduced numbers, but constructed on different principles, on the principles of our old tribunal structure, that is, without lay judges. This is a screaming defect in that it pulls down the whole system. Yet there is no other way practically to handle the problem.

He then explained the necessity of an apparatus "which would be sufficiently elastic to execute the shock task which would probably

[12] *Ibid., biulleten' No. 1*, p. 30.
[13] *Ibid.*, p. 23. The speech was rewritten and published as an article later. See N. Krylenko, "Reforma sudoustroistva," *Ezh. sov. iust.*, No. 37–38 (October 13–20, 1922), pp. 1–5.

be presented in the immediate future." He expressed the hope that
it would be possible soon to remedy this defect. He found reason
to praise the new system over the old because it provided at least
centralization and leadership through which it would be possible
to establish a single line of policy and abolish the dualism which
had existed up to that time in the judicial institutions.

THE NEW GENERAL COURTS

The experience of the preceding five years was reflected in the
general court system established by the 1922 judiciary act.[14] There
were to be several levels of courts in each of which cases might be
tried. Only the cases concerned with simple matters and involving
private disputes rather than the community as a whole were to be
heard by the people's court constructed along lines which had
become familiar to all, namely, with a bench of one professional
judge and two lay judges.

The cases of greater public importance in that they involved interests of the general public although not the very life of the regime
itself were to be tried by a less popular form of court devoid of
lay judges. While it was called in the judiciary act a "people's court,"
it could have been said that it was something else because the
bench was occupied by no one except the professional people's
judge. This form of court was not entirely new to the Soviet system.
There had been authority since 1918 in the people's judge sitting
alone to consider cases in which the court was needed as little more
than a registration bureau. In 1918 a single professional judge had
been permitted to record divorce and to register facts such as
family relationship when the action involved no contest. In July,
1922, the authority of the single judge had been expanded by the
newly adopted Code of Criminal Procedure of the Russian Republic[15] to include jurisdiction over moderately serious criminal
cases. The judiciary act of October 31, 1922, put this expanded jurisdiction in the statute relating to court structure. An additional crime

[14] Judiciary Act, RSFSR, October 31, 1922, [1922] I *Sob. Uzak. RSFSR*, No.
69, item 902.
[15] Code of Criminal Procedure, RSFSR, effective July 1, 1922, [1922] I
Sob. Uzak. RSFSR, No. 20–21, item 230, Art. 26.

was added soon after to the scope of the single judge's authority.[16]

Jurisdiction of the judge sitting alone extended to cases involving resistance to military service by committing injury to one's body or by forging documents or by bribing officials or by changing one's name or by using religious conviction as a pretext or by using any other artifice, buying up of commodities in which trade was limited or forbidden, and actions falling within the general classification of the Criminal Code as crimes involving the protection of health, safety, and public order.[17] This latter category was defined by the Criminal Code as the preparation of poisons, the failure to inform officials of the illness or death of cattle, violation of health regulations in the construction of buildings, violation of regulations concerning the movement of transportation, violation of the commands given by local police when issued to protect the public, the possession of firearms, violation of the rules requiring the protection of workmen from moving parts of machines, residing under documents belonging to another person, departure without permission from an abode in which residence was required by an administrative or court order, violation of the laws on the reproduction and distribution of printed items, violation of the laws on the use of print shops and lithographing, failure to make the required reports on the work of cooperative or private enterprises, public violation by religious groups in conduct of their ceremonies and of the freedom of movement of their fellow citizens.

The idea of including within the hierarchy of general courts a more learned and experienced court to try the criminal cases endangering the very life of the regime as well as the more complicated civil cases was carried into the new act in a form reminiscent of the "special sessions" established in the summer of 1920. The new, more experienced court was to be called the "provincial court." Its jurisdiction was not established by the judiciary act but was to be found in the codes of procedure. Since the Code of Criminal Procedure which had been enacted shortly before the

---

[16] This was done in the 1923 revision of the Code of Criminal Procedure, RSFSR, February 15, 1923, Art. 25, [1923] I *Sob. Uzak. RSFSR*, No. 7, item 106.

[17] Code of Criminal Procedure, RSFSR (1922), Art. 26. In the 1923 revision it became Art. 25.

judiciary act had not anticipated the creation of a provincial court, the definition of its jurisdiction had to wait until a revision of the code in 1923, at which time a Code of Civil Procedure was also enacted.

Jurisdiction of the provincial court when it was finally defined by the procedural codes was rather similar to that of the old "special sessions" and of the revolutionary tribunals. It was to try criminal cases[18] involving state crimes, instigation of religious prejudice of the masses for the purpose of overthrowing the new government, actions designed to prevent the proper functioning of the administrative apparatus of the state as defined in Chapter 1, Part 2, of the Criminal Code (with a few exceptions), criminal activities of state officials as defined in Chapter 2 of the Criminal Code (with a few exceptions), and a few "economic crimes" (defined as failure to maintain in good condition state property entrusted to one's care, failure to perform a contract concluded with a state agency), intentional or negligent killing, encouragement to suicide of a minor or one unable to understand the meaning of his actions, unlawful restraint of a person by means dangerous to life or health, or the commitment to a hospital for mental illness of a healthy person for reasons of a personal character, sexual relations with minors, theft of state property, armed robbery or the use of physical or psychological force in a robbery, and intentional damage to property by fire or flooding or by other means dangerous to the public.

The civil cases reserved for the jurisdiction of the new provincial courts were defined[19] as those in which the amount of the claim exceeded 500 gold rubles, suits against a state agency or state official for damages caused by illegal or improper acts performed in the course of their duties and suits for the return of property which had been improperly converted, suits against a county executive committee or against a city soviet in a city of the county, if brought against the organization as a whole rather than against individual members, and suits arising out of partnership agreements, copyright, patent, trade marks, firm names or protected industrial patterns.

---

[18] Code of Criminal Procedure, RSFSR (1922), Art. 26.
[19] Code of Civil Procedure, RSFSR, July 7, 1923, Art. 23, [1923] I *Sob. Uzak. RSFSR*, No. 46–47, item 478.

Civil actions were to be brought before the provincial court if they concerned a request to be excused from military service because of religious beliefs[20] or in protest against the state notary because of action or failure to act or because of delays in the state notary's office.[21]

The new provincial courts were at greater distance from the masses than the people's courts, but they retained a link. They were to have lay judges on the bench with the professional judge. For a time in the discussion of the character of the provincial court, it had been debated whether there should be lay judges at all. Krylenko reported to his listeners in the Central Executive Committee[22] that a whole series of disputes among the draftsmen had been occasioned by discussion of the form of the provincial court when sitting as a court of original jurisdiction. In the provincial revolutionary tribunals which were being supplanted by the new court, there had been no lay judges. In the council of people's judges which was also being supplanted there had been lay judges. The new provincial tribunal in assuming duties from both sources might have adopted either system.

The decision was finally made to place lay judges upon the bench of the provincial court when it tried cases as a court of original jurisdiction. In Krylenko's words the decision was dictated by two desires: to maintain the unity of the entire court system by patterning both courts of original jurisdiction upon the same arrangement, and to carry out the Communist party's program of 1919 which had called for the attraction of the largest number of people possible into the judicial process.

Lest his listeners lose sight of the fact that the considerable attention given in his speech to the new provincial court did not suggest the eclipse of the simpler people's court, Krylenko declared that most of the cases would be tried by the people's court and not by the provincial court. He cited in proof of that fact the statistics which showed that 92 percent of all cases in courts of original jurisdiction were being tried by the people's courts at the time.[23] The people's courts were, therefore, the courts with which the bulk of the people would be dealing in the settling of their disputes.

[20] *Ibid.*, Arts. 226–30.   [21] *Ibid.*, Arts. 231–34.
[22] *RSFSR—IV sessiia VTsIK, biulleten' No. 1*, p. 27.
[23] *Ibid.*, p. 26.

THE NEW JUDGES

The qualifications to be required of judges had worried Krylenko at the January conference when he had proposed an amalgamation of the general courts and the revolutionary tribunals. He could not imagine that the judges in the general courts, at least at the lowest level, could be expected to be educated politically sufficiently to escape local influences and sentimentality in deciding cases of political concern to the regime. He had urged his co-workers to consider an improvement in the quality of judges, both professional and lay, in the new courts which he was proposing.

The improvement in quality of judges remained a matter of concern to Krylenko in October as evidenced by his speech to the Central Executive Committee. He declared that matters of the greatest political importance were the qualifications to be required of a people's judge, the manner of selection and recall, the agency to which the judges were to be responsible, and the routine to be used in selecting lay judges. He declared frankly to his listeners that experience had shown that not all citizens were qualified to be people's judges, especially at the time when civil law relationships were being revived.[24]

To assure the selection of acceptable persons as judges the draft had been prepared, Krylenko said, to permit only those having the right to vote to be chosen. This could assure the elimination of nonproletarian elements. This had been the rule of the 1920 act, but Krylenko made it sound like an innovation. Further, professional qualifications were to be assured by a new requirement that the candidate for the bench must have had not less than two years of responsible work in a state, public, professional, or Communist party position, or he must have served for at least three years as a people's judge. Existing cadres of judges would be screened against these requirements. The 1920 act had also required experience of the type prescribed by the 1922 draft, but it had set no minimum duration for such experience.

The professional people's judges were to be appointed by the provincial executive committees for a term of one year on the

[24] *Ibid.*, p. 24.

nomination of the provincial court or of the People's Commissariat of Justice. There was to be no limit on reappointment. A judge might be removed before the expiration of his term by the appointing authority with notification of the reasons to the People's Commissar of Justice in person. Krylenko said that he felt confident that if a provincial executive committee refused to remove a judge in whom the Commissar of Justice had lost confidence, there would always be a place to which the Commissar might appeal, but except for such circumstances the recall power should be in the same agency to which the appointing power had been given. Krylenko made it clear that recall might occur for reasons having nothing to do with any crime committed by the judge. If there were crime, there was to be a trial. A convicted judge would not remain qualified for reappointment at any time to the bench, whereas a recalled judge might be reappointed if the circumstances warranted.

By these provisions on the appointment and recall of judges, it became clear that the policy makers of the Commissariat of Justice had found it desirable to depart completely from the principle of the framers of the fundamentals which had existed since 1917, with the slight limitations established in the summer of 1920.

The officials of 1922 concluded, apparently, that judges were never again to be the creatures of the local soviets, appointed and recalled solely by them. The system of 1920 under which the county and city soviets appointed judges subject to veto by the provincial executive committee seemed, apparently, too risky for those now making policy. Judges under the 1922 procedure were to be subject to the control of the central authorities in Moscow, although for purposes of convenience in administration, or perhaps to placate those who still dreamed of the advantages of local autonomy, they were in the ordinary course to be appointed and recalled by provincial authorities. These provincial authorities were by no means as close to the people as were the local soviets which had held the appointing power under the 1920 act, but they were only half-way up to the central authorities. As such they may still have retained some of the aura of the local communities for those who disliked complete centralization. A provincial capital such as Novosibirsk must have seemed to many Siberians much closer both geographically and sentimentally to their problems than Moscow.

The supervision of the people's judges which had been provided up to that time by the councils of people's judges in each province was declared by Krylenko to have proved itself inadequate. His disapproval of the existing system was laid to the fact that the various councils of people's judges were not themselves under any central authority. With the abolition of the provincial councils of people's judges contemplated in the 1922 act and the creation of new provincial courts, to which reference has already been made, an opening developed, in Krylenko's opinion, for supervision by these courts. Supervision was to include "review, inspection, instruction, financial and statistical accounting, and appellate jurisdiction over all of their decisions." In Krylenko's words, there was thus created "a strong fist, a judicial center." [25] It was to be far more all-embracing in its authority over the local people's courts than had been the department of justice of the provincial soviet up to that time, which had been sharing with the provincial council of judges authority over the local courts to the confusion of all because of the lack of precise limits on the jurisdiction of each of the two supervising agencies.

The qualifications to be demanded of the lay judges gave Krylenko further trouble. In 1920, when the matter had been the subject of major discussion, the decision had been taken to open the panels from which lay judges were to be drawn to all citizens. Only in the "special sessions" of the people's courts with their jurisdiction over complex cases were the panels restricted to those who had evidenced in practice that they understood their political role. In the face of strong opposition against a broad base for the lay-judge system, the officials of the Commissariat had nevertheless chosen to support a system which would give to the rank and file an important part in the judicial process.

Krylenko was prepared to reverse the policy established in 1920. No all-inclusive lay-judge system found favor with him. He declared to the Central Executive Committee that the problem of struggling with the illegal distilling of liquor remained a serious problem to the regime, and yet the average lay judge refused to treat it as a serious crime. If it was a serious crime in the eyes of the policy makers, he said, then it was not immaterial who could serve as a

[25] *Ibid.*, p. 25.

lay judge. Krylenko pointed with pride to a provision of the draft that lay judges would have to be drawn from the population in accordance with a new formula: 50 percent from working-class circles, 25 percent from the armed services, and 25 percent from representatives of the villages, namely, the peasants. He said nothing of the retention in the draft of the 1920 formula that all citizens of either sex having the right to vote might serve as a lay judge. He seems to have assumed that the quota system described in a subsequent article of the draft made statement of the general principle as unimportant as statement of the general principle that the court system remained a unitary one.

The selection of lay judges within the designated quotas was to be made from panels to be prepared in each county seat by an allotment commission composed of a member of the county soviet's executive committee, the deputy provincial prosecutor, and two people's judges of the county to be chosen as the most seasoned and firm. The committee was to obtain the names for its panel by setting quotas for each category of lay judges at the rate of two hundred persons to serve during the year in each of the people's courts of the county and asking the factory committee of the trade unions and the headquarters of trade unions comprising persons not engaged in factories, to prepare a list to meet the quota assigned. The lists were then to be posted, and any citizen had the right to protest the inclusion of a name within a limited time. The county commission would also have the right to exclude any name that seemed undesirable to it. Krylenko thought that the system would assure stable courts.

Krylenko's plan suffered in some degree in the legislative committee of the Central Executive Committee. When the draft finally emerged as law, the changes were disclosed as a reduction in the allotment committee's size by requiring the inclusion of only one local judge instead of two, and the addition to the list of the agencies to be asked to prepare the lists for the allotment committee of the people's courts of the county, the military commander of the local troops, and the village executive committees of the county.[26] The most important amendment was a change in the formula for selecting class groups. While the working-class group was to remain

[26] Judiciary Act, RSFSR, Arts, 19–21.

at 50 percent of the total on the panel, the peasants were increased in importance to receive 35 percent of the places, while the armed services were reduced to 15 percent to make room for the increase in the peasant representatives. Perhaps Krylenko and his colleagues had not counted on the continuing strength of the peasant deputies in the Central Executive Committee.

Both professional and lay judges in the provincial courts were to be required to meet higher qualifications than those set for the judges in the people's courts. The professional judges at the provincial level were to include the president, two deputy presidents (one for civil cases and one for criminal cases), and twelve other judges. The president and his deputies had to meet the minimum requirements of a candidate for people's judge plus service for at least three years as a people's judge or as a member of a revolutionary tribunal. To provide some flexibility, the Commissariat of Justice was authorized to make exceptions.

Professional judges were named by the provincial executive committee for one-year terms, subject to a veto in the Commissariat of Justice. The latter might also propose its candidates. Judges could be recalled by the provincial soviet's executive committee before the expiration of their term, but never without the consent of the Commissariat of Justice, unless they had been convicted by a court or disciplined by action in the Supreme Court of the Republic. If the provincial soviet's executive committee refused to replace a candidate for president or deputy president vetoed by the Commissariat, the latter could seat its substitute without action of the provincial executive committee.

Lay judges in the provincial courts were to be chosen from a panel of names prepared at the request of the provincial court by a committee to be composed of a representative named by the provincial soviet's executive committee, two judges of the provincial court, the provincial prosecutor, and three members of the provincial council of trade unions. Each provincial court was to be provided with a panel of 200 names, not more than 175 of whom had served for not less than two years in public and trade-union organizations, and at least 25 of whom were people's judges. These people's judges were to serve in the capacity of lay judges for civil cases which were brought before the provincial court. Both criminal and civil benches when trying cases as a court of original jurisdiction were to be composed of one professional judge and two lay judges. When sitting as a court of appeal from decisions of the people's courts, the bench was to be composed of three professional judges.

Krylenko noted that the provincial courts would also have a disciplinary bench of three judges to maintain in the decisions of the people's courts the line of the central Soviet authorities.[27] This seemed necessary, in Krylenko's opinion, especially in housing matters or in suits to recover property. He felt it necessary to make certain that no judge issue a decision which might be formally correct but which would in substance violate the spirit of Soviet policy. Apparently, to Krylenko it was important not only to reverse such undesirable decision but to discipline the judge concerned so that he would not repeat his error.

The fifteen professional provincial judges were to sit together as a "plenum" to consider recommendations to the highest legislative authorities of the Republic as to desirable orders to be issued on the interpretation of the law or as to changes in the law itself. Krylenko pointed out that this was a new right and that it was limited to matters raised by concrete cases. It could not be exercised in general terms but had to be tied to a matter raised in a specific instance.

THE SPECIALIZED COURTS

The specialized courts provided for in the judiciary act of 1922 were not discussed in detail by Krylenko in his speech to the Central Executive Committee. Judging by his derogatory remarks about the violation of the unitary court system created by their existence, he was not happy about them and considered them to be temporary bodies soon to become unnecessary. He hailed the proposed reduction in the number of them and the subordination of all to the Supreme Court.[28]

One of the specialized courts was really only a variation of the people's court. This was the "labor session" of the people's court. Under provisions of the act[29] the "labor session" was to be attached to the provincial court and to be composed of one professional judge

---

[27] *RSFSR—IV sessiia VTsIK, biulleten' No. 1*, p. 28.
[28] *Ibid.*, p. 29.   [29] Judiciary Act, RSFSR, Art. 92.

and two permanent lay judges, one to be named by the provincial council of trade unions and one by the department of labor of the provincial soviet's executive committee. The court was ordered to operate in accordance with the usual rules for the people's courts. Its professional judge was to be named and recalled in the same manner as the nonspecialized professional judges.[30] Its jurisdiction was over all violations of the Code of Labor Laws, and its decisions were appealable to the provincial court in accordance with the rules applying to appeals from the nonspecialized people's courts. Its affairs were subject to supervision by the provincial court in the usual manner.

It will be seen that its unique character was confined to the fact that it was to specialize in a single type of case, and its lay judges did not rotate at very brief intervals as was the rule for the regular lay judges in the people's court but sat permanently, one representing labor and the other that department of the state administrative apparatus which had to do with labor matters.

The military and military-transport courts were to operate under the control and supervision of the Commissariat of Justice and the Supreme Court of the Republic.[31] The Supreme Court was charged with the task of organizing these courts. The military courts were to be organized at three levels, in military districts or on fronts, in army corps, and at the division level. The military-transport courts were to be established in the cities of Moscow, Petrograd, Kharkov, Rostov-on-Don, Omsk, Tashkent, and Smolensk. This listing of cities constituted a reduction in their number from the previously existing situation.

The personnel of the military court was to be composed at each level of a president, his deputy, and four members. These were named at all levels by the Supreme Court's military college from a list of candidates prepared by the military council for the district or front, or by the commanding officers. Consent for the military college of the Supreme Court to designate judges at the top level had to be given by the "Revolutionary Military Council of the Republic."

The judges of the military-transport court were also to be composed of a president, a deputy, and four members nominated by the Peoples' Commissariat of Means of Communication to the Supreme

---

[30] *Ibid.*, Art. 93.   [31] *Ibid.*, Arts. 85–91.

Court's military-transport college and named by the latter with the consent of the Commissariat.

Judges in both types of military court were subject to discipline by the Supreme Court, and to removal at any time on advice by the Supreme Court to the appropriate military revolutionary committee or the People's Commissariat of Means of Communications.

No lay judges were to sit either in the military courts or in the military-transport courts. The absence of lay judges in these courts displeased Krylenko. He said it was a defect which pulled down the whole system, but there was no escaping it under conditions of the time. It was a defect which also displeased the historian of the first six years' experience with the court system when he wrote in 1923.[32] He felt one year after the reform that the omission of lay judges had been a serious breach in the principle established for the general courts, even for the provincial courts. He noted that both the military and the military-transport courts had jurisdiction over civilians. The military courts were given jurisdiction not only over men in uniform, but also over civilians who committed the crimes of espionage, refusal to appear for military service when called, ill-intentioned refusal to perform a contract with the state, and systematic theft from state warehouses, when these crimes endangered the strength of the army.[33] The military-transport courts had jurisdiction over any act linked with violation of the rules for the proper operation of rail and water transportation.[34] Both types of cases were no more important than those placed within the jurisdiction of the provincial court, and yet the bench in the provincial court when sitting as a court of original jurisdiction had to include lay judges.

The military courts seemed to the historian to require special thought because military problems were special, but he believed that in peacetime, at least, a way could be found to choose lay judges under some exceptional method which would take into consideration the military considerations involved. For the transport courts, which seemed to him to be only a specialized form of the provincial court, he found no reason whatever for excluding lay judges if they could

[32] See Ia. L. Berman, *Ocherki po istorii sudoustroistva RSFSR s predisloviem N. V. Krylenko* (Moscow, 1924), pp. 64–65.
[33] Code of Criminal Procedure, RSFSR (1923), Art. 27.
[34] *Ibid.*, Art. 28.

be permitted to sit in the provincial courts. The historian explained the absence of lay judges on the ground that there was unnecessary fear of and lack of confidence in the institution of the lay judge.

The "land commissions" to decide disputes over the use of the land,[35] and the "arbitration commissions" to hear disputes between state agencies in the commercial field [36] had already been established by separate decrees enacted before the judiciary act was brought forward for discussion. The judiciary act incorporated these decrees by reference,[37] but provided further that each system would be subject to supervision by the People's Commissariat of Justice, the Supreme Court, and the Prosecutor of the Republic, and at the local level by the provincial court and the provincial prosecutor.

The arbitration commissions are beyond the scope of this study since they dealt with disputes between state agencies and were of no direct concern to the individual, although reference will be made to them again in consideration of a unified civil procedure, but the land commissions concerned closely the citizen. Under their special statute the land commissions emerged as a three-step system to decide all manner of disputes over the use of the land. Their jurisdiction was extended to claims by groups or by individuals, and concerned boundaries, deprivation of the right to use in the circumstances provided by law, appropriation of use for purposes of highways and improvements, and also disputes within families over the division of land use when the family separated into its component parts.

The concept of a divided system in which there was a court close to the people to hear their personal disputes, and another court one or two stages removed from the people for disputes in which a state agency was concerned found reflection in the land commissions as it had in the court structure of 1922. Commissions were to be organized in each volost, or group of villages, under the control of the executive committee of the volost soviet. The next higher level was to be at the county level, and then there was to be also a land commission

[35] Order on the Procedure for Hearing Land Disputes, May 24, 1922, [1922] I *Sob. Uzak. RSFSR*, No. 36, item 428.
[36] Statute on the Procedure for Deciding Property Disputes between State Offices and Enterprises, September 21, 1922, *ibid.*, No. 60, item 769.
[37] Judiciary Act, RSFSR, Art. 94.

in the province. Each was to be organized by the executive committee of the soviet at the level concerned and to be held responsible to the same executive committee.

The volost land commission was given jurisdiction over all conflicts within the group of villages constituting the volost when the dispute concerned the use of land by the villages themselves, or by associations of peasants, or by individual peasants. The county land commissions had jurisdiction over conflicts between volosts over the use of the land and over conflicts in which a state farm, a collective farm, a state enterprise, or a state office was a party. The provincial land commission was to hear disputes between counties over the use of the land, and all disputes between a local community and a state enterprise or office of national importance if the dispute arose out of the regulations concerning the use of the land.

Appeals lay to the county land commission from the decisions of the volost land commissions, and to the provincial land commission from decisions of the county commissions. Rules of procedure for trials were to be the same as those in effect in the people's courts. Parties were to be permitted to have the aid of an attorney. The members of the land commissions were to enjoy the same rights as people's judges.

Members of the land commissions at the volost level were to be a president, chosen from the membership of the executive committee of the volost soviet and two other members, one elected by the volost soviet and the other named by the volost committee of poor peasants. All members had to be approved by the executive committee of the county soviet. At the county and provincial levels the members were to be a president named by the county or provincial soviet's executive committee and two other members, one of whom was to be the deputy chief of the county or province soviet's land distribution department and the other a judge of the people's court.

THE SUPREME COURT OF THE REPUBLIC

The pinnacle of the court hierarchy was to be occupied by a new Supreme Court of the Republic.[38] For some years there had been a supreme revolutionary tribunal which had controlled all the revolu-

---

[38] *Ibid.*, Part III.

tionary tribunals, and since March, 1921, there had been a department within the Commissariat of Justice which had supervised the work of the general courts under the title of "supreme court control." This department had not been conceived as a supreme appellate court, but rather as a control point through which uniformity in the work of the courts might be established by a sampling process. In practice, as has been indicated by a review of the cases, the department became a supreme appellate tribunal, accepting appeals from below.

Krylenko explained [39] to the Central Executive Committee that the new Supreme Court of the Republic would combine the work of the supreme revolutionary tribunal and of the department of supreme court control of the Commissariat of Justice, as the latter had come to operate. In short, it would be a supreme appellate tribunal, but with additional powers. It would also set aside decisions of any court on its own initiative. It would discipline judges in the lower courts. It would issue rulings interpreting the codes. It would even try cases of an unusually important character as a court of original jurisdiction. It would not, however, gather statistics on the work of the courts, nor inspect the courts, nor remove judges, for these and other administrative functions relating to the business of running the courts would remain with the Commissariat of Justice.

Unlike the Supreme Court of some lands, including the United States, the Russian Republic's Supreme Court would be organized in colleges, specializing in the various types of cases coming before the court. It would have appellate colleges for civil and criminal cases coming up from the provincial courts, as well as colleges specializing in the affairs of the military courts, and the military-transport courts, colleges for the trial of cases as a court of original jurisdiction, and a college for disciplining judges. Cases would be heard by benches of three professional judges chosen from the appropriate college. There were to be no lay judges within the Supreme Court structure.

All thirty judges of the new Supreme Court of the Republic would meet together as a "plenum" to issue rulings on interpretation

[39] *RSFSR—IV sessiia VTsIK biulleten'* No. 1, p. 28.

of the codes. Krylenko declared that there was no desire to reestablish the powerful supreme court of the Russian Empire, known as the "senate" with its authority to interpret any law whatever. The new Supreme Court was to be limited in its right of interpretation to the codes of substantive law and of procedure alone.[40]

To assure close relationship between the new Supreme Court and the Commissariat of Justice, there was established the requirement that the Prosecutor of the Republic, who functioned within the Commissariat at the time, be present at plenary meetings of the Supreme Court. In Krylenko's words, this would assure that "the link between actual court practice and the policy to be followed by the court would in reality be the closest possible." No principle of separation of powers between judiciary and executive could be permitted to mar the progress of the plans of the Communist party leadership which was focusing its attention at the time on the executive aparatus. If the Prosecutor of the Republic disagreed with a decision of the plenary session of the Supreme Court, he could take the matter to the Central Executive Committee as the highest authority on the policy to be applied by the courts.

To organize and conduct the affairs of the body of judges, there was established in the new Supreme Court an executive committee, called a "presidium." Its members were the president, the deputy president, and the chief of each college within the court. The concept was later to be introduced into the provincial courts as well, with the result that the administration of affairs and ultimately policy making for courts above the level of the people's courts were concentrated in a small number of judges to the exclusion of the rank and file of the bench.

There was marked by the introduction of the "presidium" system another departure from the concept of the early days when the council of people's judges, which had been the sole court of appeal at the time, had been composed of the judges of the judicial district without differentiation as to gradation of political reliability. While it was possible to argue that efficiency required an administrative committee within each court, the fact of concentration of power cannot be overlooked. It required less effort to direct the policy of a

[40] *Ibid.*, p. 29.

court with such an administrative committee than would have been required to convince a large group composed of all judges of the various colleges.

Members of the Supreme Court were to be named by the Presidium of the Central Executive Committee. The president, the deputy president, and the presiding judges of the civil and criminal colleges and of the military and military-transport colleges were to be named by the Presidium of the Central Executive Committee on its own initiative. The members of the military college would be nominated by the Revolutionary Military Council of the Republic, while the members of the military-transport college would be nominated by the People's Commissariat of Means of Communication. All other judges would be nominated to the Presidium of the Central Executive Committee by the People's Commissariat of Justice. Only the appointing authority could dismiss any of the judges.

The procedure for appointing judges to the Supreme Court of the Republic was revealed by Krylenko to have been in dispute in the drafting committee. Some had argued that to give the court high prestige, judges should be named each year by the Central Executive Committee at its first meeting following the Congress of Soviets, which was then meeting on an annual schedule. Krylenko had thought this a source of impossible limitation on necessary change when so many judges were involved. Apparently, he wanted to have judges removable in easier fashion when requested by the commissariats concerned, and replaced with new judges. The solution of the judiciary act as set forth above seems to have been the acceptable compromise.

In removing judges, the commissariats were not left free to act alone, but they could recommend. Their recommendation was taken to the steering committee, called the Presidium, of the Central Executive Committee, rather than to the whole Central Executive Committee itself. Presumably, the smaller steering committee was readier to accept the recommendation of the commissariats than was the Central Executive Committee as a whole. As a result of this arrangement the judges could have had no illusions about the necessity of their responsiveness to policy suggestions emanating from the commissariats.

Original jurisdiction of the Supreme Court was established over specified classes of criminal and civil cases. Those of a criminal character[41] were defined as "cases of exceptional importance, referred for trial by the Presidium of the Central Executive Committee or by the plenum of the Supreme Court, or by the Prosecutor of the Republic, or by the head of the G.P.U. Cases referred by the latter two officials could be transferred for trial to any of the provincial courts. The cases referred by the other two authorities could not be avoided by the Supreme Court itself.

In addition to cases individually referred for trial, the Supreme Court had original criminal jurisdiction in all cases in which the criminal defendant was a member of the Central Executive Committee accused of a crime relating to his official duties, a member of the Council of People's Commissars or a member of an advisory council ("college") of any of the various commissariats, a member of the presidium of the Supreme Council of National Economy, a member of the Revolutionary Military Council of the Republic, a member of the Supreme Court of the Republic, a deputy prosecutor of the Republic, a member of the advisory council of the G.P.U., an ambassador or other official accredited by the Soviet government to a foreign government.

The Supreme Court could take jurisdiction over or assign to any provincial court a charge against the following persons: provincial prosecutors and their deputies, members of the executive committee of the provincial soviet, and members of the provincial court.

In accordance with the same principle high army officers, as well as members of the revolutionary tribunals and revolutionary prosecutors when accused of crimes subject to the jurisdiction of the military tribunals were made subject to trial only by the military college of the Supreme Court of the Republic.

Civil jurisdiction as a court of original jurisdiction was also conferred upon the Supreme Court of the Republic by the Code of Civil Procedure.[42] Suits against people's commissars or against officials having equivalent rank and also suits against the executive committee of a provincial soviet as a whole could be brought only in the college for civil cases of the Supreme Court. The college was not

[41] Code of Criminal Procedure, RSFSR (1923), Art. 499.
[42] Code of Civil Procedure, RSFSR, Art. 24.

required to keep the case, for the Supreme Court was authorized to transfer any suit filed in its civil college to the provincial court sitting at the domicile of the defendant or to any other provincial court.

By these provisions the draftsmen adopted a practice familiar to some other legal systems in which categories of high officials and parliamentary deputies may be made defendants only in the highest court of the land. Since no lay judges were to be permitted in the Supreme Court's colleges when sitting as courts of original jurisdiction, there was further emphasis in this exclusion of lay judges at the Supreme Court level upon the departure being made in the judicial reforms from the principle of popularity.

The separation from the people caused by the exclusion of lay judges from the Supreme Court's colleges was not to last, however. The Commissariat of Justice proposed an amendment of the law in 1923 to introduce lay judges when the Supreme Court's colleges sat as courts of original jurisdiction. The Commissariat's spokesman before the Central Executive Committee said only that 48 lay judges would be placed upon a panel for use in the Supreme Court "in the interest of achieving uniformity in our system." [43] The Decree of July 7, 1923,[44] adopting the proposal was followed soon by a decree[45] providing that the lay judges be approved by the Presidium of the Central Executive Committee of the Republic and that their names be published in the official newspaper of the Central Executive Committee. Obviously, the lay judges in the Supreme Court were to be selected with more than usual care.

REFORM IN THE SMALLER REPUBLICS

The new judiciary act had hardly been enacted for the Russian Republic before a movement being fostered at the time by the Communist party throughout all the republics began to have influ-

[43] See Brandenburgskii in *RSFSR—II sessiia VTsIK, X sozyva* (*Stenografcheskii otchët*) (Moscow, 1923), p. 62.
[44] Order on Changes and Additions to the Judiciary Act, RSFSR, July 7, 1923, [1923] I *Sob. Uzak. RSFSR*, No. 48, item 481, amending Art. 103.
[45] Decree on the Procedure for Requiring People's Lay Judges to Perform Judicial Duties in Court Sessions of the Supreme Court, September 28, 1923, *ibid.*, No. 79, item 765.

ence upon the court structure. This movement was to lead to federation.

The Communist party had taken steps during the summer of 1922 to prepare the way for federation in order to bring about its political aim of an international proletarian state and to meet the practical requirements of military defense through union and economic integration through abolition of state frontiers.

Prior to the move toward formal federation the various republics, which had arisen since the Revolution of 1917 to incorporate the principal minority ethnic groups of the old Empire in a pattern of professedly independent states, had established their own court systems. These had been patterned closely upon the system of the Russian Republic as it had evolved up to the time at which the sister republic came into being. Once a republic had adopted the Russian pattern, it kept pace with the changes made by the Russians.

Most of the new republics formed on the Russian pattern made no pretense of independent thought in evolving their court systems. They adopted the Russian laws as their own within a few months after the Russians acted. Only the Ukrainian republic showed some measure of independence occasionally in drafting its laws and devising its legal institutions, but even the Ukrainian deviations were not consequential. In August, 1922, the Ukraine had finally been forced to accept public dictation as to the operation of its courts. A statute[46] adopted by the Russian Republic and published in its official gazette required the Ukrainian military courts to apply the Russian Republic's Criminal Code and Code of Criminal Procedure. If such dictation had occurred previously, it had been conducted through Communist party channels out of sight of the general public. Now the subservience of the Ukraine was publicized for all to see.

With a pattern of conformity with Russian thinking thoroughly established for the Ukrainians as well as for their less numerous fellows in Belorussia, Armenia, Azerbaidzhan, and Georgia, it was to be expected that the smaller republics would merely adopt the

---

[46] Decree on Changes in the Organization of Tribunals of the Ukraine, August 10, 1922, [1922] I *Sob. Uzak. RSFSR*, No. 51, item 643.

Russian Republic's judiciary act of October 31, 1922, as their own. In fact this happened, but with the usual delays. In this instance the delays accounted for a curious incident. The smaller republics were able because of the delay to present a judiciary act incorporating the influence of formal federation upon the judicial structure of the republic well before the Russian Republic amended its own act in 1924.[47]

The Ukrainian Republic presented the first example of the effect of federation upon a republic's judicial structure. It omitted from its judiciary act, which was adopted on December 16, 1922,[48] any provision for colleges for military and military-transport cases within its Supreme Court. In the articles of the Ukrainian act establishing the military and military-transport courts, it was declared that organization of, and subsequent supervision over, these specialized courts was to lie in the similarly named colleges of the Supreme Court of the Union of Soviet Socialist Republics. On December 16, 1922, no such formal union yet existed. It came into being only on December 29, 1922, by treaty between the Russian, Ukrainian, Belorussian, and Transcaucasian Republics.[49] The latter was a federation of the Armenian, Azerbaidzhan, and Georgian Republics created for the purpose of bringing the Transcaucasian peoples into the Union as a group rather than individually.[50] While the treaty of union of December 29, 1922, provided that there would be a federal supreme court,[51] the constitution establishing the court did not appear for some months.[52]

[47] Order on Additions to and Changes in the Judiciary Act, RSFSR, October 16, 1924, [1924] I *Sob. Uzak. RSFSR*, No. 78, item 782, par. 22. The original Art. 55 of the 1922 Judiciary Act had become Art. 94 by virtue of the amendment of July 7, 1923, lengthening the act. Hence the 1924 amendment refers to Art. 94 and not Art. 55.

[48] Judiciary Act, Ukrainian SSR, December 16, 1922, effective February 1, 1923, [1922] I *Sobranie Uzakonenii i Rasporiazhenii Raboche-Krest'ianskogo Pravitel'stva Ukrainy*, No. 54, item 779.

[49] For text of treaty, see SSSR—*I s"ezd sovetov Soiuza sovetskikh sotsialisticheskikh respublik (Stenograficheskii otchët s prilozheniiami)* (Moscow, 1923), pp. 8–11.

[50] The Constitution of the Transcaucasian Socialist Federated Soviet Republic had been adopted December 13, 1922. For text, see *Istoriia sovetskoi konstitutsii v dekretakh i postanovleniiakh sovetskogo pravitel'stva 1917–1936* (Moscow, 1936), pp. 223–32.

[51] Art. 12 of the treaty.

[52] Constitution adopted provisionally by the Second Session of the Central Executive Committee, USSR, First Convocation, July 6, 1922, and ratified by

To look at the record of Ukrainian legislation, one would think that the Ukrainian legislators had prepared for federation of the various republics and the creation of a federal government two weeks before it became a fact. This would not have been hard to do, because a draft federal constitution had been approved by the Communist party and was in circulation during the autumn of 1922. The Ukrainians certainly knew what was planned,[53] and they seem to have decided to act in accordance with this information.

Another explanation of the Ukrainian action can also be made, and it is given credence by the fact that the Russian Republic had not taken federal plans into account in its judiciary act adopted at the end of October, even though the Russian Republic's leaders were the prime movers toward federation. It may be that the Ukrainians changed the text of their judiciary act between the date of its adoption and the date of its publication in the official collection of Ukrainian laws in the last issue for the year 1922. This issue bears the actual publication date of January 18, 1923. It may have seemed wise to the Ukrainians to take advantage of the delay in publication of their official gazette to bring the new statute into conformity with what was to be the new judicial structure rather than to adopt a pattern identical with that of the Russian Republic only to change it within a few months.

The republics which were smaller than the Ukraine promulgated their judiciary acts even later than the Ukraine, and this delay gave them the opportunity to follow her example. The Belorussian Republic adopted its statute on the pattern of the Ukrainian Republic on March 30, 1923,[54] although it seems to have established its courts under the Russian Republic's statute before that time. This is suggested by a January 29, 1923, order[55] of the Belorussian Com-

---

the Second Congress of Soviets of the USSR at its third sitting, January 31, 1924. For text, see *Istoriia sovetskoi konstitutsii*, pp. 256–67. Chapter VII (Arts. 43–48) is entitled "On the Supreme Court of the USSR."

[53] The Seventh All-Ukrainian Congress of Soviets had declared on December 13, 1922, its class solidarity with the workers and peasants of Russia, Belorussia, and the Transcaucasian union and the existence of a factual unity and demanded strengthening and deepening of the union. See *ibid.*, pp. 234–35. It had also adopted a resolution listing 16 articles of a proposed basis for a constitution, see *ibid.*, pp. 237–39.

[54] Judiciary Act, BSSR, March 30, 1923, [1923] *Sobranie Uzakonenii i Rasporiazhenii Raboche-Krest'ianskogo Pravitel'stva BSSR*, No. 4, item 40.

[55] *Ibid.*, No. 1–2, item 22.

missariat of Justice requiring that all people's judges be examined during the first half of 1923 on the new judiciary act. It is most unlikely that the judges would have been admonished to study an act which had not yet been enacted by their own republic. They must have been applying the Russian act at the time.

The Belorussian statute of March 30, 1923, presented one variation from the pattern of the Ukraine. The Belorussians were to have no provincial courts. This omission was presumably due to the fact that the Belorussian Republic of the time was no larger than some of the provinces of the Russian and Ukrainian Republics. Because of its small size the Belorussian Republic had no administrative subdivisions organized as provinces. Its counties were directly subordinate to the central governing apparatus of the Republic. To parallel the administrative structure, the people's courts might have been made responsible only to the Supreme Court of the Belorussian Republic. Such a parallel structure was not, however, created.

The expectation of elimination in the Belorussian Republic of the level represented in the large republics by the provincial court was not fulfilled. The Belorussian judiciary act created a single intermediate court between the people's courts and the Supreme Court of the Republic. This court was called a "superior court." The purpose seems to have been to relieve the Supreme Court of the Republic of the burden of trials as a court of original jurisdiction and to reduce the number of appeals from the people's courts. The Supreme Court was left free to perform its supervisory function like the supreme courts in the larger republics and to take the relatively few appeals from the intermediate court sitting as a court of original jurisdiction.

The three smaller republics south of the Caucasus adopted a structure similar to that of the Belorussian Republic.[56] These republics had previously followed without alteration the pattern set by the Russian Republic, and they continued to do so, although they now went through the formality of adopting their own judiciary acts and codes of substantive and procedural law. Their judicial structure

[56] This has been assumed in the absence of full records from examination of the official gazette of the Azerbaidzhan republic which contains several amendments to its Judiciary Act, although the act itself does not appear in the gazette.

was complicated by the fact that when they had federated in the Transcaucasian Republic on March 13, 1922,[57] they had provided for the creation of a federal supreme court within their own three-way federation. With creation of the U.S.S.R. in which their three-way Transcaucasian federation participated with the Russian, Ukrainian, and Belorussian Republics to create the U.S.S.R., there was planned a system in which there were two supervising courts above the supreme courts of each of the three republics south of the Caucasus. Actually the Supreme Court of the Transcaucasian federation was not brought into existence.

THE FEDERAL SUPREME COURT

Federation of the various republics in a Union brought about the promulgation of a new federal constitution. In marked contrast to the constitutions of the republics which formed its constituent parts, except for that of the newly created Transcaucasian federation, the new constitution of the U.S.S.R. contained a chapter on the federal Supreme Court.

It will be recalled that the draftsmen in the Russian Republic of 1918 seem to have thought at one time of including provisions on the court system in their first constitution, but none were placed in the final draft. Since no reasons for the omission were given, it has been impossible to indicate why the courts, of all of the branches of government in the fledgling Russian Republic, had no constitutional standing. Since they were not included within the constitution, they had existed only by virtue of statute.

The U.S.S.R. constitution of 1923 included a chapter on the court defining the jurisdiction and structure of the new Supreme Court in some detail.[58] Perhaps the new approach to the court represented by the inclusion of the subject in the constitution symbolized the new approach to law. While the draftsmen of 1918 had been imbued

---

[57] The Communist parties of the three republics, creating the Transcaucasian Federation, voted for federation on November 29, 1921, but the Central Executive Committees of the republics voted for union only on March 12, 1922. See A. I. Denisov, ed., *Istoriia gosudarstva i prava, chast' II* (Moscow, 1948), pp. 84–85. These decisions preceded adoption of the constitution of the federation by several months.

[58] Chap. VII.

with the idea that courts and law would soon "wither away" with progress toward socialism, the men of 1923 had revised the time schedule.

No withering of the state and of its courts was expected in the foreseeable future by those who were entering upon the New Economic Policy. In consequence, it may have seemed reasonable to the constitutional draftsmen of 1923 to place in a single federal document a description of the new federal state apparatus in all of its branches, legislative, executive, and judicial. There was added reason to do so in that the republics who were joining the federation may still have had some concern about the federal government's prospective influence upon their national cultures. Although their Communist parties appear to have developed strong leadership positions which would have prevented any nationalist revolt in the republics, their leaders may have thought that there was no need to make their task harder by antagonizing the national minority groups among the masses. Stalin later suggested as much when he explained to some Americans that ultimate union had become possible only because the national minorities had been permitted to go their own way until experience proved to them that strength lay in union.[59]

The new federal Supreme Court was to have jurisdiction over five types of problem: it was to give the republic courts guiding instructions on the application of all-union law; it was to hear protests brought to it by the federal prosecutor against decisions of the supreme courts of the republics as violating federal law; it was to advise the Central Executive Committee of the federal government on legislation of the republics believed to violate federal law; it was to decide disputes arising between the republics, and it was to have original criminal jurisdiction over crimes committed by members of the federal government's Central Executive Committee and Council of People's Commissars when acting in their official capacities.

The college pattern of organization which had become familiar in the organization of the supreme courts of the republics was introduced into the federal Supreme Court. It was to have military and military-transport colleges which would assume all administrative

[59] See Joseph Stalin, "Interview with the American Labor Delegation" (1927), in *Leninism* (English translation; Moscow, 1933), II, 382.

functions as well as appellate control over the lower courts of this type, and it was to have civil and criminal colleges to follow the work of the republic supreme courts in these fields. When a suit was brought by one republic against another, or a criminal prosecution was entered against a high federal official, special benches were to be constituted for the trial.

Eleven judges of the Supreme Court were to meet as a "plenum" from time to time. This plenum was to be composed of the four presidents of the supreme courts of the four republics forming the federation, and one representative of the newly created federal G.P.U. The six other judges, holding their posts independently of their positions as representatives of the four republic supreme courts or of the federal G.P.U., were to be named to the court by the Presidium of the Central Executive Committee of the federal government.

A Supreme Court Act was adopted on November 23, 1923,[60] to provide detail not placed in the pertinent articles of the federal constitution. It clarified as being within the jurisdiction of the court civil suits and criminal prosecutions of exceptional importance when they concerned the interests of two or more republics. This breadth of authority had not previously been evident in the constitution's provisions for jurisdiction over disputes between republics and prosecution of high officials. Likewise, it enlarged the plenum of the court by adding to the provision that each of the four republic supreme courts would have a representative in the plenum a note to the effect that until such time as the Transcaucasian Republic should organize its Supreme Court, there would sit representatives of the supreme courts of the Armenian, Azerbaidzhan, and Georgian Republics.

The benches of the colleges hearing protests from civil and criminal decisions of the various republic supreme courts were to be composed of three judges, one of whom was to be a member of the plenum. By this provision it was made evident that the court would include on its staff judges not having seats in its plenum. In fact this

<hr/>

[60] [1923] *Vestnik TsIK, SNK i STO*, No. 10, item 311. Revised by Order of July 14, 1924, entitled "Instruction [*nakaz*] to the Supreme Court of the Union of Soviet Socialist Republics," [1924] I *Sobranie Zakonov i Rasporiazhenii Raboche-Krest'ianskogo Pravitel'stva SSSR*, No. 2, item 25. For revised text see *Sistematicheskoe sobranie zakonov SSSR* (Moscow, 1926), IV–V, 82.

happened, but all such judges were professionals, for lay judges were not introduced into the Supreme Court until later.⁶¹ No precise total number of Supreme Court judges was set by statute.

A prosecutor for the Supreme Court was to be named by the Central Executive Committee of the U.S.S.R. He was instructed by the statute to provide the Supreme Court with conclusions on all matters before it, and to prosecute all criminal cases over which the Court had original jurisdiction. The subordination of the Supreme Court to the Central Executive Committee was symbolized by the further authorization of the prosecutor to protest to the Central Executive Committee any decision of the Supreme Court's plenary session with which he could not agree.⁶² This provision again made clear that the judicial branch of government, at the federal level as well as at the republic level, was not to be independent of the policy makers in the branch dealing primarily with legislation. There was to be no separation of powers in the sense championed by Montesquieu.

A FEDERAL JUDICIARY ACT

The federal government acted in the autumn of 1924 to establish the basic principles for the judiciary throughout the republics and within the federal apparatus as well.⁶³ The statute of October 29,

---

⁶¹ Statute on the Supreme Court of the USSR and the Prosecutor of the Supreme Court of the USSR, July 24, 1929, [1929] I Sob. Uzak. RSFSR, No. 50, item 445. By section 14 there was created a panel of 25 lay judges named annually by the Presidium of the Central Executive Committee of the USSR, 12 of whom were selected from nominees of the Presidiums of the Central Executive Committees of the Union republics and 13 of whom were selected from nominees of the Supreme Court of the USSR. One lay judge from the panel was to sit with the professional judges in hearings conducted by the civil and criminal colleges or in special court sittings.

⁶² Constitution of the USSR (1923–1924), Art. 46. *Istoriia sovetskoi konstitutsii v dekratakh i postanovleniiakh, sovetskogo pravitel'stva, 1917–1936* (Moscow, 1936), pp. 255–67.

⁶³ For the discussion within the Central Executive Committee at the time of adoption of the basic principles, see *SSSR—II Sessiia TsIK (Stenograficheskii otchët)* (Moscow, 1924), pp. 197–206, 404–61, 589–97. Krylenko again protested the description of the Soviet court system as "unified," pointing to the variation in court structure in the provinces and to the specialized courts. See *ibid.*, p. 406. He also protested what he interpreted as a tendency to dictate to the republics on too many detailed matters, but he was voted down on this point. See *ibid.*, p. 461.

1924,[64] in twenty-four articles established the existing system of courts in federal law. No republic could thereafter depart from the general principles of the statute without subjecting itself to an action before the Supreme Court to determine whether its departure constituted a violation of federal law. Experimentation in the future was to be limited and to require federal approval. Yet the general principles did not concern details.

Examples of the areas left for experimentation to the republics were these. Judges in the courts of the republics might be chosen as the republics might decide. While candidates for judges were to be required to have had experience in public, Communist party, or court work, the federal rules did not establish any specific period of duration of the experience. The definition of the circumstances in which a single people's judge might sit without lay judges to try a case was left to the republics. The republics might decide the type of case in which the provincial courts or the supreme courts of the republics were to have original jurisdiction. The republics were to be free to establish their court investigating agencies and their court marshals as they wished, but the colleges of advocates and the notaries were to be organized in accordance with general principles established by federal law alone.

The military and military-transport courts were removed from the system of republic courts and made subject solely to the Supreme Court of the U.S.S.R. Since there was not created in the federal system a Commissariat of Justice of the U.S.S.R., the Supreme Court of the U.S.S.R. had responsibility for these military courts not only for the correctness of their decision but also for their organization and administration as well. In effect there came into existence a self-contained system of federal courts with lower instances functioning throughout the republics but beyond the reach of the republic officials. A sharp line had been drawn in the preceding years between the courts having to do with matters believed to concern the very life of the regime and the courts having to do with settlement of disputes between citizens not related to survival of the state. The new federal judiciary act reaffirmed the separation of the two systems. The less vital matters were to remain, under the federal

[64] Order on Basic Principles of the Judicial System of the USSR and of Union Republics, [1924] I *Sob. Zak. SSSR*, No. 23, item 203.

judiciary act, within the jurisdiction of the republics, subject to such control by the federal government as might be established in the form of statutes purporting to enact "fundamental principles."

It will be seen that centralization had been increased by federation, but not to the exclusion of administration by the republics of the apparatus having to do with most disputes in Soviet society. The preservation of republic commissariats of justice subject to no higher commissariat of justice in the federal government stood in 1923 and 1924 as the symbol of the federal-state relationship envisioned by the policy makers. Policy would be made on basic issues relating to the judicial system by the federal government, but administration would be left to the republics. To this there was to be one exception, namely, in those fields which were believed to concern the very life of the state. For these fields even administration would be conducted by federal authorities through the Supreme Court's colleges for military and military-transport affairs.

BUILDING FOR THE YEARS

The judicial reforms of 1922 were thought to have created a system which would remain unchanged for many years. Krylenko summarized the reform in an article published at the end of 1922 by saying, "The new judicial system has been built seriously and for a long time." [65] He felt that his expectation of stability was merited by the departure made by the draftsmen from what seemed to Krylenko to be the unworkable features of the earlier laws. He noted particularly the decentralized structure of the earlier courts and their reliance upon the general public for their personnel. He believed that because of these policies the courts had been too lenient for the needs of the new regime, with the result that the government had found it necessary to develop the Cheka to quell opposition with a very strong arm. Had the courts of 1917 been less subject to the pressure of public opinion, the undesirable features represented by the Cheka would have been avoided, in Krylenko's opinion.

The 1922 reforms were declared by Krylenko to have been the

[65] N. V. Krylenko, "Sudebnaia reforma," *Sovetskoe pravo*, No. 3 (1922), p. 62.

result of a compromise. The new court was placed between the police activity represented by the Cheka and the trial of a case with procedural safeguards. As a result of this compromise the new courts seemed to Krylenko to have lost the base for leniency. Control over them had been centralized to assure that they would not slip back to a lenient attitude. Yet the courts were not to act arbitrarily as the Cheka had done. They were to be required to function on the basis of written law, rather than revolutionary expediency, and their procedure was designed to provide a defendant with the opportunity of presenting his case.

The compromise of 1922 was expected by Krylenko to make it possible for the court system to meet pressures from both sides. The courts could protect the regime, and they could provide a fair trial. For this reason the court structure was expected to remain unchanged for a long time.

The introduction of the federal structure suggested to a different writer at the outset of 1923 that there was to be no stability in the court structure.[66] He expected centralization of court matters in the federal government to continue with a consequent reduction in the autonomy of the courts of the republics. He noted that the federal government had already established a law on the structure of the prosecutor's office in each republic from which no departure was to be permitted. Further, he noted the Russian Republic's dictation to the Ukrainian Republic's military tribunals in the decree of August 10, 1922, to which reference has been made above.

The supreme courts of the republics were expected by this author "to express themselves as sections or branches within a harmonious system of federal courts." The future of the supreme courts of the republics was expected to be similar to the development which had been witnessed in the four free states forming the Union of South Africa. A federal system of law to be administered by the federal court system was thought to be inevitable, and the beginning of it was already believed to be evident. In short, the various republic courts were expected to be absorbed within the federal system, and federal codes of law were expected

[66] V. Durdenevskii, "Na putiakh russkomu pravu," *ibid.*, No. 1 (4) (1923), pp. 28–29.

to replace those which had been enacted in the Russian Republic just prior to the author's article.

The author of this forecast of increasing authority in the federal government had been a member of the Constitutional Democratic party before the Revolution. He was noted also for his knowledge of comparative law. He was not, therefore, as politically responsible as Krylenko or as unwilling to relate foreign experience to possible Soviet development. It may be the irony of history that it is he, Durdenevskii, who has survived to write and advise the Soviet legal profession to the present day while Krylenko was purged in 1937, never to appear again.

Chapter 7

THE WATCHMAN

THE REPRIEVE to private enterprise granted in 1921 was expected
to create a class of bourgeoisie who would require watching. To the
policy makers of 1922 it seemed inevitable that this class would
seize every opportunity to utilize its newly granted freedom to
benefit itself at the expense of society generally. Fraud, speculation,
and even attempts to regain political power were anticipated as
commonplace during the period of reprieve. The workingmen and
peasants were expected to bear the brunt of the bourgeoisie's efforts
at self-enrichment.

Some state official was thought necessary under the new conditions to perform the task of bringing to court those who went so
far in their efforts to grow rich as to endanger public order. Such an
official was expected to have to intervene even in civil suits when
an unprincipled capitalist with a clever lawyer appeared to be
gaining an unfair advantage over a member of the working class.
The problem of the draftsmen of 1922 was to create an institution
which might serve as a watchman to sound the alarm when the
public interest was threatened.

Thinking for some years before 1922 had been moving in the
direction of a state prosecutor, but there was resistance to the
idea. The recollection of the prosecutor of prerevolutionary times
was still fresh. He had been considered the scourge of the Imperial
forces of law. As in all other instances, the Soviet reaction was to
seek something different for their own system. The planners of
1917 in their effort to start afresh had been prepared to leave the
watchman function to the public generally. It was expected that
socially conscious individuals would step forward either on their
own initiative or when instigated by a trade union or a cooperative
association or the Communist party to initiate court action against

the misfit. No permanent state official was designated in the first decree on the courts to perform the accusatorial function.

The informal arrangements of 1917 soon became unbearable to the judges. They found in practice that they needed assistance. To meet their demands a civil-service panel was created by the People's Court Act of 1918. It made available a pool of persons on a salary from which a court might select an accuser and a defender when the situation required. In spite of high hopes expressed for the civil-service idea, the scheme proved to be unworkable, and dissatisfaction spread. By 1920 there were many voices demanding a change.

Thinking ran in the direction of a professional prosecuting staff separate from the agency providing defense attorneys. The People's Court Act of 1920 took the step and placed the accusatorial function in a new institution to be organized in each province by the provincial executive committee's department of justice. The department would determine the number of accusers required and would nominate candidates for appointment by the executive committee of the provincial soviet. When a judge needed help, he would file his request with the provincial department of justice, and an assignment would be made. It was characteristic that the judge called for help before the accuser was assigned.

Conditions were such that the prosecuting function was performed on a haphazard basis. The state still relied on the socially minded individual or agency to bring illegal activity to the attention of the judge. By this time there had been developed a local police, but it seems to have been inadequate to the prosecuting function. There was also the Cheka, but it was concerned with political cases and mass control through terror. It was not operating in the sphere of routine violation of law. Further, it rarely took its cases to court.

PLANNING STATE PROSECUTION

A sharp debate broke into the open in early 1922 as to the structure to be desired in an agency designed to prosecute. There seems to have been no doubt among the persons concerned with law enforcement that a prosecuting agency was necessary to perform two functions: (a) to instigate criminal proceedings, and (b) to provide general supervision of all state agencies so that laws would be observed in the conduct of affairs. The debate concerned not the functions to be performed but the best way of fitting the new agency into the state pattern.

A draft statute was published by the Commissariat of Justice early in January, 1922,[1] under which an Office of State Prosecutor would be established within the Commissariat of Justice to be headed by a Prosecutor of the Republic, and to function at the local level through "people's prosecutors" attached to the departments of justice in the executive committees of the provincial soviets. Krylenko took issue immediately with the structure proposed in the draft.[2] He revealed that the college of the Commissariat had approved the draft by a majority of one, and he declared himself determined to explain the minority's position so that the matter might be discussed fully in the Fourth Congress of persons engaged in the administration of justice when it convened at the end of January.

The long-debated issue of centralization or decentralization was revealed as the nub of the conflict between the two factions within the Commissariat. Krylenko struck a blow on behalf of the minority's case for centralization. He based his arguments upon what he felt to have been a growing danger within the judicial system, namely, pressure upon the courts for decisions in accord with the desires of the head of the department of justice of the provincial soviet's executive committee. He believed that if the proposed draft were adopted, the same pressure would be exerted by the provincial department of justice head upon the provincial office of the prosecutor.

The provincial department of justice's head had been enabled to exercise influence upon the judicial system in Krylenko's opinion by the fact that the president of the provincial council of people's judges, although chosen by the council itself, could not hold his position until confirmed by the provincial executive committee. Further, he could be removed by the confirming authority. If the prosecutor at the provincial level, although not subject to confirmation in his position by the provincial executive committee

---

[1] "Proekt dekreta o gosudarstvennoi prokuratura, razrabotannyi Narkomiustom," *Ezhenedel'nik sovetskoi iustitsii*, No. 1 (January 1, 1922), p. 12.

[2] N. Krylenko, "K kritike proekta o prokurature," *ibid.*, No. 3 (January 15, 1922), p. 2.

under the terms of the proposed draft, were nevertheless named by the college of the Commissariat of Justice on the nomination of the provincial department of justice, the danger of influence from provincial sources was believed by Krylenko to be great. He felt the danger especially serious in the performance of the second function of the new office, namely, the general supervision of all state agencies to assure legality in their actions.

Krylenko argued that protection from the wrath of local officials subjected to criticism by the prosecutor was inadequately assured by the provisions for naming and removal of prosecutors by the college of the Commissariat of Justice. Further, Krylenko was alarmed because under the proposed system the provincial prosecutor was to be required to file his complaints against local administrative authorities and even his complaints against illegal action of the provincial executive committee itself with the provincial executive committee. To be sure, in the latter instance, the complaint was to be forwarded to the Commissariat of Justice, as were the periodical reports of the provincial prosecutor filed with the provincial executive committee, but Krylenko expected that if such reports and complaints had to pass through the hands of the provincial administrators, there was no possibility that the provincial prosecutor would act boldly in defense of the law. Krylenko noted that the head of the provincial department of justice was almost always a member of the provincial executive committee, as were the presidents of the council of people's judges and of the revolutionary tribunal. Complaints against these key officials of the law-enforcing apparatus would, in effect, be made known to them in time to conceal evidence or take other precautions before the investigation from above began. Krylenko concluded his analysis by saying, "supervision over the observance of law ought to be planned seriously or not at all."

The issue seems to have revolved in part around the future of the departments of justice of the executive committees of the provincial soviets. Krylenko ridiculed the majority for its cry that if the prosecutor were separated from the department there would be no reason for the latter to continue. He asked, "What of it?" Krylenko asked also why the preservation of the provincial departments of justice was so necessary that the prosecutor was to be "castrated" so that he could not in fact do anything.

The proposal of Krylenko was to abolish the provincial departments of justice. The provincial prosecutor would be named under his scheme at the center in Moscow. He would be authorized to attend meetings of the executive committee of the provincial soviet with the right of "consultative vote," which meant that he might advise but not vote. In contrast to the draft's provisions, the prosecutor under Krylenko's plan would route his reports and complaints directly to the prosecutor's department in the Commissariat of Justice. He would perform his functions in the people's courts through a staff of his own choosing and directed by his deputy in each local county seat. This deputy would also see to the proper maintenance of the local places of confinement and to the application of the penalty of compulsory labor without confinement.

If the provincial departments of justice were abolished, Krylenko wanted the courts to report directly to the first department of the Commissariat of Justice rather than through the provincial executive committee. The courts would have their own administrators and budgets. This would put them beyond the administrative reach of the prosecutors, who could perform their supervisory function only through complaints in their periodical report to the Commissariat or through their right of appeal to higher courts.

At the top level there would also be a change in the draft statute under Krylenko's plan. He found the same evils at the top level as he had found at the provincial level. The draft provided apparent protection to the Prosecutor of the Republic against pressure from administrators, for he was to be appointed by the Central Executive Committee of the Republic, but the Prosecutor of the Republic was to be a member of the college of the Commissariat of Justice to which he had to make his reports and complaints against illegal activities including those of the officials of the Commissariat. Krylenko demanded that the Prosecutor of the Republic be made superior to the college of the Commissariat and be given direct access to the Central Executive Committee.

An arrangement such as that proposed by the majority suggested to Krylenko that the Prosecutor of the Republic might try to compete with the Commissar of Justice. To avoid such tension between the two highest officials in the executive arm of the law-enforcing apparatus, Krylenko proposed that the responsibilities of the Prosecutor of the Republic be fused with those of the Commissar of Justice, who would become at the same time Commissar of Justice and Prosecutor of the Republic. Such a solution would place the new Prosecutor above the college of the Commissariat and would give him a seat on the Presidium of the Central Executive Committee. Krylenko indicated that he would not propose the abolition of the post of Commissar of Justice as he had proposed the abolition of the provincial departments of justice "because no one was speaking for such abolition," but it was clear that in his compromise the new function would almost swallow the old.

The majority struck back at Krylenko's scheme through its spokesman, A. Y. Estrin. The majority's spokesman was later to become a primary mover in preparing the draft criminal code of 1930, which reflected his school of thought's expectation that the state was beginning to wither away. Apparently, even in 1922 Estrin resisted centralization because he thought it to be a move away from the development of local initiative which he considered essential to the ultimate placing of responsibility for the maintenance of order upon the individual citizen. In the eyes of the school to which Estrin belonged, and to which even Krylenko was recruited in the 1930's when Stalin's regime of centralization had indicated more clearly the trend toward authoritarianism, the ultimate withering away of the state would occur only if the citizens were led by degrees in the direction of taking greater responsibility for their own affairs. The method of creating responsibility was expected to be through participation in local government.

Estrin argued for the retention of the departments of justice of the executive committees of the provincial soviets.[3] He believed the new economic policy to be raising many new problems which had to be settled as part of a complex single policy rather than separately, and the provincial departments of justice were necessary for this purpose of coordinating policy. While the need for orderly prose-

---

[3] "Otdel iustitsii, prokuratura i prochie organy iustitsii (tezisy tov. Estrina)," *ibid.*, No. 4 (January 22, 1922), p. 8.

cuting obviously called, in Estrin's opinion, for the creation of a
new agency to perform the function, the new prosecutor's office
could not be permitted to replace the provincial departments of
justice, because by its very nature it was not able to perform all
of the department's functions, in particular the administration of
the program of correctional labor without imprisonment, the organization of the notarial offices and of the appellate instances of
the court system.

The provincial prosecutor was not expected by Estrin to be
so much under the thumb of the provincial department of justice
that he could not perform his duties. Estrin admitted that the
provincial prosecutor would have to submit his complaints under
the proposed draft to the college of the department of justice of
the provincial executive committee, but there seemed to Estrin
ample protection of independence in that the prosecutor who did
not agree with the college could then submit the complaint to the
full executive committee of the provincial soviet or to the prosecutor's department in the Commissariat of Justice in Moscow. It
was also a guarantee of independence to the provincial prosecutor
in his opinion, in that only the Commissariat of Justice could dismiss
the prosecutor, and any criminal charge against him had to be
heard in the Supreme Court of the Republic.

Retention of the provincial prosecutor within the college of the
provincial department of justice, in which there also sat the president
of the council of people's judges of the province and the president
of the revolutionary tribunal, seemed to Estrin to assure that a
single line of policy would be established in all agencies in the
struggle against crime. This would not mean in Estrin's view that
any individual case would be decided under pressure from the
provincial executive committee. Estrin anticipated that each agency
involved in the disposition of a case would act independently in
determining the position it would take within the framework of
common policy.

At the county level, Estrin would preserve the county bureaus of
justice so that they might continue to organize and instruct the
people's courts of the county and maintain the investigating apparatus. The prosecutors at the county level would under the
majority draft be named by the provincial prosecutor and be con-

firmed by the provincial soviet's executive committee. No influence of county officials upon them would be possible.

PUBLIC DEBATE OF THE PLAN

Both Estrin and Krylenko were chosen to present their views to the Fourth Congress of persons engaged in the administration of justice at its sitting during the evening of January 27, 1922.[4]

The substance and conclusion of the discussion has already been presented in the general consideration of the Fourth Congress, but the details bear consideration at this point. They indicate the split of opinion at the time on the relationship to be desired with central and local authorities. The resolution of the question was to influence permanently the method of settling disputes in Soviet society.

Krylenko spoke first to establish the need for an office of state prosecutor to assure that citizens could do what they were permitted to do and to see that those who violated the law were punished. The system of prosecution then in existence was characterized by Krylenko as being completely casual. To avoid this condition, he said that there must be a centralized apparatus in which the prosecutors would be named and held responsible by central authorities.

The prosecutors were also to have the function of preventing violation of law, Krylenko declared, and for this reason they must be completely independent of those agencies which might interfere with the performance of their functions, namely, the provincial executive committees. Krylenko explained that the constitution did not prevent independence of provincial authorities. It did not require that prosecutors be named by them. With establishment of the provincial prosecutors he expected the provincial departments of justice to have no further usefulness.

Estrin presented the opposite view, declaring that the prosecutors must function through the provincial departments of justice, in accordance with the thesis he had expressed earlier. When he finished, one Smirnov supported Krylenko in opposition to the

---

[4] "Doklad tov. Krylenko o prokurature," *ibid.*, No. 5 (January 29, 1922), pp. 11–12.

provincial departments of justice, saying that in most cases they were agencies around which there whirled intrigue and quarrels, making them utterly worthless. Another speaker declared that the provincial departments played no part in the defense of revolutionary legality because the courts were unable to act independently of the local officials. Apparently, the local politicians prevented prosecution of themselves.

In closing his side of the debate, Estrin ridiculed his opponents as expecting the prosecutor to be an Atlas bearing the whole burden of law enforcement upon his shoulders. This was impossible, in Estrin's view, because the court itself was a part of the picture. Estrin thought that the departments of justice would be necessary at least temporarily to effect the changes in the courts proposed by the Fourth Congress, if for no other reason. He reminded his listeners that a Criminal Code was being introduced, which would require serious reorganization. The applicability of criminal law was closely linked with local conditions, and the prosecutor would have to be close to these conditions to perform his duties properly. Such a link could be maintained only through the provincial departments of justice.

Commissar Kurskii spoke to save the local agencies of his Commissariat of Justice, saying that the provincial executive committees were the "legislative arm of the government" on the provincial level. Since the Commissariat of Justice played the most active part in the legislative process, it was clear that it must have its representatives in the provincial executive committees. The prosecutors could not bear the burden of preparing legislation, and the provincial executive committees would have to create some sort of new juristic agency if the provincial departments of justice were to be abolished. Kurskii thought it possible that some day the provincial departments of justice might be liquidated but not at a time when a judicial reform was in process, and probably not until all administrative departments of a provincial executive committee were combined. He seems to have had in mind an ultimate step toward simplification of administration of which many Communists of the time were dreaming.

Krylenko repeated his thesis again at the close, and his voice carried the day. The congress voted to adopt the proposal of its

presidium under which the prosecutors would be named and removed only by central authorities in Moscow; they would sit in
the provincial soviets' executive committees with the right to speak
but not to vote; and as long as the provincial departments of justice
might exist, the prosecutor would not be subject to any of their
resolutions.

The prosecutors were also to be made responsible for the supervision of the investigating agencies and of the local police.[5] The
investigating apparatus was to remain tied administratively to the
courts. It was to be organized by investigating districts. The district
investigator was to make sure that the inquests and house searches
conducted by the police met with the requirements of law. At the
provincial level there would be an investigator for the more
important cases, to be named by the Commissar of Justice and to
investigate cases referred to him by the provincial prosecutor, the
provincial executive committee, and the "special session" of the
council of people's judges. The provincial prosecutor would supervise the provincial investigator.

The debate was not ended with the resolution of the Fourth
Congress. It broke out in even more fundamental form when the
members of the Central Executive Committee of the Republic
gathered on May 17, 1922, to enact the draft prepared by the
Commissariat of Justice.[6] Some of the members questioned the
use of the term "prosecutor" as having odious prerevolutionary
connotations and proposed a manufactured term meaning "the
fortress of legality." Some questioned the expediency of creating
such an agency. Some spoke against the centralization of authority,
pointing to England as having achieved the most progressive
victory in developing local government. These speakers feared that
a centralized prosecutor's office would attempt to control completely
the activity of the provincial executive committees and the agencies
of local administration. Some considered the draft a vote of no
confidence in the provincial executive committees.

Mikhail Kalinin attempted to calm all fears and point out the
reasons for centralization in a speech saying that the prosecutor as

[5] For resolutions of the congress, see "Rezoliutsii s"ezda," *ibid.*, p. 13.
[6] For a summary, see A. Ia. Vyshinskii, *Sudoustroistvo v SSSR* (Moscow,
1940), pp. 278–80.

conceived in the draft was the best institution yet devised up to that time. Further, there was no reason to shun the name, because the tsarist prosecutor had been different in serving the tsarist government. He believed the time had come when an institution of this kind in some form or other had to be introduced.

While the question of the desirability of the new Office of Prosecutor seems to have been settled relatively easily, the matter of the relationship between the provincial administration and the provincial prosecutor brought forth one of the most serious matters of policy to face the leadership of the time. Lenin found it necessary to refer the matter to the Politburo of the Communist party, as the innermost policy-making agency of the land.

THE POLITBURO INTERVENES

Lenin revealed in his letter of May 20, 1922, to the Politburo that the Communist party caucus in the Central Executive Committee contained a majority in opposition to the proposal to appoint provincial prosecutors from Moscow and to hold them responsible solely to Moscow.[7] The majority wanted to maintain the principle of "dual-subordination" as it existed generally throughout the provincial administrative apparatus, namely, subordination on the one hand to the central authorities represented by the Commissariat concerned with the type of work being performed locally, and on the other hand subordination to the provincial executive committee on which the local administrator sat. The majority also was reported as rejecting the right of the provincial prosecutors to protest any decision of local administrative authorities generally and of the provincial executive committee.

In his characteristically vigorous way, Lenin declared that it was hard to imagine an argument to defend such a clearly wrong point of view. He had heard in support of the view only that dual subordination was necessary to prevent the emergence of bureaucratic centralism and to protect the provincial administrative authorities against the assumption of a supercilious attitude by the central

---

[7] See V. I. Lenin, "O 'dvoinom' podchinenii i zakonnosti," in *Sochineniia* (4th ed.; Moscow, 1951), XXXIII, 326; also published in *Sovetskaia prokuratura v vazhneishikh dokumentakh* (Moscow, 1956), p. 202.

administrators. To this argument Lenin asked: "Is it supercilious to demand that observance of law be the same throughout the whole Republic?" Having set the problem before the Politburo, Lenin entered upon his argument.

The basic error in the proponents of dual subordination was thought by Lenin to be their failure to see that the prosecutors were not like the other administrators. He admitted that dual subordination was desirable in situations when real differences between provinces had to be taken into consideration. Agricultural conditions, industrial development, and administrative problems certainly differed in the various provinces. To overlook these differences would be bureaucratic centralism, for the appreciation of differences was the basis for all rational work.

The prosecutors were to be distinguished from the heads of the land, industrial, and other departments in that they were not administrative authorities, and they had no vote in any administrative decision. Their sole task was to see to the really uniform comprehension of law throughout the Republic regardless of local differences and local influences.

Local conditions were not to be left out of consideration because of the proposed centralization of the Office of Prosecutor, Lenin stated. When a violation of law was discovered, the prosecutor was to take the case to court. The courts were local agencies, chosen by local soviets. The courts in reaching their decision were required to follow the uniform law of the republic, but they were also required in setting the penalty to take into account local circumstances. A court might say that although the law had been violated in a given case, certain circumstances known to the local community, as explained by testimony in court, obliged the court to recognize the necessity of reducing the penalty applicable to a given individual or even to acquit him.

Lenin thought it also wrong to say that a provincial prosecutor should have no right to protest decisions of a provincial executive committee because the agency known as the Workers'-Peasants' Inspection was doing so. Lenin reminded the Politburo that this agency was judging matters not only on the basis of conformity to law but on the basis of the wisdom of a decision. The prosecutor was to examine only for conformity to law, and he could not set aside a decision. His only way of being effective was to protest it to appropriate authorities.

The part local pressures were playing upon state administration seems to have been well known to Lenin. He declared that there was no doubt that the country was in a sea of illegality and that local pressures were the primary opponents of establishing conformity to law. Even within the Communist party, as revealed in the periodic cleansing of membership, there had been found attempts to influence decisions, yet the Communists were much better informed as to the importance of law than were local officials generally. This fact seemed to Lenin to make it clear that subordination solely to the central authorities was necessary. Only there did he expect to be able to find people who could resist local pressures because they were close to the party agencies which represented the maximum guarantee against local and personal influence, namely, the Orgburo, the Politburo, and the Central Control Commission of the party. The Control Commission was thought to be especially fitted since its members were prohibited to sit in any other place, whether it be commissariat or state agency, and thus they were immune to influence from the administrative side.

It seemed possible to Lenin that the central authorities might make an error in some of their decisions relating to prosecution, but this error would be uncovered in Lenin's opinion by the local Communist party agencies who could take measures to have it corrected. He felt that to argue for dual subordination was to take what he called the absurd position that there were available for the position of prosecutor enough exemplary men who would not play ball with local administrators.

The Politburo accepted Lenin's proposal that the Office of Prosecutor be freed of any local influences, and the Central Executive Committee then adopted the proposed draft on May 26, 1922.[8] The statute was enacted not only in the Russian republic,[9]

[8] See Lenin, *ibid.*, XXXIII, 474–75, editorial note No. 80.
[9] Statute on Prosecutor's Supervision, May 28, 1922, [1922] I *Sobranie Uzakonenii i Rasporiazhenii Rabochego i Krest'ianskogo Pravitel'stva RSFSR*, No. 36, item 424.

but in almost identical wording in the Ukrainian Republic on July 12, 1922.[10]

THE STATUTES ENACTING THE REFORM

The Statute on the Office of Prosecutor incorporated the provisions which had been espoused by Krylenko. The Commissar of Justice became concurrently the Prosecutor of the Republic and chief of the Office of Prosecutor within his Commissariat. Assistant prosecutors were to be named and recalled by the Central Executive Committee of the Republic on the recommendation of the Prosecutor. Provincial prosecutors were to be named by the Prosecutor of the Republic and to be transferred or removed solely by him. As an apparent gesture of conciliation to the local officials, the Prosecutor of the Republic was directed to select his candidates for the post of provincial prosecutor both from his staff at the central office and from a list of candidates advanced by the provincial authorities. Within each province the work was to be distributed among assistant prosecutors named by the Prosecutor of the Republic on the recommendation of the provincial prosecutor.

Provincial prosecutors were authorized to attend all meetings of provincial executive committees and to present to provincial executive committees proposals that orders issued by them or agencies subordinate to them be repealed or amended as violating law or superior orders. In the event of refusal to repeal or amend, the provincial prosecutor might appeal the matter to the Council of People's Commissars or to the Presidium of the Central Executive Committee of the Republic through the channel of the Prosecutor of the Republic. The offending order was not to be suspended, however, pending a decision at the center.

By these provisions it became evident that the provincial ad-

---

[10] June 28, 1922, [1922] I *Sobranie Uzakonenii i Rasporiazhenii Raboche-Krest'ianskogo Pravitel'stva Ukrainy*, No. 28, item 440. The Ukrainians added to the powers of the office "participation in civil trials." The Belorussian statute offered wider variations in the text. See decree of June 26, 1922, [1922] *Sobranie Uzakonenii i Rasporiazhenii Raboche-Krest'ianskogo Pravitel'stva BSSR*, No. 5, item 83. The Azerbaidzhan statute followed the Russian pattern, see decree of July 11, 1922, [1922] *AzSSR*, No. 7, item 241. All four statutes may be compared in *Sovetskaia prokuratura v vazhneishikh dokumentakh*, pp. 212–24.

ministrative authorities had been brought completely under the supervision and control of the central authorities. One may speculate that Lenin and his closest advisers had intended at all times to achieve complete centralization of authority. The record suggests, however, that centralization was not the result of prior design which had become possible of achievement only in 1922. The record suggests that Lenin found himself facing in 1922 near chaos in the provincial governments. Local officials seem to have been intoxicated with power and to have assumed the right to govern as they wished without following directions from headquarters. When this insubordination was coupled with venality, nepotism, and interchange of favors, it became doubly undesirable. Lenin was prepared to descend with the full force of the central agencies of the Communist party upon the provincial authorities to prevent a continuation of such activity. The establishment of the Office of Prosecutor was his answer to the problem.

What Lenin did not see, or perhaps was unwilling to admit, if one accepts the conclusion that centralization was not Lenin's desire from the outset of his regime, was that he had opened the way for subsequent authoritarians to establish their power at headquarters through the channels he had created. In attempting to make the local authorities conform to the law, he had silenced them and removed any possible restraint from below upon abuse of power at the top. While local government can provide a source of inefficiency and abuse of political power in any political system, it can also provide a brake upon the emergence of a tyrant at the top from whom even greater evil can flow than from a whole circle of provincial tyrants. In seeking to avoid one evil, it is hard to avoid the other and greater evil. The measures taken in 1922 within the Russian republics prepared the way for what was to come and may be considered an object lesson in the dangers to be found lurking in measures designed to control abuse of power on the local level by strengthening the central authorities.

The court functions of the prosecutor defined in the decree were those which had been anticipated by proponents of the decree: instigation of court proceedings against violators of the law, supervision of police inquests and examinations by the state investigators, preparation of indictments, nol-prossing of suits at any stage in the proceedings when the charges seemed to lack substantiation, prosecuting cases before the courts, appealing or protesting decisions, and verifying the legality of detention of all persons in all places of detention, including those maintained by the political police. For the first time in the five-month discussion of the function of the prosecutor, there was reference to his right to participate in civil suits as well as criminal prosecutions. This appeared in the form of a laconic declaration in the statute without amplification. It remained for the Code of Civil Procedure to provide details of this function.

Krylenko's other demand that the provincial departments of justice be abolished was also complied with. Decrees in both the Russian and Ukrainian Republics abolished these institutions and transferred their former functions to other agencies.[11] While the prosecutors had been given a large part of the department's activities, its supervisory functions over the law-enforcing agencies would have been left untended, had no action been taken. The presidium of the provincial council of people's judges was given the nonprosecuting functions. These included organization of, and supervision over, the various people's courts, the investigators, the marshals, and the notarial offices throughout the province. A supervisory function was also to be performed over the colleges of advocates, the legal consultation points, and the commissions for handling offenses of juveniles. The council of people's judges was required to make periodic reports on the performance of these functions to both the provincial executive committee and the People's Commissariat of Justice in the republic's capital.

By this decree the council of people's judges in each province became not only a court but an administrative office for most of the affairs concerning the enforcement of law within the province. This task was emphasized by a supplementary article of the decree which filled in details on the general functions, making it clear that the organizational function with respect to courts, included the

---

[11] Decree on Abolition of the Provincial Departments of Justice [*Gubiust*] and their County Agents [*Ubiust*] and on the Procedure for Putting the Prosecutor's Office into Operation, September 6, 1922, [1922] I *Sob. Uzak. Uk.*, No. 39, item 588. A comparable decree has not been found for the RSFSR, but the change was made, as indicated by the redistribution of functions to be referred to later in the chapter.

nomination to the provincial executive committee of candidates for the position of professional judge in the people's court and also the maintenance of panels from which the lay judges were to be chosen. It also included the recommendation to the provincial executive committee of recall of unsatisfactory judges. It was explained further that all functions previously performed by the council of people's judges in collaboration with the former provincial department of justice would now be performed by the council of people's judges alone.

To avoid the confusion which Commissar Kurskii had foreseen in expressing opposition to abolition of the provincial departments of justice which had been performing a quasi-legislative function in interpreting and systematizing decrees and orders of the government for the convenience of the provincial executive committee and its various departments, the decree provided for the transfer to the Commissariat of Justice in the republic's capital of such functions.

One has the impression that the decree abolishing the provincial departments of justice required the transfer to the various provincial councils of people's judges of the staff serving the former provincial departments of justice. The reform would, therefore, have eliminated little more than the head of the former provincial department of justice. It certainly would have encumbered the work of the courts with many administrative details for which courts are usually not held responsible had there been no transfer of staff. The very fact that years later, in 1939,[12] the decree was reversed to reestablish the provincial departments of justice suggests that the measure was taken out of a sense of exasperation with the conduct of affairs by

---

[12] The change was made by decree of the Presidium of the Supreme Soviet of the RSFSR, April 21, 1939, put into effect by a statute on the Administrations of the People's Commissariat of Justice, RSFSR, in the Provincial Soviets of Deputies of Toilers, June 1, 1939, [1939] *Sobranie Postanovlenii i Rasporiazhenii RSFSR*, No. 8, item 26. A return to the previous status of judicial rather than administrative supervision was initiated by the Tadzhik Republic by decree on November 17, 1958, when the republic's Ministry of Justice was abolished and supervision over all activity of the provincial and people's courts as well as over the advocates and the notaries was transferred to the Republic's Supreme Court. See *Kommunist Tadzhikistana*, November 19, 1958, p. 3. This reversion to earlier practice may have been a trial in one republic prior to general acceptance in others if it proved successful. Such a general return had been urged by the Vice President of the USSR Supreme Court in May, 1958. See N. Morozov and I. Perlov, "Ob organizatsii sudebnoi sistemy," *Izvestiia*, May 18, 1958, p. 4.

the provincial departments as they had been operating. The heads of these departments seem to have been arrogating to themselves all functions relating to the enforcement of law within the province, including the judicial function in that they were dictating to the provincial courts. To eliminate the evil the leadership of the state was prepared to establish a burdensome administrative structure which was to hamper the work of the courts and create eventually an evil which seemed even greater than the one that had brought about the decree.

With the reform of the judiciary in October, 1922, and the transfer of the judicial functions of the provincial councils of people's judges to the newly created provincial courts, the administrative duties established for the councils of people's judges at the time of the abolition of the provincial departments of justice also passed to the newly created provincial courts.[13] To replace the county bureaus of justice, which had been the administrative agencies of the provincial departments of justice on the county level, there was established in 1923 a "county agent of the provincial court." [14] This official was to perform all the administrative and financial duties of the provincial court at the county level. He was to be chosen by the plenum of the provincial court from among the people's judges of the county and to rank as a member of the provincial court.

The reorganization of the Commissariat of Justice to bring within it the Office of the Prosecutor of the Republic and to exclude the provincial and county departments of justice was enacted in statute on February 1, 1923.[15] The distribution of administrative functions between the courts, the Commissariat, and the Office of the Prosecutor of the Republic within the Commissariat was incorporated in

[13] See Judiciary Act, RSFSR, October 31, 1922, Part II, [1922] I *Sob. Uzak. RSFSR*, No. 69, item 902.

[14] Decree on Changes in and Additions to the Judiciary Act, RSFSR, July 7, 1923, [1923] *ibid.*, No. 48, item 481, Chap. XI. By the same decree there were added to the Judiciary Act as integral chapters the previously enacted separate statutes on advocates and notaries. The subordination of these agencies to the provincial courts rather than to the provincial departments of justice was indicated. Compare Statute on Institution of Advocacy, May 26, 1922, sec. 43, [1922] *ibid.*, No. 36, item 425, with decree of July 7, 1923, sec. 39.

[15] Statute on the People's Commissariat of Justice, February 1, 1923, [1923] *ibid.*, No. 10, item 120.

the federal judiciary act of October 29, 1924.[16] By this all-union decree the relationships between the various agencies engaged in the enforcement of law were stratified, with but few changes, until the next fundamental reform of 1938 incorporating the plan established by the second constitution of the U.S.S.R., adopted in 1936.

Federation in 1923 made no change in the structure of the prosecutor's office. Although a prosecutor was created within the Supreme Court of the U.S.S.R., he was limited to prosecuting cases brought before that court and to protesting its decisions to the highest authorities of the federal government. He was not related through any administrative channel with the work of the prosecutors of the various republics and their subordinate provincial prosecutors.

THE RIGHT TO INTERVENE

In development of the authority established by the statute on the Office of Prosecutor of 1922 to intervene in civil suits, the Code of Civil Procedure was adopted on July 7, 1923.[17] The prosecutor was given the right both to instigate a civil suit or to intervene at any stage in the procedure if such a step was required "to protect the interests of the state or of the toiling masses." [18] He was to have the right to obtain a copy of any document in the case and to review the record and to make notes.[19]

The court might call for a prosecutor at any stage of the proceedings, and the call was mandatory upon him.[20] If the interests of a state agency or enterprise were brought into a case in which the state agency or enterprise was not represented, the court was required to notify the agency and also the prosecutor.[21] If a case

---

[16] Basic Principles of the Judicial System of the USSR and of the Union Republics, October 29, 1924, [1924] I *Sobranie Zakonov i Rasporiazhenii Raboche-Krest'ianskogo Pravitel'stva SSSR*, No. 23, item 203.

[17] Code of Civil Procedure, RSFSR, July 7, 1923, [1923] I *Sob. Uzak. RSFSR*, No. 46–47, item 478.

[18] *Ibid.*, Art. 2. He was also given the right to bring a civil suit when it seemed necessary at any point during criminal proceedings. See Code of Criminal Procedure, RSFSR, May 25, 1922, Art. 58, [1922] *ibid.*, No. 20–21, item 230. In the revised code of February 15, 1923, this became Art. 54; see [1923] *ibid.*, No. 7, item 106.

[19] Code of Civil Procedure, (1923), RSFSR, Art. 11.

[20] Art. 12.   [21] Art. 172.

was taken on appeal by one of the parties to a higher court, the prosecutor had the right to file a written opinion or to appear for personal argument at the court sitting at the time of the appeal.[22] Even after an appeal, or after the expiration of time to appeal, the Prosecutor of the Republic or one of the provincial prosecutors might ask the Supreme Court of the Republic to exercise its right of review,[23] and the Prosecutor of the Republic or one of the provincial prosecutors acting through the Prosecutor of the Republic might obtain the file on a case and request a reversal of an appellate decision if he thought that the interests of the state or of the toiling masses so required. There was no limit of time upon the filing of this request.[24]

In criminal proceedings the prosecutor was given similar rights of intervention. In addition to the customary role of state agent to decide whether prosecution should be commenced[25] and to conduct the accusation before the court,[26] the prosecutor was given the right by the code of criminal procedure to file with a higher court a protest against a sentence.[27] This right might be exercised not only on behalf of the prosecution but also on behalf of a defendant who seemed to the prosecutor to be unable to protect his own interests against a court which had not been alert to them.

Even after an appeal had been disposed of by a college of the Supreme Court of the Republic the Prosecutor of the Republic might ask for a review by the full membership of the Supreme Court sitting as a plenum.[28] To permit such intervention the Prosecutor of the Republic was authorized to demand from any court at any time the file of any case and to suspend execution of the sentence during the period of examination.[29]

To perform the many functions assigned to the new Office of Prosecutor a large staff was planned.[30] In addition to the Prosecutor of the Republic, who was also to be the People's Commissar of Justice, there were to be in the Russian Republic one Deputy Prosecutor of the Republic, four prosecutors to head the four sections of the office, four to handle affairs of the Supreme Revolu-

[22] Art. 224.   [23] Art. 252.   [24] Art. 254.
[25] Code of Criminal Procedure, RSFSR (1923), Chap. XIX.
[26] Art. 8.   [27] Art. 349.   [28] Art. 438.   [29] Art. 440.
[30] "Iz deiatel'nosti Narodnogo Komissariata Iustitsii," *Ezh. sov. iust.*, No. 26–27 (July 17–24, 1922), pp. 22–23.

tionary Tribunal (which was still in existence when the plan was prepared), thirty military prosecutors to work in the revolutionary tribunals of the republic, sixty provincial prosecutors, eight investigators for the most important cases, twelve assistants to the prosecutor, and the necessary clerical staff. At the provincial level the provincial prosecutor was to have a staff of three deputies to attend to matters at the provincial capital, and one deputy for each county seat, three prosecutors to be available as consultants and the necessary clerical staff. All of this apparatus was to begin functioning not later than August 1, 1922, and as early as possible where suitable persons were available for appointment.

On July 25, 1922, Commissar Kurskii called the prosecutors together in Moscow to discuss with them the role they were to play. He told them that it would be naive to imagine that all the evils of the court system would disappear solely out of fear of the prosecutor's eye.[31] The courts would have to be improved from within. In this comment the Commissar may have been indicating his irritation at the emphasis being placed upon the new office of prosecutor as a cure-all. From his point of view bad judges could not do better solely because they were watched. They would have to be improved in quality before any real progress could be expected.

The role of intervenor puzzled an author in the Ukraine, writing in the autumn of 1923.[32] He found it impossible to imagine that a prosecutor might intervene to prosecute a criminal action or to bring a civil action as defender of the interests of the state and of the toiling masses without acquiring a subjective interest in the case. He quoted Cicero to the effect that a wise orator prepares his speech without thinking of any subsequent necessity for a different position. He argued that a prosecuting attorney who appeared as a party could not be other than subjective. The author was prepared, however, to distinguish the role of the prosecutor when he intervened to present legal conclusions in a case in which the prosecutor was not a party to the action, or when he intervened to bring a case to the attention of the Supreme Court after the

[31] "Khronika: voprosy iustitsii na vserossiiskom soveshchanii prokurorov," *ibid.*, No. 29–30 (August 10–17, 1922), p. 26.

[32] N. Zil'bershtein, "Prokuratura i grazhdanskii protsess," *Vestnik sovetskoi iustitsii*, No. 7 (November 1, 1923), p. 179.

appeal had been concluded. Under such circumstances the author expected the prosecutor to intervene on behalf of impartial objective truth. He was to intervene as an expert witness on a legal question.

Having concluded that a prosecutor might intervene in a case in either of two different capacities, as a party to a suit or as an expert on the law, the author argued that when the appearance had been in the capacity of party, any subsequent attempt to intervene in a supervisory capacity should be forbidden. The author could not imagine how an objective role might be assumed after the subjective role of criminal prosecution or of civil plaintiff had been concluded.

The editors of the official Ukrainian law review in which the author was permitted to express his views found it desirable to add editorial footnotes to the article. They stated that a Soviet prosecutor, even when appearing as a party, must demonstrate his impartiality, as if he were presenting conclusions as an expert rather than the argument of a partisan. The editors found that under their conception of the impartial character of a prosecutor's participation in a trial, there was no reason to forbid protesting of a decision in a supervisory capacity to the Supreme Court when the prosecutor has previously appeared as a party, "because the office of prosecutor both when giving its conclusions and when appearing as a party in a civil suit or in supporting a criminal accusation, acts in all circumstances and at all times as a representative of the state and not as a defender of private interests." To complete their argument the editors added that they expected a similar impartial attitude from lawyers in the case, "for both prosecutor and lawyer in the spirit of Soviet law are aids to the court and not hired servants of the parties."

The argument of the editors stems from the Soviet view that the state in a capitalist economy is the repressive apparatus used by the minority ruling class to preserve its power over the masses. As such, the state is presumed to hire a prosecutor to perform the partisan function of representing the interests of the ruling class. In Soviet theory the Soviet state is not partisan, nor can its prosecutor be partisan, since it is presumed to represent the entire population's interests, because of the elimination of capitalism and the consequent elimination of any basis for class struggle. Some might find the position of the Soviet editors of 1923 implicit in the Soviet court structure from the date of its creation in 1917. The judge at that time had been looked upon as rather similar to the wise man of the primitive community, who was expected to decide a dispute in the interests of the entire community rather than in the interests of a ruling class. Accusers and defenders were expected to step forward from the community itself, not as paid representatives retained by a party, but as honest impartial citizens interested in aiding the court in the exploration of all of the facts so that a decision conforming to the requirements of the preponderant majority of the community might be possible. The judge was not conceived to be a referee in a test of wits but a chairman of a committee of citizens including accusers and defenders to probe the matter fully.

The editorial footnotes to the Ukrainian author's article indicated the path of thought which was to become official as years passed. Prosecutors were professedly impartial, although with the passage of time the difficulty in believing this to be so seems to have required recognition. The role of intervenor to protest a decision to a higher court was placed solely upon the prosecutors of the Republic, and subsequent to the creation of a Federal Prosecutor in 1933 upon his office as well. As a result, the men who had to participate in the trial itself were not to be expected to take a position at a higher stage in the procedure in opposition to that assumed in the forum in which they had appeared in the first instance.

By creating the function of impartial intervention, the Soviet policy makers attempted to distinguish their institution of prosecutor from the institution to be found elsewhere. What they failed or refused to anticipate was that other factors besides capitalism might also create selfish interests. Lust for power, belief in the superior wisdom of those with education in historical materialism, or whatever it may be that has motivated Soviet concentration of authority in a very few has prepared the way for partisanship in Soviet ruling circles. The prosecutor, as a vital arm of the apparatus of compulsion, has not been able to adhere, and perhaps could never have adhered, to the impartial role assigned to him by the 1922 decree on the prosecutor and the 1923 procedural codes.

EXAMPLES FROM PRACTICE

The first record of activity of the newly created Office of Prosecutor in the Commissariat of Justice of the Russian Republic indicated that attention was being given to advising on the application of unclear provisions of criminal and civil law.[33] Three questions were asked and answered. One concerned the applicability of the Criminal Code's articles punishing the violation of state monopolies and of regulations concerning gold and foreign currencies to a sale of goods for hard currency. The answer was in the affirmative, and the argument in support of the conclusion was based upon a decree making the purchase and sale of gold, silver, platinum, and foreign currency a state monopoly and upon a second decree providing that only state enterprises and cooperative associations were permitted to accept such currency for goods, and they were obligated to deliver any such currency to the State Bank.

The applicability of a 1920 statute authorizing the presidium of a provincial soviet's executive committee to forbid residence in an area declared subject to martial law was the matter raised in the second question. It was asked whether a specific individual might be barred from an area when military action was not in process. The Prosecutor's Office replied that since 1922 the decree on exile of participants in counterrevolutionary activity had centralized the exiling authority in the Commissariat of Internal Affairs. The provincial executive committees were directed to refer cases involving denial of the right to reside to the Commissariat of Internal Affairs with a full statement of the reasons why action was desired.

The right to levy execution upon a bank account of a state enterprise to satisfy a judgment for wages was raised in the third question. The Prosecutor's Office declared that execution might be levied if the enterprise had been placed upon a business accounting basis under the provisions of the new public corporation law, but no execution might be levied upon state property if the employing agency was not operating on a business accounting basis but under appropriations made to it as an arm of a state administrative bureau.

[33] "V otdele prokuratury Narodnogo Komissariata Iustitsii," *Ezh. sov. iust.*, No. 43 (November 25, 1922), p. 17.

A statistical summary of the work of the prosecutors in the Russian Republic during the year 1923[34] revealed that as the opponents of the independent role established by statute for the prosecutors had expected, friction had developed in the relationships evolving between the provincial prosecutors and the provincial executive committees to which they were not made responsible under the decree. Examples given in the review included cases of two county soviets in Tula Province which had refused to send to the provincial prosecutor for verification the orders issued by the executive committee. The executive committee in the Pribaikal Province had tried to force the provincial prosecutor to become a department of the executive committee. In Saratov Province a county executive committee had attempted to interfere with the work of the courts in the county, and this had brought a conflict with the prosecutor. In Perm Province there had been a dispute over the arrest under orders from the prosecutor of a member of a city executive committee. Two distant executive committees were reported to have declared that they alone understood local conditions, and they had refused for months to agree with the concept of the presence within the province of a prosecutor independent of their control.

Most of the conflicts between prosecutors and executive committees were said to have been settled without reference to authorities above the provincial level, but eight had been sent to the Office of the Prosecutor within the Republic Commissariat of Justice for solution. Some had even been taken by the Prosecutor of the Republic to the Central Executive Committee of the Republic for resolution. The subject matter of these most difficult disputes indicates the type of problem before the prosecutors. One was a protest of the provincial prosecutor against orders of the Tersk Provincial Executive Committee declaring five dwellings which had been returned to owners under the policy of the N.E.P. "houses of the soviet." The occupants had been evicted. The prosecutor had also protested against measures adopted by the same executive committee to prevent illegal distilling of liquor. One had been an appeal from a prosecutor's protest against the Kursk

---

[34] "Obshchii obzor deiatel'nosti prokuratury v 1923 g.," *ibid.*, No. 51–52 (December 31, 1923), pp. 1192–98.

Provincial Executive Committee's order increasing payments in kind for services rendered by the provisional government and another had been an appeal against the arrest under orders of the same executive committee of the chief of the telephone exchange in one of the provincial cities. Two protests had been against orders of the Perm Provincial Executive Committee to sell fifty pianos which presumably had been confiscated from private owners, and to introduce an admissions tax. The final protest had been against an order of the Nizhegorod Provincial Executive Committee municipalizing some buildings.

All differences between provincial prosecutors and provincial executive committees were said to have been resolved by the end of 1923, except in the provinces of Penza, Arkhangelsk, and Novo-Nikoliaevsk. Some indication of the numbers of interventions against local executive committees is provided by statistics in six provinces. They vary from Simbirsk, in which the protests had been only 2 against orders of the provincial executive committee and 14 against orders of county executive committees, to Novo-Nikoliaevsk, in which 28 provincial orders had been protested and 15 county orders.

Attendance at meetings of local state agencies occupied much time of the staffs of the local prosecutors' offices. In Kaluga Province 502 meetings had been attended and reports on matters of doubtful legality arising in these meetings had been requested in "more than one hundred cases." Criminal proceedings had been instigated in various circumstances, numbering 35 in Votsk Province, 21 in Nizhegorod, "more than ten" in Tambovsk, 7 in Voronezh, and 5 in Kalmyk.

Complaints from citizens as to violations of their rights had been numerous. They had totaled, throughout 1923, 3,108 in Saratov Province, 2,976 in Viatka, 2,436 in Smolensk, and 2,371 in Tula. Less than 10 percent of the complaints had been found to require no action by the prosecutor.

Court intervention in the capacity of supervisor had required 427 appearances in the sessions prior to trial at which motions were heard and at the trial itself in Viatka province, 208 appearances in Simbirsk, 403 in Vitebsk, 195 in Kuban-Black Sea, and 249 in Kostroma. Post-trial review of criminal cases with a view to protesting the court decision to a higher court had been initiated in

246 cases in Pskov Province, 219 in Briansk, 182 in Chernovets, 120 in Novgorod, and 318 in Simbirsk. Similar post-trial review in civil cases had occurred much less often, amounting to only 53 cases in Viatka Province, 41 in Tersk, 42 in Orlov, and 29 in Smolensk. It was said that "very few" protests had been filed with the Supreme Court of the Republic by the prosecutors against decisions of the colleges of the provincial courts.

Party membership and social background were revealed in the same report. Of the provincial prosecutors, only 2.4 percent were not members of the Communist party in 1923, while only 21.1 percent of their staffs were not party members. The social origin of the provincial prosecutors indicates that few came from the laboring classes, only 22.1 percent being recorded as of peasant origin, 17.5 percent as of working-class origin, and the balance of "remaining origins." These would presumably have been primarily the professional classes of prerevolutionary Russia. The statistics on educational qualifications indicated that 26.7 percent of the provincial prosecutors had received a legal education, 17.5 percent had a university nonlegal education, 26.7 percent had high school education, while 29.1 percent had only grammar school education. All provincial prosecutors had worked previously in some aspect of the law-enforcing activities of the Soviet state, and 60.4 percent of them had been engaged in such work for more than three years, which made them veterans of the early period.

THE IMPACT OF FEDERATION

Federation of the several republics at the end of 1922 had no evident immediate impact upon the organization of the Prosecutor's Office as it had upon the structure of the courts. There was established by the federal constitution no Prosecutor of the U.S.S.R. To be sure, there was created by the constitution within the Supreme Court of the U.S.S.R. a Prosecutor of the Supreme Court of the U.S.S.R.,[35] but he was provided with no administrative link with the prosecutors of the several republics. His functions were limited by the constitution to giving conclusions on all questions coming before the Supreme Court for decision, to prosecuting cases tried

[35] Constitution of the USSR, 1923–1924, Art. 46.

by that court, and to protesting to the Presidium of the Central Executive Committee of the U.S.S.R. decisions by the plenum of the Court with which he could not agree.

The authority of the Prosecutor of the Supreme Court of the U.S.S.R. was defined more precisely in the statute of the Supreme Court of November 23, 1923,[36] to indicate that he was the officer of the court who would initiate before it hearings on the conformity of orders, decisions, and sentences of Supreme Courts of the several republics with federal law or the interference of such actions with interests of other republics, yet he was not given administrative authority over prosecutors in the republics.

Even with the "Basic Principles for the Judiciary of the U.S.S.R. and of the Union Republics" of October 29, 1924,[37] there was no change in the status of the prosecutor of the Supreme Court of the U.S.S.R. He remained apart from the prosecutors of the several republics, although his subordinates operating within the military tribunals and transport tribunals which had been brought under the administrative control of the Supreme Court of the U.S.S.R. by the steps already discussed in the preceding chapter were instructed by the "Basic Principles" to govern their relationships with the Prosecutors of the Republics and their staffs in accordance with the special statutes relating to these tribunals and the Supreme Court statute.[38] It was recognized that there would have to be constant interchange of views and information between local prosecutors in the two systems of courts, for they would be dealing with individuals who would be tried in the federal or republic system of courts depending upon the nature of their offense. There was, however, to be no federal control over the prosecutors operating in the courts of the republic, for they were independent.

Looking back on the 1924 "Basic Principles" from a distance of sixteen years, Andrei Vyshinskii was to find them greatly different

[36] Statute on the Supreme Court of the Union of Soviet Socialist Republics, November 23, 1923, [1924] I *Sob. Uzak. RSFSR*, No. 29–30, item 278. The statute appears in the RSFSR collection of laws with other decrees promulgated earlier by the USSR Central Executive Committee and approved by the Second Congress of Soviets of the USSR, October 24, 1924. The Prosecutor's authority is defined in Part VII. For text, see also *Sistematicheskoe sobranie deistvuiushchikh zakonov SSSR* (Moscow, 1926), IV–V, 82.

[37] [1924] I *Sob. Zak. SSSR*, No. 23, item 203.

[38] *Ibid.*, sec. 21, note 2.

in substance from the 1922 statute on the Prosecutor's Office.[39] He found in them a broadening of functions establishing the unquestioned authority of the Prosecutor's Office. A comparison of the authority of the office as established by the 1922 statute and the 1924 "Basic Principles" indicates that the latter law did indeed make more specific the functions of the office, but one would have thought that the implications of the more general words of the 1922 statute went as far as the authority granted specifically in 1924, yet Vyshinskii did not think so.

Vyshinskii thought also that the 1924 law had been a great improvement over the 1922 law because it had made more specific the highly centralized character of the office in each republic. He criticized the 1922 statute for having permitted the local soviets to nominate their candidates for the position of provincial prosecutor, even though the 1922 statute had provided that dismissal, transfer, and suspension of prosecutors could be effected only by the Prosecutor of the Republic. He liked the wording of the 1924 law which had said that "The Prosecutor's Office shall be organized on the basis of centralization and subordination solely to the Prosecutor of the Republic." [40] He thought that this left no doubt as to the independence of the prosecutors from local influences.

Vyshinskii may have had in mind the difficulties which had been met in 1923 in forcing the provincial executive committees to accept the authority of the provincial prosecutor, for those difficulties have been shown by the authors of the time to have been very real. He had to admit, however, that even though the 1924 law tried in more explicit terms than the law of 1922 to indicate the complete independence of the prosecutors from the local soviets and local Communist party officials, it had not succeeded in its aim. He reported that at least up to the time of the date of the decree of June 25, 1932,[41] stressing the necessity of preserving law and order, there had been many attempts of local soviets and local Communist party organs to intervene in the affairs of the employees of the prosecutors' offices. The June 25, 1932, decree had declared:

---

[39] A. Ia. Vyshinskii, *Sudoustroistvo v SSSR*, pp. 286–87.

[40] Basic Principles, October 29, 1924, sec. 14, par. 2.

[41] Decree on Revolutionary Legality, June 25, 1932, [1932] I *Sob. Zak. SSSR*, No. 50, item 298.

For the purpose of further strengthening revolutionary law and order, and improving and uplifting the importance of the judicial and prosecutor's agencies it is categorically forbidden to remove or transfer people's judges except on resolution of a provincial executive committee, while district prosecutors may be removed or transferred only on the decision of a provincial prosecutor or of higher agencies of the Prosecutor's Office and of the Peoples' Commissariat of Justice.[42]

To Vyshinskii the great importance of this statement of principle was without question, for without it he foresaw a return to what Lenin had feared, namely, variation within the law between province and province, depending upon the type of local influence brought to bear upon the prosecutors to follow a provincial "line" or point of view.

While the Soviet policy makers seem to have been willing to experiment with autonomy of the prosecutors within each republic for a good many years after formal federation of the republics, they indicated on June 20, 1933, that an end had come to such experimentation. On that date the Central Executive Committee and Council of People's Commissars of the U.S.S.R. adopted a decree settling once and for all the question of centralization.[43] A Prosecutor's Office of the U.S.S.R. was established with general direction over the activities of the prosecutors' offices in the several republics.[44] The basis was laid for the highly centralized system of prosecutor's offices incorporated in the second constitution of the U.S.S.R. adopted in 1936 [45] and continued to the present day.

[42] *Ibid.*, sec. 6.

[43] Decree on the Establishment of the Prosecutor's Office of the USSR, [1933] I *Sob. Zak. SSSR*, No. 40, item 239.

[44] The prosecutor's offices in the republics remained within the administrative structure of the republic People's Commissariats of Justice. They were not removed from the Commissariats until the decree of July 20, 1936, [1936] I *Sob. Zak. SSSR*, No. 40, item 338, placed them under the direct administrative control of the Prosecutor of the USSR.

[45] For text of Constitution of the USSR, December 5, 1936, see *Izvestiia*, No. 283, December 6, 1936. The structure of the Prosecutor's Office of the USSR was reorganized to prepare to bear its heavy burden by Decree on the Structure of the Prosecutor's Office of the USSR, November 5, 1936, [1936] I *Sob. Zak. SSSR*, No. 59, item 450.

Chapter 8

PROFESSIONALIZING THE BAR

EXPERIMENTATION with the structure of the bar had resulted during the first four years of the new Soviet state in no acceptable pattern of organization. Complete informality as it had been tried in the early months had proved to be inadequate. The citizens had not come forward in the courtroom out of a sense of duty to defend the interests of relatives or neighbors unable to protect themselves. The unlimited opportunity provided by the first decree on the courts for representation in court seems to have opened the gate to practice by former members of the Imperial bar rather than to have encouraged relatives and friends of an accused or an aggrieved plaintiff to appear.

The Imperial bar might have been eliminated by banning all representation in court and by requiring the judges to act alone in exploring the facts of a case. Some of the early Soviet enthusiasts who were seeking new ways of conducting the business of government were quite prepared for such a radical departure from familiar patterns, but the thoughtful judges refused to take such a position. They felt that they needed help in exploring facts. They were ready to discard their inherited dislike of lawyers because they felt that under the new circumstances brought by the Revolution lawyers would become different. The bar could be expected to help the court rather than to take a position which they believed had usually been in the interest of the client alone.

The necessity for legal assistance in complicated cases had been recognized within three months of the Revolution. A college from which persons might be selected by a court both for the prosecution and for the defense had been established by the second decree on the courts. It had provided aid to judges in the newly created district courts hearing cases carried over from prerevolutionary court calendars and new suits for large damages. Still the great mass of cases in the peoples' courts had been heard without benefit of lawyers. The bar, such as it was, had cut a very small figure in the procedure of the court room.

The first novel experiment had been to create a civil-service panel from which accusers and defenders would be selected. A regular salary was paid to those on the panel, and they held themselves in readiness for a call. To the Communists charged with the administration of the court system at the time, the concept of such a civil-service function seemed to fit their political theory. The system had been accepted in the People's Court Act of 1918, but its popularity had been short lived. Within nineteen months the Commissar of Justice had come back to the platform to expose the abuses which had arisen under the civil-service system and had called for a change. The salary concept was discarded, and the accusers were separated institutionally from the defenders.

Legal aid as a labor duty of those with legal education had been the next experiment. All who could be presumed to understand the law were registered, and from the registry were selected for brief periods of time those persons who were needed to assist in the conduct of a law suit, civil or criminal. No fees were to be paid by the parties, for the lawyers were to continue to receive their usual wages from their regular employers, and if self-employed, they were to be paid a per diem from public funds. The labor-duty system was made the rule in the People's Court Act of 1920.

Throughout all of the experimentation it was always provided that relatives might appear for a party, as well as representatives of labor unions or of a factory committee to which the party might belong. In this feature there was retained a symbol representing the original idea of the tribunal of primitive society before which parties would be accused and defended by blameless citizens sensing their social duty to assist the local wise men in preserving social order. The Soviet court had already passed by 1920 well beyond the primitive tribunal which had appealed so strongly to Commissar Kurskii in the early years, but symbols still meant a great deal to the Communist leaders.

The leaders were unwilling to accept the fact that their system of legal institutions was becoming complicated and was moving away from the influence and control of the people on the farms and in the factories. They clung to recitals of concepts no longer possible of application such as the single-court system and the determination of applicable legal rules by reference to an ill-defined concept called "revolutionary conscience." The preservation of access to the court-room for the relative and friend of a citizen in trouble seems to have been one more of the aspirations to which the Communist leadership wished to hold. The policy makers were moving toward a professional bar, but they did not want to establish for it a monopoly of representation.

The development of economic policy in the direction of limited private enterprise became the straw that broke the back of the revolutionary concept of legal representation without professional organization. Everyone seems to have anticipated that the courts would be flooded with actions, both civil and criminal. The bourgeoisie in whom the Communists had no faith whatever were expected to litigate actively. It was also expected that the bourgeoisie would misuse their newly granted privileges, and that they would have to be prosecuted so as to protect what was to be left of the socialism inaugurated by the Revolution. Under such circumstances the whole question of legal representation in court required re-thinking, and the Fourth Congress of persons engaged in the administration of justice, meeting in January, 1922, was asked to make suggestions. It was the general opinion of those present that what was needed was a professional bar to be established in a college of defenders tied to the courts. The courts would supervise and discipline, but the bar would be sufficiently autonomous and independent to elect its executives from its own membership. State salaries for lawyers were not to be reinstituted, nor was their work to be a labor duty entirely without pay. Legal representation was to be the profession of persons admitted to practice after examination of their qualifications and for whose maintenance there were to be charged fees of the clients. To avoid a relapse into what was thought to be one of the evils of the fee system lawyers were to be admonished that they must perform free of charge legal services for those unable to pay. To provide control over fees charged of financially responsible clients a tariff was to be established.

While the conferees in January, 1922, were prepared to move toward a professional bar structured in a pattern familiar to prerevolutionary lawyers, they wanted still to retain some of the informality of the early revolutionary years. They spoke in favor of the right of relatives to appear, and also of the right of appearance of representatives of trade unions and other social organizations to which the accused might belong.

LEGISLATION OF 1922

A skeletal decree was introduced into the meeting of the Central Executive Committee of the Congress of Soviets of the Russian Republic on May 15, 1922. The spokesman for the Commissariat of Justice, Ia. Brandenburgskii, informed the legislators that the details of the new organization of the bar would be worked out in a special regulation to be reviewed by the Commissariat of Justice and the Council of People's Commissars, and this regulation would be brought eventually to the Central Executive Committee for enactment as a statute.[1]

Brandenburgskii's expectation was only partially fulfilled. The skeletal decree was enacted as planned on May 26, 1922,[2] but the regulation providing detail was promulgated on July 7, 1922,[3] only by the Commissariat of Justice without the anticipated action by the Central Executive Committee. On some points the Commissariat revised what the Central Executive Committee had done. The obvious irregularity of such revision of law by an administrative agency annoyed one of the prerevolutionary lawyers who was by that time supporting the regime and who wrote his analysis of the new bar in the journal published in aid of the practicing lawyer.[4]

The new "colleges of defenders" were to be organized in each province under the terms of the decree of May 26, 1922, by the provincial departments of justice. In this provision there was a departure from the recommendations of the advisory conference of

[1] *RSFSR—Biulleten' III sessii Vserossiiskogo Tsentral'nogo Ispolnitel'nogo Komiteta, IX sozyva,* (*Stenograficheskii otchët*), *zasedanie ot 15 maia 1922 g.* (Moscow, 1922), p. 33.

[2] Statute on the Institution of Advocacy, May 26, 1922, [1922] I *Sobranie Uzakonenii i Rasporiazhenii Rabochego i Krest'ianskogo Pravitel'stva RSFSR,* No. 36, item 425.

[3] Regulations on the Institution of Advocacy, July 7, 1922, *Ezhenedel'nik sovetskoi iustitsii,* No. 24–25 (July 3–10, 1922).

[4] A. S. Tager, "Zametki ob advokature," *Pravo i zhizn',* Book I (1923), p. 44.

January, for the participants in the latter had suggested that the lawyers be attached to the courts. Membership at the outset was to be proposed by each provincial department of justice to the presidium of the provincial soviet's executive committee. After the initial list of charter members had been approved in this manner, further members were to be admitted with less formality. The presidium of each provincial college of defenders was to receive applications for membership and to pass upon them. Admission was to be immediate when the presidium of the college acted, but the presidium of the college was required to notify the presidium of the provincial soviet's executive committee of the admission, and the latter might subsequently order the expulsion of the newly admitted member. In this fashion there was given to the lawyers themselves the right to control their own membership after the charter members had been determined, but the regime did not release the lawyers completely from control. There was preserved a means of reversing through the provincial soviet the action of the lawyers.

The lawyers were to be permitted to choose their own leaders, for the decree provided that the presidium of the college should be elected by the general meeting of members of the college. As might have been expected under the system of influence created by the Communist party, the election within the general meeting was not to be conducted without planning by the Communists. A report of the first meeting of the college in Moscow states without concealment that the first presidium was nominated by a faction composed of those members of the college who belonged to the Communist party. Of the nine persons elected, five were Communists and the other four were from the "group of so-called peoples' lawyers." [5]

The presidium of the college was given by the decree the usual powers of an executive committee, namely, to see to the performance by the members of their duties as members, to exact disciplinary fines, to disburse funds from the treasury of the college, to organize the offices in which legal advice would be given to the public, and to determine the cases in which no fee would be charged and those

---

[5] "Otkrytie deiatel'nosti moskovskoi kollegii zashchitnikov," *Ezh. sov. iust.,* No. 37–38 (October 13–20, 1922), p. 38.

in which a fee would be charged according to the tariff. Only in one instance was there to be an appeal from the presidium's ruling, namely, in the case of the exaction of a disciplinary fine. In such cases the aggrieved party might appeal the ruling to the provincial soviet's executive committee.

Members of the colleges were not to be permitted to hold salaried positions in state offices or industrial enterprises, except as teachers in law schools. To avoid any confusion over outside activities, it was provided that the exclusion did not extend to prohibition of the holding of elective office within the system of soviets. Members were to be paid through fees, but the decree established three categories of clients with regard to fees. Persons found by a people's court to be penniless were to be charged no fee; persons who were wage earners in positions as clerks in state or private offices or workmen in state or private enterprises were to be charged for the services within the limits set by a tariff of fees, and persons outside the other two categories were to be charged in accordance with whatever agreement might be reached between the attorney and the client. Each lawyer was to be taxed a percentage of his fees for maintenance of the college and of its consultation offices. The percentage was to be fixed by the Commissariat of Justice.

To indicate that the new bar was not being given a monopoly of representation in court the decree recited the familiar provision of the early years that close relatives and members of trade unions and other public associations to which a party before a court belonged were to be permitted to appear in court as a representative of a party. It also permitted other persons to appear with the special consent of the court having jurisdiction over the case.

Fear lest the new bar obtain a monopoly of representation had caused a sharp debate in the Central Executive Committee over the right of appearance. When the draft of the Commissariat of Justice was brought in for enactment, the legislators indicated the tenacity with which they held to their earlier concepts of a system of legal representation open to the nonprofessional. To meet this point of view but to bring it within bounds, a provision had been inserted by the Commissariat of Justice in the draft statute on the new bar reading: "In exceptional circumstances other persons having the special confidence of the court may also be permitted to defend." [6] In this provision the Commissariat indicated that it was prepared to go beyond the circle of relatives and representatives of trade unions and other public associations, but it was not prepared to go very far.

The limits of the Commissariat's position had been made clear in a statement by its spokesman before the Fourth Congress of workers in the field of justice in January, 1922. The spokesman had declared that the very popular author Maxim Gorkii or some other person having without question the confidence of the court and having no professional relationship to the legal system would be permitted to appear if he were asked by a party and if he had something to contribute to the case.[7] The narrowing in this way of the circle of persons authorized to appear in aid of a party was sharply criticized in the Central Executive Committee in May. It was said that the creation of the college of defenders should not be permitted to deprive any blameless citizen having full legal rights to appear as a representative of a party before the courts, and that no special privileges should be created for the members of the college of defenders.

The limited proposal of the Commissariat was stricken from the draft, and it was provided that "other persons shall be permitted to defend but only with special permission of the court." This form was, apparently, expected to keep the door open for persons with no monumental reputation comparable to that of the Revolution's romantic hero, Maxim Gorkii. Nevertheless, the door was not opened to all. The control of the court over appearances of attorneys was preserved, and in this fact the faction favoring restrictive practices found its opening. The proponents of the open-court policy of the early days claimed a victory, as indicated by the argument of a Soviet commentator in 1926 that the Central Executive Committee's decision of 1922 had settled the matter. Any blameless person having full legal rights was thought authorized to appear as an advocate unless there were some special reason for excluding him, such as the special character of the trial making the participation of a person, even one having the confidence of the court, unsuitable.[8]

The courts seem to have been unprepared for a broad interpreta-

[6] E. S. Rivlin, *Sovetskaia advokatura* (Moscow, 1926), p. 30.
[7] *Ibid.*, p. 31.   [8] *Ibid.*

tion of the authority to admit any blameless person to appear before them. Judicial reluctance to open argument to all was manifested in the rulings of subsequent years. The lay representative was not popular with many of those guiding state policy, and the legislation of 1922 appears to have been regarded by what might be called the traditionalists as but a temporary defeat of the restrictive policy for which they fought.

Nothing was said in the decree of May 26, 1922, about the qualifications to be required of applicants for membership in the colleges. This important provision was left for the supplementary regulation issued by the Commissariat of Justice on July 7, 1922. It was there established that the following persons might apply: (1) persons who had worked in agencies concerned with the administration of Soviet law for not less than two years; (2) persons who passed an examination in legal theory and practice to be conducted by a three-man examining commission composed of the president of the council of people's judges, one other member of the council of people's judges, and a member of the presidium of the college of defenders. Persons otherwise qualified were to be denied admission to the college if they had not reached the age of majority, if they were deprived under the constitution of the right to vote and to be elected to agencies of the soviets, if they were standing trial for crime, if they had been limited in their civil rights by a court sentence, or if they had previously been expelled from a college of defenders. Any person denied admission might appeal the denial to the presidium of the provincial soviet's executive committee.

Not all decisions were left to the presidium of the college. The general meeting was stated in the Commissariat's regulation to have the right to discuss matters of general concern to the college; to determine the amount of the tax upon fees with which the expenses of the college were to be met, and to work out the general plan under which the offices for giving legal advice to the public would be set up and operated.

UKRAINIAN IMPROVEMENTS

The Ukrainian Republic adopted almost identically worded rules for the establishment and operation of the colleges within its boundaries. Being, as usual, some months behind the Russian Republic in enacting legislation, the Ukrainians seem to have decided that it would be advantageous to combine in one decree the substance of both the Russian Republic's skeletal decree and of its Commissariat of Justice's regulation. The Ukrainian decree of October 2, 1922, includes, therefore, all that was necessary to understand the operation of the colleges in one document.[9]

The Ukrainian decree provides more precision in the functions of the various agencies of the college than is to be found in the Russian decree and regulation. For example, the admission of members remains in the hands of the presidium of the college subject to the right of the presidium of the provincial soviet's executive committee to expel, but the Ukrainians have added that the provincial soviet's executive committee must make its decision within one month, or its silence will have the force of an acceptance. The minutes of general meetings of members of the college were ordered sent within three days to the presidium of the provincial court and to the provincial prosecutor. Election of the presidium of the college was to be valid only if at least half of the members of the college were present at the general meeting held for the purpose.

The presidium of the college was given an additional power of importance by the Ukrainian decree: it was authorized to suspend or expel members of the college, subject to the usual appeal of the aggrieved party to supervising authority. It was also authorized to take measures to see that cases in charge of members who became ill, died, or expelled would be assumed by a substitute.

The Ukrainian decree takes note as well of an event subsequent to enactment of the Russian Republic's statute—namely, the abolition of the provincial department of justice and the substitution of the provincial court as the administrative agency for judicial matters. The Ukrainian decree made the provincial court the supervising agency for the college of defenders. As has been indicated, the abolition of the provincial department of justice by the judiciary acts of 1922 in the various republics came about as the result of what seems almost to have been a feeling of spite on the part of Krylenko and his colleagues against the chairmen of these depart-

[9] Statute on the Institution of Advocacy, October 2, 1922, [1922] I *Sobranie Uzakonenii i Rasporiazhenii Raboche-Krest'ianskogo Pravitel'stva Ukrainy*, No. 43, item 630.

ments. The change was not the result of a desire to strengthen judicial control. In consequence, the transfer of control to the new provincial courts from the departments of justice can hardly be interpreted as an effort to assure the colleges of defenders of protection against the administrative mind. The new provincial courts were to be no less administrative than the old provincial departments of justice had been, and the bar had not, in fact, become attached to a court in the sense contemplated by the members of the Fourth Congress of juristic workers when they had met in January, 1922.

The Russian Republic was not to amend its statute on the bar to reflect the change in structure of the courts until the following year. Although the Russian lawyers may have cooperated with the Ukrainians in developing the Ukrainian refinements, it was not until July 7, 1923,[10] that the Russians introduced the revised skeletal statute into their Republic's judiciary act. The Russian Republic's amendments indicated that control over the bar had in fact already passed to the provincial court from the provincial department of justice. The amended statute suggested also that the Russian Republic's authorities had found it necessary to provide, as the Ukrainian Republic had provided, that the provincial soviet's executive committee must either act quickly in barring admission of new members or be taken to have approved a candidacy, for the Ukrainian provision on the subject was incorporated in the Russian statute without change. Further, the provincial soviet's executive committee was given the right to dismiss at will any of the previously approved members of the college, in the same manner as this right had been established by the Ukrainian decree.

Commentators explained that the right to dismiss at any time a previously approved member of the college had been included in the 1923 amendment because of the experience of the first year of application of the 1922 statute. One month was said to have proved to be an inadequate time to discover whether a newly admitted member was undesirable as a lawyer, and for that reason it had been necessary to extend the probationary period indefinitely.[11] It was also declared that some of those admitted as charter members of

[10] Decree on Changes in and Additions to the Judiciary Act, RSFSR, July 7, 1923, Chap. VI, [1923] I *Sob. Uzak. RSFSR*, No. 48, item 481.

[11] "Kakie izmeneniia v polozhenie o sudoustroistve vneseny narkomiustom v sessiu VTsIK?" *Ezh. sov. iust.*, No. 25–26 (July 5, 1923), p. 577.

the colleges by the presidiums of the provincial soviets' executive committees had been found to be bad, but even greater numbers of those admitted subsequently by the presidiums of the colleges had not been up to the standards required of Soviet officials.[12] This fact was said to have given rise to a practice of dismissal of college members by the provincial soviets' executive committees after the expiration of the one-month period even though the 1922 statute had given no such authority to the executive committees. The 1923 amendment was, therefore, to bring the law into accord with the necessities of the situation as they had emerged in practice.

Employment of lawyers in salaried posts outside the college seems also to have been a matter of concern at the time, for the Russian Republic's amendment of 1923 added to the category of permissible employment a new second category. Members of the college were to be allowed under the new rule to retain college membership even though they might be employed as legal advisers to state offices and enterprises, but only when such permission was recommended by the presidium of the college and when the request for permission was supported by a request from the state office or enterprise concerned. Finally, the approval of the provincial court was required. Since this provision had not been anticipated in the Ukrainian legislation, it must have shown itself desirable in subsequent experience.

The prosecutors in the Russian Republic became a controlling agency over disciplinary decisions of the presidium of each college by the Russian amendment of 1923, emulating the earlier Ukrainian legislation. Under the 1923 Russian amendment a prosecutor might appeal a disciplinary decision to the provincial soviet's executive committee. While this arrangement limited the authority of the new bar generally to police itself, it may have provided some protection to an individual member of a college of defenders who was being punished solely because he had antagonized local officials. The prosecutors had been made independent of the provincial soviets by the statute creating them in 1922, and they were under no compulsion to curry favors locally. Their intervention may have been able to force the soviet to correct a hostile decision of the local bar

[12] S. Askarkhanov, "Voprosy sudoustroistva na poslednei sessii VTsIK," *ibid.*, No. 31 (August 9, 1923), p. 703.

leaders, for a prosecutor could reach over the head of local authorities in the event that there developed within a province a cabal refusing to follow policy set in Moscow.

The severe shortage of legally trained personnel to staff the new colleges and to perform duties as legal advisers to the new public corporations which were being created in 1923 to operate state-owned industry, railroads, mines, and distribution outlets is evidenced by the Russian Republic's amendment of 1923 to its statute on advocates. The shortage is further indicated by reports of the organization of various colleges soon after the adoption of the new decrees in the various republics.

IMPLEMENTATION OF THE
NEW POLICY

The first meeting of the college of defenders in Moscow on October 8, 1922, brought together only 205 lawyers out of the 320 licensed to practice by the Moscow Soviet.[13] Moscow was not only the most populous city within the country; it was also the center in which most of the newly created public corporations had their head offices. In communities farther from the center the number of lawyers was much smaller. For example, in the Tyumen Province in the Urals only 11 persons had been approved as charter members of the provincial college of advocates up to September 20, 1922.[14] The first general meeting of members of the Tyumen college was held on December 24, 1922. It was declared that the original 11 had been chosen from 45 applicants. A reporter for the province indicated that there was a shortage of talent, for among the persons with theoretical or practical training part had been blackballed in the selection process, part were busy as legal advisers to public corporations, and part were not sufficiently well fitted for the work.

The Akmolinsk Province reported that it had only 10 charter members of the college by October, 1922. There were only 4 persons found qualified to serve in the important city of Petropavlovsk.[15] All

---

[13] "Otkrytie deiatel'nosti moskovskoi kollegii zashchitnikov," *ibid.*, No. 37–38 (October 13–20, 1922), p. 38.

[14] "Advokatura na urale," *ibid.*, No. 46–47 (December 30, 1922), p. 41.

[15] "Kollegiia zashchity," *ibid.*, p. 41.

members of the Akmolinsk college had legal education, but none belonged to the Communist party. Some applications had been received from Communists, but the candidates were still awaiting examination.

Questions were asked about the statute on the colleges soon after its publication. Writing in the lawyer's magazine, one of the members of the old bar who had accepted the principles of the new regime tried to describe the limits of the power of the provincial executive committee over the college.[16] He reminded his readers that the spokesman for the Commissariat of Justice had told the Central Executive Committee of the Russian Republic's Congress of Soviets when the legislation had been introduced that the colleges were to have definite autonomy. This seemed to him to provide the basis for interpretation of the power of the control agency. He declared that the right of the provincial executive committee to veto an applicant was limited to what the statute said. It did not extend to forcing upon the college acceptance of an applicant which the college did not want. He felt that his interpretation was supported further by the fact that the Commissariat's spokesman had told the legislators that more control than the veto was not required because the bar had changed greatly in character from prerevolutionary times and now had a definite inclination to work with Soviet authority.

The right of the provincial executive committee to set aside a decision of the college either on its own initiative or on the protest of the provincial prosecutor was also examined by the critic. He thought that this right must obviously be limited if the bar were to be autonomous. He found what he thought was a limitation by concluding that the revocation might be ordered only if the college had violated a provision of the law. It could not be directed against a decision of the college or of its presidium when that decision had been based upon a matter of judgment of the expediency of the situation.

In these two comments on the limits of control over the college one senses that the author was repeating what he thought obvious so as to discourage excesses on the part of the control agencies. He

[16] Tager, "Zametki," p. 43.

and his fellow lawyers were probably rather suspicious of the control agencies, and his comments may have been designed to express that suspicion in as palatable a form as possible.

On the matter of financial support for the colleges the author was more outspoken. He thought that the state treasury should bear the cost of establishing the consultation points to be of service to the people generally. He noted that the statute provided for maintenance of these points out of a tax on fees. He remarked that the fees might vary greatly from province to province with the result that the number of consultation offices would necessarily vary greatly. This basis for establishing consultation offices seemed to him to be a purely fortuitous one and not a rational one for planning the creation of a net of legal-advice centers, yet such centers were, the author indicated, of great importance to Soviet leaders. The author seems to have been trying to appeal to Commissar Kurskii's previously expressed desire to provide for a system of courts which would be close to the people in every village and hamlet. He suggested that if the popular courts were to be effective, they should be accompanied by equally well distributed legal-consultation offices. Such a large net of offices as would be required could not in his opinion be financed out of a tax on fees.[17] The critic asked for an annual allocation from the state budget.

The literal limitation in the statute upon a lawyer's appearances in courts and tribunals of the province within which the lawyer lived seemed to the critic also ill advised. He remarked that this limitation could lead to the development of an appellate bar which he considered to be an evil of other systems of legal procedure. The appellate court was often beyond the boundaries of a given province, and the limitation on appearances could prevent a lawyer who had tried the case from taking it up to the distant appellate court. Further, the limitation could operate to the disadvantage of some of the new public corporations or of the central organization for the League of Cooperatives. These had their main offices in Moscow, yet they did business throughout all provinces of the Republic. It seemed obvious to the critic that business would have to be conducted without attention to geographical boundaries, and so he

[71] It was later reported from Kharkov Province that the tax was 7 percent on fees. See "Iz zhizni khar'kovskoi gubernskoi kollegii zashchitnikov," *Vestnik sovetsoi iustitsii,* No. 2 (August 15, 1923), p. 44.

called for adoption of a rule that would make clear that lawyers admitted to one provincial college might practice before the courts of other provinces without the necessity of living in the other provinces.

Any limitation on numbers of persons to be admitted to the colleges, which limitation seemed to the critic to be implied in the regulation issued by the Commissariat, was thought to be unwise. It was admitted that limitation had attraction to those who hoped to obtain large fees, but the critic argued that the lawyers before the Revolution had not sought to improve their incomes by elimination of competition, and there was no reason for the new lawyers to want to do so. The critic also thought that specialization should be allowed, because life had become complicated, and a lawyer could not be expected to be familiar with all branches of law any more than a doctor could be skilled in all branches of medicine.

Branch offices in the counties, as permitted by the regulation, also attracted the attention of the critic. He recognized that such offices were necessary to the efficient functioning of the colleges, but he cautioned that they must be limited in their powers. They should always act as agents of the provincial college, and should never be permitted to arrogate to themselves any policy-making functions. The critic went further to say that a presidium of a college could not be permitted to transfer to a county bureau any of its rule-making functions or its disciplinary functions. The county bureaus could only do such things as receive applications for membership in the college to be acted upon by the college, or gather evidence to be used in disciplining a member. It could neither admit nor discipline. It could collect the tax on fees of members to finance the consultation offices, and it could assign lawyers to specific cases.

The critic ended his article by saying that the creation of a Prosecutor's Office and of a bar by the 1922 decrees had strengthened the parties in court proceedings, and that this strengthening was desirable. It would increase the "health" of Soviet court life. Clearly, the lawyers of the past who had thrown their support behind the new regime felt happy that a professional bar had been authorized. It suggested reestablishment of a vigorous adversary procedure such as they had known before and which they thought essential to a fair trial. They accepted the necessity of governmental control over the bar, but they hoped that the control permitted by the law would not be abused. They were prepared to accept the new statute and regulation as they stood, but they could find a few points at which they hoped that eventually the statute on advocates would be improved.

ORGANIZING THE MOSCOW BAR

The presidium of the Moscow college began to work the day after its election on October 8, 1922.[18] It named three secretaries to see to the implementation of its decisions and to prepare for meetings of the full presidium. It named an office manager to attend to house-keeping details including the accounting of funds. Two committees of four members each were also named, one to attend to the disciplining of members and the other to be concerned with planning the establishment of consultation offices throughout the province.

The committee on consultation offices drafted rules for establishment and conduct of the offices. The draft was submitted to the general meeting of members and finally sent to the provincial council of people's judges for approval. Control over the offices was to remain in the presidium but to be exercised in fact through the committee. A weekly meeting of managers of consultation offices was to be held to discuss problems and suggest action. In addition members of the presidium were to be sent on circuit during the initial period to see personally what was being done and to decide what improvements in procedures might be recommended. Consultation offices were to be set up not only for general practice in geographical districts but also for specialized fields. There were to be specialized consultation offices for peasant affairs, for civil and administrative matters, for the legal protection of children, and for provincial matters taken before the Supreme Court of the Republic. Consultation was also to be provided in prisons. The inadequate number of lawyers available prevented establishment of consultation offices in every county, and to meet the need teams of three were created to travel on circuit through the counties to provide legal advice.

The optimum number of lawyers for Moscow Province had been

[18] "Rabota mosovskoi kollegii zashchitnikov," *Ezh. sov. iust.*, No. 46–47 (December 30, 1922), p. 38.

set by the Moscow soviet at 350. It was indicated that during the first two months 320 places had been filled. Four persons had subsequently vacated their places, so that 34 vacancies remained for which there were 850 applicants. A long and tedious period of testing was expected. The report gave clear indication that the number of lawyers available for the many tasks to be performed was completely inadequate even for the capital city. Apparently it was not expected to be easy to obtain an increase in the existing limit on numbers, for the suggestion was made that before the number could be raised statistics on the cases in the province requiring lawyers would have to be prepared and presented to the Moscow soviet so that it could measure the need.

Assignment of a lawyer in a case in which one was requested free of charge or on the limited fee basis established by the tariff was to be made in the following manner: when the case was in the people's court, the assignment would be made by the consultation office in the county concerned, but when the case reached the appellate level the choice would be made by the consultation office attached to the appellate court, unless a lawyer who had tried the case below continued with the case on appeal. In cases before the special sessions of the council of people's judges or before any of the revolutionary tribunals, the assignment of a lawyer would be the task of the presidium of the college itself, thus assuring, presumably, what was expected to be a responsible political choice.

Disciplinary matters were to be handled by the disciplinary committee of the college. The committee established a uniform diary into which the lawyer was to write his activities and place his time charges so that his relations with clients could be audited easily. It forbade all advertising by lawyers in newspapers, and designated the form of professional card which might be placed on the door of a lawyer's home. Disciplinary action was to be taken by the committee, and sent forward for review by the presidium of the college only if the committee split in its opinion, or if the matter was deemed to be of great importance requiring review even when the committee had been unanimous.

When the report of the operations of the Moscow college is read in the light of the criticism leveled at the statute and regulation on the bar as it has been reviewed above, it is evident that some of the developments feared by the critic were coming to pass. A limit on numbers in the college was being set by the provincial soviet, with the result that the work of the college was being hampered. An appellate bar was coming into existence, although the dangers foreseen by the critic were being avoided in part by extension to the trial lawyer of the privilege of remaining with a case as it was carried up on appeal if he wished to do so. On the other hand some of the dangers anticipated seem not to have been felt by the Moscow college. There was no complaint about inadequate funds to establish consultation offices. The complaint was over inadequate numbers of persons. There was no requirement that all lawyers be in general practice, for specialized consultation offices to be concerned with matters concerning peasants, children, and civil and administrative law were being formed.

LIMITATIONS ON NUMBERS
OF LAWYERS

The complaint against policies which resulted in limitation of numbers of members of the college was also raised by reporters from the Ukraine.[19] The Kharkov college reported "about 100 members" by mid-July, 1923, after two and a half months of operation. Of these, 75 were in the city and only 25 in the country districts of the province. Sixty applications had been received since the charter members had been admitted. Nine of the applicants had been accepted without examination, 20 had been admitted to the examination, and one had been rejected. The remaining 30 applications had not yet been examined.

The report suggested that difficulty was being faced in recruiting new members because members of the college were being required by the Commissariat of Finance to buy a license to conduct private practice just as if they were a merchant. This requirement seemed to the reporter to be out of keeping with the role assigned to the new colleges. He could see no reason why a lawyer should be classed in the unpopular category of "commercial" if he were to

---

[19] "Iz zhizni khar'kovskoi kollegii zashchitnikov," *Vestnik sov. iust.*, No. 2 (August 15, 1923), p. 44.

be required to provide without charge legal advice to the public, if he were to be called a "responsible official" in the statute on the judiciary, and finally if the presidium of the college were to be permitted to use the Soviet state's insignia in its institutional seal. The "commercial" classification was said to drive out of the organization the very people who were wanted, presumably because they would not as Communists accept a position which threw them into a category against which they as Communists had fought the Revolution.

Communists had, apparently, been joining in spite of the "commercial" category into which the College had been placed by the Commissariat of Finance. The Kharkov presidium of seven contained four Communists. Ekaterinoslav's college had 30 Communists out of 126 members. Perhaps these Communists were aware that the position of the Commissariat of Finance was not realistic, and that it would ultimately have to be reviewed in the light of the political importance of the colleges.

The political importance of the colleges was manifest in a subsequent report of the categories of persons served by the consultation offices of the Kharkov college during May and June, 1923.[20] This showed that of 807 cases, 205 had been requests for aid from white-collar workers, 117 had come from employed workmen, 65 had been brought by invalids, 67 by unemployed persons, 65 by artisans, 76 by merchants, 129 by housewives, 57 by peasants, and 22 by students. Such a report suggested that the bar was not engaged primarily in protecting the bourgeoisie as some had thought it would be. When the total of 807 cases is compared with the 700 reported as having been handled without a fee in what appears to have been about the same period, the financially advantageous cases seem to have been about 12 percent of the total.

Similar statistics from Chernigov and Poltava Provinces showed concentration of work on cases of workers, clerks, and peasants.[21] Out of 376 cases in Chernigov Province from February through June only 35 were taken on behalf of private enterprisers. Of the

[20] "Na mestakh: v kharkovskoi kollegii zashchitnikov," *ibid.*, No. 4 (September 15, 1923), p. 104.
[21] "Na mestakh: v chernigovskoi kollegii zashchitnikov"; also "Na mestakh: v poltavskoi kollegii zashchitnikov," *ibid.*, p. 105.

376 cases, 134 had been taken without charge, 94 had been charged a full fee, in accordance with a private agreement between client and counsel, and the balance had been charged at the tariff rate for workers and clerks. Poltava Province's college reported that only 5 cases had been brought by private enterprisers out of 165 brought during the first few months of operation.

Civil cases were almost everywhere in the majority of those in which lawyers gave advice or appeared. Kharkov's college reported 696 civil cases out of its total of 807; Chernigov's college reported 169 civil cases, 153 criminal cases, and 34 administrative cases; Poltava's college reported 116 civil cases, 38 criminal cases and 11 administrative cases. Criminal cases were in the majority, however, in Ekaterinoslav Province, with 401 cases out of the 422 entered on the books of the college between March and the end of July.

Some hint as to the reason for the small number of cases in some provinces relating to private enterprisers is to be found in the report for 1923 from Vladimir Province in the Russian Republic.[22] The legal advice bureaus were denying legal advice to persons deprived under the provisions of the constitution of electoral rights. Nothing in the law supported this position, for it had been provided expressly that persons with property could obtain legal aid on payment of a fee. Presumably many of those with property were merchants or were employing labor for profit under the respite granted private enterprise by the New Economic Policy. Although they could not vote or be elected to office under the rule of the constitution, they had civil rights, and these must have included the right to counsel. If the provincial college was refusing to give advice entirely, it was either misunderstanding the intent of the legislators or leaning over backward to avoid any taint of association with the bourgeoisie.

The control agencies seem to have aroused some antagonism in the Ukraine. The Poltava college reported that two of the persons admitted to membership had been vetoed as being "unsuitable." The college was, apparently, unhappy about this action, for a question had been sent to the Commissariat of Justice to

[22] "Na mestakh: iuridicheskie konsul'tatsii," *Ezh. sov. iust.*, No. 27 (July 12, 1923), p. 617.

ask for reasons. There is no indication that the Commissariat replied. Another author hinted that the provincial courts were taking disciplinary matters into their hands. He wrote an article to say that they had no right to discipline members of the college, although he did not go so far as to say that they were already acting as disciplinarians.[23] He limited himself to an argument based upon his interpretation of the statute, saying that the definition of the members as "responsible officials" did not make the lawyers employees of the court in the sense that they could be disciplined by it. He even used the Commissariat of Finance's classification of law practice as a "free profession" for purposes of taxation to support his point. In doing so he sought to turn to the college's advantage a tax classification against which Ukrainian lawyers have been seen to have been struggling in an effort to rid the bar of the political taint of being bourgeois in its activities.

THE RIGHT TO COUNSEL

The legislators of 1922 were not prepared to give to an accused citizen the right to counsel in all circumstances. Their concern on this score seems to have been more with preservation of secrecy than with fear lest lawyers use their skill to outwit judges and prosecutors to the detriment of the state. Protection against the skillful attorney of a class enemy was being provided in companion statutes by permitting the prosecutor to enter even a civil case at any stage of the proceedings, and by providing not only for appeals but for periodic review of the work of the lower courts without appeal. The one danger against which the draftsmen could not protect the state by these provisions was revelation of facts to an attorney who would remain free in the community after execution of sentence against his client to whisper what he had learned to those who might use the information in an attempt to unseat the regime.

The first Code of Criminal Procedure,[24] which was adopted a day before the new statute on the college of advocates, followed

---

[23] I. A. Khmel'nitskii, "Gubsud ili kollegiia zashchitnikov," *Vestnik sov. iust.*, No. 5 (October 1, 1923), p. 126.

[24] Code of Criminal Procedure, RSFSR, May 25, 1922, [1922] I *Sob. Uzak. RSFSR*, No. 20–21, item 230.

the pattern of protection against the revelation of secrets as it had been developing during the preceding years. No lawyer was to be permitted under any circumstances to assist the accused during the period of preliminary investigation, nor could a defendant before a revolutionary tribunal demand counsel under all circumstances.

The preliminary investigation had been put beyond the reach of lawyers by the People's Court Act of 1920, when the investigation was taken out of the hands of a board of three investigators and placed in the hands of a single man. In this act, as it was later explained, the policy makers had sought to preserve the secrecy which had been made possible by the elimination of all but one investigator.

Having established secrecy in 1920, the policy makers seem to have found it undesirable in 1922 to threaten secrecy by opening the preliminary investigation to members of the bar. Their refusal to do so is the more remarkable because with the 1922 legislation the bar was being organized as a formal institution in which disciplinary action awaited those who abused their privilege to the detriment of the state. Perhaps because they did not wish to attract attention to what must have seemed to some a lack of faith in the integrity of the new college of defenders, the authors of the 1922 Code of Criminal Procedure provided no explicit exclusion in so many words. They simply failed to provide for a lawyer's presence at the preliminary investigation. Counsel was to be named only after the termination of the preliminary investigation when the trial court met in preparatory session to determine whether the case was ready for trial.[25] This provision was said by an historian of the bar to have indicated that no counsel would be permitted earlier than the time indicated.[26]

The secrecy reason for excluding counsel from the preliminary investigation was not given by the historian in his attempt to explain the phenomenon. He chose to bring forth other arguments. He said that the investigation was conducted on an inquisitorial basis rather than an adversary basis, and this made counsel unnecessary.

[25] *Ibid.*, Art. 247. In the revision of February 15, 1923, this became Art. 243, [1923] *ibid.*, No. 7, item 106.
[26] Rivlin, *Sovetskaia advokatura*, p. 35.

Such an argument left untouched the age-long complaint of those who have been arrested that they need the help of counsel at the very start to help them prove their innocence at a time when they rarely understand the opportunities open to them.

The specter of the innocent but unprotected defendant is seen to have worried the historian, however, in spite of his assertion that the preliminary investigation's inquisitorial form excluded the possibility of counsel, for he added another argument. He stated that counsel was not necessary at the investigation stage because the newly created office of prosecutor had been charged with the protection of defendants as well as with their prosecution. This argument took no notice of the doubt, which a Ukrainian author is shown to have expressed, that prosecutors can divest themselves of the burden of prosecution to consider the possibility that one whom they have accused may be innocent.

The final argument presented by the historian in support of the exclusion of counsel from the preliminary investigation was that the new procedural code had provided the accused with the opportunity to appeal to a court any apparent illegality of the preliminary investigator's procedures. This argument also rang false, for an untutored and often illiterate accused can hardly have been expected to have known without the aid of counsel which of the actions of the investigator were illegal.

The lack of persuasiveness of the arguments presented seems to have worried the historian, for he suggested after completing his defense of the draftsmen that he would have favored the right of the accused to consult with counsel during the period of the preliminary investigation if not to have counsel actually present at the sessions conducted by the preliminary investigator. The author wanted to draw a distinction between consulting with counsel at a time when the accused was not actually before the preliminary investigator himself and being present as counsel at the preliminary investigation. He felt sufficiently strongly about this to suggest that the code be amended to provide at least for the right of consultation outside the investigation chamber.

Continuing suggestions through subsequent years from the pens of Soviet procedural specialists that counsel be permitted to attend the preliminary investigation imply that Soviet legal technicians, as opposed to those Communist party members who have been charged with the formulation of policy, have never been pleased with the law of exclusion. These authors seem always to have nurtured doubts that an accused person can understand his rights and utilize them without help to protect himself. As the years have passed and the peril of revelation of secrets has diminished with the dying out of members of the old bar and their replacement by young men trained under the Soviet regime, the hand of the procedural reformers has been strengthened. There was much writing in the late 1930's and again after the war in favor of counsel at all stages of Soviet criminal procedure.

The exclusion of counsel from trials before the revolutionary tribunals seems to have rested upon a similar desire for secrecy. . The exclusion was not absolute in this instance, however. The code declared that an attorney was never to be required as an absolute right of an accused, but it was for the bench in each case to decide whether the case was sufficiently important or involved sufficiently complex facts or had special political and social interest.[27] If any of these factors were found, the bench might request the presence of both an accuser and a defender to assist it in finding and interpreting the facts. If the defendant refused an attorney, this refusal was not to be permitted to prevent the presence of an accuser.

Provisions such as these excluding counsel unless found desirable by the revolutionary tribunal must be read in the light of the jurisdiction of these tribunals. At the time of enactment of the Code of Criminal Procedure the revolutionary tribunals still had their wide jurisdiction over the public generally as well as over the army and transportation. It was they who tried the highly political cases in which security was a primary issue, and secrecy could have been a factor of importance in keeping from enemies the extent of opposition to the regime within the new Soviet republics.

The Supreme Revolutionary Tribunal was given the same rights by the 1922 Code of Criminal Procedure as the inferior revolutionary tribunals to exclude or admit attorneys. When it sat as a court of original jurisdiction, it was directed to function under

[27] Code of Criminal Procedure, RSFSR, (1922), Art. 415.

the same rules of procedure as the lower tribunals.[28] When it sat as a board of appellate review, it was authorized even to exclude the parties themselves from its examination of the file.[29]

Outside the area influenced by the leadership's craving for security the lawyer was given a strong position by the new Code of Criminal Procedure. While no guaranty of the right of counsel was expressed in so many words, it seems to have been implied by the many provisions relating to his appearance and his function. The clearest statement of the right was in an article dealing with multiple defendants, providing that if the interests of the defendants conflicted, no single attorney was to be permitted to represent them. The article ended with the provision that if the interests conflicted "there must be named a special lawyer for each person before the court." [30]

The full force of the command that there be an attorney for each member of a group of defendants with conflicting interests was reduced by the general articles on attorneys. One of these general articles[31] provided that defenders were to be required only in four situations: (1) when the charge was sufficiently serious to require trial before a people's court with six lay judges, (2) when the accused was already detained under guard, (3) when there was an accuser in the case, and (4) when the accused was blind, deaf, or generally lacking in physical capacity to perceive correctly what was transpiring. Even these situations, however, seem to have occasioned no requirement that an attorney be present when an accused was arraigned before the standing bench of a people's court for speedy trial because of an admission of guilt on the part of the accused or because in the opinion of the examining authorities the evidence was incontrovertible.[32]

A trial was to be adjourned until another attorney might be found if a designated attorney failed to appear in a case in which the code required his presence.[33] The client could not be forced to accept any one who might be designated to advise him. Under the code provisions, he had to express his willingness to accept a substitute, if the substitute were not of his own choosing. Notice of an attorney's failure to appear had to be sent by the court to

---

[28] Art. 455.   [29] Art. 443.   [30] Art. 255 (Art. 251 in the 1923 revision).
[31] Art. 59.   [32] Art. 398.   [33] Art. 272 (Art. 268 in the 1923 revision).

the college to which the attorney belonged, and disciplinary action had to be instituted.

Attorneys were given sufficient procedural rights by the new code to permit them to perform their functions as counselors and participants in the trial. They were authorized to consult with their client as soon as they were named, even if their client was in prison; to familiarize themselves with the file on the case and to take notes.[34] They could not be called as witnesses in the case[35] nor could any witness be permitted to appear as a representative.[36] They could examine the defendant[37] and cross-examine the witnesses presented by the prosecution.[38] They were to be given the right always to speak last without limit of time in the presentation of their final argument so long as their speech was relevant,[39] and to rebut any reply which might be made by the prosecution to their final argument.[40]

Appearance of an attorney on appeal to the council of people's judges was authorized in an article giving attorneys the right to speak on such an occasion.[41]

The classes of persons who might appear as representatives of a party were defined in the Code of Criminal Procedure[42] in the same manner as in the statute on the college of defenders. Since the code was adopted one day before the statute on defenders, the provisions in the code on this subject were the ones over which the debate already referred to had occurred, and the resolution of the debate in favor of denying a monopoly of representation to the colleges of defenders, to which reference has been made, was reflected in both documents.

PROCEDURAL REVISION IN 1923

The enactment of a new judiciary act in October, 1922, five months after the adoption of the Code of Criminal Procedure,

[34] Art. 256 (Art. 252 in the 1923 revision).
[35] Art. 65 (Art. 61 in the 1923 revision).
[36] Art. 60 (Art. 56 in the 1923 revision).
[37] Art. 287 (Art. 283 in the 1923 revision).
[38] Art. 291 (Art. 287 in the 1923 revision).
[39] Art. 308 (Art. 304 in the 1923 revision).
[40] Art. 311 (Art. 307 in the 1923 revision).
[41] Art. 356 (Art. 410 in the 1923 revision).
[42] Art. 57 (Art. 53 in the 1923 revision).

required considerable revision of the 1922 code. The creation of provincial courts to absorb the jurisdiction of the former councils of people's judges as well as of the general revolutionary tribunals, and the establishment of a new Supreme Court of the Republic to assume the court control duties formerly placed in the Commissariat of Justice introduced new institutions for which provision had to be made. The position of the lawyer in the new judicial structure erected over the people's courts had to be defined.

One change was made by the new code of 1923 in the provisions regulating the appearance of lawyers in the people's courts. The circumstances in which a lawyer was required to be present were reduced in number. While courts still were required to appoint a lawyer to defend an accused if an accuser were present, and to protect the blind, deaf, and generally incompetent, they were no longer required to see to the presence of a lawyer if an accused were already detained under guard.[43] There is no literature to indicate why the change was made. It would seem to have been substantial, for a prisoner would assuredly have had less opportunity to arrange for the presence of a lawyer than an accused who was still at large. The 1922 requirement that a lawyer be present whenever an accused was already in a detention house or prison could have been during its short life of real advantage to defendants if it was enforced.

Counsel was not required under the 1923 code in the serious type of case formerly tried by the people's court with six lay judges sitting with the professional judge, as he had been under the 1922 code. The 1922 judiciary act had abolished the former seven-man tribunals of the people's courts, with the result that the elimination of the requirement of a lawyer in cases coming before the former seven-man tribunal looks at first glance to have been nothing more than a revision of the procedural code to take account of the abolition of the former tribunal. It was more than that, however, for much of the jurisdiction of the former seven-man courts was continued in the newly created provincial courts. It was they who tried under the new procedural code charges of murder, mayhem, arson, and banditry. These had formerly been tried by the seven-

---

[43] Code of Criminal Procedure, RSFSR, February 15, 1923, [1923] I *Sob. Uzak. RSFSR*, No. 7, item 106, Art. 55.

man people's court. While the transfer had carried jurisdiction to
the provincial courts, it had not included the provision that counsel
be required in such cases in the provincial courts. In consequence,
persons charged with serious crimes were put in a less advantageous position by the 1923 code as regards compulsory assignment
of counsel than they had been before the revision.

A handicap of still another fashion developed out of the transfer
of jurisdiction over serious crimes from the people's court to the
provincial court. While counsel was always permitted in the people's courts, although not required except in the situations indicated,
counsel was not always permitted before the provincial courts.
Under the new code of 1923 there was no absolute right of counsel
before the provincial courts when they sat as courts of original
jurisdiction.[44] The judges were authorized to decide for themselves
whether they wished to have the aid of counsel. This had been
the rule of the 1922 code for the revolutionary tribunals, and with
the absorption by the provincial courts of the general revolutionary
tribunals, the exclusionary rule was also absorbed. The new code
gave a defendant before a provincial court some protection, for
it provided that counsel must be admitted if there were to be an
accuser, but if there was no accuser, there was no absolute right
of counsel, even if the defendant requested counsel to aid in the
preparation and defense of his case.

Appeals from the people's courts to the provincial courts were
made the beneficiaries of a rule more advantageous to the appellant than was the rule of the same court when sitting as a
court of original jurisdiction. The code permitted counsel to appear
and to speak before the provincial court on appeal.[45] If the case was
carried up to the Supreme Court of the Republic, the same right
to representation by counsel existed, but the appellant was handi-
capped. The code required no summons of the parties nor even
notice to them, except in the form of a posting at the courthouse
of a notice of the calendar for each day twenty-four hours before-
hand.[46]

Both the 1922[47] and the 1923[48] codes of criminal procedure

[44] Art. 381.   [45] Art. 410.   [46] Art. 435.
[47] Code of Criminal Procedure, RSFSR (1922), [1922] *ibid.*, No. 20–21,
item 230, Art. 361.
[48] Code of Criminal Procedure, RSFSR (1923), Art. 415.

provided appellate protection for a defendant deprived of the right to counsel in those cases in which it was guaranteed by the code. Thus, it was cause for setting aside a sentence and for a new trial if counsel had been denied by a trial court in violation of the code.

Civil procedure lacked secrecy problems if one may take the contrast between the 1923 Code of Civil Procedure[49] and the 1922 and 1923 Codes of Criminal Procedure as indicative of such an attitude. No article of the Code of Civil Procedure guaranteed that counsel would be permitted in every case and at every stage of the procedure, but the right was implicit in the provisions for appointment of counsel and for his activity. A party to a civil suit was given the right to conduct a case either in person or through a representative,[50] and a subsequent article listed as possible representatives members of the college of defenders.[51]

Counsel was not limited to members of the college, for as in the case of criminal proceedings a party was permitted to have as his representative an agent of the trade union to which he belonged. If it was a group, it might have its officer or permanent employee. A party might even have any other person if permitted by the court.[52] There was to be no monopoly of representation granted to the new college of defenders. An argument even was made that any one selected as counsel by a party might appear regardless of what the court thought. This argument rested upon what seems to have been an overriding provision in a preceding article authorizing a party to choose as his representative any one he might wish,[53] subject to the exclusionary provision relating to minors, persons deprived of rights under a court sentence, persons under guardianship, persons who had been excluded from colleges of defenders, and judges, lay judges, investigators, and prosecutors.[54]

Counsel was authorized by the code to inspect all documents filed in a civil case, to take notes, and to request copies on payment of the usual clerk's fee.[55] He had to authenticate his authority by exhibition of a power of attorney,[56] and this power had to state specifically that he could compromise a case, admit responsibility of

---

[49] Code of Civil Procedure, RSFSR, July 7, 1923, [1923] I *Sob. Uzak. RSFSR*, No. 46–47, item 478.
[50] Art. 12.   [51] Art. 16.   [52] *Ibid.*   [53] Art. 12.   [54] Art. 20.   [55] Art. 11.
[56] Art. 17.

a client, transfer his authority to another, consent to transfer of the dispute to arbitration, or receive property or money on behalf of a client only if the power of attorney authorized such activity.[57]

The right of counsel in civil appeal could be exercised more easily than in criminal appeal. Counsel was not only authorized to be present in both the provincial courts and Supreme Court.[58] Counsel had a right to considerable advance notice, for the provincial court was required to serve notice upon a party of an impending appeal in the same manner as notice was to be served of a trial itself, namely by registered letter with return receipt requested or by process server from the local police office or from the office of the local soviet's executive committee. In the Supreme Court of the Republic notice was to be published in the official journal of the Commissariat of Justice not later than two weeks before the appellate review, and notice was also to be posted at the courthouse itself. There was no limited twenty-four-hour notice as was the rule in criminal appeal.

Costs of counsel were to be awarded a winning plaintiff in an amount representing 5 percent of the judgment. Should the defendant win, he was to be awarded costs in the amount of 5 percent of the amount which had been claimed as damages by the plaintiff.[59]

"UNDERGROUND PRACTICE"

Reports on the first full year of operations began to appear in the press at the end of 1923. They indicated that a very few men were carrying a monumental load. The Yaroslavl college reported only 39 members for the whole province.[60] This small band had made 650 appearances without fee during the year. The shortage of licensed lawyers had resulted in very little attention to citizens in the village communities, with the result that a considerable "underground" practice had been initiated by persons not belonging to the college. Such activity was said to have had a bad effect upon the progress of adjudication because the unlicensed attorneys were taking cases which should not have been pressed; they were

---

[57] Art. 18.   [58] Art. 242.   [59] Art. 46.

[60] "Na mestakh: V iaroslavskoi gub. kollegii zaschitnikov," *Ezh. sov. iust.*, No. 45 (November 17, 1923), p. 1048.

dragging them out and were avoiding the tax levied upon members of the college for permission to do business.

The Orienburg college had only 11 members.[61] These had conducted 3,068 oral consultations during the year and had prepared papers in 1,807 instances. There had been 189 appearances in court in civil or criminal cases for which no fee had been charged. The general meeting of the college had been held seven times during the year, while the presidium had met 31 times.

The official year-end report[62] of the Commissariat of Justice on the work of the first six months of 1923 repeated the same complaint of inadequate numbers of licensed lawyers. While the population of cities was found generally throughout the Russian Republic to have been adequately supplied with legal advice, the peasants of the villages were found to have had almost no access to members of the colleges. In addition to the problem of inadequate numbers there was the problem of inadequate political education. The Commissariat found that there were extremely few Communists among the members of the colleges, and the provincial courts seemed to have been paying too little attention to building up the colleges in constructive ways.

The provincial courts had been, apparently, developing a policy of disciplining members of the colleges, as had been feared by commentators soon after the colleges had been created, and as had been hinted months earlier in the Ukraine. The Commissariat's report listed nine disciplinary proceedings conducted by provincial courts against members of colleges of defenders throughout the Republic.[63] These statistics confirmed a report of some months earlier that the provincial courts had been disciplining members of the colleges in violation of the provision of the statute placing disciplinary authority in the presidiums of the colleges alone, except for the right of expulsion.[64]

The annual reports complained of "underground" practice, and this presumably posed a real problem. Nothing could be done about

[61] "Na mestakh: orenburgskaia kollegiia zashchitnikov," *ibid.*, p. 1049.
[62] "Svodnyi otchët o deiatel'nosti gubernskikh i oblastnykh sudov RSFSR za I-e polugodie 1923 g.," *ibid.*, No. 51–52 (December 31, 1923), pp. 1177–92.
[63] *Ibid.*, p. 1181.
[64] Vl. Trapeznikov, "Ditsiplinarnaia otvetstvennost' zashchitnikov," *ibid.*, No. 40 (October 11, 1923), p. 922.

prohibiting practice by persons not members of the colleges, for the statute on the college and the codes of criminal and civil procedure had been adopted in a form permitting "other persons" to appear as representatives of a party if the court gave special permission. The near-monopoly of legal representation which had been proposed by the Commissariat of Justice for the new colleges of defenders had been specifically rejected in debate by the legislators in the Central Executive Committee. The door had thus been left open for unlicensed persons to do legal work, so that any campaign against irresponsible action had to be conducted on an individual basis rather than on a group basis.

The people's courts seem to have been resisting the policy established by the law, for they took the position that "other persons" need not be admitted in actions before the court if the facts of the case were "clear." [65] The courts are reported to have been urged to take this position by plaintiffs in personal injury actions. The argument of plaintiffs was that to admit unlicensed persons as defenders was to acknowledge weakness on the part of the court. Exclusion of informal defenders on the ground that the case was "clear" was indicated by the commentator who exposed the situation as being utterly without foundation in law, but he admitted that the court had a problem. The court could not know personally every one who might be proposed as a defender. It was impossible to tell whether there was legitimate reason to refuse consent to appear on the ground that the person put forward by a party was irresponsible or even an enemy of the new regime. To meet this problem the commentator suggested that the court be permitted to require from the candidate a written statement that there were no impediments to his appearance. Presumably, the author wanted to make possible a subsequent prosecution for lying to a state official if the impediments became evident at the trial or on some subsequent occasion.

The Moscow Provincial Court issued a circular requiring that any one, presented as a defender under the provision of the code permitting "other persons" to appear, must be known personally to the court, or must merit special confidence because of the position

---

[65] I. L., "Kto mozhet byt' zashchitnikom," *ibid.*, No. 9 (March 6, 1923), p. 190.

he had in society or because of his special relationship to the person he wished to defend.[66] Soon after, the same court told the people's courts under its jurisdiction that "other persons" must not be admitted unless it could be determined whether they were trying to circumvent the code's provisions on representation.[67]

Criminal prosecution of an "underground" practitioner was ordered by a Ukrainian provincial court as its remedy against undesirable practice.[68] The case presented a glimpse of legal activities at the time and deserves to be reported in some detail. Suit had been brought in the People's Court by a young woman for breach of promise to marry for which she claimed 5,000 rubles damages to compensate her for the disgrace she had suffered and 500 rubles as wages for one month's work. In her allegation the woman claimed that she had been promised marriage and in reliance on the promise she had entered the defendant's home as his wife. After one month he had not only refused to register the marriage but had expelled her from his home.

The trial court found for the plaintiff on both claims, saying that although the Soviet statutes provided for no right of recovery for disgrace yet, in application of "revolutionary conscience, the socialist concept of law and local custom" the defendant must be required to pay for twenty-five days of housework at 20 rubles a day and 75 rubles for the disgrace which had been suffered. From the decision the defendant appealed to the Kharkov Provincial Court.

An affirmance of the decision for the plaintiff on the claim for wages was given, but the claim based on disgrace was rejected. It was said in the appellate court's opinion that the trial court had used not a socialist concept of law in reaching its decision but local custom inherited from the epoch of capitalist structure of society. The courts were authorized to apply local custom in the view of the Provincial Court but only when there was no specific law on the subject. The Provincial Court admitted that there was no specific law on the subject of breach of promise for marriage, but

---

[66] Circular No. 45, February 7, 1923. Quoted in Rivlin, *Sovetskaia advokatura*, p. 30.

[67] Circular No. 57, 1923 (precise date not given). Quoted in *ibid.*

[68] See *Chertenkova* v. *Karamza*, "Sud i zhizn': isk za 'beshest'e'," *Vestnik sov. iust.*, No. 5 (October 1, 1923), p. 132.

it felt that the very idea was in conflict with the spirit of Soviet family, marriage, and civil law. It recited the principle of the Family Code to the effect that registration of marriage did not create a marriage but only recorded what the parties had agreed to consummate. Registration was necessary under the law only to provide for legal consequences of a marriage and not for the existence of the marriage. Accordingly, there could be no disgrace in voluntary cohabitation without registration.

The Provincial Court berated the People's Court for bowing to the psychology and prejudices of the man in the street. Disgrace was possible only if human dignity had been impaired, and there was no impairment of dignity either in law or ethics in cohabitation without registration. Further, if there had been any impairment of human dignity, it could not have been rectified in a civil suit but only in criminal prosecution of the offender. The Provincial Court declared that it was only under capitalist conditions that injury to human dignity could be measured in money in a civil suit. Human dignity was said to be on such a high pedestal in Soviet society that even a minimal impairment or attempt at impairment was to be punished severely under the Criminal Code.

Having settled the point of substantive law the Provincial Court turned its attention to the lawyer in the case. It noted that both the plaintiff's complaint in the People's Court and the subsequent appeal to the Provincial Court by the defendant had been signed by the same person as representative. The court declared that the individual had indicated by signing the appeal that he understood that the basis for the original complaint which he had also signed was contrary to the spirit of Soviet legislation. The court ordered its agent in the county concerned to determine the identity of the representative. If he proved to be a member of the college of defenders, disciplinary action was to be initiated, and if he proved to be an unlicensed practitioner, he was to be prosecuted under the criminal law as having signed legal papers which he had no right to sign. The court ended its opinion by ordering a copy of its opinion sent to all people's courts in the province for their information and guidance.

The historian of the bar cited the case to indicate another transgression of the law on advocacy by the courts, for there was no prohibition in the law against signing legal papers.[69] All Soviet citizens had been given the right. While the historian thought that the case provided reason for punishment because of the kind of advice which had been given, it did not in his opinion reflect correctly the rule of law relating to representation by persons not members of the college of defenders. The court had tried to exclude all unlicensed attorneys from practice by its decisions, whereas it should have limited itself to punishment of the individual who had been guilty of barratry.

A CANON OF ETHICS

A Canon of Ethics was adopted and published by the Kiev College of Defenders in October, 1923.[70] It established in its opening paragraph the duties placed upon the newly organized bar in the following words:

A defender is the aid of the court in its effort to discern the truth in court and to reach a just decision; the defender is, therefore, required to illumine the case, guiding himself above all else by the interests of the toilers and of Soviet justice. Conscious failure to cite laws, diminishing the right of an adversary, and also chicanery, procrastination, etc. are contrary to the concept of achievement of the calling of a defender.

Four sections set forth the duties of the defender in his relationship to the court, to the college of defenders, to the client paying no fee, and to the client from whom a fee in accordance with the tariff or a full fee in accordance with a private agreement was to be charged.

In his relations with the court the defender was admonished not to take advantage of a gap in the law to the benefit of his client but to guide himself by what he believed to be the interests of the Revolution in assisting the court to fill the gap by creating a judicial precedent. He was required to show respect to the court, but the court in return was expected to show respect to him, and if the court did not do so, the defender was authorized to ask that the record show the derogatory remark of the court so that an

---

[69] Rivlin, *Sovetskaia advokatura*, p. 44.

[70] "V kievskoi kollegii zashchitnikov: nakaz chlenam kollegii o normakh professional'noi etiki," *Vestnik sov. iust.*, No. 5 (October 1, 1923), p. 139.

appeal might be taken if it was of such a character as to have hampered him in performing his duties. He was also authorized to inform the presidium of the college.

Respect for all other participants in the trial was also required. The defender was forbidden to use to his advantage any personal friendship he might have enjoyed with any of the members of the court.

In relations with the college of defenders the member was required to show respect for colleagues and to execute any order of the college's presidium, subject to his right to appeal its validity to the general meeting of members. His every action which could reflect upon his honor, whether in court or outside of it, could be made the subject of a disciplinary action. Some activities were forbidden entirely, these being brokerage, selling on a commission, loaning money at interest, selling goods as a merchant, any manner of speculation, and the purchase of a client's claim even when the purchase price was to be paid only out of whatever judgment might be obtained.

Relations with clients paying no fee had to be conducted with "special attention to performance of the defender's obligation." A disciplinary penalty would be exacted if it became apparent that the record of a case had not been studied or its preparation had been slighted. On assignment to a criminal case the defender was required to study it immediately and to call for the assignment of additional defenders if the varied interests of the parties required more than one defender. No case could be transferred to another defender without the consent of the presidium of the college. Acceptance of a fee from a person having the right under the law to a free defender was cause for exclusion from the college.

Conduct of cases for which a fee was to be charged in agreement with the client or under the tariff was subject to a special set of rules. Clients could not be obtained through the services of a runner or by advertisements or by printing professional cards for general distribution, or by disclosing a defender's connections. No case which was clearly unjust could be accepted, nor could a defender enter any case which would lower his dignity as a servant of Soviet justice.

Having accepted a case the defender was required to use all

legal means to advance the interests of his client, but if he concluded that the claim was dishonest, he was required to withdraw and to notify the court of his action. Disciplinary action was to be taken against any defender who showed serious ignorance of the law by failing to act before a statutory period expired or who caused unnecessary procedural delay, or who consciously perverted the meaning of a law or of a fact or who conferred with witnesses outside of court.

Financial arrangements with a client had to be made before services were begun and had to be explained and stated so clearly that there could be no misunderstanding. If a client had the right to pay a fee in accordance with the tariff because he was an employee, his right under the tariff had to be explained, and there could be no solicitation of an additional fee. If money was received in advance for expenses, there had to be a subsequent accounting. Fees, when not governed by the tariff, were to be fixed in consideration "not only of the size of the property interest of the client or the degree of punishment with which he was being threatened, but also in consideration of the amount of work necessary to conduct the case."

DECISIONS ON LEGAL ETHICS

The Moscow College of Defenders published in 1925 a volume of the decisions of its Presidium on legal ethics.[71] Taking the form of a report to the general meeting by one of the members of the committee, and grouping the types of actions under ten headings, the volume gave a picture of the activities of the bar in the areas treated by the canons of ethics.

The duty to accept a request to defend an individual was illustrated by an account of the refusal of a member of the college to take up to the Supreme Court on appeal a conviction of a client.[72] The client's wife had reported that when she requested further legal aid she had been informed that there was no basis for appeal. She felt, however, that the lawyer had refused only because he was dissatisfied with his fee. The disciplinary commission of the college

[71] V. I. Veger, *Ditsiplina i etika zashchitnika* (Moscow, 1925).
[72] *Case of Libson, ibid.,* p. 12.

had reprimanded the lawyer and ordered him assigned to a rural district for six months. The Moscow Provincial Court's Presidium had protested the punishment as too mild to the Moscow Soviet's Presidium and the latter had ordered a review of the case by the Presidium of the College of Defenders.

The protest of the soviet's presidium was based not only upon the mildness of the penalty but also upon that part of the penalty that made an assignment to rural work a penalty. The soviet's presidium remarked that legal aid to village communities was one of the most important aspects of a college of defenders' work. Rural service was not to be degraded by being made a punishment for an offending member of the college. No mercenary motive was found by the presidium of the college in its review of the reasons for refusing to take the case up on appeal, but the Presidium concluded that no good member of the college would have been so tactless in explaining his conclusion on the merits of an appeal as to leave in the mind of a client's wife a feeling that the real issue was one of a fee. This failure to make his position clear was found to reflect not only on the lawyer but upon the entire college to which he belonged. It was said that "he should have dissipated by a proper explanation the shadow which under any other circumstances fell inescapably upon the college of defenders." The presidium ordered expulsion from the college for one year, refusing to make it permanent as the soviet's presidium had requested because exclusion would have prevented the lawyer's obtaining any government or public position, and such a penalty would have been too severe.

The duty to know the law was illustrated by a case in which a young newly accepted member of the college had appeared before an assembly of seventy peasants with a city group attempting to spread good will among the peasants.[73] His task had been to explain the land law. After reading from the code he had received questions as to why the local land tax was higher than that provided by the code. He was unable to answer and proposed that the question be held until the following day when the tax inspector was expected to be present. The tax inspector did not come, however, and the peasants went away feeling that they had been made the subjects of discrimination. The presidium noted that there was a

---

[73] *Case of Varshavskii, ibid.*, p. 13.

special order of the Council of Ministers which was unknown to the young lawyer, and which set a special rate of tax for the Moscow Province.

In his own defense the young lawyer argued that he had expected to discuss land usage and not taxation, which required special knowledge of local conditions and statistics. The presidium of the college ordered a simple reprimand because of the youthful inexperience of the lawyer, but it used the opportunity to explain that the lawyer should have been aware of the special order on taxation and he and his colleagues should have anticipated questions concerned with local matters and should have planned their appearance before going to the village.

The duty to live in exemplary fashion was illustrated by a case in which a divorced wife complained of outrageous treatment of herself and her children by a former husband who was a member of the college of defenders.[74] Her charge was that her former husband had been niggardly with payments for maintenance, had absented himself at a sanitarium during a very hard period when she and the children had been ill with scarlet fever, had urged her to leave the country and go to her mother abroad, had refused to pay the cost of a summer in the country for the family, and finally had notified the police of a missing winter overcoat which the wife had pawned to obtain funds for the summer in the country. As a result of the notice to the police there had been a search of the house followed by an interrogation of the wife in the presence of the children whom she had found it necessary to bring to the police station for want of any one with whom to leave them.

The former husband in his defense presented a long story of hardship as the result of which the disciplinary commission had concluded that he had been in the right formally, but it found that he had been morally wrong in notifying the police of the missing overcoat. His notification had given rise to the search and the interrogation in the presence of the children. The commission thought that he should have been tactful and should have avoided the unhappy scene. His actions had discredited not only himself but the college to which he belonged. His penalty was set at six month's suspension from membership. A further penalty

[74] *Case of Grosman, ibid.,* p. 16.

of severe warning had been given to a woman member of the college who had acted as his intermediary in many of the relations with his family and who had been present at the search of the house.

The presidium of the college on its review of the record found it desirable to reduce the penalty to a severe warning on the ground that the interests of the children would be affected adversely if their father could earn no fees for six months. The woman lawyer's penalty had to be reduced to a reprimand to make it less than that of the principal offender.

The duty to act within the limits of authority granted a member of the college was illustrated by a case brought on complaint that a member had in representing his client entered a home and attempted to obtain information about a prior conviction of a suspected giver of false testimony.[75] The complaint alleged that the member had threatened to put the accused's wife in prison if she did not give the information. In his defense the member indicated that he had been asked by his client, a public organization, to verify the statement of a woman who was heard on a previous occasion of marital discord to declare that her husband had once been convicted. The husband on a subsequent trial for a different offense had denied any such conviction when it was raised in consideration of his character. He had been acquitted of the alleged second offense, but the public organization had wanted to determine whether a prosecution for lying to an official was not in order, and so it had asked its counsel to investigate. The member declared that as soon as he learned that the woman was now on good terms with her husband and would not discuss the matter, he had left her home.

The presidium found that there had not in fact been any threat to imprison the woman if she refused to talk, but that the member of the bar should have anticipated that there would be a sorry scene if he entered the home with such a question and that he should have refused his client's request to conduct the interview. A warning was issued.

The duty to show respect to an opponent at a trial was illustrated

[75] *Case of Murav'ev, ibid.*, p. 21.

by a case involving an allegation that a member of the college had insulted a prosecutor.[76] The presidium found that the prosecutor had been attempting to show the shady character of a defendant who with others was accused of bribery of officials by exposing her irregular marital relations. He argued that the woman was receiving maintenance from her husband, and at the same time was supporting a second man. Her lawyer sought to meet this attack upon his client's character by referring to the new Soviet attitude toward marriage. He had concluded in his argument that the woman's position was correct in substance because she loved both men dearly.

The final remarks in defense of the client had included the words interpreted as insult.

She is a good woman, and I base this conclusion on the relations of both men to her. There has been nothing perceived that could arouse our indignation. Marriage relationships have been reconsidered greatly by us. A woman is no longer property. Soviet marriage has liberated her. Jealousy and hatred on the part of a husband toward his former wife and her subsequent husband seem primitive. What does the prosecutor want, that there be jealousy and hatred between these three persons? That is not required. This situation represents the contemporary attitude toward marriage relationships.

The attorney had then turned toward the prosecutor and had spoken the words, "He recognizeth not his own kind." The presiding judge had immediately intervened to say that the lawyer should confine himself to the facts and refrain from giving a lecture. To this the lawyer had replied: "Wait, citizen judge, the prosecutor has been saying things he does not believe."

The presidium of the college concluded that the member had expressed correct ideas, but in a tactless form, which had been made worse by phrases which made them appear to be an impermissible slur upon the prosecutor. The presidium thought it obvious that the lawyer had not intended to insult the prosecutor, and it accepted the lawyer's explanation that his tongue had slipped in the heat of debate. It concluded that in spite of the heat of debate the lawyer should not "wander on" in court with such impermissible phrases, and it ordered that a reprimand be given.

[76] *Case of Aronovich, ibid.,* p. 23.

Appropriate conduct towards a client was made the issue in a case in which a lawyer was charged with having been overly cordial to the accused in the presence of the court after termination of a case.[77] It was claimed that he shook hands with his client so fervently before leaving the courtroom that he gave the impression that he was making a public demonstration against the court's decision of guilt. It was also claimed that he had used impermissible arguments in defending his client against a charge of violation of the labor law in her employment of young girls. It was said that in his defense he indicated lack of appreciation of the class nature of his client's offense.

The accused lawyer explained that his handshake in open court had been caused by the necessity of leaving the courtroom abruptly to hurry to another in which he was expected, and his farewell had not been intended as a demonstration of sympathy. The presidium held that since his record in other cases had been exemplary, and since the handshaking did not seem to have been intended as a demonstration against the judges, the attorney did not deserve a severe penalty, but it informed the man that it took notice of his lack of proper class analysis of the offense of his client. Presumably the lawyer was expected to accept this as a warning against lack of sufficient respect for the principles of the Revolution in defending clients in the future.

Absence of tact was illustrated by several cases as the next category of ethical offenses. The college's presidium seemed determined to prevent harming the prestige of the profession through tactless action. It punished a woman attorney for implying that her time and skill could not be compensated adequately by the small amount offered by a client as a fee to discuss matters going beyond the original case assigned to her on a no-fee basis.[78] The presidium said that she should have explained that she was not allowed to accept a fee in a case assigned to her without fee, and should not have given the impression that her reason was otherwise for rejecting the offered fee. The presidium also found inexcusable the woman's failure to obtain a power of attorney, so that she was prevented from appearing for her client when the case was called unexpectedly during the absence of the client from the building.

[77] *Case of Shemetov, ibid.,* p. 25.   [78] *Case of Fishkes, ibid.,* p. 28.

Fee matters seem to have been embarrassing to the presidium, for it warned another attorney who had told a client in response to a question asked on behalf of a friend that a fee would probably be 50 chervontsy, a very high figure in those days, to handle the friend's case if he were to seek an attorney from the college. The presidium said that this remark gave the impression that fees were fixed without regard to the rules of the college and solely on the basis of the personal whim of the advocates.[79]

Lack of tact was also found and made the occasion for a warning in a situation where an attorney had served a summons personally upon a fellow member of the college while making an insulting remark about the manner in which his opponent was conducting the case. The presidium thought that the usual process server should have been used, and that no personal remarks were called for.

A tactful approach to local officials was recommended in a case in which an attorney had appeared for consultations in a village near Moscow on market day and had not reported to the local judicial and administrative officers of the village prior to beginning his work.[80] The lawyer's defense that he had to hurry his consultations to permit him to return home to children who had scarlet fever was thought to mitigate his offense, but the presidium said that the attorney's record was such that it indicates that in the future he could be expected, unless warned on the point, not to organize his work in such a way as to avoid unnecessary complications.

Participation as an arbiter in a dispute brought criticism upon a college member because he had given the impression that he was partisan in the dispute which he had been asked to share in deciding.[81] The presidium thought the probabilities of a charge of partisanship were great in any arbitration, and so it hailed a ruling made after the date of the attorney's service prohibiting participation by attorneys as members of arbitration panels. Yet in spite of the obvious temptations toward partisanship in arbitration proceedings it thought that in this case the partisan character of the representation had been so grave as to give rise to what seemed to

[79] *Case of Orlovskii, ibid.,* p. 30.   [80] *Case of Meerovich, ibid.,* p. 33.
[81] *Case of Petushkov, ibid.,* p. 34.

be otherwise inexplicable misunderstandings in the conduct of the arbitration.

Both attorneys in another case were found to have violated legal ethics in their relationships in and out of court.[82] A severe reprimand was issued to the attorney who had threatened his colleague's client in a loud voice in a dininghall that if payment was not made voluntarily, it would be twice as large later, and who subsequently said that the colleague's client when he appeared to testify was really not a clerk in a cooperative but a capitalist saloon-keeper who had merely gone through the form of making his business appear to be that of a cooperative. Under the government's attitude of the time the cooperative form of doing business was favored over that of the individual enterpriser, and many individuals were accused of trying to conceal the real character of their business by bringing together some inactive colleagues in a paper cooperative. The attempted slur might really, therefore, have discredited the witness. Spurred on by this pressure from his opponent and the latter's attempt to discredit the witness, the other attorney permitted himself to say at the trial: "I declare categorically that Belova's attorney is telling a pure untruth; as if he did not know that the witness is a former clerk in a cooperative!" For this improper imputation of falsehood, the second attorney was called upon to note the impropriety of his words.

Charges against members of the college on grounds of drunkenness, failure to appear in cases assigned to them, mishandling of cases, lack of proper interest in the proletarian cause because of hostile class origin, and improper speeches in defense of clients were examined in the final part of the presidium's report. In all cases the presidium found the complaints ill founded and dismissed the charges against the attorneys to give the impression that the presidium was not being driven politically to accept criticism of the bar without examination. The last case in the report reveals, however, the difficulty faced by the new college from overly zealous citizens intent upon pressing what they believed to be the interests of the proletariat without the impediment of intervening defense attorneys.

Six members of the college had appeared in defense of a group

[82] *Case of Levin and Erastov, ibid.,* p. 38.

of 33 defendants accused of systematic theft of commodities from state warehouses. The prosecutor had addressed the lawyers as a group with such phrases as "Why did you come here?" and then, turning to one of the lawyers, the prosecutor had remarked, "That attorney works in dirty fashion; he plays with marked cards." The attorney who had been singled out for attention then asked the court to order the prosecutor's speech inscribed in full in the record, and the court so ordered, but this was not done. Later the lawyer who had asked for inclusion of the speech in full was taken before the disciplinary commission. The presidium found on hearing the other lawyers in the case that the speech of the prosecutor had in fact been as critical and insulting as claimed, and that under the circumstances the retort of the accused attorney provided no reason to punish him.[83]

LEGAL ETHICS AND SOVIET SOCIAL THEORY

A reflection of the torment through which conscientious lawyers were going in an effort to establish a system of legal ethics appropriate to the new society in which they found themselves is given in a thin volume, *Truth and Falsehood in Criminal Defense*, published in 1927.[84] After indicating that the problem was as old as the bar itself and had been treated *in extenso* on many occasions before the Revolution in Russia and in other lands as well, the author set forth sixteen principles to guide the lawyer in the new Russia.

Lawyers were warned not to accept a case if a client asked them to distort facts or to betray secrets learned from another client.[85] The retainer was to be rejected also if the lawyer knew that he might have to be a witness against his client.[86] In answer to the difficult question of whether the lawyer ought to reject the case of an individual known to be guilty the author suggested consideration of a case published by the newspaper *Izvestiia* on April 4, 1925, which seemed to illustrate the problem. A lawyer was reported to have refused a court assignment to defend the

---

[83] *Case of Pinchevskii, ibid.*, p. 62.
[84] N. N. Polianskii, *Pravda i lozh' v ugolovnom zashchite* (Moscow, 1927).
[85] *Ibid.*, p. 41.   [86] *Ibid.*, p. 42.

ringleader of a gang because he thought the ringleader guilty. The lawyer had represented the other members of the gang and argued that they should be shown clemency because they were illiterate and did not understand their actions. Rejection of the defense of the ringleader seemed wrong to the commentator for an attorney practicing under Soviet conditions because "Soviet law leaves for the defense when the guilt of the accused has been established still more scope than prerevolutionary law, since punishment is to be chosen with more regard than under pre-revolutionary law to the personal record of the accused and to the circumstances which gave rise to his crime." [87] Having concluded that a lawyer should accept a court assignment to defend a person known to be guilty, the commentator had no difficulty in deciding that a lawyer should also accept a case voluntarily on a retainer to try to help a guilty person obtain clemency.

If the lawyer took the case without knowledge of the client's guilt but found during the trial that the evidence of guilt was so persuasive as to convince the lawyer that he was arguing a lost cause, the lawyer was advised to withdraw from the case if the client would permit it, or if not, to continue but only to argue in mitigation of the penalty.[88]

It was one thing to defend a guilty person in an effort to obtain clemency and another to join with the prosecutor in castigating the defendant. The commentator rejected as unsound an article in a contemporary legal journal approving the action of a lawyer who in his closing speech supported the prosecutor's demand for a sentence of ten years' imprisonment.[89] The charge had been seduction of young girls, and the defending counsel had been moved to say that there was no reason for a lesser sentence for such a truly dangerous criminal. The commentator took the view that the lawyer's code of ethics forbad conscious injury to a client's case even in the name of justice.

The desirability of preserving the adversary system of court procedure under Soviet conditions seems to have been accepted fully by the commentator, for he argued that a lawyer should never introduce evidence or inform the court of circumstances which

[87] *Ibid.*, p. 46.   [88] *Ibid.*, p. 60.   [89] *Ibid.*, p. 48.

would increase the chances of a conviction or reflect unfavorably upon his client.[90] Such a view suggests that a judge should not be helped to discover what he was unable to learn from the prosecutor or from his own investigation. Yet this doctrine was not without limits, for the commentator admonished his readers never to misrepresent a situation consciously. Thus, it was said to be unethical to refer in court to the unblemished record of a client whom the attorney knew to be a recidivist although the court had no knowledge of prior offenses. Perhaps to reassure those fledgling Soviet lawyers who were intimidated by the proclivity of many ardent revolutionaries, not excluding some prosecutors and judges, to presume the guilt of defendants of bourgeois origin, the commentator declared that a good lawyer would not cease to argue the innocence of a client until there was incontrovertible evidence of guilt, even though the lawyer might have a strong but nevertheless unsubstantiated sense that his client was guilty in spite of a denial of guilt.

Further evidence of confidence in the efficacy of the adversary procedure appears in the commentator's support for legal argumentation by a lawyer who was not himself convinced of the finality of what he was presenting as the proper interpretation of the law.[91] The bar was reminded that it was the judge's duty and not that of the lawyer to weigh all of the legal arguments and to draw the final conclusion as to what the law really was. The lawyer should present to the judge any plausible interpretation so that a final decision might be made with all possibilities in mind. The complicating factor presented by the presence in print or in the record of another case of an interpretation of the law by counsel contrary to the one which seemed desirable in the interest of the present client was met squarely by the commentator. While agreeing that a change in position on the interpretation of the law might be supported logically as being permitted because it was in the interest of the client, the commentator thought that legal ethics forbade such a change in viewpoint. To permit a change on any other basis than that of a real change in thinking on the subject or because of a series of judicial decisions holding against a prior view seemed to the commentator

[90] *Ibid.*, p. 49. [91] *Ibid.*, p. 53.

to allow the public to draw the conclusion that a lawyer plays only a role in a drama, and that he changes his views on the meaning of the law as easily as an actor changes his costume.

The calling of a witness or the presentation of documentary evidence, even at the request of a client, if it was known that the witness would give false testimony or that the document was a forgery was declared to be an outright violation of professional ethics.[92] This rule was not to be interpreted to exclude a doubtful witness or a doubtful document.

A client who opposed the presentation of evidence which the lawyer believed essential to the defense was to be told that the Code of Criminal Procedure permitted withdrawal from a case unless the court ordered the contrary, and even in the latter situation counsel was permitted to petition for replacement.[93] Yet if replacement was not permitted or if it was manifestly too late to withdraw without prejudicing the client's defense, the lawyer was advised to consider that his position was that of a necessary participant in the work of a court seeking the truth. Under such a conception of the lawyer's function, he had to refuse to countenance the client's desires in the matter of evidence and do whatever seemed necessary to save him from an undeserved penalty.

The most difficult decision of all for an attorney was said to be that presented by the client who confessed his guilt to the attorney on a charge which the prosecution could not prove with the evidence before it. Should the attorney withdraw? The question had seemed so difficult to the commentator that he had written to the bar in Brussels, Paris, Berlin, and London.[94] From the replies which he had received and which he set forth the commentator concluded that he found most suitable to Soviet conditions the position taken by the General Council of the Bar in London. The Secretary of the General Council had informed the Soviet commentator that in a case brought before the General Council in 1915 the recommendation had been made that if counsel received a confession of guilt from a client before the defense was undertaken, it was undesirable for him to proceed. He should propose to the client that he approach another lawyer. Yet if counsel felt that the confession was not conclusive because of the mental state of the client or some other cir-

[92] *Ibid.*, p. 61.   [93] *Ibid.*, p. 63.   [94] *Ibid.*, p. 76.

cumstance in the case, the defense might be undertaken, but never to the extent of lying or conniving in a fraud.

The English reply had been brought for discussion before a meeting in the "House of Scientists" on February 23, 1926, by the Soviet commentator, and two points had been made in opposition to adoption of the English rule. First, since a Soviet judge must establish his "inner conviction" as to the truth on the basis solely of what was presented in court, and since the prosecutor cannot accuse the defendant on the basis of a confession which has not been placed with the material in the dossier, why should a defense attorney be held to some other standard? Secondly, it was argued in opposition to the English view that it might result in a whole series of rejections if the accused confessed to each new lawyer in turn. The commentator believed that the first objection bore on its face the reason for its rejection, while the second might be avoided if the accused did not repeat his confession. Apparently, the commentator thought that a perceptive person would not repeat the same mistake twice if he wanted to obtain counsel. In spite of his feeling that the second objection was purely theoretical, the commentator continued to argue that if the accused persisted in his desire to confess, some lawyer would have to be prepared to make a compromise between his duty as a lawyer to defend and his duty to protect the secret confided by his client. What that compromise might be, the commentator did not say.

Representation upon appeal presented some problems. Suppose that a lawyer concluded after examination of the record of the trial that the finding of guilt had been supported by the evidence. Could he reject a request for representation on an appeal? Just such a question was suggested by a 1924 decision of the Moscow Province College of Defenders, and the latter had held that there was a duty to argue an appeal even in such a case. The commentator agreed with the holding but he found himself moved by his feeling that an attorney could not be permitted to pass judgment by weighing the evidence appearing upon a record of a trial. His duty was to determine whether there had been a sufficient violation of procedure to merit an appeal and not to serve as a substitute for an appellate judge.[95]

[95] *Ibid.*, p. 82.

The legal ethics report closes with the unusual problem presented to an attorney who learns during the trial that his client, who seeks civil damages in a slander action from one who has charged him with having committed a crime, did in fact commit the crime charged.[96] Withdrawal from the case was said to be tantamount to proclaiming the guilt of the client, and to providing evidence on the basis of which the former client might be tried, convicted, and executed. The commentator thought that there was no ethical action possible except withdrawal even though prosecution of the former client might follow.

What was the general duty of a Soviet lawyer in the light of the specific situations which had been reviewed? The commentator declared that first of all a Soviet lawyer must avoid any action that would cast his high calling in the light of a money-making business.[97] He must always speak the truth. He did not face the conflict on this issue which was thought to exist in the capitalist world between professional ethics and a higher norm of social ethics which counseled him to "lie to save" those whom the majority of society believed to be "casualties of justice." Adherence to the higher social ethic was thought to be justified under capitalism for a lawyer representing a workingman before a bourgeois class court because there was believed to be a class conflict presented by the situation. Such a class conflict was declared to be absent when a Soviet citizen stood before his judges, and so there was no longer justification for lying to the court. The bar was told that it should have confidence in the court because that court was representative of the people and not of the state against the people, as the commentator presumed a court to be in a capitalist state.

The lingering fear that while courts would expect full respect from the new Soviet bar, the members of the latter might not receive similar respect from the Soviet judges found expression in the final sentences of the commentary. The author pleaded with the Soviet judges to realize that the lawyer who defended his client was not opposing the workers' state but performing his duty to that state. The Soviet lawyer was performing a duty owed to the achievement of justice in his country, and this duty was the more compelling be-

---

[96] *Ibid.*, p. 86.   [97] *Ibid.*, pp. 88–91.

cause the authority of Soviet law itself depended upon the respect created for justice.

THE INFLUENCE OF FEDERATION

Federation of the various Soviet republics at the end of 1922 had no formal impact upon the organization of the college of defenders for fourteen years, although the colleges in each of the republics conformed in fact to the pattern established first in the Russian Republic in 1922. The 1920's constituted a period during which the idea seems to have been prevalent that the administration of most of the apparatus of the law should be left to the republics without the superior formal control of a federal Ministry of Justice. The newly created federal Supreme Court was given no authority over the bar. The provision of legal aid to the public was considered a republic function to be performed by republic commissariats of justice through the intermediary of the provincial courts.[98]

In its directing capacity the Commissariat of Justice of the Russian Republic issued a series of circulars on the tariff to be charged for services rendered to those who qualified for tariff fees as workers and clerks[99] and established the subjects in which candidates for the colleges should be examined, namely the structure of state agencies, court procedure, criminal, civil and land law.[100] The Commissariat evidenced its displeasure with the course of events in 1924 by issuing an instruction to the provincial courts outlining steps to be taken to improve the legal aid being given to the public.[101] It was declared that above all else the quality of the personnel of the colleges should be raised by adding to their membership workers from local Communist party and trade-union organizations. Emphasis was to be placed upon recruitment of members of the working class who had the requisite training in law, government, party, or

[98] Statute on the People's Commissariat of Justice, February 1, 1923, sec. 3(b), [1923] I *Sob. Uzak. RSFSR*, No. 10, item 120.

[99] Circulars attached as appendices to the July, 1922, Regulations of the College of Defenders and also circular No. 200 of October 6, 1925, *Sbornik tsirkuliarov narkomiusta RSFSR za 1922–1925 gg.* (Moscow, 1926), pp. 123–24 and 126.

[100] Circulars attached to Regulations, Appendix No. 3, *ibid.*, p. 124.

[101] Circular No. 61 of April 23, 1924, *ibid.*, p. 125.

trade-union work. The provincial courts were ordered to pay more attention to the colleges and to require prompt submission of reports from the colleges with special reference to their legal aid to the public.

Lack of confidence in the colleges on the part of state agencies and the Communist party members who guided them appears to have been the outstanding feature of the life of the colleges in the formative years. This lack of confidence continued even beyond those years, for again in 1931 the Commissariat of Justice of the Russian Republic issued a circular on the matter of legal aid to the public.[102] Emphasis was placed upon developing this service by concentrating the efforts of the trade unions upon its establishment in the fast growing workers' settlements around new factories and in the collective farms. The provincial courts were accused of doing nothing to press the colleges into extending their services, leaving many inhabited places without even one person qualified to give legal advice.

Again in 1933 the Commissariat turned its attention to improving legal aid to workers and collective farmers, but on this occasion their directive made no mention at all of the colleges.[103] It told the trade unions to organize legal consultation offices to provide legal aid to trade union members in cooperation with the local prosecutors, local agents of the Commissariat of Justice, members of the disciplinary factory courts, and social activists. The colleges continued to function in accordance with the institutional pattern created in 1922, but their popularity was not great. Just as the commentators of the 1920's had feared, those charged with administration of the law came increasingly to belittle the role of professional counsel and to rely on the judges, the prosecutors, and those who might come forward from the trade unions to protect the interests of the accused. Only in civil suits where considerable sums of money were involved did the parties retain lawyers with any regularity, and even these suits were often conducted by the parties alone with the help of interrogation by the judges.

The expression of renewed interest in the orderly administration

---

[102] Order of December 9, 1931, in *Sbornik tsirkuliarov i raz"iasnenii Narodnogo Komissariata Iustitsii RSFSR* (Moscow, 1934), p. 33.
[103] Directive of June 16, 1933, *ibid.*, p. 34.

of the law which was to begin to appear in 1934 in connection with the preparations for adoption of a new constitution of the U.S.S.R. found its reflection in new concern for the colleges of advocates. Law professors began to argue as they had in the early 1920's that lawyers were necessary to the proper conduct of a lawsuit because they aided the prosecutor and the judges. The leading specialist in criminal procedure stated the lawyer's task in the trial as being "aid to the court in the most correct and many-sided investigation of the case and as legal aid to the accused in utilizing the procedural rights given him by the law." [104] The leading authority on civil procedure likewise emphasized the important role of the lawyer in a civil proceeding as "an aid to the court in the struggle for socialist legality and also to give legal aid to the broad masses of the toilers." [105] He referred in support of his statement to a Russian Republic Supreme Court order of December 13, 1933.[106]

Although the lawyer seems to have been emerging from the relatively low state to which he had sunk in the legal hierarchy in the late 1920's and early 1930's, his new importance was not to bring with it greater freedom of action. The colleges were to become subjected to federal control by legislation preparing the way for adoption of a new federal constitution. A People's Commissariat of Justice was created for the first time in the federal government by decree of July 20, 1936.[107] Its charter, as published in December, 1936,[108] disclosed that among the functions of the new Commissariat would be "general guidance and supervision of the giving of legal aid to the population." Since the new federal Commissariat of Justice was of the type required to operate through commissariats of similar name in each of the republics, there was no direct operating control placed in the arm of the federal government, but there had by the new decree been established a formal means of coordinating

[104] M. S. Strogovich, *Ugolovnyi protsess* (*pod red. A. Ia. Vyshinskogo*) (1st ed.; Moscow, 1934), p. 75.

[105] A. F. Kleinman, *Grazhdanskii protsess* (1st ed., Moscow, 1934), pp. 17–18.

[106] *Sovetskaia iustitsiia*, No. 7 (1934), p. 23.

[107] Order on the Organization of a People's Commissariat of Justice, USSR, July 20, 1936, [1936] I *Sobranie Zakonov i Rasporiazhenii Raboche-Krest'ianskogo Pravitel'stva SSSR*, No. 40, item 338.

[108] Charter of the People's Commissariat of Justice, USSR, December 8, 1936, *ibid.*, No. 62, item 455, sec. 2(e).

functions within the republics. Coordination seems previously to have been provided by the less formal means of sharing of experience through Communist party channels.

The new People's Commissariat of Justice in the federal government was slow to exercise its coordinating function over the colleges of defenders, but by decree of August 16, 1939,[109] the Council of People's Commissars approved a new statute prepared by the federal Commissariat of Justice of the U.S.S.R. establishing the rules to be followed in creating colleges and in conducting their affairs. A new name, "advocates," replaced the Revolution's term "defenders," but the institution was continued along the lines established by the various Soviet republics in legislation of 1922 and 1923. The colleges had, apparently, come to stay, but they were still not trusted to govern their own affairs without the intervention of the Commissariat of Justice. Refusal of a governing board of a college to admit an applicant to membership or to exclude a member might still be appealed to the Commissar of Justice of the Republic,[110] and the Commissar of Justice of the U.S.S.R. and the various commissars of justice of the republics established for themselves the right to expel a member of the college without reference to the college itself.[111] It was this latter right of expulsion by the commissars of justice which was to draw the fire of the reformers after Stalin's death in 1953 in their effort to remove from the central authorities the right to punish lawyers whom colleagues at the bar were not prepared to punish.[112] It remains to be seen whether Communist party officials can bring themselves to trust the lawyers of the present time sufficiently to let them keep their own house in order without prodding from the central authorities in the present-day ministries of justice.

[109] Statute on the Institution of Advocacy, USSR, August 16, 1939, [1939] *Sobranie Postanovlenii i Rasporiazhenii Pravitel'stva SSSR*, No. 49, item 394. Regulations issued by the People's Commissariat of Justice, USSR, are collected in NKIuSSSR, *Sovetskaia advokatura* (Moscow, 1942).

[110] Statute on the Institution of Advocacy, USSR, 1939, sec. 11.

[111] *Ibid.*, sec. 12.

[112] See account of personal interview with the President of the Moscow College of Advocates in Harold J. Berman, "Law Reform in the Soviet Union," *American Slavic and East European Review*, XV (1956), 188.

Chapter 9

PROCEDURE TO THE FORE

A PLEA for early codification of procedure and of the law generally opened the year 1922. To an author in the journal of the Commissariat of Justice, codification spelled an end to the methods used during the early years of the new era.[1] He hastened to add that he was not criticizing what had been done in the recent past, for the early methods had their place under the special conditions of the civil war. Nor did he mean "to relegate revolution to the archives" by pressing for codification. "The revolutionary concept of law must run like a red thread through every criminal sentence or civil judgment: it is only being limited by written norms, it is not being abolished."

To those who had formed impressions from court practice alone, without reading the decrees and regulations of the preceding years, the plan to codify may have seemed to mark a sharp departure from existing policy. To those versed in the instructions and statutes, however, the codification plans could not have come as a shock, for simple procedural rules had been prescribed in writing since the first instruction issued to the local people's courts by the Commissariat of Justice on July 23, 1918.[2] The People's Court Act of 1918 had subsequently shown that policy makers did not want procedural requirements ignored, for the act had commanded the reviewing court to order a new trial on finding substantial violations or incorrect application of decrees. The importance to be given procedure was further emphasized by the requirement that reviewers strike down "especially, violation of the forms of court procedure."

Although procedural rules had been becoming a part of the

[1] I. Slavin, "Sud i novaia ekonomicheskaia politika," *Ezhenedel'nik sovetskoi iustitsii*, No. 1 (January 1, 1922), pp. 6–7.
[2] See Chap. I, *supra*, p. 26.

legal system in the years before 1922, practitioners would have had reason to doubt the sincerity of early efforts to sanctify procedure, for practice had tended to ignore the rules. This irregularity was indirectly admitted by the first author for 1922, for in pleading for acceptance of the need for codified procedural law, he found it necessary to declare: "Now that the objective conditions of civil war are changing, there are no obstacles to realizing in Soviet Russia in the very near future the complete protection of the individual in court." [3]

Fear lest citizens misinterpret the codification of procedure as bringing a return to what were remembered as unnecessary delays, formalities, and paper work in the law of the Empire seems to have haunted those responsible for preparing the new procedural codes. On the one hand the Revolution was hailed as having swept away all of the old order including the Imperial court procedure and as having replaced the former rules "by an examination of the cases with the simplest formalities deprived of all remnants of the former external solemnity and detailed dissection of the problem." On the other hand it was recognized that simplicity had created some harmful consequences, for "the means of investigating the case, the technique of court procedure, had been reduced to a primitive explanation of the matter to the persons before the court, which, in the majority of cases decided the matter at that very first sitting." [4]

An examination of hundreds of cases had disclosed to the officials that only a very small percentage of trials required more than one sitting. Speed of decision had resulted in one notably harmful feature, in that the work of review had been hampered by the inadequacy of the record of the trial, for the minutes were often too short and too incomplete to permit effective review.

The speed of trials had also resulted in reducing an accused person's opportunity to defend himself because he had been given no time to bring in witnesses or produce evidence. He had been forced to rely solely on what he might be permitted to say himself to the judges. Many citizens even thought that nothing more had been required of them, for they had become confident that the

[3] Slavin, p. 6.
[4] Grig. Ryndziunskii, "Izlozhenie sudebnykh protokolov i reshenii," *Ezh. sov. iust.*, No. 7 (February 12, 1922), p. 5.

court would decide in their favor if only it could hear their statement of the case. In civil cases the courts were accused of giving the defendant very little opportunity to present his argument, on the ground that there seemed to be no reason to rehearse facts which seemed clear enough as the plaintiff presented them. Courts had given the impression that any new intervention was to be deplored as delaying the case and as introducing red tape. All requests for adjournment of the hearing to obtain evidence had been overruled in the desire to finish the matter at one sitting. Judges had abused their right to conduct the case and had shown too little self-restraint in their effort to get on with the matter. In an effort to eliminate paper work, the judges had been inclined to eliminate all documentary evidence and complaints, so that when the trial was finished, there was nothing in the record but the minutes of the trial prepared by the judge himself and including only what impressed him rather than a summary of all that went on. It was indicated that the minutes often contained only the simple statement, "The plaintiff stated his complaint, and the defendant presented his denial."

The stage was being prepared for new procedural severity, for judges were advised to follow the old maxim, "Make haste slowly," and "to observe those necessary procedural rules which make for completeness and self-restraint without which it is impossible to inspire respect for a court and confidence in the correctness of its decision." [5] Procedural rules were being popularized as necessary to the success of the Revolution and no longer in opposition to what the Communists hoped to achieve.

Mikhail Kalinin as president of the Central Executive Committee of the Russian Republic set the theme of respect for procedure in aid of the state on the highest official level in his speech on the evening of January 28, 1922, to the Fourth Congress of persons engaged in the administration of justice.[6] He ridiculed those who because of their familiarity with the methods of struggle both in battle and in the "indirect" political sphere thought that a plea for return to legality meant a return to the bourgeois point of view. He admitted frankly that in the preceding four years "legality"

[5] *Ibid.*, p. 6.
[6] "Rech' predsedatelia VTsIK tov. M. I. Kalinina," *ibid.*, No. 5 (January 29, 1922), p. 6.

had not been given the importance it deserved, but he declared that "at the present moment it has for us very great importance." Then he called upon the experience of the states of Western Europe to buttress his argument. He suggested that his listeners consider a "classic country like England." He noted that the English government was obviously large, strong, and powerful and controlled colossal forces, yet the government was meticulous in conforming to procedural forms. He asked his audience why this should be. He argued that, of course, the government as a bourgeois government brings influence to bear upon the court, yet it conforms to procedural requirements. In his view the English government presented the picture it did, "only because the court is one of the powerful instruments of the bourgeois state, and by conforming to the procedural forms they fix firmly in the consciousness of the masses respect for the court, so that when an individual goes before a court there is a well-known respect shown him, which is absorbed by Englishmen with their mothers' milk." He drew the conclusion that what was useful for the bourgeois state was also useful for the state of the working class and the peasantry.

To soften his remarks and remove some of what might have been interpreted as cynicism, Kalinin added that, of course, the new proletarian state differed from the bourgeois state not solely because it was a proletarian master rather than a bourgeois master but because as a proletarian state it had the interest of the whole people at heart. It was engaged in creating the ideal society in which there would be ideal relationships between citizen and citizen and also between citizen and state. The court had its place to fill in creating the ideal society, for it had not only to settle quarrels, it had to inculcate the principles of the new society in the subconsciousness of the working and peasant masses.

Specific recommendations as to the details of court procedure did not appear in Kalinin's speech, for he spoke only in generalities except to express his view that the jurisdiction of local administrative bodies should be reduced in favor of the people's courts in the settling of disputes over use of land. The congress itself adopted no resolutions on procedure, having centered its attention on the institutions of the court, the prosecutor, and the bar generally. The drafting of criminal and civil procedural codes seems to have been left to Kurskii and his colleagues in the Commissariat of Justice without instructions. No advice was sought publicly from lawyers generally on criminal procedure in subsequent months in the pages of the journal of the Commissariat, although civil procedure was subjected to public comment, as will be shown subsequently. Nothing on procedural matters appeared in the Commissariat's journal until the May session of the Central Executive Committee of the Russian Republic except a brief circular indicating that the Commissariat was remaining alert to procedural problems.[7] In that circular bearing date of April 13, 1922, the Commissariat instructed courts to arrange their calendar calls so as to save the time of parties and witnesses. They were asked to call only a few cases for a given hour and to hold to the calendar except in situations of emergency.

A NEW CODE OF CRIMINAL PROCEDURE TAKES FORM

Although the published record is bare of information showing how a procedural code was being prepared within the Commissariat, the third sitting of the Ninth Convocation of the Central Executive Committee provided the forum for the disclosure of a complete draft of a code of criminal procedure.[8] Krylenko took the floor as rapporteur on the code for the legal commission of the Central Executive Committee. He announced that it was unnecessary to read the draft as a whole because most of the 481 articles were technical, and all matters of principle had been discussed in the legal commission without opposition, "except for five or six articles, of which two are matters of principle." This characterization of the dissent proved to be an understatement, for in the discussion that followed more than a dozen matters were raised, and all seem important.

In summarizing the debate for the readers of the Commissariat's

---

[7] Circular No. 33, April 13, 1922, on the Procedure for Summoning the Accused, the Injured Parties, etc. to Court Sittings, *Sbornik tsirkuliarov Narkomiusta RSFSR za 1922–1925 gg.* (*Deistvuiushchikh na 15 iiulia 1926*) (Moscow, 1926), p. 145.

[8] *RSFSR—III sessiia Vserossiiskogo Tsentral'nogo Ispolnitel'nogo Komiteta, IX sozyva, mai 1922 g., Stenograficheskii Otchët, biulleten' No. 11, 27 maia 1922 g.* (Moscow, 1922).

journal a reporter later wrote that Krylenko had characterized the code as the systematized practice of all local courts, and that in consequence the principles would be assimilated without any difficulty.[9] To the reporter the highlights of the code were to be found in the extension to each individual of an opportunity to defend his rights. The code was characterized as a kind of declaration of rights, for the individual could now protect himself against a violation of law. The basic points were designated as the limitation placed upon the time during which persons might be imprisoned awaiting trial, the clarification of responsibility for interrogation so that persons would not sit in jail while various agencies passed the case from desk to desk, and the requirement that the indictment be presented at least twenty-four hours before the trial and without exception.

No debate was reported as having occurred "unless the intervention of comrade Larin is such." Larin was said to have opposed the monopoly given the bar as defenders, as well as the special jurisdiction established for crimes by responsible officials, and the designation of the national language to be used at the trial. The journal's readers were given no idea of the opposition which actually developed from Larin and others to some of Krylenko's points. That opposition is revealed in the transcript of the session.[10] Krylenko faced hostile critics on several points. It was so strong that he succeeded in overcoming it in one instance only by persuading the presiding officer to put the question in a manner which required a vote on rejection of an entire article rather than on its amendment in limited form.[11]

The continuation of revolutionary tribunals and transport courts alongside the system of people's courts evoked criticism reflecting the desire of many to simplify the court system. This issue has been discussed in a prior chapter and need not be reviewed here. The purely procedural points which excited criticism had to do with the right to ask for a closed trial, the national language to be used at the trial, the time for presentation of an indictment to the accused, the procedure for filing requests for mercy, the length of

[9] S. Z-tsev, "III sessiia VTsIK," *Ezh. sov. iust.*, No. 18 (May 20, 1922), p. 8.
[10] *RSFSR—III sessiia VTsIK, biulleten' No 11.*
[11] *Ibid.*, pp. 3–4, in the exchange between Krylenko and Larin over the text of Article 30.

time before a sentence of death might be executed after notice
had been given to higher authority, and the right of the Supreme
Court Control to demand a case for review in the absence of an
appeal.

The issue of secrecy of trials was raised only obliquely, for there
was no opposition to the draft's provision that doors might be closed
in the event that it was found necessary by the court to exclude the
public to preserve military, diplomatic, or state secrets or to protect
a party or witness from publicity in a sex case. The proposal made
in opposition to Krylenko was that there be added a note to the
article permitting the state security police, known as the G.P.U.,
to make a request to close the doors. Krylenko thought the specifica-
tion of this right of the G.P.U. unnecessary because anyone had
the implied right to make the request under the general provision
giving the court discretionary right to close the doors in the circumstances indicated.[12] Krylenko's view was upheld in a voice vote,
and the note was omitted, although it was to reappear in the revision of 1923.

The national-language question was raised in a proposal to
eliminate from the draft any reference to Russian as the language
of the trial. It was urged that the pertinent Article 22 provide
solely that the trial should be conducted in the language of the
majority of the population in a given locality. The argument was
that to mention Russian specifically as the principal language, even
when there was subsequent provision for another language when
the majority of the population of a given locality was not Russian,
reflected a "great-power tendency." The legal commission was reported as having opposed this amendment on the ground that
there was no such great-power tendency reflected in the draft. The
only purpose of reference to Russian was to indicate that the
Russians constituted the majority of the population generally within
the Republic, and it was reasonable to refer to Russian as the usual
language of a trial. The amendment was rejected.[13]

The time set for delivery of an indictment[14] was to be changed
from the existing rule of twenty-four hours in the revolutionary
tribunals and seven days in the people's courts to three days for
both, but part of the committee had categorically refused to accept

[12] *Ibid.*, pp. 1–2.   [13] *Ibid.*, p. 2.   [14] *Ibid.*, p. 9.

the prolongation of time for the revolutionary tribunals. Krylenko reported that a first compromise had been tried, namely, to reduce the period to forty-eight hours under conditions of "battle." This first effort at compromise had failed, and a substitute was offered, namely, to permit a reduction "to forty-eight hours in exceptional circumstances and when approved by a court ruling setting forth the nature of the circumstances." Krylenko added his view that if a reduction were to be permitted, it ought to be to as little as twenty-four hours. A proponent of the three days' proposal spoke up to remind the deputies that many people were not capable of examining the indictment even of a simple case in a short time, much less of a complicated case, and they certainly could not call witnesses in so short a time. In spite of this protest the forty-eight-hour rule in exceptional cases was adopted.

Requests for mercy after a sentence of death by a revolutionary tribunal were discussed by a deputy who declared that many comrades had been executed unjustly without having had an opportunity to obtain a review of their conviction. Krylenko argued that under existing practice permitting despatch of a telegram to the Central Executive Committee of the Republic asking for mercy, every convicted person sent such a telegram, and the execution was delayed "forever." He argued for limitation upon this right,[15] but he was voted down by deputies who knew, apparently, that there had been excesses by local revolutionary tribunals and that execution had not been stayed forever.

As to the delay prior to execution of a sentence of death, it was argued in debate that the telegraph system worked badly, and that the draft's proposal to require a delay of only twenty-four hours after notification to the Supreme Revolutionary Tribunal before executing the sentence was unrealistic. It was proposed that the period of waiting be extended to seventy-two hours. Krylenko agreed, and the longer period was accepted.[16]

The right of the Supreme Court Control within the Commissariat of Justice to request any case in process before the people's courts, the councils of people's judges, or the revolutionary tribunals was added to the draft as a result of the debate.[17]

A month's reflection upon the work of the Central Executive

[15] *Ibid.*, p. 10.   [16] *Ibid.*, p. 14.   [17] *Ibid.*, p. 12.

Committee at its May sitting caused an author in the July 7 issue of the Commissariat of Justice's journal to say that the new Code of Criminal Procedure made it possible "for every literate worker and peasant to take upon himself with a peaceful mind the hard duties of a judge." [18] The author was happy that the new judges would not have to absorb the whole code before beginning their work, for the arrangement of the code by stages in the trial made it possible in his view to use the code as a manual to be consulted as each step was taken. "The judges do not have to learn the code by cramming but by testing their every act and every order."

Adoption of the new code was not, however, to be interpreted as requiring the undoing of all that had been done in opposition to its principles. Lest there be a wave of reversals, the July author told his readers that all directing agencies should proceed cautiously and not change court decisions which were correct in substance although not in the form prescribed by the new code. He felt that it would be some time before the workers in the legal institutions understood the new laws. By this advice the Commissariat indicated that while policy called for the establishment of a procedure which would cause the public to develop faith in the courts, as Kalinin had proposed, there was to be no acceptance of the doctrine of the English courts which Kalinin was trying to emulate, namely, that one cannot be sure of what the substance of a case really is if procedural requirements are not observed.

A PROCEDURAL BILL OF RIGHTS

The Code of Criminal Procedure was approved by the Central Executive Committee of the Russian Republic on May 25, 1922, to become effective July 1, 1922.[19] Its "Part I" sounded like the bill of rights which had been promised. No one could be deprived of freedom or imprisoned except in the situations defined in the law and in accordance with the procedure established by law.[20] Every judge and prosecutor who found within his jurisdiction someone

[18] A. Lisitsyn, "Ugolovno-protsessual'nyi kodeks," *Ezh. sov. iust.*, No. 24–25 (June 30–July 7, 1922), p. 1.
[19] [1922] I *Sobranie Uzakonenii i Rasporiazhenii Rabochego i Krest'ianskogo Pravitel'stva RSFSR*, No. 20–21, item 230.
[20] Art. 5.

imprisoned without proper authority or in excess of the period permitted by law was to release that person immediately.[21] A judge or prosecutor who learned that someone within his jurisdiction was imprisoned in an improper place or under improper conditions was to take measures to see that the requirements of the law were adhered to.[22] A preexisting civil judgment in the case was to have effect in the criminal action only to establish an event, and not the guilt of the accused.[23] All court hearings were to be public, except when military, diplomatic, or state secrets required closing of the doors, or in cases involving sex crimes.[24] Even when the case was heard in camera, the sentence had to be announced publicly.[25] An accused was to have the right to an interpreter and to receive the indictment and other documents in the trial in his own language.[26] A record was required at all stages of the procedure, including a statement of the substance of any testimony, signed by the witness concerned.[27] Within three days after preparation of the record the parties who participated had the right to file their comments on its completeness and truth, and the court was required to decide the merits of the objection.[28]

Criminal procedure was divided in the parts which followed into seven stages: (1) initiation of proceedings, (2) short inquiry by organs of detention, (3) preliminary investigation, (4) transfer to court, (5) trial, (6) judicial review, and (7) execution of the sentence.

The elements of these seven formally named stages were not new, for most of them had been inaugurated by the first procedural rules adopted in July, 1918. The code of 1922 represented but a refinement of a procedure which had been developing ever since abandonment of the concept of an informal court composed of an elder of the village or Communist party wise man authorized to take what measures he thought necessary to keep the peace. Procedural practice had already moved far from the lack of rules with which the judge of 1917 had been faced. He had enjoyed the help of no prosecutor nor investigator to prepare the case. He had been expected to rely upon an enraged citizenry for the initiation of proceedings and upon his own resources for investigation, helped

[21] Art. 6.   [22] Art. 7.   [23] Art. 13.   [24] Art. 19.   [25] Art. 21.
[26] Art. 22.   [27] Art. 82.   [28] Art. 86.

as he might be by any social organizations that felt it their duty to gather evidence against the accused and by any relatives or friends of the accused who came to the defense by assisting in the gathering of whatever could be found to support his plea of innocence or for mercy. Previous chapters in this study have shown that the primitive concept of judicial procedure had collapsed under the burden of practice.

One relic of the informal past appeared in the new code in spite of the inauguration of formality. A judge was still authorized to take the initiative in instigating proceedings,[29] in setting the case for trial without the prior intervention of any other agency,[30] in informing the accused of the charge against him,[31] and in questioning him as to his desires for his defense.[32] Yet this simplified procedure, which had been the rule in the first months after the Revolution, now became the rare exception, for the new code required the conduct of a preliminary investigation by someone other than the judge in all cases where the crime was so serious that law required it to be tried either by a revolutionary tribunal or by a judge and six lay judges. While a judge might decide to dispense with such an independent preliminary investigation in lesser cases, he had to issue a written reasoned decision explaining why he felt it unnecessary to have the case prepared by others before trial.[33] This requirement would normally dissuade the cautious judge from assuming the investigating function.

Complaints might still be filed with a judge by an enraged citizenry represented by a public organization such as a labor union or cooperative, or by a citizen,[34] but the judge no longer was the sole recipient. The usual route of complaint was to the police, the prosecutor, or a preliminary investigator. On receipt of an oral or written complaint,[35] which could not be rejected out of hand even if the alleged crime had been committed outside of the official's territorial jurisdiction,[36] the recipient prepared a decision on the measures to be taken. If the decision was against proceeding, the complainant had to be advised, and he had seven days to appeal the refusal to the appropriate court whose decision was final.[37] If the decision was in favor of proceeding, preliminary investigation

[29] Art. 96.   [30] Art. 237.   [31] Art. 101 (4).   [32] Art. 260.   [33] Art. 110.
[34] Art. 96.   [35] Art. 97.   [36] Art. 99.   [37] Art. 100.

was commenced, or a court took jurisdiction directly.[38] With what seems to be a desire to discourage the satisfaction of personal grudges, the code required those who filed oral complaints to sign a statement of the complaint as prepared by the official to whom it was made, and the warning had to be given that the uttering of false testimony was a criminal offense.[39] An anonymous complaint could serve as instigation of proceedings only after a secret investigation by the police of its merit.[40]

Certain charges had to be dropped when received, namely, those against a person who had died (unless the charge was that the false testimony of the person against whom the charge had been brought or the criminal action of a judge had resulted in an unjust conviction), those against a person amnestied by name or in a general amnesty of persons who had committed a specified type of crime, those against which a period of limitation had run, and those unsupported by the complaint of the injured party, if that complaint was required.[41]

In explanation of the last category the code established that for taking the law into one's own hands, unpublished or published personal insults, slander, libel, and mild forms of battery no prosecution might follow unless the injured party brought a complaint and did not reach a reconciliation before execution of the sentence.[42] If a prosecutor concluded that there was a public interest involved, he might enter such a case to prevent its termination in the event of reconciliation.[43] For the more serious crimes of intentional bodily injury, rape, statutory rape, intentional violation of patents or trademarks no proceedings could be commenced without the complaint of the injured party, and even if reconciliation occurred the proceedings could not be dropped.[44] This second category differed from the first in that a prosecutor was not asked to exercise discretion as to whether a public interest was concerned. The code declared the public interest, but the sensibilities of the injured party were considered in that no proceedings could be instigated without complaint. The difference lay only in the effect of reconciliation.

In later years a commentator explained that when rape was committed by several persons or as a vestige of a tribal custom, the

---

[38] Art. 101.   [39] Art. 97.   [40] Art. 98.   [41] Art. 4.   [42] Art. 10 (par. 1).
[43] Art. 10 (par. 2).   [44] Art. 11.

wishes of the injured party could not be considered paramount because the crime had become cloaked with a public interest.[45] The fact that the commentator found it desirable to make such a statement suggests that practice went beyond the code's provisions, perhaps on the legal basis that such crime was analogous to banditry or its equivalent and justified prosecution even if the woman refused to expose what she probably thought shameful, or—in the tribal situation—routine.

THE POLICE INQUIRY

Arrest and subsequent detention seem to have worried the draftsmen of the code. The provisions appear to have been drawn to pacify those who were demanding legality in police activities, yet they avoided any risk to the security of the regime. Strict-sounding rules of conduct were established for the police, but the means of making them effective were scant. Thus, detention was to be permitted only when necessary to prevent the escape of a suspected person, and then only if the individual had been caught in preparing or committing a crime or immediately thereafter; when the injured party or a witness designated a person as having committed a crime; when evidence of the crime was found on the person or in the home of the suspect; when the suspect had no permanent home or place of work; and when the identity of the suspect could not be established.[46]

To enforce these limitations upon the police the code required that the agency making the arrest inform a judge or a court within twenty-four hours, stating the reason for the detention.[47] This gave the judge an opportunity to perform his duty to release anyone found within his jurisdiction unlawfully detained. If the arrest was not approved within forty-eight hours after receipt of notice by a judge, an investigator or a court, that person had to be released. If the crime was so serious as to require preliminary investigation under the rules of the code, the police had to notify the prosecutor and a preliminary investigator of the action.

In the procedure established for approval of the arrest the drafts-

[45] M. S. Strogovich, *Ugolovnyi protsess* (Moscow, 1938), p. 108.
[46] Code of Criminal Procedure, RSFSR (1922), Art. 105.
[47] Art. 106.

men seem to have sought to throw around a suspect some of the protection afforded by the warrant in common-law countries but there was a difference in that approval was required only after the fact rather than before.[48] Further, there was created no procedure equivalent to the writ of habeas corpus to assure that the matter of arrest and detention would be brought to the attention of a judge. Practice soon showed that the procedure was inadequate in restraining an overly zealous police.

Further protection of a suspect was attempted in a requirement that detention, even when authorized, could continue for only one month, after which the file had to be passed on to the prosecutor if no crime seemed to have been committed, or if the crime appeared to be of a serious type. The file went directly to a court if the crime was such that a penalty no greater than a year of deprivation of freedom might be meted out.[49] During the period of detention the police, the agency of criminal investigation, or the state political police[50] could not only collect any real evidence which might seem pertinent to the case,[51] but they were also authorized to interrogate the accused and witnesses and to make any searches and seizures deemed necessary to prevent destruction or concealment of evidence of the crime.[52]

In a final attempt to restrain overly zealous police officials, the draftsmen ended their chapter on police inquiry with an article placing the whole process under the control of the prosecutor to whom any protest against illegal activities of the police might be made and in whom resided the right to intervene at any moment to inform himself of the proceedings and to propose lines of conduct.[53]

To many western minds control over the police by a prosecutor seems no control at all, but it is possible that organization of opposition within the committee to such a provision would have been difficult, for proponents could refer to the arguments already disclosed when the new prosecutor's office was created, namely, that the Soviet prosecutor was supposed to be of a special type. He had been defined in the statute creating the office as an agent seeking not solely the conviction of the accused but the orderly conduct of prosecutions, which was interpreted to require as much attention

[48] Art. 6.   [49] Art. 107.   [50] Art. 102.   [51] Art. 103.   [52] Art. 104.
[53] Art. 109.

to the possible acquittal of the accused as to his conviction. It bears repeating that to western trained lawyers such considerations have seemed more theoretical than real, but they probably provided the basis in the minds of Soviet policy makers for establishing the prosecutor's supervisory role as a means of preventing police excesses and brutality.

THE PRELIMINARY INVESTIGATION

The preliminary investigation which was commanded in serious cases and recommended in all [54] was patterned upon that found in countries adopting the civil-law forms of procedure. To conduct this stage there already existed the appropriate agency which was the outgrowth of the investigating commissions created in July, 1918, and replaced by individual investigation under provisions of the People's Court Act of 1920. The investigator was charged with the task of investigating not only those circumstances which tended to incriminate the accused but also those which tended to exculpate him, and also to search for facts which would minimize his offense as well as those which would maximize it.[55] To make such an investigation possible the investigator was required not only to interrogate the accused [56] but to call any witnesses that he or his accuser might designate,[57] and to prepare a written reasoned statement in the event that he refused to do so.[58] The accused and his accuser were authorized to be present in person at all investigative activities and interrogations, and to put questions to witnesses and experts.[59] Yet in the event that the investigator concluded that their presence would help them to conceal the truth or to learn prematurely information which had to be kept secret to facilitate later stages of the investigation he could exclude them.[60] In this effort to protect security the door was opened to abuse.

Interminable investigation was to be hampered by the requirement that within twenty-four hours of receipt of information of commission of crime if an arrest had occurred, and forty-eight hours in other cases, the investigator begin his investigation and send a notice to the prosecutor of that fact.[61] The investigation itself had

---

[54] Art. 110.   [55] Art. 113.   [56] Art. 111.   [57] Art. 114.   [58] Art. 116.
[59] Art. 117.   [60] *Ibid.*   [61] Art. 112.

to be completed within two months, unless the prosecutor extended
the time at the request of the investigator because of the im-
possibility of completing the investigation within the two months
allowed.[62]

Excesses of the investigator were in the first instance the concern
of the prosecutor who was declared the supervisor of the investigation,[63] but the accused had some rights of appeal to a court. He
could ask the removal of the investigator if he were a relative of
the parties or otherwise interested in the case, and the petition had
to be answered by the court to which the investigator was responsible or by the court where he had his office within three days
of receipt of the petition.[64] The accused was, however, at the mercy
of the investigator, in such an appeal, for the petition could not
be filed directly with the court but only through the agency of the
investigator. In an effort to prevent suppression of the petition by
the investigator, the code required him to transmit it to the court
within twenty-four hours.[65] Further effort to protect the accused
against his investigator took the form of a special chapter of the
code devoted to appeals against his activities.[66] By these articles
the accused, or witnesses, experts, bondsmen, and other interested
parties might appeal to the court to which the investigator was
responsible or the court where he had his office if they believed
their rights to have been infringed. In this instance the petition
might be filed directly as well as through the investigator, and it
could be oral as well as written. The petition had to be filed within
seven days of the act complained against, unless the complaint was
against slowness generally, and the court had to decide the matter
within seventy-two hours. The investigator was required to give
his view of the matter within twenty-four hours of receipt of the
complaint. Filing of a complaint did not suspend the investigation,
for it continued until the decision on the complaint was handed
down.

The setting forth of many apparent safeguards against arbitrary
action by preliminary investigators may have satisfied those who
feared for the future of legality under the new code, but on sober
reflection they could have noted that the most important protection
of all had been omitted, namely, the right to counsel at the stage of

[62] Art. 119.   [63] Art. 121.   [64] Art. 125.   [65] *Ibid.*   [66] Chap. 18.

preliminary investigation. As has been indicated earlier, no article denied the right to counsel specifically, but the implication of the code was that counsel might be called only to prepare for trial.[67] No lawyers were in fact permitted to assist a client before that time so that in practice the implication of denial of counsel was made clear.

Since it would have been a rare individual who could have understood his rights or could have had the courage to demand observance of the code by the man from whom mercy might have been expected in the absence of criticism, the various provisions gave very limited protection against one who was prepared to exceed his authority for whatever reason. Soviet lawyers later admitted as much but nothing was done to remedy the situation during Stalin's life, and even after his death the preliminary investigation remained the unpublicized pretrial determination of guilt or innocence which the draftsmen made of it in their code, except when the accused was a minor. In the new fundamental principles adopted by the federal parliament in December, 1958, a juvenile delinquent was accorded the right to an attorney during the preliminary investigation.[68]

The indictment prepared at the end of the preliminary investigation was to be in a form familiar to Continental systems generally. It appeared to be far more than the accusatory act of a state official charged with prosecution, as it would be in modern England or of a grand jury as it would be generally in the United States. It was the work of an official of the court, charged formally with the task of being not prosecutor but impartial fact finder, seeking to exculpate the accused if the facts indicated innocence. It set forth in detail not a prima facie case against the accused as would be the true bill of a grand jury at common law but a reasoned statement of evidence in his favor as well as against him, keyed to a record of the proceedings in which the statements of the defendant and of his witnesses were set forth, together with those of the accusers. When the investigator transmitted to the prosecutor the indictment[69] or conclusion that the investigation had produced insufficient evi-

---

[67] See Arts. 247 and 250.

[68] Law on the Approval of the Fundamental Principles of Criminal Procedure of the USSR and of the Union Republics, December 25, 1958, *Vedomosti Verkhovnogo Soveta SSSR*, No. 1 (933) (January 1, 1959), item 15, Art. 22.

[69] Code of Criminal Procedure, RSFSR (1922), Art. 215.

dence to merit the trial,[70] he completed his function and was ready for his next case.

Fear on the part of some of the draftsmen that delays would occur during the period of detention prior to trial proved to be well founded, as indicated by circulars of the Commissariat of Justice issued soon after adoption of the code. On June 8, 1922, the Commissariat asked all agencies to advance out of the order in which they were filed complaints of the Central Executive Committee of the Republic, or of the Council of People's Commissars or its economic administrative arm, the Council of Labor and Defense, so that investigations might be completed "in the shortest period possible." [71] On June 30, 1922, the Commissariat found it necessary to ask courts and tribunals to take cases instigated by the Workers'-Peasants' Inspection "in swift order," calling as witnesses members of the staff of the inspection ministry who had made the investigation and notifying the ministry of the day of the trial so that personnel might be assigned to prosecute the accused.[72]

Shocking violations of the rules were disclosed in a circular of February 17, 1923,[73] in which the Commissariat of Justice noted that the criminal-inspection service of the Republic had found that arrested persons were being held in unsanitary conditions without artificial illumination and even without a pot of boiling water and bread; that they were being detained for more than the permitted period; that in the journal maintained by the police there was often missing the first name and patronymic of the arrested person; that the order for arrest was given no number and was not communicated to higher authority within the time required by the code; and that in some cases nothing appeared about the arrested person except the order for arrest. To put a halt to such violations the Commissariat

[70] *Ibid.*, Art. 206.

[71] Circular No. 44, June 8, 1922, on the Procedure for Hearing Cases Instigated by the All-Russian CEC, the Council of People's Commissars and the Council of Labor and Defense, quoted in A. B. Vroblevskii, *Postateinyi kommentarii k ugolovno—protsessual'nomu kodeksu RSFSR* (Moscow, 1923), p. 101.

[72] Circular No. 54, June 30, 1922, on the Procedure for Hearing Cases Instigated by Organs of the Workers'-Peasants' Inspection, *ibid.*

[73] Circular No. 31, February 17, 1923, on Measures to Bring Order into Criminal Searches, the Preparation of a Record of a Case and the Preservation of Material Evidence, and also the Detention of Arrested Persons, *ibid.*, pp. 109–10.

ordered more frequent checks on detention houses and the preparation of a model police blotter on which facts would be entered and from which notice could be sent to the prosecutor.

Conduct of the investigation appears to have been faulty at times, for one author reported that the suspected person was sometimes not questioned at all during the period of his detention with the result that clarification of the case was often impeded and the person detained had no idea of the complaint against him.[74] A handbook for prosecutors ordered them to see that police investigators limit their searches to those required by real necessity, and that only in extreme circumstances they detain individuals in an effort to disclose the crime.[75]

The two extremes of laxness and overzealousness on the part of preliminary investigators were also revealed in reports. Laxness was indicated when the Supreme Court Control struck down a conviction because the defendant had not been interrogated, and no indictment had been prepared and presented as required by the code.[76] The trial court had proceeded solely on the basis of preparatory material submitted by the political police, the G.P.U., and this was not enough in a serious case since the code required preliminary investigation. Overzealousness to the point of brutality in the conduct of preliminary investigation was disclosed by an order of the Supreme Court Control to the effect that a confession of the accused at the preliminary investigation or even at the trial could not always be taken as uncontestable proof of guilt, the more so if the accused charged that it had been obtained by compulsion.[77]

TRANSMISSION TO COURT

Having received the recommendation of the preliminary investigator to terminate prosecution or to proceed with trial, the prosecutor made his decision as to the advisability of the recommendation. He might decide that the case should not be dropped,

[74] M. Grodzinskii, "Dopros obviniaemogo v novom protsessual'nom kodekse," *Pravo i zhizn'*, No. 3 (1922), p. 56.
[75] M. Kobalenkov, "Rukovodstvo dlia prokuratury," quoted in Vroblevskii, *Postateinyi kommentarii*, p. 109.
[76] Case No. 24-v, quoted in *ibid.*, p. 118.
[77] Supreme Court Control, Decision in Criminal Case No. 980, 1920, quoted in *ibid.*, p. 131.

in which event he had to present his opposition to the court, and this he could do with argument in person.[78] If he thought the case insufficiently prepared, he could return it to the investigator for further attention.[79] If he thought the recommendation for trial ill founded because of lack of facts or of law, he could oppose the recommendation personally before the court.[80] If he was in complete agreement with the recommendation for trial, he could transmit the indictment to court with a recommendation that it proceed to summon the defendant, or he could substitute a new indictment prepared by himself to accord more closely with his own conclusions.[81] He might also change the list of persons to be called as witnesses as it had been appended to the indictment by the preliminary investigator,[82] and he could indicate whether he would argue the case himself or send a deputy.[83] If the court was not content with a deputy, it could order the prosecutor to appear in person.

The court which received the prosecutor's conclusions met in preparatory session to consider the indictment. This session was treated by the code as a distinct stage of the proceedings, namely, that of "transfer to court." The bench at such a preparatory session was composed of the professional judge sitting alone, but if he concluded that the indictment should be quashed, he was required to associate with himself two lay judges so that a full court might make such a decision.[84] If necessary in the judge's view, the case might be returned for further investigation,[85] or if it was a matter solely of the formulation of the conclusions, the judge might change them without reference back to those who had drawn them.[86] If the indictment satisfied the judge, a decision to proceed was issued in the name of the court.[87] Not later than within seventy-two hours before the time set for trial, a copy of the indictment had to be presented to the accused.[88]

During the entire time from the commencement of the investigation to trial the suspected person could have been detained, for the code permitted this as the most extreme form of assuring the presence of the suspect at his trial. Less severe measures were also authorized in the form of a personal undertaking or bond not to

[78] Code of Criminal Procedure, RSFSR (1922), Art. 230.
[79] Art. 231.   [80] Art. 232.   [81] Art. 233.   [82] Art. 234.   [83] Art. 235.
[84] Art. 237   [85] Art. 241.   [86] Art. 244.   [87] *Ibid.*   [88] Art. 249.

depart from the jurisdiction, an undertaking supported by a surety or by a pledge of property or money to appear, or house arrest. It was the preliminary investigator's task to decide whether any of these measures were required when the charge came to him.[89] The prosecutor could continue these measures while he was reviewing the work of the preliminary investigator, and then in his report to court he indicated his view as to what measures should be applied while awaiting trial.[90] In its decision to proceed to trial the court included its order as to measures to be taken to assure the presence of the defendant.[91] Appeals against such an order could be filed with the Council of People's Judges within fourteen days of the order,[92] but there was no appeal if the order was issued during the trial because of failure of a defendant to appear when called.[93]

THE TRIAL

Flanked by his two lay judges the professional judge entered the courtroom as all stood in respectful attention for the beginning of the drama of the trial. At the left of the bench stood the court secretary prepared to draft the record of the proceedings on which appeal might be based. In front of the bench usually stood a prosecutor or his representative and beside him the attorney to whom the defendant had a right once the indictment had been received and to whom he could tell his full story.[94] In contrast to the courtroom in common-law lands, but in keeping with the traditions of the Continental jurisdictions of which the new Soviet court was one, the table before the judges had upon it what was often a very large file containing not only the indictment but the full record of the preliminary investigation. Tied together in simply bound folders with numbered pages keyed to the charges of the indictment were the signed statements comprising the testimony of witnesses who were to appear at the trial, as well as the investigator's conclusions drawn from any visits he might have made to the scene of the crime. Also present were any documents, weapons, or other material evidence.

For the Soviet draftsmen, just as for all Continental jurists, the

[89] Art. 147.   [90] Art. 235.   [91] Art. 246.   [92] Art. 350.   [93] Art. 351.
[94] Art. 256.

trial was not expected to present the surprises so characteristic of a trial at common law. Except for those few minor crimes which were brought before a judge without preliminary investigation the subject with which the court had to deal at the trial had already been explored extensively. The proceedings which constituted the trial were but an additional stage in the series of proceedings which had been developing since the police had first become suspicious or had made an arrest. Part III of the code called the trial "Proceedings in the People's Court." The type was larger than that used for the eight chapter headings which fell within the part. The arrangement was unique, for no other part had a heading at all. The reader of the other parts was left to his own analysis to find the reason for the grouping of chapters which occurred therein. The effect created by the enlarged type for the trial suggests a desire on the part of the draftsmen to emphasize the proceedings in the people's court as the focal point in the affair, preceded by the preparatory steps and followed by the review, but in actuality the trial was little more than public verification of the conclusions reached in the preparatory stage. The court reheard witnesses to determine their credibility and examined documents and other real evidence to ascertain whether three heads in consultation would conclude what the preliminary investigator and the prosecutor had already concluded, namely, that the accused was guilty.

Procedural guarantees to the accused introduced the chapter on the court sitting. He found restated his right to counsel and to investigate personally or through counsel the "case," which meant the file of the preliminary investigation.[95] He could ask the professional judge prior to trial to subpoena witnesses, experts, and evidence, and his request had to be granted if the judge found the explanation given by the accused sufficient to suggest relevancy. If the request was denied, the judge had to issue a reasoned opinion.[96] It was not sufficient excuse to refuse the request if there seemed already to be enough testimony on the subject planned for the trial. Like all other rulings of the court as to the conduct of the trial to which the accused took exception, it had to be included in the record of the proceedings for possible subsequent review on appeal.[97]

[95] Art. 256.   [96] Art. 257.   [97] Arts. 258 and 261.

Interminable trials with their many strains upon the accused and their prolongation of his detention were prohibited by a requirement that the proceedings continue without interruption except for intermissions, and no other case could be heard during such intermissions.[98] Trials could be held in the absence of the defendant if the penalty could not exceed six months deprivation of freedom. If the charge were more serious, as indicated by the penalty prescribed under the articles concerned, the defendant had to be brought in unless he agreed to trial in his absence or refused to accept summons or concealed himself.[99] Even in minor cases when the defendant's presence was not required by the code, the court was instructed to hear argument from those interested as "parties," which meant the prosecution, the injured person, and any representative of the defendant, as to the desirability of proceeding without him, and the order to proceed or to adjourn the proceedings had to be inserted in the record for possible subsequent review.[100]

If a prosecutor was expected and he failed to appear, the case was adjourned unless a substitute could be found, as was also the rule if a named attorney did not appear.[101] Absence of the injured party who was accusing the defendant resulted in quashing the indictment if it was one of the offenses for which proceedings were not permitted without support of the person injured.[102] If a civil plaintiff who had joined a civil suit with the criminal prosecution because the same facts were involved failed to appear, the civil suit was dismissed without prejudice to reinstatement if the criminal prosecution were adjourned and later resumed.[103]

Having determined who was present, the court was ready to begin. The identity of the accused was established, and he had to be asked whether he had received a copy of the indictment.[104] The presence of witnesses and experts was verified,[105] and any last-minute requests for additions to the roster were considered in the same manner as before trial,[106] the proceedings being adjourned if necessary until the witnesses could appear.[107]

Witnesses were then to be called solemnly before the court to be advised of their duty to tell all that they knew and warned that

[98] Art. 262.   [99] Art. 269.   [100] Art. 270.   [101] Art. 272.   [102] Art. 274.
[103] Art. 273.   [104] Art. 268.   [105] Art. 275.   [106] Art. 276.   [107] Art. 277.

in the event of false testimony they would be subjected to criminal prosecution. The code required that they then be excluded from the room and prevented from comparing notes with other witnesses during the proceedings.[108] Experts could remain in the courtroom unless the court thought it necessary to exclude them as well.[109]

No oath was required of witnesses,[110] for the reasons already disclosed in an earlier chapter, namely, because it was officially thought to violate the principle of separation of church and state to require such an oath, and probably, unofficially, because it was thought unseemly to require an oath in a state directed by a political party which denied the existence of God. The Criminal Code which existed at the time subjected the giver of false testimony in official interrogation to a penalty of deprivation of liberty for a period of up to one year.[111]

The accused was also told again of his rights to explain anything he wished at any moment during the trial and also to interrogate witnesses, experts, or co-defendants directly or through an attorney.[112] The names of the three members of the court were then announced and the accused and the injured party were advised of their right to challenge any of them on the ground of interest in the case.[113] Such a challenge was to be decided after the withdrawal of the challenged judge by the two judges remaining, and a negative vote of either was enough to support the challenge.[114]

With the stage set, the judges in place, and the courtroom in order, the professional judge was directed to read the indictment, or in the absence of such, the prosecutor's charge or the complaint of the injured party, or the presiding judge's own statement of the charge against the accused.[115] The substance of the charge was then repeated in colloquial terms which the accused could be expected to understand, and he was asked whether he pleaded "guilty" and wished to say something immediately.[116] The prosecution and defense were then asked for the plan which they wished to follow in presenting their versions of the case, and if these met the court's pleasure, argument began.[117]

---

[108] Art. 278.   [109] Art. 279.   [110] Art. 57.

[111] Criminal Code, RSFSR, [1922] I *Sob. Uzak. RSFSR*, No. 15, item 153, Art. 90.

[112] Code of Criminal Procedure, RSFSR (1922), Arts. 281 and 292.

[113] Art. 282.   [114] Art. 51.   [115] Art. 283.   [116] Art. 284.   [117] Art. 285.

A plea of "guilty" released the court from any duty to take evidence, unless one of the parties requested that this be done. With no further duty to prove the charge the court turned immediately to the statements of prosecution and defendant to assist it in sentencing the defendant.[118] If the plea was "not guilty," the accused might make a statement immediately, or after each witness had testified or after all had testified.[119]

In the light of explanation years later that a defendant might refuse to testify,[120] although it was admitted that the question was almost academic since he rarely refused to take the stand, one article of the code seems unclear. It provides that interrogation of the accused shall be conducted by the presiding judge and the lay judges, and then by the prosecution, the civil plaintiff, the defense attorney, and other defendants in that order. It provides further that "Interrogation of the accused in the absence of co-defendants shall be permitted only in exceptional cases, if the interests of disclosure of truth so require." [121] Such an article suggests that there could be interrogation, although no article of the Criminal Code provided for punishment in the event of failure to testify. Perhaps the draftsmen thought it unnecessary to raise the issue because the effect of any refusal to testify would be so great upon the judges that there was a psychological sanction against those who withheld testimony in that they might fear heightened penalty in the event of a finding of guilt. Whatever the draftsmen may have thought, their treatment of the matter was to be criticized later as inadequate protection of the accused's right to remain silent.

Witnesses were to be questioned by the one on whose behalf they were called and then by the opposition,[122] including the judges.[123] In this authorization to the judges to put questions lay further evidence of the fact that a Soviet judge was not a referee of an adversary proceeding but an active participant in the examination at the trial. No witness could leave the room on completing testimony without the specific consent of the presiding judge,[124] and witnesses might confront each other and examine each other in the event of contrary testimony.[125] The witnesses were

---

[118] Art. 286.   [119] *Ibid.*   [120] Strogovich, *Ugolovnyi protsess*, p. 180.
[121] Code of Criminal Procedure, RSFSR (1922), Art. 287.
[122] Art. 291.   [123] Art. 293.   [124] Art. 295.   [125] Art. 294.

permitted to refresh their memories from notes,[126] but if they testified as to the substance of documents, these had to be introduced in evidence, and at the order of the court made a part of the record.[127]

The character of the trial as a verification of the preliminary investigation was suggested by the provision that witnesses had to be called to testify again at the trial to what they had told the preliminary investigator, but in the event that they did not appear on subpoena[128] or changed their stories or lost their memory of what had been said, their prior testimony could be read into the court record.[129] Prior testimony of co-defendants who were dead or of a defendant who was absent might be read into the record also if requested by one of the parties or by the court.[130]

Expert testimony was to be given orally but then reduced to writing for the record.[131] If the experts disagreed or were unclear, the court on its own initiative or that of one of the parties might call additional experts.[132] The court might itself proceed to any place whose inspection seemed necessary at any moment in a trial, and it might go as a body or delegate one of the judges to take the view.[133] If the presentation of evidence ended with what the court believed to be inadequate proof when more could possibly be found, a recess could be called at the request of one of the parties or on the court's own initiative until such evidence could be brought in, or the case could be returned to the police or preliminary investigator for further action.[134]

Following completion of the gathering of evidence, the court was instructed to call upon the parties for their summing up; first the prosecution, then the injured party, and finally the lawyer for the defense or the defendant himself.[135] New evidence could not be produced in these speeches, but more evidence might be requested, and the court had to decide whether it was necessary.[136] The prosecutor could withdraw his case at this time if he so desired because of insufficient proof of guilt.[137] Rebuttals of concluding speeches were permitted to all, in one more round,[138] and then the defendant was offered the opportunity to make his final personal statement,[139] which might be as long as he wanted and

---

[126] Art. 296. [127] Art. 297. [128] Art. 301. [129] Art. 300. [130] Art. 299.
[131] Art. 302. [132] Art. 304. [133] Art. 305. [134] Art. 306. [135] Art. 308.
[136] Art. 309. [137] Art. 310. [138] Art. 311. [139] Art. 313.

concern any subject he chose. He could not be questioned by anyone, although if his speech disclosed new material requiring in the court's view new investigation, such an investigation might be ordered.[140] Both prosecution and defense had the right to give the court just before the judges retired a proposed formulation of the sentence, but the court was not bound to follow it.[141] This closed the proceedings, and the three judges retired to prepare their decision.

No one might enter the consultation room while the three judges deliberated, and the court secretary and any additional judges were specifically named as excluded.[142] No part of the preliminary investigation or any other material was permitted to the judges unless it had been put into the record at the trial.[143] The sentence as read to the accused had to include not only a finding of guilt and a statement of the penalty, but who would pay court costs and how the civil suit, if any, was decided.[144] It also had to contain information on right to appeal.[145]

The decision of the court was that of a majority, and any dissenting judge might prepare a written opinion to be attached to the decision but not to be read in court.[146]

The sentence was executed only after expiration of the time to appeal, or following a decision of an appellate court in support of the sentence.[147] During the period of appeal, such measures as might seem necessary were ordered by the court to assure that the defendant did not leave the jurisdiction.[148]

JUDICIAL REVIEW

A house is only as strong as its foundations, and experience was to show that the victory of those draftsmen who were struggling for legality in Soviet judicial proceedings could be snatched from them. Two weak points in the procedure were present, both of them almost inescapable. The first and most important was the structural disadvantage created by the fact that prior to the trial there had been a full preliminary investigation which was looked upon not as the simple preparation of a prima facie case which

[140] *Ibid.*   [141] Art. 314.   [142] Art. 321.   [143] Arts. 322, 323.
[144] Arts. 324, 338, 339.   [145] Art. 340.   [146] Art. 329.   [147] Art. 346.
[148] Art. 345.

might be disproved at the trial but as a full hearing by an official responsible to the court and directed to be impartial in his sifting of the evidence so that exculpatory evidence as well as accusatory material might be thoroughly balanced with no less rigor than was to be shown at the trial which was to follow.

It has been admitted again and again, and especially after Stalin's death by Soviet specialists in criminal procedure, that there has been a tendency of investigators to lean in the direction of accusation, a tendency which could not be corrected by a defense attorney because no such attorney was permitted at this stage of the proceedings.[149] With such a bias, the case was bound to take a direction toward a finding of guilt by the investigator unless the charges were patently trumped up by an injured person or the police. When the judges at the trial opened the volumes of record placed before them by the preliminary investigator and the prosecutor, they were tempted to do no more than the code required, namely, verify what they had received. To be sure there was at this second stage a defense attorney in many cases to question points which had not been questioned earlier and to throw new light upon circumstances or to suggest other possible interpretations of facts, but with the attitude toward defense attorneys that has already been shown to exist in spite of official calls for respect of the task to be performed by counsel, this intervention was often without effect. Accumulated evidence against the accused seemed too weighty to be overridden by judges who had little time to search out for themselves new materials, in spite of the code's authorization that they do so. The normal pattern was to approve what had been discovered by the investigator, as has been admitted by those Soviet authors who have written in criticism in later years.[150] An appellate court called upon to review the trial would have been unusually astute if it had been able to detect bias of the sort indicated in the face of what appeared to be a strong case for the prosecution, particularly when the court's investigation was restricted to the record and to a determination of error.

A second limitation upon the effectiveness of the appellate court

---

[149] M. P. Shalamov, "K voprosu ob otsenke soznanie obviniaemogo," *Sovetskoe gosudarstvo i pravo*, No. 8 (1956), pp. 44–50.

[150] M. Ia. Savitskii, "Zadachi i polozhenie zashchitnika v sovetskom ugolovnom protsesse," *Sov. gos. i pravo*, No. 7 (1955), pp. 92–99.

arose out of the fact that its review was limited to the record. Unlike some Continental courts of appeal, it had no right to go beyond the record and to recall witnesses to permit it to formulate its own conclusions of their credibility. The record was the appellate judges' only source of information. The code required the keeping of a record, and it specifically mentioned certain things which had to be inscribed within it, but it could not command the education of enough court secretaries to fill the positions adequately. It was even hard to find in those early days enough trained people to be judges and prosecutors, and the position of court secretary was considerably less attractive in pay scale and prestige. In consequence, relatively incompetent people filled the positions, with the result that court records were often inadequately prepared and hardly the material with which an appellate court, no matter how able, could rectify errors committed at the trial. The record was never a stenographic record of all that had transpired and rarely even the summary of a person who knew enough about judicial procedure to select wisely what needed to be recorded.

The new code's provisions on judicial review must be considered in the light of these two vitally important but imponderable shortcomings of the situation.

In keeping with the terminology established by the second decree on the courts of February, 1918, the new code spoke of "cassation" and not of "appeal." Civil-law traditions of the Continent give special meaning to these words, unlike the meaning given them in Anglo-American common law.[151] By adopting the term "cassation," the draftsmen intended to convey the meaning of a review of the record without rehearing of witnesses and examination of material evidence.[152] The higher courts were not to be excluded from evaluation of the evidence, however. On the contrary, they were authorized to consider the conclusions of the trial court to determine whether the conclusions were reasonable in light of the evidence presented, but they had to limit themselves to the record. Since the American courts are similarly limited but bear the name

---

[151] See René David and Henry P. DeVries, *The French Legal System, An Introduction to Civil Law Systems* (New York, 1958), p. 35.

[152] To explain the difference and present arguments against adoption of the Continental type of appeal, an editorial reviewed foreign systems for Soviet readers. See "Za Rubezhom: ob apelliatsii v ugolovnykh delakh," *Ezh. sov. iust.*, No. 1 (January 9, 1923), pp. 22–23.

of appellate courts, the word "appeals" is used in this study as it is more familiar to the American reader than the Continental term. Its use may be thought by the Continental lawyer inappropriate to an explanation of the type of review performed by the Soviet judicial reviewing authorities.

Limitation of the superior courts to a review of the record did not exclude the parties from their reviewing session. Under the codes' provisions, the parties had to be summoned, although their failure to appear did not prevent review of the case.[153] The parties or their representatives were not permitted, however, to open the argument. One of the judges of the reviewing court who had studied the record presented his report of the situation. Thereafter, the party who had filed the appeal or protest presented any comments he might wish to make, and the opposing party answered. The prosecutor was to be asked for his conclusions, but the opportunity to say the final words had to be given to the defendant or to his attorney.[154] The parties were permitted to file written briefs or to argue points not raised in the original appeal, but not after the prosecutor had completed his final summation.[155]

The draftsmen seem to have been determined to avoid excessive formality in the appellate procedure, for they authorized the reviewing court to go beyond the specific points raised on appeal to review the entire case, and to take action without limitation to the points raised.[156] They were seeking for what they conceived to be the truth. They were not preparing the stage for a referee in a battle of wits between a prosecutor and a defense attorney.

Setting aside a sentence was authorized in four situations: (1) if the investigation at the stage of preliminary investigation or at the trial had been inadequate to disclose every fact that might have an influence on the sentence, including those that might suggest that the crime had been committed by someone else; (2) if there had been substantial violation of the rules of the procedural code; (3) if there had been violation or incorrect application of the Criminal Code; or (4) if there were clear injustice in the sentence.[157]

The key to maintenance of conditions at a trial permitting a defendant to assert the rights given him by the code lies in an

---

[153] Code of Criminal Procedure, RSFSR (1922), Art. 355.
[154] Art. 356.   [155] Art. 356 (note).   [156] Art. 358.   [157] Art. 359.

authorization to set aside a sentence following a trial which had violated procedural rules. The Soviet draftsmen showed that they had moved far from the 1917 approach which had presumed that procedural rules were unnecessary to determine truth, and from the approach of the first of the years that followed, when it was presumed that procedural rules were desirable but that it might be possible to reach a just decision even with their violation. In 1922 the draftsmen were prepared to say that procedure was so vitally important to determination of truth that violation of procedural rules was cause for reversal. Still they left an opening for the judges to decide that not all procedural violation was cause for reversal but only "substantial" violation. In this indication that procedural violation must be "substantial" to require retrial, the draftsmen followed the pattern set by all legal systems including those of the common law, but they faced the difficulty of pointing the way for a system not old enough to have established a tradition of what was substantial or a body of judges with a second sense on this score. To meet this inadequacy, they sought to clarify the requirement by stating positively what was a substantial violation under any circumstances.

The conditions requiring reversal for substantial violation of procedure were listed as being: an improperly constituted bench of judges at the trial; refusal of the trial court to terminate proceedings when circumstances required it, such as death of the accused, reconciliation in those cases where there could be no prosecution unless the complaint were sustained, absence of any complaint from the injured party when such a complaint was required to permit prosecution, laches, amnesty, absence of facts constituting a violation of the Criminal Code; or a trial without the presence of the defendant or his attorney in those cases where presence was mandatory.[158]

The direction to set aside a sentence for incorrect application of or violation of the Criminal Code was followed by a definition of what constituted error. The definition contained the obvious circumstances, but it terminated with the admonition that a sentence in which such errors occurred should not be set aside unless the error had given rise to a sentence which was wrong. Thus, if the

[158] Art. 361.

reviewing court found that a crime other than the one for which the accused had been prosecuted had been committed, and the sentence would have been appropriate to the newly identified crime, there should be no new trial.[159] In short, there was iterated the major principle of the past which still seemed to have great importance, that criminals were not to be permitted to escape punishment because of lack of skill on the part of prosecutors or trial judges.

A touchy point in the authority granted to any reviewing court is the authority to set aside a sentence because of clear injustice. Such authority can open the door to error, for it places the reviewing judges in the position of the trial court, and such a position is generally thought undesirable for judges who have not had the benefit of seeing the witnesses and judging for themselves whether they seemed to be telling the truth. Systems of law which limit reviews to the record often permit setting aside of a sentence on such grounds, but the question remains whether there should be a new trial or whether the reviewing judges can assume the authority of establishing some new sentence which they think appropriate to the situation as they understand it.

Soviet draftsmen defined the circumstances under which clear injustice might be found, as when a sentence is not supported by any facts, and when a sentence does not go beyond the boundaries set by the law for the crime committed but still seems to be inappropriate to the special circumstances of the case.[160] After such a finding, the case had to be remanded for new trial, by which requirement the draftsmen cast their lot with those who deny to the appellate court the right to prescribe a new sentence after setting aside the old.

New trial was the remedy for all vitiated sentences, except those issued by courts without jurisdiction and those where an amnesty had been improperly applied or those where there had been no basis for trial at all.[161] The reviewing court in the first situation might leave the sentence in effect if it thought that the result had been correct even though the court had assumed improper jurisdiction,[162] or in the case of improper application of an amnesty it might adjust the sentence in accordance with the terms of the

---

[159] Art. 362.   [160] Art. 363.   [161] Art. 366.   [162] Art. 365.

amnesty,[163] and, of course, it might terminate proceedings if there was no basis for trial at all.[164] On remanding for new trial, the reviewing court was required to give a full explanation to the trial court to permit it to proceed correctly on retrial.[165] It was added that the new sentence following retrial might be appealed in the usual manner.[166] The decision of the reviewing court, ordering retrial, might be appealed to the Supreme Court Control within the Commissariat of Justice.[167]

The psychological discouragement of defendants' appeals, created by the English system which permits a reviewing court to increase a penalty on an appeal, was rejected by the Soviet draftsmen of the 1922 code. The reviewing court could not increase a penalty when a defendant appealed, and even the court on retrial was limited, for the draftsmen provided expressly that if the first sentence was appealed by the defendant, the sentence could not be increased on retrial.[168] By this provision it appeared that the burden was placed on the prosecutor of obtaining as severe a sentence as he felt necessary at the first trial, or of protesting a sentence to a reviewing court before the defendant decided to appeal, for if the defendant appealed, there could be revision only downward.

Such a conclusion as to the prosecutor's burden, sound as it might seem to western minds, is not appropriate to the Soviet system by virtue of the fact that the Soviet draftsmen introduced in their system an "audit" procedure. Under this procedure the state is always given a second chance, even if a decision has become final in the absence of appeal or after affirmance on appeal. Through this procedure the Soviet draftsmen indicated their continuing fear of full stability of law, even though their new code had as its public purpose the introduction of stability.

THE AUDIT PROCEDURE

The audit procedure authorized the president of the reviewing court, at this time the council of people's judges, or the provincial prosecutor or the prosecutor attached to the reviewing court, to demand any case at any stage of its proceedings so that the council

---

[163] Art. 366.   [164] Art. 364.   [165] Art. 367.   [166] Art. 371.   [167] Art. 372.
[168] Art. 370.

might audit those proceedings.[169] If the case was actually in process of trial, the trial proceeded to the sentence, but otherwise proceedings below would be halted while the dossier was sent forward for audit. The prosecutor attached to the reviewing court prepared a report on the matter and presented it to the president of the reviewing court. If both agreed that there was no reason to intervene, the case was returned to progress along its normal course, but if there was disagreement between prosecutor and president, the matter went to the presidium of the reviewing court, which was authorized either to return the case to the people's court with appropriate comments to govern further proceedings, or in the event that a sentence had been pronounced, the matter was sent for decision to the Supreme Court Control in the People's Commissariat of Justice.[170] The draftsmen added that the audit procedure might commence at any time. In short, the interests of the state were of such importance in their view that necessary measures to protect the state should be permitted, no matter how tardy the state's officials were in noticing the danger.

Such unlimited opportunity for reconsideration was not extended to reopening of cases because of newly discovered evidence, for the draftsmen provided that an acquittal might be reopened only within one year from the time of discovery of the new evidence but not even in such circumstances if they occurred five years following the date when the sentence had become final. Only the prosecutor might call for reopening of an acquittal, but the sentenced individual, his attorney, his relatives, or social organizations to which he had belonged or still belonged, as well as the prosecutor might petition for reopening of a case which had ended in a conviction.[171]

The Supreme Court Control of the People's Commissariat of Justice was given the function of examining the prosecutor's report on the necessity for reopening the case,[172] or the appeal of the petitioning parties in the event that the prosecutor found no reason for reopening the case in response to the petition.[173] The Supreme Court Control then reached a final decision and wrote an opinion.[174]

---

[169] Art. 373.　　[170] Art. 374.

[171] Arts. 379 (reopening on new evidence), 381 (reopening of acquittal or case ending in conviction).

[172] Art. 383.　　[173] Art. 384.　　[174] Art. 385.

In the event that the Supreme Court Control decided in favor of a new trial, the case was returned for repetition of the proceedings from the start, in accordance with the rules of the code.[175]

The Supreme Court Control was given authority to examine cases not only when brought before it because of newly discovered evidence or on appeal or protest from a council of people's judges[176] but also on its own initiative, for it could demand that any case be sent to it, no matter where it might be within a people's court, a council of people's judges, or a revolutionary tribunal,[177] and it could set aside a sentence not only for clear violation of law but also in the event of "clear conflict between the sentence or decision and a guiding fundamental of Soviet legislation and the general policy of the workers'-peasants' government." [178] Decisions on this basis were declared to be binding on all people's courts and revolutionary tribunals.[179] In short, there was continued by the code the procedure of supreme control over all legal activities, as it had emerged in the years of trial and error. The code marked the permanent abandonment of the concept of the early years which left to each locality determination of appropriate law and procedure. Soviet jurisprudence was made subject to the control of a single supreme center, which was guardian not only of the law but of state policy, with which rigid application of the law might conceivably create conflict.

THE RULES OF EVIDENCE

Rules of evidence had seemed hateful things to those who created the first Soviet courts in 1917. They abolished them entirely, leaving the wise man who was then the judge to decide for himself what he would hear and what he would think of it. To the common-law lawyer such an approach to the problem of evidence is cavalier. It suggests absence of any real appreciation of the varying qualities of evidence and the desirability of setting up some principles to govern its introduction at a trial so that no one may be convicted on the basis of hearsay or circumstantial situations.

With the progress of the Soviet court structure away from revolutionary primitiveness to complexity, and with the increasing

---

[175] Art. 387.   [176] Art. 461.   [177] Art. 465.   [178] Art. 466.   [179] Art. 467.

espousal of adherence to procedural rules, it might have been expected that the attitude toward evidence would change. Yet it did not, and the draftsmen were able to place in their new code the simplest of provisions. They provided that "a court is not limited by any formal rules of evidence, and from this fact it follows that in accordance with the circumstances of the case it may permit the introduction of this or that evidence or demand evidence from third persons for whom the demand is obligatory." [180]

Although this article presents a principle which may seem distinctly revolutionary and Soviet-inspired to the Anglo-American lawyer, it coincides with some Continental attitudes. An eminent French authority has found it possible to say that "in reality, there is no French 'law of evidence,' " and to provide as proof of the fact the absence of any important study of the law of proof for over a hundred years in France.[181]

The Soviet draftsmen, in view of the Continental attitude toward evidentiary rules, could remain completely within the spirit of their revolution against formalities and at the same time hold to the tradition of western civil law. This was so because of the rejection of the jury system in the courts of the new Russia, and because of its absence except in the French *cours d'assises*, trying certain criminal cases.[182] It is common knowledge that the Anglo-American rules derive from the necessity of protecting what were once untutored jurors from hearing oral testimony of a hearsay character, and that there is no similar fear in the modern common-law countries of letting a judge hear such evidence when he is sitting without a jury.

Having adopted the Continental rule admitting all evidence, the Soviet draftsmen left for the writers of treatises a discussion of what was necessary to reach a conclusion of guilt. In years to follow Soviet authors adopted the French concept[183] that a judge must establish an "intimate conviction" of guilt before he convicts,[184] and there need be no statutory or customary definition of what type of evidence or what amount of evidence creates this intimate conviction.

---

[180] Art. 61.   [181] See David and DeVries, *French Legal System*, p. 74.
[182] *Ibid.*, p. 76.   [183] *Ibid.*
[184] See A. Ia. Vyshinskii, *Teoriia sudebnykh dokazatel'stv v sovetskom prave* (2nd ed.; Moscow, 1946), Chap. V.

To this concept of complete freedom of evaluation of evidence, the draftsmen created one exception, and that had to do with documents. If a claim or charge rested upon a document, there could be no proof of the document by oral testimony.[185] If a witness read from a document, it had to be shown to the parties, and, if the court so decided, made a part of the record of the trial.[186] With an eye to creation of a record which might be meaningful on appeal, the draftsmen also required that although experts had to give testimony orally in court, their opinion had to be reduced to writing and made a part of the record.[187] In this way the inefficient court secretaries were relieved of a function they were incapable of performing, and the reviewing authority was assured of the presence of important conclusions in the record.

It was to require years for the Supreme Court Control and its successor, the Supreme Court of the Republic, to establish through a line of judicial decisions some indication of the pattern of evidence necessary to convict. While no formal rules were created by these decisions, it became clear through a host of decisions remanding for new trial that courts had to sift evidence with care and seek the best in terms not unfamiliar to a common-law lawyer.

THE REVOLUTIONARY TRIBUNALS

Although the code makers were seeking to stabilize procedure to strengthen the Soviet regime by currying favor among their own people and western workmen beyond their boundaries, they still had to prescribe for the revolutionary tribunals. The political authorities had shown their lack of confidence in stabilized procedures in early 1922 when they had decided to continue the revolutionary tribunals at the side of the regular courts. The code makers had been compelled to find a way of compromising between the order they sought to establish in the courts and the essentially free rein which the politicians wanted to preserve in the revolutionary tribunals. The spirit that motivated retention of the revolutionary tribunals still exercised influence over the regular courts, for the draftsmen had found it necessary to leave numerous openings for

---

[185] Code of Criminal Procedure, RSFSR (1922), Art. 297.
[186] *Ibid.*   [187] Art. 302.

political intervention in the progress of a case through the court system. These openings have already been reviewed, and they have been seen to run from the right of intervention in any case at any time by the prosecutor and the Supreme Court Control to the less obvious but no less real possibilities offered by the fact that an accused was denied counsel at the important stage of preliminary investigation.

The influence of one system upon the other did not, however, run only in one direction. The temper of the country was turning against arbitrary procedures as they had developed in the revolutionary tribunals. Controls had been introduced in these bodies as well as in the regular courts over the years, and there had even been considerable support for a proposal that they be abolished entirely. The draftsmen must have sensed the trend of opinion even among the Communist party members, for discontent was on the verge of boiling over. Within a few months the revolutionary tribunals were to be absorbed into new provincial courts under control of a newly created Supreme Court and subject to the requirements of the Code of Criminal Procedure, albeit with some of the exceptional features created for the revolutionary tribunals during their years of activity. Under the circumstances of 1922 the draftsmen could talk about restraint for the revolutionary tribunals even though in fact they created little of novelty for them.

The restraining influence of 1922 showed itself in the opening article of the pertinent chapter of the 1922 Code of Criminal Procedure which declared: "Procedure in the revolutionary tribunals shall be defined by the rules established for the conduct of cases in the people's courts," [188] but the exceptional character of these political courts was then recorded by a few closing words in the article, "with the exceptions defined in the following articles." There followed forty-six articles of exceptions, chief among which was the authorization to the tribunals to exclude counsel from the hearings,[189] authorization to the preliminary investigator to omit preliminary investigation and to rely upon the police inquiry alone in cases where he thought the matter clear,[190] authorization to the tribunal to omit at the trial repetition of any testimony which had been given at the preliminary investigation or police inquiry and

---

[188] Art. 413.   [189] Art. 415.   [190] Art. 419.

which was of such a nature as "to admit of no doubt of its truth," [191] authorization to the tribunal to rely for its opinion on evidence not reviewed at the trial,[192] and to refuse to hear the defendant's explanation,[193] limitation on the tribunal's rights to send a matter back for reinvestigation except in those cases in which the tribunal finds that the material is so scanty that it cannot in any way be augmented at that very sitting,[194] reduction of the time allowed for appeal from the fourteen days permitted in the people's courts[195] to forty-eight hours from the time of receipt of the sentence in written form, which must have been within twenty-four hours of its oral announcement,[196] while in wartime there was to be no right of appeal at all.[197]

Uniformity of policy was sought by provision for a supreme tribunal with a "cassational college" to hear appeals from sentences and protests by prosecutors. If the sentence had been one of death, a decision of the supreme tribunal had to issue within one week of receipt of the appeal or protest.[198] In contrast to the rule applicable below, requiring that the accused be present before the revolutionary tribunal at the trial except in those circumstances permitting trial *in absentia* in a people's court, the supreme tribunal was not required to summon the accused,[199] although it had to post a calendar stating whether the accused might attend the argument. Since the code prescribed that the appeal be argued in public,[200] it is evident that an alert attorney might have brought his client to the courtroom, if the client were fortunate enough still to be at liberty.

For the accused, the decision of the cassational college was final, but a prosecutor might protest it to the plenum of the supreme tribunal within twenty-four hours after its issuance,[201] and the sentence could not be executed pending the decision of the plenum. The case might be returned for retrial, but if the supreme tribunal believed it desirable, it might reduce the penalty to the appropriate one allowed by the Criminal Code for the offense committed, or in circumstances when there seemed no appropriate reduced penalty, it could send a recommendation to the Presidium of the Republic's Central Executive Committee, namely, to the interim legislative

[191] Art. 424.   [192] Art. 429.   [193] Art. 430.   [194] Art. 431.   [195] Art. 350.
[196] Art. 433.   [197] Art. 434.   [198] Art. 442.   [199] Art. 443, par. two.
[200] Art. 443, par. one.   [201] Art. 446.

authority, for the designation of what amounted to a penalty by special legislation.[202]

The president of the supreme tribunal had the same powers of audit as were given to the presidents of the councils of people's judges.[203] To permit this audit to occur, the code required that every sentence of death be communicated immediately to the supreme tribunal, even if there were no appeal or protest, giving the facts of the hour and minute of the pronouncement of sentence, a brief summary of the accusation, and the name, age, class origin, and social status of the sentenced individual.[204]

Cases of exceptional importance either as to subject matter or rank of the accused were to be tried in the supreme tribunal as a court of original jurisdiction,[205] and from such decisions there was no appeal.[206] Only audit procedure was available to set them aside. As has already been indicated with regard to supreme control over the work of the system of regular courts, the Supreme Court Control of the People's Commissariat of Justice was given jurisdiction over the entire system of revolutionary tribunals as well as over the regular courts. In this way, the opponents of the continuation in 1922 of revolutionary tribunals sought to satisfy their desire for a single system of courts without a separate arm for political crimes.

KRYLENKO'S EVALUATION OF 1922

Krylenko reviewed his work of 1922 in a series of lectures given to the law students in Moscow in 1923.[207] He was not happy with the Code of Criminal Procedure. The defect lay in his view in the increasing complexity of the law.

I note that the transition from 97 articles in the People's Court Act, containing everything on the structure of the courts and on procedure, to 450 articles in the Code of Criminal Procedure, 226 articles in the Criminal Code, 350 articles in the Civil Code and about 100 articles in the Judiciary Act—this is a little too much. All of this has created extraordinary complexity in our court work, and our immediate task will be its simplification.[208]

---

[202] Art. 445.   [203] Art. 448.   [204] Art. 450.   [205] Arts. 456, 458, 459.
[206] Art. 455.
[207] N. V. Krylenko, *Sudoustroistvo RSFSR* (*Lektsii po teorii i istorii sudoustroistva* (Moscow, 1923)).
[208] *Ibid.,* p. 161.

Criticism of the Code of Criminal Procedure was made more specific later in the lecture, for Krylenko declared: "The defects of the Code of Criminal Procedure lie not only in the fact that a large number of articles are surplus, but also in the fact that it is too demanding in the categorical requirements of its articles; it provides too many details for court procedure—that is its inadequacy." [209]

Krylenko was unwilling to condemn the code in its entirety, and it would have been remarkable if he had criticized substance, for he had been one of the principal architects. He concluded his comments on the code with a note of approval. "Since it introduces order into court procedure it is a plus, and necessary for us."

In Krylenko's summary it was evident that procedural norms had been introduced with a will to make them a fundamental part of the Soviet legal system. Yet there was still a lingering hope that they could be simplified, not to the extent of 1917, or even of 1920, but to something less complex than what they had become in the new Code of Criminal Procedure. This hope was not to be realized, however, for the code adopted in 1922, as modified but not simplified in 1923, was to outlast Stalin's regime and to be submitted to revision only in 1958 with the general reworking of the codes at that time.

[209] *Ibid.*, p. 162.

Chapter 10

A SECOND STEP IN
PROCEDURAL REFORM

RECONSTRUCTION of the court system by law of November 11, 1922,[1] to eliminate the revolutionary tribunals, to reform the councils of people's judges into provincial courts with jurisdiction extended to cases formerly tried by revolutionary tribunals, and to create a supreme court outside the People's Commissariat of Justice necessitated redrafting of the Code of Criminal Procedure.

Krylenko had declared the obvious in his concluding remarks at the meeting of the Central Executive Committee which had adopted the Judiciary Act in November.[2] In presenting a draft enabling law to bring the new Judiciary Act into effect on January 1, 1923, Krylenko inserted a paragraph directing the Presidium of the Central Executive Committee to commission the People's Commissariat of Justice to rework the Code of Criminal Procedure to conform to the new Judiciary Act. His paragraph declared: "This is necessary in view of the fact that courts will take the place of the tribunals." By this phrase Krylenko pointedly singled out for comment that element of the new judiciary law which constituted his victory over proponents of the dual system previously existing. There were certainly other features of the new court structure which required revision of the Code of Criminal Procedure, but perhaps none of these seemed as important in his eyes as that for which he had fought hardest.

The legislative commission of the Central Executive Committee had in mind only a minor review of the Code of Criminal Procedure,

[1] [1922] I *Sobranie Uzakonenii i Rasporiazhenii Rabochego i Kres'tianskogo Pravitel'tsva RSFSR*, No. 62, item 902.

[2] *RSFSR—IV sessiia Vserossiiskogo Tsentral'nogo Ispol'nitelnogo Komiteta, IX sozyva, 23–31 oktiabria 1922 g.*, (*Stenograficheskii otchët*) *biulleten'* No. 8, 1 noiab. 1922 g. (Moscow, 1922), p. 5.

for the enabling law concluded with a phrase which, although it sounded like no more than a description of what had to be done, must have been meant by the members of the Central Executive Committee to be an order. This phrase read: "Conforming changes of a purely editorial character must be introduced in the procedural code, without touching the whole procedural structure." Speed seemed essential, for the paragraph ended with the expressed desire that a revised Code of Criminal Procedure be brought into effect with the new Judiciary Act on January 1, 1923.

Lenin reemphasized the importance of speedy codification in a speech following Krylenko's. He declared: "You all, of course, understand well that other states unfortunately do not know such speed of legislation as we have. We shall see whether they will not also in the not distant future have to give attention so as to catch up at least a little bit in these matters with Soviet Russia." [3]

Speed seems to have been the order of the day, and this may have been reason enough for leaving to the Presidium of the Central Executive Committee and to the Commissariat of Justice the reworking of the Code of Criminal Procedure without the necessity of presenting the draft to a full meeting of the Central Executive Committee, but the result was to overlook the opportunity afforded by review to correct inadequacies noted in the first code.

EARLY REACTION TO
PROCEDURAL REFORM

Inadequacies were not concealed from public view during the period of reconsideration, however, and many of them were exposed in the journal of the Commissariat of Justice itself. One of the people's judges began writing his criticisms in the Commissariat's journal not long after the first Code of Criminal Procedure had been adopted.[4] He singled out three points for comment: (1) the time for challenging members of the court, (2) the moment at which witnesses called in a case were to be sent out of the courtroom to await their turn on the stand, and (3) the instructions on

---

[3] *Ibid.*, p. 13.

[4] Sergei Simson, "Spornye voprosy ugol.-protsess. kodeksa," *Ezhenedel'nik sovetskoi iustitsii*, No. 26–27 (July 17–24, 1922), p. 6. Continued in *ibid.*, No. 33 (September 9, 1922), p. 7.

the preparation of a record of court proceedings. In his comments he showed that at least one trial court judge was thinking seriously about procedural details and their importance in protecting the accused. He ridiculed the new code's provision that a challenge to members of the court was to be permitted only after decisions had been made as to whether to place the accused under guard, on what to do if the accused or the accuser, counsel, witnesses, or experts had not appeared, on whether to seek additional evidence in the case beyond that presented by the record of the preliminary investigation and after an explanation had been given to the accused of his right to participate in the proceedings. The judge said that a challenge at this point came too late, for a challenged judge should not determine these essential matters. He urged that there be a return to the rule of the 1920 People's Court Act when the challenge was presented as soon as the court opened and before decisions were made on any matters whatever.

The presence of witnesses in the courtroom, while it was being decided whether proceedings might be continued in the absence of the accused, the accuser, counsel, civil plaintiff, and injured party, as permitted by the new code, seemed to him harmful because it permitted witnesses to overhear discussion which might influence their own subsequent testimony, especially when there was discussion of whether an absent witness was really required. The critic preferred the formulation of the 1918 People's Court Act providing for the immediate exclusion of witnesses from the courtroom after they had reported and before any consideration of other matters.

The objection to the new rules on preparation of the court record laid bare the obvious fact that these records were inadequate for an appeal. The judge quoted a circular of the Moscow Council of People's Judges issued in 1922 saying:

Records are written in a very non-fastidious handwriting; often instead of a short but precise and objective recording of the procedural progress of the events of the court sitting in a given case, they have as their substance selections from phrases written down at random, whose reading can in no case provide either an account of the original procedural developments of the court hearing at first instance or make it possible to draw any more or less firm conclusion concerning the procedural side of the case.[5]

[5] *Ibid.*, No. 33, p. 7.

He thought that the new code was inadequate to meet the difficulties, because it provided different requirements for the recording of various aspects of the case. In one article some important elements were "required" to be recorded,[6] while in another article it was provided that equally important elements "are noted,"[7] the latter verb being a less imperative form in the Russian language, as it is also in the English translation. He thought all of the listed elements critical to decision in the ultimate appeal, and he urged that the matter be rectified by provision of a standard form of record in which printed headings and blank spaces would indicate what information needed to be preserved to make the record useful. Only in this way could he see any opportunity of overcoming the chaotic, nonprofessional type of work then being carried on by court secretaries.

Sharp criticism of the new code's provisions on questioning of the accused appeared at the same time in the journal of the practitioners.[8] An author stated the principle with which he started to reason, saying that the accused must be given the same rights as the accuser if there were to be real adversary procedure, and that it was no answer to argue that class justice required an exception. He insisted that the question was not how to deal with an enemy of the ruling class, but rather whether a given accused individual was in fact such an enemy. Having stated his principle he examined the new Code of Criminal Procedure and found it wanting. He singled out for criticism the articles on questioning of the accused,[9] saying that under their provisions the police would not be required to question a person under arrest for a whole month, leaving him without information as to the reason for suspicion. Further, the code left the impression that the interrogation by the police was devoid of formality, but if this were so, it would be harmful to the suspected person because any statements made during the interrogation could be introduced at the trial. Under such circumstances, in the author's view, there should be known guarantees similar to those applicable

---

[6] Code of Criminal Procedure, RSFSR [1922], I *Sob. Uzak. RSFSR,* No. 20–21, item 230, Art. 85.

[7] *Ibid.,* Art. 84.

[8] M. Grodzinskii, "Dopros obviniaemogo v novom protsessual'nom kodekse," *Pravo i zhizn',* No. 3 (1922), pp. 56–65.

[9] Code of Criminal Procedure, RSFSR (1922), Arts. 104, 107.

during the stage of investigation by the preliminary investigator.

The preliminary investigation itself was inadequately treated in the critic's view because there was no requirement that the suspected person be informed of his right to remain silent and to refuse to answer questions. Finally, when there were several defendants at a trial, each to be examined in turn, there should be complete disclosure to each of what the others had said during any period of exclusion of an accused, and even these exclusions of one or another of the defendants from the courtroom should occur only in exceptional circumstances. One good thing was said for the new code. It required that in recording testimony the question be placed in the record with the answer. The critic hailed this provision, for it seemed obvious to him that answers could be understood fully only when weighed with the question that was asked.

Less organized criticism appeared in a series of questions published with answers in the Commissariat's journal. Some thought the revolutionary tribunals had been given too many continuing privileges, while others thought that the privileges of the revolutionary tribunals should have been extended to the people's courts. Thus, one questioner[10] asked why the new code failed to establish a strict category of cases in which the accused must have counsel, just as was established for the people's courts. The answer was simply that the old special statute on the revolutionary tribunals had given the tribunals the right to decide at any moment in the trial that the case was sufficiently clear to stop proceedings and to withdraw from the hearing room, and also to hear a case without participation of an accuser or a defense attorney. It was explained that traces of this old rule had been carried over as an exception into the new code,[11] and this accounted for the absence of any circumstances in which counsel was made compulsory in revolutionary tribunals. With the history of Commissariat opposition to the continuation of revolutionary tribunals outside of the court system in mind, the reader may conclude that the Commissariat was unhappy that the revolutionary tribunals preserved their special privileges, but it had been politically impossible to set aside a rule which had become fixed in practice.

[10] I. S., "Diskussionaia stranitsa po primeneniiu ugolovnogo i ug.-prots. kodeksov," *Ezh. sov. iust.*, No. 39–40 (October 27–November 4, 1922), p. 25.

[11] Code of Criminal Procedure, RSFSR (1922), Art. 28.

The reverse criticism appeared in a question[12] asking why the people's courts were denied the right granted to revolutionary tribunals to exclude both an accuser and defense counsel and also to refer in their sentence to documents not introduced in the trial.[13] Again the answer referred to the fact that these privileges had been reproduced from the past and were now permitted as exceptional to the revolutionary tribunals "in the interest of strengthening them as especially warlike court organs." The editor in his answer wished, apparently, to emphasize the contrast, for he said, "This question discloses exceptionally well the sharp difference between the court prerogatives of the people's court on the one side and of the revolutionary tribunals on the other."

Rules of evidence seem to have caused misunderstanding of a primitive nature. It was asked [14] whether the testimony of a witness unable to come for interrogation because of illness might not be admitted as a written document in a case for which there had been no previous police interrogation or preliminary investigation. The answer was "Certainly not!" Then the editor declared that such written testimony might outweigh the testimony taken by the investigating authority from other witnesses, and this would be unjustified because it would have been given under circumstances in which the investigating organ could not have taken the initiative in putting the questions.

What to do in the event of absence of parties, witnesses, and experts seems to have worried another questioner,[15] for he asked what reasons for failure to appear on summons could be considered valid. The editor explained that the new code established no grounds for validity of failure to appear, but left it for the judge to decide in each case whether the absence was justified.[16] Furthermore, there might be an appeal from his decision by analogy to the code provision permitting appeals from decisions on similar absences by the preliminary investigator.[17]

What to do in the absence of the court secretary from the trial was the subject of another question.[18] He asked whether the

[12] I. S., "Diskussionaia stranitsa," p. 25.
[13] Code of Criminal Procedure, RSFSR (1922), Arts. 429–30.
[14] I. S., "Diskussionaia stranitsa," p. 26.   [15] *Ibid.*, p. 25.
[16] Code of Criminal Procedure, RSFSR (1922), Arts. 134, 165.
[17] *Ibid.*, Art. 216.   [18] I. S., "Diskussionaia stranitsa," p. 25.

presence of a secretary was necessary, and whether his absence might be reason for an appeal. The editor explained that the deciding factor was whether the absence of the secretary resulted in harmful consequences. If the appellant did not allege inaccuracy of the court record because of the secretary's absence, then there need be no reversal. The editor went further to provide a rule of thumb for appeals for procedural violations. He declared:

In general every procedural violation is evaluated from the point of view of the degree of distortion of the perspective of the case, or detraction from the prestige of the court because of the given violation, or of ignoring of the rights of the parties (such as participation of the secretary in the judges' deliberation room, clear inequality of the parties in the proceedings because of the fault of the court president, etc.), and the evaluation of the material is the province in each situation of the cassational court.

A people's judge in the Moscow Council of People's Judges asked whether a judge who heard the case in the court of original jurisdiction could serve as reporter when the case appeared before the council of people's judges on appeal.[19] He stated that in one case the council of people's judges had disqualified such a judge "to avoid a misunderstanding." The editor declared that the new code provided no direct answer to the question, but he noted that one article[20] of the new code disqualified a judge of first instance from the court of second instance when a case he had tried came up on appeal. Reasons for such a rule were stated, and the implication was left, but not specifically stated, that the council of people's judges should exclude a judge of first instance from the position of reporter when the case reached it on appeal.

The editor was less charitable with a questioner[21] who asked whether a judge called upon to reframe an indictment under the rule of the new code permitting a court to reframe an indictment if it disagreed with the charge[22] would thereafter be disqualified from deciding the case because he had participated in an investigatory function. The editor said, "This is an absurd question," and

---

[19] I. Slavin, "Diskussionaia stranitsa po primeneniu ugolovnogo i ug.-prots. kodeksov," *Ezh. sov. iust.*, No. 37–38 (October 13–20, 1922), p. 29.

[20] Code of Criminal Procedure, RSFSR (1922), Art. 48.

[21] I. S., "Diskussionaia stranitsa po primeneniu ugolovnogo i ug.-prots. kodeksov," *Ezh. sov. iust.*, No. 41 (November 11, 1922), p. 18.

[22] Code of Criminal Procedure, RSFSR (1922), Art. 244, par. 2.

went on to reject the suggestion by saying that the judge acted as a member of the whole court, and if he were disqualified, the whole court would be disqualified. This seems by implication to have been an impossible conclusion from the editor's point of view.

A people's judge in the Altai Mountains was incensed because he no longer seemed to be permitted to reduce measures taken by the police to assure the presence of a suspected person at his trial.[23] The editor confirmed that the new code had changed the rule, although without explicit exclusion. It had merely listed the right of a judge to continue measures or to increase measures of restraint,[24] and then the editor read a little lecture on statutory interpretation, saying that when an article permitting certain acts is silent on others, it means that the unmentioned acts are not permitted.

Various time limits set in the new code worried judges. One asked [25] whether a court had to assemble within three days to hear a complaint against the court record. The editor explained that the new code required only the filing of the complaint within three days,[26] so that the time limit was not made binding on the court. Yet the editor thought it advisable to add that the court must "hasten the review," and further, it must not permit the parties to submit for inclusion in the record written statements of testimony which had not in fact been presented in court.

A twenty-four-hour time limit set by the code for filing notice of arrest[27] raised a question[28] as to whether there would be consequences for the police if its notice failed to reach a distant court investigator or a prosecutor within twenty-four hours of an arrest. The editor explained the duty as being only to send the notice by the fastest possible method without delays in paper work in the office. A warning was given that persons guilty of delays would be held personally responsible.

The right of a party to be present at the various stages of procedure before trial seemed unclear to questioners. One asked [29]

---

[23] I. S., "Diskussionaia stranitsa," *Ezh. sov. iust.*, No. 41, p. 28.
[24] Code of Criminal Procedure, RSFSR (1922), Art. 251, par. 5.
[25] I. S., "Diskussionaia stranitsa," *Ezh. sov. iust.*, No. 41, p. 29.
[26] Code of Criminal Procedure, RSFSR (1922), Art. 86.
[27] *Ibid.*, Art. 106.
[28] I. S., "Diskussionaia stranitsa," *Ezh. sov. iust.*, No. 41, p. 17.
[29] *Ibid.*, p. 18.

whether a suspected person had to be called by the preliminary investigator. The editor replied, "Certainly not," and explained that the code permitted an investigator to exclude or include parties during the investigation as he thought desirable.[30] Similarly, another questioner[31] asked whether parties had to be summoned to appear at the preliminary sitting of the court when arrangements were made for the trial which was to follow. The questioner seemed to favor such a summons, for he asked, "How otherwise can it be known whether, for example, the parties are being held under guard?" The response informed him that the code required only that the record of the sitting note whether the parties were present,[32] and that no provision was made for summoning them. This indicated that the judge had only to decide whether to permit the parties to be present if they appeared without summons. The questioner may have had in mind the possibility of instituting a modified form of the Anglo-Saxon writ of habeas corpus at this point, for a requirement of summons would have necessitated producing the accused had he been in jail, and the judge could then have heard any complaint of the accused that he had been improperly arrested while awaiting trial.

Challenges to the jurisdiction of the court inspired several questions. Under Article 44 of the new code any case sent by one court to another for lack of jurisdiction in the first court had to be tried by the receiving court, even if it thought itself to be without jurisdiction, although after it had sentenced the criminal, it might refer the matter to a higher court for a decision by way of review of the legality of its action. An early questioner[33] asked why the receiving court was required to decide the matter before it could raise the question of jurisdiction with a higher court. The editor explained that the first decree after the Revolution had forbidden transfers of cases from one court to another for lack of jurisdiction because there had been endless disputes between courts over jurisdiction under the Empire, and this was an evil which the first decree had sought to avoid. The new code was merely continuing the early effort to prevent endless transfers of jurisdiction.

[30] Code of Criminal Procedure, RSFSR (1922), Art. 117.
[31] I. S., "Diskussionaia stranitsa," *Ezh. sov. iust.*, No. 41, p. 18.
[32] Code of Criminal Procedure, RSFSR (1922), Art. 83.
[33] I. S., "Diskussionaia stranitsa," *Ezh. sov. iust.*, No. 39–40, p. 26.

The matter was raised again later when a questioner asked whether it was required under Article 44 that a case be sent to a higher court on a challenge to jurisdiction.[34] The editor explained that such referral was to be only after a decision had been reached and by way of review and not appeal before rendering of the decision. Then the editor added angrily, "You must read the law attentively."

Challenges to jurisdiction were shown to be more complicated than the preceding two answers indicated in a question and answer presenting greater detail.[35] The questioner asked whether one of the parties might challenge jurisdiction if a court had assumed jurisdiction and had made no order on the subject because of oversight. Further, if a challenge were in order, at what moment must it be declared—during the hearings, or after they had been completed and the party was making his summation? To this question the editor replied that it was not clear what kind of jurisdiction was in dispute. It might be a dispute as to whether another court had jurisdiction or it might be a dispute over whether the same court should sit but in another form, as, for example, with two lay judges instead of six. If it were the first situation, the proceedings had to be stopped immediately at whatever stage they might have reached and the case had to be sent to the court deemed proper. If it were the second situation, the proceedings should be continued if trial had already reached the verification of evidence and if the parties did not object,[36] and if it were a matter only of a smaller bench, the code required that the proceedings be continued to the end regardless of the party's wishes.[37]

Deficiencies noted in application of the new code were made the subject of a special study.[38] The author declared that some deficiencies must be corrected within the briefest time. His major concern seems to have been with thefts of timber from state

---

[34] I. S., "Diskussionaia stranitsa," *ibid.*, No. 41, p. 18.

[35] *Ibid.*, p. 17.

[36] Code of Criminal Procedure, RSFSR (1922), Art. 42.

[37] *Ibid.*, Art. 43.

[38] K, "Chem neobkhodimo dopolnit' ug.-protsess. kodeks," *Ezh. sov. iust.*, No. 39–40 (October 27-November 4, 1922), pp. 26–27. This view was later sharply criticized on the ground that the forest wardens often made errors, and so the accused should always be present in court at the trial to defend himself. See Pavlovskii, "Diskussionaia stranitsa po primeneniiu ugolovnogo i ug.-prots. kodeksov—o lesoporubkakh," *Ezh. sov. iust.*, No. 19 (May 17, 1923), p. 442.

forests, for he thought the code had permitted an error in not listing this crime as one for which a judge sitting alone might sentence an offender. Further, he thought this offense should be included within those for which a sentence might be given even when the accused did not appear for trial. His reasoning was that the new code had provided that an accused be present whenever his offense might be punished with a penalty of more than six months imprisonment or required a bench containing six lay judges. He noted that an examination of the Criminal Code showed that there were very few crimes for which penalties of less than one month were applicable, which meant that with very rare exceptions the presence of the accused was required in criminal trials. For the illegal cutting of timber this requirement seemed to him unnecessary, since the parties thought it useless to come to court when apprehended since they knew they had no defense, and since it was very hard to travel, even when necessary to appear as a defendant in court. Failure of the accused to appear necessitated a new summons, waste of paper in new court records, and, most importantly, it was without purpose. The critic noted that if it were recognized that such cases ran to hundreds, one could imagine how much unnecessary work was caused. His proposal was to extend Article 269 of the new code to require the presence of the accused only if the possible penalty were one year or more.

Further criticism was leveled at the new code for refusing to permit a single judge to dismiss a case if he found no elements of a crime when reviewing the matter before trial. The old statute on the people's court had permitted such action, but the new code permitted a single judge only to initiate investigation, and denied him the right to discontinue investigation when sitting alone without his lay judges. It was asked why this restriction was necessary at the very time that the professional judge's powers were expanded by the new code, especially since he was being given the right to issue court orders when sitting alone. The author urged return to the old principle.

Opposition to the new rule on reconciliation concluded the survey of inadequacies in the new code. It was noted that the new rule forbade the dropping of an accusation of theft of personally owned property after reconciliation, while the practice of the past had permitted such dismissal. The author concluded:

Such practice is not contrary to revolutionary concepts of law, which have considered property crimes to be the result of social inequality. From the point of view of bourgeois law property crimes have a public-law character, since they undermine the foundations of property ownership. The Revolution has recognized this point of view to be prejudiced. The more so, since the Russian people have looked upon those cases in the same way as cases in which there may be reconciliation, and, consequently, it is often the case that the criminal is 'forgiven' for having caused the property loss. There is no reason to protect private property against the wishes of the owner himself.

DREAMS OF SIMPLIFICATION

A direct appeal to utilize the authority given to revise the Code of Criminal Procedure to take into account not only the creation of new courts but the possibility of reversing the trend toward rigid procedures opened the issue of the Commissariat's journal for November 25, 1922.[39] The author decried the emphasis which had crept into Soviet criminal procedure on the keeping of records not only at the trial but in the preliminary investigation and the requirement that sentences state their reasons. "All of this is not only guiding rules but obligatory requirements of law, whose violation is an occasion for cassation. When there also falls on the head of the court a Code of Civil Procedure, the burden of requirements for the worker-judge will become unbearable." The author declared that no one who loved and knew the work of the court could fail to wrack his brains to find a way of simplifying procedure, to reduce formalities to a minimum.

Here was a fundamental objection to all that was being done to formalize procedure; a voice crying out in the pages of the law journals for a return to the primitive court of 1917. It had not been many months since Commissar Kurskii had himself taken a position in favor of simplicity, but he had been forced to withdraw from this position with the development of events. Perhaps he still held some

[39] A. Lisitsyn, "Nuzhno uprostit' sudoproizvodstvo," *ibid.*, No. 43 (November 25, 1922), pp. 1–2.

of his old views, at least to the extent that he believed a corrective necessary, for he permitted publication of the criticism on the front page of his own journal, but the march of events suggests that the article was the whiplash of a dying dragon. Simplicity had gone forever, and the drafting committee in the Commissariat was to pay no attention to the author's plea, although the torch was taken up months later in the very issue of the Commissariat's journal which published the first excerpts of the revised code.[40] This time the complaint was not so fundamental but against red tape in general, and specifically against a requirement for registration of complaints at the office of the prosecutor which created double entries. By early 1923 the procedural requirements of records had been firmly established, and criticism could lie only against making two records of the same thing.

Delays in drafting the revised code prevented realization of Krylenko's expectation that it would be ready for use on January 1, 1923, when the new court system became effective. Makeshift arrangements to apply the old code to the new courts became necessary. The Commissariat of Justice published an instruction[41] terminating the sending of requests for review to the Supreme Court Control within the Commissariat, since it had to go out of existence on January 15, two weeks after the date on which the new court structure was supposed to have become effective, but continuing the review procedure for criminal cases as it existed in the council of people's judges under the now outdated Code of Criminal Procedure.[42] Presumably what was meant was that the procedure to bring review jurisdiction into action would be the same as under the outdated code, although the body which would now conduct the review would be the new provincial court rather than the council of people's judges, which had been superseded. These courts were actually being established, as evidenced by publication of the minutes of the first meeting of the Moscow Provincial Court, giving no date, but presumably during January, judging

[40] Bogomolov, "K voprosu ob iskorenenii volokitstva," *ibid.*, No. 6 (February 13, 1923), p. 128.
[41] "Iz deiatel'nosti Narodnogo Komissariata Iustitsii," *ibid.*, No. 1 (January 9, 1923), p. 14.
[42] Code of Criminal Procedure, RSFSR (1922), Arts. 373, 374.

from references within the minutes.[43] A circular of the Commissariat of Justice under date of February 2, 1923, outlined ten points of a procedure for protesting sentences of trial courts and decisions of provincial courts relating to them to the new supreme court. These rules were to remain in effect "until the Code of Criminal Procedure in its new form enters into force." [44]

The first publication[45] of the new code was limited to that chapter which had to do with jurisdiction of people's courts, provincial courts, military courts, and military-transport courts. The editors showed themselves so rushed in their desire to put this in print that the regular number of the Commissariat's journal bearing the date of February 13, 1923, was delayed for a few days to print the selection, which was approved by the Presidium of the Central Executive Committee only on February 15, 1923,[46] to become effective immediately.

THE REVISION OF 1923

The revised code showed itself to be primarily an amendment of the May, 1922, version. Lenin's admonition that codification must be speedy seems to have been taken to heart to such an extent that no attempt was made even to improve upon the language, for the revisers let slip an erroneous verb,[47] an erroneous gerund,[48] and two erroneous cases[49] as they had appeared in the first code. Not until years later were the proper forms indicated by an industrious editor in a republication.[50]

[43] "Khronika: Pervyi plenum moskovskogo gubsuda," *Ezh. sov. iust.*, No. 4–5 (February 6, 1923), p. 109.

[44] Circular No. 17, on the Procedure for Protesting the Entry into Force of Sentences of the Cassational Colleges of the Provincial Court by Way of Audit, February 2, 1923, *ibid.*, No. 4–5 (February 6, 1923), p. 118.

[45] "Vypiska iz ugol.-prots. kodeksa," *ibid.*, No. 6 (February 13, 1923), p. 142.

[46] Code of Criminal Procedure, RSFSR, [1923] I *Sob. Uzak. RSFSR*, No. 7, item 106.

[47] *Ibid.*, Art. 17. This had been Art. 17 in the 1922 text.

[48] *Ibid.*, Art. 405. This had been Art. 441 in the 1922 text.

[49] *Ibid.*, Arts. 261 and 293. These had been Arts. 265 and 297 in the 1922 text.

[50] See corrections placed in brackets in S. A. Golunskii, ed., *Istoriia zakonodatel'stva SSSR i RSFSR po ugolovnomu protsessu i organizatsii suda i prokuratury 1917–1954 gg.: Sbornik dokumentov* (Moscow, 1955), pp. 187 ff. and 251 ff.

The new code contained some changes other than those necessitated by the revised structure of the courts. These suggested that the draftsmen had seized the opportunity offered by the necessity of revision to perfect some points of detail and also to resume the battle over rights of the accused, although they gave little attention to the complaints against the old code which had been published in the Commissariat's journal during the months of their deliberations.

The details corrected in the new code were inconsequential, although the inadequacies which they were intended to correct had probably plagued some of the courts. There were measures to assure the protection of material evidence. Thus, evidence that had to be saved was ordered packed carefully,[51] and if it could not be kept in the investigator's office, it was to be described in detail, photographed and sealed.[52] Delays at the trial were to be reduced when a lay judge had to retire. The new code permitted the trial to proceed without repetition of previously submitted evidence if there had been a substitute lay judge in the courtroom throughout the proceedings, and he did not ask for a fresh start.[53]

The resumed battle over rights of the accused was evidenced by new provisions designed to assure that he knew of his rights, but there was a transfer from the defense attorney to the prosecutor of some of the burden of seeing that the courts observed the rules. To western minds this transfer could not but reduce the opportunities to make use of protective rules, although under Soviet concepts of the dual function of prosecutors, it may have seemed to some that there was no negation of the very efforts that were being made to strengthen the position of the accused.

Improvement of procedures to assure that an accused knew of his rights was sought by addition of a requirement that the minutes of the investigation and of the trial contain declarations that the accused had been informed of his right to give his explanation at every stage of the proceedings, and also that he be informed of the procedure to be followed in filing an appeal and the time limits for such an appeal.[54] Under the Soviet theory that the procedural code is, in a measure, a checklist for an inexperienced

---

[51] Code of Criminal Procedure, RSFSR (1923), Art. 68. Compare Art. 72 in 1922 text.

[52] Art. 67. Compare Art. 71 in 1922 text.

[53] Art. 42. Compare Art. 46 in 1922 text.   [54] Art. 80.

judge to help him through the trial, the inclusion of these provisions may have increased the likelihood that the notifications would be made. Further, to reduce the possibilities of after-the-fact minutes, the 1923 revision required that the minutes be signed by the president of a court and its secretary.[55]

The shift of controls from the defense attorney to the prosecutor was evident in provisions reducing the occasions when the presence of a defense attorney was mandatory,[56] and increasing the occasions when a prosecutor had to be notified of restraints placed upon a suspect. The elimination of the defense attorney has already been discussed in a preceding chapter and need not be repeated here.

The prosecutor was pushed to the fore in the role of protector of the innocent with a series of provisions relating to the powers of the police. He had to be notified immediately by the police if a search or interrogation of suspects or witnesses was undertaken.[57] When the investigator opened a case, he had to notify the prosecutor if he planned to request court permission to proceed when the whereabouts of the suspect were unknown.[58] The prosecutor had to be notified when measures to assure the presence of the suspect at investigation or trial were to be taken,[59] and any measures ordered by the prosecutor had to be put into effect by the investigator, who, if he disagreed, had no recourse but to appeal to a court after he had performed the order.[60] The prosecutor had to be present at a search of quarters of diplomatic representatives of foreign states along with the representative of the Commissariat of Foreign Affairs previously required.[61] The prosecutor became a check on the leniency of the investigator, for the latter now had to notify him if dismissal was to be recommended because of insanity of the accused at the time he committed the crime.[62]

Procedure governing police activities was differentiated in the new code between ordinary police interrogation and conduct of full investigation in those circumstances when the preliminary investigator was not brought into the case.[63] When the police performed the full investigative function, it was now made clear that

[55] *Ibid.*   [56] Art. 55.   [57] Art. 99. Compare Art. 104 in 1922 text.
[58] Art. 133. Compare Art. 136 in 1922 text.
[59] Art. 146. Compare Art. 149 in 1922 text.
[60] Art. 148 (note). Compare Art. 151 in 1922 text.
[61] Art. 178. Compare Art. 181 in 1922 text.
[62] Art. 197. Compare Art. 200 in 1922 text.   [63] Art. 98.

the officers had to follow the code's provisions on preliminary investigation.[64] By the new rules the police had to notify a court within twenty-four hours of detention of a suspect, giving the reasons for its action. Within another forty-eight hours the court had to approve detention or order the individual freed. To these improved rules designed to protect the suspect from police arbitrariness there was added an ominous caveat, declaring that the security police of the G.P.U. were not bound by the Code of Criminal Procedure, but were subject to special rules for that agency.[65] Such rules were never made public. In this change, Krylenko lost the battle he had won in 1922, when he had successfully kept the exception out of the code.

Restrictions were added by the 1923 code to those already in force on a preliminary investigator. In 1922 he had been given twenty-four hours if there had been no arrest.[66] By the 1923 revision the time in both instances was cut to "immediate" action.[67] Together with this restriction there went provisions releasing an investigator from some of the control previously exercised. In 1922 he could not refuse to undertake investigation if an injured party requested it in one of the serious cases listed in the code without giving a written reason for refusal.[68] In 1923 this requirement was eliminated. The investigator's freedom of action was further enhanced by elimination of the 1922 provision permitting the suspect and the injured party to be present at all stages of the preliminary investigation to ask questions of witnesses or to make explanation unless specifically excluded by the investigator on the ground that presence would interfere with the conduct of the investigation or disclose prematurely facts which should remain secret during the investigation.[69] Since the 1922 provision left the investigator free to exclude undesirables, complete elimination of the article in 1923 suggests that the draftsmen recognized that the old rule placed the investigator under a burden of justifying his action, and they wanted to give him untrammelled freedom of action. To this conclusion there needs to be added one reminder—that the prosecutor is always obligated to watch over the work of the preliminary

[64] Arts. 101–4.   [65] Art. 104 (note).
[66] Code of Criminal Procedure, RSFSR (1922), Art. 112.
[67] Art. 110 (1923).   [68] *Ibid.*, Art. 110 (1922), Art. 108 (1923).
[69] Art. 117 (1922).

investigator. The 1923 code reemphasized this fact by adding a clause to the article on the work of the preliminary investigators for the serious cases to be tried in the new provincial courts. The article stated that the preliminary investigator must perform "under the closest supervision of the appropriate prosecutor." [70]

Enhancement of the prosecutor's role was effectuated by the 1923 code also at the expense of the court. Thus, under the terms of 1922 complaints against the work of the investigator had to be reported either to a court or to a prosecutor within twenty-four hours.[71] The 1923 code eliminated the court as a recipient.[72] With this change, which seems so vital to a common-law lawyer, there was an accompanying blow, in that the 1922 provision permitting a complainant to argue orally before the court in support of his complaint[73] was simply dropped, for the prosecutor was required to offer no such opportunity. Both of these changes represented a step toward the complete incorporation of the corps of preliminary investigators within the office of prosecutor. While the formal transfer did not occur until 1928,[74] the way had been prepared.

Although the court was losing its position in 1923 as a controlling factor over the work of the preliminary investigators, the prosecutors were not bereft of all restraint from above. The 1923 code added a provision that a trial prosecutor must make his decision on whether to forward a case to court within two weeks of receipt of the report of the preliminary investigator or obtain the permission for an extension of time from the provincial prosecutor.[75] In the 1922 code there had been no time limit set on the period during which a trial prosecutor might meditate.[76]

The procedure for the trial was changed only slightly in 1923 from what had been prescribed in 1922, but again the prosecutor was brought further to the fore. He was now authorized to be present at any time he wished during the preliminary sitting of

---

[70] Art. 384 (1923). Compare Art. 418 in 1922 text.

[71] Art. 221 (1922).   [72] Art. 217 (1923).   [73] Art. 223 (1922).

[74] Order of People's Commissariat of Justice, RSFSR, March 15, 1928. The text has not been found, but see commentary on it in P. Akhimov, "Sledstvie i prokuratura," *Ezh. sov. iust.*, No. 14 (April 16, 1928), pp. 422–25. See also circular of People's Commissariat of Justice on the Manner of Appointing, Dismissing, Accounting and Reporting of Investigation, July 17, 1928. *Ibid.*, No. 26 (July 17, 1928), p. 755.

[75] Code of Criminal Procedure, RSFSR (1923), Art. 227.

[76] Art. 223 (1922).

the professional judge designed to make the decisions necessary to the proper conduct of a trial.[77] The court was also strengthened by being given greater authority to control the presentation of the case for the accused. In 1923 there was eliminated [78] the provision denying to the court the right to limit the number of witnesses to be called by the parties or to select from the list of witnesses or experts proposed by the parties the ones it wished to hear.[79] It may be that the part of the old article which remained was sufficient to cover this point, for it denied to the court the right to refuse to summon witnesses or experts proposed by the parties on the ground that the case was already clear enough. Yet the fact of elimination of the specific paragraph on limitation of numbers suggests that the emphasis upon restraint which had previously been strong had been withdrawn.

The accused's position was slightly improved by the 1923 court in respect to his right to be present at the trial. In 1922 the presence of the accused was not required unless the possible penalty was six months' imprisonment.[80] In 1923, his presence was required if there was possible imprisonment of any duration, unless, as had been the case in 1922 as well, he concealed himself from the court or expressed directly his desire to be absent from the trial.[81]

The judges were given a bit more freedom than had been theirs under the 1922 code. A paragraph was added in 1923 saying that the conclusion of experts was not binding upon a court, although if it was not followed, there must be a reasoned explanation given either in the sentence or in a separate opinion.[82] A paragraph of the 1922 code was removed to increase the judge's freedom in formulating its inner conviction as to guilt. In 1922 the codifiers had required the court to insert in the descriptive part of the sentence the facts discovered at the trial which the court concluded to be fundamental to its decision.[83] The deletion of this requirement in 1923 left the court free merely to state its conclusions without supporting facts.[84] A practice was developed later which indicated that the higher courts could not be restrained from reviewing the

---

[77] Art. 248 (1923). Compare with Art. 252 in 1922 text.
[78] Art. 254 (1923).   [79] Art. 258, par. 2 (1922).   [80] Art. 269 (1922).
[81] Art. 265 (1923).
[82] Art. 298 (1923). Compare with Art. 302 in 1922 text.
[83] Art. 338, par. 2 (1923).   [84] Art. 334 (1923).

evaluation of evidence by the trial court, and by 1950 the Supreme Court of the U.S.S.R. issued an order saying, "In sentences there must be set forth the motives on the basis of which the court reached its conclusion of guilt or innocence with regard to each defendant. In this there must be set forth concretely the evidence placed by the court as the basis for conviction or acquittal of the accused with the motives of the court for accepting the evidence. In rejecting any evidence in the case which supports the accusation or exculpation of the accused, the court must state in the sentence why that very evidence was rejected by it." [85] Any other attitude toward stating evidence in a sentence precludes review, and it must be assumed that in 1923 the draftsmen wished to limit review to errors and policy and exclude reconsideration of the evaluation of evidence.

The liberation of the trial court from extensive review of some of its findings was further extended by elimination in 1923 of another procedural requirement relating to appeal. In 1922 the codifiers had provided that any appeal which failed to charge formal violation of the rights of a party by the trial court and appealed solely against the substance of a sentence, although having no validity as an appeal, nevertheless put the reviewing court on notice to examine the matter as one of audit, under the usual rules for audit, and the petition for appeal had to be attached to the record.[86] In 1923 the draftsmen eliminated the requirement that the faulty appeal should be made a part of the record,[87] thus presumably removing from the eyes of the auditing court whatever the party may have had to say as to his reasons for objecting to the sentence as a whole without charging error.

There was recognition that court secretaries were inadequate to their positions, for in 1923 the codifiers eliminated the provision of 1922 to the effect that a violation of the rules of procedure was not to be considered as having occurred at the trial unless it appeared in the minutes.[88]

While procedure in the new provincial courts when they sat as

---

[85] Order of the Supreme Court of the USSR, No. 13/9/U, July 28, 1950, printed as annotation to Chap. XXIV, *Code of Criminal Procedure RSFSR* (Moscow, 1956), p. 180, par. 5.
[86] Code of Criminal Procedure, RSFSR (1922), Art. 354.
[87] Art. 350 (1923).   [88] Art. 432 (1922) and Art. 399 (1923).

courts of first instance was established in the same pattern as had previously been created for the revolutionary tribunals, that is with many exceptions from the more protective procedures of the people's courts, the 1923 code improved the lot of the accused in some measure. Thus, the time allowed for appeal from its sentences was increased for the defendant to seventy-two hours from the time of receipt of a copy of the sentence[89] instead of the forty-eight hours established in 1922.[90] The authorization in 1922 code to the Supreme Revolutionary Tribunal to list those tribunals operating in places where fighting was occurring from which there might be no appeal was dropped,[91] although there was retained from the new provincial courts the same right formerly granted to all revolutionary tribunals during time of military operations to ask that no appeal be permitted even in those cases where it might otherwise be permitted.[92] This provision authorized a protest to the provincial executive committee against permitting an appeal from a sentence of death, and it was for the reviewing authority to decide whether the danger was as great as found by the provincial court requiring immediate execution of the convict without appeal. In no event could the reviewing authority reconsider the finding of guilt.

The appellate work of the new provincial court was subject to little change in procedure from what it had been for the old council of people's judges, although there were some novelties which may have operated to the detriment of the convicted person. Thus, there was a shortening of the definition of what was to be considered as error below. The 1922 definition had included as an example of inadequate investigation "failure to investigate all possible factual reasons, circumstances, and persons guilty of committing the crime." [93] The 1923 code simply eliminated the example,[94] leaving the basic definition of error the failure to investigate any facts necessary to the sentence. To support the elimination of 1923 as inconsequential it is necessary to conclude either that within one year the judges had come to understand what complete investigation required or that they had understood the requirements in 1922 and the first codifiers had inserted surplusage. The 1923 code eliminated

---

[89] Art. 400 (1923).   [90] Art. 433 (1922).   [91] Art. 434 (1922).

[92] Art. 406 (1923), Art. 435 (1922).

[93] Art. 360 (1922).   [94] Art. 414 (1923).

another 1922 provision which had defined an unjust sentence as one including two factors: (1) when it was completely without proof in that it contained no support in the facts of the court hearing, and (2) when the penalty, although not exceeding the limits of the law nevertheless was sharply out of keeping with the situation.[95] The first of these was removed,[96] probably because of the revision of the code already considered under which the sentence was no longer to be required to set forth facts.

The convicted person lost in 1923 his right to appeal the decision of the reviewing court to the supreme court,[97] for under the 1923 version the decision of the provincial court on appeal from a people's court was final.[98] It was thereafter subject only to audit by the new supreme court, which meant that the prosecutor but not the convict could call it to the attention of the higher authority for reconsideration.

Procedure for the newly created Supreme Court of the Republic was inserted in the 1923 code to replace that previously established for the Supreme Court Control of the People's Commissariat of Justice.

Completion of the revision in early 1923 did not end experimentation with the text. The draftsmen returned to the Central Executive Committee at its session held at the end of June, 1923, to request amendment, but Krylenko sought to arouse as little excitement as possible, by inserting but two paragraphs in a rather long speech on proposed amendments to the Criminal Code.[99] He said that there were no changes in the Code of Criminal Procedure, except for purely technical articles to eliminate red tape in the procedure for submitting a case for audit to the provincial prosecutor. Under the old procedure the people's court responded to the prosecutor's request for audit by forwarding the file to him through the provincial court. The draftsmen wanted to permit the people's court concerned to deal directly with the prosecutor and to forward the case to him without the intervention of the provincial court. While the matter may have seemed only technical to the draftsmen, it strengthened the hand of the prosecutor and was one more step

---

[95] Art. 363 (1922).   [96] Art. 417 (1923).   [97] Art. 372 (1922).
[98] Art. 426 (1923).
[99] *RSFSR—Vtoraia sessiia VTsIK, X sozyva, stenograficheskii otchët i postanovleniia* (Moscow, 1923), p. 56.

in the progression of steps toward a powerful prosecutor's office with direct access to the various agencies of the law.

The prosecutor's hand was further strengthened when the legal committee made its report through Krylenko at the end of the sitting.[100] Further amendments were proposed, one to extend to the prosecutor of the military and military-transport colleges of the Supreme Court the right to demand the file of any case in the tribunals subordinate to the college for audit. Previously this right had been solely in the president of the college.

Other amendments, slipped into the revising statute adopted by the session,[101] gave to the provincial court original jurisdiction over crimes involving intentional serious bodily injury, eliminated the Workers'-Peasants' Inspection agency as an investigating organ, and most importantly amended the article relating to jurisdiction over juveniles to forbid prosecution of children from 14 to 16 years of age unless the commission for juvenile cases concluded that measures of a medical-pedagogical character were inapplicable to the situation.

UKRAINIAN PROPOSALS FOR REVISION

Months after the Russian Republic had put the finishing touches on its revision of the first Code of Criminal Procedure and had enacted it as law in February, 1923, the Ukraine was still waiting to complete its revised code. The Ukraine's original code, as adopted on September 13, 1922,[102] had been almost identical with the one first adopted by the Russian Republic. Only two substantial changes over the Russian text had appeared, and one was inevitable. The Ukrainian language was placed alongside the Russian as an official language of court proceedings.[103] The other substantial change was a refusal to follow the Russian example of including rape on the list of crimes which would be prosecuted only if the injured

[100] *Ibid.*, pp. 247–48.
[101] Decree on Changes in and Additions to the Code of Criminal Procedure, July 10, 1923, [1923] I *Sob. Uzak. RSFSR*, No. 48, item 480.
[102] Code of Criminal Procedure, Ukrainian SSR, September 13, 1922, [1922] I *Sobranie Uzakonenii i Rasporiazhenii Raboche-Krest'ianskogo Pravitel'stva Ukrainy*, No. 41, item 598. A Russian translation was published by the People's Commissariat of Justice, Ukrainian SSR, in a pocket edition in 1925.
[103] *Ibid.*, Art. 22.

party complained.[104] Inconsequential changes were corrections of
some of the grammatical errors made by the Russians in their first
code,[105] and a correction of an erroneous cross reference which the
Russians had let slip.[106] The Ukrainian revisers of 1923 faced, therefore, essentially the same text as the Russians had revised some
months earlier.

The Ukrainians seem to have felt less bound to follow the
Russian model on the revision than they had felt in drafting their
first code. It was this spirit of innovation that inspired a Ukrainian
commentator to declare that under the guise of revising the Code
of Criminal Procedure to take into account the changes in the structure of the courts the authors of the draft had gone far beyond the
limits set by the new judiciary act and far beyond the revisions
already made in the second Russian code.[107] In his view the draftsmen had introduced in their revision a whole series of errors having
nothing to do with changes required by the judiciary act. His attack
upon the draft began to appear in the journal of the Ukrainian
Commissariat of Justice on September 1, 1923, with a footnote
provided by the editor to reveal the troubles of the authorities. The
editor disclosed that the Ukrainian Commissariat of Justice had
prepared a revision of the first code on the basis of the Russian
Republic's revision of February 15, 1923, and that this draft had
been approved with inconsequential changes by the "Little Council
of People's Commissars," but that thereafter the draft had been
withdrawn from the legislative channel "until final decision of the
question of the Supreme Court of the U.S.S.R., and of other constitutional questions with which is linked the organization of the
court structure and court procedure in each of the countries joining
in union."

The Ukrainian's criticism was said to be directed against his own
people, but examination of the details shows it to have been aimed
largely at the Russian draftsmen, for his opposition was primarily to
points being copied by the Ukrainians from the revised Russian

[104] *Ibid.*, Art. 11.
[105] *Ibid.*, Arts. 17, 219, 265, 297, but the draftsmen overlooked the erroneous
gerund in the RSFSR Code, Art. 441.
[106] *Ibid.*, Art. 4, par. 1.
[107] Viktor Erivman, "Proekt izmenenii ugol. prots. kodeksa Uk. SSR," *Vestnik
sovetskoi iustitsii*, No. 3 (September 1, 1923), p. 71 and *ibid.*, No. 4 (September 15, 1923), p. 106.

code. He felt displeased with the increased authority given the prosecutor over the investigatory stage and with the elimination of the court from the list of agencies having authority (1) to decide conflicts of jurisdiction between investigators,[108] (2) to transfer venue of investigations,[109] (3) to extend the period of arrest to permit completion of an investigation,[110] and (4) to hear complaints against acts of the investigators.[111] In all of these situations the prosecutor was to be the sole controlling authority.

Reduction of the circumstances requiring the presence of a defense attorney also angered the Ukrainian author, for he noted that with the elimination of the old form of people's court having six lay judges before whom a defense attorney was always required, the occasions requiring presence of a defense attorney were being reduced substantially.[112] He revealed a practical situation, however, after making his point, by adding that the presence of a defense attorney was not always helpful to the accused, for in cases in which no prosecutor appeared opposite a defense attorney the judges sensed a duty to prosecute with the result that the adversary character of the proceedings was lost, and the bench became partisan.

The weakening of the adversary character of proceedings seemed to the critic evident in the elimination of the former article[113] granting to the accused and the injured party the right to be present at the preliminary investigation to ask questions of witnesses and experts. He also decried removal of the former procedural guarantee[114] requiring release of an arrested person if a court or an investigator failed to approve the arrest within forty-eight hours of notification.

All of these features had been introduced in the Russian revision of 1923. The exclusively Ukrainian variations which were being criticized were in reality very few in spite of the critic's opening statement to the contrary. Such Ukrainian changes as there were related to jurisdiction of courts. The crime of taking law into one's own hands[115] was being removed, as it had been in the Russian

---

[108] Code of Criminal Procedure, RSFSR (1922), Art. 130.
[109] Art. 127.   [110] Art. 162.   [111] Arts. 216–18.   [112] Art. 59.
[113] Art. 117.   [114] Art. 106.
[115] Criminal Code, Ukrainian SSR, August 23, 1922, effective September 15, 1922, [1922] I *Sob. Uzak. Uk.*, No. 36, item 553, Art. 103.

revision, from the list of crimes prosecuted only on complaint of the injured party and dismissed at any moment if reconciliation occurred.[116] Yet, unlike the Russians, the Ukrainian draftsmen planned to transfer this crime to the category for which prosecution occurred only on complaint of the injured party but for which there could be no subsequent dismissal even if reconciliation were to occur. The Russians in their revision had placed this crime among the great bulk of offenses over which neither the desire to prosecute on the part of the injured person nor subsequent reconciliation could be decisive for the prosecutor in reaching his decision on whether to proceed with the case. To the Ukrainian critic the Ukrainian decision was illogical, for in his view a crime, deemed to be sufficiently dangerous to be excluded from those for which prosecution occurred only if the injured party complained, acquired a public character which could not be dissipated by subsequent reconciliation. Having made his point, the critic weakened its effect, for he found it necessary to admit that the proposed Ukrainian compromise was expedient, since it was hardly worthwhile to consume the time of the public authorities with neighbors' disputes over the ownership of kitchen knives if there were no complaint at all.

Rape seemed to the critic to require transfer from the category into which it had been placed in the first code. At this point the critic permitted himself to praise the Ukrainian draftsmen for proposing to follow the Russian model. In the first Ukrainian Code of Criminal Procedure rape had been treated as a crime of public character, prosecuted without regard to the desire of the injured woman to proceed with prosecution. The draftsmen now proposed to place this crime in the category of those prosecuted only with the consent of the injured party, but not dropped even if reconciliation should occur. To the critic it was wise to follow the Russian model, for the publicity relating to a prosecution for rape had often caused as much suffering as the act itself. This justified withholding prosecution unless the woman involved was willing to testify. Also, change in the classification might, in the critic's view, reduce the number of unfounded prosecutions, for he believed it to be true

[116] Code of Criminal Procedure, RSFSR (1922), Art 10; compare Art. 10 in 1923 text.

that it was often the case that intercourse had occurred with consent, although circumstances required that a public announcement of rape be made. If women could drop the charge before prosecution, the real interests of justice would be served. The implication is left with the reader that women could vindicate their honor by making it known to the village that they had not consented, without requiring the state to proceed to prosecution on the basis of evidence which was usually falsified to protect reputation in the community.

Redistribution of the jurisdiction of the various courts over crime, made necessary by the abolition of the people's court with six lay judges, had provided the opportunity to reconsider the rating of seriousness given by the first Ukrainian code to various crimes. The critic saw no reason for demoting to the people's court with two lay judges crimes such as the execution of abortion without proper medical preparation, the intentional causing of serious bodily injury, the intentional causing of less serious bodily injury from which permanent injury to health or lengthy loss of the function of some organ of the body resulted, and kidnapping of a child. For these serious crimes the critic preferred the jurisdiction of the new provincial courts. On the other hand he saw no reason for giving to the provincial courts such crimes as refusal to accept a document written in the Ukrainian language, or the hampering of teaching in a native language, escape of a person under arrest, exchange of foreign money or valuables at an unauthorized place within 15 versts from the state frontiers, theft from state enterprises under serious circumstances, and intentional disruption of transport. The people's court seemed to him to be a suitable place for trials of such issues.

In spite of the Ukrainian draftsmen's progress toward preparation of a revised Code of Criminal Procedure, nothing was enacted until 1927.[117] The Ukrainians seem to have been able to function under a code which had become obsolete in its jurisdictional section with the 1922 change in the structure of the courts. The first Ukrainian

---

[117] Code of Criminal Procedure, Ukrainian SSR, July 20, 1927, effective September 15, 1927, [1927] I *Sob. Uzak. Uk.*, No. 36–38, item 168, republished in Russian with amendments to 1957. See D. S. Karev, ed., *Ugolovno-protsessual'noe zakonodatel'stvo SSSR i soiuznykh respublik, sbornik (Osnovnye zakonodatel'nye akty)* (Moscow, 1957), pp. 91–142.

code of 1922 was republished in 1925 with a notation on the cover that it contained amendments to March 1, 1925, but there was not a single change from the wording of the code as originally adopted. Judicial decisions also support the conclusion that a makeshift arrangement was in effect. Thus, the College for Criminal Cases of the Ukrainian Supreme Court cited articles relating to procedure in the abolished revolutionary tribunals as applicable to procedure in the newly created provincial courts in three of its decisions in September and October, 1923.[118]

The other republics acted more quickly than the Ukraine to enact codes similar to that of the Russian Republic. Thus, the Belorussian Republic adopted its code in 1923,[119] as did the Georgian Republic[120] and the Armenian Republic.[121]

JUDICIAL EXPERIENCE WITH PROCEDURE

Judicial decisions within the Russian and Ukrainian Republics indicated during 1923 that the trial courts were not appreciating the seriousness attached to the new rules of criminal procedure. The trial judges had not yet caught the spirit of reform and were

[118] See Decisions of the Ukrainian Supreme Court, Nos. VI, VII, and VIII, *Vestnik sov. iust.*, No. 9 (December 1, 1923), p. 242.

[119] The Belorussian SSR relied wholly upon the codifiers of the RSFSR for its code of criminal procedure. On June 24, 1922, it extended the application of the Russian Republic's 1922 Code of Criminal Procedure to the Belorussian Republic. [1922] *Sobranie Uzakonenni i Rasporiazhenni Raboche-Krest'ianskogo Pravitel'stva BSSR*, No. 5, item 81. After the Russian Republic had enacted the revision of 1923, the Belorussian Republic again extended its application to Belorussian territory, albeit with amendments to nine articles. Decree of March 30, 1923, [1923] *Sob. Uzak. BSSR*, No. 4, item 41. A text with amendments to 1957 is published in Russian in Karev, ed., *Ugolovno-protsessual'noe zakonodatel'stvo*, pp. 145–88.

[120] The Georgian Republic adopted its code of criminal procedure by decree of August 17, 1923, [1923] *Sobranie Uzakonenni Rasporiazhenni Raboche-Krest'ianskogo Pravitel'stva GSSR*, No. 53, item 1. A Russian translation is published in Karev, *Ugolovno-protsessual'noe zakonodatel'stvo*, pp. 218–62. The Azerbaidzhan Republic adopted temporary rules on jurisdiction on February 13, 1923, to be applied until promulgation of Codes of Civil and Criminal Procedure. [1923] *Sobranie Uzakonenni i Rasporiazhenni Raboche-Krest'ianskogo Pravitel'stva AzSSR*, No. 2, item 112, and its code. Its current code with amendments to 1957 is published in Karev, pp. 265–306.

[121] Code of Criminal Procedure, Armenian SSR, September 28, 1923, [1924] *Sobranie Dekretov Armianskoi SSR*, No. 5, item 24. A revision adopted June 22, 1934, is published in Russian in Karev, *Ugolovno-protsessual'noe zakonodatel'stvo*, pp. 328–65.

tempted to proceed without full regard to the requirements established in the interest of accurate determination of guilt. The college for criminal appeals in the Supreme Court of the Russian Republic found it necessary to set aside a series of convictions and to order new trials because the facts had not been examined sufficiently. Thus, a conviction of a group of railway workers for negligence causing the collision of two trains was set aside because the trial court had failed to examine the engineer of one of the trains in spite of the fact that his testimony was crucial to an understanding of the situation.[122]

A conviction for accepting bribes and bringing discredit upon the security police, the G.P.U., was set aside because the trial court had examined as its sole witness a man suffering from serious nervous disorders and had thus violated the procedural rule prohibiting the examination of witnesses suffering from physical or psychological handicaps.[123]

A conviction of a couple for conducting a bandits' raid was set aside because the sentence contained no descriptive part and no statement of the precise articles of the Criminal Code which had been violated.[124] In this instance, the accused had argued that the trial court had failed to take into consideration the proletarian origin of the accused, the serious economic conditions of the time which had been accentuated by unemployment, the absence of recidivism, and military service before the Revolution. The college of the Supreme Court found it impossible to determine what the trial court had considered because of the violation of the code's requirement of a complete sentence, including a statement of the class origin of the convicted person. Further, no finding had been given of the articles of the Criminal Code found to have been violated. The court had only attached to its sentence a copy of the indictment. In this situation the college found it desirable to lecture the trial court, and it wrote:

In discussing the question of the sentence, it is first necessary to formulate precisely on the basis of the facts of the court investigation exactly of what the accused has been found guilty, and then to find the article of

---

[122] *Case of Lagutenko, Ezh. sov. iust.*, No. 23, (June 14, 1923), p. 541.
[123] *Case of Kotov and Travin, ibid.*, pp. 541–42.
[124] *Case of Kulikov and Ivanova, ibid.*, p. 542.

the Criminal Code corresponding to such a formulation. Guilt for 'violating articles' as the tribunal wrote in this case cannot be.

Inadequate examination of the situation was cause for remanding of a case involving a charge of instigation of murder of a housing administrator so as to get control of the administration of an apartment house.[125] The appellant argued that he had not counseled murder, that the court had been influenced against him by a newspaper campaign conducted after the murder, and that the punishment of ten years' solitary confinement did not correspond to the seriousness of his offense, being the same penalty as was meted out to the actual murderer. The college of the Supreme Court found that the evidence supported the conclusion that there had been only indirect influence upon the murderer, for the instigator had not anticipated in urging ouster of the manager that the murderer would actually kill him. Further, the formulation of the accusation had not been as precise as required by the code.

Failure to provide an interpreter for the final plea of a defendant before a court, one of whose three members did not understand the defendant's language, was found to be cause for retrial of an individual who had been acquitted of a charge of abuse of authority in the conduct of the Moscow administration of forced labor and the concentration camps under its jurisdiction.[126] The case had reached the Supreme Court on the protest of the prosecutor against the acquittal, and it indicated that in this instance the procedural requirement normally considered to be a protection of an accused had been turned to his disadvantage in upsetting or at least threatening to upset his acquittal.

Hampering the filing of appeals in violation of the procedural code provided the Supreme Court with an opportunity to be severe with a court while remanding a case for retrial when it was found that the accused had not been permitted counsel although a prosecutor had been present.[127] The college warned:

In view of the fact that in this case the Supreme Court has been presented by the Amur tribunal with a second example of withholding of an appeal of a convicted person . . . the cassational college orders that the appeal

[125] *Case of Volkov and Naumov, ibid.*, pp. 542–43.
[126] *Case of Katsev, Mark, et al.*, No. 546a, *ibid.*, No. 17 (May 3, 1923), p. 398.
[127] *Case of Panteleev*, No. 146c, *ibid.*, No. 20 (May 24, 1923), p. 469.

must be sent with the file to Moscow to the Supreme Court within twenty-four hours of its receipt, and that rejection of the appeal may not be permitted, and it warns that if a delay in forwarding an appeal reoccurs, the case will be transferred to the disciplinary college for punishment of the president of the Amur tribunal, or the instigation of criminal proceedings (in the event of the execution of the sentence without permitting an appeal).

Shifting of jurisdiction plagued the courts in spite of the strict limitations adopted by the code in an effort to stop it. An author complained that it was not exceptional for a case to travel for whole years from one court to another in search of a court organ competent to try it.[128] He remarked, "Such a situation cannot help but reduce the authority of the proletarian court and paralyze its work." Then he explained the rule of Article 26 of the Code of Criminal Procedure.

The Ukrainian Supreme Court was experiencing similar problems in clarifying the meaning of the new procedural code. Question was raised as to whether a conviction for sexual relations with an immature person must be set aside since the trial was public in violation of the code's requirement of secrecy in sex cases.[129] Neither party had raised the matter of secrecy at the trial. The Supreme Court held that although the code's requirement of secrecy had been violated, there was no reason to set aside the sentence if the issue had not been raised at the trial. This was evidence that no one had felt his or her rights infringed by the violation of the code.

A similar decision was handed down refusing to set aside a conviction because the provincial court had failed on its own initiative to look at real evidence and examine documents as required by the code. Yet since the attorneys had not objected during the trial and the sentence was correct in substance, the Supreme Court left the sentence as it stood.[130]

The court's right to exclude evidence if it seemed to it unneces-

---

[128] K. P., "Neskol'ko slov o podsudnosti ugolovnykh del," *ibid.*, No. 22 (June 7, 1923), pp. 512–13.

[129] *Case of Roshchin-Insarov*, No. 297–1923, *Vestnik Sov. Iust.* No. 8 (November 15, 1923), pp. 215–16.

[130] *Case of Omel'iants et al.*, No. 253 R. 2.–1923, *ibid.*, No. 9 (December 1, 1923), p. 242.

sary was upheld in a case in which a court had refused to proceed with the interrogation of witnesses and had met the requirement of the code that it write its reasons for refusal into the record.[131] In the same case the trial court had even refused to permit the parties to speak in summation, and the Supreme Court indicated that the code permitted such refusal if the court thought the matter already well enough clarified.

The Donets Provincial Court's failure to record the moment at which a copy of a sentence had been handed the convict in violation of the code's requirement was given as reason for the Supreme Court's inability to determine whether an appeal had been filed within the time limit set by the code and, therefore, cause for remanding.[132]

Amnesty problems beset the courts, for the supreme courts of both republics found that trial courts had been uncertain when they were required by an amnesty to apply the code's provision and drop a given case. A provincial court in the Ukraine applied the amnesty proclaimed on November 7, 1922, in honor of the fifth anniversary of the Revolution to free a rapist. The Supreme Court found this error because between October, 1922, and December, 1922, that is, both before and after the amnesty, the accused had raped a neighbor five times during the final months of his own wife's pregnancy. The court declared: "To apply an amnesty it is necessary that both the beginning and the end of the crime occur before the date of the amnesty."

The complicated problem of applying an amnesty when a civil suit was joined with the criminal prosecution brought forth a decision from the Russian Republic's Supreme Court that in spite of the amnesty the case must be heard to a conclusion to determine the civil suit, but the criminal case would not proceed to sentence.[133]

Challenges to the personnel of the bench had been expected by the code's draftsmen to concern only one of its members. When a

---

[131] *Case of Itskovich and Mikhalevich,* No. 229 R. 2–1923, *ibid.*

[132] *Case of Denichenko,* No. 296–1923, *ibid.*, pp. 242–43.

[133] Protocol No. 18, September 21, 1924, *Sbornik deistvuiushchikh raz"iasnenii Verkhovnogo Suda RSFSR, izdannykh za vremia s 1923 g. do 1 ianvaria 1929 g. s predisloviem P. I. Stuchka* (Moscow, 1930), p. 301.

challenge was presented against the full bench of three judges, the Supreme Court found it necessary to issue a circular saying that the challenged bench should itself decide the issue by a majority vote using as a guide the articles of the code defining the qualifications necessary to service as a judge. An appeal against such a decision could lie to a higher court in the usual manner.[134]

The impartiality required by the code of investigators was placed in doubt by the Supreme Court in its annual report for 1924. Practice was showing, according to the report, that the work of the investigators and of the provincial courts in this regard was far from satisfactory, for 40 percent of the sentences which had been set aside by the Supreme Court's college for criminal appeals had been stricken because of failure to investigate a matter thoroughly. There had been examples of failure to call eye-witnesses, ignoring of a suspect's request that witnesses who might establish innocence be summoned, and failure to examine documents crucial to a decision of the case. There had even been failure to observe the code's requirements that if a witness or document was not examined, the reasons be given, for the investigator and judges in most cases had been content to say that any given evidence was "substantial" or "not substantial" for the case. Such an explanation was inadequate. The court ended its report with the charge:

In general, practice has demonstrated that in the work of courts and investigating organs there is in the most extreme degree a harmful, completely impermissible accusatory leaning, an accusatory approach to the case. To demonstrate all of the danger of this leaning it is enough to recall that the consequences of such a leaning strikes first of all at the poorest part of the population.[135]

The inexperience of courts with codified law led some judges to believe that without regard to the code they could still take such cases as they wished. The Commissariat of Justice of the Russian Republic had to caution them early in 1924 in a circular warning courts to take only such cases as involved criminal activities provided for by some article of the Criminal Code. It was explained that courts were not distinguishing between cases which should involve only fines levied by an administrative organ and

---

[134] Circular No. 43, July 2, 1923, *ibid.*, p. 308.
[135] *Ibid.*, p. 313.

those requiring prosecution. Judges were ordered to drop immediately any cases which should not be before them.[136]

In spite of the new procedures with their frequent indications of limits of time within which action had to be taken, cases began to accumulate in the people's courts. The Commissariat sought to correct what the code could not provide for by issuing a circular ordering the provincial courts to follow matters in the people's courts closely, assigning additional judges or changing boundaries of judicial districts so as to balance the case load.[137] In each review the higher courts were to search out reasons for delays below and to bring disciplinary action when necessary. They were to confer with postal authorities to improve the delivery of court letters and with the police to assure the correct service of summons.

The people's courts were admonished to see that no case waited even one day to be heard when it was ready, and to establish a realistic plan or calendar based upon a study of the number of cases that could be heard in a day. The judges were to be critical when counsel asked for additional time to call witnesses or to prepare. Finally the courts were asked to make sure that no cases got lost or misplaced in the files.

It was evident from reports of practice in the field of criminal procedure that the conflict between a desire for simplicity and the necessity to establish an order designed to achieve uniformity of treatment and speed of action was being decided in favor of regimentation. While the higher courts were being increased in importance as supervisory agencies, there was emerging the concept of a powerful prosecutor with authority transcending the ordinary role of a prosecutor. The courts remained the agencies to decide matters of guilt and innocence, but the cases which came before them had been so completely prepared by investigators and prosecutors who supervised them and decided when violations of pretrial procedure had occurred that the accused appeared before the judges with a psychological barrier to vault. In this fact is to be found a major characteristic of the criminal procedure created by the draftsmen of 1922 and accentuated by the draftsmen of

[136] Circular No. 14, January 17, 1924, *Sbornik tsirkuliarov Narkomiusta RSFSR za 1922–1925 gg. (deistviushchikh na 15 iiulia 1926 g.)* (Moscow, 1926), p. 151.
[137] Circular No. 247, December 8, 1925, *ibid.*, pp. 143–45.

1923. It was a characteristic so firmly imbedded that it was to survive even the reforms after Stalin's death, even though there were at all times voices raised against it, urging a revision of procedure, at least sufficiently to make of the investigators agents independent of the prosecutor and institutionally established in a manner more likely to assure that they would be able to execute the nearly impossible task placed upon them by the Code of Criminal Procedure of acting as much in the interests of the suspect as of the accusers, the task created by Article 3.

THE FIFTH CONGRESS OF PERSONS ENGAGED IN THE ADMINISTRATION OF JUSTICE

One of the recurring opportunities for periodic review of the judicial process was offered in March, 1924, by a Fifth Congress of persons engaged in the administration of justice. The Fourth Congress in 1922 had set the stage for the codification that followed, and some of the members attending the fifth thought that its convening indicated that the time was ripe for an extensive revision of the Code of Criminal Procedure. For the first time since the codification process had been initiated Krylenko[138] was not chosen to review criminal procedure, but the task was given to a newcomer, Andrei Y. Vyshinskii. It was the same Vyshinskii who was later to achieve world-wide notoriety as the severe prosecutor in Stalin's trials of his enemies in the late 1930's. After assuring his audience that "the struggle for revolutionary legality in the field of law is linked with the struggle for the best form of judicial procedure since the latter assures the success of the former," Vyshinskii presented the Commissariat's proposals.[139]

Vyshinskii was prepared to change radically the role of the police, the preliminary investigators, and the prosecutors. He saw no reason to restrict the police to the conduct of searches and seizures but proposed that they be increased in authority so that there would be no real difference between them and the preliminary

---

[138] Krylenko spoke only about salary levels of persons engaged in the administration of justice. See session of March 15, 1924, *Ezh. sov. iust.*, No. 12–13 (March 20–27, 1924), p. 286, and about the audit work of the provincial courts, *ibid.*, pp. 295 and 297.

[139] Morning session, March 13, 1924, Report of Vyshinskii, *ibid.*, pp. 279–280.

investigators, at least for crimes of limited importance. He then proposed that the preliminary investigators be given the right to conduct the prosecution of cases in court after completing their investigation. He thought that such a change in their role would be in the interest of "economic, rational, and swift progress of the case from the police examination to trial." He complained that the investigators had functioned poorly in that their work had been one-sided, incomplete, inadequate in the assembling of evidence, and "most importantly, their conclusion rests not on the objective facts as disclosed by the testimony of the accused, experts, documents, etc., but on subjective elements." To remedy this situation he proposed that the investigator be limited strictly in the time allowed for performance of his duties; that the prosecutors be restricted in extending the limits of time set for investigators, and that the investigators be instructed in means of avoiding the inadequacies. Further, the code should be amended to permit the accused to inform himself of the facts disclosed during the investigation so as to reduce the possibility that there would be introduced at the trial evidence which the prosecution would have no time to verify. Finally, he proposed that there be established personal responsibility of investigators and prosecutors for inadequacies in the investigation.

The trial itself was also subjected to criticism by Vyshinskii. He thought it necessary to find a way of improving it so as not to lose time, but his proposals suggest that he was prepared to save time by reducing the opportunities of the accused to present his case. Thus, he urged that the accused be permitted to present the facts of the case in an opening statement only if he pleaded guilty. The existing situation under which an accused was asked in all cases to tell his story before interrogation began seemed to Vyshinskii to lose much time. Vyshinskii also proposed that the article of the code permitting a party to demand full verification of material be revised to permit only one of the judges to make such a demand. He opposed the existing rule that a case be returned for continuation of the preliminary investigation if new evidence were disclosed at the trial, saying that a court should be permitted to examine this evidence if it felt that it would not be overburdened by the investigation. He would save time by permitting the court to refuse to hear the final arguments of the prosecution and defense if it thought them unnecessary, and finally, he would revoke the code's prohibition to a trial court to refer in its sentence to evidence or documents not disclosed at the trial.

Vyshinskii's proposals are reported as having stirred up a "lively discussion." [140] Issue was taken with his proposal to increase the powers of the police to that of an investigating organ on the ground that the police should be limited to the conduct of searches. Some were opposed to increasing the powers of the investigator, especially if he were to be permitted to conduct the prosecution in court. It was feared that this obligation would lead the investigator to search for accusatory material and to depart from the rule that he investigate a case from all sides. Finally, it was said that the investigator was already so burdened that he should not be asked to do more.

Those who looked upon the occasion as an opportunity to seek complete revision of the code criticized Vyshinskii's address. They demanded more changes than he had proposed. They wanted the code simplified radically by generalizing many of its articles, and by transferring others to a ministerial instruction. In this series of remarks there was heard again the recurring cry of despair over the complex development of Soviet criminal procedure from the simple form in which it had been introduced.

In spite of the lively discussion and the strong opposition evidenced by the reporter's account, the theses[141] advanced by Vyshinskii were adopted as a resolution of the congress[142] to serve as suggestions to the Commissariat in the preparation of amendments to be submitted to the Central Executive Committee. An unsigned editorial [143] expressed satisfaction with the congress and contrasted it with the Fourth Congress because "They did not debate at it any general problems, absorbing the whole field in their perspective or questioning the existing structure of judicial agencies or foretelling its destruction down to its very roots." The editorial thought that on the contrary, "almost all resolutions were based on, first of all, the statement of one fundamental fact, namely that the given judicial system is for the given moment and for the

---

[140] *Ibid.*, pp. 280–81. [141] *Ibid.*, pp. 299–300. [142] *Ibid.*, pp. 306–7.
[143] "Itogi V s"ezda," *ibid.*, p. 267–68.

given circumstances the only possible and the only correct system." The editor was pleased that there was no criticism of the system with regard to its fundamental principles, but "the polemics had been directed to its possible evolution." The only misfortune of the session was that it had disclosed a "regrettable antagonism between the provincial courts and the Prosecutor's Office." This was said clearly to be due to three factors: the prosecutors had an audit procedure separate from that of the provincial courts; they were centralized in structure; and the central Office of the Prosecutor was somewhat separated from the administrative work which had been undertaken to establish the provincial courts. In these comments the Commissariat of Justice indicated its continuing displeasure at the independence which the prosecutors were gaining over the courts. Although the prosecutors were structurally within the Commissariat, the prosecutor's status as a separate department, responsible only directly to the Commissar at the top rather than through the usual channels seems to have given prosecutors a feeling of aloofness. This feeling was being strengthened with each succeeding revision of the code, but the Commissariat's officials seem generally to have been unhappy about its existence. Perhaps they foresaw the eventual maturity of the Office of the Prosecutor, when it would be separated from the Commissariat and created as the most powerful agency of law in the land, relegating the Commissariat of Justice to a less prominent position.

Economizing on time had been Vyshinskii's keynote, and the Commissariat set out to reduce the length of the period between sentencing of a criminal and the moment at which all subsequent proceedings would terminate. In a report of activities[144] published two months after the Fifth Congress the time spent on retrial of a case after Supreme Court reversal was disclosed as having been subjected to study. A substantial revision of procedure was proposed. Remanding for new trial was to be eliminated when the Supreme Court of the Republic thought immediate revision of a sentence necessary in view of the facts disclosed in the record of the trial in the provincial court or military tribunal.[145] Revision could only reduce the severity of a sentence, however, and the

---

[144] "Posle s"ezda," *ibid.*, No. 19–20 (May 10–17, 1924), pp. 439, 442.
[145] Code of Criminal Procedure, RSFSR (1923), Art. 437.

reduction might not be less than the minimum allowed by the appropriate article of the Criminal Code.

Further economizing on time was to be effected by eliminating some of the cases that had been coming to the Supreme Court of the Republic for audit. This was to be done by revising the code's procedure permitting transmission of audit made by a provincial court of a people's court's sentence to the Supreme Court for a second audit.[146] Under the proposed revision, the audit of an appellate college of a provincial court, instigated by the protest of a prosecutor, would require no second audit if the court agreed with the prosecutor. Only if there were disagreement would the plenum of the provincial court be called to hear the issues, and only if the disagreement between court and prosecutor persisted would the matter go to the Supreme Court's appellate college for a final audit. By this amendment the provincial court's authority to forward any decision to the Supreme Court for audit was to be replaced in many cases by the mere filing of its decision with the supreme court for its information. Presumably, an overworked Supreme Court could be expected to be content to lay aside the matter without more than a glance if it found agreement on the inferior level of audit between the provincial court and the prosecutor, and, thus, time would be saved.

KURSKII'S PROPOSED AMENDMENTS

Commissar Kurskii published his detailed proposals for amendment of all codes one month prior to the opening of the session of the Central Executive Committee called to consider them. With an introductory explanation, he disclosed the principles governing the changes.[147] They were his old slogans, namely, simplification of legal procedures and widening of the jurisdiction of the people's court as the court nearest to the people.

Simplification of the procedures was to be accomplished by the two measures already announced soon after the Fifth Congress of persons engaged in the administration of justice to eliminate re-

[146] *Ibid.*, Art. 426.
[147] D. I. Kurskii, "Ob"iasnitel'naia zapiska k proektu izmenenii i dopolnenii ugolovno-protsessual'nogo kodeksa RSFSR," *Ezh. sov. iust.*, No. 35–36 (September 9–16, 1924), p. 825.

trials when the only error had been in application of the law to well-established fact and to reduce the number of audits following the termination of the usual appellate procedures. The additional measures of simplification were those proposed by Vyshinskii at the Fifth Congress. The authority of the police to conduct the full investigation in all but the most complex and serious cases was to be expanded [148] and it might even conduct the investigation in serious cases if the investigator saw no reason to intervene. The work of the police as an investigating agency was, however, to be reviewed by the investigators when the police concluded that a case should be dropped.[149] In the original form of the 1923 code it was the prosecutor who had to review the material when the police thought no elements of crime had been uncovered or the guilty persons had not been found. Generally the supervision of the investigatory work of the police which had been placed in the prosecutor by the 1923 text[150] was now to be in the office of the investigators, although supervision of the investigators remained in the prosecutor,[151] who replaced the court as the agency to hear any challenge to the investigator by the person subjected to investigation.[152]

The court was not eliminated completely from review of the investigation, for the proposed amendments included one to eliminate the formerly existing limitation on the authority of the court when it met before trial to determine whether a *prima facie* case had been made out and the case was really ready for trial. Under the 1923 version, the court was denied the right at this stage to look at more than the indictment, for it could not examine the report of the preliminary investigator. In 1924 this limitation on the court was to be removed.[153]

Vyshinskii's restrictions on the right of the accused to tell his story immediately after the reading of the indictment, unless he pleaded guilty, were incorporated in the proposals.[154] Speed was also encouraged in that the court was authorized to verify new evidence introduced for the first time at the trial without return

---

[148] The existing rule was in the Code of Criminal Procedure, RSFSR (1923), Art. 108.

[149] This was permitted by the Code of Criminal Procedure, RSFSR (1923), Art. 105.

[150] *Ibid.*, Art. 107.   [151] *Ibid.*, Art. 118.   [152] *Ibid.*, Art. 122.

[153] *Ibid.*, Art. 263 (note).   [154] *Ibid.*, Art. 280.

of the case to the preliminary investigator for examination.[155] Speed
was at such a premium that it was sought even at the expense of
the rights of the accused in those cases in which the court was
authorized to sentence immediately without hearing the evidence.
Under the 1923 text, the accused on receipt of his sentence had
the right to demand of the court a hearing on the facts.[156] Under
the 1924 revision, he could only appeal. Kurskii thought this innovation a time saver, and explained that the number of crimes
subject to treatment in this summary fashion were to be increased.
They were to be those, however, which were not complicated and
for which imprisonment was not permitted by the Criminal Code.

Expansion of the jurisdiction of the people's court as the court
nearest to the people was to be accomplished by narrowing the
list of crimes set forth in Article 26 as subject to the exclusive
original jurisdiction of the provincial court. Kurskii said he wanted
both to save the time of the higher court for appellate work and
as an administrative center for court work within the province, and
to make the lower court the forum for all offenses relating to the
way of life of the people. The specific offenses so transferred to
the people's court included murder under circumstances of strong
emotion, killing while exceeding appropriate limits of self-defense,
unintentional killing or killing under a suicide pact made with a
minor or one incapable of controlling his acts, deprivation of freedom under conditions dangerous to health or life or causing pain,
theft of cattle, robbery committed with the use of force so long as
the force did not endanger life or health, assumption of authority
reserved to state officials, and opposition to state officials by individuals so long as no force was used.

By his proposals Kurskii sought to achieve some part of his continuing aim of a low-level tribunal manned by local people and at
no great distance from every village as the major agency for
settling disputes in Soviet society. This desire was firmly held by
him, and he had departed from it reluctantly in 1922 under pressure
of those who thought his people's courts ill prepared to understand
the seriousness of major offenses. In 1924 the time seems to have

[155] *Ibid.*, Art. 312.
[156] *Ibid.*, Art. 370.

been ripe for him to reassert his views and present the amendments necessary to effect them.

AMENDMENTS OF 1924

Kurskii's dream of a popular court applying simple procedure was reechoed at the session of the Central Executive Committee of the Russian Republic before whom the drafts were brought in October, 1924.[157] The stage was set for discussion of the eighth item on the agenda when Kurskii rose on October 14 to discuss crime and the work of his courts.[158] He was optimistic that the courts could cope with the enormous volume of cases coming before them if a few amendments were adopted. His figures showed that the year 1924 had begun with 122,000 criminal cases and 85,000 civil cases on the dockets of the people's courts awaiting trial. During the first six months of 1924 the people's courts of 32 provinces had received 441,000 criminal cases and 143,000 civil cases. Each people's judge was hearing 95 cases a month, so that the backlog on June 30 had been 148,000 criminal and 94,000 civil cases.

Analysis of the types of crime suggested measures to reduce the case load on each court. By all odds the most widespread offense was the stealing of wood from state forests, but a close second was the illegal distilling of liquor. Novgorod Province reported that 25 percent of its crimes were thefts of timber, while 26 percent were illegal distilling. Briansk showed 46 percent as thefts of timber and 11 percent illegal distilling. To solve this problem Kurskii suggested that forests must be protected better so that would-be thieves were kept out of them, while the illegal liquor business would have to be cut by eliminating from men's minds the desire to make private profit, which in Kurskii's eyes was a bourgeois approach requiring eradication. From the point of view of judicial reform, all that Kurskii had to suggest was that the presidium of the executive committee in each county and the administrative department of each provincial executive committee be authorized to

---

[157] *RSFSR—VTsIK, XI sozyva, vtoraia sessiia, stenograficheskii otchët* (Moscow, 1924).

[158] *Ibid.*, pp. 325–28.

fine forest thieves so as to relieve the people's courts of some of the burdens placed upon them.

Detailed consideration of the court structure and procedure was left for Professor Ia. Brandenburgskii to develop.[159] He noted that all proposed changes had been discussed both in the judicial organs and in the recently convened Fifth Congress of persons engaged in the administration of justice. He repeated the by now popular refrain, saying, "All these changes have been called forth by the needs of our practical work and are based on the fundamental idea of possible simplification of our court, especially of our court procedure." He was not prepared to suggest that all holes had been plugged, for there was still to be plenty of trouble which he laid not at the door of lack of leadership, for there were many Communist party members in the courts, but to the existence of too great an abundance of procedural rules for a judiciary composed 80 percent of workers and peasants.

An apology preceded the presentation of detail, for Brandenburgskii was not about to propose the extensive simplification he advocated. He said frankly: "The great task presented to us is to simplify our court procedure, and that means simplifying the rules which must be observed in conducting a court trial. This work, unfortunately, at the present moment is not yet presented to the session of the All-Russian Central Executive Committee." Still, he continued to hold out hope for the future in adding, "Without any doubt, you may be confident of it, it will be prepared for the next session." History proved him wrong, for no change of a radical nature in the direction of simplification was to be made in the Russian Republic's code during Stalin's lifetime, except for trials of terrorists,[160] and of counterrevolutionary "wreckers and diversionists," [161] to which attention will be directed at the end of this

---

[159] *Ibid.*, pp. 332–40.

[160] Decree on the Introduction of Changes into the Existing Codes of Criminal Procedure of the Union Republics, December 1, 1934, [1934] I *Sob. Zak. SSSR*, No. 64, item 459. This was incorporated in the Code of Criminal Procedure, RSFSR, by decree of December 10, 1934, [1935] I *Sob. Uzak. RSFSR*, No. 2, item 8.

[161] Decree on Introducing Changes into the Existing Codes of Criminal Procedure of the Union Republics, September 14, 1937, [1937] I *Sob. Zak. SSSR*, No. 61, item 266. This was incorporated in the Code of Criminal Procedure, RSFSR, by decree of February 2, 1938, [1938] I *Sob. Uzak. RSFSR*, No. 3, item 38.

chapter. What simplification occurred, in a general way, came only when codes were enacted in the new Central Asian republics, as will be indicated subsequently in this study, and even this simplification had to be repudiated soon after as the cause of confusion.

Having restated the government's constantly expressed desire for simplification, Brandenburgskii turned to the jurisdiction of courts and repeated what had been said at the Fifth Congress in March, namely, that the burden on the provincial courts must be reduced and the authority of the people's courts enhanced. This could be done by listing more crimes over which the people's courts would have original jurisdiction. He then suggested that other matters could be left for consideration in committee.

The committee brought in its recommendations on October 16.[162] In Kurskii's words the changes recommended by the Commissariat of Justice had all been accepted. Brandenburgskii revealed that the committee had asked the Presidium of the Central Executive Committee to work out a draft for further expansion of the jurisdiction of the people's courts.[163] This was a renewed plea for popularization of the courts so that the provincial courts would not be the place of trial for so many types of cases. A second revelation was that the note excluding the G.P.U. from the operation of the general rules of the Code of Criminal Procedure had been proposed not by the Commissariat but by the majority of the committee's members.[164] In this comment the Commissariat again showed itself to be on the side of restraint over the security police, while the politicians on the Central Executive Committee were still consumed with fear lest power be snatched from them by an artful band of plotters. For them observance of criminal procedure was all right so long as it was not permitted to threaten their positions. They seemed to be drawing a distinction between murder, rape, and bodily injury on the one hand and political intrigue on the other. The Commissariat officials probably also drew the same distinction, but they knew because of their legal education that their drafts had provided enough opportunities to permit a prosecutor and judge to catch the political dissenter without having to give a security police *carte blanche*. They may also, because of their edu-

---

[162] *RSFSR—VTsIK, XI sozyva, vtoraia sessiia*, p. 429.
[163] *Ibid.*, p. 438.   [164] *Ibid.*

cation, have been influenced in some measure by their recollections of the history of the French Revolution from which the conclusion could be drawn that danger lurks in the shadows even for the leaders of a revolution as it feeds on forces driven by passion and equipped with power over which there is no control.

The debate over the committee's proposals presented one of the increasingly rare opportunities to see a victory for the Commissariat moderates over the fearful politicians.[165] The issue was brought forward by the committee's recommendation that there be no appeal from court orders made during the trial, but rather that they be subject to revocation only if found on audit, that is, when the higher court on its own initiative or the initiative of a prosecutor was moved to examine the record of a case. A deputy rose to disclose that there had been sharp division in the committee on this point. Emboldened by this intervention Brandenburgskii let it be known that he personally favored the right of appeal to the provincial courts against court orders of this nature, and that his view was that of the government, although as reporter for the committee he had found it necessary to report a contrary view. The matter was put to a vote on the floor and Brandenburgskii's position was sustained, and the amendment to Article 370 made accordingly. The draft contained in the report was then adopted as law.[166]

In reporting on the work of the session to its employees, the Commissariat of Justice published in its journal Brandenburgskii's summary.[167] After noting that all had gone as recommended by the Commissariat, except for the addition of the note exempting the G.P.U. from the provisions of the Code of Criminal Procedure,[168] he disclosed that the deputies had chosen the opportunity to adopt three resolutions on policy and to ask that these serve as guides for the preparation of future amendments. First, the deputies spoke in favor of broadening by degrees the jurisdiction of the people's courts. Second, they favored terminating before trial unimportant violations of law out of a desire to save time and trouble for the

---

[165] *Ibid.*, pp. 440–41.

[166] Law on Additions to and Changes in the Code of Criminal Procedure, RSFSR, October 16, 1924, [1924] I *Sob. Uzak. RSFSR*, No. 78, item 784.

[167] Brandenburgskii, "Sudebnye voprosy na 2–i sessii VTsIK, XI sozyva," *Ezh. sov. iust.*, No. 39–40 (October 9–16, 1924), pp. 919–20.

[168] Code of Criminal Procedure, RSFSR (1923), Art. 107 (note).

state agencies. Third, they ordered that there be no release before trial of persons deemed to be especially socially dangerous, and in particular horse thieves. He indicated that the peasant deputies had forced adoption of the third resolution because they felt that the public would lose confidence in the law enforcing agencies if a horse thief were released after arrest under existing provisions of the code solely because there was no reason to fear that he would flee the jurisdiction.

Not until 1925 were the two latter recommendations put into effect, the horse-thief exception in February,[169] and the *de minimis* rule in May.[170] At the May session of the Central Executive Committee, which lasted but two days, the government spokesman seems to have found it necessary to remind his listeners that the initiator of the amendments to the codes was likely to be the Presidium of the Central Executive Committee, but he put it in palatable form by saying, "You know that changes in the codes, in accordance with our law, can be made only by sessions of the All-Russian C.E.C., but the law permits the Presidium in the intervals between sessions to introduce in the event of extreme necessity corresponding changes in our codes." [171]

There may have been some who wondered how the measure of extreme necessity was to be determined, especially when they looked at what was offered. It was the action of the Presidium amending the code to provide for arrest of persons even when there was no fear that they flee the jurisdiction. It had undoubtedly been initiated by the resolution of the preceding session on horse thieves, but it went much further to list a large number of articles of the Criminal Code, for violation of which a person might be arrested on order of the investigator without the necessity of finding that flight was to be anticipated. In the explanation of the government spokesman these were the serious crimes, commission of which made of an individual such a social danger that he could

---

[169] Decree Amending Art. 158 of the Code of Criminal Procedure, February 23, 1925, [1925] I *Sob. Uzak. RSFSR*, No. 13, item 94. Further amended, July 6, 1925, *ibid.*, No. 49, item 372.

[170] Order on Additions to and Changes in the Code of Criminal Procedure, RSFSR, May 5, 1925, amending Art. 4a, *ibid.*, No. 29, item 217.

[171] *RSFSR—VTsIK, XI sozyva, tret'ia sessiia; Stenograficheskii otchët* (Moscow, 1925), p. 5.

not be left at large awaiting conclusion of the preliminary investigation even though he could not flee.[172] An outsider can understand the possible danger, yet if it had gone for nearly two years without causing concern except for horse thieves, it is hard to see why it could not have waited for resolution until the regular sitting of the Central Executive Committee in May. The *de minimis* rule had been held over, yet it was a much less controversial issue on which the Presidium might have acted on the basis of the resolution adopted at the October session of the Central Executive Committee. Perhaps this action may be taken as evidence that the Presidium was beginning to build up its reputation as the principal actor in the legislative process, while its parent body was becoming more of a mass gathering at which accomplished facts were presented for ratification, leaving only very broad issues for debate.

FEDERAL PRINCIPLES OF CRIMINAL PROCEDURE

When federation had been accomplished in 1923, it had been designed to influence criminal procedure as well as other aspects of the legal system. Under the first federal constitution the four constituent republics had conferred upon the federal government the right "to establish the fundamentals of structure of the judicial agencies and of judicial procedure."[173] A committee had been ordered established by resolution adopted on Kurskii's motion at the meeting of the federal government's Central Executive Committee in November, 1923.[174] Composed of two representatives to be named by the Presidium of the Central Executive Committee of each republic, it had to prepare and present a draft to the Presidium of the federal government's Central Executive Committee for enactment by the full Central Executive Committee at its next session. This time schedule was not met, for the draft came before the Central Executive Committee only at its sessions of October, 1924.[175]

---

[172] *Ibid.*, p. 10.

[173] Art. 1 (o), Constitution of the USSR, [1923] I *Sob. Uzak. RSFSR*, No. 81, item 782.

[174] *SSSR—Tret'ia sessiia Tsentral'nogo Ispolnitel'nogo Komiteta Soiuza sovetskikh sotsialisticheskikh respublik; Stenograficheskii otchёt* (Moscow, 1924), pp. 67–68.

[175] *SSSR—2 sessiia, II sozyv—TsIK Soiuza sovetskikh sotsialisticheskikh respublik; Stenograficheskii otchёt* (Moscow, 1924).

The government's spokesman, Vinokurov, opened his report with reassurance to his listeners that one fundamental principle had been followed, namely that the courts of the federation were to be class courts, and he quoted Lenin to the effect that "the court is an organ of authority of the proletariat and of the poorest peasantry." [176] He showed that this rule had long since been put into practice, for the statistics on the courts in the Russian Republic showed that 87 percent of the people's judges were of worker or peasant social origin; 61 percent of the preliminary investigators were of similar origin; and 72 percent of the judges in the provincial courts were likewise. They were subject to strong party leadership, for 75 percent of the people's judges were members of the Communist party, while 80 percent of the provincial judges were members of the party.[177]

The similarity between the codes of criminal procedure of the various republics was found "to give the opportunity to draw from them a number of 'propositions' of all-union importance." [178] Vinokurov found this uniformity no surprise since the codes reflected the class structure of society. He thought the phenomenon no different than that created by the copying of the French Code Napoléon by other countries having bourgeois social structure.[179] In this he footnoted the Marxist theory of law and chose to ignore the fact that a principal reason for similarity was the common leadership of all republics by members of the Communist party which recognized no ethnic boundaries and which had been working since the founding of the several Soviet states for unification of policy.

The federal principles were to be essentially those of the existing codes, except for a few changes, one being the requirement that detention of a suspect be limited to two months, with an additional month on approval of the prosecutor.[180] This limit was said not to be found throughout all codes, and was being inserted in the federal fundamental principles "so that prisons will not be overloaded and so that cases will not become pickled." The arguments of some who had proposed limits at the time of adoption of the Russian code, based upon a more liberal concept of personal rights,

[176] *Ibid.*, p. 197.   [177] *Ibid.*, p. 199.   [178] *Ibid.*, p. 207.   [179] *Ibid.*, p. 198.
[180] *Ibid.*, p. 209.

seem in this passage to have been replaced by an argument based upon physical capacity of prisons and the inefficiency of effective prosecution of cases long dormant. A further change suggested by the federal principles was the elimination of release on money bail to be replaced by release from detention only on the undertaking of workers' or peasants' organizations that an accused would appear for his trial if released during the period of waiting. To permit money to enter this situation was in the government's view to open the door to the rich "Nepmen" to avoid detention in jail.

Other features of the general principles were to coordinate the judicial systems of the various republics by providing the rule that sentences in one republic were to be compulsory in all others and by providing a principle to be applied in the event of conflict of procedural rules between republics.[181]

Debate on these proposals took an unexpected turn. Protests were not registered against the details but rather against the principle of federal adoption of fundamentals. Krylenko rose after the government's speech to initiate a violent attack upon it as violating the federal constitution.[182] Waving a copy of a Communist party resolution calling for respect of the republics, he declared that he now saw centralization occurring at the expense of the republics. He noted that already the status of the advocates and of the notaries had been established by federal law. He proposed reworking to the very roots the general principles appearing in the government's draft. He was followed by a vigorous speech in support of the draft by Antonov-Saratovskii,[183] but when the latter sat down, one Reikhel rose to criticize the draft as being not just basic principles but "fundamentals plus eleven legislative acts or series of them . . . plus all that the Union sees fit." [184] Kurskii followed to show himself a centralizer by saying that he had always been for unification of principles, and he had wanted the general principles to become the general parts of each republic's code to be followed by a special part in which much would be established by the federal government.[185]

The debate waxed so hot that the presiding officer, Mikhail Kalinin, exercised his prerogative to intervene with some of his

---

[181] *Ibid.*, p. 213.   [182] *Ibid.*, pp. 406–14.   [183] *Ibid.*, p. 414.
[184] *Ibid.*, p. 421.   [185] *Ibid.*, p. 422.

simple peasant wit. He declared: "Seven jurists have spoken from the tribune and these jurists have led us into such a jungle that I warrant no one has understood anything of the argument." [186] To this statement the record shows "applause." Not all had been fooled, for the same Larin who had been the thorn in Krylenko's side on previous occasions rose to say that although not a jurist he knew what had been going on, for the matter was a political one, and he was a man of politics. He found the issue to be a simple one, namely how strong should the federal government be?

Although the debate continued, it was at last brought to a close by a cryptic statement disclosing the attitude of the federal government to the federal-republic relationship created by the 1923 constitution. Vinokurov said simply:

Once you have created the Union, you have created unity; it must be defended. It is impossible, we cannot permit that there be established foreign trade while judicial procedure is achieved completely independently without the influence of that foreign trade. For law always protects material interests. To say otherwise is to stand on a purely idealistic point of view. . . . The question is only whether it is needed or not needed; expedient or not expedient. But it is said that there is a violation of the Constitution. This is to speak nonsense. In the Constitution it is not forbidden to work out fundamentals, and these fundamentals we can understand broadly or narrowly.[187]

In short, the constitutional relationship between the federal and republic governments was to be whatever the federal legislature said it was. Perhaps Vinokurov thought that it was enough that one of the chambers of the Central Executive Committee had been organized to provide equal representation to each of the republics. Certainly there was no judicial review of the constitutionality of laws to which Krylenko could appeal.

After Vinokurov's final speech the issue was put before each chamber of the bicameral Central Executive Committee separately to be adopted without further comment, although the matter was referred to committees of each chamber for editing. This took more time than had been expected, for at the final sitting of the deputies Krylenko as spokesman for the committees could only say that there had been a division of opinion on criminal procedure between committees of the two chambers, and he would have to

[186] *Ibid.*, p. 428.   [187] *Ibid.*, p. 461.

ask the deputies, since they had confidence in the conciliation commission which settled disputes between the two chambers, to authorize the Presidium of the Central Executive Committee to approve the text as it would issue from that conciliation commission without reference back to both chambers for ratification. His proposal was accepted, so that the final act approving the fundamental principles was adopted only after the deputies had gone home. The Presidium placed its approval upon the law on October 31, 1924.[188]

Thirty-two articles comprised the federal law.[189] They were a restatement of the fundamentals already underlying the code of the Russian Republic, except for one point on which the government had dwelt, namely the fixing of the maximum term for detention. The other point emphasized—the abolition of money as bail—seems to have been lost in committee. Because of the close parallel between the Republic codes and the federal government's principles, no wave of sweeping amendments followed in each of the republics. Criminal procedure had become essentially fixed in form, to remain until 1958 with no critical changes from the federal government, except for those of 1934 and 1937 simplifying procedure in trials of terrorists and counterrevolutionary "diversionists and wreckers," to be discussed below with reference to Stalin's influence on the law.

Summarizing the federal principles of 1924, a Soviet historian[190] has selected twelve points for attention: (1) criminal proceedings shall be initiated by the prosecutor, court agencies, and organs of investigation and of the police; (2) investigatory proceedings shall be under the supervision of the prosecutor; (3) inviolability of the person shall be protected by the supervision of the court and of the prosecutor over the correct application of detention and arrest during investigation; (4) court sessions shall be public; (5) the case shall be heard in the language of the majority of the local

[188] Order Approving Drafts of (1) the Fundamental Principles of Criminal Legislation of the USSR and of the Union Republics; and (2) Fundamental Principles of Criminal Procedure of the USSR and of the Union Republics and (3) Statute on Military Crimes, October 31, 1924, [1924] I *Sob. Zak. SSSR*, No. 24, item 204.

[189] The Fundamental Principles of Criminal Procedure of the USSR and of Union Republics, October 31, 1924, *ibid.*, item 206.

[190] M. A. Chel'tsov, *Ugolovnyi protsess* (Moscow, 1948), p. 158.

population with protection of the interests of orality of the court and of the rights of the accused; (6) the accusation shall be sustained by the prosecutor and by representatives of social organizations; (7) the accused shall have broad rights to defense in the court investigation; (8) the court investigation shall be based on direct evidence; (9) the evidence shall be evaluated by the court on the basis of his inner conviction without regard to any formal rules of proof; (10) there shall be cassational-revision procedure for the review of sentences without verification of facts established by the court of first instance; (11) increasing of the penalty shall be prohibited on second examination of the case unless the sentence was protested by the prosecutor on grounds of its lack of severity; (12) review of the sentence through an audit procedure shall be permitted for reasons of substantial violation of the forms of judicial procedure or of substantive law.

The primary event closing the formative years of Soviet criminal procedure was this adoption of the federally established fundamentals, based upon the experience of the Russian Republic. Powerful forces seemed at the time to be giving lip service to simplification, but it had not occurred. The Central Executive Committee of the Russian Republic had resolved that efforts be made to simplify, but nothing had followed. One plaintive cry of criticism was raised at the end of 1924, when Professor A. Estrin complained that the Central Executive Committee "had far from solved the problem of creating the most economic procedure" in its resolutions of 1924.[191] They remained but pious expressions of desire.

Not until 1929 was there an indication that the codifiers had been experimenting in their studies with a simplification of the procedural code. Organization of a new republic provided the opportunity to work on a *tabula rasa*. The Uzbek code which appeared at that time was greatly reduced in length, from the 465 articles of the Russian Republic's model to 175 articles.[192] Later the creation of another new republic, the Turkmen, provided a second opportunity to simplify, and the codifiers achieved the

[191] A. Estrin, "Kak uluchit' i uprostit' nash ugolovnyi protsess," *Ezh. sov. iust.*, No. 49 (December 19, 1924), pp. 1177–78.

[192] Adopted by decree No. 133, June 29, 1929, [1929] *Sobranie Uzakonenii i Rasporiazhenii Raboche-Krest'ianskogo Pravitel'stva Uz. SSR*, No. 24, item 95. A Russian translation of the text with amendments to 1957 appears in Karev, *Ugolovno-protsessual'noe zakonodatel'stvo*, pp. 192–214.

adoption of a similarly simplified code of 180 articles.[193] The triumph of the simplifiers came in 1935 with the adoption of the shortest code of all, that of the Tadzhik Republic, with only 154 articles,[194] but it was triumph before capitulation, for at that very moment the tide began to run against the simplifiers.

Estrin and those with whom he associated were denounced for their efforts to weaken Soviet criminal law and procedure.[195] In 1937 they disappeared from their posts at the time of the purges of Stalin's enemies. An introductory comment to the official 1938 republication of the Turkmen code declared that the inadequacies of the code arose "principally from its excessive shortness, explained by the fact that there had been removed from its text everything that had formerly been considered 'procedural technicality.'"[196] It was later claimed that because of the shortness of their codes the authorities in the republics which had served as the experiment in simplicity had been forced to refer frequently to the code of the Russian Republic for aid in solving procedural problems.[197] The Russian Republic's code of 1923 became, therefore, a model with the equivalent of the force of law even in those republics which had departed radically from it in an effort to turn back the clock to something approaching the simplicity of the first years of Soviet judicial activity before the introduction of complexity in the codifying process of 1922 and 1923. The death knell had been sounded for simplicity.

To this conclusion of the campaign for simplicity there was one crucial exception, namely that for the political trial. Under 1934 amendment, adopted at the time of the assassination of the secretary of the Leningrad Communist party's Executive Committee, and 1937 amendment, adopted at the height of Stalin's purges, many

[193] Adopted September 11, 1932. For Russian translation of text with amendments to 1957, see *ibid.*, pp. 369–96.
[194] Adopted August 15, 1935. For Russian translation of text with amendments to 1957, see *ibid.*, pp. 310–24.
[195] For selections from authors denouncing the simplifiers for their conception of the withering away of the state, see *Soviet Legal Philosophy*, translated by Hugh W. Babb, with introduction by John N. Hazard (Cambridge, Mass., 1953). Detail on matters of criminal law are given in John N. Hazard, "Reforming Soviet Criminal Law," *Journal of Criminal Law and Criminology* (Chicago, 1938), Vol. 24, pp. 157–69.
[196] Quoted in *40 let sovetskogo prava* (Leningrad, 1957), I, 608.
[197] *Ibid.*

of the procedural protections established in 1923 were withdrawn for those indicted for terrorist acts and as counterrevolutionary "diversionists and wreckers." [198] Terrorists could have no attorney at the trial, and no appeal thereafter. They could not even demand to be present. Counterrevolutionaries received their indictment twenty-four hours before trial, could not appeal, and were to be executed immediately if their plea for mercy were denied. In short, the Code of Criminal procedure was waived in such cases in a gesture of maximum simplification and return to utter primitiveness.

Not until Stalin's death did the proponents of orderly proceedings find it possible to reassert their point of view, aided in all probability by a world public opinion and a domestic public opinion enraged by the excesses of the Stalin regime. The police were curbed in a decree abolishing the special boards of the Ministry of the Interior,[199] which had previously had the power to exile for periods of up to five years persons deemed to be "socially dangerous," and without observance of any published procedural requirements.[200] In 1956 a federal decree[201] removed from the Code of Criminal Procedure the 1934 and 1937 amendments. Thereafter, there was no legal way of avoiding the requirements of the code. Complexity of procedural detail was again the rule not only for the cases arising from the usual social tensions but also for the cases based upon politically inspired violence against state officials and general politically inspired unrest.

[198] Citations, *supra,* footnotes 160 and 161.

[199] The decree has not been published but it has been identified in an unsigned editorial in the law review of the Institute of Law of the Academy of Sciences USSR as having been promulgated in 1953. See "Za povyshenie roli pravovoi nauki v kodifikatsii sovetskogo zakonodatel'stva," *Sov. gos. i pravo,* No. 1 (1956), p. 3. The importance of this abolition is commented upon by Harold J. Berman, "Law Reform in the Soviet Union," *American Slavic and East European Review,* XV (1956), 183–85.

[200] Decree on Special Boards in the People's Commissariat of Internal Affairs of the USSR, November 5, 1934, [1935] I *Sob. Zak. SSSR,* No. 11, item 84.

[201] Decree on the Abrogation of the Order of the Presidium of the CEC, USSR, of December 1, 1934, "On the Procedure for Conducting Cases Concerning the Preparation or Commission Terrorist Acts" and the orders of the CEC, USSR, of December 1, 1934, and September 14, 1937, "On Introducing Changes into the Existing Codes of Criminal Procedure of the Union Republics," April 19, 1956, [1956] *Vedomosti Verknovnogo Soveta SSSR,* No. 9 (851), item 193.

Chapter 11

CIVIL PROCEDURE
CAPS THE CLIMAX

FEAR of a renascent bourgeoisie consumed the codifiers as they turned to preparation of a Code of Civil Procedure. The New Economic Policy introduced by Lenin to restore the war-ravaged economy compelled amplification of procedural opportunities to settle civil disputes, but it also opened the door in Soviet eyes to the domination of the proletariat by private producers and tradesmen. Stabilization of law to foster private commerce and industry seemed inescapable, but stability created dangers in the eyes of the politicians. Both in the discussion at the time of publication of the draft Code of Civil Procedure and in the government's presentation of the draft to the Russian Republic's Central Executive Committee for enactment the first item of concern was protection against abuse of civil procedure by the new bourgeoisie.

The danger inherent in stability of law and departure from the flexibility of the earliest years had already been recognized by the codifiers in creating the Office of Prosecutor. This office had been conceived as that of a watchman destined to make certain that the bourgeoisie remained in its place. The same danger had inspired the draftsmen of the Civil Code[1] as they toiled simultaneously with the procedural experts. In its initial article the Civil Code was to provide that "Civil rights shall be protected by law, except in instances when they are exercised contrary to their socio-economic purpose." The procedural draftsmen had to consider the desirability of similar precautions.

[1] Civil Code, RSFSR, October 31, 1922, effective January 1, 1923, [1922] I *Sobranie Uzakonenii i Rasporiazhenii Rabochego i Krest'ianokogo Pravitel'stva RSFSR*, No. 71, item 904. The civil codes of all union republics are published with amendments to 1957 in I. B. Novitskii, ed., *Grazhdanskoe zakonodatel'stvo SSSR i soiuznykh respublik* (Moscow, 1957).

The Russian Republic's Commissariat of Justice began to publish chapters of the proposed code in installments in August, 1922, with an editorial note urging readers to submit comments for publication. The editors promised that suggestions would be transmitted to the college of the Commissariat to be considered in a revised draft.[2] For the first time the Ukrainians had influenced the Russians, for they had taken the initiative, with publication of a prior draft, and the Russians are said to have profited by their experimentation.[3] Yet they were not to hold their initial advantage, for the Russians were the first to enact a Code of Civil Procedure, and the Ukrainians fell back to their accustomed place. They announced eventually completion of the work of their drafting committee with "general adoption of the Code of Civil Procedure of the R.S.F.S.R. with a few very unimportant changes having no substantial importance." [4]

PROTECTION AGAINST BOURGEOIS CLEVERNESS

Precautionary measures against the bourgeoisie took a form at the start similar to that initiated in the draft of the Civil Code. The codifiers introduced their procedural draft with Article 2, declaring:

The people's court shall provide defense and protection to legal rights of parties turning to it on condition that in establishing these rights they shall have acted in good faith. This shall be presumed generally in all cases, but the presumption may be rebutted in any given case by evidence submitted by the opponent as well as by all persons interested in the matter.[5]

[2] "Proekt grazhdanskogo protsessual'nogo kodeksa," *Ezhenedel'nik sovetskoi iustitsii*, No. 29–30 (August 10–17, 1922), p. 20. Subsequent installments appeared in Nos. 31–32, 33, 35, 36, 37–38, and 39–40 of that year, and Nos. 1, 2, 4–5, and 7–8 of 1923.

[3] N. I. Avdeenko and M. A. Kabakova, "Grazhdanskoe protsessual'nogo prava," published in *40 let sovetskogo prava* (Leningrad, 1957), I, 653 (footnote 36).

[4] "Raboty soveshchaniia po podgotovke grazhdanskogo protsessual'nogo kodeksa Uk. SSR," *Vestnik sovetskoi iustitsii*, No. 5 (October 1, 1923), p. 136. But compare the less subservient tone of A. Semenova, "Grazhdanskii protsessual'nyi kodeks Ukrainskoi sotsialisticheskoi sovetskoi respubliki," *Ezh. sov. iust.*, No. 41 (October 23, 1924), pp. 972–74. The Ukrainian code had been promulgated on September 3, 1924, to become effective October 1, 1924, [1924] I *Sobranie Uzakonenii i Rasporiazhenii Raboche-Krest'ianskogo Pravitel'stva Ukrainy*, No. 16–17, item 156.

[5] *Ezh. sov. iust.*, No. 29–30 (August 10–17, 1922), pp. 20–21.

Article 3 of the draft declared: "There shall be no defense of rights exercised with the exclusive and obvious intention solely to cause harm to the other party." Article 10 said: "The parties are required to utilize all of the procedural rights belonging to them in good faith. Every misuse and declaration having as its purpose delay or obfuscation of the proceedings shall be excised immediately by the court, and the parties shall be deprived of the right to use these rights in the future." Sanctions were to be provided through an authorization to the court to fine any party found guilty of conducting the case in bad faith or flouting court orders, and the court was authorized even to sentence an offender to the obligation to pay the fine from future wages and to remain at his employment for a given period of time sufficiently long to assure payment.[6]

Introduction of precautionary measures which would have permitted in effect the nullification of the code whenever a judge thought a party to be without clean hands aroused immediate opposition. An author broke into print in the Commissariat's journal within three weeks of publication of the first installment of the draft. He apologized for writing before the whole draft had been disclosed, but he found himself moved by indignation to make immediate comment on the opening articles.[7] He noted that no Code of Civil Procedure in Western Europe had similar provisions in its text, nor had there been such a provision in the tsarist code. He admitted that the German and Swiss Civil Codes had contained provisions requiring that rights be exercised in good faith to be protected, but these provisions were only in the Civil Codes. He thought such precautions had no place in a procedural code, for three reasons: all new codifications should follow a general plan which is logical and the basis for evolution in a given field of law, and for a procedural code there should be nothing but procedural norms; further, since the Civil Code would have such provisions, it was courting disharmony if a similar idea were to be incorporated in the procedural code in a possibly slightly different form; and finally, practice in application of such articles might be other than expected, for judges might go as far as to refuse to accept a suit,

[6] Draft Code of Civil Procedure, RSFSR, Art. 11.
[7] N. Vavin, "K proektu grazhdanskogo protsessual'nogo kodeksa," *ibid.*, No. 33 (September 9, 1922), pp. 9–10.

and this would prevent determination of the facts without which no accurate decision in the matter could be made.

Doubt that the court could determine whether rights were being abused unless a hearing were held motivated a second author to question the wisdom of the proposed Articles 2 and 3. If the articles were to remain, he thought it necessary to provide some manner in which a court might determine what the contested rights were and reestablish those that had been violated.[8]

Lack of clarity in the draft worried a third author, particularly in view of the fact that the code would have to be administered by young Soviet jurists chosen from the workmen and peasants.[9] He began his criticism with Article 10, proposing that it set forth at least the principal procedural rights of the parties to be observed if an exhaustive list could not be included, for the judges were asked to deprive parties of these rights if they misused them, and they should be told what the codifiers had in mind. Further, it was not clear whether the codifiers wanted the parties themselves deprived of the rights or only their representatives, the lawyers. An opposite view followed when an author chose to omit comment on the opening articles because he thought that they gave rise to no doubts as to their meaning, thanks to the fullness with which they were written.[10]

Debate over the Code of Civil Procedure dragged on into 1923, and the draft remained unfinished, to the apparent embarrassment of the Commissariat of Justice. Commissar Kurskii found it necessary to issue an instruction[11] on January 4, 1923, establishing the principal norms of civil procedure to be applied until the code should be published. In its opening section it declared that since the new Civil Code and Judiciary Act adopted by the fourth session of the Central Executive Committee had become effective on

---

[8] Sambur, "Zametki k proektu grazhd. protsessual'nogo kodeksa," *ibid.*, No. 34 (September 16, 1922), p. 15.
[9] A. Krashkevich, "Zametki k proektu grazhdanskogo protsessual'nogo kodeksa," *ibid.*, No. 39–40 (October 27-November 4, 1922), pp. 27–28.
[10] L. Reshetnikov, "Zametki k proektu grazhdanskogo protsessual'nogo kodeksa," *ibid.*, No. 42 (November 18, 1922), p. 17.
[11] Circular No. 4 on the Basic Norms of Civil Procedure, January 4, 1923, [1923] I *Sob. Uzak. RSFSR*, No. 8, item 107 and *Ezh. sov. iust.*, No. 1 (January 9, 1923), pp. 26–29.

January 1, 1923, the commissariat found it necessary to order continued application of the old People's Court Act of 1920, as modified by subsequent circulars, and to continue in force existing tables of court costs and fees. The instruction introduced new rules for jurisdiction made necessary by the coming into being of the court revision, and a skeletal statement of the order of events in the civil proceedings before the court.

Criticism of the draft's precautions against misuse of procedural rights had its effect, for the Commissariat removed from the bill submitted to the Central Executive Committee in June, 1923, most of the criticized articles. Gone were Articles 2 and 3 authorizing courts to protect rights only if exercised in good faith and forbidding protection of rights exercised exclusively and obviously with the intention of causing harm to the other side. Only the first draft's Article 10 remained, requiring that parties exercise their rights in good faith and authorizing courts to excise any document having as its aim delay and obfuscation, but the concluding phrase to which objection had been taken was omitted. The final form of the code no longer authorized the court to deprive an offending party of the right to exercise his rights in the future.

The government spokesman before the Central Executive Committee, Professor Ia. Brandenburgskii, took pains to point out, however, that the new code had the proletariat at heart.[12] He called attention to the fact that the draftsmen had approached with the greatest care the matter of execution of judgments on assets of state agencies and against wages of laborers. The new code was relatively short, containing 317 articles in contrast to five times as many articles in the old prerevolutionary code. Finally, the code made it very clear that the court was to find its law only in decrees and orders of the central and local governmental organs and in the general policy of the workers'-peasants' government.[13] It was not to rely on custom. To have permitted reliance on custom would, in the government's view, have permitted reliance on rules of conduct which had their origin in prerevolutionary circumstances, for five years had been too short a time since the Revolution

[12] Brandenburgskii, in *Vtoraia Sessiia, VTsIK, X sozyva, zasedanie vtoroe,* pp. 38–47.
[13] Code of Civil Procedure, RSFSR, [1923] I *Sob. Uzak. RSFSR,* No. 46–47, item 478, Art. 4.

to give rise to new customs. Prerevolutionary custom had passed into history since the coming into effect of a new social-economic structure. Further, the court must develop existing norms of the code in logical manner by extending the code's principles if it found a gap in the law, and not rely on custom which would bear no relation to the spirit of the new code.

No reference to "revolutionary consciousness" appeared in the new code. Although this concept was praised as having been of great utility when there had been no firm laws, there were not only firm laws in 1923, but there were codes of such laws. No need was recognized to continue the inconvenience which had appeared in the past in practice with the application of the principle of "revolutionary consciousness." The new codes had incorporated within them the best from practice of the period of application of the general principles. Reference to "revolutionary consciousness" was thought less valuable under the new conditions than reference to the general policy of the workers'-peasants' government. A judge, presumably, would look not into his own mind to create a rule that he thought right, as he would have done under the earlier provision, but he would try to fathom the intent of the government.

Whether the Soviet state had a peculiar measure of interest in civil procedure not to be found in bourgeois states seemed hard for Brandenburgskii to clarify. He explained that in all states, whether bourgeois or non-bourgeois, the interest in criminal and civil procedure differed, for in criminal trials the dispute was not over the right to commit an act but only as to whether the act prohibited by the Criminal Code had been committed. In contrast a civil suit put in issue the question of right to act as a party had acted. In a criminal trial in order to establish whether an act had been committed it was necessary to conduct a preliminary investigation, searches, seizures, and arrests. In a civil case no such steps were necessary.

The state's interest in civil proceedings in a bourgeois society was, therefore, limited to making certain that a dispute was settled correctly, but not in all cases would it be concerned. The state would set in motion the procedure of the courts only if one of the parties to the dispute requested it. If a creditor having a debtor's note in his hands wanted "to throw it upon the ground," the state was not concerned. No one was to be required to go to court as a plaintiff unless he wanted to. The Soviet state in Brandenburgskii's view was to follow this much of the usual pattern of state concern. To make this policy clear to all, the final draft declared, "A court shall enter upon the trial of a case only on complaint of a party interested in it." [14]

Yet a Soviet code could not stop there, for the interests of the working class, represented by the Soviet state, seemed to require a corrective to the old familiar rule that the state had no interest unless a party requested a court to hear his complaint. In view of this special interest the draftsmen inserted as a second sentence to follow the familiar rule the right of the prosecutor to begin a case or to intervene at any moment if the protection of the interests of the state or of the toiling masses required. Brandenburgskii explained that the Council of People's Commissars had added this provision to the draft presented by the Commissariat, taking into consideration the conditions in which all were then living. It was quite possible that a party having a right to bring suit might not act because of dependence upon the wrongdoer or for some other reason. In such cases the prosecutor needed to intervene as the representative of state authority.

The conventional relationship between a civil cause of action and criminal prosecution, familiar as it must have been to Soviet lawyers, needed to be stated, apparently, for some years later the Leningrad provincial court found it necessary to set aside a criminal conviction of several members of a cooperative association for failure to pay up their membership subscriptions.[15] The trial court had assumed that since cooperatives were being encouraged as a means of restoring the economy, and were therefore of importance to the state, the delinquent members had committed crimes against the state. For the provincial court their delinquency gave rise only to a right in the other members to bring civil suit against them on their obligations.

The principle that generally the state was interested only if an aggrieved party thought it desirable to seek redress in a court

[14] *Ibid.*, Art. 2.

[15] Case of *Emelian, Ksenofontova, Zakharov, et al.*, Protocol No. 25 (July 17, 1931), *Sudebnaia praktika Verkhovnogo Suda RSFSR*, No. 13 (September 30, 1931), p. 14.

explained, in the government spokesman's view, the reason for the code's general attitude toward events after suit had been started. The plaintiff was left free to increase or decrease the amount he demanded. He could drop the case, but if he did so, he could not reintroduce the case at a later date. This arbitrary exclusion was explained as necessary only to avoid court delays.

Application of the principle that the plaintiff was to determine whether to sue was not, in the government spokesman's view, to be allowed to create a misunderstanding of the role of the judge at the trial of a civil claim. The parties were not to be recognized as operating exclusively within the confines of the principle of adversary procedure. Maintenance of a position for the judge as arbiter of a contest in which the parties presented such evidence as they chose and drew such conclusions as they wished seemed intolerable in the spokesman's view in a workers'-peasants' country. It was a position rejected formally by Decree No. 3 on the courts in July, 1918. The new regime intended to follow the 1918 rule and to depart completely from Article 367 of the tsarist code which had denied to the judge the right on his own initiative to demand that one or another party produce evidence. "We stand in diametric opposition to such a point of view," declared the spokesman.

We require the judge to take an active part in civil procedure. We have structured our procedure in such a way that in all probability we shall meet the most desperate and evil criticism from Western European bourgeois science. We have structured it so that the workers and peasants who turn to a court with whatever civil claim may be confident in advance that they will find in the judge himself defense and protection of their interests.[16]

The participation of the judge in vigorous fashion seemed especially necessary in the spokesman's view because the preponderant majority of cases would be tried in the people's courts and without the help of free legal aid, since the state was not in a position to provide it. Only the judge could give aid in such cases. The draft had been prepared, therefore, with provisions to the effect that when a worker or peasant entered court, the judge would first of all interrogate the plaintiff, would himself plan the presentation of the claim, would himself on his own initiative ask of any agency that

[16] Brandenburgskii, *Vtoraia sessiia, VTsIK*, p. 43.

could give certification of a fact that it provide it, and would himself summon witnesses if that proved to be necessary. Further, he
would tell the plaintiff what evidence was necessary to prove the
claim, he would confront witnesses and take a view of any place
pertinent to an event, and he would name experts and do whatever
else was necessary to evaluate evidence. This would "emphasize the
'keystone of the procedure,' the activity and independence of our
judges."

In concrete terms the freedom of the judge to act as he wished
in clarifying a case was established by the authorization to the
judge to admit whomever he wished as a representative of a party
to a case; to suspend the running of any statutory period of limitation; to summon a defendant for pretrial interrogation if necessary
to establish his poverty or inability to work, and generally to do
everything required to discover the real truth. Only by making
such efforts did the government spokesman think it possible to
keep the court high in the esteem of the people. Determination of
the facts in full was to be preferred over shortening, simplifying,
and reducing the cost of procedure. Only by doing so would it be
possible to keep the parties from turning away from the court to
arbitration to settle their disputes.

The government's assurances that the workers would not be
betrayed by the new Code of Civil Procedure fell on the deaf ears
of one deputy.[17] He rose in his seat to express his fears that the
Nepmen bourgeoisie would misuse the code. He thought that every
deputy must know from his own experience how clever the Nepmen
were in using Soviet laws with great art to protect their own interests and keep the workmen from defending themselves. The
lawyers for the Nepmen were using the law so cleverly that all the
provisions designed to help the workmen were of no avail, and the
courts were tripping up the workers in their own legislation instead
of openly defending the interests of the toilers against the exploiters.
To this critic the government's spokesman had given the impression
that all was well, and that it would become even better if the code
were adopted. On the contrary he thought that the courts, because
of the very nature of their work, would isolate themselves from the
guidance of the Communist party and link themselves more closely

---

[17] Preobrazhenskii, *ibid.*, pp. 47–48.

to the letter of the law. In consequence he thought it especially important that every article of the new code be scrutinized with care so that no article could be read with two meanings.

The Commissariat had sought to forestall such criticism by attaching an explanatory note to the draft presented to the deputies. In that note the draft had been extolled as creating a simple and uncomplicated system, noting the principal stages of the flow of civil procedure and establishing only

those requirements which constitute the foundation of every civil procedure and whose violation inescapably detracts from each court decision, depriving it of the authoritative importance and force necessary to a court decision and at the same time providing the circumstances for court practice in civil matters to mark out the path of further development of Soviet civil procedure, discarding those norms which are recognized as superfluous, and broadly developing those principles which prove themselves to be necessary for the proper work of the court.[18]

This approach and the telling remarks of the government's spokesmen, prepared as they undoubtedly were with the support of the Communist party, seem to have overcome the moving criticism playing upon the emotions that had brought the Revolution to a successful conclusion in 1917. The government's draft was adopted with but changes in detail. Under date of July 10, 1923, the Central Executive Committee enacted the Code of Civil Procedure as law to become effective September 1, 1923.[19] For the first time in Soviet experience civil procedure had been separated from criminal procedure and established in a code of its own. Thus, there was rounded out the new quadrumvirate of codes—criminal and civil, criminal procedural and civil procedural—which together with the Judiciary Act provided the foundation of the Soviet legal system.

THE GENERAL PRINCIPLES
IN THE NEW CODE

The plan of the new Code of Civil Procedure indicated that as with the Code of Criminal Procedure the draftsmen had sought to

[18] A. F. Kleinman, *Grazhdanskii protsess* (2nd ed.; Moscow, 1935), p. 9.

[19] [1923] I *Sob. Uzak. RSFSR*, No. 46–47, item 478. An official list of laws repealed by enactment of the code was published by the Central Executive Committee and Council of People's Commissars under date of November 26, 1923, *Ezh. sov. iust.*, No. 47 (December 6, 1923), p. 1100.

write a handbook which might be followed as the inexperienced judge progressed through the civil trial. Five parts established: (1) general principles including rules regulating representation in court, jurisdiction, fees, fines, limitations of time, and summonses; (2) steps in presenting a suit and in trying it; (3) special proceedings relating to the administration of decedent's estates, enforcement of arbitral awards, deposits, court orders issued in conformity with documents requiring no trial, divorce, release from compulsory military service because of religious conviction, and complaints against the actions of state notaries; (4) appeal and review of decisions; and (5) execution of judgments and decisions.

The general principles, in addition to including the measures discussed at length by the government spokesman on presentation of the draft, namely those designed to protect the proletariat from artful bourgeois lawyers[20] and to assure application of proper state policy to a dispute,[21] established a general rule of conflicts of law providing that the law of the place of contracting or of the commission of an act should govern unless the Russian Republic had a treaty providing for some contrary solution with the jurisdiction involved.[22] If foreign law needed to be proved, the court might ask the People's Commissariat of Foreign Affairs to communicate with the government concerned for an opinion on the matter.[23] The language of the court was to be that of the majority of persons living at its seat, and interpreters were to be provided when necessary.[24] Civil suits for damages arising out of injury caused in the commission of a crime might be presented if they had not already been decided during the criminal trial.[25] All parties had the right to inspect originals of any documents in the case and to make notes and obtain copies on payment of the tax and costs.[26]

Representation in court was introduced by an article authorizing the court to summon the prosecutor if he seemed necessary.[27] The plaintiff and defendant were authorized to present their case personally or through a representative, unless they had been declared incompetent or were limited by law in their competence, in which case only a representative could appear.[28] "Collectives"—that is, state agencies, corporations, partnerships, cooperatives, and other

---

[20] Code of Civil Procedure, RSFSR, Arts. 5, 6.
[21] Arts. 3, 4.   [22] Art. 7.   [23] Art. 8.   [24] Art. 9.   [25] Art. 10.
[26] Art. 11.   [27] Art. 12.   [28] Art. 13.

associations—acted as plaintiffs or defendants through their duly constituted organs.[29] Representatives might be any person selected voluntarily by a party, or those named by law for the incompetent.[30] Choice was not limited to members of the bar, but could be extended to officials of a trade union to which a party belonged, officials of a collective group, or any person admitted by the court for the purpose.[31] Through this provision the hostility of Soviet policy makers to creation of a monopoly of representation for the bar, a hostility which has already been discussed in detail, was evidenced, although it did not take the form of giving the court complete freedom in its admission of representatives, for one had to be at least eighteen, without limitation of rights by court sentence, without a record of having been expelled from a college of advocates, and not a judge, investigator, or prosecutor except in cases where the latter was brought into the case in accordance with the code's provisions.[32] A representative had to be provided with a power of attorney by his principal, setting forth his authority.[33]

Jurisdictional articles established the people's court, as has already been indicated, as the primary court for civil suits,[34] but created in the provincial court jurisdiction over suits exceeding 500 gold rubles in amount or brought against a state organ or official for improper administrative acts, or against county executive committees or city soviets, or arising out of a partnership agreement, or copyright, patent, or trademark.[35] The Republic's Supreme Court, through its College for Civil Cases, was made competent to try cases brought against a people's commissariat, or a central office comparable to a commissariat, or against a provincial executive committee as a whole, although the college might transfer the case or a category of such cases for trial to a provincial court, selected with regard to the domicile of the parties or other circumstances.[36]

The domicile of the defendant or his place of permanent work established jurisdiction for suit,[37] and if this was not known, suit might be brought at his last-known place of residence or the situs of the property.[38] If a dispute arose out of the performance of a contract, suit might be brought at the locus of performance,[39]

[29] Art. 14.   [30] Art. 15.   [31] Art. 16.   [32] Art. 20.   [33] Arts. 17, 18, 19.
[34] Art. 21.   [35] Art. 23.   [36] Art. 24.   [37] Art. 25.   [38] Art. 26.
[39] Art. 28.

while those relating to the use of the land, or to sale of property in satisfaction of a judgment, or to inheritance were to be brought at the situs of the property.[40] If there were alternatives, the choice of jurisdiction was left to the plaintiff.[41]

Disputes over jurisdiction between courts were as unpopular in civil cases with the draftsmen as they had been in criminal cases, with the result that the code forbade them.[42] A court finding that it was without jurisdiction in a given case returned the complaint to the complainant with its opinion on proper jurisdiction so that the matter might be presented to the appropriate court.[43] If the party objected, he might appeal the rejection of jurisdiction to the provincial court.[44]

Money matters were then put before the judge as he turned the pages of the new code. Costs to a plaintiff were established in four categories: (1) a court tax, (2) a stamp tax, (3) a chancery tax, and (4) expenses in conducting the case.[45] Every claimant and counterclaimant paid a tax in the first category as a percentage of the amount of the claim (1 percent on claims from 10 to 50 gold rubles, 2 percent on claims from 50 to 500 gold rubles, and 3 percent on claims in greater amount). Claims of less than 10 rubles and those having no money value were excused from tax. Appeals were to be charged at one half the rate set for initiating suit.[46]

The basis for computation was the amount of the claim or counterclaim as given by the party introducing it,[47] although the court might intervene to define the amount if the figure set by the interested party was clearly out of keeping with the real amount sought.[48] In maintenance cases the claim was arbitrarily fixed as the total of the payments sought for one year, except when the claim was for indefinite payments or for life, in which case the total for three years was used for tax purposes. If the amount could not be determined before trial, the court was to set an arbitrary figure, not less than 10 rubles, and to fix the correct amount later when the trial indicated the sum claimed.[49] If the claim was reduced in amount, no refund was to be made, but if it was increased, an additional tax was levied.[50]

[40] Art. 29.   [41] Art. 30.   [42] Art. 33.   [43] Art. 31.   [44] Art. 32.
[45] Art. 34.   [46] Art. 35.   [47] Art. 36.   [48] Art. 37.   [49] Art. 38.
[50] Art. 39.

The stamp tax was not fixed by the code, but was to be charged at whatever rate might be set from time to time by special statute.[51] The chancery tax was levied on all copies, papers, written evidence, and other documents filed in the case at the rate of 10 gold kopeks per page.[52] Expenses incurred in conducting the case were to include the cost of witnesses, which was set at their regular wage for the time spent in court, and if they requested it, they might also receive compensation for the full time they were away from work at the average rate of wage in the given locality plus transportation to and from the court.[53] Fees for experts were to be fixed by the court at the time of summons.[54]

There were favored parties excused from the payment of all four categories of expense—namely, state organs and enterprises excused from payment of production taxes, plaintiffs claiming wages or maintenance, and toilers recognized by the trial court as having insufficient resources to pay the taxes.[55]

Funds necessary to bring the parties, witnesses, and experts to court as well as to pay the costs of any court travel required to survey the circumstances of the cause of action were payable in advance by the party requesting the appearance or the travel.[56] If initiated by the court in performance of its duty to see that no stone was left unturned, both parties were required to pay the cost in equal shares. At the end of the case, the loser paid costs of conducting the case including the court tax in proportion to the extent to which the claim was satisfied against him.[57] Thus, a defendant who successfully resisted all or part of the claim would recover from the plaintiff the percentage of his costs proportional to the extent of his victory. Such costs to be recovered included costs of representation by an attorney or other agent in an amount of 5 percent of the judgment or, in the defendant's case, of the amount he was not required to pay to the plaintiff. Costs incurred by the court in investigation of the facts on its own initiative by calling witnesses and experts were charged to the parties in proportion to the part of the complaint satisfied against them.[58] Appeals against rulings of the court on the amount of fees might be taken during a seven-day period after the determination.[59]

[51] Art. 40.   [52] Art. 41.   [53] Art. 42.   [54] Art. 44.   [55] Art. 43.
[56] Art. 45.   [57] Art. 46.   [58] Art. 47.   [59] Arts. 48 and 249.

The court was fortified in its power to require the presence of witnesses or the parties by power to fine them in an amount of from 3 to 10 rubles, depending upon their wealth, and, if they repeated, by compelling them to appear in the company of the police and by a fine of double the amount.[60] If they refused to testify on appearance for reasons found unsatisfactory by the court, they might be fined from 10 to 50 gold rubles.[61] Persons in possession of documents found necessary to the case by the court were to be fined from 10 to 50 gold rubles for refusal to produce them even if they were not parties to the case.[62] The draftsmen of the code in these articles rejected the request of a commentator who had proposed in the discussion period that guidance be given as to what were unsatisfactory reasons for failure to testify.[63] He thought that without at least some examples set by the code, a wide variety would occur in practice. The draftsmen seem to have been prepared to take their chances.

Periods set as limitations on actions were defined in familiar terms so as to exclude a holiday if a term expired on such a day,[64] to provide that date of mailing was conclusive in meeting the requirement of the period,[65] and to provide that documents received after the running of the prescriptive period were not to be examined.[66] If the code set no specific period, the court might set one,[67] although in such case it could be extended by the court at the request of a party if this seemed desirable.[68]

Summonses had to be sent by registered mail with return receipt requested, or by messenger, police officer, or the appropriate village executive committee.[69] If none of these methods were available, it might be given to one of the litigants for delivery. Delivery of summons outside the country was to be entrusted to the People's Commissariat of Foreign Affairs.[70] A summons had to contain the name of the court, the place and time to appear, the names of the parties and identification of the matter concerned, a request that all evidence in the matter be presented, and a statement of the penalties for failure to appear.[71] To assure that the summons was

---

[60] Arts. 49 and 51.   [61] Art. 50.   [62] Art. 52.
[63] Reshetnikov, "Zametki," p. 17.
[64] Code of Civil Procedure, RSFSR, Art. 57.
[65] Art. 59.   [66] Art. 65.   [67] Art. 53.   [68] Art. 61.   [69] Art. 66.
[70] Art. 67.   [71] Art. 68.

actually served, the process server had to return to the court to inform the court personally of the service and to present a receipt signed by the receiver of the summons with a notation of the time of service.[72] In the event that the process server was himself a litigant in the case, the signature of the recipient of the summons had to be verified by the local police office, or by the house administration or office in which the recipient lived or had his permanent place of work. A summons might also be left with relatives or a house administration or office if the person summoned was not available to the server,[73] and if any refused to accept it, the server was to notify the court on his return.[74] If the actual place of residence was unknown, the court might set the case for trial on receipt of a note from the housing administration of his last known place of residence that it had received the summons.[75]

PRESENTATION OF A CLAIM
AND THE TRIAL

The general principles in the first part of the code provided the worker-peasant judge with background thought to be necessary to apply the detailed rules that were to follow in the second part of the code devoted to the trial. The general principles occupied 74 articles. The provisions for the trial were to require 116 more, constituting the heart of the code. Here were to be found instructions for each succeeding step required of the judge.

Emphasis was placed upon documents, the court being directed to begin examination of a civil case only if there was a written complaint. Recognition of the fact of illiteracy and lack of understanding of the law made necessary, however, acceptance also of an oral complaint in the people's court[76] to be prepared in written form subsequently by the judge or court secretary and signed by the judge and complainant.[77] A complaint had to be informative, setting forth the precise name of the plaintiff, and of his agent if the latter was to appear, the full name of the defendant, the permanent place of work and the residence of both plaintiff and defendant, the circumstances on which the complaint was founded,

[72] Art. 69.   [73] Art. 70.   [74] Art. 71.   [75] Art. 72.   [76] Art. 75.
[77] Art. 77.

a statement of the evidence supporting the suit, and the relief desired, including the amount requested.[78] If initiated in a provincial court or the Supreme Court, the complaint and supporting documents had to be in copies sufficient for all defendants.[79] Before summoning the defendant the court might call plaintiff's witnesses or request documents from those in a position to provide them if they were necessary to prosecution of the case and if because of their nature the defendant could have no objection to their introduction.[80]

If a plaintiff feared that assets would not be available to satisfy such judgment as he might obtain, he might request the court to take measures to assure that the defendant did not conceal or dissipate his assets while awaiting the decision,[81] but this might be done only if the documents presented a prima facie case.[82] The court might in return require the plaintiff to deposit in court sufficient funds to cover defendant's costs should he defend successfully.[83] The opposing party need not be called to the hearing on security. If the claim was filed by a state agency against a private enterprise, the court might appoint a conservator to observe the proper conduct of affairs in the enterprise.[84] The court was authorized to take possession of sufficient of the defendant's property to secure the amount sought,[85] but the defendant might obtain release of the property upon deposit of a required sum of money into court.[86]

Court orders concerning the securing of complaints could be appealed within the usual seven-day period for appeals of court orders, but during the period of appeal the property seized remained under the court's jurisdiction.[87] The defendant might subsequently recover losses incurred by him as a result of the seizure should he be held to have been in the right.[88]

Having assembled the documentation, the full three-judge court entered directly upon the trial in open court.[89] In contrast to criminal procedure, there was no formal period of review by the professional judge sitting alone before trial to make certain that all was in order. There was no special "stage" for preliminary preparation of the case. Within a few years the absence of such

[78] Art. 76.   [79] Art. 78.   [80] Art. 80.   [81] Art. 82.   [82] Art. 83.
[83] Art. 84.   [84] Art. 88.   [85] Art. 87.   [86] Art. 89.   [87] Art. 91.
[88] Art. 93.   [89] Art. 94.

a specific "stage" was found to be the cause of loss of time in trials, because sittings of the full court had had to be adjourned several times while additional evidence was gathered.[90] An amendment of 1929[91] provided that the single professional judge might call both the plaintiff and defendant before him to hear what they would say at the trial, to notify the prosecutor and public organizations if he thought them likely to be interested in the outcome, to summon additional witnesses or to demand additional documents from both sides, in exceptional cases to obtain from witnesses unable to attend the trial their written testimony, to transfer the case to another court if the one before which it had been brought did not have jurisdiction, to set a more realistic value on the claim if the plaintiff had not stated its true value, to relieve the indigent from the duty to pay fees, to fine witnesses for refusal to attend or to produce documents, to dismiss the case for want of any showing of right, to obtain testimony from witnesses living at a distance from the court, and to join suits which should be heard together. Only after all of this had been done was it to become necessary to call the full three-judge court into session to hear the case. All of these actions prior to the 1929 amendment were to be taken by the full three-judge bench at the opening of the proceedings.

The trial section of the code opened with general matters. Publicity and orality were made the rule,[92] but the doors might be closed if the public interest was thought to require secrecy, or if the facts related to the intimate life of the parties, or if the court on its own initiative or at the request of one of the parties in which the court concurred found secrecy to be necessary for all or part of the hearings.[93] In any event the ultimate judgment had to be announced publicly.[94]

Parties might challenge the members of the bench as they could in criminal proceedings,[95] and a judge might withdraw on his own motion if he thought himself interested in the case.[96]

The review of the substance of the case opened with a request by the court to the parties to present their full case with reference

[90] Kleinman, *Grazhdanskii protsess,* p. 27.
[91] Order on Amendment of Articles of the Code of Civil Procedure, RSFSR, November 20, 1929, [1929] I *Sob. Uzak. RSFSR,* No. 87–88, item 851, amending Art. 80.
[92] Code of Civil Procedure, RSFSR, Art. 94.
[93] Art. 95.   [94] Art. 96.   [95] Art. 102.   [96] Art. 104.

to all evidence they wished to present.[97] New evidence not announced to the court at the time the hearings began might be admitted only if the court recognized the presence of important circumstances which had prevented the timely presentation of the evidence.[98] At any moment that the court thought the case to be clear enough, it could terminate the hearing and give judgment.[99]

RULES OF EVIDENCE

Rules of evidence were more extensive than they had been in the Code of Criminal Procedure. In contrast to the earlier code's simple provision permitting the court to hear any evidence it wished in the process of establishing an inner conviction as to the truth of the matter, the Code of Civil Procedure enforced the requirements of the Civil Code for certain types of agreements. In those situations for which the Civil Code established specific forms for the conclusion of contracts,[100] parole evidence in proof of an obligation was declared to be nonadmissible.[101] To enforce the stamp tax on documents, the code required payment of the tax and fines immediately upon presentation of an unstamped document,[102] the document being impounded until payment. Although the code made no provision as to whether a document was admissible in evidence without payment, a subsequent commentator[103] declared that such a document did not lose its evidentiary character because of nonpayment of the stamp tax, but it seems that proceedings were halted until the tax was paid. An appeal against the order to pay was permitted in the usual manner.[104]

Exclusion of evidence was also permitted if the court found it lacking in relevancy to the case,[105] and to facilitate the determination of relevancy the party presenting a witness was required to

[97] Art. 105.   [98] Art. 106.   [99] Art. 108.
[100] Civil Code, RSFSR, Arts. 29, 72, 90, 138, 153, 265, 266, 297.
[101] Code of Civil Procedure, RSFSR, Art. 128.
[102] *Ibid.*, Art. 147.
[103] B. Shekhter, *Grazhdanskii protsessual'nyi kodeks RSFSR, prakticheskii postateinyi kommentarii (obshcheiiskovoe proizvodstvo)* (Leningrad, 1926), p. 105.
[104] Code of Civil Procedure, RSFSR, Art. 147 (note).
[105] Art. 120.

indicate the facts to be proved by the witness.[106] If a document was challenged as a forgery, it had to be set aside although it remained as evidence in the case until proof was presented successfully to deny its authenticity,[107] at which point it was withdrawn from the case and the court opened criminal proceedings against the forger.[108]

Although the burden was placed on the party presenting a claim to prove it,[109] the Soviet concept of an active court was reflected in a provision that evidence might be gathered by the court on its own initiative even to the point of taking a view.[110] The court might require the parties to present additional evidence, or it might decide that no evidence was required to prove a matter over which it would take judicial notice.[111] No presumptions were established by the code, although their absence was soon to arouse the Supreme Court to action. In 1925 the court established that all property whose ownership was in dispute was to be considered the property of the state until the contrary was proved.[112]

The same rules as those provided by the Code of Criminal Procedure applied to the examination of witnesses. They were to be required to testify when called,[113] unless their testimony would in the court's opinion disclose a state secret or office secret of a party; or unless the court decided on the request of one of the parties that a witness was interested in the outcome or was in some extraordinary relationship to a party.[114] They were to be warned of prosecution for lying;[115] they were to be excluded from the courtroom until questioned;[116] each was to be questioned singly,[117] in the order established by the court;[118] they were to remain in court after questioning until released, and to be available for subsequent questioning[119] or for a confrontation with other witnesses who had presented contrary evidence.[120] If witnesses lived in another town, they might be questioned by the court at their home, but if they later appeared in court, they were to be permitted to testify again.[121]

[106] Art. 131.   [107] Art. 149.   [108] Art. 151.   [109] Art. 118.   [110] Art. 121.
[111] Art. 120.
[112] Explanation of Plenum of Supreme Court, RSFSR, June 29, 1925, cited in Kleinman, *Grazhdanskii protsess*, p. 34.
[113] Code of Civil Procedure, RSFSR, Art. 129.
[114] Art. 130.   [115] Art. 132.   [116] Art. 134.   [117] Art. 133.   [118] Art. 135.
[119] Art. 137.   [120] Art. 138.   [121] Art. 139.

A document might be subpoenaed [122] when the party wishing to obtain it proved to the court's satisfaction that it was necessary to the case and also presented credible reasons for believing that it was in the custody of the person indicated.[123] Documents as a rule were to be delivered directly to the court, and a copy would be given to the party concerned.[124] A commentary published in 1926 shows that practice was soon simplified in that the court might give to the party concerned a subpoena signed by the court to be presented to the person or state agency believed to have the document.[125] This procedure, requiring less attention by the court to the mechanics of preparation of the case, was to be followed unless in the court's view a conflict was likely to develop when the subpoena was presented. Under such circumstances the court might demand the document itself.[126]

Documents were not to be conclusive proof, but might be contested,[127] except in circumstances provided by law. A commentator explained that documents beyond reproach were official ones issued by state agencies and those notarized by a state notary, although forgery might always be claimed.[128]

No rules were established by the code as to how evidence should be weighed, but eleven years later an author summarized court practice as having developed in the image of Soviet class ideology. He wrote:

In evaluating evidence the decisive elements are not the subjective-individualistic impressions of the judges, but the objective value of the evidence, taken in dialectical union with all of the circumstances of the case in their entirety. The approach of the court to evidence must be based upon social-class analysis of the role and testimony of the witnesses, on the analysis of the true class relationships under which the given case arose. Thus, the evaluation of evidence in Soviet civil procedure is characterized by the following elements: (1) a class approach to evidence, (2) a dialectic method of evaluation, (3) an objective character of evaluation as a counterweight to bourgeois subjectivism.[129]

---

[122] Art. 140.   [123] Art. 141.   [124] Art. 142.
[125] Shekhter, *Grazhdanskii protsessual'nyi kodeks,* p. 100.
[126] *Ibid.*
[127] Code of Civil Procedure, RSFSR, Art. 146.
[128] Shekhter, *Grazhdanskii protsessual'nyi kodeks,* p. 103.
[129] A. F. Kleinman, *Grazhdanskii protsess* (1st ed.; Moscow, 1934), p. 37.

Experts were looked upon as means of court verification and evaluation of evidence rather than as witnesses presented by the parties. They appeared on summons by the court,[130] although they might be challenged by one of the parties as lacking in authority or as having an interest in the outcome of the case.[131] Their opinions might be oral or written, but if oral, they had to be reduced to writing and signed,[132] and they had to state the reasons for their conclusions.[133] Recognition of the experts as a means of verifying evidence rather than as producing testimony themselves was emphasized by the code by juxtaposing with the articles on experts and in the same chapter of the code the rules for taking a view. Under these rules the entire court or a single member of it might visit the locus of an event,[134] together with experts[135] and parties,[136] if the latter wished to attend. A record of the visit had to be prepared and signed by all of those present to which there had to be attached any diagrams, maps, photographs or other bits of evidence.[137] Experts had their place, therefore, to help the court, for as the commentator later explained, "One cannot, in fact, it is impossible to ask that the judges have knowledge in all fields: medicine, bookkeeping, architecture, caligraphy, etc." [138] Since experts were invited by the court to help it, the parties could not compel their presence. According to the commentator, it was to be noted that the court "might" call an expert. It was not "required" to do so, and the parties could not do more than propose that an expert be called. Further, an expert's conclusion was not binding upon the court, for the court alone had the right to evaluate the evidence.[139]

The role of the expert as the agent of the court rather than of the parties was later reemphasized by an author who wrote:

In bourgeois procedure there exists what is called the "parties' experts": the parties present a statement to the court as to whom they agree to select as experts, and the court is required to call the persons named by the parties. . . . In Soviet procedure the court has the right to reach its decision even without naming experts if on the bench there are persons

---

[130] Code of Civil Procedure, RSFSR, Art. 152.
[131] Art. 153.   [132] Art. 155.   [133] Art. 157.   [134] Art. 160.   [135] Art. 156.
[136] Art. 161.   [137] Art. 162.
[138] Shekhter, *Grazhdanskii protsessual'nyi kodeks*, p. 110.
[139] *Ibid.*

(the people's judge, a member of the court, lay judges) having enough knowledge to elucidate special questions.[140]

A record had to be kept not only of a visit to the locus of an event, but of the entire trial as well as of every event outside the hearing bearing upon the matter.[141] It was not, however, a stenographic record, but rather a summary prepared by the court secretary. It was required to state the place and time of the trial, the membership of the court, whether the parties had appeared, the substance of what was said by witnesses and the objections raised by the parties and the court's responses, evidence presented, and documents.[142] The summaries of witnesses' testimony had to be signed by the witnesses concerned, as well as by the parties and the court.[143] All participants in the case had the right to examine the record and within three days to enter their remarks. The president of the court was then required to review the remarks and make the corrections necessary.[144]

To the commentator of 1926 the most frequently violated rule of the code relating to the record was that it be signed by all members of the court, and this he thought to be the result of the different rules for the record in a criminal case where only the president of the court need sign. He noted also that in contrast to criminal procedure, the record in a civil case had to be signed by the witnesses as to their own testimony and by the parties, whereas in the criminal case the secretary of the court signed for all.[145] This contrast in the rules of the two types of procedure was not to last in practice, for in 1929 the code was amended to require that the record be signed only by the president of the court and the secretary.[146] Perhaps the secretary had been so slow in transcribing his notes that when he was ready lay judges were not available to give signatures because they had left the court to be replaced by those called for the next trial, while the witnesses had gone home. Although such a change in the rules may have made for convenience, it can hardly have contributed to accuracy. It is

---

[140] Kleinman, *Grazhdanskii protsess*, p. 35.
[141] Code of Civil Procedure, RSFSR, Art. 109.
[142] Art. 110.   [143] Art. 111.   [144] Art. 112.
[145] Shekhter, *Grazhdanskii protsessual'nyi kodeks*, p. 78.
[146] Order on the Amendment of Articles of the Code of Civil Procedure, RSFSR, November 20, 1929 [1929] I *Sob. Uzak. RSFSR,* No. 87–88, item 851.

significant that it coincided with the end of the New Economic Policy, which suggests that when the pressures of private enterprisers were lifted, the procedures designed to protect the Nepmen were sacrificed to speed and the oft-expressed desire for simplification.

Concealment or destruction of evidence was to be blocked by petitioning, during a trial or before it, the professional judge to take measures to protect it.[147] If circumstances required quick action, or if the prospective defendant had not yet been determined, the opposing party need not be summoned,[148] but the evidence had to be described, the circumstances requiring protection detailed, and its probative value explained.[149] No appeal was permitted from the court's order declaring the protective measures.[150]

Routine rules permitted the joining of co-plaintiffs and co-defendants,[151] the admission of third persons having an interest in the outcome,[152] and the combining of several suits between the same parties.[153] If during the proceedings a state agency was brought into the matter, the court had to notify it as well as the prosecutor's office.[154]

Judgment was to be given on the majority vote of the three judges, none of them being permitted to abstain.[155] The judgment had to be in written form, signed by all three judges,[156] and state the time of issuance, the names of the judges and of the participants, the subject of dispute, the basis for decision and the laws followed by the court in reaching decision, the requirements placed upon the defendant and the manner of execution, the procedure for appeal, and the distribution of costs.[157]

Generally the decision was to be announced at the end of the court sitting, but in complex cases up to three days might be taken to formulate a decision.[158] In any event the judgment had to be announced publicly.[159] The court could not give judgment in an amount exceeding the plaintiff's claim if the figure had been stipulated by the parties or was an amount fixed in a contract, note, or tariff.[160] If there were several defendants or plaintiffs, their

---

[147] Code of Civil Procedure, RSFSR, Art. 123.
[148] Art. 126.   [149] Art. 125.   [150] Arts. 127 and 188.   [151] Arts. 163–66.
[152] Arts. 167–71.   [153] Art. 173.   [154] Art. 172.   [155] Art. 174.
[156] Art. 175.   [157] Art. 176.   [158] Art. 177.   [159] Art. 178.   [160] Art. 179.

shares had to be indicated.[161] Execution of the judgment might be accelerated or retarded as the circumstances seemed to require,[162] and if the judgment concerned the performance of a specific act or delivery of a specific chattel, the time for performance was to be set.[163] The untutored nature of the judges may explain the unusual precaution taken by the code in providing that the judgment be given only by the judges who had been seated at the trial. One can conjure up a picture of a courtroom from which the court had withdrawn at the end of the trial to reach its decision and immediately one of the judges had died of a heart attack. It might have been tempting to substitute a lay judge called for a subsequent case. That such a temptation was present is suggested by the 1926 commentator who warned his readers against such action, saying that if one of the judges is suddenly taken ill or dies, the case must be reheard *de novo*. No other judge could be brought in to complete the bench for preparation of the judgment.[164]

EXECUTION OF JUDGMENT

Execution of the judgment was on the basis of an order, known in the West as an exequatur, issued by the court, which became effective immediately unless the defendant were a state office or enterprise.[165] In the latter case execution was not required before completion of the time to appeal, or, if an appeal were taken, upon decision on appeal.[166] Likewise, if an individual defendant declared that he could not be restored to his former position if he should win an appeal, execution would be stayed.[167]

Execution of judgment was the task of the marshal. The office of marshal had been reviewed in the general reorganization of the courts in 1922, and the Commissariat of Justice had been directed to establish it,[168] but the formal introduction of a chapter on the office into the Judiciary Act occurred only three days prior to the adop-

---

[161] Art. 183.   [162] Art. 182.   [163] Art. 180.

[164] Shekhter, *Grazhdanskii protsessual'nyi kodeks*, p. 139.

[165] Code of Civil Procedure, RSFSR, Art. 186.

[166] *Ibid.*, Art. 187.   [167] *Ibid.*

[168] Statute on the People's Commissariat of Justice, February 1, 1923, sec. 3 (a), [1923] I *Sob. Uzak. RSFSR*, No. 10, item 120.

tion of the Code of Civil Procedure.[169] Under the provisions of this chapter, the office was to be made subordinate to the provincial courts.[170] In a note to the key article it was provided that functions of a marshal might be performed by the local police or a volost executive committee, and this seems to have been an important extension of the office, for the Commissariat of Justice on August 16, 1923, issued a circular directing such agencies to perform marshal's duties subject to the guidance and control of the people's courts.[171]

Although the marshals were to be employed and dismissed by the order of the president of the provincial courts,[172] complaints against their activities were to be lodged with the people's court whose judgment they were executing,[173] and they were made subject to the Criminal Code or to disciplinary action depending on the seriousness of their offense.[174] Prosecutors who wished to protest their activity filed their complaint with the provincial court.[175]

The ranks of the marshals could be filled only with persons of good standing,[176] as indicated by the fact that they had not been convicted by a court or excluded from a public organization, were not deprived of electoral rights under the provisions of the constitution excluding the bourgeoisie from the electoral process, and had not been noted during the civil war for disloyal relationships to Soviet authority or belonging to anti-Soviet political parties. Finally, they had to have had at least a year's experience in some position in the agencies administering Soviet law or its equivalent under the supervision of the provincial court.[177] In short, the marshal had

[169] Decree on Changes in and Additions to the Judiciary Act, RSFSR, July 7, 1923, *ibid.*, No. 48, item 481.

[170] *Ibid.*, Art. 45.

[171] Circular No. 167 on Regulations for Execution by the Organs of the Militia of Civil Judgments of the People's Courts, August 8, 1923, *Ezh. sov. iust.*, No. 32 (August 16, 1923), pp. 740–41.

[172] Decree on Changes in and Additions to the Judiciary Act, July 7, 1923, Art. 46.

[173] Code of Civil Procedure, RSFSR, Art. 270.

[174] Decree on Changes in and Additions to the Judiciary Act, July 7, 1923, Art. 50.

[175] *Ibid.*, Art. 51. [176] *Ibid.*, Art. 47.

[177] Krylenko later ridiculed this requirement of experience since no experience was required of a candidate for a judgeship. See N. V. Krylenko, *Sudoustroistvo RSFSR (Lektsii po teorii i istorii sudoustroistva)* (Moscow, 1923), p. 188.

to be an experienced person with a class background which would assure his attentiveness to the class interests of the proletarian elements.

The marshal's task was to present the exequatur to the debtor and to demand performance.[178] He was saved the burden of personal service, for the exequatur might be mailed to the debtor at his last-known address, if he had been present in court personally, or through a representative at the trial.[179] If his address was unknown, the creditor might ask the court for appointment of a representative of the debtor to make payment from such assets as might be within the jurisdiction.[180] Time for performance was set as at not longer than seven days, unless some other time was set in the judgment itself.[181] Generally the marshal was to search for property within his own district, but if necessary, he might levy upon property anywhere within the same county or city.[182] If property were concealed, the marshal might conduct a search of the debtor's home or storehouse, but only in the presence of the local police and the housing administration.[183] Levies were to be made only during a working day unless there was fear that property would be removed or dissipated, in which event a night or holiday levy would be permitted on the decision of the people's judge.[184] The marshal was not authorized to delay or abandon attempts to levy upon property without court order or without the request of the creditor.[185]

If property of the debtor proved to be insufficient to satisfy all claims of various parties, payment was to occur in the following order: wages and maintenance claims; claims of state agencies; and, thereafter, there was to be equal division among the remaining creditors.[186] Division of the assets had to occur within three days after they came into the hands of the marshal,[187] but if there were a dispute over the distribution, it was to be settled by the people's judge. If he approved the account submitted by the marshal, there could be no appeal, but if he altered it, there might be an appeal to the provincial court within seven days.[188]

If there had been a deposit of funds at the opening of the trial to assure payment if judgment were given, satisfaction of the judg-

---

[178] Code of Civil Procedure, RSFSR, Art. 257.
[179] Art. 258.   [180] Art. 259.   [181] Art. 260.   [182] Art. 261.   [183] Art. 263.
[184] Art. 264.   [185] Art. 265.   [186] Art. 266.   [187] Art. 267.   [188] *Ibid.*

ment was effected from the deposited fund and the balance returned to the debtor.[189] All expenses of execution were to be borne in the first instance by the creditor, although he could obtain repayment from the funds of the debtor when they were subsequently obtained.[190]

On completion of the execution, the marshal returned the exequatur to the issuing court with a notation of execution.[191]

LEVY UPON PROPERTY AND GARNISHMENT

Levy upon property in satisfaction of a judgment had worried the draftsmen, for they wished to avoid what they thought had been the inequities of the bourgeois world. They wanted to avoid further impoverishment of workers and peasants, not only to keep them from becoming a public charge, but because the spirit of the Revolution would be judged by such practical things as the treatment accorded debtors during the period of neo-capitalism established by the New Economic Policy. As has been seen, the problem of executing judgments was on the mind of the government when it introduced the new Code of Civil Procedure into the Central Executive Committee for enactment. The provisions on the subject have importance not only for technical reasons but as indication of the impact of political considerations upon procedural law.

The chapter of the code concerned with levies upon property opened with prohibition of levies on property necessary to the life of the debtor: his clothing and housekeeping items, his tools of production and the instruments required in his profession or his artisan's shop, his agricultural implements, one cow, one horse, and fodder for three months, his seed grain in an amount suitable to the size of his farm plot, and unharvested produce.[192]

Even such explicitness in protecting debtors proved inadequate, for within two years the Commissariat of Justice found it necessary to issue an instruction with 42 articles detailing the procedure for execution of judgments.[193] Noting reports of widespread failure to

[189] Art. 268.   [190] Art. 269.   [191] Art. 262.   [192] Art. 271.
[193] Circular No. 134 on the Procedure for Executing Judgments, July 3, 1925, *Sbornik tsirkuliarov Narkomiusta RSFSR za 1922–1925 gg.* (*deistviushchikh na 15 iiulia 1926 g.*) (Moscow, 1926), pp. 235–42.

observe the rules and especially those protecting the toiling peasantry and foreigners, and believing that the cause was partially the lack of completeness and clarity of existing laws, the Commissariat reminded the courts that its 1923 instruction and the rules of the code must be observed. Still, it had to be admitted that part of the cause for violations was not only ignoring of rules, but it lay at the feet of inadequate numbers of marshals and a local police which was too busy with other matters to give attention to what seemed to be of secondary concern. To meet this problem the Commissariat ordered the provincial courts to increase the number of marshals, especially in county districts, in proportion to the number of executions to be handled and the distances to be traveled, and to do so out of local budgets. After setting the general rules the Commissariat turned to detail.

The trouble seems to have been with levies upon property of an entire peasant household for the debts of an individual member. The commissariat ordered that levies on such communal property be permitted only if it was in satisfaction of a judgment against the whole household. If only a single member was the debtor, even though he might be the head of the household, the levy could be only on such property as might be for his personal use. Property of the community fund might be taken only to the extent that it could be distinguished under the usual rules for partition of family funds, and then only if the claim were for maintenance of a child living outside the family. Although it was not mentioned, such a child would probably have been one born out of wedlock to one of the male members of the family who had fallen in love with but not married the village belle.

Peasant householders living in a commune or artel, that is as a member of one of the early types of collective agricultural groups favored by the state, were given an additional privilege in that their houses and barns could not be levied upon if serving their agricultural needs.

A careful record was to be maintained under the rules of the code when property was levied upon, for an inventory had to be prepared,[194] with full information as to the case involved and the

---

[194] Code of Civil Procedure, RSFSR, Art. 275.

description and value of each item,[195] if necessary with the help of an expert.[196] Claims of third persons to ownership of an item had to be recorded.[197] Unless it seemed necessary to remove the property immediately from the debtor's possession, he was permitted to hold it[198] and even to use it if it was not reduced in value as a result of such use.[199]

Within not less than seven days nor more than a month,[200] and presumably after any appeals against the work of the marshal had been settled, the marshal sold the property at public auction,[201] after three days notice of sale published in the local press,[202] or it was sold on the market if it was a commodity designed for commerce.[203] If the property had been pledged as security for a debt, the pledgee was to be notified so that he might protect his interests.[204] The sale was to be recognized as not having occurred if no one appeared to buy, if the bid was less than the value set on the item, or if a bidder failed to pay.[205] In such an event the creditor might ask within three days that the property be delivered to him in satisfaction of the judgment and at the value set in the inventory to an amount necessary to satisfy his claim.[206] If the creditor did not wish the property for himself, the marshal was obliged to announce a second sale within one week, and the property went to the highest bidder without restriction.[207]

Garnishment of wages was to be permitted only to the extent that they exceeded whatever had been set as the minimum wage for the given community by the proper authorities in accordance with the rules of the Code of Labor Laws.[208] The balance could be garnished only to the extent of 50 percent if it were for maintenance of members of the debtor's family, and to 20 percent for other claims, but such percentage restrictions did not apply to bonuses. An employer who refused to deliver the garnished wages was himself responsible for the amount sought.[209]

Deposits with third persons or state agencies might also be attached by the marshal,[210] subject to a fine of 100 gold rubles for refusal to deliver the property.[211]

[195] Art. 276. [196] Art. 279. [197] Art. 277. [198] Art. 280. [199] Art. 281.
[200] Art. 303. [201] Art. 300. [202] Art. 304. [203] Art. 301. [204] Art. 305.
[205] Art. 314. [206] Art. 315. [207] Art. 316. [208] Art. 289. [209] Art. 291.
[210] Arts. 292–94. [211] Arts. 295.

PROCEDURE ON APPEAL

Appeals against judgments were permitted to the provincial court against decisions of the people's courts within two weeks and to the Supreme Court of the Republic within one month against decisions of the provincial courts sitting as courts of original jurisdiction.[212] Reasons for appeal had to be stated,[213] these being violation, or incorrect application, of existing law including failure of the court to interpret properly the policies of the workers'-peasants' government, and also if the decision was found to be clearly contrary to the facts found by the court at the trial.[214]

The trial court received the notice of appeal and sent it within three days with the file to the superior court for review, and notified the respondent at the same time.[215] The latter had a week to reply.[216] The parties were then summoned to appear for the appeal, or in the Supreme Court the case was set for hearing on its public calendar not less than two weeks prior to the hearing date.[217] Failure of a summoned party to appear was no cause for not proceeding.[218]

At the hearing the prosecutor had the right to file a written statement of his conclusion or make an oral argument.[219] The court was not limited to the errors stated in the appeal,[220] and in its decision it might alter the judgment in whole or in part, or terminate the case, or remand it for new trial.[221] Reasons had to be given for the action taken.[222] If the appellate college of the Supreme Court thought it necessary to obtain an interpretation of the law prior to deciding the matter, it might ask for such an interpretation from the full plenum of the court.[223]

SPECIAL PROCEEDINGS

Apart from the procedures established for the routine civil claim, the code provided in a special section procedures for the settling of decedent's estates, the enforcement of arbitral awards, making

[212] Art. 235.   [213] Art. 236.   [214] Art. 237.   [215] Art. 239.   [216] Art. 240.
[217] Art. 242.   [218] Art. 243.   [219] Art. 244.   [220] Art. 245.   [221] Art. 246.
[222] Art. 248.   [223] Art. 249.

deposits in court, divorce, exempting from military service because of religious scruples, and complaints against the actions of a notary.[224] The distinguishing feature of all but the last two of such procedures was that the professional people's judge sat without lay judges to decide the matter,[225] although he was subject to the same rules of procedure in hearing the matter as if he had been hearing the usual complaint, and if a dispute between the interested parties arose, he was required to associate with himself two lay judges to decide it.[226] In the latter two circumstances jurisdiction was in the provincial court,[227] in accordance with the rule already established by the Judiciary Act.

The distinguishing feature of the special proceedings was, therefore, the anticipation that there would be no disputed facts to be settled between two citizens. Even divorce was placed in this category because most of the cases were expected to be those in which both parties agreed to divorce, and even if they had not, the law at this time permitted either one to obtain separation if he wished, so long as provision was made for custody and maintenance of the children of the marriage.[228]

The work of the Russian draftsmen was adopted without change by the Ukrainians as has already been indicated. It was soon established as the code of the Belorussian Republic, although with some additions.[229] The Armenians also followed the Russian pattern.[230]

THE FIFTH CONGRESS OF PERSONS ENGAGED IN THE ADMINISTRATION OF JUSTICE

In their general review of the functioning of all aspects of the new legal system created to meet the conditions of the New

---

[224] Art. 191.   [225] Art. 192.   [226] Art. 193.   [227] Arts 226 and 231.

[228] Code of Marriage, the Family, and Guardianship, RSFSR, Art. 87, [1917–1918] I *Sob. Uzak. RSFSR*, No. 76–77, item 818.

[229] Code of Civil Procedure, Belorussian SSR, July 26, 1923, [1923] *Sobranie Uzakonenii i Rasporiazhenii Raboche-Krest'ianskogo Pravitel'stva BSSR*, No. 13–14, item 116. A Russian translation with amendments to 1957 is published in V. P. Chapurskii, ed., *Grazhdanskoe protsessual'noe zakonodatel'stvo SSSR i soiuznykh respublik* (Moscow, 1957), pp. 145–75.

[230] Code of Civil Procedure, Armenian SSR, September 23, 1923. A Russian translation with amendments to 1957 is published in Chapurskii, *Grazhdanskoe protsessual'noe*, pp. 359–93.

Economic Policy, officials of the Commissariat of Justice, meeting with a cross section of individuals in a Fifth Congress of persons engaged in the administration of justice on March 14, 1924, examined the progress of civil procedure. Professor A. G. Goikhbarg, who had gained renown as the leading figure drafting the Civil Code, took the floor to present the Commissariat's view, in a speech entitled, significantly, "Class Politics in Civil Procedure."[231]

Class politics was indeed Goikhbarg's primary concern. After noting that all Soviet laws were shot through with class principles, he pointed out that the draftsmen of the procedural code had thought this not enough. They had obligated the judge to base his decision on the class principle and to look upon the parties to a dispute differently, depending on whether they came from one or another class. This principle he found established by Article 4 of the Code of Civil Procedure. Goikhbarg's interpretation of this article must have come as a surprise to some of his listeners, since it had not been the subject of discussion at the time of the presentation of the first draft in any such terms. It had been looked upon in 1923 as an article permitting the court to fill gaps in the law rather than to set aside the principles of the code whenever their application would seem to bring about a result harmful to the proletarian element in a dispute.

The draftsmen had cut out of their draft its original Articles 2 and 3 authorizing courts to protect rights only if exercised in good faith and forbidding protection of rights exercised exclusively and obviously with the intention of causing harm to the other side. They had retained as Article 6 of the new code only the draft article requiring that parties exercise their rights in good faith, an expression in positive terms rather than the negative terms of the rejected articles. Now Goikhbarg was reading something new into the code in requiring judges to disregard the law. He said:

If, in examining a concrete case, the court sees that the general normative laws when applied in practice to the given case would lead to a result violative of proletarian politics, he cannot apply existing laws but must

---

[231] "Doklad t. Goikhbarga po p. 7 povestki dnia 'Klassovaia politika v grazhdanskom protsesse; O spetsial'nykh sudebnykh uchrezhdeniiakh'," *Ezh. sov. iust.*, No. 12–13 (March 20–27, 1924), pp. 284–85. For a less official account of this speech, see A. Fradkin, "V Vserossiiskii s"ezd deiatelei sovetskoi iustitsii (Osnovnye momenty), *Pravo i zhizn'*, No. 3–4 (1924), p. 114.

lift himself up to the general wellsprings of proletarian politics. Therefore Article 4 of the Code of Civil Procedure must be a foundation-stone article, and the court must turn to it in every decision.

He went further to say that on the appeal the higher court was authorized to set aside a judgment incorrectly applying the law, and this was stated as including specifically Article 4. In consequence he thought his position well taken, and urged the provincial courts to use their power to educate the people's courts and the citizens generally "especially in cases close to life, where more than anywhere else class interests come into conflict and where application of the letter of the law sometimes leads to very bad results." He ended his discussion of class politics by saying, "One must not hold to the letter of the law, for if one does so it is easy to liken oneself to a Talmudist."

Goikhbarg's view was not to go unchallenged, for less than two years later the College for Civil Cases of the Supreme Court of the Russian Republic issued Instruction No. 1 in 1926 in opposition.[232] In that instruction the Supreme Court's College declared that decisions were being found in which Article 4 was being applied when there were provisions in the law precisely on the point in issue. It gave as an example a judgment rejecting on the basis of Article 4 a claim of various plaintiffs to have established their right to living space in a housing cooperative at the minimum rate set by an order of the Moscow Soviet. The Supreme Court's College said, in keeping with the view of the draftsmen of 1923: "It must be remembered that Article 4 of the Code of Civil Procedure does not give the right to a court to refuse to apply to a case laws or regulations of the workers'-peasants' government directly relating to the given case, if there are such." Then the Supreme Court softened the rule by adding that if it became necessary to decide a disputed question on the basis of the general foundations of Soviet law and the general policy of the workers'-peasants' government, the court cannot limit itself to reference to such general principles, but it must set forth in detail in its judgment exactly what general principles it had in mind so that its finding could be reviewed by a higher court.

[232] *Sbornik deistvuiushchikh raz"iasnenii Verknovnogo Suda RSFSR* (Moscow, 1930), p. 166.

Goikhbarg's view was, therefore, to be challenged by the highest court within less than two years of its stating, but among his colleagues at the Fifth Congress he had support, for the resolution on this point, after citing specifically articles 4, 5, 179, 237, "and others" of the Code of Civil Procedure as reflecting the concept of protection to be afforded the workers'-peasants' government and the toiling masses, declared:

The Congress considers the primary task of the Supreme Court and of the provincial courts to be the correct instruction of courts in the application of the articles listed in deciding property disputes, and, in particular, calls special attention to application of Article 4 of the Code of Civil Procedure, as the one giving the concrete method of deciding individual cases when there is a collision of the formal law and principles of the class policy of the proletarian court.[233]

The resolution in favor of Goikhbarg's position was not indicative of the thinking of all of those present, if one may judge from some of the questions asked of the speaker. One voice wanted to know, "Does the class origin of the parties determine the existence of class politics in civil procedure, or is the determinant the interests of the class as a whole, since the interests of any given individual may conflict with the interests of the national economy?" In the question the speaker was asking whether the court was to look at the background of the parties or at the substantive issue involved. Goikhbarg took a cautious line in replying. He said: "In such a situation the governing point of view must be that the right to be protected shall be the one which is more expedient in the interests of the national economy." He seems in this answer to reject a judgment based solely on the class origins of the parties. Yet he added that judicial decisions had gone in two extreme directions, one trying to find the answer to all questions by examining the code and the other paying no attention to the code but trying to find the answer to all questions in a rule of expediency. To Goikhbarg the latter was undesirable because it made of the court a policy-creating organ. Having taken a middle position, Goikhbarg avoided clarification by taking refuge in generalities:

We must find a way under N.E.P. conditions, under conditions of class conflicts, to achieve a class line in civil procedure. We must raise the

[233] "Rezoliutsii V-go Vserossiiskogo s"ezda, VII," *Ezh. sov. iust.*, No. 12–13 (March 20–27, 1924), pp. 308–9.

question of methods of judicial activity both in the field of application of law as well as in the collection and evaluation of evidence. The substance of these methods must lie in the decision of questions in conformity with the circumstances.

His questioner must have left the room with a feeling that the class origin of a litigant was a major item to be proved and considered in evaluating evidence for the light it could be expected to throw on the honest or dishonest character of the claim before the court, even though the court was directed to consider the interests of the class as a whole in reaching its decision and not to vote arbitrarily against the creditor when the debtor was a worker or peasant. The result may have been the same in court practice of the time regardless of which approach was used, but Goikhbarg wanted the record to show a desire on his part to avoid vindictiveness against capitalists as such, at least during a period when they were being encouraged because Lenin had thought neo-capitalism necessary for the good of the nation as a whole.

RENEWED EMPHASIS ON UNIFICATION OF COURTS

Broadening the jurisdiction of the regular courts was the second point in Goikhbarg's report to the Fifth Congress.[234] His colleagues had frequently expressed their desire to reduce the number of special courts, and now it was Goikhbarg's turn to revert to Kurskii's old theme of a unitary-court system. Goikhbarg turned to disputes between state enterprises which were at the time being decided by a special tribunal called the Supreme Arbitration Commission, to which reference has been made during consideration of the 1922 court reform. Goikhbarg said that the special tribunal had been created because it was thought that such disputes should be heard by a body authorized to decide each case on the base of expediency rather than law. Under his interpretation of the broad power to decide matters between individual disputants on the basis of expediency under Article 4 of the Code of Civil Procedure, he thought it unnecessary any longer to separate the cases of state enterprises from those of private individuals. He found also that

[234] "Doklad t. Goikhbarga," *ibid.*, p. 285.

there was added reason for union in that the Arbitration Commission was in its decisions applying the rules on contract law to disputes between state agencies. It was being as legal as the courts. In short, he was saying that the state enterprises were being held by their own special tribunal to the strict rules of the Civil Code on contracts, while at the same time the people's courts were abiding less and less by the letter of the law in disputes between individuals, so that there was now little difference between the two approaches. Both types of disputes could be brought together into a single-court system in which the arbitration tribunals would continue to exist, but within the court system rather than as independent agencies subject to control by the People's Commissariat of Justice and the courts which had not in fact exercised any control.

A similar expansion of jurisdiction of the regular courts to include the work of the land commissions brought Goikhbarg's speech to a close. Such a dream had been expressed at the time of the drafting of the judiciary act, but it had not been realized, and the land commissions had been left to continue as agencies of the local soviets with a pattern of organization already discussed in connection with the 1923 judiciary act. Goikhbarg agreed with the proponents of unification that unity was to be desired in principle since the land commissions heard disputes over the use of the land, and these often involved conflicts between the rich and poor peasants. Still, he felt that it was not yet time to consider their abolition in favor of the people's courts, for the reason that there were not yet sufficient resources to increase the number of people's courts to decide such cases.

The resolutions[235] adopted by the congress in response to Goikhbarg's jurisdictional proposals accepted his view that the arbitration tribunals should no longer be independent but should be brought immediately within the general court system by analogy to the "labor sessions" of the people's courts before which disputes over employment were coming. As for the land commissions, the Fifth Congress showed its impatience and resolved to recommend that there be commenced the step-by-step transfer of land-use disputes from the commissions to the people's courts depending upon the conditions in each locality and bearing in mind the number of

[235] "Rezoliutsii," *ibid.*, p. 309.

disputes heard by each commission. The congress wanted the transfer completed by January 1, 1925.

The temper of the jurists of the Russian Republic in early 1924 as they reviewed the experience of the first six months under the Code of Civil Procedure was one of impatience with the continuing variety of courts engaged in settling civil disputes in Soviet society. They wanted unification of the courts as much as it had been wanted since the inception of the Soviet legal system. They saw no reason for separate tribunals to hear disputes over land use, or even for separate tribunals to hear disputes between state enterprises. Their ideal was one set of general courts for all with three steps applying the new procedural law with precision, but not to the exclusion of attention to politics. On this latter point they were divided. The more powerful element associated with the Commissariat of Justice wanted to retain flexibility of "class justice" to such an extent that a court might depart from procedural law as well as substantive law when the protection of a worker or peasant seemed necessary in the interest of the community even if the law seemed to require otherwise. Yet there were voices in the assembly who feared such an approach lest it open the door to prejudiced opinions in favor of a worker merely because he was a worker. They wanted to be certain that judges limit their departure from the law to circumstances in which the interests of the new society as a whole were endangered. Perhaps they could imagine circumstances which might require the rejection of the heartfelt cry of a peasant defendant for protection from a tradesman in the interest of sanctity of contract as an element necessary to the restoration of the impoverished economy of the entire country.

While accepting the necessity for flexibility to prevent hardship on peasants and workers in extreme cases because of the strict application of substantive law, some of the voices at the Fifth Congress and in the press refused to extend the concept of flexibility to the procedural field. They wanted to be sure that a judge knew the facts before he tried to apply the principles of law or policy to the substance of the dispute, and they felt that setting aside of procedural requirements would obscure the facts. Procedure had not been invented to conceal the issue or to defeat the ignorant party because of its complexity. It had been designed by Soviet experts to provide every aid to the ignorant in presenting their case, and it had as its purpose clarification of detail in the interests of a society ruled by proletarian elements. It was not a hostile but a friendly procedure in this view, and there was no reason to provide escape clauses. The rejection by the political authorities of such clauses, except for Articles 4 and 10 of the Code of Civil Procedure, had made that clear, and even these articles were to be applied restrictively. Professor Goikhbarg's suggestion to the contrary had come as a surprise to some in the hall at the Fifth Congress. It was more a warning of a tendency which was to become dominant in the early 1930's when the N.E.P. was being washed away in the flood of forced collectivization and dekulakization than a statement of official policy in the mid 1920's, as evidenced by the Supreme Court decision in 1926 to the contrary.

The importance given to procedural law in the second year of the N.E.P. did not blind Krylenko to his dream of the distant future, and in that dream he restated the faith of the Communist party of which he was an unusually militant member. In addressing his students in 1923 he asked them how they imagined their court would look under the ideal conditions of Communist society.[236] He replied that if they expected to find a court at all they were wrong, for a court was an instrument of state power and in Communist society the state would have withered away. But in the meantime, during the period of "volatilization," there would once again emerge on top the general humanitarian principles reflected in the program of the Communist party. Moral measures would probably be applied to those who defected from observation of the rules of a given social order. These would be conditional sentences, social censure, expulsion from the community, denial of the right to participate in social and political organizations, and deprivation of political rights. He expected that there would reappear the principles found in the People's Court Act of 1920. The various levels of courts would be abolished; the breaking up of the court system into different types of tribunals would be abandoned; dependence upon central authorities would be no more; and the first principle of guidance would be ethics, which under conditions being created by a socialist economy would be

[236] Krylenko, *Sudoustroistvo RSFSR*, pp. 207–8.

much stronger than they were in 1923. Then in all probability there would return the principles of the People's Court Act, the principles of "simplicity, beauty, closeness to the people and directness." These were Krylenko's perspectives for the future. The system of 1922–23, of which he was a chief architect, he summed up in a motto he would inscribe above each Soviet court, namely the old Roman maxim, *dura lex, sed lex,* which he translated into Russian for his listeners as "severe law, fierce law, yes, even blood-spattered law, but still law."

Chapter 12
REFINING PROCEDURE IN PRACTICE

SIMPLIFICATION had been the closing note of the Fifth Congress of persons engaged in the administration of justice in March, 1924, but the policy had to be put into practice if it were to remain more than a dream. The Commissariat of Justice had shown itself ready in the past to follow the suggestions of the first four congresses, so much so that to an outsider it cannot but seem that the delegates used their advance knowledge of what the Commissariat was planning to prepare their resolutions. At the Fifth Congress the Commissariat had been instructed in precise terms to amalgamate the state arbitration tribunals and the land commissions with the general courts and to broaden the jurisdiction of the lowest link in the court system, namely the people's courts. These decisions had not been hedged about with conditions which would have to be met before the steps could be taken. They were expressed with clarity as firm desires of those engaged in administering the Soviet legal system not only in the Commissariat but on the bench, in the Prosecutor's Office and at the bar. The Commissariat had called the meeting for discussion of what was deemed necessary to improve the procedural situation prior to making proposals for amendment of the codes, and, presumably, its experts sat down after the sessions to put the resolutions into effect.

The first indication of what was being done in the commissariat appeared a month prior to the meeting of the Central Executive Committee of the Russian Republic. The Commissariat published its proposals, including those for amendment of the Code of Civil Procedure in the issue of its journal dated September 9–16, 1924.[1] In its explanatory note accompanying the drafts the Commissariat

[1] "Izmeneniia i dopolneniia kodeksov zakonov RSFSR vnosimye NKIu na utverzhdenie 2-oi sessii VTsIK, XI sozyva," *Ezhenedel'nik sovetskoi iustitsii*, No. 35–36 (September 9–16, 1924), pp. 838–41.

responded to one of the major desires of the Fifth Congress in declaring its intention to widen the jurisdiction of the people's court in the civil field as well as in the field of criminal procedure. This would be accomplished by raising the existing top limit on civil claims heard by the court from 500 gold rubles to 1,000 gold rubles. To quiet the fears of any who might have thought the judges incapable of dealing with larger amounts, the Commissariat stated that the average commercial agreement was within this price range so that the cases would be routine and not exceptional, and, further, judges, both lay and professional, having the usual qualifications, could be expected to decide them properly.

While the proposed amendment sounded like an innovation, it was really only a request for approval of what had already been done, for on July 28, 1924,[2] the Presidium of the Central Executive Committee and the Council of People's Commissars had already issued a decree making the change. It had, apparently, been thought desirable to act promptly after the Fifth Congress to effect this reform without waiting for completion of the full set of changes to be proposed for all codes to the September meeting.

The proposals to amalgamate the arbitration tribunals and the land commissions with the people's courts as they had been made in the resolutions of the Fifth Congress went unheeded. Both of these sets of tribunals were left outside the general court system by the September reforms in what is a noteworthy departure by the Commissariat from its erstwhile practice of following the wishes, if not even inspiring the wishes, of the delegates to the congresses of juristic workers. To be sure, there had been some warning that the delegates had gotten out of hand on this issue, for Goikhbarg had hinted at the possibility of refusing to accept the proposals when he had said in his concluding remarks that although he agreed in principle to amalgamation of the land commissions with the people's courts, he feared that the time was not yet ripe for union because of the inadequate number of people's courts available to hear the large number of disputes concerning use of the land. Since Goikhbarg must have been speaking for

[2] Decree on Amendments to Arts. 11, 23(a), and 246 of the Code of Civil Procedure, July 28, 1924, [1924] I *Sobranie Uzakonenii i Rasporiazhenii Rabochego i Krest'ianskogo Pravitel'stva RSFSR*, No. 70, item 688.

the Commissariat and not solely for himself, it is small wonder that when the commissariat reviewed the situation in the light of the Fifth Congress' resolutions, it concluded that no change in the land commissions should be made.

The decision not to amalgamate the land commissions was to last, for in 1928 [3] when the federal government reconsidered land law in keeping with the federal constitution's authorization to establish general principles of land use, the opportunity to change policy was let pass. The federal statute left in effect the legislation of the republics on the settling of disputes over use of the land and this meant that the republics' systems of land commissions remained in operation. The sentiment of the jurists of 1924 was thus overruled. The Russian Republic even strengthened the independence of the system by reorganizing its Special College of Supreme Control over Land Disputes by statute of July 26, 1926.[4] The Special College was continued outside the court system, subordinate directly to the Presidium of the All-Russian Central Executive Committee. Its task was to oversee the prompt and correct operation of the various land commissions and to serve as a supreme tribunal to which protests against decisions of these commissions might be taken for reversal not only on the ground that the decision was contrary to facts or to law, but also if it violated the interests of the workers'-peasants' government and the toiling masses. Apparently the land commissions had become so ingrained in the Soviet pattern of administration that they were not to be uprooted in order to establish conformity to a general pattern of simplicity in the structure of the dispute-settling agencies.[5] A unitary-court

[3] Decree on General Principles for Use of the Land and Land Distribution, Art. 63, December 15, 1928, [1928] I *Sobranie Zakonov i Rasporiazhenii Raboche-Krest'ianskogo Pravitel'stva SSSR*, No. 69, item 642.

[4] Decree on Approval of the Charter for the Special College of Supreme Control for Land Disputes, RSFSR, July 26, 1926, [1926] I *Sob. Uzak. RSFSR*, No. 49, item 369.

[5] Land commissions were abolished on October 10, 1930, following intensification of efforts to do away with land use by individual peasant families in favor of use by collective farms, the reason being given that land commissions were no longer necessary. See Decree on the Abolition of Land Commissions and the Special College of Supreme Control for Land Disputes, RSFSR, and the Procedure for Settling Land Disputes, October 10, 1930, [1930] I *Sob. Uzak. RSFSR*, No. 51, item 623. By this decree jurisdiction over land-use disputes between persons who had been allocated plots for use was placed in village soviets. If the issue in dispute was the right to allocation, the county-

system remained a goal, but it could not be put into practice even by those in the Commissariat who wielded considerable influence.

STATE ARBITRATION COMMISSIONS

The history of the state arbitration commissions provides further evidence of the great strength of the group that thought it necessary to sacrifice unity of court structure for specialization. Created in 1922[6] in recognition of a feeling that the law and procedure to be applied in the settlement of disputes between state enterprises should not be the same as that applied in settling disputes between private citizens, they had functioned in each province and also in the center of government at Moscow, the latter body being called a Supreme Arbitration Commission and having jurisdiction over disputes between enterprises, at least one of which was classified as a "central enterprise," and also over complaints against decisions of the provincial commissions brought by public authorities, or even appeals by the parties themselves, provided that in the latter instance the sum involved in the dispute exceeded 5 million rubles.

The provincial commissions were attached to the provincial economic boards, whose task it was to oversee the operation of state enterprises at the time. The close relationship of the commissions to the executive is evident from the fact that the provincial economic boards might set aside a decision of the provincial arbitration commission, although they had then to inform the Supreme Arbitration Commission in Moscow and send forward the file for review.

---

executive committee had jurisdiction, with appeal from its decision to the land department of the provincial executive committee and from there to the provincial executive committee as a whole or to the executive committee of an autonomous republic, if the province were organized on an ethnic basis as an autonomous republic. A court, thereafter, refused to take jurisdiction over a dispute between a member of a collective farm and the collective farm over the right to use a private garden plot allocated to the member's use. Jurisdiction was held to be in the land agencies and not in a court. See *Dogadin v. Collective Farm "Krasnyi Pakhar,"* Decision No. 155, *Sudebnaia praktika Verkhovnogo Suda SSSR*, Issue VI (XII) (1944), p. 28.

[6] Statute on the Procedure for Deciding Property Disputes between State Offices and Enterprises, September 21, 1922, [1922] I *Sob. Uzak. RSFSR*, No. 60, item 769.

The criticism of the Fifth Congress had no effect on the continuation of the arbitration commissions. On the contrary, very soon after the criticism[7] there was created at the top of the system in the newly established federal government a Supreme Arbitration Commission of the U.S.S.R. This new supreme body was given jurisdiction over disputes between enterprises, one of which was included on the official list as "all-union" in status, or one of which was a local enterprise deemed to have national importance and whose head requested arbitration, or both of which were local enterprises of local importance but located in different republics. In the latter case one of the directors had to ask the Supreme Arbitration Commission to assume jurisdiction.

Not until 1931[8] was the dream of the unifiers fulfilled on this score, when a decree of the federal government abolished the various state arbitration commissions, declaring in its preamble that the purpose was "to strengthen the unity of the judicial system of the U.S.S.R." Under the decree disputes then being heard by the commissions were to be transferred to the general courts. If one of the parties was an enterprise of the federal government or of all-union importance, the Supreme Court of the U.S.S.R. was to take jurisdiction. If the enterprises were in different republics, the federal Supreme Court might also take jurisdiction, although in this situation it would do so only if the parties did not agree to trial before the Supreme Court of one of the republics. To equip the courts to hear such disputes, it was required that the two lay judges called to the court for the case be persons working in economic organs of the state. In this way a compromise was reached between those who wanted to continue specialized consideration of a dispute and those who sought unity of the system of institutions deciding disputes of all kinds. The burden on the courts was reduced in some measure by another element of the compromise, for the law permitted settlement of a dispute between two enterprises under the same ministry by the minister, but it forbade creation within the ministry of an arbitration commission. There

---

[7] Statute on the Arbitration Commission under the Council of Labor and Defense of the USSR, May 6, 1924, [1924] I *Sob. Uzak. RSFSR*, No. 62, item 618.

[8] Decree on the Abolition of the Arbitration Commissions, March 4, 1931, [1931] I *Sob. Zak. SSSR*, No. 14, item 135.

seems to have been fear lest there creep back into the Soviet legal system specialized agencies to hear cases between state enterprises on a basis in any way similar to that of a court.

The victory of the unifiers was short-lived, for within two months the tables were turned. On the books appeared the statute of May 3, 1931,[9] re-creating state arbitration as an integrated system in the federal government, the republics and the provinces, attached at each level to the executive agency for the area concerned. Thus was created a system which has survived to the present day although not without criticism from some Soviet jurists who have argued that there should be unity of law, if not of judicial institutions. This thesis was argued repeatedly after 1937, when drafting of a new civil code commenced, it being said that the law relating to contracts between public corporations should be included in the civil code, even with exceptional characteristics if necessary, and not remain outside the code in separate enactments. In this argument, which has continued without resolution to the year 1960, there has been rehearsed some of the same concern as that which moved the Fifth Congress of juristic workers. There are Soviet jurists who still want a unitary system of law and courts with as few exceptional rules and institutions as possible.

REFINEMENT OF PROCEDURAL DETAIL

While attempts to achieve unity in the court system and to strengthen the lowest level as proposed by the Fifth Congress met with only limited support on the part of the Commissariat of Justice when it presented proposals to the Central Executive Committee for enactment, the Commissariat was not without ideas of its own.[10] All of its points had already been presented to the Presidium of the Central Executive Committee for approval, and their reappearance in the draft of the Commissariat published before the full meeting of the Central Executive Committee was only to present a composite picture of the amendments being made to the original text of the 1923 code. The requirement of publication

[9] Statute on State Arbitration, May 3, 1931, *ibid.*, No. 26, item 203.
[10] D. I. Kurskii, "Ob"iasnitel'naia zapiska k proektu izmenenii grazhdanskogo protsessual'nogo kodeksa RSFSR," *Ezh. sov. iust.*, No. 35–36 (September 9–16, 1924), pp. 838–41.

of the Supreme Court's calendar in the journal of the Commissariat was eliminated to leave only the requirement of posting in the courthouse. The reason given was that the journal often appeared late and made conformity with the code's original requirement of two weeks' prior notice impossible of fulfillment. An appellate court was now to be permitted to revise judgment on appeal so long as the revision was limited to changes arising out of incorrect application of the law and did not relate to the merits of the case as decided by the trial court.

Issuance of an exequatur on a protested bill of exchange without trial of the facts was to be permitted so as to speed recovery by the State Bank on bills which it had discounted because the State Bank as the state's note-issuing authority backed these notes by bills of exchange in its portfolio. It needed, therefore, to have its assets in as liquid a form as possible, and this necessitated elimination of the requirement of full trial of the issues when payment was refused. Another proposal offered protection to the assets of consumers' cooperatives by adding to the list of items exempt from execution the debtor's share in a cooperative if his contribution had already been incorporated in the assets of the cooperative and used in the business. Here was evidence of the desire to favor the community represented by the cooperative over the individual creditor of a cooperative member, and as such it may have been symbolic of the beginning of a turn away from full protection of creditors, whose rights had been built up by adoption of the early legislation of the New Economic Policy.

Further evidence of a tendency to favor the weak is found in a proposed change in jurisdiction for suit. Actions for maintenance of dependents were to become tryable at the residence of the plaintiff rather than solely at the residence of the defendant under the usual rule.

Proposals of the Commissariat were adopted by the Central Executive Committee at its session of October 16, 1924,[11] with such general acceptance that Professor Brandenbursgkii found cause for rejoicing. In his review of the work of the session[12] he noted

[11] Decree on Additions to and Changes in the Code of Civil Procedure, RSFSR, October 16, 1924, [1924] I *Sob. Uzak. RSFSR*, No. 78, item 783.

[12] Ia. Brandenburgskii, "Sudebnye voprosy na 2-i sessiia VTsIK, XI sozyva," *Ezh. sov. iust.*, No. 39–40 (October 9–16, 1924), pp. 919–20.

that the Commissariat's proposals had been adopted almost in full, but he also hailed the initiative of the Central Executive Committee in placing cooperatives on a par with state enterprises as preferred creditors in the event of insolvency, and also the extension of Chapter XXII of the Code of Civil Procedure to include provision for private arbitration tribunals. This extension had been presented by the government for enactment after approval by the Council of People's Commissars a few days earlier, on October 9, 1924, its purpose being to accommodate to N.E.P. conditions the existing law on private arbitration.

The record[13] shows that Brandenburgskii had presented the Commissariat's proposals to the assembled deputies, emphasizing only one point with regard to civil procedure, namely the extension of jurisdiction in the People's Court to 1,000 ruble claims. He repeated the consoling advice from the pages of the Commissariat's journal that this was an average claim and there was nothing to be feared from what appeared to be addition of greater responsibility to the work of the lowest court's judges. He thought the other proposals simple enough in themselves, noting as an example that a change in method of summoning parties was solely to bring it into conformity with the method of summoning parties in the code of criminal procedure.

When the committee on juridical problems returned with its report on the Commissariat's proposals Brandenburgskii declared[14] that all proposals had been accepted, except to add to the group of creditors to receive preferred treatment on the liquidation of an enterprise the cooperatives. He also disclosed that the committee had decided to incorporate in the code the statute on private arbitration tribunals recently adopted by the Council of People's Commissars.

OPPORTUNITIES FOR PRIVATE ARBITRATION

The existing law on private arbitration was a heritage of the first months of the Revolution, the statute on the subject having

---

[13] *RSFSR—Vtoraia sessiia Vserossiiskogo Tsentral'nogo Ispolnitel'nogo Komiteta, XI sozyva* (*stenograficheskii otchët*) (Moscow, 1924), pp. 340–41.
[14] *Ibid.*, p. 442.

been enacted February 16, 1918.[15] Stuchka's *Encyclopedia of Law* twelve years later sought to justify the exceptional procedure in Marxist terms.[16] It claimed that in many societies arbitration tribunals provide a newly rising class, not yet having an influence in state affairs, and seeking to govern its affairs without reference to the reactionary courts of a dying regime, with a means of regulating the relationships developing in its midst. The tribunals, when seen in such a light, were an expression of lack of confidence in the old regime, in its courts and in its law. On the other hand such tribunals could be the outgrowth of necessity when new relationships only beginning to crystallize had not yet received necessary legal formulation as life surged forward at a swift tempo, as the result of which the disputes arising out of these new relationships could not be resolved in the state's courts. Still, in both cases the arbitration tribunals were seen as a manifestation of lack of confidence in, and of lack of satisfaction with, the state's courts. Consequently, the state found it necessary to counter the negative feature of the arbitration tribunals by bringing them under state control, causing them to be less of a family affair, less of a counterweight to state courts and bringing them closer in greater or lesser degree to the general system of state courts. Under such circumstances, according to the encyclopedia, arbitration tribunals lost their negative feature in a noticeable degree and served to relieve the regular courts of some of the burden placed upon them.

Considered within this framework of thought the arbitration tribunals had been authorized in the new Soviet Russia of 1918 "to relieve the new courts, created by the Revolution, of concern for the old inheritance," to use the words of the encyclopedia. Their limited place in social relations was indicated by the disputes excluded from their jurisdiction. They could not hear disputes over employment contracts or over matters of social insurance. They could not attempt to settle personal feuds arising out of reprehensible acts for which criminal prosecution might follow without regard to the desire of the aggrieved party to forgive. They were, then, for commercial disputes and those relating to damage to

15. Decree on a Three-man Arbitration Court, February 16, 1918, [1917–1918] I *Sob. Uzak. RSFSR*, No. 28, item 366.

[16] S. Trushchitskii, "Treteiskii sud," in P. Stuchka, ed., *Entsiklopediia gosudarstva i prava* (Moscow, 1930), p. 918.

property and for quieting personal animosity occasioned by the exchange of insults. In short, they could be permitted to relieve the courts of the burden of settling social conflicts, but only if those conflicts were not close to the heart of the new social order which the state was engaged in creating.

The 1918 decree on arbitral tribunals had permitted the parties to a dispute to establish an *ad hoc* tribunal, each party naming one member, and the two members choosing the third. Since the basis for jurisdiction was agreement of the parties, the submission (*compromis*) to the tribunal had to be in writing and signed by the parties before witnesses. If no date was set for termination of the matter and issuing of the award, four months was to be the maximum life of a tribunal unless the parties agreed to an extension. The award was to be filed for safekeeping, together with the submission and the dossier with the local court, the latter charging the regular court fees and taxes. If one of the parties requested court assistance in executing an award, the court was to issue an exequatur. Appeal lay to the congress of people's judges as the court of second instance at that time, and this body, if it set aside an award, forwarded the matter to the appropriate people's court for trial. A party who in the course of a hearing before a tribunal wished to change the arbitrator named by him might petition the local people's court to permit the naming of a substitute within seven days. If none was named within the time limit, the people's judge might name one on request of either party to the dispute. Arbitration was permitted, even if the case had gone to court, if both parties requested subsequent transfer to a tribunal.

Because of this already existing system of relationship between arbitration tribunals and the people's courts, the draftsmen of the Code of Civil Procedure had found it necessary to include in 1923 within the part relating to special procedure a chapter on the enforcement of arbitral awards. This chapter had followed the lines of the 1918 law, except to add that before issuing an exequatur to enforce an award, the people's judge had to establish that the award was granted in accordance with the requirements for the creation and functioning of arbitration tribunals and was not contrary to law. A party might appeal a decision refusing an exequatur to the provincial court.

With the 1924 extension of the chapter on enforcement of arbitral awards, the state introduced more details into the regulation of these tribunals. While the outline was the same as in the 1918 law, it was now provided that the judges might be more than one for each side as long as the number named by the parties was equal; the submission to arbitration had to be executed before a notary; not every one might serve as an arbitrator but only those who had not been deprived of civil rights by a court for crime, or were not under investigation or being tried by a court, or had not been deprived of the right to serve as a judge either by court or disciplinary decision; judges might not be changed during the hearings and a party might refuse to continue the proceedings if it became evident that one of the arbitrators was interested in the outcome and this was unknown when he had first been accepted as a member of the tribunal; on death or absence of an arbitrator the parties might agree, if they wished, to a substitution of a new member of the tribunal by the party who had named the now absent arbitrator; fees were to be charged at only one half the usual rate for court cases and documents were to be exempt from the stamp and chancery taxes; no formal rules of procedure were to be enforced, except that no decision could be rendered without having summoned the parties and having heard their explanation; neither party might withdraw after submission except in the event of allegations of favoritism of a judge; the decision had to be rendered within one month unless some other period had been set in the submission; awards were to be made on a majority vote and had to be in writing with disclosure of the substance of the decision as well as the costs to be charged to the parties; the award had to be signed by all arbitrators, and if any refused, the reason for refusal had to be indicated on the face of the award; a criminal prosecution was to be commended if the proceedings disclosed crime; the award was to be announced in open session to the parties and signed by each. If either refused, the president was to note that the objectors had been informed of its substance.

Arbitration tribunals were also authorized in the statute on commodity exchanges of August 23, 1922, creating for the neocapitalist conditions of the N.E.P. a system of agencies comparable to those existing generally in capitalist economies to provide a regulated market. Under the Soviet conception, these agencies were juridical persons having their own governing body but created under the supervision of the economic arm of the central government or of one of the provincial economic councils. Among the powers granted was that of settling disputes between members through arbitration functioning in accordance with the rules for arbitration tribunals, but a problem was presented by the fact that not only private enterprises and cooperatives belonged.

Membership included state enterprises. Since such enterprises were subject to the state arbitration system rather than the regular courts, the decision of a commodity-exchange arbitration tribunal had to be taken to the state system for enforcement rather than to a regular court. The revision of the statute on commodity exchanges made by federal decree of October 2, 1925,[17] eliminated state enterprises from jurisdiction of the tribunal, but it made no reference to application of the rules of arbitration tribunals, except to preserve the primary feature of control—namely, that execution of an award was possible only through the regular courts. No change in this was made by the revision of April 17, 1928,[18] although the formula was altered to provide that the rules of the Republic should apply to the issuance of exequaturs, and those rules continued to require court action. The arbitration commissions continued until the commodity exchanges in which they functioned were abolished by decree of February 6, 1930,[19] in the final liquidation of the neo-capitalist institutions which had served the purposes of the N.E.P.

Revision of the Code of Civil Procedure in October, 1924, brought no end to attempts to improve it. At its sitting in May, 1925,[20] the Central Executive Committee turned its attention again to civil procedure along with criminal procedure. The government's spokesman, Iakhontov, disclosed that practice had shown the neces-

[17] Statute on Commodity and Stock Exchanges and on Stock Departments in Commodity Exchanges, part VII, October 2, 1925, [1925] I *Sob. Zak. SSSR*, No. 69, item 511.
[18] Statute on Commodity and Stock Exchanges and on Stock Departments in Commodity Exchanges, part V, April 17, 1928, [1928] *ibid.*, No. 23, item 204.
[19] Decree on the Abolition of Commodity Exchanges and Stock Departments within Them, February 6, 1930, [1930] *ibid.*, No. 10, item 120.
[20] *RSFSR—3-aia sessiia VTsIK, XI sozyva (Stenograficheskii otchët)* (Moscow, 1925).

sity of amending the rules on execution of judgment and sale of property in its satisfaction.[21] The code had permitted issuance of an exequatur immediately after the trial court's decisions without waiting for the result of the appeal.[22] This had made the appeal useless, and so it was proposed to suspend execution until after the appeal, except for some exceptional cases requiring immediate execution, these being listed as judgments for wages, judgments enforcing documents as listed in Article 210 of the code, primarily those bearing notarial confirmation, and judgments based on acknowledgment in court of the obligation.[23]

The list of property excluded from levy in satisfaction of judgment was to be enlarged to add participating shares of members of consumers' cooperatives,[24] this being necessary to strengthen the position of such cooperatives in performing their service to the economy.

The third proposal gave rise to brisk debate. The government recommended that on sale of property in satisfaction of a judgment, the marshal be permitted to transport it elsewhere for sale if no bidders could be found on the spot even though the debtor might object.[25] From the floor came an angry protest against applying this rule in the villages. It would be costly economically to transport the property, and it would give rise even to political difficulties among the peasants.[26] The opponent anticipated that the state would levy upon large and small animals to pay taxes, and this would give rise to agitation against the Soviet authority. The debate waxed so hot, in spite of Iakhontov's cry that he must have been misunderstood, that the proposal was defeated on the floor. The record shows that the provision had already been adopted by the Presidium of the Central Executive Committee on December 1, 1924.[27] As a result of the special action on this matter,

---

[21] *Ibid.*, p. 15.

[22] Code of Civil Procedure, RSFSR, [1923] I *Sob. Uzak. RSFSR*, No. 46–47, item 478, Art. 186.

[23] *Ibid.*, Art. 187. For law introducing these amendments, see Decree on Additions to and Changes in the Code of Civil Procedure, RSFSR, May 5, 1925, [1925] I *Sob. Uzak. RSFSR*, No. 29, item 214.

[24] Code of Civil Procedure, RSFSR, Art. 271.

[25] This was to be a note incorporated as a paragraph in *ibid.*, Art. 302.

[26] *RSFSR—3-aia sessia VTsIK*, p. 23.

[27] Order on Addition to Art. 302 of the Code of Civil Procedure, RSFSR, December 1, 1924 [1924] I *Sob. Uzak. RSFSR*, No. 89, item 906.

the collection of laws was made to carry a law revoking the December 1 action[28] but a law was adopted creating such a rule for the remote Chechen Autonomous Province.[29] The story was not to end with this, for on June 6, 1925, the Presidium and the Council of People's Commissars decreed that the provision permitting transport and sale in other markets be reinserted, this time in broader form, not limited in applicability just to the Chechen Autonomous Province but extended "to distant places with weakly developed economic life." [30] This form was still less extensive than that adopted on December 1, 1924, and revoked in May, 1925, by the Central Executive Committee, for it could not be applied everywhere. Still, it went farther than the measure actually adopted by the deputies. The moral was clear for those who noted the sequence. It was becoming hard for groups of deputies to suppress a desire of the government when the latter thought the measure necessary and the opposition weak.

A fourth proposal extended the prosecutor's authority to intervene in civil suits not only when a state agency protested but at any time when the interests of the state as a whole seemed in his opinion to be endangered.[31] Further, the prosecutor was to be given the right to suspend execution of a civil judgment, just as he could of a criminal sentence while he was protesting the decision to a higher court.[32]

FEDERAL CONCERN WITH CIVIL PROCEDURE

Numerous subsequent decrees appear in the collection of laws, notably in 1929 [33] as the New Economic Policy drew to a close, but

[28] Order Revoking the Order of the CEC and Council of People's Commissars, RSFSR, of December 1, 1924, on Addition to Art. 302 of the Code of Civil Procedure, RSFSR, May 5, 1925, [1925] *ibid.*, No. 29, item 216.

[29] Order on Addition to Art. 302 of the Code of Civil Procedure, RSFSR, of a Note 2 for the Chechen Autonomous Province, May 5, 1925, *ibid.*, No. 29, item 215.

[30] Decree on Addition of a Note to Art. 302 of the Code of Civil Procedure, RSFSR, June 6, 1925, *ibid.*, No. 43, item 312.

[31] *RSFSR—3-aia sessiia VTsIK*, p. 19.

[32] This proposal was incorporated in an amended version of Code of Civil Procedure, RSFSR, Art. 254, by Decree on Additions to and Changes in the Code of Civil Procedure, RSFSR, May 5, 1925, par. 4, [1925] I *Sob. Uzak. RSFSR*, No. 29, item 214.

[33] Order on Amendment of the Code of Civil Procedure, RSFSR; November 20, 1929, [1929] *ibid.*, No. 87–88, item 851.

there has never been a statute providing federal guidance on principles similar to that established for criminal procedure. The republics have been left free to enact such laws as they wished, although the record shows that their Communist party leaders had already become so habituated to following the example of the draftsmen in the Russian Republic that there was no great variation. Even the simplifiers who had experimented with criminal procedure kept their hands off the codes of civil procedure. The Uzbek Republic's code, which appeared in 1927,[34] was slightly longer than that of the Russian Republic as it stood at the time, while that of the Tadzhik Republic as adopted in 1929 [35] was the same as its Uzbek predecessor. The Turkmen Republic's code of 1929 [36] was significantly longer, reflecting a desire on the part of the draftsmen to improve clarity by splitting long articles into parts, but most of its wording was identical with the Russian model, as it had been amended at the time of the Turkmen promulgation.

That the federal government was satisfied with the Russian Republic's model is suggested by a long order adopted by the Supreme Court of the U.S.S.R. on October 28, 1935,[37] filling in some measure the gap left when the federal government had failed to enact a set of general principles for civil procedure soon after its organization. By this order the Supreme Court called for the strictest adherence to procedural norms by all courts of all republics and enumerated by reference to the code of the Russian Republic those articles

[34] Code of Civil Procedure, Uzbek SSR, September 20, 1927, [1927] *Sobranie Uzakonenni i Rasporiazhenii Rabochego-Krest'ianskogo Pravitel'stva Uz. SSR,* No. 35, item 221. Russian translation with amendments to 1957 published in V. P. Chapurskii, ed., *Grazhdanskoe protsessual'noe zakonodatel'stvo SSSR i soiuznykh respublik* (Moscow, 1957), pp. 179–231.

[35] Code of Civil Procedure, Tadzhik SSR, December 19, 1929; Russian translation with amendments to 1957 published in *Chapurskii, Grazhdanskoe protsessual'noe,* pp. 326–56. The enabling act declared that since the Tadzhik Republic had been formed from the Uzbek Republic, the latter's legislation in effect at the time of formation of the Tadzhik Republic would have force in the new republic until revoked or amended. The date of separation from the Uzbek Republic was given as December 5, 1929.

[36] Code of Civil Procedure, Turkmen SSR, April 15, 1929, [1929] *Sobranie Postanovlenii Turkmen SSR,* No. 5–6, item 42. Russian translation with amendments to 1957 published in Chapurskii, *Grazhdanskoe protsessual'noe,* pp. 397–442.

[37] Order No. 52, October 28, 1935, Supreme Court USSR, A. N. Vinokurov, ed., *Sbornik postanovlenii i raz"iasnenii Verkhovnogo Suda Soiuza SSR* (Moscow, 1936), pp. 66–70.

which it thought most important, among them Article 5, requiring the judges to take the initiative in helping the weaker side in a civil case to present materials sufficiently well to establish equality with the stronger side.

Six months later the Prosecutor's Office of the U.S.S.R. published a long circular[38] in implementation of the Supreme Court's order, calling attention to the Prosecutor's duty under Article 2 of the Russian Republic's Code of Civil Procedure to intervene by way of supervision at any stage in the procedure to eliminate inadequacies in the courts.

In these two documents coming ten years after the end of the formative years in Soviet jurisprudence the federal government indicated its concern with the preservation in all republics of a uniform practice in application of their nearly uniform codes. The occasion calling forth this concern seems to have been the flood of civil cases then reaching the courts, for the Prosecutor's circular informs its readers that in the Russian Republic alone they had totaled in 1935 two million, and a similar high level of litigation is indicated for the other republics.

PROBLEMS ARISING IN COMMODITY EXCHANGES

The neo-capitalism of the New Economic Policy, even though sanctioned by Lenin and fortified by a complex system of rules governing settlement of disputes by a variety of courts and less formal tribunals, sat uneasily on the minds of officials of the Commissariat of Justice and of those deciding cases of conflict. The role of the private arbitration commissions in the commodity exchanges was one of the most debated, being on the extreme edge of the juridical concessions made by the new regime to the forces of capitalism. It was here that the neo-capitalists were most nearly free to conduct their affairs as they wished with little control on the part of the state. Apparently, they pressed their luck beyond the point of toleration in their desire to be completely free, for the jurisdictional competence of these commodity-exchange tribunals

[38] Circular No. 25/22, April 7, 1936, Prosecutor's Office USSR, A. Ia. Vyshinskii, ed., *Sbornik tsirkuliarov i raz"iasnenii prokuratury Soiuza SSR* (Moscow, 1936) pp. 132–34.

was the subject of some discussion. A case[39] before the Supreme Arbitration Commission in December, 1922, opened the problem to public view.

The dispute had arisen between two state enterprises doing business on the Nizhegorod commodity exchange. They had reached an agreement on September 9, 1922, under which Khlebo-produkt would deliver to Vladtorg 50,000 poods of rye during September at a price of 435 rubles per pood. The agreement was registered on the commodity exchange and thus brought under its rules.

Vladtorg made a down payment of 7 million rubles at the time of signing the agreement, but it received no rye at that time. The second required payment was sent ten days later to the Moscow office of the seller, but it was not accepted on the ground that the agreement had not been legally entered into because the power of attorney of the seller's agent did not authorize him to sign an agreement alone but only in company with the seller's general agent for Nizhegorod Province. The buyer then turned to the arbitration tribunal of the commodity exchange to settle the dispute. Under the award the seller was found obligated to make delivery of 50,000 poods in accordance with the terms of the agreement of September 9.

Since the value of the ruble was falling rapidly at this time of mounting inflation, even the buyer seems to have realized the necessity of revision of the contract, for the agents of the parties met and reached a new agreement on October 30 under which the seller would deliver 16,000 poods against the down payment of 7 million rubles at the price originally agreed upon, but the balance would be delivered at a new price of 700 rubles a pood, on payment of the full purchase price later in the day.

The payment was not made, the home office of the buyer arguing that it had not authorized its local agent to substitute a new agreement for the old without the confirmation of the home office. The seller thereupon refused to make delivery, and the buyer turned to the Supreme Arbitration Commission of the Russian Republic to obtain execution of the award of the commodity exchange's arbitra-

[39] *Vladtorg v. Khleboprodukt*, "Praktika Vysshei Arbitrazhn. Kommissii pri STO," *Ezh. sov. iust.*, No. 1 (January 9, 1923), pp. 19–21.

tion tribunal requiring the seller to deliver the full amount at the September 9th price. The seller then interposed the defense that the award had been issued after a hearing to which it had not been summoned, although its agent had been notified and had been present.

The jurisdiction of the arbitration tribunal of the commodity exchange was the first matter reviewed. The Supreme Arbitration Commission noted that under the statute on commodity-exchange arbitration tribunals an effort was to be made first to conciliate the parties to a dispute, and only if that failed would there be a hearing, the limits of the hearing being those set in the agreement of the parties to arbitrate. The award was to be executed voluntarily, but if it were not, the matter was to be referred to the commodity exchange's governing board to take the appropriate disciplinary measures. The Supreme Commission noted that the commodity-exchange tribunals were not courts of the state, so that any decision of the governing board had no state sanction. Arbitration in the commodity exchanges had to be looked upon like regular private arbitration under existing legislation.

Since the legislation governing private arbitration at the time was the 1918 decree on arbitration tribunals, the Supreme Commission examined the early decree. It held that although the commodity-exchange tribunals did not correspond completely to the arbitration tribunals governed by the 1918 decree, their differences were only formal so that the force of their awards must be determined by way of analogy to awards of the arbitral tribunals dealt with in the 1918 decree. Since the parties were state enterprises, jurisdiction for review of the award was in the Supreme Commission and not the regular courts, and the Supreme Commission was prepared to make the review to determine the legality of the award, both as to the form of the procedure followed in reaching decision as well as to substance.

Having concluded that the arbitration tribunals of the commodity exchanges were subject to judicial review, and that it had special competence since the parties were state enterprises, the Supreme Arbitration Commission found that notice to the seller's agent had been inadequate for purposes of the hearing. Consequently the commodity exchange's tribunal had not established its jurisdiction, and its award could not be enforced. It, therefore, became necessary for the Supreme Arbitration Commission to examine the substance of the dispute itself. This it proceeded to do, finding that a commercial enterprise holding out a given person as its agent could not later claim that his power of attorney was limited so that he could not conclude the usual agreements of the trade; the seller had recognized this agent's authority on earlier occasions to make similar agreements to the one in dispute; his authority had been confirmed by silence, for the seller had never informed any of the parties to its agreements that they required a second signature; as evidenced by the statement of the commodity-exchange governing board, the same agent had made three other subsequent agreements with his signature alone and these had not been contested; and, finally, the agent remained in the employ of the seller, which gave reason to conclude that the seller did not look upon his actions as illegal and incorrect. Thus, the contract of September 9 had to be found binding on the seller.

The revision of October 30 was, however, a valid revision of the September 9 contract, and so the Supreme Arbitration Commission decided that performance should be carried out on the basis of the amendment to the original contract. Still, there had been further devaluation of the ruble with a rise in the price of rye, so that the original prices were unrealistic. This required looking at the internal meaning of the contract, which was evident from the fact that the original price had been increased by the October amendment to take into account the devaluation of the ruble. The Supreme Commission then developed a formula to compute a fair price which would give the buyer the advantages he had sought to obtain by the September agreement, namely 20 percent reduction from the regular market price, and this formula should be applied on the day of delivery of the bills of lading to establish the price to be paid.

This case formed part of the evidence leading an author ten months later to conclude that matters were not satisfactory with the arbitration tribunals in the commodity exchanges.[40] He thought that they were attempting to create more power than they had. By

[40] B. Shekhter, "O birzhevykh arbitrazhnykh kommissiiakh (Byt im ili ne byt)," *ibid.*, No. 42 (October 26, 1923), pp. 967–68.

the rules they had adopted they were declaring their decisions final and not subject to appeal. They had even consented to hear cases arising outside of the exchanges. They held public hearings, and summoned parties and witnesses. Arbitrators and representatives of the parties might be challenged and removed. They issued awards in which they accepted or rejected a suit and awarded costs to the winner. In short, they had become in the critic's view like the pre-revolutionary commercial courts of the tsars and there were no two ways about such a conclusion. They had even copied word for word the rules of the old commodity-exchange tribunals. They pretended that their decisions were final, when by statute it was clear that they could be appealed to the courts and had to be appealed if they were to be enforced on any basis other than as a moral obligation.

The continuing value of such arbitration tribunals in commodity exchanges was questioned by the critic. If they were desirable, he proposed elimination of reliance on moral obligation to execute an award, and creation in them of the right to enforce their awards. If they did not meet the needs of life and were only tolerated as indifferent bodies with decisions devoid of any judicial meaning, they ought in his view to be abolished. This should be done not only in the interests of the persons and enterprises who turned to them but also in the interests of the state, "since every useless substitute for a court is at the present time harmful for the state." The critic's own choice was clear, for he ended his diatribe with the words, "We need no stage sets."

Less violent but no less firmly rooted criticism came from another pen.[41] The independence of the arbitration tribunals in the commodity exchanges was thought to be too great in this view, for they had no link at all with the courts unless it became necessary to enforce an award. They followed not the law of the land but commercial practice, and this was the practice of prerevolutionary times, a practice which was castigated as being the "practice and methods of the bourgeoisie." The Code of Civil Procedure had rejected custom as a source of law, and Professor Brandenburgskii had emphasized this rejection in introducing the draft of the code

[41] N. Petukhov, "Birzhevoi arbitrazh," *ibid.*, No. 49 (December 20, 1923), pp. 1131–32.

for enactment. The author concluded that even though the statute
on commodity exchanges had permitted them to establish arbitration
tribunals with the rights of arbitration tribunals generally, "this did
not mean that they did not have to conform in their work to the
general procedural laws of the U.S.S.R. and of the over-all policy of
the worker-peasant state."

Fear lest the arbitration tribunals of the commodity exchanges
get out of hand finally emerged in the Supreme Court of the Russian
Republic, for in June, 1926, it issued a Protocol declaring that until
a special instruction should be adopted regulating procedure in
these tribunals, they would be required to guide themselves by the
general norms of the Code of Civil Procedure.[42] By this protocol the
tribunals were put on notice that their awards would not be enforced if a court, upon being asked to issue an exequatur, discovered
a violation of the principles of the code, including presumably
those relating to conformity of a decision to the over-all policy of the
workers'-peasants' state.

PRACTICAL PROBLEMS IN THE
GENERAL COURTS

Practice in the general courts was demonstrating the passivity of
judges in fulfilling their role as aids to the workers. An author in
reviewing the work of the first months of application of the new
code of civil procedure concluded that the judges were not giving
enough attention to the possibility of participation in the case from
its very beginning when the plaintiff appeared with his complaint.[43]
The result was evident in the repeated adjournment of hearings
with consequent delays in settling disputes. The people's courts
were found to have been the worst offenders, and to have been
negligent in their duties as these duties were established by the
code, even in cases in which workers brought complaints which
they in their ignorance were unable to substantiate because, being

[42] Protocol No. 10, Supreme Court, RSFSR, June 28, 1926, *Sbornik deistvuiushchikh raz"iasnenii Verkhovnogo Suda RSFSR* (Moscow, 1930), p. 210.

[43] E. Dombrovskii, "Deistviia Suda po priniatiiu k proizvodstvu i naznacheniiu
k razboru del po grazh. prots. kodeksu," *Ezh. sov. iust.*, No. 49 (December 20,
1923), pp. 1137–38.

without a lawyer, they did not know even how to request the summoning of witnesses and experts.

Practice in the general courts, insofar as it can be deduced from collections of explanations published at the end of the N.E.P. by both the Russian and Ukrainian Republics' Supreme Courts and the annual volumes of decisions in the Russian and Ukrainian Republics indicates the type of problem faced by judges in protecting the helpless under Article 5 of the Code of Civil Procedure. The Ukrainian Supreme Court spoke in a dramatic protocol of February 9, 1925,[44] concerning failure of a court to seek evidence beyond that presented by the parties to determine the ownership of a disputed merchant vessel. In the view of the plenum of the Supreme Court the trial court had violated its duty "to try in every way possible to clarify the real rights and mutual relationships of the parties." The issue of ownership had been raised in an action to recover a fine for smuggling contraband into the port of Mariupol. The case is the more remarkable because the party to be protected was a bourgeois foreigner, the vessel being of Turkish registry and flying the Spanish flag.

At the hearing before the customs authorities the captain declared himself to be the owner of the vessel, but later when the vessel was libeled to assure payment of the fine, the captain sought to free the vessel by claiming that the owner was not himself but a Spanish citizen named Moses Sasson. He offered in proof of title a bill of sale executed in the Spanish consulate in Constantinople in 1922. The Prosecutor of the Republic took the case for a decision as to ownership to the Donets Provincial Court which held that the bill of sale of the ship "Iski-Dunnia" from one Gavilzade to Moses Sasson and the Spanish consul's certificate to the effect that the name was changed to "Moses" did not of themselves prove that Moses Sasson was the owner at the time that the vessel was libeled by the Mariupol custom house to assure payment of the fine. This conclusion was strengthened by the fact that the captain was in possession; had declared himself the owner before the customs

[44] *The Steamship "Moses,"* Protocol No. 3, Plenum of the Supreme Court, Ukrainian SSR, February 9, 1925; L. Dubinskii, compiler, *Voprosy grazhdanskogo prava i protsessa v postanovleniiakh plenuma Verkhsuda USSR* (Kiev, 1928), pp. 171–74.

authorities, and presented no documents subsequently to prove that he was a lessee. The court argued further that even if Sasson were the owner, he was liable to the fine as an accessory since the customs investigation had disclosed that the ship had false walls with secret hiding places. This indicated to the court that the owner knew of the purpose for which the vessel was to be used by a lessee. In view of these findings, the court dismissed the suit brought in the name of Moses Sasson to have his right of ownership in the vessel established, charging him costs.

On appeal to the Supreme Court brought by Sasson, the Court's College for Civil Cases concluded that the investigation of the Provincial Court had been adequate; that there was insufficient proof of ownership in Sasson; and that the decision below had been entirely correct and was in accord with the interests of the state. The Prosecutor protested the decision to the plenum of the Supreme Court, which held that rejection of the plaintiff's suit to establish ownership on the ground that he had not presented negative evidence to the effect that he had not sold the vessel after acquiring it was contrary both to the law and logic. As to the argument that Sasson was an accessory, the court said he had not been found to be such by the custom-house authorities, and the Provincial Court had no right to go beyond the administrative finding.

Having concluded that the bill of sale was inadequate proof of ownership, the Provincial Court should, in the Supreme Court's view, have demanded from the parties a document from the port of registry of the vessel certifying the owner and also the charter-party indicating whether the vessel had been leased to the captain. The plenum of the Supreme Court ended its declaration by stating that the mere fact of the plaintiff's foreign citizenship and residence abroad as well as a more or less well-founded supposition that he was engaged in smuggling did not release the provincial court from its duty under Article 5 of the Code of Civil Procedure to try to determine the real rights of the parties.

The Russian Republic's Supreme Court presented a tragedy as its contribution to the law of Article 5.[45] Suit had been brought

---

[45] *Vasil'eva v. Matveev*, Protocol No. 2, Plenum of the Supreme Court, RSFSR, January 16, 1928, *Sbornik deistvuiushchikh raz"iasnenii Verkhovnogo Suda RSFSR*, pp. 152–53.

for maintenance of a child born out of wedlock in the Chuvash Autonomous Republic, a unit within the Russian Republic. At the time of the birth on November 14, 1923, the mother registered her uncle as the father, but on December 3, 1923, asked that the designated father be changed to Ivan Matveev. On changing the registration she commenced suit against Matveev for maintenance of the child. The people's court, on discovering that two different men had been registered as the father, rejected the suit without even summoning the uncle because of the plaintiff's conflicting testimony.

The prosecutor of the Chuvash Republic protested the judgment, stating that since the people's court had been concerned with a semi-literate woman as plaintiff, it should have taken the initiative to clarify all circumstances of the case; that it was a Chuvash custom when a child was born out of wedlock to register as the father the nearest relative of the mother, in this case, the uncle, so that the lowly cultured woman, not knowing the regulations for registration of births, had followed her native custom. The plenum of the principal court for the Chuvash Republic rejected the protest of the prosecutor primarily because it found the woman literate, and "since she lived at a railway junction, she could not be found to be inexperienced and unaware of the law"; because there were no especially substantial violations of the law in the people's court's decision, and because the year's limit on time to protest had expired. The prosecutor protested again, this time to the college for civil cases of the Supreme Court of the Russian Republic, but the college left the decision as it was, feeling that the case had been clarified sufficiently. The President of the Supreme Court then put the matter before the plenum of his court.

Remanding of the case for new trial to a people's court was found necessary by the plenum. It declared that the court was bound under Article 5 of the Code of Civil Procedure to take the initiative in investigating all circumstances of the case because under Soviet law maintenance of a child is for the benefit of the child and not of the mother. Not only had it failed to take the required initiative, but it had rejected the suit only because the mother had registered the child first under the name of some one other than the defendant and at a time when the old customs, according to the prosecutor's protest, were still current. If the court had thought the uncle the father, it should have summoned him and not just rejected the suit. The plenum thought it too formal an approach to the case on the part of the college of the Supreme Court to reject the protest merely because the matter had already passed through two instances below, especially when there was a dispute as to whether the woman had been literate and acquainted with the law on registration of births. Further, there had been no copy of the birth certificate, but only a statement as to what it contained, and the plenum instructed all courts to avoid delays by obtaining the birth certificates and not to rely on testimony about them, for experience had proved that the facts testified to were often contested.

The extent to which the Soviet court intended to depart under Article 5 from the principles of adversary proceedings to establish truth was demonstrated in a case provided with an official headnote reading:

A Soviet court must always remember that a trial under the Code of Civil Procedure is not the former purely adversary proceeding, and it must apply broadly Article 5 of the Code of Civil Procedure, not relying to decide the case on formal elements, but it must examine from all sides the true mutual relations of the parties, liquidating these, if possible, within the same lawsuit and eliminating the necessity of liquidating the relations by bringing a new suit.[46]

The headnote appeared over a suit brought by a citizen claiming to be a member of a partnership for examination of the account books of the partnership to determine his share on liquidation. The defendants argued that the plaintiff was not a partner but a creditor and that his loan had been repaid on liquidation. The Moscow Provincial Court as the trial court had held for the defendants, saying that the plaintiff had not proved his status as a partner and consequently had no right to examine its books, he having failed to show that he had met the requirements of the partnership articles of participation in the work of the partnership for the

---

[46] *Lif* v. *Shtiller, Kalashnikov, Brikoshin, Rikhter, and Raifman*, Case No. 31433–1924, Cassational College for Civil Cases, Supreme Court, RSFSR, *Verkhovnyi Sud RSFSR, opredeleniia grazhdanskoi kassatsionnoi kollegii Verkhsuda RSFSR za 1924 god* (Moscow, 1925), pp. 17–20.

period prior to admission as required in a resolution of its general meeting. He had not assumed obligations of a partner by filing the required assumption of obligations, nor had he proved that he had not been expelled illegally from the partnership or been refused membership illegally. The trial court had stated its supposition that the plaintiff had refused to become a partner and had chosen the moment of liquidation to assert his claim only to share in its profits. In reversing the decision below, the college for civil cases of the Supreme Court seems to have been of the view that the trial court should have aided the plaintiff to present evidence of the kind necessary to prove his case, and in any event it should have made certain that his claim as creditor was adjudged in the same suit if partnership was not found, so that he would not have to bring a second suit if it had not been paid.

A similar position was taken in a case involving suit for court expenses brought by the defendant after having been vindicated by the court in a suit for delivery of 2,366 poods of flax or its value of 16,325 rubles 40 kopeks brought by the Tver Provincial Producing Commission against the Tver Provincial League of Cooperatives.[47] The trial court had rejected the original claim because of inadequate proof, but it had adjudged costs because the defendant had not claimed them. In hearing the appeal on the failure to give costs the college for civil cases of the Supreme Court said:

The principle of adversary procedure applicable in the prerevolutionary court is foreign to Soviet civil procedure, and, contrariwise, the law (Article 5 of the Code of Civil Procedure) has imposed the principle of self-help on a court. This principle of the Code of Civil Procedure has been imposed so broadly that in certain circumstances (Article 179 of the Code of Civil Procedure) it is permitted that a court in reaching its decision in the case with regard to the circumstances disclosed in court may even go beyond the plaintiff's claim. In such circumstances, not to speak of the cases when for example a legally illiterate peasant does not ask for repayment of expenses incurred in paying his representative at the trial won by the peasant, but also when a party having been informed of his rights does not present such a claim, the failure to include in the judgment reimbursement of court expenses except in those cases when the party himself refuses them would be in conflict with the funda-

[47] *Tverskoi Gubprodkom* v. *Tverskoi Gubsoiuz*, Case No. 31847–1924, Cassational College for Civil Cases, Supreme Court, RSFSR, *ibid.*, pp. 54–55.

mental principles of Soviet civil procedure and especially of Article 176 of the Code of Civil Procedure, Section "G," by which allocation of court expenses is an inescapable part of the court's judgment.

Article 5 obviously could not be used to create a right that did not exist. Such a conclusion emerges from the dismissal of a suit brought by one Janson against a state railway in the Far East for the purchase price of some firewood.[48] His request for payment had been rejected by the railway on the ground that by order of the Far Eastern Revolutionary Committee, dated March 3, 1923, all indebtedness of Soviet state agencies for the years 1921–22 within the territory governed by the committee was annulled. The seller then brought suit arguing that the order of annullment had not been published properly, nor did it relate to obligations of the railway. The railway's representative admitted at the trial that reference to the order of March 3, 1923, had been a misunderstanding, but that in any event there was no obligation to pay since the wood had been obtained not by purchase but by requisition. The Primorsk Provincial Court rejected the suit on the ground that under date of October 23, 1923, the Far Eastern Revolutionary Committee had annulled even indebtedness of state agencies for wages of workers and clerks and to pay this claim regardless of whether the wood had been obtained by purchase of the Far Eastern Revolutionary Committee would have violated the general policy of the Committee.

Article 5 of the Code of Civil Procedure was made the basis, in part, of the appeal, the appellant arguing that the court had violated the article by not discussing the character of the relationships between the parties. To this argument the college for civil cases of the Supreme Court had a simple answer: The Far Eastern Revolutionary Committee's order of September 22, 1923, to which, incidentally, no one had referred previously, had freed state enterprises from the obligation to pay private persons all debts incurred before nationalization of these enterprises, and so the plaintiff had no standing in court.

While cases criticizing the lack of initiative shown by courts in helping the parties are the most numerous to be found under

[48] *Janson* v. *Upravlenie Ussuriiskoi Zhel. Dor.*, Case No. 31804–1924, Cassational College for Civil Cases, RSFSR, *ibid.*, pp. 46–47.

any article of the code in the volumes of Supreme Court decisions, they were only a small part of the total appellate activity. Perhaps this is because the courts at the time were busier with errors of commission than with those of omission. Such an explanation is suggested by Stuchka's introduction to the volume of circulars issued by the Russian Republic's Supreme Court in 1925.[49] As president of the court he noted that the center of difficulty for the court was moving by degrees from criminal law and criminal procedure. He thought this phenomenon explicable only because practice in criminal cases was being put right to a much greater extent than in civil cases. This was not by chance, in his opinion, for the work in civil law was at least a year behind that in criminal law, and every day life was bringing forth new questions in civil law requiring an answer.

Procedural matters seem to have gained interest for the practitioners only slowly, for the index to the Russian reports in 1924 provided no listing of cases applying the Code of Civil Procedure in spite of numerous decisions concerning it.[50] Only the articles of the Civil Code were indexed. By 1925 the attitude had changed, for the two volumes for that year indexed cases applying 57 articles of the Code of Civil Procedure in the first half of the year and 46 in the second half.[51]

JUDGMENTS IN SEARCH OF GENERAL POLICY

The college for civil cases of the Supreme Court of the Russian Republic had four matters during the year 1925 requiring application of the much-debated Article 4 defining the law by which a court was to be guided in the absence of sufficient legislation on the matter. This article was the last weapon left in the hands of the school favoring retention of the primitive law of the early postrevolutionary period, and the way it fared before the Supreme

[49] *Verkhovnyi Sud RSFSR, sbornik tsirkuliarov i vazhneishikh raz"iasnenii plenuma Verkhsuda RSFSR za 1924 god* (Moscow, 1925), pp. 3–4.
[50] *Verkhovnyi Sud RSFSR, opredeleniia grazhdanskoi kassatsionnoi kollegii Verkhsuda RSFSR za 1924 god.*
[51] *Verkhovnyi Sud RSFSR, opredeleniia grazhdanskoi kassatsionnoi kollegii Verkhsuda RSFSR za 1925 god,* Issue I (Moscow, 1925), and Issue II (Moscow, 1926).

Court clarifies the fine line being drawn between elements of primitiveness and a stable, well-defined legal system.

The right to make a contract creating a monopoly right to present a dramatic production came under judicial scrutiny.[52] The well known author Alexei N. Tolstoy and his co-author, P. E. Shchegolev, concluded a contract with the Leningrad Theater Administration on November 5, 1924, giving the latter exclusive right to present their play *The Empress' Conspiracy* in Leningrad and Moscow for a two-year period, receiving therefore 500 rubles plus the usual author's royalties. Later, on February 3, 1925, the two authors made a second contract with the Moscow theater Komediia giving it exclusive rights to presentation of the drama in Moscow for a two-year period. Premières of the play occurred simultaneously on March 12, 1925, in Leningrad at the Grand Dramatic Theater and in Moscow at the Komediia. The Leningrad Theater Administration filed suit against the two authors and the Moscow producer in the Leningrad Provincial Court on March 21, 1925, requesting a declaration of nullity of the contract made with the Moscow theater and recognition of the Leningrad Administration's monopoly right in Moscow. The Leningrad plaintiff reserved the right to sue for damages arising from the Moscow presentation by the Komediia.

The plaintiff's monopoly rights under the contract were upheld by the Leningrad court in a judgment declaring that the dispute was to be decided under provisions of the law on copyright existing at the time of conclusion of the contract, namely the law of November 26, 1918, and the instruction of the Commissariat of Education issued thereunder; under existing law authors had a right to create monopoly rights to present unpublished dramatic productions; and this production should be considered as unpublished, although the existing legislation nowhere established a definition of what constituted publication of a drama. Such a finding was possible in application of Article 4 of the Code of Civil Procedure by examining the statute establishing fundamentals of author's rights. In that statute a distinction was drawn between

---

[52] *Leningradskoe Teatral'noe Upravlenie* v. *Tolstoi, Shchegolev and Shlugleit*, Case No. 32054–1925, Cassational College for Civil Cases RSFSR, *ibid.*, Issue I, pp. 272–78.

productions which had appeared and those which had not. Since Tolstoy's and Shchegolev's play had not been printed, the court held that it was an unpublished work. The contract with the Komediia was found to be without effect because it had been concluded in error, since the authors had given their consent to conclusion of the contract only on condition that the Leningrad Administration would agree, but for lack of legal information they had failed to include this condition in the contract. In recognizing the monopoly right in Leningrad, the court declared that the monopoly would terminate if the drama should be printed before the end of the two year period.

Reversal occurred in the Supreme Court's college for civil cases because of failure to apply Article 1 of the Civil Code and for faulty application of Article 4 of the Code of Civil Procedure, since the provincial court had not interpreted properly the policy of the workers'-peasants' government. To determine the rights in the situation it was necessary to take into consideration the decree of November 26, 1918, recognizing scientific, literary, musical, and artistic productions as state property. The policy of the workers'-peasants' state was made clear by the November 26, 1918, decree, namely to socialize the largest number of productions possible, to make them more easily available to the toiling masses in the broadest way possible, and only as an exception was the right granted to authors to withhold their unpublished works. This had in mind primarily literary productions, as evidenced by the fact that a special instruction was issued to govern dramatic productions, authorizing production of published ones without the author's consent. The court thought the policy clear to spread culture. There was a second policy matter, this being that the state was opposed generally to monopolies except those placed in the state, "for every monopoly right, as long as it is not in the hands of the state, serves the purpose of creating the maximum profits, and thus would separate art from the toilers." The interpretation of the Leningrad Provincial Court was found to be especially undesirable since the play in question had an "agitational character," and it would be wrong to take an interpretation which would keep off the stages of the workers' theaters in the two greatest industrial centers a play of such value. Such a means of exploiting one's rights had to be held to be a violation of Article 1 of the Civil Code as being in conflict with the social-economic purpose for which rights of contract were given. In application of Article 4 of the Code of Civil Procedure the Supreme Court's college could not agree with any interpretation of the nature of publication of plays which would keep off the stage a play which had not been printed, for a large number even of the old plays had not been printed, yet they must be available to the toiling masses.

An action to set aside a marshal's levy upon property of a debtor was brought by a state enterprise claiming that a part of the property belonged not to the debtor but to it by virtue of the fact that it was in the debtor's possession for the purposes of sale under a commission contract.[53] The Moscow Provincial Court rejected the suit at its sitting on September 29, 1924, on the ground that the contract was one of sale and not commission since by its terms the company having possession of the goods was obligated to bear all risks of damage, or loss by theft, fire, and other causes, and the company had also given the state enterprise a note for the full payment for the goods. This decision was made in application of Article 4 of the Code of Civil Procedure in the absence of any article specifically on the point.

Reversal occurred in the college for civil cases of the Supreme Court on the ground that the provincial court had improperly interpreted Article 4 of the Code of Civil Procedure. To be sure, so the Supreme Court's college held, there was nothing in the Civil Code on commission contracts, but they were well known in commerce. The policy of the state was to be determined by examination of a decree of January 2, 1923, providing that middlemen between state enterprises and private individuals might be only commission companies registered in the prescribed manner. From this it could be concluded that "a commission contract was permissible under certain circumstances and when there had been compliance with the specific requirements of the law." Further, the evidence indicates that it was not a sale, since in the ordinary custom of commerce the risk of loss was transferred under such commission contracts without transferring property in the goods,

---

[53] *Mostrikob* v. *Tovarishchestvo Manufaktura,* Case No. 33668–1924, Cassational College for Civil Cases, Supreme Court, RSFSR, *ibid.,* pp. 14–17.

and the promissory note should have been found to be only a guarantee of a conditional nature, and not evidence of sale.

Competing claims of creditors came before the Supreme Court's college for civil cases again some months later, when a decision of the Irkutsk Provincial Court was appealed.[54] The lower court had refused at its sitting of June 12, 1925, to accept a request of the liquidating commission for the Angin Consumers' Association to approve the membership of the commission and to order removal of the marshal's levy upon the property made on behalf of several creditors so that the property might be sold by the liquidating commission. The court gave as reasons its conclusion that there were no substantive and procedural norms of law concerning the method of proceeding with insolvencies. The appeal was based on Article 4 of the Code of Civil Procedure, it being argued that the court was obligated to decide the matter raised by the complaint, and it had been incorrect to say that there was no guidance in the law since the decree of May 20, 1924, on consumers' cooperatives anticipated their liquidation because of insolvency. Failure to decide the matter would cause the state in the person of state enterprises and cooperatives great losses as creditors of the association.

Reversal of the Irkutsk Provincial Court's decision was the action of the Supreme Court's college for civil cases, the college finding that there was an explanation of the Supreme Court of the Russian Republic dated June 29, 1925, covering the procedure, as well as the statute on consumers' cooperatives, and there was no reason for refusal to decide the matter. The matter was returned to the lower court.

Competing claims of creditors gave rise to the fourth case, interpreting Article 4 of the Code of Civil Procedure.[55] On this occasion the Bank for Cooperatives had sought to have established its rights as a preferred creditor in property of a peasant-producers' cooperative, Ural Stone. The Bank had opened a credit for the cooperative on September 10, 1924, secured by a list of goods in warehouse valued at 20,000 rubles and subsequently by secured

[54] *Case of Liquidating Commission for the Affairs of the Angin Consumers' Association,* Case No. 32580, Cassational College for Civil Cases, Supreme Court, RSFSR, *ibid.,* Issue II, pp. 63–66.

[55] *Sverdlov Branch of the Vsekobank* v. *Ural'skie Kamni,* Case No. 32729, Cassational College for Civil Cases, Supreme Court, RSFSR, *ibid.,* pp. 109–10.

notes in the amount of 13,000 rubles. At the request of the co-operative the security in storage was released and substitution made of goods "in circulation" (available for sale), as inventoried in Schedule No. 38 in the amount of 20,000 rubles' value, the Bank retaining the right to have these goods transferred for safekeeping to such other person or enterprise as it might designate. When the cooperative was in process of liquidation, the Bank demanded of the liquidating commission that it deliver the listed pledged goods to it. The request was refused until rights to the goods were determined by the court, and the action was brought by the Bank to have its rights as pledgee established. The Ural Provincial Court at its sitting of May 4, 1925, held that although there was no law specifically on the point of pledges of goods in circulation, in application of Article 4 of the Code of Civil Procedure, it was necessary to recognize this as a pledge of property since the policy of the state in favor of pledges was evident in the provisions relating to pledges of property under lock and seal. The court refused to accept the argument of other creditors that since the form of pledge of property in circulation was not provided for by the Bank charter and since the property was not under lock and seal, it could not be a pledge.

The decision of the Ural Provincial Court was affirmed, it being said that the appellant had sought to establish an improper interpretation of the Civil Code to exclude the pledge of property in circulation, for although the Civil Code contained nothing directly on the subject, such a form of pledge was permissible for inclusion in the arrangements for a credit under Article 92 of the Civil Code, and it was a form fully opened up with developing trade, especially in the granting of credits to cooperative agencies of commerce.

None of these cases go so far as to support the extreme view of Professor Goikhbarg that a court might disregard a norm and "lift itself up to the general well-springs of proletarian politics." In each case there was a real gap in the law. The court sought only to fill it, and it did so by analyzing related matters to find an expression of policy. Only in the copyright case did it set aside a contract for violation of policy against monopolies, but it did so by direct attack through Article 1 of the Civil Code. Its use of Article 4 of the Code of Civil Procedure was to find a meaning for "publication" of a drama in the absence of a definition in the law. This is not making use of the opening created by Article 4 to nullify a specific definition in the law. It adhered to the policy urged by the first opponent of the draft of the code back in 1923 who rushed into print before the full text had been published to register a protest against procedural manipulation to achieve class results. He wanted such possibilities reserved to the substantive matter of the Civil Code itself, and it was exactly there that the copyright decision of 1925 was placed, when Article 1 was used to set aside the contract.

This view of the reserve with which the court treated the matter is strengthened by the fact that in the volumes of decisions for 1924, 1925, and 1926 there is no reference to Article 6 of the Code of Civil Procedure under which parties are required to utilize procedural rights honestly. It will be remembered that when the draftsmen took out of the code their original articles permitting a court to refuse to recognize procedural rights exercised solely to cause harm to the other party, the excision occurred because of sharp criticism of these articles for making possible easy nullification of the procedural code. There was agreement only on leaving in the code as Article 6 in the final version the requirement of good faith. Apparently the proponents of stable law as they prepared the draft in 1923 felt little fear lest the proponents of primitiveness utilize Article 6 to reverse what must have looked to the lawyers among them like the course of history. The practice of the years 1925 and 1926 suggests that they had judged rightly, for Article 6 was not appearing as the basis for appeal to escape from procedural regularity.

To this conclusion there is, however, a sharply contrary piece of evidence in the form of a paragraph in the annual report of the college for civil cases of the Russian Republic's Supreme Court covering activities in the year 1925. It may be significant that this annual report was delayed for over a year in publication, appearing only in two issues of the Commissariat of Justice's journal for January 31 and February 7, 1927. This tardy appearance put it near the end of the period of the New Economic Policy when the handwriting was already appearing on the wall for the neo-capitalists of the N.E.P. The report introduced the matter of Article 6 after a paragraph declaring that Soviet law could not accept the principle of bourgeois law that no one may plead ignorance of the law, for under Soviet conditions there were many who were ignorant. The court had in every case to take into consideration the social situation of the parties and the degree of their cultural development and other facts. Having said this, the court, apparently in contrast, turned to discuss those who consciously sought to spin out the trial. For these the college "advised courts to apply Article 6 broadly." This advice was supplemented by the following:

The application of this article is especially expedient with regard to those parties and their representatives who, being really very familiar with the laws, use them for evil purposes by means of filing appeals against court rulings, etc., through which they create delays and spin out the trial over a long period as in former times.[56]

This paragraph may be taken to mark the beginning of a return to lessening respect for procedural requirements, such as was to characterize the later period of "liquidation of kulaks as a class," or it may be interpreted as a reassertion of the ever-present policy of keeping procedural principles within the place conceived for them, namely as a means of determining facts subject always to the precautionary measures thought to be necessary to prevent the clever bourgeois malefactor from tricking a court into measures which would result in cheating a worker or peasant out of his lawful right to protection.

The paucity of literature on Article 6 suggests that it was not being reasserted as a major plank of a new policy of primitiveness of procedure. A commentary[57] provides under the article only two items, one the paragraph from the Supreme Court college's 1925 report and the other a paragraph from a circular of the Commissariat of Justice advising courts to be alert against officials of state offices and public organizations lest they use quibbling methods in the

---

[56] S. Aleksandrovskii, "Doklad o rabote GKK Verkhsuda RSFSR za 1925 g.," *Ezh. sov. iust.*, No. 5 (February 7, 1927), p. 144.

[57] S. V. Aleksandrovskii and V. I. Lebedev, *Grazhdanskii protsessual'nyi kodeks RSFSR s postateino-sistematizirovannimi materialami* (4th ed.; Moscow, 1929) pp. 19–20. This book appears with a substitution of S. N. Abramov for S. V. Aleksandrovskii in the fifth edition (Moscow, 1931), but it is printed in part from the fourth edition plates with the same two paragraphs of commentary as in the fourth edition (see pp. 67–68).

conduct of lawsuits.[58] The courts were instructed to notify the employing office so that the official might be disciplined. Here was assertion of a situation quite the reverse of what had been expected by the draftsmen, for it was not the bourgeoisie of the N.E.P. who were delaying trials but public servants against whom no one had previously raised a voice. Article 6 was not mentioned, however, in the circular, and it seems possible that the commentator drew his own conclusions as to its applicability in selecting the circular as an annotation for his volume.

Returning to the reported decisions of 1925, it becomes evident that next to castigation of trial judges for laxness in taking the initiative to clarify every aspect of a matter when the parties had not presented sufficient evidence, the most frequently protested matter appearing in the opinions of the Supreme Court's college for civil cases was the insufficiency of judgments which failed to state the basis for decision. Eighteen opinions in 1925 referred to this problem. That it was a lesson soon to be learned is suggested by the falling off of such references to two in the year 1926. Examination of one of the 1925 cases will indicate what was the matter.

An action to set aside a contract of sale as harmful to the state and in violation of law tempted the court to act without explaining itself.[59] Perhaps it thought the circumstances obvious and requiring no detailed explanation. Certainly the complaint of the provincial prosecutor asking for the declaration of nullity painted a picture which would have brought swift action in the early years of the Revolution, with few questions asked. The charge was that in July, 1924, citizen Soskin concluded in the city of Kharbin, China, a contract to buy the barge "Refrigerator" from The Association for the Fish Industry. The prosecutor claimed that the deal was one of the means being used to dispose of Russian ships to foreigners since Soskin had since 1920 been engaged as a middleman to sell Russian ships to Chinese capitalists, and especially to the firm Utun, thus helping to weaken the Russian commercial fleet.

[58] Circular No. 192, People's Commissariat of Justice, RSFSR November 9, 1927, *Ezh. sov. iust.*, No. 47 (December 5, 1927), pp. 1484–85.
[59] *Amur Gubprokuror* v. *Soskin*, Case No. 33766–1924, Cassational College for Civil Cases, Supreme Court, RSFSR, *Verkhovnyi Sud RSFSR, opredeleniia grazhdanskoi kassatsionnoi kollegii Verkhsuda RSFSR za 1925 god*, Issue I, pp. 147–49.

Soskin's attorney explained before the Amur Provincial Court at its session of September 9, 1924, that sales of Russian vessels abroad had been occurring through the Kharbin firm Soskin & Co. in 1918 but that Soskin had not been a member of that firm and consequently he could not be held responsible in 1924 for what the firm did in 1918, and secondly that the sale had been in accord with the law. The provincial court found that by decree of November 21, 1917, the sale abroad of Russian vessels had been prohibited regardless of the citizenship of buyer and seller in view of which the contract had to be found illegal and the object of the sale had to be confiscated by the state, and so the vessel was declared the property of the Russian Republic and the sale voided.

Soskin appealed on the ground that the judgment set forth not facts but only an assumption. There had been no evidence in the case that Soskin intended to transfer the vessel abroad since he had ordered it to sail only as far as the mouth of the Sungara River, which was within the Russian Republic's boundaries. As a second point, the sale had been concluded legally with the specially empowered representative of the Russian Republic at Kharbin. Soskin was himself a citizen of the Russian Republic, and had been owning barges for two and a half years. Further, the decree of November 24, 1917, had been revoked by the decree of August 8, 1924, on the rules for selling commercial vessels, and this permitted sales to foreigners, and further, the Administration of Water Communications could always keep the barge within the country by simply refusing to grant an exit permit. Finally, the judgment confiscating the barge violated the Civil Code.

The judgment was set aside and the case remanded for new trial by the college for civil cases because of violation of Article 176 of the Code of Civil Procedure in that the provincial court's position was then completely without foundation. It did not set forth the basis for the decision, for Soskin's membership in the firm of Soskin & Co. in 1918 had not been confirmed, nor had it been shown that the sale was illegal since the act itself was not illegal unless concluded in the presence of a number of circumstances which had to be established by the provincial court since these were the bases for the prosecutor's action to set aside the sale as illegal.

This case on the extreme fringe of political toleration suggests that Stuchka and his colleagues in the Supreme Court were determined to proceed in an orderly fashion to establish facts. There were no longer to be presumptions of illegality merely because the parties were suspicious characters of the commercial world. The Supreme Court judges were prepared to take precautions to see that the helpless and especially the ignorant were provided with aid in presenting their case by a court that was willing to take the initiative, but they were not willing to let the lower courts act on suspicion to such an extent that they might without fear of reversal decide matters without full investigation.

The Supreme Court had reason to caution the lower courts, for few judges in the people's and even the provincial courts yet had legal education. The civil department of the Moscow Provincial Court, which must have been one of the best in the country because of the importance of the capital, reported during the first half of 1925 that "the next task is to raise the quality of work both in the trial and appellate departments." [60] The personnel of the court was reported to be 80 percent from worker and peasant stock and without special legal education. It was proposed that the younger comrades who had served less than one or two years have their study of law organized under the guidance of the more experienced comrades in a systematic fashion and with examinations by the presidium of the court.

This inexperienced court had a great volume of cases, for in the first half of 1925 there had been 11,887 appeals heard in contrast to 5,861 during the first half of 1924, and the court had been falling behind by about 7 cases each court day. To meet this crisis the court had organized "Saturdays" during which they had called in judges from the criminal division as well as substitute judges and clerical officials of the court, and at these sittings they had disposed of as many as 400 cases, so that by August there were no cases without a hearing date set. Eighteen judges had been permanently assigned at the time of the report, and this was expected to make it possible to maintain a normal tempo, which it was thought could dispose of a maximum of 30,000 cases in 1925. Even this would be

[60] Moskalenko, "Itogi i vyvody raboty grazhdanskogo otdela moskovskogo gubsuda," *Ezh. sov. iust.*, No. 44–45 (November 16–23, 1925), pp. 1384–86.

far too small a capacity, in the court's view, if high fees, which were keeping commercial cases from court, were reduced, and the court believed that these fees should be reduced. In consequence the court foresaw the possibility of being overwhelmed by a flood of cases if commercial disputes were to be filed without limitation, for only a quarter of the matters then being heard fell in the commercial category. Statistics indicated that the major problem before the Moscow Provincial Court at the time was housing, disputes over living space constituting 44.3 percent of the appeals from the people's courts. The second category concerned disputes over employment, totaling 15 percent of the appeals. Appeals from decisions on maintenance accounted for 11.7 percent of the cases. No accounting was given of the remaining 2 percent.

It was over courts such as this that the Supreme Court of the Russian Republic had to preside: courts with judges of limited legal education and with strong emotional attachment to the class from which the great majority of them came; courts with crushing numbers of cases to be heard requiring crisis work even on holidays and with no foreseeable expectation of lessened numbers of appeals. The situation as it stood at the end of the formative years must be considered in the light of the conditions of the time.

The report for 1925 by the college for civil cases of the Supreme Court of the Russian Republic laid bare the trying conditions of work.[61] The number of cases was mounting alarmingly. The college had heard 3,783 cases in 1924, whereas a year later the total had jumped 40 percent to 5,342. It was a much sharper increase than on the criminal side of the court where the total had risen only 22 percent in the same period, going from 13,207 to 16,092 cases.

To meet the burden the college was resorting to specialization by judges on the court, and to establishing priorities for hearings, so that the most urgent matters might be decided quickly, these being appeals against court orders and rulings. Right behind these were

---

[61] S. Aleksandrovski, "Doklad." The report is printed in two parts, the first being headed by an order signed by P. I. Stuchka as President of the Supreme Court, RSFSR, ordering distribution to all provincial courts as an aid in accordance with the order of the Presidium of the Supreme Court, RSFSR, January 7, 1927. See *Ezh. sov. iust.*, No. 4 (January 31, 1927), p. 108 and *ibid.*, No. 5 (February 7, 1927), p. 142.

to come cases involving claims for personal injury, maintenance of children and divorced spouses, employment problems, and evictions from living space. After these were to come all other types of cases but first among these were to be appeals against refusal to exempt from military service on claim of religious objection.

Stuchka's court declared a major problem to be continuing struggle against the harmful traditional habits of jurists of the old social system, which traditions were still to be found among court workers. Another problem was the increasing inadequacy of the work of the trial courts, for the rate of reversals had increased in 1925 over 1924 so that it stood at 47.6 percent of all cases heard either on appeal or on audit. An especially sore point was procedure, for of the reversals 62.6 percent concerned procedure and only 37.4 percent substantive law. Basic errors of procedure fell in the areas of assumption of jurisdiction when by law the matter should have been decided by an administrative agency (especially common with matters of nationalization of dwellings), accepting as plaintiffs persons not sufficiently interested as parties, faulty application of Article 4 concerning the law that should govern, inadequate activity in taking the initiative in exploring the matter as required by Article 5 so as not to limit decisions to consideration of the social position of the disputants but to consider all aspects of the case, and finally failure to apply Article 6, as has already been discussed earlier.

In closing its annual report for 1925 the college reminded its inferior courts that although these central features of Soviet procedure had substantial importance for the correct conduct of procedure, it was nevertheless necessary to remember "that in the interest of procedure itself the court must preserve that minimum of formality which the Code of Civil Procedure had established, for example in the summoning of the parties, interrogation of witnesses, etc." The court then made its final point, the point of those who had fought hard to establish order in the Soviet courtroom to replace the primitiveness of 1917. It said: "This is the duty of the court, for otherwise, the failure to observe the minimum formalities established by law puts the quality of the decision of the court in doubt." Then the college threw a parting gift to the primitives by adding: "Nevertheless, in spite of all of this, never must formalism be placed above the basic reason for procedure—the determination of material truth."

Stuchka's court was carrying water on both shoulders, but there was a clearly heavier load on one. There was no doubt that it was a class court in that it favored openly the class for whom the Revolution had been fought, and it was applying a civil code directing courts to set aside the substantive law when the public interest seemed to require such action. Yet, the court's policy was not, except in glaring cases of abuse, to set aside procedural law to such an extent that no one could determine what had really occurred and what were the real interests of the parties and the public in the dispute.

Settling disputes in Soviet society required, in the court's view, as evidenced by its decisions and its final report of the formative years, more than an automatic reflex in favor of arguments designed to arouse proletarian emotions. The new jurisprudence was expected to be reasoned and not emotional, for in the element of reason lay the long-range interest of the new Soviet state. This was the message left by the judges of the Supreme Court on the pages of their collected decisions in contrast to some of the militantly class-conscious sentiments expressed by the politicians and even by Goikhbarg and Vyshinskii on the tribune of the Fifth Congress of persons engaged in the administration of justice.

Chapter 13

FROM SIMPLICITY TO COMPLEXITY AND FORMALITY

THE FORMATIVE YEARS of the Soviet legal system, as they have emerged in this study, witnessed a transition from a simple, almost primitive, court to a complex set of tribunals reminiscent of those to be found elsewhere on the continent of Europe. To the Soviet jurist of 1925 the words of enthusiasm of Commissar of Justice Kurskii lauding the Soviet court of 1919 as primitive in structure and activity must have looked strange indeed. Gone were the days when a village elder or revolutionary enthusiast sat with his neighbors to hear their disputes and to resolve them without the help of state officials such as prosecutors or professional attorneys licensed to practice their profession in aid of client and court. Gone were the days when the judge acted without benefit of code of law or procedure but solely with regard to his revolutionary conscience, using his knowledge of human nature, such Marxist theory as he might have absorbed, and some residue of tsarist law as guides.

The courts of 1925 were professional. Their judges often lacked formal legal education, but their full-time occupation was the bench, and they now had the assistance of full-time prosecutors and bar. They were guided by codes of law which defined the principles to be applied in settlement of a dispute, and by codes of procedure which told them just what to do at every stage of the proceedings to determine the facts. They acted with knowledge that if they erred there was a higher court to set aside what they had done and to order a new trial, usually before some other court of the neighborhood.

The emergence of a complex judicial system applying formal rules worried many of the Soviet jurists, so they sought to differentiate the system they had created from that of other lands, to claim that it was unique in all the world. Their justification for originality lay in reassertion that their judges, their prosecutors, their bar, and the law and procedure with which these agents worked were close to the masses, the proletariat, and that these officials were inspired by the spirit of the "October Revolution." There was proud reference to what were claimed as the special features of the Soviet system: to the presence of lay judges on the bench with the professional judge having the right to share equally in deciding issues of law and fact; to the existence of prosecutors ready to intervene even in civil cases to protect not only the obvious interests of the state but the general interest in preventing a party from winning an unjust suit because of relatively more astute counsel or unqualified judge; to the broad authorization given the judge to take the initiative in searching for the truth.

Much was made of these elements claimed as Soviet innovations and most particularly of the role of the judge. His task was contrasted with what was described as the "bourgeois model." He was required to be active. He was not to be permitted to assume the position of an arbiter in a battle of wits between parties and their representatives. He was bound by no rules of evidence in criminal cases. He could examine anything or go anywhere to improve his understanding of the facts. He had only to create by whatever manner he pleased his own intimate conviction as to what had actually happened and what should be done to set the matter right. Even in civil cases the rules of evidence were few and related solely to enforcement of formalities established by the Civil Code for certain agreements.

To the American common-law lawyer such features may suggest that the orientation of Soviet officers of the law had indeed been changed from that of the judges, prosecutors, and lawyers of their acquaintance. To the jurist of the civil-law world the claim of innovation falls on deaf ears, for the lay-judge system is a German institution; the intervening prosecutor is to be found in several civil-law countries, and the actively inquiring judge freed from reliance on the parties for his facts is the key figure of the Continental trial. What the Soviet draftsmen retained after seven years of evolution to differentiate their revolution-born system from those of other lands lacked novelty, except for those tending to see a difference in kind in a difference of degree. Unmistakably the Soviet draftsmen had left open the door to arbitrary action with less legal restraint than is usual in civil-law procedures, and without question the Soviet law officials had exhibited a certain revolutionary fervor in the performance of their duties. Because of this they sometimes reached unexpected results. Still, Soviet legal institutions had much in common with those of other civil-law states, as has become evident in the pages of this inquiry.

For the outside world the revolutionary fervor of 1917 and 1918 stamped a strong impression on those seeking to characterize the Soviet legal system. Attention was focused in these years on the revolutionary tribunals as extraordinary political bodies designed to apply the rough hand of the Revolution to those who opposed the Bolshevik plans for change, or who were presumed to be enemies because of their social origin. The West was shocked especially by the Cheka, that militant body of the security police created by Lenin to protect the regime against its obvious enemies, but soon expanded in its authority so that it was striking terror into the hearts even of loyal Communists running afoul of those of their colleagues intent upon gaining personal power.

The pages of this study disclose the emergence of dissatisfaction among legally trained Bolshevik policy makers with the revolutionary tribunals and the Cheka. Krylenko, in presenting to the legislators in 1921 a proposal to audit all work of the revolutionary tribunals at a central place, bemoaned the fact that the 1920 attempt to restrict them had failed "because under the conditions of the epoch it is hard in the extreme degree to build courts distinguished by stability." [1] The jurists have been seen as adept after the first two years at seizing every opportunity to reduce the extraordinary authority of the revolutionary tribunals and the Cheka.

Fortunately for the not-too-numerous jurists the Cheka had antagonized not only the legally trained but the deputies to the Ninth Congress of Soviets and even many in the Communist party's ranks so that Commissar Kurskii was able at the close of

[1] N. V. Krylenko, Speech at Third Session of Central Executive Committee, Eighth Convocation. May 31, 1921, *RSFSR—I-IV sessiia Vserossiiskogo Tsentral'nogo Ispolnitel'nogo Komiteta VIII sozyva, stenograficheskii otchët (31 dekabria 1921 g., 19–20 marta 1921 g., 30–31 maia 1921 g., 5–7 oktiabria 1921 g.)* (Moscow, 1922), p. 185.

1921 to join a powerful coalition of forces voting for dissolution of the Cheka and transfer of its judicial authority to agencies which the Commissar of Justice and his colleagues expected to be able to control.

Even the revolutionary tribunals finally fell before the attacks of the officials of the People's Commissariat of Justice intent upon eliminating tribunals outside the court system, and in their place there was developed an extension of jurisdiction of the intermediate courts, augmented by a new set of "military tribunals," responsible to the Supreme Court of the federal government and bound to apply the Criminal Code and the Code of Criminal Procedure on pain of reversal by the Supreme Court.

With the abolition of the Cheka and the revolutionary tribunals there remained plenty of opportunity for flexibility and emotional vindictiveness under the elastic provisions of the codes, but the courts that had absorbed the extraordinary tribunals were now subject generally to rules applicable to the people's courts, although they still enjoyed exceptions. Notable among these was the right of the intermediate court to exclude counsel from the trial.

As the formative years closed, it must have seemed at least to most of the lawyers, that the turbulence of the Revolution had passed and that a legal system worthy of the name was in process of creation, applying the class approach to be sure, and allowing for exceptional procedure in political cases, yet charged with the task of making certain that facts were actually established and punishments meted out only to those who violated the rules of social intercourse established as requisite to the creation of a society structured on lines of Marxist inspiration. The extraordinary measures created for state protection through the Cheka and the revolutionary tribunals were giving way to routines designed to settle disputes in a way not unfamiliar to other societies, and it was to these routines that jurists were devoting their attention.

While jurists with knowledge of history sometimes speculated privately on the resurgence of terror, none wrote in the law reviews or warned publicly that within a few years the police officers of the abolished Cheka might roam the land in new uniforms and under a new name to dominate the lives of millions in the campaign to exterminate the kulaks as a class. Certainly few would have expected that ultimately the heirs of Stalin would find it necessary at their Twentieth Communist Party Congress in 1956 to denounce his perversion of the legal system created in the formative years.[2]

The task undertaken at the outset of this study was to test with Soviet data the thesis that modern man can settle his disputes with simplicity as the Russian revolutionaries so evidently hoped to be able to do. It is tempting to conclude from the record that the formative years of the Soviet community have proved the necessity in all modern societies for complex structures of courts and fixed rules of procedure if disputes are to be settled without social unrest. Within a very few years the Soviet legal system had moved from a primitiveness reminiscent of tribal societies to sophistication. What had taken centuries in Western Europe, and even in old Russia itself, had been repeated in the new Russia in less than a decade. Men who had expressed their desire to avoid all formalities in the settling of disputes found themselves engaged in creating what they had set out to destroy. Politicians justified this effort as essential to the well being of the state.

Can it be that the motivating force for this remarkable change in attitude was the force of social development alone? The answer to this intriguing question is clouded, as was anticipated in the preface to this volume, by the coincidence of a desire to create a new primitiveness and the presence among the Communists of considerable numbers of sophisticated experienced individuals, especially among those who guided the legal destinies of the Revolution.

Note must be taken of the educational and professional background of the men whose names stand out prominently in the pages of the minutes of meetings of the Central Executive Committee of the Russian Republic and in the law reviews of the Commissariats of Justice in the Ukrainian and Russian Republics. The first acting Commissar of Justice, P. I. Stuchka, was a lawyer, destined to prepare the first rules of court procedure and ultimately as President of the Russian Republic's Supreme Court to influence notably the observance of these rules. I. N. Shteinberg, who occupied the

---

[2] For an English translation of the major speeches, including the denunciatory speech of Anastas I. Mikoyan and the off-the-record speech of Nikita Khrushchev, see Leo Gruliow, ed., *Current Soviet Policies—II: The Documentary Record of the 20th Communist Party Congress and Its Aftermath* (New York, 1957).

Justice Commissar's position as a Left Socialist Revolutionary for the brief period of coalition government by Bolsheviks and Left Socialist Revolutionaries, was an impassioned proponent of orderly procedures in the creation of socialism.

D. I. Kurskii, who replaced Shteinberg in 1918 after a brief second interlude with Stuchka, was also a lawyer.[3] He had around him in the People's Commissariat of Justice men who knew the law of the Russian past, and some of whom had studied in Western Europe. They were revolutionaries in their loyalties to the political regime of Bolshevism, but they seem to have been imbued at the same time with a desire to progress in orderly fashion toward Communism. They felt the need for violent repression of those who had opposed their revolution, and their Marxist training led them to believe that the opponents were moved by more than individual intellectual opposition. They believed them to be opposed as members of a recently defeated ruling class, and, therefore, potential enemies, even if they had done nothing as yet individually to retard the progress of the regime. For such actual or potential enemies, the jurists of the Commissariat were prepared to tolerate, or in some cases abet, flexible procedures as temporary, to be abandoned after what they believed to be the brief spell before the state might wither away, or begin to wither away.

These legally trained men, although reduced by the Communist approach to politics to a role more nearly approaching that of the technician than policy maker, exerted considerable influence on the course of events. The record shows that it was Kurskii's voice which rose to call a halt to the chaos of divergent judicial decisions issuing from judges bound to no uniform rules. It was Kurskii who began to analyze the decisions and to select those that pleased him and to reject those that did not. Well before code making began the Commissar tried to bring uniformity by suggestion to local judges, and here was the beginning of rule making from on high. In this Kurskii was abetted by Lenin, himself trained in the law, who denounced the wide variation of practice in the various provinces and demanded that uniformity be established.

[3] A photograph and contemporary biography of D. I. Kurskii appear in *Ezhenedel'nik sovetskoi iustitsii*, No. 34 (August 30, 1923) p. 793.

Kurskii admitted in 1924, in addressing the Central Executive Committee, that he was himself a centralizer, and it may be that he and his colleagues had intended to bring about centralization from the very start but felt themselves impelled to let revolutionary fervor run its course before restoring central authority, which was associated in many minds with tsarist autocracy. Whatever the motivation the record is clear and voluminous. Kurskii began soon after his appointment to issue orders and write articles looking toward uniformity and centralized control. There emerged rules of substantive law and procedure in increasing complexity.

The era of code making began in earnest with 1922, and it coincided with the introduction of the New Economic Policy. It is this coincidence which gave rise to much speculation both within the U.S.S.R. and abroad that complexity of the legal process was forced on unwilling jurists as part of the general policy of neo-capitalism implicit in the N.E.P. Lenin did not try to conceal what he was doing on the economic side. He recognized that the Soviet economy was almost bankrupt by mid-1921, and he announced a drastic retreat. Its major feature was the restoration of the open market to the peasantry, but this move carried with it the restoration of private enterprise generally, although in limited form. Everyone seemed to take for granted that private enterprise could prosper and achieve what Lenin hoped would be possible in rehabilitation of the destitute economy only if it were accompanied by stable law. The code makers were set to work to provide the legal framework thought necessary to the success of the new economic program.

The innovating policies of 1921 opened the door of opportunity, as the record demonstrates, to many of the non-Communist lawyers of the tsarist period, who had eked out a living in precarious fashion during the first years of the Revolution. They emerged to publish their own law review and to seek admission to the new bar. They sought to guide the development of law in the direction of what it had been in the past, at least as to form. In published utterances they expressed their loyalty to the political and economic aims of the regime, but they sought to reestablish the attitude of "legality" to all that had to do with the courts.

Spurred on by the various forces desiring reform, the code makers set out to reduce the flexibility available to local courts and to create stability in the law and its instrumentalities.

The result of the drafting process showed that it built upon the experience of the early years, which had indicated a move in the direction not only of complexity and formality, but in the direction of establishing instruments and procedures of familiarity to Western lawyers. On this base, it was not difficult to erect a structure which was even further oriented toward the legal systems of civil-law countries of Western Europe and of the world generally. Draftsmen admitted publicly that they were using as models the codes of Western Europe, and in one historic instance they warned against the strictest adherence to the provisions on tort law in the Civil Code because these had been taken from the French civil code and could be presumed to favor the social structure of the land for which they had originally been devised.[4]

Some Soviet jurists of the time were prone to lay the increasing complexity of their institutions and procedure to the neo-capitalism for which they were asked to draft laws. They resisted acceptance of any thesis suggesting their new society required a complex legal system to settle disputes. They preferred to believe, or at least to pretend to believe, that simplicity had not been lost forever. In apparent response to this demand Kurskii and his colleagues assured the deputies in the Central Executive Committee of the Russian Republic that thought was being given to ultimate simplification of the proposals and that at a later session, if not at the next ensuing session, amendments would be proposed to undo some of the very work which was being presented for adoption as law in 1922 and 1923. Kurskii even went so far as to tell his confidants in the Commissariat of Justice that what was being done in 1922 to prepare a civil code was to create a system of law sufficiently familiar to the capitalists of Britain and France to induce them to invest in rehabilitation of the new Russia.[5]

[4] See annotation to Civil Code, RSFSR, [1923] I *Sobranie Uzakonenii i Rasporiazhenii Rabochego i Krest'ianskogo Pravitel'stva RSFSR*, No. 46–47, item 478, Art. 403, excerpted from Protocol No. 10, Plenum of the Supreme Court RSFSR, June 28, 1926. This annotation was edited to omit reference to French origin in the 1937 and subsequent reprints of the Civil Code.

[5] See D. I. Kurskii, Speech at Fourth All-Russian Congress of Persons Engaged in the Administration of Justice (1922), published in D. I. Kurskii, *Izbrannye Stat'i i Rechi* (Moscow, 1948), pp. 70–73.

Yet, while concluding that the New Economic Policy had indeed been the cause of much of the complexity sweeping away the last vestiges of flexibility and simplicity so dear to revolutionary hearts, the architects of the new codes could not bring themselves to dissociate what they were doing from the current of the Revolution to which most if not all of them were committed. This attitude is nowhere so well expressed as in the lectures delivered soon after completion of the first codes by Kurskii's colleague, N. V. Krylenko.

Krylenko, on whom had been placed the burden of guiding the 1922 and 1923 draft codes through the Russian Republic's Central Executive Committee, had no doubts whatever about preservation of the aims of the Revolution in what had been done. He told his law students in early 1923[6] that it was error to think that the creativeness of the codification period was inspired by the capitalist policies of the New Economic Policy. In scorn he wrote:

Many who cannot tell the difference between form and content still say that all of this raging torrent of legislative creativeness has been called forth exclusively by the N.E.P., that N.E.P. has come along and cannot live without precise legal norms, and so the precise legal norms have appeared. Some even go farther and say that N.E.P. has come, not so much as a new economic policy but as Western Europe, and in order to exhibit wares to Western Europe—for that reason Russia needs precise legal norms, legal order, a legal life, legality, and other good but empty words."

Krylenko thought that those who saw N.E.P. as the cause of everything evaluated improperly what had happened in 1917. Such a view, he said, saw only the denunciation of bourgeois norms, and the creation of the Cheka with extraordinary powers. It generalized to conclude that all law had been denied by the Revolution; that all respect for law had been scornfully rejected. For persons holding such opinions Krylenko produced his famous invective, declaring: "This can be said only by people who have lost so completely their balance wheel, and most of all, respect for our collective creativeness that there is no possibility of talking to them." He then rehearsed the developments since 1917, noting that the fundamental elements of criminal procedure and of the special part of the criminal code had been incorporated in Decree No. 1 on the courts, and these had

[6] N. V. Krylenko, *Sudoustroistvo RSFSR* (*Lektsii po teorii i istorii sudoustroistva*) (Moscow, 1923), Lecture No. 12, pp. 159–60.

been enlarged in 1920 in the guiding fundamentals of criminal law and again in the People's Court Act of 1920.

In Krylenko's thinking "N.E.P. provided only the atmosphere, facilitating it is true and hastening the exposure of this inescapable phase of development of our court work, but it never did more than that. It never foreordained the content of the work."

Krylenko's position was, therefore, that the Soviet legal system was born in 1917 in primitive form, but like the simple caterpillar, it carried within itself the complex structure of the butterfly which was to emerge inevitably when the time was ripe. The N.E.P. was in this view but an early spring, hastening the emergence of Soviet law in its full complexity from the cocoon. It was not a predatory bourgeois insect slipped stealthily past an unwary proletarian border guard to lay eggs from which a new generation of insects would hatch to eat the fledgling Soviet larvae before they had been permitted to mature.

Viewed in the light of the record, the complexity and formality of 1925 seems to have been influenced strongly in the specific form it assumed by the education and experience of the men who had drafted the codes, but the necessity of complexity and formality of some kind had been felt in increasing proportions since the spring days of 1918 following the first blush of revolutionary revulsion against all that had stood for law and order in the past. The formative years had proved to men who expected to avoid complexity and formality that there was no alternative. All they could hope for by 1925 was that, given time to think and experiment, they might devise less detailed rules and a simpler set of institutions to achieve the order they had found necessary to their aim. They expected to have the opportunity to develop their system further in subsequent years when the retreat of the N.E.P. had achieved its purpose of creating abundance and when the base had been laid for an economic system capable of providing for each according to his needs.

Disclosing the detailed progress of the ensuing years will be more difficult than discovering the facts of the formative years, for the materials indicating conflicts of ideas and sometimes even the statutes themselves have not all been published. Still, the outline of what can be expected is generally known. The draftsmen of 1922, inspired by the termination of the N.E.P. and the extension of economic planning and state monopolization of industry, and distribution, set about the preparation of simplification of the procedures they had created in earlier years. Krylenko and Pashukanis began to draft new codes in 1927[7] to reverse the trend toward formality initiated by their earlier work. The influence of this approach upon the codes of criminal procedure in the republics of Central Asia has already been sketched. To the men in the Commissariat of Justice in the late 1920's, it was time to think of the withering away of the state, of that ultimate condition envisaged by Engels as the inevitable result of expropriation of the bourgeoisie. Simplification of institutions and procedures seemed realistic and not Utopian, not because society was expected to revert to the simplicity of tribal life but because a public satiated with abundance of goods, lacking any reason for social protest, and educated to understand the beneficial results to be expected from self-imposed discipline would require increasingly less guidance and compulsion in performing social duties.

The experiment in simplification embarked upon after the close of the formative years was nipped in the bud by Joseph Stalin. He had no interest in such a development. He was seeking power without limitation, either from personal predilection for power as Lenin suggested might be the case in his warning to the Party written on his deathbed,[8] or out of a feeling that the Soviet peoples were too childlike and their economy too underdeveloped to permit relaxation of pressures in the face of what seemed to be threat of annihilation from the great capitalist powers. Whatever the motivation, Stalin found it desirable to eliminate the school of jurists which had created the Soviet legal system in the 1920's only to proceed to preach a restoration of primitiveness in 1930 and the revocation of the base of state authority necessary to assumption of absolute power.

Stalin found it unnecessary to abolish the legal system created by the judiciary act and procedural codes of 1922 and 1923 to achieve

[7] N. V. Krylenko, "K proektu novogo UPK," *Ezh. sov. iust.*, No. 47 (December 5, 1927), p. 1457. The draft was published beginning at p. 1473.

[8] For English translation of the text together with the drama of its suppression within the Communist party, see E. H. Carr, *A History of Soviet Russia, The Interregnum 1923–1924* (New York and London, 1954), pp. 258–59, 359–61.

his aim, for he was able to build alongside the judicial structure created by those statutes a parallel instrumentality of terror. The Cheka, which had been anathema to Commissar Kurskii and his colleagues, and which had continued to function under various names and with varying powers after Kurskii had succeeded in pushing it into the background at the beginning of 1922, reemerged as the security police of the People's Commissariat of Internal Affairs. Its power was extended through the creation in 1934 of special boards to sentence persons suspected of being "socially dangerous." In reaching these decisions the special board had to observe neither Criminal nor Procedural Codes.

Stalin supposed it necessary also to dispose of the leaders among those who had been planning simplification of the law in anticipation of the withering away of the state. In 1937 he declared Pashukanis an enemy of the people, and ultimately executed him. Soon after, Krylenko was treated likewise to be followed by others of the simplifiers, including Professor Estrin. Stalin's henchman, A. Y. Vyshinskii, who accepted the role of prosecutor in support of Stalin's purge, sought to establish a theoretical base to justify the purge ordered by his master. He declared that these men who had drafted the codes of 1922 and 1923 had tried to reverse the Revolution and restore capitalism by utilizing old forms. He said nothing of his own share in the drafting process. Even the memory of P. I. Stuchka, who had died in the interim, suffered disgrace in removal of his name from the title of the Moscow Juridical Institute to which it had been attached in his honor soon after his death. The sweep of the surviving "heroes" of the formative years of Soviet jurisprudence had been nearly clean. The irony was that although the pioneers were ousted and sometimes executed because they had started to undermine the base of Stalin's power, the public explanation for their disgrace was given as their work in 1922 and 1923 in creating a legal system on the model of the past.

To the legal scholars who were left after the purging of Pashukanis and Krylenko and their lesser-known colleagues in 1937 the new policy of Stalin was disheartening. Some of them followed in Vyshinskii's shadow to justify the doctrine of arbitrary power, but many waited for the day when they might reassert their belief that there was nothing incompatible between building Communism and conducting an orderly judicial system which would revere procedure and provide institutions capable of assuring its application. They had to await Stalin's death in March, 1953, before they were able to state their case with full force. At that point the highest politicians within the Communist party had been so frightened by Stalin's reign of terror that for a spell there was unity of thought between the men of the legal profession and the politicians of the party. A wave of discussion of legal reform swept the Soviet law reviews and even resulted in rectification of some of the worst abuses, notably the abolition in September, 1953, of the special boards of the Ministry of Internal Affairs, and the return to the courts of all jurisdiction to try and punish.

The events after Stalin's death throw new light on the formative years of Soviet jurisprudence. They suggest that at times there was a cleavage in approach to the legal system between the men who guided the destinies of the U.S.S.R. in the Politburo of the Communist party and the men who worked in the legal system, whether in the courts, the procuracy, the administrative mechanism of the Commissariat of Justice, or the bar. The supreme politicians demonstrated their mistrust of formal restrictions on the exercise of arbitrary power. They wanted to preserve flexibility for themselves, as well as the instruments to utilize this flexibility so as to have a free hand to rule as they wished, and this meant ruling without restraint. As with potentates of the past, and strong men of the present, Soviet supreme politicians seem to have wanted to accomplish programs in their own way. The emphasis was upon ends with little thought to the corrupting potentialities of uncontrollable means. The obvious necessity of fast industrialization of the U.S.S.R. to meet the challenges of economically and militarily strong contemporary states strengthened the determination of the highest Soviet politicians to keep for themselves loopholes in the general pattern of law, which they mistrusted, but which advisers told them they must countenance in the name of the humanity which they championed or at least in the interest of propaganda advantage among the peoples of the world.

In opposition to the supreme politicians there stood most of the men of the law. In a sense, they were not in opposition, for they were largely, but by no means entirely, members of the Communist party, and as such they were pledged to achievement of the same ends as the supreme politicians. Yet within the area revealed in the record they were in opposition. They pushed forward whenever the opportunity was presented to do so without losing their heads to the supreme politicians in a quiet but unending effort to create limitations on arbitrary powers. They sought what they often called "legality." They professed on every occasion that it was a "revolutionary legality" or "socialist legality" they hoped to achieve. By this they tried to indicate their acceptance of goals, their willingness to work for an economic and social structure which would be quite different from that of the tsarist past or contemporary western Europe and the Americas. Yet, their emphasis was upon "legality," for as men of the law some felt that there was virtue in order, while others knew that there was political advantage to be gained in espousing order, for such espousal tended to placate society and reduce the expense of government. The lesson taught by the utilitarians had been learned that legally enforced order economizes the material cost of power.

Viewed in this perspective the formative years of the Soviet legal system represent a period when the stage was being set for what was to become an unresolved contest between methods favored by the supreme politicians and those championed by the men of the law. In the turbulence of the Revolution, the men of the law often joined with the mob to tear down the old order, but they were soon at work creating a new order in their own way by the painstaking placing of steps in the path to "legality."

The lawyers were thrown back again and again in their campaign to humanize their system, and sometimes they found it necessary to mouth phrases more royalist than those of their "kings," but they kept on with their work, although some fell permanently into the camp of the dictator. Most of them showed themselves working not to oust the regime under which they lived and for which many had given their careers but to perfect it. Kurskii provided a key note when he told his colleagues in May 1918 that the role of revolutionary repression was "not one of revenge but of defending the conquests of the Revolution for which the workers and peasants have paid with their blood." [9] The words needed saying, for the masses and many of their fiery leaders were vengeful, and it took a cool head to think as Kurskii did.

By the end of the formative years Kurskii's views were gaining favor and may even have achieved the upper hand. At least, the jurists must have thought that they had convinced the supreme politicians that the way of law and order had much to offer even those in a hurry, or, at the minimum, this way had to be followed because it had become too popular to be resisted openly by those accumulating power.

[9] D. I. Kurskii, Speech at Fourteenth Sitting of the Central Executive Committee, Fourth Convocation, May 27, 1918, *RSFSR—Protokoly zasedanii Vserossiiskago Tsentral'nago Ispolnitel'nago Komiteta 4-go sozyva (stenograficheskii otchët)* (Moscow, 1920), p. 345.

Bibliography

KEY TO JOURNALS

Ezh. sov. iust. = *Ezhenedel'nik sovetskoi iustitsii* [Weekly of Soviet Justice], Moscow.
Pravo i zhizn' [Law and Life], Moscow.
Prol. rev. i pravo = *Proletarskaia revoliutsiia i pravo* [The Proletarian Revolution and Law], Moscow.
Sov. gos. i pravo = *Sovetskoe gosudarstvo i pravo* [Soviet Government and Law], Moscow.
Sov. pravo = *Sovetskoe pravo* [Soviet Law], Moscow.
Vestnik sov. iust.: Vestnik sovetskoi iustitsii [Messenger of Soviet Justice], Khar'kov.

LEGISLATIVE HISTORY

RSFSR. Vserossiiskii Tsentral'nyi Ispolnitel'nyi Komitet: Protokoly Zasedanii (Stenograficheskii Otchët) [All-Russian Central Executive Committee: Protocols of the Meetings (Stenographic Minutes)].
Sozyv II—1917 (October 27–December 29)
Sozyv IV—1918 (March 20–June 14)
Sozyv V—1918 (July 15–November 4)
Sozyv VII—1920 (February 2–October 23)
Sozyv VIII—1920–21 (December 31, 1920–October 7, 1921)
Sozyv IX—1921–22 (December 29, 1921–October 31, 1922)
Sozyv X—1922–23 (December 28, 1922–November 3, 1923)
Sozyv XI—1924–25 (October 7, 1924–May 6, 1925)
Sozyv XII—1925 (May 11–October 24, 1925)
RSFSR. Vserossiiskii S"ezd Sovetov RSFSR: Stenograficheskii Otchët [All-Russian Congress of Soviets: Stenographic Minutes].
II S"ezd—1917 (October 25–26, 1917)
III S"ezd—1918 (January 10–18, 1918)
IV S"ezd—1918 (March 15–16, 1918)
V S"ezd—1918 (July 4–10, 1918)
VI S"ezd—1918 (November 6–9, 1918)
VII S"ezd—1919 (December 5–9, 1918)
VIII S"ezd—1920 (December 22–29, 1920)
IX S"ezd—1921 (December 23–28, 1921)
X S"ezd—1922 (December 23–27, 1922)
XI S"ezd—1924 (January 19–29, 1924)
XII S"ezd—1925 (May 7–16, 1925)
RSFSR. S"ezdy Sovetov RSFSR v postanovleniiakh i rezoliutsiiakh: Sbornik dokumentov s vvodnymi stat'iami i predisloviem sostavitelei pod obshchei redaktsiei A. Ia. Vyshinskogo [The Congresses of Soviets

of the RSFSR in Orders and Resolutions: A Collection of Documents with Introductory Articles and a Preface by the Compilers under the General Editorship of A. Ia. Vyshinskii]. Moscow, 1939.

SSSR. Tsentral'nyi Ispolnitel'nyi Komitet SSSR: Stenograficheskii Otchët [Central Executive Committee of the USSR: Stenographic Minutes].

Sozyv I—1923 (July 6, November 6–12, 1923)

Sozyv II—1924–25 (February 2, October 17–29, 1924; March 2–7, 1925)

SSSR. S"ezd Sovetov SSSR: Stenograficheskii otchët s prilozheniiami [Congress of Soviets USSR: Stenographic Minutes with Appendices].

I S"ezd—1922 (December 30, 1922)

II S"ezd—1924 (January 26–February 2, 1924)

III S"ezd—1925 (May 13–20, 1925)

SSSR. Postanovleniia pervogo s"ezda sovetov SSSR [Laws of the First Congress of Soviets of the USSR]. Moscow, 1923.

SSSR. S"ezdy Sovetov SSSR v postanovleniiakh i rezoliutsiiakh [The Congresses of Soviets of the USSR in Orders and Resolutions]. Ed. by A. Ia. Vyshinskii. Moscow, 1939.

SERIAL PUBLICATION OF
LAWS AND ORDERS

RSFSR. Sobranie Uzakonenii i Rasporiazhenii Rabochego i Krest'ianskogo Pravitel'stva [Collection of Laws and Orders of the Workers'-Peasants' Government]. Part One. Moscow, 1917–38.

RSFSR. Sobranie Postanovlenii i Rasporiazhenii Raboche-Krest'ianskogo Pravitel'stva RSFSR [Collection of Decrees and Orders of the Government of the RSFSR]. Moscow, 1939–49.

Ukrainian SSR. Sobranie Uzakonenii i Rasporiazhenii Raboche-Krest'ianskogo Pravitel'stva Ukrainy [Collection of Laws and Orders of the Workers'-Peasants' Government of the Ukraine]. Kharkov, 1919–25.

Belorussian SSR. Sobranie Uzakonenii i Rasporiazhenii Raboche-Krest'ianskogo Pravitel'stva Sotsialisticheskoi Sovetskoi Respubliki Belorussii [Collection of Laws and Orders of the Workers'-Peasants' Government of the Socialist Soviet Republic of Belorussia]. Minsk, 1923–25.

Azerbaidzhan SSR. Sobranie Uzakonenii i Rasporiazhenii Raboche-Krest'ianskogo Pravitel'stva Azerbaidzhanskoi Sotsialisticheskoi Sovetskoi Respubliki [Collection of Laws and Orders of the Workers'-Peasants' Government of the Azerbaidzhan Socialist Soviet Republic]. Baku, 1921–25.

SSSR. Sobranie Zakonov i Rasporiazhenii Raboche-Krest'ianskogo Pravitel'stva Soiuza Sovetskikh Sotsialisticheskikh Respublik: Otdel Pervyi [Collection of Laws and Orders of the Workers'-Peasants' Government of the Union of Soviet Socialist Republics: Part One]. Moscow, 1924–38.

494   *Bibliography*

SERIAL PUBLICATION OF LAWS
AND ORDERS (*Continued*)

SSSR. Vedomosti Verkhovnogo Soveta Soiuza Sovetskikh Sotsialisti-cheskikh Respublik [Messenger of the Supreme Soviet of the Union of Soviet Socialist Republics]. Moscow, 1938–59.

SSSR. Sobranie Postanovlenii i Rasporiazhenii Pravitel'stva Soiuza Sovet-skikh Sotsialisticheskikh Respublik [Collection of Decrees and Orders of the Government of the Union of Soviet Socialist Republics]. Moscow, 1938–49.

COLLECTIONS OF STATUTORY MATERIALS

Dekrety o Sudie Rabochago i Krest'ianskago Pravitel'stva [Decrees on the Court of the Workers'-Peasants' Government]. Publication of the Commissariat over the Abolished Petrograd District Court and Circuit Court. Petrograd, 1918.

Dekrety o Sudie Rabochago i Krest'ianskago Pravitel'stva [Decrees on the Court of the Workers'-Peasants' Government]. Collection compiled by the President of the Petrograd District People's Court, Legran. A Publication of the Petrograd Soviet of Worker and Red Army Deputies. Petrograd, 1918.

Sobranie Uzakonenii i Rasporiazhenii Rabochego i Krest'ianskogo Pra-vitel'stva: Sistematicheskii sbornik vazhneishikh dekretov 1917–1920 [Collection of Laws and Orders of the Workers'-Peasants' Government: Systematic Collection of the Most Important Decrees 1917–1920]. Moscow, 1920 (on cover: 1921).

Severo-Zapadnoe Promyshlennoe Biuro VSNKh: Sbornik dekretov i postanovlenii po Novoi Ekonomicheskoi Politike [North-West Industrial Bureau of the Supreme Council of People's Economy: Collection of Decrees and Orders on the New Economic Policy]. With a Foreword by R. Arskii. 2 vols. Petrograd, 1921–22.

Rossiiskaia Sotsialisticheskaia Federativnaia Sovetskaia Respublika. 1917–1922 g.: Sistematicheskii sbornik dlia sudebnykh deiatelei [Russian Socialist Federated Soviet Republic. 1917–1922: Systematic Collection for Court Officials]. Vol. I. Compiled by O. B. Barsegiants, Consultant to the Department of Justice of the Moscow Soviet of Worker and Peasant Deputies. Petrograd, 1922.

Sistematicheskoe Sobranie Zakonov RSFSR Deistvuiushchikh na 1-e Ian-varia 1928 goda (7 Noiabria 1917 g.–31 Dekabria 1927 g.) [System-atic Collection of Laws of the RSFSR in Force on January 1, 1928 (November 7, 1917–December 31, 1927)]. Under the general editor-ship of and with an Introduction by Ia. N. Brandenburgskii, member of the College of the People's Commissariat of Justice RSFSR. 2 vols. Moscow, 1928–29.

Sistematicheskoe Sobranie Deistvuiushchikh Zakonov Soiuza Sovetskikh

Sotsialisticheskikh Respublik [Systematic Collection of Laws in Force in the Union of Soviet Socialist Republics]. 5 vols., Supplement, and Index. Moscow, 1926–27. (Vols. I–II, IV–V, 1926; Vol. III, Supplement I and Index, 1927.)

BOOKS

Aleksandrovskii, S. V. and V. I. Lebedev. Grazhdanskii protsessual'nyi kodeks RSFSR s postateino-sistematizirovannimi materialami [The Code of Civil Procedure, RSFSR, with Material Systematized by Articles]. 4th ed. Moscow, 1929.

Berman, Harold J. Justice in Russia: An Interpretation of Soviet Law. Cambridge, Massachusetts, 1950.

Berman, Ia. L. Ocherki po istorii sudoustroistva RSFSR s predisloviem N. V. Krylenko [Essays on the History of the RSFSR Judicial System, with an Introduction by N. V. Krylenko]. Moscow, 1924.

Carr, E. H. A History of Soviet Russia. Vol. IV: The Interregnum, 1923–1924. New York and London, 1954.

Chapurskii, V. P., ed. Grazhdanskoe protsessual'noe zakonodatel'stvo SSSR i soiuznykh respublik [Legislation of the USSR and of the Union Republics on Civil Procedure]. Moscow, 1957.

Chel'tsov, M. A. Ugolovnyi protsess [Criminal Procedure]. Moscow, 1948.

David, René. Traité Elémentaire de Droit Civil Comparé: Introduction à l'Etude des Droits Etrangers et la Méthode Comparative. Paris, 1950.

David, René, and Henry P. DeVries. The French Legal System: An Introduction to Civil Law Systems. New York, 1958.

David, René, and John N. Hazard. Le Droit Soviétique. Vol. I: Les Donneés Fondamentales du Droit Soviétique, par René David. Paris, 1954.

Dekrety Sovetskoi vlasti [Decrees of Soviet Authority]. Vol. I. Moscow, 1957.

Denisov, A. I., ed. Istoriia gosudarstva i prava [A History of the State and Law]. Part II. Moscow, 1948.

——Istoriia sovetskogo gosudarstva i prava [A History of the Soviet State and Law]. Moscow, 1949.

DeVries, Henry P. See David, René and Henry P. DeVries.

Dubinskii, L., comp. Voprosy grazhdanskogo prava i protsessa v postanovleniiakh plenuma Verkhsuda USSR [Questions of Civil Law and Procedure in Orders of the Plenum of the Supreme Court of the Ukrainian SSR]. Kiev, 1928.

Golunskii, S. A., ed. Istoriia zakonodatel'stva SSSR i RSFSR po ugolovnomu protsessu i organizatsii suda i prokuratury 1917–1954 gg.: Sbornik dokumentov [A History of the Legislation of the USSR and the RSFSR on Criminal Procedure and the Organization of the Court and the Prosecutor's Office, 1917–1954: Collection of Documents]. Moscow, 1955.

BOOKS (*Continued*)

Gruliow, Leo, ed. Current Soviet Policies—II: The Documentary Record of the 20th Communist Party Congress and Its Aftermath. New York, 1957.

Gsovski, Vladimir. Soviet Civil Law: Private Rights and Their Background under the Soviet Regime. 2 vols. Ann Arbor, Michigan, 1948–49.

Guins, George C. Soviet Law and Soviet Society. The Hague, 1954.

Hazard, John N. Law and Social Change in the U.S.S.R. London, 1953.

——See also David, René, and John N. Hazard.

Istoriia sovetskoi konstitutsii v dekretakh i postanovleniiakh sovetskogo pravitel'stva, 1917–1936 [History of the Soviet Constitution in Decrees and Orders of the Soviet Government, 1917–1936]. Moscow, 1936.

Karev, D. S., ed. Ugolovno-protsessual'noe zakonodatel'stvo SSSR i soiuznykh respublik, sbornik (osnovnye zakonodatel'nye akty) [The Criminal Procedural Legislation of the USSR and of the Union Republics: a Collection (The Fundamental Legislative Acts)]. Moscow, 1957.

Kelsen, Hans. The Communist Theory of Law. New York, 1955.

Kleinman, A. F. Grazhdanskii protsess [Civil Procedure]. 1st ed.; Moscow, 1934. 2d ed.; Moscow, 1935.

Kozhevnikov, M. V. Istoriia sovetskogo suda 1917–1956 gody [History of the Soviet Court 1917–1956]. Moscow, 1957.

Krylenko, N. V. Lenin o sude i ugolovnoi politike, k desiatiletiiu so dnia smerti, 1924–1934 [Lenin on the Court and Criminal Policy, on the Tenth Anniversary of His Death, 1924–1934]. Moscow, 1934.

——Sudoustroistvo RSFSR (Lektsii po teorii i istorii sudoustroistva) [The Judicial System of the RSFSR (Lectures on the Theory and History of the Judicial System]. Moscow, 1923.

Kucherov, Samuel. Courts, Lawyers and Trials under the Last Three Tsars. New York, 1953.

Kurskii, D. I. Izbrannye stat'i i rechi [Selected Articles and Speeches]. Moscow, 1948.

Lebedev, V. I. See Aleksandrovskii, S. V., and V. I. Lebedev.

Lenin, V. I. Selected Works. Moscow, 1935. Vol. VI.

——Sochineniia [Works]. 3d ed. Moscow, 1928–37. Vol. XXII. 4th ed. Moscow, 1949–51. Vols. XXV, XXXIII.

——The State and Revolution. Moscow, 1935.

Narodnyi Komissariat Iustitsii, SSSR. Sovetskaia advokatura [The Soviet Institution of Advocacy]. Moscow, 1942.

Novitskii, I. B., ed. Grazhdanskoe zakonodatel'stvo SSSR i soiuznykh respublik [The Civil Law of the USSR and of the Union Republics]. Moscow, 1957.

Obnorskii, S. P., ed. Slovar' russkogo iazyka [Dictionary of the Russian Language]. Moscow, 1949.

Polianskii, N. N. Pravda i lozh' v ugolovnom zashchite [Truth and Falsehood in Criminal Defense]. Moscow, 1927.

Rappard, William E., Walter R. Sharp, Herbert W. Schneider, James K. Pollock, and Samuel N. Harper. Source Book on European Governments. New York, 1937.

Rivlin, E. S. Sovetskaia advokatura [The Soviet Bar]. Moscow, 1926.

Sbornik deistvuiushchikh raz"iasnenii Verkhovnogo Suda RSFSR, izdannykh za vremia s 1923 g. do 1 ianvaria 1929 g. [Collection of Explanations in Force of the Supreme Court of the RSFSR, Issued during the Period from 1923 to January 1, 1929]. With an Introduction by P. I. Stuchka. Moscow, 1930.

Sbornik tsirkuliarov i raz"iasnenii Narodnogo komissariata iustitsii RSFSR [Collection of Circulars and Explanations of the People's Commissariat of Justice RSFSR]. Moscow, 1934.

Sbornik tsirkuliarov narkomiusta RSFSR za 1922–1925 gg. [Collection of Circulars of the People's Commissariat of Justice of the RSFSR for 1922–1925]. Moscow, 1926.

Schlesinger, Rudolf. Soviet Legal Theory: Its Social Background and Development. New York, 1945.

Shekhter, B. Grazhdanskii protsessual'nyi kodeks RSFSR, prakticheskii postateinya kommentarii (obshcheiiskovoe proizvodstvo) [The Code of Civil Procedure of the RSFSR, a Practical Commentary by Articles (General Procedure for Suit)]. Leningrad, 1926.

Sorok Let sovetskogo prava [Forty Years of Soviet Law]. 2 vols. Leningrad, 1957.

Sovetskaia prokuratura v vazhneishikh dokumentakh [The Soviet Prosecutor's Office in the Most Important Documents]. Moscow, 1956.

Soviet Legal Philosophy. Translated by Hugh W. Babb, with an Introduction by John N. Hazard. Cambridge, Massachusetts, 1953.

Steinberg, I. N. In the Workshop of the Revolution. New York, 1953.

Strogovich, M. S. Ugolovnyi protsess (pod red. A. Ia. Vyshinskogo) [Criminal Procedure]. Edited by A. Ia. Vyshinskii. 1st ed. Moscow, 1934. 4th ed. Moscow, 1938.

Stuchka, P. I. Narodnyi sud v voprosakh i otvietakh [The People's Court in Questions and Answers]. Moscow, 1918.

——Revoliutsionnaia rol' prava i gosudarstvo [The Revolutionary Role of Law and the State]. 2d ed. Moscow, 1923.

Sudebnaia praktika Verkhovnogo Suda SSSR [Court Practice of the Supreme Court of the USSR]. Issue VI (XII), Moscow, 1944.

Veger, V. I. Ditsiplina i etika zashchitnika [The Discipline and Ethics of a Defender]. Moscow, 1925.

Verkhovnyi Sud RSFSR. Opredeleniia grazhdanskoi kassatsionnoi kollegii

BOOKS (Continued)

Verkhsuda RSFSR za 1924 god. [Supreme Court, RSFSR. Decisions of the Cassational College for Civil Cases of the Supreme Court RSFSR for 1924]. Moscow, 1925.

Verkhovnyi Sud RSFSR. Opredeleniia grazhdanskoi kassatsionnoi kollegii Verkhsuda RSFSR za 1925 god. [Supreme Court, RSFSR. Decisions of the Cassational College for Civil Cases of the Supreme Court RSFSR for 1925]. Issue I: Moscow, 1925; Issue II: Moscow, 1926.

Verkhovnyi Sud RSFSR. Sbornik tsirkuliarov i vazhneishikh raz"iasnenii plenuma Verkhsuda RSFSR za 1924 god. [Supreme Court RSFSR. Collection of circulars and important explanations of the plenum of the Supreme Court of the RSFSR for 1924]. Moscow, 1925.

Vinokurov, A. N., ed. Sbornik postanovlenii i raz"iasnenii Verkhovnogo Suda Soiuza SSR [Collection of Orders and Explanations of the Supreme Court of the USSR]. Moscow, 1936.

Vroblevskii, A. B. Postateinyi kommentarii k Ugolovno—Protsessual'nomu kodeksu RSFSR [Article-by-article Commentary on the Code of Criminal Procedure of the RSFSR]. Moscow, 1923.

Vsesoiuznaia Kommunisticheskaia Partiia (Bolshevikov) v rezoliutsiiakh i resheniiakh s"ezdov, konferentsii i plenumov TsK [All-Union Communist Party (Bolsheviks) in Resolutions and Decisions of Congresses, Conferences, and Plenums of the Central Committee]. 5th ed., 2 vols. Moscow, 1936.

Vyshinskii, A. Ia. Sudoustroistvo v SSSR [The Judicial System in the USSR]. Moscow, 1940.

——Teoriia sudebnykh dokazatel'stv v sovetskom prave [The Theory of Evidence Submitted in Court under Soviet Law]. 2d ed. Moscow, 1946.

Vyshinskii, A. Ia., ed. Sbornik tsirkuliarov i raz"iasnenii prokuratury Soiuza SSR [Collection of Circulars and Explanations of the Prosecutor's Office USSR]. Moscow, 1936.

Zelitch, Judah. Soviet Administration of Criminal Law. Philadelphia, 1931.

ARTICLES

"Advokatura na urale" [The Institution of Advocacy in the Urals], *Ezh. sov. iust.*, No. 46–47 (December 30, 1922).

"Akademicheskaia khronika, pravovoe otdelenie fakul'teta obshchestvennykh nauk Moskovskogo Gosudarstvennogo Universiteta" [Academic Chronicle, the Legal Department of the Faculty of Social Sciences of the Moscow State University], *Pravo i zhizn'*, No. 3, 1922.

Akhimov, P. "Sledstvie i prokuratura" [The Investigating Office and the Office of Prosecution], *Ezh. sov. iust.*, No. 14 (April 16, 1928).

Aleksandrovskii, S. "Doklad o Rabote GKK Verkhsuda RSFSR za 1925 g." [Report on the Work of the Cassational College for Civil Cases of the Supreme Court of the RSFSR for 1925], *Ezh. sov. iust.*, No. 5 (February 7, 1927).

Askarkhanov, S. "Voprosy sudoustroistva na poslednei sessii VTsIK" [Questions of the Judicial System at the Last Session of the All-Russian Central Executive Committee], *Ezh. sov. iust.*, No. 31 (August 9, 1923).

Avdeenko, N. I., and M. A. Kabakova. "Grazhdanskoe protsessual'nogo prava" [The Law of Civil Procedure], in Sorok Let Sovetskogo Prava. Vol. I. Leningrad, 1957.

Berman, Harold J. "Law Reform in the Soviet Union," *American Slavic and East European Review*, XV (1956).

Berman, Iak. "K voprosu ob ugolovnom kodekse sotsialisticheskogo gosudarstva" [On the Question of a Criminal Code for a Socialist State], *Prol. rev. i pravo*, No. 2–4 (12–14) (February–April, 1919).

Bogomolov. "Ka voprosu ob iskorenenii volokitstva" [On the Question of Eradicating Red Tape], *Ezh. sov. iust.*, No. 19 (May 17, 1923).

Braginskii, M. "Ispolnenie sudebnykh reshenii" [Execution of Court Judgments], *Ezh. sov. iust.*, No. 2 (January 8, 1922).

Brandenburgskii, Ia. "Sudebnye voprosy na 2-i sessii VTsIK, XI sozyva" [Judicial Questions at the Second Session of the Central Executive Committee, XI Convocation], *Ezh. sov. iust.*, No. 39–40 (October 9–16, 1924).

Cherliunchakevich. "Otchët o dieiatel'nosti miestnykh narodnykh sudov goroda Moskvy za pervuiu tret' 1918 goda" [Report on the Activity of Local People's Courts of the City of Moscow for the First Third of 1918], *Prol. rev. i pravo*, No. 2 (August 15, 1918).

"Chetvërtyi Vserossiiskii s"ezd deiatelei sovetskoi iustitsii, doklad tov. Krylenko o prokurature" [The Fourth All-Russian Congress of Workers in Soviet Justice, Speech of Comrade Krylenko on the Office of Prosecutor], *Ezh. sov. iust.*, No. 5 (January 29, 1922).

"Chetvërtyi Vserossiiskii s"ezd deiatelei sovetskoi iustitsii, doklady tov. Lunina i tov. Krylenko o sudoustroistve" [The Fourth All-Russian Congress of Workers in Soviet Justice, Speeches of Comrades Lunin and Krylenko on the Judicial System], *Ezh. sov. iust.*, No. 5 (January 29, 1922).

"Chetyrekhletie moskovskogo narodnogo suda" [The Fourth Anniversary of the Moscow People's Court], *Ezh. sov. iust.*, No. 1 (January 1, 1922).

"Doklad t. Goikhbarga po p. 7 povestki dnia 'Klassovaia politika v grazhdanskom protsesse: o spetsial'nykh sudebnykh uchrezhdeniiakh' " [The Seech of Comrade Goikhbarg on Item 7 of the Agenda, 'Class Politics in Civil Procedure: On Special Judicial Institutions'], *Ezh. sov. iust.*, No. 12–13 (March 20–27, 1924).

ARTICLES (*Continued*)

"Doklad t. Lisitsyna o poriadke rassmotreniia zemel'nykh i zhilishchnykh del" [Speech of Comrade Lisitsyn on the Procedure for Hearing Land and Housing Cases], *Ezh. sov. iust.*, No. 6 (February 5, 1922).

"Doklad tov. Krylenko o prokurature" [Speech of Comrade Krylenko on the Office of Prosecutor], *Ezh. sov. iust.*, No. 5 (January 29, 1922).

Dombrovskii, E. "Deistviia suda po priniatiiu k proizvodstvu i naznacheniiu k razboru del po grazh. prots. kodeksu" [The Activity of the Court in Undertaking and Setting Cases for Trial in Accordance with the Code of Civil Procedure], *Ezh. sov. iust.*, No. 49 (December 20, 1923).

Durdanevskii, V. "Na putiakh russkomu pravu" [On the Rails to a Russian Law], *Sov. pravo*, No. 1 (4) (1923).

Erivman, Viktor. "Proekt izmenenii ugol. prots. kodeksa Uk. SSR" [The Draft Amendments to the Code of Criminal Procedure of the Uk. SSR], *Vestnik sov. iust.*, No. 3 (September 1, 1923); No. 4 (September 15, 1923).

Estrin, A. "Kak uluchit' i uprostit' nash ugolovnyi protsess" [How to Improve and Simplify Our Criminal Procedure], *Ezh. sov. iust.*, No. 49 (December 19, 1924).

Fradkin, A. "V Vserossiiskii s"ezd deiatelei sovetskoi iustitsii (Osnovnye momenty) [The Fifth All-Russian Congress of Persons Engaged in the Administration of Justice (Basic Points)], *Pravo i zhizn'*, No. 3–4 (1924).

Grodzinskii, M. "Dopros obviniaemogo v novom protsessual'nom kodekse" [Interrogation of the Accused in the New Procedural Code], *Pravo i zhizn'*, No. 3 (1922).

Hazard, John N. "Reforming Soviet Criminal Law," *Journal of Criminal Law and Criminology*, XXIV (Chicago, 1938).

I. L. "Kto mozhet byt' zashchitnikom" [Who May be a Defender], *Ezh. sov. iust.*, No. 9 (March 6, 1923).

I. S. "Diskussionnaia stranitsa po primeneniiu ugolovnogo i ug.-prots. kodeksov" [Discussion Page on the Application of the Criminal Code and the Code of Criminal Procedure], *Ezh. sov. iust.*, No. 39–40 (October 27–November 4, 1922); No. 41 (November 11, 1922).

"Itogi V S"ezda" [Report of the Fifth Congress], *Ezh. sov. iust.*, No. 12–13 (March 20–27, 1924).

Ivanov, V. A. "Organizatsiia suda i prokuratury" [Organization of the Court and of the Prosecutor's Office], in Sorok let sovetskogo prava 1917–1957 [Forty Years of Soviet Law, 1917–1957]. Leningrad, 1957. Vol. I.

"Iz deiatel'nosti Narodnogo Komissariata Iustitsii" [From the Activity of the People's Commissariat of Justice], *Ezh. sov. iust.*, No. 26–27 (July 17–24, 1922).

"Iz deiatel'nosti Narodnogo Komissariata Iustitsii" [From the Activity of the People's Commissariat of Justice], *Ezh. sov. iust.*, No. 1 (January 9, 1923).

"Izmeneniia i dopolneniia kodeksov zakonov RSFSR vnosimye NKIu na utverzhdenie 2–oi sessii VTsIK, XI sozyva" [Changes and Additions to the Codes of Law of the RSFSR Presented by the People's Commissariat of Justice for Approval by the Second Session of the C.E.C., XI Convocation], *Ezh. sov. iust.*, No. 35–36 (September 9–16, 1924).

"Iz zhizni khar'kovskoi gubernskoi kollegii zashchitnikov" [From the Life of the Kharkov Provincial College of Defenders], *Vestnik sov. iust.*, No. 2 (August 15, 1923).

Kabakova, M. A. *See* Avdeenko, N. I., and M. A. Kabakova.

Kadich, A. R. "O narodnom sudie (iz lichnykh vpechatlienii)" [Concerning the People's Court (from Personal Impressions)], *Prol. rev. i pravo*, No. 2 (August 15, 1918).

"Kakie izmeneniia v polozhenie o sudoustroistve vneseny norkomiustom v sessiu VTsIK?" [What Changes Were Made in the Judiciary Act Introduced by the People's Commissariat of Justice into the Session of the Central Executive Committee?], *Ezh. sov. iust.*, No. 25–26 (July 5, 1923).

Khazin, Ia. A. "Sudebnaia khronika, iz praktitki Moskov. soveta narodnykh sudei" [Court Chronicle from the Practice of the Moscow Council of People's Judges], *Pravo i zhizn'*, No. 1, 1922.

Kh. "Chem neobkhodimo dopolnit' ug.-protsess. kodeks" [What Must be Added to the Code of Criminal Procedure], *Ezh. sov. iust.*, No. 39–40 (October 27–November 4, 1922).

Khmel'nitskii, I. A. "Gubsud ili kollegiia zashchitnikov" [The Provincial Court or the College of Defenders], *Vestnik sov. iust.*, No. 5 (October 1, 1923).

"Khronika" [Chronicle], *Prol. rev. i pravo*, No. 5–6 (October 1–15, 1918).

"Khronika" [Chronicle], *Prol. rev. i pravo*, No. 8–9–10 (November 15–December 15, 1918).

"Khronika: pervyi plenum moskovskogo gubsuda" [Chronicle: The First Plenum of the Moscow Provincial Court], *Ezh. sov. iust.*, No. 4–5 (February 6, 1923).

"Khronika: voprosy iustitsii na vserossiiskom soveshchanii prokurorov" [Chronicle: Questions of Justice at the All-Russian Meeting of Prosecutors], *Ezh. sov. iust.*, No. 29–30 (August 10–17, 1922).

Kobalenkov, M. "Rukovodstvo dlia prokuratury" [Guidance for the Prosecutor's Office], in Vroblevskii, Postateinyi kommentarii k Ugolovnom Protsessual'nomu kodeksu RSFSR [Article-by-article Com-

ARTICLES (*Continued*)

mentary on the Code of Criminal Procedure of the RSFSR]. Moscow, 1923.

"Kollegiia zashchity" [Colleges of Defense], *Ezh. sov. iust.*, No. 46–47 (December 30, 1922).

"Konstitutsiia sovietskoi vlasti" [The Constitution of Soviet Authority], *Prol. rev. i pravo*, No. 3–4 (September 1–15, 1918).

K. P. "Neskol'ko slov o podsudnosti ugolovnykh del" [Some Words about Jurisdiction of Criminal Cases], *Ezh. sov. iust.*, No. 22 (June 7, 1923).

Krashkevich, A. "Zametki k proektu grazhdanskogo kodeksa" [Remarks on the Draft Code of Civil Procedure], *Ezh. sov. iust.*, No. 39–40 (October 27–November 4, 1922).

Krylenko, N. V. "K kritike proekta o prokurature [In Criticism of the Draft on the Prosecutor's Office], *Ezh. sov. iust.*, No. 3 (January 15, 1922).

——"K proektu novogo UPK" [On the Draft of a New Code of Criminal Procedure], *Ezh. sov. iust.*, No. 47 (December 5, 1927).

——"Reforma sudoustroistva" [The Reform of the Judicial System], *Ezh. sov. iust.*, No. 37–38 (October 13–20, 1922).

——"Sudebnaia reforma" [Court Reform], *Sov. pravo*, No. 3 (1922).

Kurskii, D. I. "Blizhaishie zadachi izucheniia sovetskogo prava" [The Next Task in the Study of Soviet Law], *Sov. pravo* No. 1 (May 15, 1922).

——"Iz praktiki narodnogo suda" [From the Practice of the People's Court], *Prol. rev. i pravo*, No. 1 (11) (January, 1919).

——"Novoe ugolovnoe pravo" [The New Criminal Law], *Prol. rev. i pravo*, No. 2–4 (12–14) (February–April, 1919).

——"Ob"iasnitel'naia zapiska k proektu izmenenii grazhdanskogo pro-tsessual'nogo kodeksa RSFSR" [Explanatory Notes to the Draft Amendments to the Code of Civil Procedure RSFSR], *Ezh. sov. iust.*, No. 35–36 (September 9–16, 1924).

——"Ob"iasnitel'naia zapiska k proektu izmenenii i dopolnenii ugolovno-protsessual'nogo kodeksa RSFSR" [Explanatory Note to the Draft Changes and Additions of the Code of Criminal Procedure of the RSFSR], *Ezh. sov. iust.*, No. 35–36 (September 9–16, 1924).

——"O edinom narodnom sude" [The Unified People's Court], *Prol. rev. i pravo*, No. 1 (11) (January, 1919).

——"Otchët otdiela sudoustroistva Narodnago Komissariata Iustitsii" [Report of the Department for the Judicial System of the People's Commissariat of Justice], *Prol. rev. i pravo*, No. 1 (August 1, 1918).

——"Reorganizatsiia organov chresvychainoi repressii i zadachi NKIu" [Reorganization of the Organs of Extraordinary Repression and the

Tasks of the People's Commissariat of Justice], *Ezh. sov. iust.*, No. 7 (February 12, 1922).

——"Zamietki o narodnom sudie" [Notes on the People's Court], *Prol. rev. i pravo*, No. 2 (August 15, 1918).

Lenin, V. I. "K voprosu ob iavke na sud Bol'shevistskikh lidcrov" [On the Matter of the Appearance of the Bolshevik Leaders before the Court], in *Sochineniia* [Works]. 4th ed.; Moscow, 1949. Vol. XXV.

——"O 'dvoinom' podchinenii i zakonnosti" [On Dual Subordination and Legality], in *Sochineniia* [Works]. 4th ed.; Moscow, 1951. Vol. XXXIII.

Lisitsyn, A. "K uprazdneniiu VChK" [On the Abolition of the VChK], *Ezh. sov. iust.*, No. 7 (February 12, 1922).

——"Nuzhno uprostit' sudoproizvodstvo" [Court Procedure Must be Simplified], *Ezh. sov. iust.*, No. 43 (November 25, 1922).

——"Ugolovno-protsessual'nyi kodeks" [The Code of Criminal Procedure], *Ezh. sov. iust.*, No. 24–25 (June 30–July 7, 1922).

Lotov, N. N. "Deiatel'nost' Samarskogo Gubernskogo Komissariata Iustitsii [Activity of the Samara Provincial Commissariat of Justice], *Prol. rev. i pravo*, No. 2–4 (12–14) (February–April, 1919).

Magirovskii, D. "Sovetskoe pravo i metody ego izucheniia" [Soviet Law and the Methods for Studying It], *Sov. pravo*, No. 1 (May 15, 1922).

Molochkov, A. "Advokaty—pravozastupniki—sud'i–assistenty" [Lawyers-Advocates-Judges' Assistants], *Prol. rev. i pravo*, No. 7 (November 1, 1918).

Morozov, N., and I. Perlov. "Ob organizatsii sudebnoi sistemy" [On the Organization of the Court System], *Izvestiia*, May 18, 1958.

Moskalenko. "Itogi i vyvody raboty grazhdanskogo otdela moskovskogo gubsuda" [Summary of and Conclusions on the Work of the Civil Division of the Moscow Provincial Court], *Ezh. sov. iust.*, No. 44–45 (November 16–23, 1925).

"Na mestakh: iuridicheskie konsul'tatsii" [At the Local Level: Legal Consultations], *Ezh. sov. iust.*, No. 27 (July 12, 1923).

"Na mestakh: orenburgskaia kollegiia zashchitnikov" [At the Local Level: The Orenburg College of Defenders], *Ezh. sov. iust.*, No. 45 (November 17, 1923).

"Na mestakh: v chernigovskoi kollegii zashchitnikov" [At the Local Level: In the Chernigov College of Defenders], *Vestnik sov. iust.*, No. 4 (September 15, 1923).

"Na mestakh: v kharkovskoi kollegii zashchitnikov" [At the Local Level: In the Kharkov College of Defenders], *Vestnik sov. iust.*, No. 4 (September 15, 1923).

"Na mestakh: v iaroslavskoi gub. kollegii zashchitnikov" [At the Local Level: In the Iaroslav Provincial College of Defenders], *Ezh. sov. iust.*, No. 45 (November 17, 1923).

ARTICLES (*Continued*)

"Na mestakh: v poltavskoi kollegii zashchitnikov" [At the Local Level: In the Poltava College of Defenders], *Vestnik sov. iust.*, No. 4 (September 15, 1923).

"Nashi zadachi" [Our Tasks], *Pravo i zhizn'*, No. 1 (1922).

"Novyi uchebnyi plan pravovogo otdeleniia fakul'teta obshchestvennykh nauk" [The New Curriculum of the Legal Department of the Faculty of Social Sciences], *Pravo i zhizn'*, No. 1 (1922).

"Obshchii obzor deiatel'nosti prokuratury v 1923 g." [General Review of the Activity of the Prosecutor's Office in 1923], *Ezh. sov. iust.*, No. 51–52 (December 31, 1923).

"O dvizhenii del v Sovete mestnykh narodnykh sudei i mestnykh narodnykh sudakh goroda Moskvy s 1-go ianvaria po 1-oe iiulia 1918 g." [On the Progress of Cases in the Council of Local People's Judges and in the Local People's Courts in the City of Moscow from January 1 to July 1, 1918], *Prol. rev. i pravo*, No. 5–6 (October 1–15, 1918).

"Organizatsiia iuridicheskikh shkol v rossii" [Organization of Law Schools in Russia], *Ezh. sov. iust.*, No. 39–40 (October 27–November 4, 1922).

"Otchët o deiatel'nosti instituta sovetskogo prava za 1921 god i 1-iu polovinu 1922 goda" [Report on the Activity of the Institute of Soviet Law for 1921 and the First Half of 1922], *Sov. pravo*, No. 2 (July, 1922).

"Otdel iustitsii, prokuratura i prochie organy iustitsii (tezisy tov. Estrina)" [The Department of Justice, the Prosecutor's Office, and Other Organs of Justice (the Theses of Comrade Estrin)], *Ezh. sov. iust.*, No. 4 (January 22, 1922).

"Otkrytie deiatel'nosti moskovskoi kollegii zashchitnikov" [The Beginning of the Activity of the Moscow College of Defenders], *Ezh. sov. iust.*, No. 37–38 (October 13–20, 1922).

Pavlovskii. "Diskussionaia stranitsa po primeneniiu ugolovnogo i ug.-prots. kodeksov—o lesoporubkakh" [Discussion Page on the Application of the Criminal Code and Code of Criminal Procedure on the Illegal Cutting of Timber], *Ezh. sov. iust.*, No. 19 (May 17, 1923).

Perlov, I. *See* Morozov, N., and I. Perlov.

Petukhov, N. "Birzhevoi arbitrazh" [Arbitration in the Exchange], *Ezh. sov. iust.*, No. 49 (December 20, 1923).

"Posle S"ezda" [After the Congress], *Ezh. sov. iust.*, No. 19–20 (May 10–17, 1924).

"Praktika Vysshei Arbitrazhn. Kommissii pri STO" [The Practice of the Supreme Arbitration Commission Attached to the Council of Labor and Defense], *Ezh. sov. iust.*, No. 1 (January 9, 1923).

"Pravovoi institut pri F. O. N. turkestanskogo gosudar. univer." [The

Law Institute under the Faculty of Social Sciences of the Turkestan State University], *Pravo i zhizn'*, No. 3 (1922).

"Predlozheniia chitatelei k razrabotke proektov UK i UPK SSSR" [Proposals of Readers for the Reworking of Drafts of the Criminal Code and Code of Criminal Procedure of the USSR], *Sotsialisticheskaia zakonnost'* [Socialist Legality], No. 1 (January, 1947).

"Preniia po dokladu tov. Krylenko o prokurature" [Discussion of the Speech of Comrade Krylenko on the Office of Prosecutor], *Ezh. sov. iust.*, No. 5 (January 29, 1922).

"Proekt dekreta o gosudarstvennoi prokuratura, razrabotannyi narko-miustom" [Draft of Decree on the State Prosecutor's Office Prepared by the People's Commissariat of Justice], *Ezh. sov. iust.*, No. 1 (January 1, 1922).

"Proekt grazhdanskogo protsessual'nogo kodeksa" [Draft of the Code of Civil Procedure], *Ezh. sov. iust.*, No. 29–30 (August 10–17, 1922).

"Rabota moskovskoi kollegii zashchitnikov" [The Work of the Moscow College of Defenders], *Ezh. sov. iust.*, No. 46–47 (December 30, 1922).

"Raboty soveshchaniia po podgotovke grazhdanskogo protsessual'nogo kodeksa Uk. SSR" [The Work of the Meeting to Prepare a Code of Civil Procedure for the Ukrainian SSR], *Vestnik sov. iust.*, No. 5 (October 1, 1923).

"Rech' predsedatelia VTsIK tov. M. I. Kalinina" [The Speech of the President of the All-Russian Central Executive Committee, Comrade M. I. Kalinin], *Ezh. sov. iust.*, No. 7 (February 12, 1922).

Reshetnikov, L. "Zametki k proektu grazhdanskogo protsessual'nogo kodeksa [Remarks on the Draft Code of Civil Procedure], *Ezh. sov. iust.*, No. 42 (November 18, 1922).

"Rezoliutsii s"ezda" [Resolutions of the Congress], *Ezh. sov. iust.*, No. 5 (January 29, 1922).

"Rezoliutsii V-go Vserossiiskogo S"ezda, VII" [Resolutions of the V Congress—No. VII], *Ezh. sov. iust.*, No. 12–13 (March 20–27, 1924).

Rodin, D. "Rabochie professional'nye ditsiplinarnye tovarishcheskie sudy (k ikh uprazdneniiu)" [Workers' Trade Union Disciplinary Comradely Courts (in Favor of Their Abolition)], *Pravo i zhizn'*, No. 1 (June, 1922).

Ryndziunskii, Grig. "Izlozhenie sudebnykh protokolov i reshenii" [The Writing of Court Minutes and Decisions], *Ezh. sov. iust.*, No. 7 (February 12, 1922).

Sambur. "Zametki k proektu grazhdanskogo protsessual'nogo kodeksa" [Remarks on the Draft Code of Civil Procedure], *Ezh. sov. iust.*, No. 34 (September 16, 1922).

Savitskii, M. Ia. "Zadachi i polozhenie zashchitnika v sovetskom ugolov-nom protsesse" [The Tasks and Status of the Defense Attorney in Soviet Criminal Procedure], *Sov. gos. i pravo*, No. 7 (1955).

ARTICLES (Continued)

Semenova, A. "Grazhdanskii protsessual'nyi kodeks Ukrainskoi sotsialisti-cheskoi sovetskoi respubliki" [The Code of Civil Procedure of the Ukrainian Socialist Soviet Republic], *Ezh. sov. iust.*, No. 41 (October 23, 1924).

Shalamov, M. P. "K voprosu ob otsenke soznaniia obviniaemogo" [On the Matter of Evaluating Confessions of the Accused], *Sov. gos. i pravo*, No. 8 (1956).

Shekhter, B. "O birzhevykh arbitrazhnykh kommissiiakh (Byt im ili ne byt)" [On the Exchange Arbitration Commissions (To Be or Not To Be)], *Ezh. sov. iust.*, No. 42 (October 26, 1923).

Simson, Sergei. "Spornye voprosy ugol.-protsess kodeksa" [Debated Points of the Code of Criminal Procedure], *Ezh. sov. iust.*, No. 26–27 (July 17–24, 1922); No. 33 (September 9, 1922).

Slavin, I. "Diskussionaia stranitsa po primeneniiu ugolovnogo i ug.-prots. kodeksov" [Discussion Page on the Application of the Criminal Code and the Code of Criminal Procedure], *Ezh. sov. iust.*, No. 37–38 (October 13–20, 1922).

——"Sud i novaia ekonomicheskaia politika" [The Court and the New Economic Policy], *Ezh. sov. iust.*, No. 1 (January 1, 1922).

Speranskii. "Narodnye zasedateli (lichnye vpechatleniia)" [People's Lay Judges (Personal Impressions)], *Prol. rev. i pravo*, No. 5–6 (October 1–15, 1918).

——"Otchët o deiatel'nosti vitebskogo gubernskogo komissariata iustitsii za period vremeni s sentiabria 1918 goda po ianvar' 1919" [Report on the Activity of the Vitebsk Provincial Commissariat of Justice for the Period from September 1918 to January 1919], *Prol. rev. i pravo*, No. 1 (11) (January, 1919).

Stalin, Joseph. "Interview with the American Labor Delegation" (1927), in Leninism. Moscow, 1933. Vol. II.

Stuchka, P. I. "Otchët Narodnago Komissara Iustitsii" [Report of the People's Commissar of Justice], *Prol. rev. i pravo*, No. 1 (August 1, 1918).

——"Proletarskaia revoliutsiia i sud" [The Proletarian Revolution and the Court], *Prol. rev. i pravo*, No. 1 (August 1, 1918).

"Sud i zhizn': isk za 'beschest'e'" [The Court and Life: A Suit for 'Dishonor'], *Vestnik sov. iust.*, No. 5 (October 1, 1923).

"Svedeniia o deiatel'nosti mestnykh narodnykh sudov i sovetov narod-nykh sudei v guberniiakh respubliki" [Information on the Activity of Local People's Courts and Councils of People's Judges in the Provinces of the Republic], *Prol. rev. i pravo*, No. 8–9–10 (November 15–December 15, 1918).

"Svodnyi otchët o deiatel'nosti gubernskikh i oblastnykh sudov RSFSR za I-e polugodie 1923 g." [The Combined Report of Activity of the Provincial Courts of the RSFSR for the First Half of 1923], *Ezh. sov. iust.*, No. 51–52 (December 31, 1923).

Tager, A. S. "Zametki ob advokature" [Comments on the Institution of Advocacy], *Pravo i zhizn'*, No. 1 (1923).

Tarnovskii, E. "Dvizhenie prestupnosti v predelakh RSFSR po svedeniiam mestnykh sudov za 1919–1920 gg." [The Course of Criminality within the Boundaries of the RSFSR according to Reports of the Local Courts for 1919–1920], *Prol. rev. i pravo*, No. 15 (December 15, 1921).

T. P. "Narodnye sudy g. moskvy i moskovskoi gub. v 1921 g." [People's Courts of the City of Moscow and of Moscow Province in 1921], *Ezh. sov. iust.*, No. 6 (February 5, 1922).

Trapeznikov, Vl. "Ditsiplinarnaia otvetstvennost' zashchitnikov" [The Disciplinary Responsibility of Defenders], *Ezh. sov. iust.*, No. 40 (October 11, 1923).

Trushchitskii, S. "Treteiskii sud" [Three-man Arbitration Court], in *Entsiklopediia gosudarstva i prava* [Encyclopedia of State and Law]. Edited by P. Stuchka. Moscow, 1930.

Vavin, N. "K proektu grazhdanskogo protsessual'nogo kodeksa" [On the Draft of the Code of Civil Procedure], *Ezh. sov. iust.*, No. 33 (September 9, 1922).

"V kievskoi kollegii zashchitnikov: nakaz chlenam kollegii o normakh professional'noi etiki" [In the Kiev College of Defenders: An Instruction to the Members of the College Concerning Norms of Professional Ethics], *Vestnik sov. iust.*, No. 5 (October 1, 1923).

"V otdele prokuratury Narodnogo Komissariata Iustitsii" [In the Department of the Prosecutor's Office of the People's Commissariat of Justice], *Ezh. sov. iust.*, No. 43 (November 25, 1922).

"Vypiska iz ugol.-prots. kodeksa" [Excerpt from the Code of Criminal Procedure], *Ezh. sov. iust.*, No. 6 (February 13, 1923).

Zaitsev, Vl. "Sudebnye dela po okhrane truda v ianvare-sentiabre 1922 g." [Court Cases on the Protection of Labor from January to September, 1922], *Sov. pravo*, No. 2 (5) (1923).

"Za podlinno nauchnuiu razrabotku korennykh voprosov nauki istorii sovetskogo gosudarstva i prava" [For an Authoritative Scientific Reworking of the Root Questions of the Science of the History of the Soviet State and Law], *Sov. gos. i pravo*, No. 6 (1956).

"Za povyshenie roli pravovoi nauki v kodifikatsii sovetskogo zakonodatel'stva" [To Raise the Role of Legal Science in the Codification of Soviet Legislation], *Sov. gos. i pravo*, No. 1 (1956).

"Za rubezhom: ob apelliatsii v ugolovnykh delakh" [Abroad: Concerning Appeals in Criminal Cases], *Ezh. sov. iust.*, No. 1 (January 9, 1923).

Zelenetskii, A. "O nashem brachnom prave" [About Our Marriage Law], *Prol. rev. i pravo*, No. 15 (December 15, 1921).

ARTICLES (*Continued*)

Zil'bershtein, N. "Prokuratura i grazhdanskii protsess" [The Prosecutor's Office and Civil Procedure], *Vestnik sov. iust.*, No. 7 (November, 1923).

Z-tsev, S. "III Sessiia VTsIK" [The Third Session of the CEC], *Ezh. sov. iust.*, No. 18 (May 20, 1922).

TABLE OF STATUTES AND ORDERS

U.S.S.R.

1923 July 6 Constitution of the USSR, 388n
1924 July 14 Instruction to the Supreme Court of the Union of Soviet Socialist Republics, 211n

Oct. 29 Basic Principles of the Judicial System of the USSR and of the Union Republics, 213n, 235n, 244n, 245n

Oct. 31 Order Approving Drafts of (1) the Fundamental Principles of Criminal Legislation of the USSR and of the Union Republics; and (2) Fundamental Principles of Criminal Procedure of the USSR and of the Union Republics and; (3) Statute on Military Crimes, 392n

1925 Oct. 2 Statute on Commodity and Stock Exchanges and on Stock Departments in Commodity Exchanges, 447n

1928 April 17 Statute on Commodity and Stock Exchanges and on Stock Departments in Commodity Exchanges (revised), 447n

Dec. 15 General Principles for Use of the Land and Land Distribution, 438n

1929 July 24 Statute on the Supreme Court of the USSR and the Prosecutor of the Supreme Court of the USSR, 212n

1930 Feb. 6 Abolition of Commodity Exchanges and Stock Departments within Them, 447n

1931 March 4 Abolition of the Arbitration Commissions, 440n

May 3 Statute on State Arbitration, 441n

1932 June 25 Revolutionary Legality, 245n, 246n

1933 June 20 Establishment of the Prosecutor's Office of the USSR, 246n

1934 Nov. 5 Establishment of Special Boards in the People's Commissariat of Internal Affairs of the USSR, 395n

1934 Dec. 1 The Introduction of Changes into the Existing Codes of Criminal Procedure of the Union Republics, 384n

1936 July 20 Organization of a People's Commissariat of Justice, USSR, 299n

Nov. 5 The Structure of the Prosecutor's Office of the USSR, 246n

Dec. 8 Charter of the People's Commissariat of Justice, USSR, 299n

1937 Sept. 14 Introducing Changes into the Existing Codes of Criminal Procedure of the Union Republics, 384n

1939 Aug. 16 Statute on the Institution of Advocacy, 300n
1953 (undated) Abolition of Special Boards of Ministry of Interior, 395n
1956 April 19 Abrogation of the Order of the Presidium of the CEC, USSR, of December 1, 1934, "On the Procedure for Conducting Cases concerning the Preparation or Commission of Terrorist Acts" and the Orders of the CEC, USSR, of December 1, 1934, and September 14, 1937, "On Introducing Changes into the Existing Code of Criminal Procedure of the Union Republics," 395n
1958 Dec. 25 Approval of the Fundamental Principles of Criminal Procedure of the USSR and of the Union Republics, 317n

R.S.F.S.R.

1917 Oct. 28 The Workers' Militia, 124n
Nov. 2 Declaration of Rights of the Peoples of Russia, 2
Nov. 24 First Decree on the Courts, 5, 34, 51
Dec. 18 Civil Marriage, Children, and Vital Statistics Registries, 67n
Dec. 19 Divorce, 67n
1918 Jan. 26 Introduction of the Western European Calendar, 2–3n
Feb. 15 Second Decree on the Courts, 9, 26, 52
Feb. 16 A Three-man Arbitration Court, 444n
Feb. 19 Nationalization of the Land, State Farms, 98n
April 27 Abolition of Tsarist Inheritance Law, 67n
July 10 Constitution of the RSFSR, 42–43
July 20 Third Decree on the Courts, 24, 33, 52
Oct. (undated) Code of Laws on Acts of Civil Status, Marriage, Family and Guardianship, 67n, 427n
Nov. 30 People's Court Act of the RSFSR, 47–57
Dec. (undated) Code of Labor Laws, RSFSR, 67, 101n
1919 Feb. 4 Statute on Revolutionary Tribunals, 79
Feb. 17 The All-Russian Extraordinary Commission (Cheka), 79n
April 3 The Soviet Workers'-Peasants' Militia, 79n
April 12 Revision of the Statute on the Civilian Revolutionary Tribunals, 79
April 12 Forbidding Voluntary Transfer of Soviet Office Workers from One Agency to Another, 81n
April 15 Camps for Forced Labor, 81n
April 23 Charter on the River Soviet Workers'-Peasants' Militia, 79n
April 24 Procedures for Issuing Passports for Abroad, 80n
May 2 Decree Declaring Petrograd, and the Petrograd, Olonets,

and Cherepovets Provinces in a State of Siege, and on Measures for the Defense of Petrograd, 80n

June 25 Introducing Labor Books in the Cities of Moscow and Leningrad, 81n

July 9 Procedures for Evacuating Local Executive Committees and Offices of Soviets, 80n

Nov. 5 Amnesty on the Second Anniversary of the October Revolution, 81n

Dec. 12 Basic Principles for the Criminal Law of the RSFSR, 82n

Dec. 19 Forbidding in the Territory of the RSFSR Distilling and Sale of Spirits, Strong Drinks, and Alcoholic Substances not Suited for Drinking, 97n

1920 Feb. 15 Charter for Village Soviets, 99

May 11 Registration of Persons with Higher Legal Education, 101n

May 18 Statute for Legal Consultation Sections in People's Commissariats and in All Central Offices, RSFSR, 102n

June 10 The Workers'-Peasants' Militia, 125nn

Sept. 16 Special Sessions of the People's Court and Standing Sessions, 115n

Oct. 21 People's Court Act of 1920, 166 ff., 131

Nov. 25 The Soviet Structure, 129n

Nov. 26 The Departments of the People's Commissariat of Justice, 124n

1921 Feb. 10 Procedure for Communicating between Local Executive Committees and the Council of People's Commissars, 131n

Feb. 22 Charter for the State General Planning Commission, 137n

March 10 Charter for Superior Judicial Control, 131n

March 21 Replacing Produce and Raw Material Assessments with a Tax in Kind, 137n

March 28 Free Exchange, Purchase and Sale of Agricultural Products in Provinces Completing Delivery of their Assessment, 138n

March 28 The Size of the Tax in Kind on Produce for 1921–1922, 138n

May 17 Guiding Directives to Organs of Authority with Regard to Small and Artisan Production and Artisan Agricultural Co-operatives, 138n

May 24 On Trade, 138n–39n

June 23 Uniting All Revolutionary Tribunals of the Republic, 173n

July 5 Procedure for Leasing Enterprises under the Jurisdiction of the Supreme Council of National Economy, 139n

July 7 Artisans and Small Industry, 139n

Aug. 25 Strengthening the Activity of Local Organs of Justice, 145n

1922 Feb. 6 Abolition of the All-Russian Extraordinary Commission and the Rules for Conducting Searches, Seizures and Arrests, 179n

May 24 Procedure for Hearing Land Disputes, 198n

May 25 Code of Criminal Procedure, RSFSR, 163, 186–88, 235n, 236n, 267n, 270n–72n, 274n, 313n–18n, 320n–27n, 330n–40n, 345n–51n, 354n, 356n–64n, 366n–67n

May 26 Statute on the Institution of Advocacy, 250n

May 26 Order Establishing a Charter for the College of Advocates, 162n

May 28 Statute on Prosecutor's Supervision, 162n, 229n

June 1 Criminal Code, RSFSR, 163n, 324

Aug. 10 Changes in the Organization of Tribunals of the Ukraine, 205n

Sept. 21 Procedure for Deciding Property Disputes between State Offices and Enterprises, 198n, 439n

Oct. 4 Establishing a Charter for the State Notary, 162n

Oct. 30 Land Code, RSFSR, 163

Oct. 30 Code of Laws on Labor, RSFSR, 163n

Oct. 31 Judiciary Act, RSFSR, 162n, 186, 193n, 195n–96n, 198n, 199n, 206n, 234n

Oct. 31 Civil Code, RSFSR, 163n, 396n

1923 Jan. 1 Judiciary Act, RSFSR, 343

Feb. 1 Statute on the People's Commissariat of Justice, 247n, 234n, 297n, 420n

Feb. 15 Code of Criminal Procedure, RSFSR, 235n, 355n–64n, 379n–82n, 386n

Feb. 15 Revised Code of Criminal Procedure, RSFSR, 187n, 197n, 203n, 235n, 236n, 268n, 272n–74n

July 7 Code of Civil Procedure, RSFSR, 163, 188n–89n, 203, 235, 275n–76n, 400n, 402n, 406n–27n, 448nn

July 7 Changes in and Additions to the Judiciary Act, RSFSR, 204n, 234n, 256n, 421n

July 10 Changes in and Additions to the Code of Criminal Procedure, 364n

Sept. 28 Procedure for Requiring People's Lay Judges to Perform Judicial Duties in Court Sessions of the Supreme Court, 204n

Nov. 23 Supreme Court of the Union of Soviet Socialist Republics, 244n

1924 May 6 Arbitration Commission under the Council of Labor and Defense of the USSR, 440n

July 6 Further Amendment of Art. 158 of the Code of Criminal Procedure, 387n

July 28 Decree of Amendments to Arts. 11, 23 (a), and 246 of the Code of Civil Procedure, 437n

Oct. 16 Additions to and Changes in the Judiciary Act, RSFSR, 206n

Oct. 16 Additions to and Changes in the Code of Criminal Procedure, RSFSR, 386n

Oct. 16 Additions to and Changes in the Code of Civil Procedure, RSFSR, 442n

Dec. 1 Addition to Art. 302 of the Code of Civil Procedure, RSFSR, 448n

1925 Feb. 23 Amending Art. 158 of the Code of Criminal Procedure, 387n

May 5 Revoking the Order of the CEC and Council of People's Commissars, RSFSR, of December 1, 1924, on Addition to Art. 302 of the Code of Civil Procedure, RSFSR, 449n

May 5 Addition to Art. 302 of the Code of Civil Procedure, RSFSR, of a Note 2 for the Chechen Autonomous Province, 449n

May 5 Additions to and Changes in the Code of Civil Procedure, RSFSR, 448n, 449n

May 5 Additions to and Changes in the Code of Criminal Procedure, RSFSR, amending Art. 4a, 387n

June 6 Addition of a Note to Art. 302 of the Code of Civil Procedure, RSFSR, 449n

1926 July 26 Approval of the Charter for the Special College of Supreme Control for Land Disputes, RSFSR, 438n

1929 Nov. 20 Amendment of Articles of the Code of Civil Procedure, RSFSR, 413n, 418n

Nov. 20 Amendment of the Code of Civil Procedure, RSFSR, 449n

1930 Oct. 10 Abolition of Land Commissions and the Special College of Supreme Control for Land Disputes, RSFSR, and the Procedure for Settling Land Disputes, 438n–39n

1939 June 1 Statute on Administrations of the People's Commissariat of Justice, RSFSR, in the Provincial Soviets of Deputies of Toilers, 233n

UKRAINIAN S.S.R.

1919 Jan. 14 First Decree on the Courts, 84n, 85n

Feb. 8 General Statute on Local Government, 85

Feb. 9 Establishing a Local Police Force, 85

Feb. 19 General Statute on the Civil Courts, 85

Feb. 20 Divorce, 91

Feb. 20 Civil Marriage and the Introduction of Books for Acts of Civil Status, 91n

Feb. 25 Legal Departments of the Provincial, County, and City Executive Committees, 87n

Feb. 25 Procedure and Conditions for Terminating Civil Suits in Process in Judicial Establishments Abolished by the Decree on the Court, 91*n*

March 1 Charter of the People's Commissariat of Justice, 88*n*

March 4 Nationalization of All Philanthropic Enterprises, 91

March 4 Forbidding Sales of Immovables, 91*n*

March 11 Abolition of Inheritance, 91*n*

March 14 Constitution of the Ukrainian Soviet Socialist Republic, 91*n*

March 14 Procedure for Examining Disputes between Employers and Workers, 91*n*

March 18 Granting Temporarily to the Council of People's Commissars Rights in the Sphere of Legislating and General Administration, 90*n*

March 20 Establishing a Section for Legal Advice within the Legal Departments of the Provincial and County Executive Committees, 88*n*

March 21 Amending Secs. 3 and 6 of the "Temporary Charter of People's Courts and Revolutionary Tribunals," 88*n*

April 15 Establishing Control-investigation and Administrative (General) Sections within the Legal Departments of the Executive Committees, 88*n*

April 16 Procedure for Reviewing Sentences of Revolutionary Tribunals, 89*n*

April 17 Establishing a Ninth Department of the People's Commissariat of Justice—the Supreme Court Control, 89

April 18 Establishing a Tenth Department of the People's Commissariat of Justice—the Supreme Court of Cassation, 89

1920 March 7 Registration of Specialists for Court Units, 101*n*

March 30 Requirement that All Orders Issued by People's Commissariats, Authorized Agencies and Departments of Executive Committees be Transmitted to the People's Commissariat of Justice and to the Legal Departments of the Respective Executive Committees, 99*n*

April 16 Persons Condemned to Social Compulsory Labor without Deprivation of Freedom, 100*n*

June 5 Using Practicing Jurists, 101*n*

July 3 Statute on Village Soviets, 100

Oct. 26 People's Court Act, 1920, 121 ff., 131

1921 March 27 Replacing Produce and Raw Material Assessments with a Tax in Kind, 137*n*

April 13 Free Exchange, Purchase and Sale of Agricultural Products in Provinces Completing Delivery of their Assessment, 138*n*

April 19 On Trade, 138*n*–39*n*

June 21 Guiding Directives to Organs of Authority with Regard to Small and Artisan Production and Artisan Agricultural Cooperatives, 138n

Aug. 8 Procedure for Leasing Enterprises under the Jurisdiction of the Supreme Council of National Economy, 139n

Sept. 14 Strengthening the Activity of Local Organs of Justice, 145n

Sept. 27 Notarial Functions, 143n

Oct. 18 Establishing Fees Payable to the Republic through the People's Commissariat of Justice, 143n

Oct. 30 Establishing Fees Payable to the Republic through the People's Commissariat of Justice, 146n

1922 June 28 Statute on Prosecutor's Supervision, 162n, 230n

Aug. 23 Criminal Code, Ukrainian SSR, 366n

Sept. 6 Abolition of the Provincial Departments of Justice [*Gubiust*] and their County Agents [*Ubiust*] and on the Procedure for Putting the Prosecutor's Office into Operation, 232n

Sept. 13 Code of Criminal Procedure, Ukrainian SSR, 364n–65n

Oct. 2 Statute on the Institution of Advocacy, 162n, 255

Dec. 16 Judiciary Act, Ukrainian SSR, 162n, 206n

1923 April 20 Establishing a Charter for the State Notary, 162n

1924 Oct. 1 Code of Civil Procedure, Ukrainian SSR, 397n

1927 July 20 Code of Criminal Procedure, Ukrainian SSR, 368n

BELORUSSIAN S.S.R.

1922 June 24 Code of Criminal Procedure, Belorussian SSR, 369n

June 26 Statute on Prosecutor's Supervision, 162n, 230n

1923 March 30 Judiciary Act, Belorussian SSR, 207n

July 26 Code of Civil Procedure, Belorussian SSR, 427n

ARMENIAN S.S.R.

1923 Sept. 23 Code of Civil Procedure, 427n

Sept. 28 Code of Criminal Procedure, 369n

1934 June 22 Code of Criminal Procedure (revised), 369n

AZERBAIDZHAN S.S.R.

1922 July 11 Statute on Prosecutor's Supervision, 162n, 230n

1923 Feb. 13 Temporary Rules on Jurisdiction, 369n

GEORGIAN S.S.R.

1923 Aug. 17 Code of Criminal Procedure, 369n

TADZHIK S.S.R.

1929 Dec. 19 Code of Civil Procedure, 450n
1935 Aug. 15 Code of Criminal Procedure, 394n

TURKMEN S.S.R.

1929 April 15 Code of Civil Procedure, 450n
1932 Sept. 11 Code of Criminal Procedure, 193n

UZBEK S.S.R.

1927 Sept. 20 Code of Civil Procedure, 450n
1929 June 29 Code of Criminal Procedure, 393n

TABLE OF CASES

Abramov, Case of, 20n
Amur Gubprokuror v. Soskin, 471n
Aronovich, Case of, 287n
Batov, Case of, 70n
Bazhenkov v. Vshivskii Village Community, 22n
Bogoliubskaia v. Bogoliubskii, 167n
Bykova v. Bykov, 22n
Chertenkova v. Karamza, 279n
Daletskii, Case of, 19n
Danilov, Case of, 19n
Denichenko, Case of, 373n
Dogadin v. Collective Farm "Krasnyi Pakhar," 439n
Drozdov v. Kalinin, 170n
Emelian, Ksenofontova, Zakharov et $al.$, Case of, 402n
Eremina v. Medvedev, 133n
Fishkes, Case of, 288n
Grosman, Case of, 285n
Itskovich and Mikhalevich, Case of, 373n
Janson v. Upravlenie Ussuriiskoi Zhel. Dor., 462n
Katsev, Mark et $al.$, Case of, 371n
Kormakov v. Vshivskii Village Community, 22n
Kotov and Travin, Case of, 370n
Kulikov and Ivanova, Case of, 370n
Lagutenko, Case of, 370n
Leningradskoi Teatral'noe Upravlenie v. Tolstoi, Shchegolev and Shlu-
  gleit, 464n
Levin and Erastov, Case of, 290n
Libson, Case of, 283n
Lif v. Shtiller, Kalashnikov, Brikoshin, Rikhter, and Raifman, 460n
Liquidating Commission for the Affairs of the Angin Consumers' Associa-
  tion, Case of, 467n
Livenshtein v. Livenshtein, 71n
L'vov v. Kondratov, 21n
Matina v. Skvortsov, 167n
Meerovich, Case of, 289n
Mogil'shchikov v. Factory Committee, 22n

Mostrikob *v.* Tovarishchestvo Manufaktura, 466n
Mukhametzianov, Case of, 166n
Murav'ev, Case of, 286n
Nesterenko *v.* Obshchesto Iugovostochnykh zh. d., 70n
Omel'iants *et al.*, Case of, 372n
Omonina *v.* Kaliaganov, 23n
Orlovskii, Case of, 289n
Panteleev, Case of, 371n
Petushkov, Case of, 289n
Pilach *v.* Pilach, 167n
Pinchevskii, Case of, 291n
Piniagin, Case of, 69n
Poliakovich, Case of, 68n
Roshchin-Insarov, Case of, 372n
Samigull and Khatir, Case of, 166n
Samokhvalov *v.* Komarov, 134n
Serafimovich, Case of, 20n
Shemetov, Case of, 288n
Smirnov, Case of, 68n
Spiridonova *v.* Chesnov, 168n
Sporova *v.* Sporov, 169n
The Steamship "Moses," 457n
Sulimov *v.* Maerov, 170n
Sverdlov Branch of the Vsekobank *v.* Ural'skie Kamni, 467n
Tverskoi Gubprodkom *v.* Tverskoi Gubsoiuz, 461n
Varshavskii, Case of, 284n
Vasil'eva, Case of, 135n
Vasil'eva *v.* Matveev, 458n
Vladtorg *v.* Khleboprodukt, 452n
Volkov and Naumov, Case of, 371n
Zemlianikova *v.* Livenshtein, 71n

INDEX

Abramov, S. N., 470
Accused, the:
  appellate protection of, 274–75
  in federal law of 1924, 393
  questioning of, 345–46
  requirement of presence of, 27, 352
  rights of, 349–50, 356–57, 360, 361, 362, 381–82
Accusers, 35, 38, 103, 218, 248
  in Ukraine, 87
  see also College of defenders, accusers, and representatives in civil suits
Acquittals, 37, 96
Adversary system of court procedure, 45, 291–96, 366, 460–61
Advocates, 162
  term "defenders" replaced by, 300
  see also Bar; Defenders
Afghanistan, treaty with, 149
Albania, Russian court pattern in, 86
Aleksandrovskii, S., 470, 474
All-Russian Central Executive Committee, 130, 183–86, 305, 383, 387
  debate of prosecutor's supervision, 226–27
  enactment of procedural codes, 441
  legislative commission of, 342–43
All-Russian congresses of Soviets, 128, 148–49, 179, 479
All-Ukrainian Congress of Soviets, 207
"All-Ukrainian Revolutionary Committee," 94
Amnesty problems, 82, 373
Antonov-Saratovskii, 390
Appeals:
  before congress of people's judges, 14, 24, 35–37, 56, 58
  against court orders and rulings in college of civil cases of Supreme Court of Russian Republic, 474
  filed with Council of People's Judges, 321
  filing of, hampered, 371–72
  inadequacies of court records for, 344–45

against investigator by accused, 316
in 1923 Code, 361, 363, 406
from people's courts to provincial courts, 274
for procedural violations, 348
representation upon, 295–96
of sentence, 327; in civil cases, 409, 426; from decisions of district courts, 10–11, of local people's courts, 7, 24, of revolutionary tribunals, 339; to Supreme Court, 363
time limit on, 120
in Ukrainian courts, 86–87, 103
Appellate bar, 263–64
Appellate colleges for audit, 380
Appellate court, 120, 133, 223, 260, 274–75
  limitations upon effectiveness of, 327–39
Arbitral awards, enforcement of, 406, 426–27, 445–46, 447
Arbitration, opportunities for private, 9, 443–49
Arbitration commissions:
  federal, 440–41
  local, 185
  provincial, 439
  state, 198, 431–32, 436, 439–41, 452–56
  see also Supreme Arbitration Commission
Arbitration tribunals, 9, 30, 431–32, 443–49
Armed services, quota of lay judges from, 193–94; see also Military service
Armenian Republic, 126
  civil procedure code, 427
  Code of Criminal Procedure in, 369
  Judiciary Act of 1922 in, 205–9 passim
  represented on plenum of federal Supreme Court, 211
Arrests, 313–15
Arskii, R., 138n

Arson cases, 141, 273–74
Artisans, effect of New Economic Policy on, 138–39
Asarkhanov, S., 257n
Attorneys, see Bar; Lawyers
Audit, 333–35, 361, 363, 380
Austria, temporary commercial agreements with, 149
Author's right, case involving, 464–66
Avdeenko, N. I., and M. A. Kabakova, 397n
Azerbaidzhan Republic, 126
 Judiciary Act of 1922 in, 205–9 passim
 represented on plenum of federal Supreme Court, 211

Babb, Hugh W., 394n
Banditry cases, 24, 180, 273–74
Bar, the:
 changing attitude of Soviet policy makers toward, 34, 106–9, 159–62, 250–54, 407, 477–79
 duties of, 281–83
 implementation of new policy, 258–62
 influence of federation on, 297–300
 professionalism and, 34, 38–39, 247–300
 salaried, 43–47, 48
 "underground practice" of, 276–81
 see also Lawyers
"Basic Principles for the Judiciary of the U.S.S.R. and of the Union Republics" of October 29, 1924, 244–46
Belorussian Republic, 58–59
 civil procedure code in, 427
 criminal procedure code in, 369
 Judiciary Act of 1922 in, 205–9 passim
Berman, Harold J., 300n, 395
Berman, Iak., 66
Berman, Ia. L., official Soviet historian, cited, 104n, 105n, 111n, 112n, 117, 119, 131, 133n, 152n–60n passim, 173n, 197–98
Black marketing, see Speculation, 24
Bodily injury cases, 65, 141, 312–13, 406
Bogomolov, 354
Bolsheviks, 12–13, 81
Bourgeoisie:
 law of, compared with Soviet law, 64

litigation by, 2, 249
 restraint of, 145–48, 396, 397–405, 470–71
 the state and, 44–45
 see also Private enterprise
Braginskii, M., 140n
Brandenburgskii, Ia., 204n, 250, 384–87, 400–404 passim, 442–43
Bredikhin, 159n
Bribery:
 attitude toward, 21
 cases involving, 24, 30, 39, 49, 52
 of officials, 21, 65, 141
Bulgaria, Russian court pattern in, 86
Bureaus of justice, county, 145, 146, 155
 duties of, 261
 investigators and, 114
 notarial desk established in, 143
 people's courts and, 115–16, 223–24
 replaced by county agent of provincial court, 234
 "special session" court for civil cases and, 144

Calendar reform, 3n, 13
Canon of Ethics, 281–83
Carr, E. H., 487n
Cases, carried over from prerevolutionary times, 1, 9–13 passim, 19–21, 33, 35, 91–92; see also Civil cases; Criminal cases
"Cassation," 10; defined, 329–30
"Cassational college," to hear appeals from sentences of revolutionary tribunals, 339
"Cassational" courts, 11, 14, 25, 131–36
Cassational-revision procedure, in federal law of 1924, 393
Cassation Court, Ukrainian, 84, 88–90, 92
Central Executive Committee, see All-Russian Central Executive Committee
Chancery tax, 408, 409
Chapurskii, V. P., 427n, 450n
Cheka, the, 79, 81
 abolition of, 179–80, 480
 amnesty cases and, 82
 investigating organs of, 158–59
 Krylenko on, 214–15
 people's courts and, 111–12
 question of elimination of, 150–51
 Stalin and, 488

Western attitude toward, 479
withdrawal of jurisdiction of certain cases from, 114, 115, 154
Chel'tsov, M. A., 392–93
Cherliunchakevich, 17n, 25n, 40n, 104, 112, 160
Civil cases:
    amount to be sought in, 56–57
    appeals in, 24
    authority of prosecutor to intervene in, 235–36
    involving rights of bona fide purchaser, 134–35
    judgments in, 406, 419–25, 463–76
    lawyers as defenders in, 36, 46
    number of judges trying, 52–53
    procedural guidance for, 25
    against village communal society, 22–23
    see also specific types of cases, e.g., Divorce
Civil law, 30, 67, 142, 148, 164, 315
Civil procedure:
    codification of, 188, 203, 232, 235–36, 275–76, 396–435, 447, 484
    federal concern with, 449–51
    in practice, 436–76 *passim*
Civil rights, misuse of, 396, 397–99, 400
Civil-service panel system, 45–46, 48, 218, 248
Civil war:
    amnesty following, 81–82
    Bolsheviks in, 94
    effects of, 78–83
    final battles of, 126
    reconstruction following, 128–75
Class policies, 3–5, 17, 428–31, 470, 480–81; *see also* specific classes, e.g., Workers
Codes, *see* Civil law; Civil procedure; Criminal law; Criminal procedure; Judicial acts
Codification, department of, in Commissariat of Justice, 124
Collective farms, 298, 424, 434, 438n–39n
College of defenders, accusers, and representatives in civil suits, 45
    consultative vote in county meeting of judges, 77
    departments of justice, and, 72–74, 75
    in People's Court Act of 1918, 48–49, 105

split by Court Act of 1920 on functional lines, 116–18
in Ukraine, 87, 89
see also Accusers; Defenders
Commercial courts, 5
Commercial relationships cases, 170–71
Commercial treaties, 149; effect of, 150
Commissariat of Internal Affairs, 179, 181, 240
Commissariat of Justice:
    attitude toward N.E.P., 451–56 *passim*
    concern with uniformity, 94, 96–103
    control over local, by central Commissariat of Justice, 72–77, 131–36
    county, 7, 76–77
    creation of federal, 299–300
    departments of, 124, 240–43
    directed to rework Code of Criminal Procedure, 342
    discontinuance of journal of, 79
    on inadequate numbers of licensed lawyers, 277
    pattern of organization of, 123–24
    proposals to Central Executive Committee for enactment of procedural codes, 441
    provincial, 7
    relationship between new Supreme Court and, 201
    reorganization of, 234–35
    section for establishment of new courts in, 7–8
    in Ukraine, 88–90
    All-Russian Congress of Provincial, Second, 44
    made Prosecutor of the Republic, 222, 230
    in Ukraine, 85, 94–95
Commodity-exchanges:
    arbitration tribunals, 446–47
    problems arising in, 451–56
Common-law system, 19, 29
Communist Academy, 18
Communist International, Congress of the, 126
Communist party:
    congresses of, 61–63, 481
    dissension within, 78, 128
    preparation of panels of defenders by, 119
Concessions, law of, 164

Confession of guilt, 294–95
Congresses of people's judges, 7, 14, 35–37, 55–56, 58, 72–74, 75; *see also* Councils of people's judges
Congresses of persons engaged in administration of justice:
  Third, 103–16
  Fourth, 147, 148–74 *passim;* continuation of revolutionary tribunals by, 178; debate over unification of courts in, 152–56; discussion on method of prosecution at, 219–24; implementation of decisions of, 162–66; Kalinin's speech to, 303–4; on question of professionalization of the bar, 249–50, 252–53
  Fifth, 376–80, 427–35
Consultation centers, 73, 124, 162; *see also* Legal-advice centers
Consumers' cooperatives, 442, 443, 446–47, 448, 467–68
Continental legal system, 317, 321, 329, 336
Contracts, 9, 14, 143, 170–71
  commission, 466–67
  creating monopoly rights, 464–66
  between private persons and government agencies, 102, 155
  of sale, 471–73
  between state agencies, 432, 441
  for violation of policy against monopolies, 468–69
Cooperatives, 406–7; *see also* Collective farms; Consumers' cooperatives
Corporations in civil suits, 406–7
Correctional labor without imprisonment, 223
Council of People's Commissars, 130
  Ukrainian, 94, 99
Councils of people's judges:
  appellate jurisdiction over regular people's courts, 55–56, 173
  right to demand any case for audit, 308, 333–35
  superseded by provincial courts, 342, 354–55
  supervision of people's judges, 192
  supreme control over, 131–36
  in three-level court system, 153–54
  in Ukrainian courts, 86–87
  see also Congress of people's judges
  ——*provincial:* abolition of, 192; in appealed cases, 103, 167–72 *pas-*

sim; college of defenders and, 119, 161; presidium of, 74, 75, 232–33; relationship to "special sessions" of people's courts, 114–16, 144
Counsel, right to, *see* Right to counsel
Counterfeiting of currency and documents cases, 24, 49, 52, 141
Counterrevolutionary "wreckers and diversionists," 65, 86, 180, 384, 392, 395
Court control department, 103, 124, 131–36
Court costs, 29–30, 57, 121, 461–62
Court executioner (or marshal), 72–74, 75, 115; *see also* Marshal
Court fees, 29, 57, 121, 406, 408–9, 446
  in Ukraine
  for fees paid to lawyers, *see under* Lawyers
Court fines, 97–98, 121, 406, 414
Court handbook (Stuchka), 30–33
Court investigator, *see* Preliminary investigator
Court records, 329, 344–45, 348, 418–19
Court travel, 151, 409, 417
Courts, 1–33, 57–61, 176–216
  aim at simplicity in, 122
  appearance of lawyers in, 273–74
  arbitration tribunals and, 445
  case load of, 375, 383
  departments of justice and, 72–74, 75
  effect of abolition of Cheka on, 180–81
  increase in authority of, 385, 386
  inexperience of, with codified law, 374–75
  judges' apathy in civil cases in, 456–63 *passim* (*see also* Civil cases)
  judiciary act reorganizing system of, 162
  jurisdiction of, 6–7, 30, 273–74, 368, 372, 380, 382–83, 397, 400, 406–8, 437–38
  Kurskii's efforts to popularize, 57–59, 180–83
  "labor sessions" of, 185, 195–96, 432
  land-use disputes transferred from commissions to, 431–32

1919 Communist party program for, 61–63
in 1922 Act, 173–75, 184, 186–89
in 1923 Code, 359–61
of 1925, 477
practical problems in, 456–63
prerevolutionary law in, 16–24
principle of initiative in, 26–27
representation in, 278, 406–7 (*see also* Defenders; Right to counsel)
review of investigation by, 381
revolutionary tribunals and, 148–56 *passim*, 183–84
rules of evidence in, 335–37 (*see also* Evidence)
specialization in, 51–57
"special sessions" of, 111, 114, 122, 123, 144–45, 154–55, 173, 177
staff of, 14, 347–48, 361
"standing" session of, 105, 111–16 *passim*, 154
supreme control over, following civil war, 131–36
systematized collection of most important decrees for 1917–20, 125
in three-level court system, 5–6, 153, 154
types of cases in, 19–24, 155, 166–72 (*see also* cases; Civil cases; Criminal cases)
in Ukraine, 84–87
unification of, 94–127, 152–56, 431–35
variation in work of, in villages and in cities, 151
see also specific functions and officials, e.g., Trials; Judges
——*local people's,* 1–33 *passim;* freedom of, curtailed, 99–103; hostility to formality in, 28–33; jurisdiction of, 12–14, 24, 47–51, 59–61, 82, 139–42, 166–72; number of, 14; preparation of panels of defenders by, 119; procedural guidance to, 25–28, 33, 301; use of lawyers in, 40–43
——*provincial;* administration of judicial matters of provincial departments of justice taken over by, 255–57; appellate work of, 362–63, 426; council of people's judges replaced by, 354–55; "county agent" of, 234; creation of, 273, 342; disciplining of members of the colleges, 267, 277; jurisdiction of, 188–89,

273–74, 385, 407, 426; number of judges in, 184, 195; procedure in, 361–62; prosecutor and, 379
Courts, commercial, 5
Courts, political, 150–52
Courts, prerevolutionary, 3
Courts, supplementary, 33
Courts, volost, 5, 149
Creditors:
competing claims of, 467–68
protection of, 442, 443
Crime, 1919 decrees specifically defining, 65
Crime of taking law into one's own hands, 366–67
"Crimes against the Individual," 65–66
Crimes involving protection of health, safety, and public order, 187
Criminal cases, 68–70
convictions in, 96, 327, 334, 363, 406
handled by provincial colleges, 266
in judiciary act of 1922, 186–87
lawyers as defenders in, 35–37, 46
number of judges trying, 52–53
in People's Court Act of 1918, 47
procedural guidance in, 25, 26–27
redistribution of, after abolition of people's courts with six lay judges, 368
right of prosecutor to intervene, 236
sentences: as read to accused, 327; conditional, 21; death, 307, 308, 362; reduction of, 36, 56, 109–11; review of, 393; setting aside of, 132–33, 330–32; suspended, 83; unjust, 363; uniformity in various republics of, 390
in Ukraine, 84, 95
Criminal law:
"a basic aid," 82–83
defined, 83
guidance from central authorities on, 65–67
need for study of, 164
Criminal procedure:
codification of, 186–88, 205, 236, 267–68, 270–76 *passim,* 305–13, 240–95
federal principles of, 388–95
Krylenko on, 485–86
in practice, 436–76 *passim*
seven stages of, 310–11

Crossing of frontier without permission, 180
Czechoslovakia, Russian court pattern in, 86

Damage suits, 70–71
David, René, and Henry P. DeVries, 319n, 336
Death, judicial recognition of, in the event of long absence, 30
Death sentence, 307, 308, 362
Debts, moratorium on payment of, 30
Decedent's estates, 406, 426–27
Defenders, 39, 87, 106
  lawyers as, 34, 43–47, 159–60, 218, 328, 357, 366
  nonprofessional, 35, 41–42, 48–49, 161–62, 247, 248–49, 252–54, 275
  term replaced by "advocate," 300
——colleges of, 38, 40–42; as centers for consultation, 109; change in structure of, 58; disciplinary matters in, 263; financial support for, 260; Fourth Congress on, 160–62; lack of confidence in, 298; in Moscow, 262–64; provincial, 250–54, 261; subjected to federal control by legislation, 299; see also Colleges of defenders, accusers, and representatives in civil suits
Defense of laches, 25
Denikin, A. I., 78, 81
Denisov, A. I., 11n, 209n
Department of justice, provincial, 72–77
  abolition of, 232–34, 255–56
  Commissariats of justice replaced by, 72
  investigating organs of, 158–59
  notarial desk established in, 143
  reestablishment of, 234
  relationship to "special session" of people's courts, 115–16
  right of review, 133
  in Ukraine, 85
Deposits in court, 406, 427
Detentions, 314, 318–21 passim, 358
DeVries, Henry P., see David, René, and Henry P. DeVries
Distillers of illegal liquor, 21, 39, 97, 112, 383–84
District people's courts:
  abolition of, 47, 48
  borough soviets and, 10

establishment of, 11–12, 33
hostility to formality in, 28–33
jurisdiction of, 10, 14–16, 24, 70–72
Kurskii's attitude toward, 23–24, 177
lawyers in, 37–39
loss of importance of, 24–25, 59–60
number of judges for, 10, 52
practice in, 14–16
procedural guidance for, 25–26
second decree instruction to, 16
supreme court control and, 11
Divorce cases, 14, 22, 30, 41, 53, 67, 406, 427, 475
  Ukrainian decrees on, 91
Documents as evidence, 416
Dombrovskii, E., 456–57
Dramatic productions, special instruction governing, 465
Drunkenness, attitudes toward, 97, 112, 115
Dubinskii, L., 457n
Durdenevskii, V., 215–16

Economic boards, provincial, 439
"Economic crimes," 188
Economic planning, extension of, 487
Economy, development of through state enterprise, 136–37
Embezzlement, 70
Employment problems, 475
England:
  commercial treaty with, 149
  defendants' appeals in, 333
  General Council of the Bar in London, 294
  indictment systems, compared, 317
  procedural forms in, 304, 309
  rules of evidence in, 336
Erivman, Viktor, 365–67 passim
Espionage, 84, 86, 180, 197
Estonia, diplomatic relations established between Finland and, 149
Estrin, A. Y., 222–25
  criticism of federal code, 393
  denunciation of, 394
  purged by Stalin, 488
Evidence:
  in civil cases, 404, 414–20
  court's right to exclude, 54, 372–73
  documents as, 416
  evaluation of, 32
  in federal law of 1924, 393

liberation from formality in taking of, 58
presentation of, 294
protection of material, 357
reopening of cases because of newly discovered, 132–36, 334
rules of, 335–37, 347
Exequaturs:
issuance of, 447, 448, 456
on protested bills of exchange, 442
Experts, calling of, 27–28; use of, 34, 417
Extortion, attitude toward, 21, 39

Factory committees, preparation of panels of lay judges by, 122–23
Family Code, 16, 133–34, 168, 280
Far Eastern Revolutionary Committee, 462
Federal-state relationship, 214, 390–92
Finland, diplomatic relations established between Estonia and, 149
Flexibility *vs.* uniformity, 94–127
Fradkin, A., 428n
Fraud, attitude toward, 21, 39

Georgian Republic, 126
adoption of Code of Criminal Procedure in, 369
Judiciary Act of 1922 in, 205–9 *passim*
represented on plenum of federal Supreme Court, 211
Germany, commercial agreement with, 149
Gifts, in excess of 10,000 rubles, prohibition of, 30
Goikhbarg, A. G.:
on amalgamation of land commissions with the people's courts, 437–38
on broadening jurisdiction of the regular courts, 431–35
on class politics in civil procedure, 428–31, 468
Golunskii, S. A., 10n
Gomulka, W., 86
Gorkii, Maxim, 253
G.P.U., *see* State Political Administration
Grodzinskii, M., 319n, 345–46
Gruliow, Leo, 481n
Guardianship, 67
Guilt, determination of, 370–71

Habeas corpus, writ of, 350
Hazard, J. N., 16n, 394n
Horse thefts, 387–88
Household property, division of, 140
Housing disputes, 135–36, 182, 475
Hungary, Russian court pattern in, 86

Iakhontov, 447–48
Imperial Code, 9; question of applicability of, 20–21
Imprisonment, 306, 309–10, 313–15, 360
Indictment, time set for delivery of, 307–8
legal system and, 489–91
Industry:
in New Economic Policy, 139–40
stabilization of law to foster, 396
state monopolization of, 487
Inflation, 143, 147
Inheritance, 30, 67, 91, 408
Institutes of law, 17, 162, 165
Investigation, department of, in Commissariat of Justice, 124
Investigation, preliminary, *see* Preliminary investigation
Investigator, preliminary, *see* Preliminary investigator
Iran, treaty with, 149
Italy, commercial agreement with, 149
Ivanov, V. A., 10n

Journals, law, 126, 140–41, 163, 164–65
Judges, 4–5, 104–5, 109–12, 477–79
attitude toward role in civil suits, 456–63 *passim*
in Code of Criminal Procedure, 348–49, 352
education of, 171
eligibility requirements for, 48, 50–51, 374
guidance to, in handbook, 31
impeachment proceedings against, 113
issuance of documents to, 147
in Judiciary Act of 1924, 213
powers of intervention, 54
reduction of authority of in Court Act of 1920, 120–26 *passim*
requirement of registration by, 101–2
responsibilities of, 311–12
right to recall, 25, 62, 105, 109–10
shortage of, 473–74

Judges (*Continued*)
  statutes for guidance of, in 1919, 61–68 *passim*
  tightening of restrictions on, 96–97
  in Ukrainian courts, 84
  see also specific Acts; Courts; *and* Congresses of people's judges; Council of people's judges
——*lay*, 52–53, 122, 154; attitude toward professional bar, 38–39; departments of justice and, 72–74, 75; panels for choosing of, 233; on provincial court bench, 189; purpose of use of, 34; in Supreme Court's colleges, 204; in Ukrainian courts, 86–87
——*professional*, 6, 34, 52–53, 154, 190–95; attitude toward use of lawyers in courts, 40–43; minimum of legal knowledge required of, 30, 477; powers of, 352; in Ukrainian courts, 86–87
Judiciary acts:
  of 1922, 176–216, 272, 487–88
  of 1923, 256–57, 487–88
  of 1924, 212–14, 235
Jury system, rejection of, 336; substitution for, 52–53
Justice, socialist concept of, 11, 16–17, 19, 48
Justices of the peace, 1, 5–7, 10, 149
Juveniles, 15; jurisdiction over, 364
Juvenile delinquency, 15, 317

Kabakova M. A., *see* Avdeenka, N. I., and M. A. Kabakova
Kadich, A. R., 1, 17, 40
Kalinin, Mikhail, 226–27, 303–4, 309, 390–91
Karelia, 80
Karew, D. S., 368n, 393n
Kerenskii, Alexander, 19
Khazin, Ia. A., 166n
Khmel'nitskii, I. A., 267
Khrushchev, Nikita, 481n
Kiev College of Defenders, Canon of Ethics published by, 281–83
Kleinman, A. F., 299n, 405, 413n, 415–18 *passim*
Kobalenkov, M., 319n
Kolchak, A. V., 78, 81
Kozhevnikov, M. V., 9n
Kozlovskii, 104
Krashkevich, A., 399
Krylenko, N. V.:
  on Cheka, 479

on code of criminal procedure, 305–9 *passim*, 342
debate between Estrin and, 224–25
draft of new codes of 1927 by, 486, 487
on effect of N.E.P. on legal system, 485–86
at Fifth Congress, 376
on ideal conditions of Communist society, 434–35
on judicial reforms of 1922, 214–15, 340–41, 358
on lay judges in provincial courts, 189
on legislative commission, 185
on method of prosecution, 219–22
on office of prosecutor, 157
presentation of draft judiciary act, 183–86
on principle of federal adoption of fundamentals, 390, 391–92
proposal for amalgamation of people's courts and revolutionary tribunals, 178–79
protest against dictation from above, 212n
purged by Stalin, 216, 488
on qualifications of judges, 190–95, 421n
on specialized courts, 195
on Supreme Court of the Republic, 200–204
on unified court system, 151–56
Kucherov, Samuel, 5n
Kulaks, liquidation of, as a class, 434, 470, 480–81
Kurskii, D. I.:
  on centralization, 72–77, 390
  on Cheka, 179, 479–80
  circular of Aug. 27, 1920, 113–16
  on civil procedure, 399–400
  on coexistence of revolutionary tribunals and people's courts, 174–75, 178
  congratulatory telegram to, 59
  on controls on judges, 109–12
  on criminal code, 148
  on development of new law, 163–64
  influence of, 482–83
  introduction of new journal, 163
  on legal defenders, 156–60
  on legislative commission, 185
  meeting with prosecutors, 237
  on people's courts, 23–24, 47, 57–59, 64–72, 105–6, 120, 148–52,

156–57, 176–78, 353–54, 380, 382–83

proposed amendments to codes, 380–83

on role of revolutionary repression, 490–91

on shortcomings of the bar, 106–9

speech in honor of fourth anniversary of founding of Moscow People's Court, 148

on value of provincial departments of justice, 225–26

Labor disputes, 97, 172

Labor duty, legal-assistance as, 101, 109, 111, 119, 248, 249

Labor exchanges, 172

Labor inspectors, attempts to bribe, 172

Labor laws, 16, 30, 67, 172, 196

Labor sessions of the people's courts, 185, 195–96

Labor unions, *see* Trade unions

Land commissions, 198–99, 432–33, 436, 437–39

Land use:
disputes over, 98, 140, 151, 182, 198–99, 408
jurisdiction in disputes over, 132
land commissions for, 185
Special College of Supreme Control over, 438–39

Language:
desire for simplification of legal, 5
national or majority, to be used in courts, 306–7, 368, 392–93, 406

Larceny, cause of, 142–45

Larin, 309, 391

Law, codification of, 66–67, 82–83; *see also specific codes,* e.g., Civil procedure

Law, international, 164

Law, prerevolutionary:
applicability to new courts, 16–19, 20–21
attitude toward, 48, 121

Law, primitive, as example for Soviet law, 64, 248, 311, 463–64, 477

Law, substantive, 90–91, 433

Law journals, 163, 164–65, 238–39

Lawyers:
appearances outside own province, 260–61
assignment to cases, 263

attitude toward college of legal defenders, 43–44

collapse of system of paid staff of, 118

in district courts, 37–39

employment of, outside college, 257

fees to, 147, 161–62, 252, 282–84, 288–89

labor duty by, 101, 109, 111, 119, 248, 249

limitations on numbers of, 262–67 *passim*

politicians and, 490–91

position in new Code of Criminal Procedure, 271–72

position in new judicial structure of 1923, 273–76

reappearance under permissive provisions of first decree, 35–37, 46

requirement of registration by, 101–2, 109

salaries to, 248, 249

shortage of, 258, 262–64, 276–77

see also Bar; College of defenders, accusers, and representatives in civil suits

Lebedev, V. I., 470

Legal-advice centers, 73, 101–2, 260, 262, 265–67

Legal aid:
Commissariat calls for improvement in, 297–98
necessity for, 118, 122, 247–48
to workers and collective farmers, 108, 298

Legal education, 17, 162, 165, 171

Legal ethics, 281–97

"Legality," 490

Legal representation, 116; *see also* Defenders

Legal tradition, influence of, 18

Legislation, department of, in Commissariat of Justice, 124

Lenin, V. I., 61n
on centralization, 78, 231
on courts, 389
creator of Cheka, 479
effort to improve economy, 483 (*see also* New Economic Policy)
influence of, 482
on legal matters, 62
on need for redraft of Code of Criminal Procedure, 343
at Ninth Congress of Soviets, 148–49
on prosecutors' supervision, 227–30

Lenin, V. I. (*Continued*)
  purge by, 128
  on tsarist courts, 3–4
Libel case, 312
Liberalism, 104, 117
Lisitsyn, A., 180–81, 309, 353
Lloyd George, David, 81, 150
Lotov, N. N., 7n
Lunin, 152

Magerovskii, D., 164
Maintenance suits, 14, 71–72, 166–69, 442, 459–60, 475
Manufacturers, small-scale, effect of New Economic Policy on, 138–39
Marriage laws, 30, 67, 141, 279–80, 287
  in Ukraine, 91
Marshal, 420–22, 424, 425, 448; *see also* Court executioner
Marx, Karl, 18
Mayhem cases, 273–74
Mikoyan, Anastas I., 481n
Military service, refusal to appear for, 65, 187, 197
  exemption from, because of religious convictions, 112, 189, 406, 427, 475
Military tribunals, 84–85, 183, 184–85, 480
  and Military-transport courts, 196–98, 213–14, 244, 306–7
"Militia," *see* Police, local system
Ministry of Internal Affairs, abolition of special boards of, 395, 489
Minors, jurisdiction of commission on, 30
Molochkov, A., 35n, 36n, 41n
Mongolian People's Republic, treaty with, 149
Montesquieu's theory of separation of powers, 43, 212
Morozov, N., and I. Perlov, 233n
Moscow:
  cassational court in, 25
  college of defenders in, 258, 262–64, 283–91
  commercial courts in, 5
  department of justice in, 74–75, 76, 77
  local people's court in, 13–14, 40
  loss of population in, 142
  military-transport court in, 196
  problem of applicable law in, 17

Moscow Provincial Court:
  circular on defenders in court, 278–79
  types of cases before, 473–74
Moscow State University, Law Department of, 165
Moskalenko, 473n
Murder:
  attitude toward, 21
  cases, 24, 39, 65, 68–69, 141, 273–74, 382

Natural law theory, 66–67
N.E.P., *see* New Economic Policy
"Nepmen," 390, 404, 419
New Economic Policy, 137–42, 483–87 *passim*
  effect on necessity for changes in law, 150, 443
  end of, 419, 449–50, 469–70
  final liquidation of neo-capitalist institutions which served purposes of, 447
  increased civil disputes and, 142–45
  influence on civil procedure, 396
  neo-capitalism of, 451
  reestablishment of the bar and, 160
  restraint against use of, by bourgeois element, 145–48
  in Ukraine, 137–39, 146–47
Norway, temporary commercial agreements with, 149
Notaries, 143, 174, 223
  state, 162, 406, 416, 427
  in Ukraine, 146–47

Oath in court, 28, 324
Officials:
  bribery of, 21, 65, 141
  crimes by, 21, 39, 86, 97, 111
  right of persons to sue, 62

Paris Commune of 1871, 4
Partnership suits, 406–7, 460–61
Pashukanis, E. B., 17–18, 153, 487, 488
Passports, issuance of, forbidden, 80–81
Patents, violation of, 312
Paternity case, 133–34
Pavlovskii, 351n
Peasantry:
  courts for, 5

New Economic Policy and, 137–39
procedural law and, 433–34
quota of lay judges from, 193–94
Penalties:
increase of, 393
right of judges to reduce, 109, 110–11
variation in, 97–98
People's Court Act:
of 1918, 47–51, 112–16, 301
of 1920, 116–27 *passim*, 117, 434–35
Perlov, I., *see* Morozov, N., and I. Perlov
Personal injury, claims for, 475
Personal insults case, 312
Personal rights, cases concerned with, 68–72
Petrograd:
civil war in, 78–80 *passim*
commercial courts in, 5
department of justice in, 74–75, 76, 77
district court in, 12, 14–15
local people's court in, 12, 14
loss of population in, 142
military-transport court in, 196
percent of acquittals in, 96
Petukhov, N., 455–56
Planning commission, state, 137
Poland:
peace treaty with, 149
Russian court pattern in, 86
Sovietization of, 126
Polianskii, N. N., 291–97
Police:
activities of, 357–58
attitude toward new court, 2
complaints to, 311–12
departments of justice and, 72–74, 75
in federal law of 1924, 392–93
as investigating agency, 313–15, 381
local system (militia), 123–25, 158, 159, 174, 226
political, 179–80
powers of, 378
prosecutor and, 357
river, 79
in Ukraine, 85
Vyshinskii on role of, 376–79 *passim*
Politburo, 227–30, 489
Political cases before revolutionary tribunals, 47

Political offenses, 79
Political rights as test of eligibility for office-holding, 50–51
Political trials, 394–95
Preliminary investigation, 16, 26, 73, 311, 315–19, 327–28
exclusion of lawyers from, 268–70
in federal law of 1924, 392–93
inadequate treatment in Code of Criminal Procedure, 346
presence of accused at, 349–50, of representative at, 119
in Ukraine, 95
Preliminary investigator, 8, 34, 174, 226, 268, 315–19
complaints to, 311–12
impartiality required by 1923 code, 374
powers of, 378
prosecutor and, 158, 357, 376, 381
restrictions on, 358–59
review of police investigations by, 381
tendency of, to lean in direction of accusation, 328
transmission to court of recommendations, 319–21
in Ukraine, 89, 146
Vyshinskii on role of, 376–79 *passim*
——*commission of*, 26, 38, 49–50, 54, 61; collegiate system abolished, 114–15, 121; consultative vote in county meeting of judges, 77; departments of justice and, 72–74, 75; revision of, 105–6
Preobrazhenskii, 404–5
Prerevolutionary cases, *see* Cases, carried over from prerevolutionary times
Prerevolutionary law, *see* Law, prerevolutionary
Private enterprise:
effect of nationalization decrees on, 108
number of cases involving, 265–66
place of, in new system, 5
reprieve for, 136–42, 217, 249, 396, 483
Procedure:
attitude toward violation of laws of, 135
Bill of Rights in, 306, 309–13
codification of, 301–41
conflict between uniformity and flexibility in, 94–127 *passim*

Procedure (*Continued*)
difference between criminal and
civil, 401 (*see also* Civil procedure; Criminal procedure)
impact of political considerations
upon laws, 396–405, 423
judicial experience with, 369–76,
436–76
Kurskii on, 148, 380–82
provisions for, in People's Court
Act, 54–55
reforms of, 342–95 (*see also* Civil
procedure; Criminal procedure)
rules adopted in July, 1918, 310
Soviet justification for, 477–79
in third decree, 25–28
in Ukrainian courts, 84
Property:
crimes, 21, 39, 65–66
division of household, 140
levy upon, 423–25, 448–49
ownership disputes, 9, 98, 168–70
prohibition of transactions concerning real, 30
Prosecutors, 217–48
abolition of tsarist office, 34
in civil suits, 235–36, 406
complaints to, 311–12
control over bar, 257–58
control over police, 314–15
court functions of, 217–18, 231–32,
359
created, 1920, 117
establishment of state office, 1922,
156–59, 162
excesses of investigator, concern of,
316, 319
in federal law of 1924, 392–93
impact of federation on, 243–46
increased importance of, 356–60,
364
investigator and, 316, 319, 358–59,
376, 381
plans for, in 1922, 218–27
Politburo on supervision of, 227–
30
power of, 375–76, 378
provincial, 241–42, 243, 332–33,
379
recommendations following preliminary investigation, 319–21
right to demand audit, 333–34
shift of controls from defense attorney to, 356–57
Soviet justification for, 477–79
staff of, 236–37

Vyshinskii on role of, 376–79
passim
Prosecutor in Supreme Court of the
U.S.S.R., 212, 235, 239, 243–44,
246
Publications, *see* Journals
Publications, department of, in Com-
missariat of Justice, 124
Public health, labor duty in, 101
Punishment, department of, in Com-
missariat of Justice, 124
Punishment, types of, in court sen-
tences, 83
Purges, 128

Rape cases, 24, 49, 52, 65, 68, 141,
312–13, 373
in Ukraine, 364–65, 367–68
Rappard, W. E., 62n
Reconciliation, 367
Reikhel, 390
Reshetnikov, L., 399, 410
Retrials, 7, 133, 332–33, 380–81
in Ukrainian court system, 87
Review:
over court decisions, 7, 10–11, 132,
173–74, 301, 327–35, 361, 363,
406
department of supreme court control, 132–33
in federal law of 1924, 393
prohibition of, of small cases removed, 58
procedure for, 55
"Revolutionary consciousness," 32,
68–72, 401, 477
Revolutionary tribunals, 8
abolition of, 342, 480
in amnesty cases, 82
civilian, 79
continuation of, 306–7
criminal cases in, 155
departments of justice and, 72–74,
75
exclusion of counsel from trials
before, 270
investigating organs of, 158–59
jurisdiction of, 24, 30, 114, 115,
154
military, 79, 155
as operative in 1922, 172–75
people's courts and, 111–12, 148–
56 *passim*, 183–84
political cases reserved for, 47
preparation of panels of defenders
by, 119

privileges of, 346
procedural rules for, 337–40
question of elimination of, 150–51, 178
requests for mercy after sentence of death by, 307, 308
in Ukraine, 86, 88–89, 95
Western attitude toward, 479
see also Supreme Revolutionary Tribunal
Right to counsel, 267–72, 316–17, 322, 371–72, 480
Rivlin, E. S.:
on exclusion of counsel at preliminary investigation, 119, 268–69
on organization of lawyers, 160–61
on representation in court, 35, 117, 252–53, 280–81
Robbery:
attitude toward, 21
cases involving, 24, 49, 52, 65, 69–70, 141, 142–45, 382
Rodin, D., 182n
Roman law, compared with Soviet law, 64
Ruble, value of, 6n
Rumania, Russian court pattern in, 86
Russian Republic:
development of federalism within, 164
experimentation in legal matters, 1–83
first constitution of, 42–43
territorial jurisdiction of criminal laws of, 83
types of civil-suit problems faced in general courts of, 456–63 *passim*
Ukraine and, 100, 113
Ryndziunskii, Grig., 302n, 303n

Sabotage cases, 86
Sambur, 399
Sanitary and safety regulations, violation of, 172
Savitskii, M. Ia., 328
Search of quarters of diplomatic representatives of foreign states, 357
Security police, *see* G.P.U.
Semenova, A., 397n
Serfs, courts for, 5
Settlements of disputes outside of courts, 8–9, 34
Sex crimes, 307, 310, 372; *see also* Rape
Shalamov, M. P., 328
Shchegolev, P. E., 464

Shekhter, B., 414n, 416–18, 454–55
Shteinberg, I. N., 8, 12–13, 482
Simson, Sergei, 343–45
Slander cases, 312
Slavin, I., 301, 302, 348
Smuggling, 180
Social duties, 101
Social insurance, 81
Social-insurance premium, failure to pay, 172
Socialist Revolutionary party, 12-13, 100
Social relationships, law as sphere of, 164
Social theory, legal ethics and, 291–97
Soviet legal system:
attitudes toward formality, 28–33, 56, 94
class approach in, 3–5, 17, 428–31, 470, 480–81
crystallization of structure of, 176–216
decrees on, 4–13, 16, 18, 19, 23–25, 33, 38, 247
effect of reprieve to private enterprise on, 137, 139–42
effects of civil war on, 64–93, 123–27, 129–31
efforts at simplification of, 34–63, 302–3
primitive law as example for, 64, 248, 311, 463–64, 477
recapitulation of, 477–91
Stalin's influence on, 487–89
uniformity *vs.* flexibility, 94–127
see also Civil law; Civil procedure; Criminal law; Criminal procedure; Judiciary acts
Soviets, 11, 38, 45, 49–50, 51, 55
borough, 10, 74–76
city, 10, 130
county, 77, 120, 191
district, 10
village, 10, 122–23
——*local:* interrelationship of central authorities and, 99–100
liquidation of affairs of evacuated, 80; office of prosecutor and, 157–58; people's courts and, 153; position of, following civil war, 129–31; powers of, 18, 98, 191; relationship to local police, 124–25; system of recall by, 109–10
——*provincial:* departments of justice of executive committees of, 220–21, 222; District People's Court

Soviets (*Continued*)
and, 10; executive committee, power of, 259–60; following civil war, 129; power of, 72–73, 120, 251, 257; preparation of panels of defenders by, 119; relationship to prosecutor's office, 158; right to ratify members of council of people's judges, 55

Speculation (black marketing) cases, 24, 30, 49, 52, 86, 97, 111, 141

Speranskii, 20*n*, 39*n*, 43*n*, 44*n*, 59*n*, 60*n*

Stalin, Joseph:
abolition of codes of 1922 and 1923 by, 487–88
death of, 489
denunciation of, 481
influence on experiment of simplification of legal system, 175, 487–89
on national minorities, 210

Stamp tax, 408, 409, 414

State, Soviet theory of, 3–4, 44–45, 238–39

State enterprises, 406–7, 432, 446–47, 452, 462

State Political Administration (G.P.U.), 179–81, 203, 211
case against, 370
exclusion of, from operation of general rules of Code of Criminal Procedure, 385–86
issue of secrecy at trials, 307
not bound by Code of Criminal Procedure, 358

Statutes of limitations, 25

Steinberg, I. N., *see* Shteinberg, I. N.

Strogovich, M. S., 299*n*, 312–13, 325

Stuchka, P. I.:
as acting Commissar of Justice, 7–8
death of, 488
on definition of law, 83
Encyclopedia of Law, 444
handbook by, 30–33
influence of, 481–82
instruction on court procedure for the local people's courts, 13, 26
introduction to volume of circulars issued by Russian Republic's Supreme Court in 1925, 463
on legal education, 51
on legislative commission, 185
on problems in civil cases, 474–76
on selection of judges, 4

Suicide pacts, 382

Summonses, 406, 410–11

Supreme Arbitration Commission of the Russian Republic, 198, 431–32, 436, 439–41, 452–56

Supreme Arbitration Commission of the U.S.S.R., 440–41

Supreme Council of National Economy, 139

Supreme Court Control, 11, 25, 200, 308
abolition of, 354
final decision by, in audited cases, 334
in reopening of cases, 334–35
reorganization of Special College of, over land disputes, 438–39
in Ukraine, 89

Supreme Court of Cassation, Ukrainian, 89–90, 92

Supreme Court of Criminal Cassation, 153–54

Supreme Court of the Russian Republic, 131–36, 177, 199–204, 273, 342
appeals to, 274, 276, 363, 426
on arbitration tribunals of commodity exchanges, 456
College for Civil Cases, 407, 429, 474–75
in Judiciary Act of 1922, 184
in Judiciary Act of 1923, 211, 363
military and military-transport courts under supervision of, 196
professional judges on, 200–201, 202
review of people's court decision, 173–74, 276

Supreme Court of the U.S.S.R., 203–4, 209–12, 213, 235, 243, 450–51; *see also* Prosecutor of the Supreme Court of U.S.S.R.

Supreme Judicial Control, Department of, 154

Supreme Revolutionary Tribunal, 154, 173, 199–200, 270, 340, 362

Surplus grain, refusal to report, 65

Tadzhik Republic, procedural code in, 394, 450

Tager, A. S., 250, 259–62

Tarnovskii, E., 140*n*, 142*n*, 155*n*

Taxes, 137–38, 254, 349, 408–9; *see also* Stamp tax

"Temporary Instruction on the Organization and Work of the Local People's Courts," 25

Terrorists, 384, 392, 395

Theft:
attitude toward, 21
types of cases, 180, 197, 383–84, 387–88
Time limit:
allowed for appeal, 362
on cases, 375, 379–82 *passim*, 389–90, 406
on detention of a suspect, 389–90
Tito, Marshal, 86
Tolstoy, Alexei N., 464
Trademarks, violation of, 312
Trade unions:
All-Russian Central Council of, 183
disciplinary tribunals, 182–83
legal aid to members of, 298
preparation of panels of defenders by, 119
preparation of panels of lay judges by, 122–23, 193–94, 196
representation by official of, in civil suits, 275, 407
representatives of, as defenders in court, 119, 248, 252, 275
Transcaucasian Soviet Federated Socialist Republic, 206
"Transfer to court," 319–21
Transportation, rail and water, 197
Transport courts, *see under* Military tribunals
Trapeznikov, Vl., 277*n*
Treason, 65, 86
Trials, 29, 321–27
of civil cases, 406, 411–23
delays in, 96–97, 111
issue of secrecy of, 307, 310
length of, 323
oversimplification of, 302–3
procedure for, 28, 54, 359–60 (*see also* Procedure)
proceedings before trial, 29 (*see also* Preliminary investigations)
rate of reversals of decisions, 475
remand for new, 11, 36, 56, 332–33 (*see also* Retrials)
right of exclusion from, 54
in Ukraine, 86, 95
Vyshinskii on, 377–78
Turkestan State University, Institute of Law in, 165–66
Turkey, treaty with, 149
Turkmen Republic, procedural code in, 393–94, 450

Ukrainian law review, 238–39

Ukrainian Republic:
abolition of provincial departments of justice in, 232
attitude toward increased powers of prosecutor, 366
centralization of authority in, 85, 87–93
civil code of, 397
civil procedure code of, 427
civil suits in general courts of, 456–63 *passim* (*see also* specific types of suits)
civil war in, 78, 92, 94–95
court developments in, 83–93
criminal prosecution of "underground" practitioners ordered by, 279–81
criticism of 1923 Code on jurisdiction of courts, 366–67
fees for civil plaintiff restored in, 146
implementation of decision of Fourth Congress, 162–66
industrial disputes, decrees on settlement of, 91
influence of Russian Republic on court system of, 85–86
influence on Russian Republic, 113
judicial decisions within, 369–76 *passim*
Judiciary Act of 1922 in, 205–9 *passim*, 230
on labor duty, 101–2
language of court proceedings in, 364
limitation of number of lawyers in, 264–65
New Economic Policy in, 137–39, 146–47
People's Court Act, of 1920, 113, 121–22
philanthropic enterprises, decree on nationalization of, 91
professionalization of bar in, 254–58
proposals for revision of Code of Criminal Procedure, 364–69
revolutionary tribunals in, 86, 88–89, 95
Soviets in, 87–88, 100, 102
see also specific phases of Soviet *legal system*, e.g., Courts; *and* specific types of cases, e.g., Counterrevolutionary cases
Uniformity *vs.* flexibility, 94–127

Union of Soviet Socialist Republics
(U.S.S.R.), 126, 206–7, 209
Central Executive Committee, 388
constitutions of, 209–10, 246, 299–
300
effect on office of prosecutor, 235,
243–46
influence on the bar, 297–300
influence of criminal procedure,
388–95
relationship with republics, 214,
390–92
on Russian Republic's Code of Civil
Procedure, 450–51
See also Supreme Court of U.S.S.R.
United States:
grand jury system in, 317
rules of evidence in, 336
U.S.S.R., *see* Union of Soviet Socialist
Republics
Uzbek Republic, procedural code in,
393–94, 450

Vavin, N., 398–99
Veger, V. I., 283n
"Village" courts, 5
Vinokurov, A. N., 389, 391, 450n
Vitebsk Province:
activity of people's courts in, 7, 60,
96
District Court of, 16
investigating commissions in, 61
Provincial Commissariat of Justice,
59
required work as penalty in, 98
Volost courts, 5, 149
Vyshinskii, A. Y., 148n, 226n, 336n,
451n
on "Basic Principles," 244–46

review of criminal procedure by,
376–80
role of prosecutor in support of
Stalin's purge, 488

"Withering away" process and court
system, 3–4, 123, 210, 222, 434,
482, 487
Witnesses, 27, 28
absence of, at trial, 347
in civil cases, 404, 410, 415
presence in courtroom of, 323–26
passim, 344
suffering from physical or psychological handicaps, 370
Work, required, as penalty, 97–98,
100–101
Work camps, 81
Workers:
disputes between, 2
illegal dismissal of, 172
legal aid for, 108, 298
quota of lay judges from, 193–94
urge to favor, in courts, 17, 433–
34
Workers'-Peasants' Inspection, 228,
364
Wrangel, P. N., 126

Yudenich, N. N., 78
Yugoslavia, opposition to pattern of
Russian court in, 86

Zaitsev, Vl., 172n
Zelenetskii, A., 141n
Zelitch, Judah, 13
Zil'bershtein, N., 237–39
Z-tsev, S., 306